Charlene D. [signature]
Genesis 50:20

Praise for

Overcoming the Narcissist, Sociopath, Psychopath, and Other Domestic Abusers: The Comprehensive Handbook to Recognize, Remove, and Recover from Abuse

There are a number of great books out there about the dynamics of domestic violence, but I've yet to read one that is more complete than this one. What makes this book different? It is more comprehensive than any book I've read on domestic violence. Charlene recognizes that people are complex, so in this book she addresses the whole person (psychological, physical, and spiritual). This book has the wisdom to change how advocates help people of faith. It has the depth to challenge the most seasoned expert in the field of domestic violence. It has the gentleness that beckons the reader into an immersive experience and the boldness to challenge existing structures of abuse advocacy. I'm thankful to know Charlene and to add this book to my list of incredible resources that I'm confident will inform and even reframe my advocacy efforts for the rest of my life.

—Neil Schori, Senior Pastor, The Edge Church, Aurora, IL
Advocate for domestic abuse victims
Former pastor to Stacy Peterson (fourth wife of convicted murderer and former Bolingbrook, Illinois, police sergeant Drew Peterson)

This book provides a much-needed resource for women, particularly women of faith, who are seeking to escape domestic abuse. In one readable yet comprehensive book, Charlene Quint covers what every woman needs to know about identifying abuse, getting out safely, healing, and moving on with her life.

—Michael Strauss, Esq., Schlesinger & Strauss,
Illinois State Bar Association Family Law Chair 2019–2020
Vice president of the board of A Safe Place, Zion, IL

In this one-stop all-inclusive book, Charlene Quint provides women in abuse a guide on how to identify abuse and abusers, get out safely, recover, and reclaim their lives. A must-read for all women in abuse or in its aftermath.

—Michael Nerheim, Lake County State's Attorney, IL

For a survivor, domestic violence is a complex continuum of hundreds—maybe even thousands—of experiences, circumstances, and decisions. There are so many, in fact, that it isn't easy to cover them all in one book. However, Charlene Quint, through her personal experience and law practice and advocacy, has done a great job of touching on the most common ones and providing succinct insights that are certain to help any survivor or member of a survivor's support system.

—Chris McMurry, Director of Theresa's Fund
Founder of DomesticShelters.org.

A must-read! Charlene Quint has written a must-read for anyone experiencing domestic abuse. Finally, a handbook addressing all three stages of rescuing yourself, finding strength, and finding your new life. This handbook will help you go from victim to successful survivor!

—Kelly Keiser, Survivor

Domestic violence is the most silenced and misunderstood epidemic of our time. An astounding 35 percent of women will at some point in their lives experience domestic violence, sexual assault, and/or stalking. Countless more experience verbal, emotional, and financial abuse. It takes great bravery for a woman to break the bonds and make a new, peaceful life for herself and her children. In this groundbreaking, all-encompassing handbook, Charlene Quint explains in plain language how to identify the signs of abuse, how abusers use power and control, what to expect when a woman leaves an abuser, practical steps to take, and how to escape while maintaining her safety and sanity. It also helps the victim in her journey to healing, taking her life back, and being all that she is designed to be. It is an invaluable resource for every woman escaping abuse, as well as the counselors, lawyers, and clergy who serve them.

—Pat Davenport, CEO and Executive Director of A Safe Place, Zion, Illinois

In this most comprehensive work, Charlene Quint helps us recognize the vast and diverse dimensions of domestic violence. Her book provides a handbook for survivors, victims, perpetrators, counselors, lawyers, and pastoral ministers to help them understand the multifaceted dynamics of domestic violence and how to respond appropriately. Her extensive and insightful commentary on sacred Scripture dispels distortions often used to justify abuse of women. This is an extraordinary contribution to the literature on domestic violence.

—Fr. Charles Dahm, OP
Director of Domestic Violence Outreach, Archdiocese of Chicago

This handbook is an incredible source of information that combines research about abuse and abusers, with a biblical foundation, firsthand accounts, and practical guidance for victims of abuse and for those who seek to provide help. It will be of great help for victims, for church leaders, and for all those who seek to understand the dynamics of abuse so that those who suffer can find safety and support.

—Steve McMullin, PhD,
Academic Dean and Director of ADC New Brunswick,
Sheldon and Marjorie Fountain Professor, Acadia Divinity College, Acadia University, Nova Scotia

This book is amazing. It's everything that a woman seeking to escape an abusive relationship will need to know. This is the one book to have when dealing with a domestic violence situation. Whether you are a counselor, medical professional, clergy, friend, family member, or target of the abuse, this is the one book that will help to clarify the situation and provide a roadmap to a better life. It instructs, educates, encourages, guides, and provides comfort and hope to women who find themselves in an abusive situation. It's a godsend.

—Susan Bacharz Guenther, LCPC, BC-TMH
Founder, Counseling for Transitions, Evanston, IL

The impact of domestic violence (intimate partner violence) on our families, children, and spouses (or intimate partners) continues to be among the leading cause of violent crimes. Spiritual leaders are known to be one of the first who receive a call for help from the person suffering from domestic violence. Ms. Quint has done a wonderful job by arming the readers with critical information to be the light in darkness on a difficult topic. This book is what spiritual leaders need to assist broken, afraid, confused, and hurt partners in finding their way to physical, emotional, and spiritual safety. All pastors, church leaders, ministers, rabbis, clergy, and other leaders who have dedicated their lives to help the hurting need this book.

—Rev. Peonita Harris, PsyD, LMFT, CSAT, CDWF
Executive Director, Cornerstone Counseling Center of Chicago

I first met Charlene Quint at a fundraiser for a domestic violence organization. We formed an instant sisterhood, having shared similar histories of abuse, escape, and recovery. Shortly after, I had the opportunity to hear her speak at an event. As I listened to her share her powerful truth, my heart was filled with inspiration and respect for her strength, her spirit, her faith, and her true passion for helping other women in similar circumstances—and there are many.

When you're trapped in an abusive relationship, it's like living in thick fog. Oftentimes you don't even recognize where you are and are unable to see a way out. This book helps change all of that and is truly unlike any other I've read on the topic. It first helps readers recognize and identify abuse and understand the thought processes of the abuser. It then goes on to provide practical information about safety planning, managing finances, finding legal assistance, and getting the emotional support essential to successfully getting through the journey of overcoming abuse.

The specific, practical advice that Charlene gives in this book alone makes it the one guide to recognizing and escaping abuse that every woman who is concerned about her well-being should have. But it goes even further, discussing the spiritual and emotional implications of abuse and divorce. She gives readers strength by reminding us of the spiritual armor God has given all of us and dispelling some myths surrounding abuse and divorce in the church. Quint provides inspiration, hope, and healing to allow women not only to remove themselves from abusive situations successfully, but to go on to live a life of joy, fulfillment, and recovery. I wish that a guide like this had existed when I went through my own journey. It is a must-read for all women who know they need help and for those who are wondering if their relationship is healthy or safe. I am truly grateful to Charlene Quint for all she does to help women overcome abuse, and I am certain this book will help and change the lives of so many.

—State Representative Joyce Mason, 61st District, IL

If you are pastor, you have people in your care who have been impacted by domestic abuse—the statistics show that this is universally true. This book will not only give you the tools to respond in God-honoring ways, but will also change your heart regarding this issue (which is too often ignored in the Christian subculture) and will pave the way for making your faith community a place of healing for victims.

—Rev. Christopher Stephens, Senior Pastor, Gurnee Community Church, Gurnee, IL

In this book, Charlene Quint has masterfully described and illustrated the experiential results of the violation of God's design through domestic abuse. Yes, it's tragic that this book is needed, but the fact of the mat-

ter is that the need is desperate because the tragedy is so large. Victims of domestic abuse desperately need the emotional, relational, psychological, financial, familial, legal, and scriptural help this book offers. My hope is that the church and society at large will hear it and stand in support of the victims. God calls us to it.
—Richard E. Averbeck, PhD, Professor of Old Testament and Semitic Languages,
Trinity Evangelical Divinity School, Deerfield, Illinois
Licensed Professional Counselor

Praise from Survivors for Charlene Quint:

Thank you for all the ways you have used your beautiful voice to extend healing and encouragement to so many! You are making a huge impact on so many lives! Keep shining! —J.Z.

Charlene, you are a most excellent friend! Beautiful and courageous and wise, and you speak truth and love, and you are truly an inspiration. I'm so thankful for you! You are an example of a woman of God. I know God gave me your voice, and you have helped me tremendously! Thank you! —L.M.

You are an amazingly strong woman. You give us all courage to know that we can make it. Also, you let us know that there is hope in Christ and hope to find true love in a relationship. —R.R.

Dear Charlene, thank you so much for guiding me to this group. I know God has used you for that and will use you for so much more! I gain so much from sharing in our group, and I hope I also can offer help and support to the other members. God Bless! —L.G.

Your strength and bravery shine through when you talk. I appreciate you stating truth so clearly. —Anonymous

You continue to inspire me! Thank you for all you do. —J.M.

For too long, women have not been heard or believed if they dared to speak their truth to the power of men. Thank you for helping me to voice my truth. —T.A.

You have a wonderful heart to serve others and to deliver God's blessings. May the light of Christ grow ever stronger within you . . . to bring hope to the hopeless and healing to the brokenhearted, in Jesus's name. You are a treasure! —A.A.

Thank you so much for your kindness, and I thank God for you too! God bless you, Charlene! —H.K.

Thank you very much. . . . The support you've given me is immeasurable. Thank you so much for everything! I pray God rains His blessing down upon you. I am truly grateful for you. —C.C.

You are such an inspiration and an example to many. Thank you for the many ways you have helped me. —R.R.

Your choice to live in freedom and bring others out of oppression is by far the clearest expression of the heart of the Father I have seen in a long time. So blessed to be with you. —N.D.

Dear Charlene, I thank God for you! You are my beautiful teacher and display God's love, strength, joy, and beauty each moment. You are walking love and a warrior for all of us and Him. You are making such a difference in my life and in many people. . . . I pray that God will always bless you and protect you. —H.K.

Charlene, I love your fighting spirit and your desire to show others the path to freedom. Stay strong. —K.K.

You have endured so much, yet you've proven that nothing can bring you down. I absolutely look up to you—you are such a voice for others. Never lose the positivity. —H.N.

Your spirit and strength is such an inspiration. Thank you for being a guide. I'll always appreciate you. —C.C.

Freedom, truth, and strength, all encompassed with God's grace. Thank you for sharing and shining on me. —D.G.

You have been a huge inspiration. A beautiful example of grace and a godly life. I learn so much from you and I'm so thankful for you! We are free—free at last! —L.M.

"Free woman" is so very apt for you. Thank you for your brace and enduring help for me and all of us. You are truly living your calling with grace and inspiration. —S.M.

You're such an inspiration to me! Your grace and spiritual life help me learn through the words of the Bible. Thank you for that gift. I am so happy to be able to celebrate my freedom with you. —K.K.

Your heart, your mind, and your spirit always draw me nearer to the Father! What a blessing you are to me! —N.D.

Whenever you share the victory in your story, I get so encouraged and validated from a Christian perspective. Thank you for sharing your story and your wisdom. —M.R.

Climbing off the abusive ledge as despair and anxiety try to keep you there has only been made possible by the unconditional love and guidance of Charlene and Chris. Amazing vessels sent by the Lord! —J.A.

Charlene, you are truly amazing! —K.B.

Endorsements for Speaking Engagements by Charlene Quint:

Renowned speaker and domestic violence survivor Charlene Quint spoke about her very real and courageous journey as an abused spouse and is a heroic role model for others. She serves as a beacon of hope for so many. I'm grateful she is willing to share her story and not only provide hope for survivors, but help them find the needed services so that they may be able to say that they, too, survived and moved on safely and successfully. It was an honor to be in her presence. Thank you, Charlene Quint. —Highland Park, IL, City Councilman

Charlene, on behalf of the Lake County Rising Committee and the Lake County State's Attorney's Office, thank you for sharing your story with the Lake County community. Your words were a blessing for those who heard you, and more than one woman was put on a path to healing because of your willingness to share your experience. I know you will continue to positively impact many lives. —S.B., Lake County State's Attorney's Office

Thank you for your support of the Highland Park-Highwood Legal Aid Clinic and women in need of guidance. You are an inspiration. —Highland Park-Highwood Legal Aid Clinic

Wow! Way to go Charlene! With three daughters, this is an issue that gives me grief/worries, no matter what talks we have! My girls are strong, but still I have seen this so many times. . . . Keep on! —M.M.

Such important education about these communities. . . . Your bravery and story are inspiring and will change lives. —B.R.

Charlene, they picked a wonderful speaker. Keep bringing the message of truth! —D.S

Thanks, Charlie, for using the gifts God gave you. You really are making a difference! —J.B.

I . . . experienced a whole range of emotions. Anger, shock, and sadness that someone I grew up with was subjected to such abuse. . . . I'm thankful that God gave you the courage to escape, protected you, and called upon you to go public with your story. . . . I have great admiration and respect for the brave, articulate woman you have become and for the way you are using your education, talents, and experiences to help others. You are doing God's work. . . . May He continue to bless you! —V.V.

Your courage, honesty, and forthrightness are an inspiration. You would most likely say, "It is all God—He gets the glory." However, you said "yes" to the assignment He has given you! . . . Through your sharing, others have gained hope and courage. —C.P.

So proud of everything that you do, Charlene, and the amazing person that you are. —K.P.

You give so much to so many! Special, special lady. —R.R.

Amazing woman with an amazing message! —J.A.

Raising awareness is key to our whole society evolving. Keep on keepin' on! I support your efforts wholeheartedly. I now understand that abuse sneaks up on the victim slowly and gradually, and the abuser oftentimes is very charismatic and manipulative and able to lie so well that he may present himself as innocent. However, you are right—if you present yourself as the victim, you should be believed and protected within the church. —J.T.

This is all truth! I appreciate you sharing all of this. —C.A.

Way to go, Charlene. Turned what you endured into helping our society as a whole. May God bless you! —J.T.

Thank you for your courage. If every time you share your story and it delivers at least one person from living in that hell . . . —J.S.

Your courage gives others strength and hope. —J.F.

God is certainly using you and using your suffering to bless others. —J.B.

Wow! Phenomenal! —S.L.

Thanks for your witness and advocacy. Grace and peace to you. —L.R.

Thank you for all you're doing! —S.V.

Awesome presentation. . . . So proud of you for standing tall and bringing much-needed attention to this. You are God's warrior. —K.M.

I count it a privilege to know you as a friend and warrior for this epidemic. —G.M.

Fabulous! —B.M.

Amazing person with an amazing message! —B.B.

You are amazing—thank you for what you do. You rock. —B.M.

Thank you, Charlene Quint, for all that you are doing to bring light to a dark subject and to share hope with so many hurting souls. —C.A.

You did a fantastic job! Thanks for making a positive impact and changing lives! —L.D.

I'm proud of you for sharing your message and sharing hope. Blessings. —E.M.

It was awesome. . . . This girl has spirit. —E.R.

Praise for Charlene Quint from University Students:

Charlene Quint . . . personified using your experience, as well as healing. What first stood out about her was her vulnerability in sharing her trauma. . . . By talking about her abuse to other women, she helped them take the first step to share what they were going through and seek help. Especially considering that she is a person of faith, and abuse is often stigmatized and considered private in the religious realm, being open about her experiences was likely all the more difficult for her, and impactful for others going through the same thing. Beyond the incredible strength she displayed by sharing her experiences, creating a law firm to fight domestic abuse and writing a comprehensive book about abuse is using the resources she uniquely has—namely, education to advocate for others who do not have a voice. Charlene Quint turned her personal healing into advocacy and action. —University Student

For the past year I have wanted to become a therapist, so when I started considering law school these past couple weeks, I knew I would want to focus on victims of domestic violence. Charlene Quint's experience only inspired me more to work with this population, and her book, with its two alternating covers, demonstrated the importance in providing as many resources as possible for these victims. —University Student

Personally, I was touched and inspired by the powerful experiences and hardships that our speakers . . . went through, particularly when Charlene Quint . . . spoke about her experiences surviving domestic abuse and leaving the private sector of law to start her own law practice representing survivors of domestic abuse. . . . It was inspiring to hear about these powerful women using the experiences they had been through as a catalyst of change to improve so many people's lives. . . . Hearing strategies about doing just that and how these powerful leaders decided on career changes or what their purpose in life is, following anger and grief, was inspiring and informative. —University Student

I was particularly inspired by Charlene Quint. . . . Hearing Charlene talk about her experience with domestic violence was deeply moving. From my own observation, I have found that people who get involved in politics because of a personal experience they have had are extremely committed to their goals and to helping others in similar situations. I thought it was inspiring to hear that Charlene is in the process of "writing the book she needed" when she was dealing with domestic violence. Many people who experience hardships allow themselves to be broken by the world—that is not the case with Charlene. Instead, she is using the pain she experienced in her own life to fuel her mission to heal others. Through her work, Charlene shows a remarkable ability to turn the darkest moments of her life into a positive force that helps many people like her. —University Student

There is a quote by Tarana Burke that I love and live by: "Trauma halts possibility; movement activates it." In our class on advocacy, I saw this quote demonstrated by Charlene Quint and our speakers. They discussed these traumas and adversities that they have experienced in their lives and how they turned their experience into action. This stood out to me because of the immense bravery it takes to do that and the power that lies in it. It is a great display of strength and resilience, and an inspiration, to bring good out of the worst things that have ever happened to you. . . . There is power in who we are and what we have overcome, and owning that power and using it for change is a force to be reckoned with. —University Student

One thing that really stood out to me was the [experience] that inspired Charlene Quint to take action. This stood out to me because she experienced firsthand what the people she is fighting for have experienced. She is coming from a place of honesty, truth, and experience when she defends victims of domestic abuse in court. It was really shocking to hear that she was left completely alone after she left her abusive husband. Even more shockingly, there were no government programs to help her. Instead of backing down and keeping quiet, Charlene Quint took her experience to make a change and ensure that no one would be abandoned by the court and government like she had been. I learned that it is essential to fight for your beliefs and that if you do so, impacting just one person's life is worth it. —University Student

Charlene Quint's personal story and her journey to the advocacy work she does now really moved me. Even just the mention that her book has an alternative cover presenting it as women's poetry, an issue I had never thought about in terms of seeking help while surviving domestic abuse, emphasized a point: those closest to the pain should be closest to the power. Charlene's lived experience informed her later career work and made her a better resource and advocate for domestic abuse survivors than anyone. Despite what she had been through, she was still able to acknowledge her privilege in having a law degree and a job that could support her outside of her abusive relationship. She turned her pain and newfound freedom into motivation to help others like her. There is nothing more inspiring and telling about resilience and commitment than a story like that. I teared up as she spoke, and she taught (or reminded) me to work from the heart. —University Student

The Comprehensive Handbook to
RECOGNIZE, REMOVE, and *RECOVER*
from *ABUSE*

OVERCOMING
THE NARCISSIST, SOCIOPATH, PSYCHOPATH, AND OTHER DOMESTIC ABUSERS

Charlene D. Quint,
J.D., C.D.V.P.

The Comprehensive Handbook to
RECOGNIZE, REMOVE, and *RECOVER*
from *ABUSE*

OVERCOMING
THE NARCISSIST, SOCIOPATH, PSYCHOPATH, AND OTHER DOMESTIC ABUSERS

Charlene D. Quint,
J.D., C.D.V.P.

ROMANS 8:28 BOOKS

© 2020 by Charlene D. Quint. All rights reserved.

Published by Romans 8:28 Books, an imprint of Redemption Press, PO Box 427, Enumclaw, WA 98022.

Toll-Free (844) 2REDEEM (273-3336)

Redemption Press is honored to present this title in partnership with the author. The views expressed or implied in this work are those of the author. Redemption Press provides our imprint seal representing design excellence, creative content, and high-quality production.

No part of this publication may be reproduced, stored in a retrieval system, or transmitted in any way by any means—electronic, mechanical, photocopy, recording, or otherwise—without the prior permission of the copyright holder, except as provided by US copyright law.

Nothing in this book is intended to provide legal advice or counseling advice. Rather, this book intends to describe generalities and provide general information. For legal advice specific to your situation, consult an experienced attorney licensed in your state. For counseling advice specific to your situation, consult an experienced licensed counselor, psychologist, or psychiatrist who is a Certified Domestic Violence Professional.

Unless otherwise indicated, all Scripture quotations are taken from the Holy Bible, New International Version®, NIV® Copyright ©1973, 1978, 1984, 2011 by Biblica, Inc.® Used by permission. All rights reserved worldwide.

Scripture quotations marked CEB are taken from the Common English Bible. © Copyright 2011 by the Common English Bible. All rights reserved. Used by permission.

Scripture quotations marked TPT are taken from The Passion Translation®. Copyright © 2017, 2018 by Passion & Fire Ministries, Inc. Used by permission. All rights reserved. ThePassionTranslation.com.

Scripture quotations marked KJV are taken from the Holy Bible, King James Version, Public domain.

Scripture quotations marked TLB are taken from The Living Bible copyright © 1971. Used by permission of Tyndale House Publishers, Inc., Carol Stream, Illinois 60188. All rights reserved.

Scripture quotations marked NASB are taken from the New American Standard Bible® (NASB), Copyright © 1960, 1962, 1963, 1968, 1971, 1972, 1973, 1975, 1977, 1995 by The Lockman Foundation. Used by permission. www.Lockman.org

Scripture quotations marked NKJV are taken from the New King James Version. Copyright © 1982 by Thomas Nelson, Inc. Used by permission. All rights reserved.

Scripture quotations marked NLT are from taken the Holy Bible, New Living Translation, copyright © 1996, 2004, 2015 by Tyndale House Foundation. Used by permission of Tyndale House Publishers Inc., Carol Stream, Illinois 60188. All rights reserved.

Scripture quotations marked NRSV are taken from the New Revised Standard Version Bible, copyright © 1989 the Division of Christian Education of the National Council of the Churches of Christ in the United States of America. Used by permission. All rights reserved.

Scripture quotations marked VOICE are taken from The Voice™. Copyright © 2008 by Ecclesia Bible Society. Used by permission. All rights reserved.

Scripture quotations marked WEB are taken from the World English Bible. Public Domain.

ISBN: 978-1-951310-00-4 (Hardback)
978-1-951310-06-6 (ePub)
978-1-951310-07-3 (Mobi)

Library of Congress Catalog Card Number: 2020906487

Contents

Acknowledgments ... xvii
Foreword by Neil Schori ... xix
Special Words from Dr. Richard E. Averback ... xxi
Poem—*Hero in an Invisible War* by Kim Karpeles ... xxiii
Introduction ... xxv
Poem—*The Battle Cry* by Charlene D. Quint ... xxviii

Part I. *Recognizing the Narcissist/Sociopath/Psychopath/Domestic Abuser*

Chapter 1. Myths and Realities of Abuse ... 31
Chapter 2. The Relationship between Domestic Abusers, Narcissists, Sociopaths, and Psychopaths ... 37
Chapter 3. The Three Phases of a Romantic Abusive Relationship ... 51
Chapter 4. The Cycle of Abuse within a Relationship ... 56
Chapter 5. The World according to the Narcissist, Sociopath, Psychopath, and Other Abusers ... 59
Chapter 6. Emotionally Healthy Relationships ... 67
Chapter 7. Emotional and Verbal Abuse ... 81
Chapter 8. Physical Abuse ... 158
Chapter 9. Financial Abuse ... 168
Chapter 10. Sexual Abuse ... 189
Chapter 11. Spiritual Abuse ... 200
Chapter 12. Other Annoying Attitudes and Behaviors of Abusers ... 219
Chapter 13. The Other Woman (and There's Always Another Woman) ... 233
Chapter 14. Confronting the Abuser and Conflict Resolution ... 236
Chapter 15. Counseling and Marriage Books ... 240
Chapter 16. Why Do They Do What They Do? ... 243

Part II. *Removing the Narcissist/Sociopath/Psychopath/Domestic Abuser from Your Life*

Chapter 17. Why Does She Stay? ... 249
Chapter 18. Realize that He Will Not Change and She Is Not the Problem ... 252

Chapter 19. What to Expect from the Abuser if She Stays in the Relationship 254
Chapter 20. What to Expect from the Abuser if She Leaves the Relationship 255
Chapter 21. What to Expect from Family, Friends when She Leaves. 265
Chapter 22. What to Expect from Children of the Abuser when She Leaves. 269
Chapter 23. Dealing with Parental Alienation and the Inevitable Harm to Children 273
Chapter 24. Co-Parenting with an Abuser 288
Chapter 25. Have a Safety Plan 290
Chapter 26. Have a Financial Plan 296
Chapter 27. Have a Legal Plan 300
Chapter 28. Have a Communication Plan 313
Chapter 29. Have a Spiritual and Emotional Support Plan. 322
Chapter 30. The Spiritual Battle. 326
Chapter 31. Redemption and The Spiritual Journey of the Exodus: From Bondage,
    Through the Desert, To the Promised Land. 336
Chapter 32. The Armor of God You Will Need for the Fight 344
Chapter 33. The Only Opinion That Matters Is God's 362
Chapter 34. What Does the Bible Really Say about Divorce from an Abuser?. 366
Chapter 35. Biblical Best Practices for the Church: How to Support the Victim
    and Hold the Abuser Accountable. 376
Chapter 36. The Most Common Mistakes that Churches and Pastors Make. 391

Part III. *Recovering from the Narcissist/Sociopath/Psychopath/Domestic Abuser*

Chapter 37. The Target of a Narcissist, Sociopath, Psychopath or Other Domestic Abuser 409
Chapter 38. Effects of Abuse on Women 413
Chapter 39. Effects of Abuse on Children. 419
Chapter 40. A New Perspective 423
Chapter 41. Lies about God and the Truth That We Are His Beloved. 426
Chapter 42. Lies That Get a Woman into Abuse and the Truth about Relationships. 438
Chapter 43. Lies that Keep a Woman in Abuse and the Truth That Sets Her Free. 445
Chapter 44. Lies That Inhibit Healing and the Truth That Heals 457
Chapter 45. Practical Steps Toward Healing 483
Chapter 46. Healing Our Children. 506
Chapter 47. New Relationships 526
Chapter 48. God Our Father, Rescuer, Redeemer, Deliverer, Warrior, Restorer, Healer,
    and Avenger 533
Chapter 49. Becoming the Woman God Designed You to Be. 548

What's Your Story? 559
Appendix. 561

Acknowledgments

I AM FIRST AND foremost grateful to Almighty God, who called me to write this book, and served as Author in Chief. Although I had known Him as Savior for many years, I now know Him as Rescuer, Redeemer, Deliverer, Warrior, Mighty to Save, Restorer, Teacher, and Healer.

This book is dedicated to the brave women who have made the decision to break the chains of abuse and start a new life of peace and love for themselves and their children. You have done the hardest job in the world. May God bless you and may this book guide you.

I am grateful to my husband, Chris, who shows me every day what the love of Jesus looks like. I am thankful to him for showing the world what a godly man looks like and for his unwavering support of this book and my work to help other women out of abuse.

I am thankful to my children and godchildren for the joy they bring and for making this world a better place.

I have grateful appreciation to A Safe Place, its CEO Pat D., therapist Nancy D., and all the staff for allowing me the privilege of walking beside women who are escaping abuse, helping them heal and watching them blossom. They are doing God's work.

I am appreciative for my Gurnee Community Church family and our Wednesday morning women's Bible study. Their love, support, countless prayers, and example of a healthy, Spirit-filled, vibrant family of believers has been a source of healing and inspiration.

I am indebted to the brave women and men who shared their stories here to help others who read this book find wholeness and healing. Thank you for being an inspiration to others: Brenda, Cathy, Charlotte, Darci, Donna, Denise, Dirk, Ellen, Hilary, Jane, Jan, Jennie, Jeannie, Joan, John, Julie, Kerry, Linda, Liz, Lori, Lydia, Madison, Maria, Natalie, Robin, Roberta, Sahira, Sally, Sherrie, and Tina. (Names have been changed to protect the survivors from their abusers.)

I am thankful for the countless prayers, words of encouragement, endorsements, and promotion of this book from hundreds of well-wishers, attorneys, domestic violence professionals, counselors, pastors, law enforcement, government officials, legislators, and survivors.

I am appreciative to Redemption Press and publisher Athena Dean Holtz for believing in this project, recognizing the need for this book, and encouraging me along the way.

I would be remiss without giving special recognition to Reverend Mike W., Steve and Lois W., Reverend David W., Garth W., Amy T. R. W., Jim and Kara M., F. L. and Judy K., Thomas V. K., Chad K., Diane W. H., Holy Cross Catholic Church of Deerfield, and Christ Church Lake Forest for opening my eyes to abusers and their loyal supporters in the church, in families, and in friends. Without the tireless efforts of the individuals listed in this paragraph, this book would never have been written.

Foreword

by Neil Schori

In 2007, even though I was still relatively new to pastoral ministry, I was pretty convinced that I had "seen it all." As the counseling pastor for a large church in the Chicago suburbs, I learned a lot about people, and I really began to believe that I had lost my ability to be surprised by the issues that plague humanity. All of my naïveté was shattered when Stacy Peterson told me at a coffee shop that her husband, Drew Peterson, had killed his previous wife, Kathleen Savio. Two months later, Stacy disappeared, and as of the time of my writing, she has not been found.

I knew nothing about domestic violence at the time, but I understood that had to change. I didn't know where to go to learn about it. Domestic violence isn't a subject that is discussed in seminaries, and divorce is often discouraged in traditional evangelical churches. So I prayed. Two years later, God answered my prayer in the form of a whirlwind named Susan Murphy-Milano. Susan challenged me in all the right ways, and before she died in 2012, she asked me to continue her legacy of helping victims and educating religious leaders on how to be safe spaces for victims.

I've been blessed beyond words by each victim I've helped and through each church that has expressed curiosity in how to change their cultures in a way that takes burdens off victims instead of continue down paths committing the typical "institutionally friendly" actions that further victimize the (already) victims of domestic violence.

Four years ago I was asked by A Safe Place, an amazing domestic violence shelter in the Chicago suburbs, to speak at a symposium. It was there that I met Charlene Quint. Charlene wears her faith in Jesus on her sleeve in an incredibly encouraging way. She's the opposite of a Bible thumper. She lives what she believes in powerfully authentic ways and serves her community as an attorney and as a volunteer at A Safe Place.

Charlene is a wealth of information when it comes to faith, the law, and loving people well. Even though she's quite learned, I'm certain that her most useful knowledge comes from the pain of the personal experience of being a longtime victim of domestic violence herself, at the hands of her ex-husband. Charlene has allowed God to transform the pain in her life in a way that will set many victims of abuse free.

There are a number of great books out there about the dynamics of domestic violence, but I've yet to read one that is more complete than this one. Charlene artfully weaved together a huge amount of information that needs to be read in parts to assimilate the jewels of life-change that she has learned.

What makes this book different? It is more comprehensive than any book I've read on domestic violence. Charlene recognizes that people are complex, so in this book she addresses the whole person (psychologically, physically, and spiritually). In chapters 1 and 2, you'll get an intro into what domestic violence is and you'll learn the connection between personality disorders and abuse. It's both eye-opening and alarming, and is a must-read for victims who have been praying and waiting for their abusers to change.

Chapters 3 and 4 speak to the cycle of abuse that is designed by abusers to keep their victims feeling off-balance and confused. If you're in a relationship that one day might seem like rainbows and unicorns and then the next day is like walking on eggshells, you'll probably see yourselves in those chapters. Don't resist it, and don't ignore the signs!

Chapter 17 asks and answers the ever-present and just-beneath-the-surface-question, Why does she stay? Charlene lists ten significant reasons that victims stay with their abusers. Number 4 is basically "her faith." It's a devastating truth that people of any faith need to wrestle with and come to conclusions that aren't harmful to the very people that faith should work for instead of against.

Chapter 25 is essential for victims of abuse to read before they leave their abusers. Charlene realistically details the particular danger that exists for victims once they finally decide to leave. This chapter is not a one-size-fits-all kind of safety planning chapter. Charlene goes into necessary and painstaking detail to speak to the differing realities that victims of abuse may experience.

Chapter 30 takes a magnificent turn to address the spiritual battle that exists in every single case of abuse. Charlene represents the Bible well and challenges the reader to look beneath the surface to see that abuse is driven by one: the Enemy of our souls, Satan himself. The remaining chapters do an amazing job of exposing the lies that abuse victims often hear that shape their views of themselves and that keep them entrapped for years after their abusers have moved on to other prey.

Charlene ends the book in the same way she started it: with a finesse in tandem with simple and practical ways to heal. This book has the wisdom in it to change how advocates help people of faith. It has the depth to challenge the most seasoned expert in the field of domestic violence. It has the gentleness that beckons the reader into an immersive experience and the boldness to challenge existing structures of abuse advocacy.

As a domestic violence victim advocate, I'm thankful to know Charlene and to add this book to my list of incredible resources that I'm confident will inform and even reframe my advocacy efforts for the rest of my life.

With Gratitude,

Neil Schori
Senior pastor, The Edge Church, Aurora, Illinois; advocate for domestic abuse victims;
Former pastor to Stacy Peterson (fourth wife of convicted murderer and former Bolingbrook, Illinois, police sergeant Drew Peterson)

Special Words

from Dr. Richard E. Averbeck

This is a very important book, but it is so terribly sad that the author had to write it. Domestic abuse is a plague on the human condition that disrupts our world and our lives. As the narrative goes in Genesis 2, God created the woman and designed marriage in response to the man's need for a companion (v. 18). He would be attracted to her as one who was his match in every way (v. 23). He would leave his family of origin and make another one with this woman, whom he would cherish as his treasured partner (v. 24). They would be fully intimate with one another, with nothing to cover up physically, emotionally, or spiritually (v. 25).

This was God's original design for marriage, and it is still His plan for us even today in the relationship between the man and the woman. According to Ephesians 5, if we live as people filled by the Spirit of God (vv. 18–20), we will submit to one another because of our reverence for Christ (v. 21). This is a spiritual matter at the core of our human spirit. This submission to one another issues in a call for the woman to submit to her husband in their marital life, showing him respect as the head of her and the household as Christ is the head of the church (vv. 22–24, 33). The call extends also to the husband, who is to give himself up for his wife as Christ gave Himself up for the church. The husband is to do everything in his power to support the shining forth of her manifold beauty to the world (vv. 25–31, citing Genesis 2:24).

Domestic abuse is a calamity of immense proportions that mutilates individuals, people, families, communities, societies, and the entire world of human relationships. It has done so since the fall into sin in Genesis 3, and we see its ugly face and effects at all levels of society today. Before the fall, the man and woman were both naked and had no shame (Genesis 2:25). After it, they felt ashamed of their nakedness, and covered up, hid, and blamed everyone but themselves for what had happened (Genesis 3:7–13). We feel the effects of the fall into sin most powerfully in the damage to our relationship with God and the relationship between men and women.

How is a woman supposed to respect a man who takes neither her nor God's design for marriage seriously? Yes, women can violate the design, but as a man, I am deeply disturbed about how much domestic abuse flows from the man to the woman. It seems that men, especially particular kinds of men, are prone to abuse their physical, financial, emotional, mental, relational, and other powers to destroy rather than elevate the woman whom

God wants them to cherish. As men, in the church and in the world as a whole, we are responsible to step up and stand up against this tragic evil in the world.

In this book, Charlene Quint has masterfully described and illustrated the experiential results of the violation of God's design through domestic abuse. Yes, it is tragic that this book is needed, but the fact of the matter is that the need is desperate because the tragedy is so large. Victims of domestic abuse desperately need the emotional, relational, psychological, financial, familial, legal, and scriptural help this book offers. My hope is that the church and society at large will hear it and stand in support of the victims. God calls us to it.

Richard E. Averbeck, PhD
Professor of Old Testament and Semitic Languages
Trinity Evangelical Divinity School, Deerfield, Illinois
Licensed Professional Counselor

POEM

Hero in an Invisible War

When she hears the garage door open,
Her hackles start to rise,
'Cause what's coming through that door,
Is always a surprise.

If she's in the kitchen
Cooking up a meal,
She knows the knives are handy,
Though she's fighting what she feels.

The news plays in the background,
She wishes their eyes could see,
'Cause if something were to happen,
They'd know who to believe.

Every survivor has a story worth telling,
A tale others need to hear;
When she finds the courage to share,
She's a hero in an invisible war.

Today was a good day,
Someone else stoked his fires;
She won't have to replace what's missing,
And lets out a small sigh.

Last week he came home empty,
And she was the one he could blame;
When you're perfect like he thinks he is,
Somebody else must shoulder his shame.

Every survivor has a story worth telling,
A tale others need to hear;
When she finds the courage to share,
She's a hero in an invisible war.

Compliant on the outside,
But there's something deep within,
Where his need for control can't reach her,
A place where he can't win.

Poem

He should know he doesn't own her;
He thinks she'll stay and try,
Even when his eyes turn black
And anger fuels his fires.

The few she's told don't believe her,
"No, he's too great a guy;
If he acts that way,
I need to see with my eyes."

Every survivor has a story worth telling,
A tale others need to hear;
When she finds the courage to share,
She's a hero in an invisible war.

The boxes were taped and loaded
With her half of the stuff;
Not much for the decades she'd spent, but
She knew it'd be enough.

She backed her car out slowly,
Pulled in front of the van,
Pressed the garage door button,
Wishing she could make it slam.

Her fight for freedom not over,
More battles for another year,
But the house filled with surprises,
Was now in her rearview mirror.

Every survivor has a story worth telling,
A tale others need to hear;
When she finds the courage to share,
She's a hero in an invisible war.

Kim Karpeles

INTRODUCTION

WOMEN IN TOXIC RELATIONSHIPS are desperate for answers. Why is he so mean? What just happened here? Why don't all the marriage books I have read work? Can our marriage be saved? I know he's high maintenance and has a strong personality, but he hasn't hit me, so this really isn't abuse, right? Will he change if we go to counseling? The counselor called him a narcissist—that can be cured, right? What happened to the Prince Charming I knew when we were dating? Why did he change after the wedding? Will Prince Charming ever come back? Is all this my fault? Why can't he just be nice? If I am nicer to him, he'll reciprocate, right? Why does he call me names and rage when he is mad? Will he hurt me again? Will he ever add me to his bank account, or will I always be on an allowance and have to give him receipts of everything I buy? Why does he make me feel like a prostitute instead of a wife when we have sex? Does the Bible really say I have to submit to his every whim? Does God command me to stay in this awful marriage? Am I the only one going through this? Are all the other husbands the same? Does he even love me? Has he *ever* loved me? Is it better to stay for the kids even if he is abusive to me, or should I get out so they don't see a dysfunctional marriage? If I file for divorce, how do I get out safely? Where would I go since I have no money? How do I ensure that the breakup of our marriage doesn't disrupt my kids' lives? What is he going to do to me if I leave? Will he treat me better if I leave? How do I find a good lawyer? Will my church and friends support me if I leave? I don't want a divorce, but I can't stay here much longer; what should I do? Now he's hurting the kids. Should I stay to protect them, or should I leave and hope he doesn't get custody? Don't they need a dad in their lives? How do I move on with my life? I know he's bad for me, so why does it hurt so much to leave? Why do I miss him? Will I ever find true love? I am afraid of the future. I feel so broken—will I ever heal? I used to be strong and confident; now I don't even know who I am—what happened to me? Will I ever be happy again? Did God send me this abuse? Is God mad at me?

This comprehensive handbook is designed to help women in abusive relationships find the answers they need and to help the counselors and pastors who serve them provide wise counsel and guidance. Organized into three sections, this book will help women recognize the signs and tactics of abuse, remove themselves safely from their abuser, and recover from abuse. I call these the "3 Rs" of abuse every woman needs to know. The book walks women through the entire process of (1) identifying abusers and abuse in all its forms; (2) escaping from abuse by being forearmed with the knowledge of what to expect from abusers and others, and how to devise plans to leave safely with as little damage as possible; and (3) healing from abuse, and building a new, abundant life.

Many women in abusive marriages do not even know what a healthy relationship looks like. She might have known a normal relationship prior to meeting her abuser, but after years of gaslighting, projection, and her abuser telling her his abuse is normal, she no longer recognizes a healthy relationship or that she is in an abusive one. For this reason, in addition to describing different forms of abuse and the characteristics of an abuser, this book also defines healthy relationships as well as healthy men and women.

Many women in abusive marriages read dozens of marriage books and waste thousands of dollars on marriage counseling only to spend years or even decades with an abuser who will not change. If you are in an abusive relationship, throw out your marriage books and fire your marriage counselor. Marriage books and marriage counseling only work for two emotionally healthy people with goodwill toward each other who want the best for their marriage and each other. Abusers are not emotionally healthy. They do not hold goodwill for their spouse, and they do not care about their marriage or their spouse, except to the extent they serve the abuser's selfish needs. Marriage books don't work for abusers. The American Psychiatric Association and domestic abuse organizations discourage marriage counseling with abusers. Women in abusive marriages need straight, no-nonsense, honest information that explains what they are dealing with, how to get out, and how to rebuild their lives. The choice to stay or leave a toxic relationship is always theirs. This book gives them the information they need to make an informed decision.

Women of faith, in particular, struggle with abusive marriages, abusers, and divorce. They often experience a great deal of guilt in an abusive marriage, and even greater guilt if they leave. Many Christian women do not even recognize their difficult marriages as abusive. This book speaks directly to women of faith. It examines what God, through Scripture, says about abuse and abusers, how to respond to people who abuse, and divorce in abusive relationships. Importantly, we discuss how to heal and become the woman God designed you to be.

Pastors and church leaders also struggle with the proper response when domestic abuse occurs in their congregations. This book is designed to help them know what the Bible says about domestic abuse and offers biblical best practices to address domestic abuse in a congregation, support the victim, and hold the abuser accountable. Domestic abuse is evil. The church needs to call domestic abuse what it is and stand up against evil, while implementing church discipline to call the abuser to repentance.

Interspersed among the descriptions and explanations are stories of real women who have overcome abuse. Their examples bring the text to life. Many women feel alone in their struggles until they talk with other women going through similar experiences. They are often surprised to discover that other abusers behave in the same way as their spouse or partner. I joke that all abusers use the same Abuser's Handbook. While a woman is in an abusive marriage, her abuser's actions can seem confusing and unexpected. However, once a woman knows who she is dealing with, abusers are surprisingly predictable.

Our main character is Charlotte, who was married for more than twenty years to a financially successful businessman in the North Shore of Chicago. They had two children together, and each had children from prior marriages. Charlotte's husband is an equal-opportunity abuser, and thus used every type of abuse, including financial, emotional and verbal, physical, sexual, and spiritual abuse.

Through their common connections with a local domestic abuse organization, we are also introduced to women who became friends with Charlotte: Kerry, Sahira, Hilary, Liz, Lydia, Sherrie, Denise, Jane, Lori, and others. The stories of two men who have been victims of abuse, Dirk and John, are also included. (All names

INTRODUCTION

have been changed to protect the survivors of abuse.) These ladies and gentlemen come from all walks of life and were married to their respective abusers for between one year and thirty years. I am eternally grateful to these brave men and women for sharing their stories so others can learn, find hope, and heal. Tragically, even during the short time that I have been writing this book, several people associated with these victims have been killed or committed suicide due to domestic abuse. One abuser took his own life, another abuser committed a murder-suicide, and one victim took her own life.

    Most importantly, this book is designed to help women heal. Healing occurs primarily through getting to know God, rejecting the lies of Satan, and replacing them with the truth of God. I am grateful to God for His gentle, and not-so-gentle, urgings to write this book. And I am beyond privileged to be able to walk with you on your journey of healing and becoming the woman God designed you to be. God wants an abundant, extraordinary, uncommon, vibrant, overflowing life for you. He designed you to be a lioness because your Daddy is the Mighty Lion of Judah. He created you to be His princess warrior, fighting evil and bringing light to the darkness, because you are the daughter of the King of Kings, mighty to save. He formed you to be a victor, not a victim. God is a redeemer, and He is on a rescue mission for *you* to take you out of the bondage of abuse and into freedom. Now let's get after it.

POEM

The Battle Cry

Wondrously and wonderfully you are made:
A precious gift, a priceless treasure.
A beautiful spirit, a contagious smile,
Loveliness without measure.

You fight an unseen fight
In a battle you did not choose.
Expect a miracle! Banish fear and doubt!
For this battle you shall not lose!

You shall conquer the foe and defeat this enemy.
You shall finish as you have started:
Indomitable, Unbeatable and Undefeatable,
Courageous and Lion-hearted!

Hope and Faith are on your side,
And Peace and Laughter and Love.
God Almighty shall break your chains
And heal you with His hands from above.

May you arise better and stronger
When this battle is done.
A fearless warrior forged in the fire,
Victorious as the war is won!

Charlene D. Quint

Part I

Recognizing the Narcissist/Sociopath/Psychopath/ Domestic Abuser

The first "R" of the "3 Rs" of an abusive relationship is recognizing the abuse and the abuser. Many women, particularly women of faith, are unable to identify abusers or abusive behaviors, and therefore do not even recognize they are in an abusive relationship. In Part 1, we dive into the details of the tactics abusers use and the characteristics of narcissists, sociopaths, psychopaths, and other domestic abusers.

CHAPTER 1

Myths and Realities of Abuse

Domestic abuse is the most denied, silenced, and misunderstood issue facing the church and society today. We choose to believe myths rather than facts to make ourselves feel better about the scourge of domestic abuse. Our legal system, local communities, family units, social networks, employers, and even our local churches overwhelmingly support the abuser rather than the victim.

Of course, no one says out loud, "I support the abuser. I approve of the fact he abuses his wife and children." That would be social suicide. We support them in a more insidious fashion. When a woman comes forward to expose the abuse she has endured, often for decades, no one wants to admit their friend, relative, coworker, client, or fellow church member is an abuser. No one wants to admit there's an abuser in their close-knit circle. That would reflect poorly on them. After all, abusers are charming and charismatic to outsiders, especially those whose favor they want to gain. Abusers look just like the rest of us—they don't generally look like Charles Manson, and they don't wear a big scarlet letter *A*. Most people simply don't want to believe the victim. What's more, if they did believe her, they would be compelled to do something. Who wants to be aligned with an abuser and rapist? If they had any moral compass, they would need to distance themselves from the abuser, terminate his employment, order supervised parenting time, remove him from the country club, and excommunicate him from the church. That kind of change takes courage and moral fortitude that, frankly, most people do not have. It is much easier to discredit the victim and accuse her of lying, mental illness, or having an affair.

After people deny the truth, they then silence the victim. "That's not a Christian thing to say. You need to stop casting aspersions on your husband." "If you can't say something nice, don't say it at all." "How dare you say something like that about my father!" "You need to forgive and forget." "No one believes you." "Saying things like that embarrasses the family. Stop it." "We don't limit who can attend church. Our church is open to everyone, including your husband, regardless of their background." "I don't see any bruises. This is normal stuff married people do. Your petition for an order of protection is denied."

Once the abuse is denied and the victim is silenced, the abuser is then embraced by the church, his family, social network, and employers, as well as the courts. Everyone can continue with their lives as if nothing had happened. The abuser is emboldened by the support of his community. Knowing he can get away with it, he escalates the abuse.

When domestic abuse is discussed, the image that often comes to mind is the video of NFL player Ray Rice punching out his then-girlfriend in the elevator and dragging her limp body into the lobby. We don't realize that many homicides and mass shootings are the direct result of years of domestic abuse and often occur when a victim tries to escape her abuser. Many churchgoers are under the misimpression that abuse consists only of hitting, stabbing, or shooting a wife or girlfriend. They believe abuse generally occurs in minority communities where the average person is poor, uneducated, unemployed, and unchurched. Churchgoers may be quite sure abuse doesn't occur in their congregation, and certainly not in white, middle- and upper-class communities where people are educated, employed, professionals, and live in lovely landscaped houses, drive fancy cars, wear designer clothes, attend church, and belong to the local country club. "It doesn't happen to people like me. It happens to those people," they tell themselves. Many pastors are ill-equipped to address domestic abuse when a woman seeks help. Too often pastors support the abuser by refusing to believe the victim or impose church discipline. The abuser is allowed to continue attending church, which then forces the victim out of her own fellowship. Many churches ignore the biblical directive to support the oppressed, to act righteously, and to speak up for those with no voice. Rather than providing a sanctuary for the mistreated sheep of the flock, the church becomes a haven for wolves.

Abuse is far more comprehensive, systematic, and calculated than most people imagine. More than simply hitting, stabbing, or shooting in a crime of passion, abuse is an inclusive set of behaviors and attitudes intentionally designed to gain and maintain power and control over others. Abusers are characterized by a lack of conscience, empathy, and remorse, and they use others for their own selfish needs. They have an insatiable need to dominate, especially over their wife or intimate partner.[1]

Domestic abuse encompasses a range of actions and attitudes, including emotional and verbal, financial, physical, sexual, and spiritual abuse. We will explore each in greater detail. The goal of all abuse is to damage another person's spirit. Thus, emotional and verbal abuse exists in all abusive relationships.[2] However, the abuse often begins with financial abuse, which is prevalent in 99 percent of abusive relationships.[3] The abuser's planning and manipulation, often spanning years, is malevolently brilliant and masterfully executed. He will often set up his diabolical financial planning and emotional manipulations twenty or more years in advance in anticipation of the inevitable divorce. Once an abuser has convinced a victim to relinquish her job, forego employment opportunities, give up on her education, and become financially dependent upon him, he has paved the way for financial abuse. Emotional and verbal abuse follow and inevitably escalate over time to physical abuse and sexual abuse.[4] When a woman values her faith and religious traditions, the physical and sexual abuse will also lead to spiritual abuse—that is, twisting the Scriptures to keep her in the abusive relationship.

Abuse is more rampant than most people imagine. While we may read of the occasional celebrity or corporate titan who has been accused of domestic abuse or sexual assault, far more abuse occurs among ordinary people whose bad behavior does not make the headlines. According to a recent survey conducted by the Center for Disease Control, an astounding 35 percent of women and 28 percent of men have experienced "rape, phys-

---

[1] "FAQ on Domestic Violence," National Center on Domestic and Sexual Violence (NCDSV), n.d. http://www.ncdsv.org/images/DV_FAQs.pdf.
[2] Adrienne Adams, "Measuring the Effects of Domestic Violence on Women's Financial Well-Being," Center for Financial Security, University of Wisconsin–Madison, CFS Research Brief 2011-5.6, https://cfs.wisc.edu/2011/05/01/adams2011/.
[3] Adams, "Measuring the Effects of Domestic Violence on Women's Financial Well-Being."
[4] Adams, "Measuring the Effects of Domestic Violence on Women's Financial Well-Being." According to the article, women suffer physical abuse in 98 percent of abusive relationships.

ical violence, and/or stalking by an intimate partner in their lifetime."[5] In addition to rape, physical violence, or stalking by an intimate partner, studies show that approximately 40 percent of women report verbal abuse, emotional violence, or coercive control by an intimate partner.[6] A recent survey indicates nearly half, 48 percent of women and a similar percentage of men, experience emotional abuse or coercive control in intimate relationships during their lifetime, including being called names like ugly, fat, crazy, or stupid; told they were a loser, a failure, or not good enough; witnessing a partner's dangerous anger; being insulted, humiliated, or made fun of; demanding to know the victim's whereabouts; making threats; and isolating the victim.[7] By way of comparison, the percentage of women who experience domestic abuse by an intimate partner is approximately equal to the percentage of people who will contract all forms of cancer combined! Domestic abuse against women is an epidemic. However, the scars are mainly unseen, and the victims are silenced and not believed; therefore, we don't recognize its widespread occurrence, support the victim, or search for a cure.

Contrary to popular thinking, domestic abuse permeates all races, ethnicities, religions, professions, educational levels, and socio-economic groups. Abuse occurs in all communities. Domestic violence is prevalent in affluent communities where power and money lead people to believe rules don't apply to them, as well as in lower-income communities. However, it is more likely to be kept silent in affluent communities—behind million-dollar homes and Porsches—because the stigma of abuse is hard to overcome, the women have no access to finances, and the powerful men behind the abuse will wreak havoc on the lives of those who dare to expose the truth.[8]

Sadly, domestic abuse is just as prevalent in the Christian and Jewish communities as in secular communities. Abuse occurs in nearly every congregation.[9] Unsurprisingly, some of the most abusive men are nominal Christians—that is, persons who claim to be Christian but who rarely or sporadically attend church.[10] In effect, these people are practical atheists—they claim to be Christian for the social or moral benefits of belonging to a group of believers, but they act in a way that proves they do not believe in a God who requires us to love others or who punishes sin. They also twist the Scriptures to justify their abuse and keep their wives in abusive marriages.

Predictably, Christian women stay in abusive relationships significantly longer than women of no faith.[11] Many Christian women don't even recognize they are in an abusive marriage. The church most often trains girls and young women to be kind, patient, giving and forgiving, selfless, unassertive, dependent, and deferring to male figures. However, we don't do a very good job of teaching our girls and women to see themselves as strong individuals made in God's image, daughters of the King of Kings, lionesses of the Lion of Judah, worthy of re-

---

[5] "Get the Facts & Figures," National Domestic Violence Hotline, n.d. https://www.thehotline.org/resources/statistics/;"Violence Prevention," Centers for Disease Control and Prevention. N.d., https://www.cdc.gov/violenceprevention/intimatepartnerviolence/index.html.

[6] M. M. Carney and J. R. Barner, "Prevalence of Partner Abuse: Rates of Emotional Abuse and Control." *Partner Abuse, 3*(3) (2012): 286–335, https://doi.org/10.1891/1946-6560.3.3.286.

[7] M. C. Black, et al., *The National Intimate Partner and Sexual Violence Survey (NISVS): 2010 Summary Report* (Atlanta, GA: National Center for Injury Prevention and Control, Centers for Disease Control and Prevention, 2011), https://www.cdc.gov/violenceprevention/pdf/nisvs_report2010-a.pdf.

[8] NCDSV, "Fact & Figures."

[9] https://www.gordonconwell.edu/blog/domestic-violence-in-the-church/. This footnote applies to both the first and second sentences of this paragraph.

[10] S. Tracey, "Patriarchy and Domestic Violence: Challenging Common Misconceptions," *Journal of the Evangelical Theological Society* 50/3 (September 2007): 573, n44.

[11] https://www.gordonconwell.edu/blog/domestic-violence-in-the-church/.

spect, capable of establishing healthy boundaries, discerning between good and evil, and lady warriors who fight for righteousness. It is little wonder abusers often target Christian women, whom they know will pray tirelessly for them, suffer in silence, and extend forgiveness for their abuse over and over again rather than call the abuse the evil it is and flee from it.

Despite the prevalence of domestic abuse in Christian congregations, the majority of clergy and congregational leaders—and even many counselors—admit they have not received adequate specialized training for responding to domestic abuse within their congregations.[12]

Many pastors simply deny that domestic abuse is a significant problem in the church worldwide and in their own congregations. In a recent Lifeway survey of Protestant pastors, about 75 percent said they know a friend, family member, or church member who has experienced domestic violence, and about 75 percent admit it's a problem in their community, but the same pastors don't believe it's a problem in their church. One of the best ways to let parishioners know the church is a safe place where victims of domestic abuse will be supported when they reach out for help is to preach about it. However, most pastors do not communicate from the pulpit or elsewhere that their church is a safe space for victims of abuse. Forty-two percent "rarely" or "never" address domestic violence from the pulpit, and 22 percent speak about it only once a year[13].

As one might expect, more than 90 percent of abusers who perpetrate the systematic, persistent, injurious violence that maintains control and power over another are men. Eighty-five percent of victims are women.[14] Although men also suffer from abuse, the effects of abuse on women are far more devastating. While we do not discount the fact that men can be the victims in abusive relationships, because the vast majority of victims are women, in this book we will use the gender pronoun *she* when referring to a victim and *he* when referring to an abuser.

The cost of domestic abuse in human lives and dollars is staggering. Each year in the US, domestic abuse is responsible for 2 million injuries, 1,300 deaths, and 5.3 million female intimate partner victims.[15] Every three years we lose more people to domestic violence than we did on September 11, 2001, when the planes hit the Twin Towers. Domestic violence is the leading killer of women worldwide. In 2017, 58 percent of female homicides in the world were caused by husbands, boyfriends, and other family members, making domestic abuse the most common killer of women.[16]

If they are not killed, abused women are more likely to develop severe health issues. Women have a higher

---

[12] "Pastors More Likely to Address Domestic Violence, Still Lack Training," LifeWay Research, Sept. 18, 2018, https://lifewayresearch.com/2018/09/18/pastors-more-likely-to-address-domestic-violence-still-lack-training/; Julia Baird and Hayley Gleeson, "How to Navigate the Research on Domestic Violence and Christian Churches: A Few Frequently Asked Questions," ABC News, updated October 5, 2017, https://www.abc.net.au/news/2017-07-24/how-to-navigate-the-research-on-domestic-violence/8738738.

[13] "Pastors Seldom Preach about Domestic Violence," LifeWay Research, June 27, 2013, http://lifewayresearch.com/2014/06/27/pastors-seldom-preach-about-domestic-violence/.

[14] Michael Kimmel, "Gender Symmetry in Domestic Violence, Violence Against Women," 8, no. 1 (Nov. 2002): 1332–1363, abstract available at https://www.ncjrs.gov/App/Publications/abstract.aspx?ID=198004.

[15] "Statistics," Hope for Domestic Violence, http://hope4dv.org/statistics/?view=mobile.

[16] *Global Study on Homicide: Gender-Related Killing of Women and Girls 2018*, United Nations Office on Drugs and Crime, 2018, https://www.unodc.org/documents/data-and-analysis/GSH2018/GSH18_Gender-related_killing_of_women_and_girls.pdf.

risk of serious health concerns, including, heart disease (70 percent), stroke (80 percent), asthma (60 percent),[17] depression, suicide, gastro-intestinal problems, neurological disorders, chronic pain, disability, anxiety, unintended pregnancy, miscarriage, stillbirth, HIV, STD's, and PTSD (post-traumatic stress disorder) due to prolonged exposure to stress and forced sex.[17]

Victims of domestic abuse collectively lose approximately eight million days of paid work per year. Domestic violence costs the US economy more than $8.3 billion, of which $5.8 billion is for medical and mental health services, and $2.5 billion is lost due to lower productivity.[18] Half of domestic abuse victims are harassed at their workplace by their abuser. Sixty-four percent of domestic violence victims have diminished ability to work due to domestic abuse, resulting in distraction, fear of discovery, harassment by their partner at work, fear of their partner's unexpected visits, inability to complete assignments on time, and job loss.[19] Over 80 percent of abuse victims report their jobs are negatively affected by abuse.[20]

Finally, we now know there is a strong correlation between domestic abuse and mass shootings. In the majority of mass shootings, the perpetrator had a history of violence against women.[21] On November 5, 2017, a man who had been convicted of domestic violence, had spent a year in prison, and had received a bad-conduct discharge from the military killed twenty-six people in the First Baptist Church of Sutherland Springs, Texas. The town of four hundred and a church community of fifty included the shooter's mother-in-law—a reminder that domestic abuse is everywhere and that the goal of an abuser is to destroy the partner who leaves him and everything she holds dear.[22]

An abusive marriage is a scary place for a woman. She may not recognize the abuse, but feels she needs to stay in the marriage. She may not know whether she should stay in a marriage and hope for the best or leave. She may want to believe her husband will change, as he has promised so many times before, but she now has a sick feeling he never will. She wonders why she still is attached to a man who has been so mean to her but can also be wonderfully nice when he wants to be. She remembers the early days when he swept her off her feet, and she wonders why those days are gone, and if they can ever come back. She wants to talk to her pastor or a counselor, but he seems unapproachable and perhaps has even told her she needs to stay in the marriage. She has seen how vindictive her husband has been to others, and wonders if she can ever escape safely. She is afraid of the future, but is more afraid she will lose her children to him. She is overwhelmed by the task before her, and she needs answers. She has no access to funds and cannot fathom how to get herself and her children out, find a safe home,

---

[17] Robert Pearl, "Domestic Violence: The Secret Killer that Costs $8.3 Billion Annually, *Forbes,* Dec. 5, 2013, https://www.forbes.com/sites/robertpearl/2013/12/05/domestic-violence-the-secret-killer-that-costs-8-3-billion-annually/#1bf20f1a4681.

[18] Pearl, "Domestic Violence."

[19] "Economic Impact of Domestic Violence," DomesticShelters.org https://www.domesticshelters.org/domestic-violence-statistics/economic-impact-of-domestic-violence#.WgXlvbpFw6Y.

[20] "How Does Domestic Violence Impact People at Work?" Canadian Labour, Oct. 22, 2019, https://canadianlabour.ca/uncategorized/how-does-domestic-violence0impact-people-work/

[21] "The Men Behind the US's Deadliest Mass Shootings Have Domestic Violence—Not Mental Illness—in Common," *Business Insider,* Aug. 5, 2019, https://www.businessinsider.com/deadliest-mass-shootings-almost-all-have-domestic-violence-connection-2017-11.

[22] Alex Horton, "The Air Force Says It Failed to Follow Procedures, Allowing Texas Church Shooter to Obtain Firearms, *The Washington Post,* Nov. 7, 2017, https://www.washingtonpost.com/news/checkpoint/wp/2017/11/06/the-air-force-says-it-failed-to-follow-procedures-allowing-texas-church-shooter-to-obtain-firearms/?noredirect=on&utm_term=.4d0c23278136.

keep the kids in school and continuing in their activities, pay for a lawyer, get or keep her job, keep her children fed with a roof over their heads, and somehow heal from the gaping wound in her heart.

Gentle reader, if this describes you, this book is for you. This book is designed to help women in domestic abuse learn how to recognize abuse and abusers, inform women of what they need to know to safely remove themselves from abuse, and equip them to recover, heal, and lead an amazing life. It is also designed to educate and equip clergy and counselors to better support victims of abuse and hold abusers accountable. God never meant for His beloved daughters to be held in the prison of abuse. He wants us to have a full, abundant life overflowing with love and joy. My prayer is that this book will guide you out of the chains of abuse and into freedom and lead you to be the woman God has designed you to be. The path will not be easy. The Enemy is at work trying to keep you chained. This is a spiritual battle from which no one goes unscathed. But God is on your side, and He will go with you and fight for you. God is on a rescue mission. Your rescue mission. There is no time to waste. Let's go.

CHAPTER 2

The Relationship between Domestic Abusers, Narcissists, Sociopaths, and Psychopaths

Abuse is perpetrated by someone who is neither normal nor emotionally healthy. Normal, emotionally healthy people have empathy, a moral compass, and a conscience, and they naturally protect, support, and nurture others. In fact, all mammals instinctively protect and support their families and members of their own communities. If abusers are neither normal nor emotionally healthy, then who are they? Can a domestic abuser be cured? Will he respond to treatment? Is it genetic or learned behavior? What characterizes an abuser? What am I dealing with?

Connection between Domestic Abuser and Cluster B Personality Disorders

The term *domestic abuser* is not a defined in the *Diagnostic and Statistical Manual* (DSM), a handbook published by the American Psychiatric Association (APA).[23] While *domestic abuser* is not a defined term in the DSM, the overwhelming majority of abusers have what the APA refers to as Cluster B personality disorders—in particular, narcissistic personality disorder and antisocial personality disorder (from where we get the terms sociopaths and psychopaths).[24] Research reveals that 80-90 percent of court-referred and self-referred wife abusers have one or more personality disorders, and that prevalence nears 100 percent as the violence becomes more severe and chronic.[25] The majority of abusers have not been diagnosed by a mental health professional. Narcissistic personality disorder and antisocial personality disorder are considered "dangerous and severe" and have impulsivity, emotional dysregulation, and violence in common. In layman's terms, the common characteristics boil down to lack of conscience (as evidenced by the lack of remorse or repentance when they have hurt, mistreated, or stolen from someone), lack of empathy (they don't care they have hurt someone's feelings), and using others for their own

---

[23] Mental health care professionals in the US and much of the world consider the DSM, with its descriptions, symptoms, and other diagnostic criteria, the authoritative guide for diagnosing mental disorders.
[24] "Your Recovery Starts Here," *Safe Relationships Magazine*, https://saferelationshipsmagazine.com/.
[25] Zlatka Rakovec-Felser, "Domestic Violence and Abuse in Intimate Relationship from Public Health Perspective," Health Psychology Research, 2014 Nov. 6; 2(3):1821, https://www.ncbi.nlm.nih.gov/pmc/articles/PMC4768593/

selfish needs. Psychologists have labeled the combination of narcissism (entitled self-importance), psychopathy and sociopathy (callousness and cynicism), and Machiavellianism (strategic exploitation and deceit) as the Dark Triad. Many people have multiple personality disorders. For example, many narcissists (whose main characteristics are grandiosity and lack of empathy) are also sociopaths (whose main characteristic is lack of conscience).[26] Frighteningly, up to 15 percent of the population has one or more personality disorders.[27] Essentially, these dark and dangerous people live among us and look like us, but we have no idea who they are until we find ourselves caught in their malevolent web.

Narcissistic personality disorder and antisocial personality disorder are considered untreatable[28] and incurable. For purposes of this book, we will use the term *SNAP* (i.e., Sociopaths, Narcissists, Abusers, and/or Psychopaths) for a person with one or more of these disorders, whether the disorder is diagnosed or not. We will use the term *abuser* for one who chooses to abuse others. The terms *SNAP* and *abuser* are often used interchangeably because so many abusers are also SNAPs. SNAPs don't see a need for treatment and do not see anything wrong with themselves. Most of them never seek treatment, and they only attend treatment when a spouse or partner gives them an ultimatum. Other mental illnesses, such as anxiety disorder or depression, negatively affect those who suffer from them, so much so that people with these disorders seek help to alleviate their suffering. A person with anxiety disorder seeks treatment to ease or eliminate the anxiety, and one suffering from depression seeks a mental health professional to lighten her outlook. However, SNAPs do not "suffer" from mental illness; rather, those around them suffer. SNAPs simply don't care about the devastating effects they have on others. Most mental illnesses are characterized by unintentional, unwanted behaviors and attitudes that negatively affect the person with the mental illness. For example, a person with depression does not want to be depressed, and a person with anxiety disorder does not want to be anxious. They are not intentionally trying to be depressed or anxious. However, narcissistic personality disorder and antisocial personality disorder are primarily characterized by intentional, dangerous behaviors and attitudes specifically designed to harm others. For example, a SNAP will intentionally dump a wife out of a car, and he will deliberately refuse to include a wife on a bank account to ensure she has no access to funds. He wants to be mean—in fact, he prides himself on being mean. These are purposeful behaviors. In spiritual terms, we would label them as sinful and evil. However, because the APA is a secular professional association, they must assign neutral labels or diagnoses.

We may be tempted to take pity upon those who have narcissistic personality disorder or antisocial personality disorder as someone who suffers from a mental disorder that they cannot help. This is a mistake. Unlike other mental illnesses that primarily affect the person with the mental illness, individuals with narcissistic personality disorder and antisocial personality disorder intentionally choose to harm their victims. Or, depending on what is most beneficial for their selfish goals, they will be on their best behavior with others. In other words, they exploit others and use people as objects to satisfy their own selfish ends.

For example, a SNAP may be cooperative with a boss he wants to impress, but he will sabotage a coworker's efforts when it would mean a promotion for himself. A SNAP can appear thoughtful and doting when dating a new girlfriend, but he will refuse to pay child support and alimony to a former wife of twenty-five years. A SNAP may feign an apology to entice a wife who has threatened to leave back into the relationship, but any positive

---

[26] *Diagnostic and Statistical Manual of Mental Disorders: DSM-5* (Arlington, VA: American Psychiatric Association, 2013) 661, 671.
[27] *Diagnostic and Statistical Manual of Mental Disorders: DSM-5*, 646.
[28] Empirical studies have shown that treatment of these personality disorders lacks clinical significance.

change in behavior will be short-lived. In other words, SNAPs choose when to appear good and when to be evil. Keep in mind: good people never try to appear evil, but evil people often try to appear good.

Below we will explore the characteristics of narcissists, sociopaths, and psychopaths as outlined in the DSM-5.

Antisocial Personality Disorder

Perhaps the most dangerous mental disorder is antisocial personality disorder, also known as sociopathy, psychopathy, or dissocial personality disorder.[29] In recent years, there's been confusion over terminology. Some psychiatrists diagnose one who has learned socially deviant behavior and acquired certain negative personality traits from his environment or early experiences as a sociopath, while others diagnose someone with socially deviant behavior and certain personality traits based on genetic, biological, and psychological factors as a psychopath. Thus, based on how the diagnosing psychiatrist views the origins and determinants of the disorder, the same person may receive a diagnosis of sociopath by one mental health expert and a diagnosis of psychopath by another. For purposes of this book, we will not make such a distinction. The terms *sociopath* and *psychopath* are used interchangeably in the mental health profession. Antisocial personality disorder is much more common in men than women[30] and is estimated to occur in approximately 4 percent of the population.[31] This disorder is characterized by a "pervasive pattern of disregard for, and violation of, the rights of others" with "deceit and manipulation central features" starting at the age of fifteen or younger.[32] Three of the following seven indications are needed for a diagnosis:

1. Failure to conform to lawful social norms (destroying property, harassing others, stealing, illegal occupations, disregard for the wishes, rights, or feelings of others)
2. Deceitfulness (deceitful and manipulative to gain personal profit or pleasure, money, sex, or power)
3. Impulsivity or failure to plan (decisions made without forethought or consideration for the consequences to self or others, sudden change of job, residence, or relationships)
4. Irritability and aggressiveness (physical fights, spousal and child abuse)
5. Reckless disregard for the safety of self or others (speeding, driving while intoxicated, accidents, high-risk or harmful sexual behavior and substance use, neglect or failure to care for a child in such a way that puts the child in danger)
6. Consistent irresponsibility as indicated by repeated failure to sustain consistent work behavior or honor financial obligations (irresponsible work behavior, unemployment despite ample opportunities, defaulting on debt, failure to pay spousal support or child support, failure to support dependents)
7. Lack of remorse (i.e. lack of conscience), as indicated by being indifferent to or rationalizing having hurt, mistreated, or stolen from another (blaming victims for being foolish, helpless, or deserving of their abuse, minimizing harmful consequences of their actions, indifference, failure to make amends for hurtful behavior, belief that everyone—including himself—is out to "help number one," and that one should stop at nothing to avoid being pushed around)[33]

---

[29] *DSM-5*, 659.
[30] *DSM-5*, 662.
[31] Martha Stout, *The Sociopath Next Door* (New York: Harmony Books, 2005), 8.
[32] *DSM-5*, 659.
[33] *DSM-5*, 659–660.

Dr. Robert Hare, a world-renowned expert on sociopaths and psychopaths, has developed a checklist of their traits—the Hare Psychopathy Checklist. It is important to know that while many criminals qualify as sociopaths or psychopaths, many more individuals who have never seen the inside of a jail cell are also sociopaths and psychopaths. Their criminal behavior has never been caught or prosecuted, or there was not enough evidence beyond a reasonable doubt to convict them. While their behavior may not be illegal, it is nonetheless immoral, such as cheating on a spouse, irresponsible use of company funds, squandering money needed for household necessities, refusal to care for their own child, or blaming victims they have mistreated with hurtful retorts like "losers deserve to lose." Psychopathy and sociopathy are a collection of related symptoms; however, not all twenty of the following characteristics need to be indicated to determine whether a person is a sociopath or psychopath. Likewise, one or two symptoms do not a psychopath make. While mental health professionals would caution mere amateurs from making armchair diagnoses, the following traits and behaviors of sociopaths and psychopaths are helpful in determining what we are dealing with:

1. Glib and superficial charm—smooth, engaging, charming, slick.
2. Grandiose (exaggeratedly high) estimation of self—arrogant, cocky, self-assured, opinionated, think they are superior to others.
3. Need for stimulation—prone to boredom, engage in risky, thrilling activities to alleviate boredom, don't finish tasks they consider routine or dull.
4. Pathological lying—deceptive, deceitful, underhanded, unscrupulous, manipulative, dishonest.
5. Cunning and manipulative—use of deceit and deception to cheat, con, or defraud others with callous ruthlessness and lack of concern for victim.
6. Lack of remorse or guilt—as indicated by being indifferent about having hurt, mistreated, or stolen from another, disdain and contempt for the victim (lack of conscience).
7. Shallow emotions—superficial emotional responsiveness, emotional poverty, interpersonal coldness despite signs of open gregariousness.
8. Callousness and lack of empathy—lack of feelings toward people, cold, contemptuous, inconsiderate, tactless.
9. Parasitic lifestyle—intentional, manipulative, selfish, financial, exploitation of others.
10. Poor behavioral controls—irritability, annoyance, impatience, threats, aggression, verbal abuse, unable to control anger or temper.
11. Sexual promiscuity—brief and superficial relations, numerous affairs, indiscriminate selection of sexual partners, several sexual relationships at the same time, sexually coerces others into sexual activity, takes great pride in discussing sexual exploits and conquests.
12. Early behavior problems—lying, theft, cheating, vandalism, bullying, alcohol use, etc., prior to age thirteen.
13. Lack of realistic long-term goals—inability or persistent failure to develop and execute long-term goals.
14. Impulsivity—inability to resist temptations, frustrations, and urges; lack of deliberation without considering consequences; foolhardy, reckless.
15. Irresponsibility—repeated failure to honor obligations and commitments.
16. Failure to accept responsibility for own actions—absence of dutifulness, antagonistic manipulation, denial of responsibility, manipulates or blames others.

17. Many short-term relationships—lack of commitment to long-term relationship reflected by inconsistent, undependable, unreliable commitments, including marital commitments.
18. Juvenile delinquency—behavior involving antagonism, exploitation, aggression, manipulation, or a callous, ruthless tough-mindedness.
19. Revocation of conditional release—revocation of probation or other conditional release (from law enforcement) due to technical violations, carelessness, low deliberation, or failing to appear.
20. Criminal versatility—diversity of behavior characterized as criminal offenses, regardless of whether arrested or convicted; taking great pride in getting away with crimes and having no consequences.[34]

Narcissistic Personality Disorder

In addition to antisocial personality disorder, narcissistic personality disorder is also a common trait of those who abuse. Narcissistic personality disorder is more prevalent in men than women and is estimated to occur in up to 6.2 percent of the population.[35] It is characterized by "a pervasive pattern of grandiosity, need for admiration, and lack of empathy" as indicated by at least five of the following characteristics:

1. A grandiose sense of self-importance (exaggerates achievements and talents, expects to be recognized as superior without commensurate achievements, overestimates ability, inflates their accomplishments, boastful, pretentious, surprised when they do not get the praise they feel they deserve, devalues the contributions of others)
2. Is preoccupied with fantasies of unlimited success, power, brilliance, beauty, or ideal love (ruminates about long overdue admiration and privilege, compares themselves favorably with famous or privileged people)
3. Believes he is special and unique and can only be understood by, or should only associate with, other special or other high-status people or institutions (believes he is superior to others and expects others to recognize him as such, attributes unique, perfect, or gifted qualities to himself and those with whom he associates, his self-esteem is enhanced by the idealized value he assigns to those with whom he associates, insists on having only the best person serving him (doctor, lawyer, hairdresser, designer, etc.), insists on being affiliated with the best institutions, devalues those who disagree or disappoint them)
4. Requires excessive admiration (self-esteem is fragile and depends upon being highly regarded by others, need for constant attention and admiration, see themselves as the center of the universe, expect their arrival to be treated with great fanfare, charming, fishes for compliments)
5. Has a sense of entitlement (unreasonable expectations of especially favorable treatment or automatic compliance with their expectations, expectations of being catered to and furious when they are not catered to, they insist they don't have to wait in line, they view their very important work or desires as so important that others should defer to them, becoming incensed if they don't)
6. Is interpersonally exploitative within relationships (they take advantage of others to achieve their own ends, their sense of entitlement combined with lack of sensitivity leads to the conscious exploitation of others, they expect to be given whatever they want, regardless of the impact on others or the cost of a

---

[34] Robert D. Hare, et al., "The Revised Psychopathy Checklist: Reliability and Factor Structure," *Psychological Assessment: A Journal of Consulting and Clinical Psychology*, 2, no. 3 (1990): 338–341.
[35] *DSM-5*, 671.

relationship, they expect great dedication and excessive work from others and employees to further their own goals without considering the cost to others, they form romantic relationships and friendships only if the other person advances their purposes and enhances their self-esteem, they usurp special privileges and extra resources they think they deserve because they are so special)

7. Lacks empathy and is unwilling to recognize or identify with the feelings and needs of others (they assume others are totally concerned about their welfare while being totally unconcerned about others' welfare, they discuss their own concerns in inappropriate and lengthy detail, they fail to recognize that others have feelings and needs, they are contemptuous and impatient with others who discuss their problems and concerns, they make hurtful remarks and do hurtful things without caring about the pain they inflict, the needs of others are seen as signs of weakness and vulnerability, they are insensitive, cold, and lack interest in others)

8. Is often envious of others or believes others are envious of him (they begrudge others who are more successful of their success or possessions, they feel they better deserve achievements, admiration, or privileges than others, they harshly devalue the contributions of others, especially if others have received praise or recognition)

9. Shows an arrogant, haughty behavior or attitude (they display snobbish, disdainful, contemptuous, or patronizing attitudes), they look down on people in positions of service (such as a waiter, attendant, childcare worker, teacher, bank teller, customer service person, secretary, receptionist, or anyone who earns less than they do), and they call them rude, clumsy, idiotic, or stupid[36]

Dr. Leon Seltzer, one of the foremost experts in the field, has formulated a list of common traits that, in addition to the DSM-5, describe individuals with narcissistic personality disorder, also known as narcissists. These qualities are listed below.

- Highly reactive to criticism. Narcissists immediately and forcefully respond to criticism or anything they assume or interpret as negatively evaluating their person or performance.
- Fragile egos. Although they outwardly appear self-confident because narcissists are highly skilled at exhibiting exceptionally high self-esteem, underneath they have a fragile ego and are insecure. Thus, they are constantly driven to prove themselves.
- Inordinately self-righteous and defensive. Narcissists need to protect their overblown but fragile ego. They cannot admit a mistake or offer a true apology. They have a "my way or the highway" attitude in leading and decision-making.
- React to contrary viewpoints with anger or rage. Narcissists expect everyone to agree with them and share their opinions. If not, they respond with personal attacks, rage, and insults.
- Projection. Narcissists project onto others the qualities, traits, and behaviors they can't or won't accept in themselves. They cannot accept that they have any deficits or weaknesses, and they accuse others of the very things they are most guilty of. By invalidating, devaluing, and denigrating others, it makes them feel better about themselves.
- Poor (or no) interpersonal boundaries. Narcissists view others as extensions of themselves who exist to serve their needs, and they put their needs above everyone else's. They espouse a "What's mine is mine

---

[36] *DSM-5*, 669–672.

and what's yours is mine" mentality. They don't view others as independent beings with their own needs, opinions, and goals to be honored. They dominate conversations about themselves, are not interested in others, and even brag about how they got away with something (a crime, an affair, how they chewed someone out, how they manipulated or conned someone)—not realizing the listener is appalled at their lack of kindness.[37]

Examples of Abusers/Narcissists/Sociopaths/Psychopaths in the Bible

While many of us prefer to focus on the role models and more uplifting portions of the Bible, we cannot forget that Scripture describes people of all types, including abusers, narcissists, sociopaths, and psychopaths. Of course, they were not labeled as such in Scripture. Rather, they were called wicked and evil; they rejected God and His moral code, placed themselves on the throne of their lives, were filled with pride, arrogance, and haughtiness, showed no empathy, remorse, or conscience, and intentionally and systematically caused destruction to others. Their actions and attitudes are now clearly considered abusive, narcissistic, sociopathic, or psychopathic. Although it is more inspirational to study the role models in Scripture, we would do well to remember that the Bible is useful for instruction, even when, or perhaps particularly when, it describes individuals who have rejected God and followed Satan's calling to steal, kill, and destroy. Below is a sampling of the SNAPs included in Scripture. These examples are included to help a woman in an abusive marriage discern the character and behavior of her abuser.

Pharaoh demanded service from the Hebrew slaves, but had no appreciation for their humanity. He treated them with extreme cruelty and showed no remorse. He refused to release his grip over them because he would have lost his free labor force. Showing kindness to them would have been perceived as weakness. As the Israelites requested their freedom, he imposed more egregious abuse to convince them that he, not the God of Israel, was in charge. When they finally left Egypt, Pharaoh did not release them out of benevolence, but because a higher authority forced his hand. The cost to retain his labor force became too high. Even after he let the Israelites go, he followed them and tried to destroy them.

A woman in an abusive marriage may feel like an Israelite in slavery to a pharaoh. He is only interested in her services and doesn't value her as a person. He shows no remorse for his cruelty. When she requests her freedom by way of a divorce, he escalates the abuse to keep her in bondage and show her he is in control. Eventually, her husband relinquishes control only when a judge, a higher authority, imposes a divorce with a court order. Leaving an abuser is a particularly dangerous time for a woman since he continues to stalk and destroy her, even after a divorce.

Saul repaid David's loyalty and friendship with evil. Although the friendship started out well, Saul eventually rejected God and was overcome with an evil spirit that tormented him. Saul falsely accused David of treason and betrayal, slandered him, and became insanely jealous of David's success, popularity, and favor with God. Saul plotted against David, hunted him down, and tried to kill him without justification. David did not wish Saul any ill will and refused to harm him even when he could have. David tried to reason with Saul and assure him that he remained loyal, but it was impossible to reason with Saul. Saul used his daughter Michal as a bargaining chip to get David to do his bidding. After they were married, Saul gave her to another man.

A woman in an abusive marriage may feel like David in a relationship with Saul. While the relationship

---

[37] Leon Seltzer, "6 Signs of Narcissism You May Not Know About," *Psychology Today*, Nov. 7, 2013, https://www.psychologytoday.com/blog/evolution-the-self/201311/6-signs-narcissism-you-may-not-know-about.

started off well, for no apparent reason her husband turned cruel, falsely accused her of infidelity and betrayal, and became jealous of her. He slandered her and falsely accused her of any number of things to her friends and network, causing them to turn against her and side with her husband. She tried to reason with him and even went to counseling, but he could not be reasoned with. Eventually, she separated or divorced. She took the high road and went out of her way to cause him no harm—she simply wanted to be free from abuse. But he stalked her, increased the abuse, and tried to destroy her. He even used her children against her. By lying to them about their mother, he turned them against her and made sure they aligned with his next wife or girlfriend.

King Ahab and Queen Jezebel were known as the most evil rulers of Israel. They rejected God and His morals, killed the temple priests, worshipped and sacrificed to Baal, had a neighbor murdered to get his land, and threatened to kill Elijah, God's prophet. Athaliah, the daughter of Ahab and Jezebel, continued their depravity. She married a king of Judah and, after he died, she murdered her own grandchildren to prevent them from rising to power, and she took over the throne herself. When one grandchild was saved by going into hiding and was crowned the next king, she accused the people who saved him of treason. In doing so, she accused the rescuers of the same thing she was most guilty of herself, an abusive tactic called *projection* (2 Kings 11).

A woman in an abusive relationship may feel as if she has married into the family of Ahab and Jezebel. Her husband completely rejects God's morals and does whatever he wants at the expense of others. He falsely accuses her of the very things he is most guilty of, including infidelity (treason), lying, and being abusive, arrogant, and unreasonable.

King Nebuchadnezzar of Babylon was arrogant and boastful of himself and his accomplishments. Known for their cruelty, the Babylonians invaded Israel, dragged the captives back to Babylon, and forced them to worship Nebuchadnezzar upon threat of death. When Shadrach, Meshach, and Abednego refused to worship the king, he threw them into the fire. Looking over his kingdom, Nebuchadnezzar praised himself for all he had accomplished—without acknowledging God. God turned him insane and let him eat grass like a donkey for seven years until he humbled himself and acknowledged God (Daniel 4). Besides King Manasseh, King Nebuchadnezzar was the only person in the Old Testament whom God zapped to turn his heart toward God.

A woman in an abusive marriage may feel like she has married her own King Nebuchadnezzar—an arrogant, prideful husband who believes he is her king rather than her equal partner. He demands that his family worship him; he makes all the decisions without input from her or the children, and he barks orders like she is an employee rather than a wife. He believes he should be the only one making decisions, that he is the monarch of his family, and that he can't have others making decisions or offering their input when he is entitled to make them. He threatens his spouse and children to ensure they follow his wishes. He believes his success is due entirely to his own wonderfulness, not God's blessings. He brags of his accomplishments and looks with contempt on those who are not as financially successful.

Most of the kings of Israel were wicked, unrepentant, and contemptuous of God and His moral standards. They were so evil that some even sacrificed their own children to their gods. Scripture describes the events leading to their downfall into malevolency. As each king took the throne and established himself as the reigning monarch, he became powerful and wealthy, which led to pride, which in turn caused his heart to turn away from the Lord and toward idols, which in turn caused the downfall of Israel and judgment from God. For example, Scripture records: "But after Uzziah became powerful, his pride led to his downfall" (2 Chronicles 26:16). Uzziah's pride was so complete that he rejected God's explicit standards of temple worship and burned incense, a task only the priests were allowed to do. But when the priests rebuked him for violating God's laws, rather than confessing his sin and seeking forgiveness, he raged at them (2 Chronicles 26:16–19). King Manasseh is the only king of Israel recorded to have had a change in heart who turned to the Lord, but only after he was dragged away as a prisoner by the Assyrians with a hook in his nose and shackles on his feet (2 Chronicles 33).

A woman in an abusive marriage may feel like she has married a king of Israel. Her husband may have been well behaved and doting while they were dating, but as soon as they married and he established his kingdom as the head of the household, his true character emerged. He was now in charge. As he became successful professionally and his wealth grew, he no longer appreciated her or God. Rather than being dependent upon God and being thankful for God's good gifts, such as his wife and family, the most important things in his life became *his* money, *his* rising career, and all the things he could buy with the money *he* made. The big house in an affluent community, fancy cars, vacation homes, club memberships, access to other wealthy and powerful people, and the prestige and special privileges money brings became his idols, his most prized possessions, his identity. He adopted the philosophy of the world: "He who dies with the most toys wins." As his heart turned away from God, it also turned away from his wife and family. These toys were not assets he acquired with his life partner; these were *his* assets. His wife was merely an add-on to his life who, like all add-ons, was replaceable. He played the starring role in the stage play of *his* life, and she was merely an extra or a supporting actress at best, not a co-star. He used pornography regularly and had numerous affairs that, along with his material possessions, boosted his fragile ego. Eventually, he had no time for his wife or children, who were sacrificed on the altar of possessions and prestige. When, in desperation, she approached her priest or pastor to discuss how far he had strayed from God and their marriage, rather than admitting his sins and repenting, her husband exploded in rage at her and the pastor for daring to even mention he was less than perfect.

In a little-known yet gruesome passage from Judges 19 and 20, an abusive Levite intentionally gave his concubine to an angry mob to be gang-raped to avoid harm to himself. A concubine was a woman who was a secondary wife to provide additional children, household help, and sexual companionship to a man. Although she did not have the rights of a wife, she nonetheless belonged to a husband and was afforded some rights, such as food and clothing. Unlike a wife, she could not get a bill of divorce from her husband. Prior to the gang rape, the concubine had left her husband and had gone back to her father's house. In Israel, a woman leaving her husband was highly unusual. We can only assume her husband was so abusive that she left and returned to the relative safety of her childhood home. Four months after she left, her husband came looking for her at her father's house and tried to convince her to return to the abusive marriage. He "spoke kindly" to her, and he ate, drank, and laughed with her father. After several days, he finally convinced both his concubine and her father to let her go back to him. The Levite's home was at least a day's walk from her father's home, but instead of leaving early in the morning so they would make it home safely by dark, the Levite insisted on leaving midday. On the way home they spent the night in a house in the territory of Benjamin. The utterly depraved men of the town gathered as an angry mob around the house and demanded the Levite come out so they could rape him. To save himself, the Levite gave them his concubine instead. She was gang-raped all night, and then she dragged herself back to the house and died on the doorstep. When he saw her lying there, knowing she had been gang-raped but not knowing she was dead, he callously told her to get up. Her husband showed no remorse or loss at her death. He tossed her body over his donkey and brought it back to his house. Instead of honoring her with a proper funeral, the husband cut up his concubine into twelve pieces and sent one to each of the twelve tribes of Israel. He then blamed the Benjamites for her rape and death, taking no responsibility himself, and started a civil war between the tribe of Benjamin and the other tribes of Israel that took the lives of 65,000 men. The tribe of Benjamin was nearly wiped out. Knowing the harm that would come to her, the Levite put his concubine in harm's way, clearing the way for the townspeople to inflict the actual harm.

A woman in an abusive marriage may feel like a concubine—a woman who is expected to serve her husband and provide sexual services but is not valued as a wife or equal partner. When she leaves, she may go back to her childhood home because she has nowhere else to go and no way to support herself. Her abusive husband follows her and stalks her to force her to return to the abusive marriage. Even though he is unrepentant, he will try to sweet-talk her into thinking things will be different. He may even apologize and cry a crocodile tear, claiming that he has missed her. He knows he needs to get the approval of her family, too, especially her dad, so he schmoozes it up with him and claims it was all a big misunderstanding. Eventually, her abuser's lies and deception convince her and her family she should try to make the marriage work, and she goes back with her husband. However, his heart hasn't changed, and she finds, as do all women who return to unrepentant abusers, that the sweet talking ends and the abuse escalates. He is still only concerned about himself. And when it comes to protecting her or saving his own skin, her husband will put her in harm's way while knowing that someone or something else will inflict harm on her. He will then claim he is an innocent victim, even though he was responsible for the damage. She will eventually die an emotional and spiritual death if she stays in the abuse, or like the concubine, a physical death.

King David's son Amnon was the spoiled, evil son of a father who did not raise his children well. Amnon burned with lust for his half sister Tamar, who had the same father but a different mother. With advice from his cousin, he manipulated a way to be alone with her by falsely claiming he was sick and asking her to care for him. He knew she had a good heart and would help him. However, when they were completely alone, he raped her, even though she begged him not to. As soon as he was done raping her, his heart immediately changed, and his lust turned to hate. According to Jewish law, a man who seduced a virgin was obligated to marry her since a young girl who was no longer a virgin was considered unworthy of marriage. When she tried to hold him to the law, he refused. He discarded her without any emotions and with no consideration of how he had defiled her and ruined her life, and he sent her away. To complete her humiliation, he had her escorted out of his house by a servant and locked the door. Even though King David heard of Amnon's crime against his half sister, he did nothing. Tamar spent the rest of her life living as a shunned woman with her brother Absalom, who eventually killed Amnon for raping his sister (2 Samuel 13).

A woman who is in an abusive marriage may feel like Tamar. During the courting phase, her husband was smitten with her and tracked her like a lion after his prey. He appealed to her good graces, lied to her, convinced her to trust him, and then used sex to show her he was in charge. Rape is a violent act designed to humiliate the victim and demonstrate his complete control over her in a most dehumanizing way. The rapist uses an act designed by God to show physical love for one another and instead uses it to degrade a person made in the image of God. After capturing his prey, he is no longer interested in her, and she is no longer useful to him. After the sex act, he discards her with the same lack of emotions as disposing of yesterday's newspaper because it is no longer useful. He is completely uncaring of the destruction he has perpetrated upon her and the lifelong harm he has inflicted. During a divorce, he completely discards her in a similar manner and moves on to his next prey.

The Bible includes plenty of real-life abusers/narcissists/sociopaths/psychopaths. While women of faith may not be accustomed to such examples, we would be wise to study the typical attitudes and behaviors of abusive individuals from these illustrations and use what we learn to know what to expect from abusers in our own lives. It is also important to understand that, with few exceptions, God did not zap the SNAPs into being good. He did not change their hearts. God allowed their own wicked hearts to become more deceived and depraved by the Enemy. (See Romans 1.) However, God did equip His people with appropriate spiritual and physical weapons to respond to evil. God works the same way today. He doesn't transform abusers into good persons, despite our prayers. But He does equip us with spiritual and physical weapons to defend ourselves, and He provides people, opportunities, and resources to allow us to flee from evil.

Descriptions of Abusers/Narcissists/Sociopaths/Psychopaths in the Bible

In addition to examples, the Bible provides a number of descriptions and warnings of SNAPs. While we often read the Bible to learn godly attitudes and behaviors, we must also be diligent in gaining discernment, the ability to identify good and evil. As Christian women, we often miss the mark when it comes to identifying unhealthy, toxic, abusive people. We are taught, almost from birth, not to say unkind things even if they are true, to think only the best of others, to overlook faults, to forgive offenses, to look for the good and ignore the bad, etc. As a result, women of faith tend to be naïve and Pollyannaish in their approach to relationships, and they miss the signs of malevolent men. While it may be advisable to overlook innocent faults and to forgive unintentional offenses, it is also imperative to identify the signs of people who intentionally, with malice, seek to harm or destroy us emotionally, verbally, financially, sexually, or spiritually.

Many naïve Christian women are under the false impression that they can and should change abusive men into kind, God-fearing men. They misunderstand the Great Commission as a license to date and marry depraved men so they can witness to them and convert them into believers. This shows a grievous and dangerous misinterpretation of the Bible and how we should go about seeking a mate. When it comes to SNAPs, verses in both the Old and New Testaments warn us to "Have nothing to do with such people" (Deuteronomy 17:7; 19:19; 21:21; 22:21, 24; 24:7; 1 Corinthians 5:11; 2 Timothy 3:5; Titus 3:10).

When we read Scripture, particularly the Old Testament, we are sometimes tempted to read it as we would an old novel—entertained by a story with plot twists, interesting characters, and surprises around every corner. This approach misses the intent of Scripture as a useful tool for teaching, rebuking, correcting, and training so we are equipped today for carrying out God's purpose in our lives (2 Timothy 3:16–17). If we are to grow in wisdom and discernment, we must read Scripture and apply it to our lives today. For the woman who is in or has been in an abusive marriage, she must understand that God is speaking to her through His Word—He is describing her abuser. He is warning her and revealing how her abuser will continue to act. He is equipping her to deal with her abuser. It's important to note that throughout Scripture, God does not reveal that He will magically change her evil, cruel, abusive husband into a model, God-fearing citizen. Rather, He will allow her abuser to continue the death spiral of destruction he has chosen for his life because he has rejected God. Thus, in Scripture, God is telling her to run from evil. He is promising her He will rescue her and redeem her. God uses Scripture to tell her He has a wonderful plan of an abundant life for her that does not include abuse.

Below are a few biblical descriptions of SNAPs, along with warnings of how we should handle them. I encourage you to turn to these passages in your own Bible to understand the context, including the prayers requesting justice and the thanksgiving of deliverance from evildoers, especially in the Psalms.

> But mark this: There will be terrible times in the last days. People will be lovers of themselves, lovers of money, boastful, proud, abusive, disobedient to their parents, ungrateful, unholy, without love, unforgiving, slanderous, without self-control, brutal, not lovers of the good, treacherous, rash,

conceited, lovers of pleasure rather than lovers of God—having a form of godliness but denying its power. Have nothing to do with such people. They are the kind who worm their way into homes and gain control over gullible women, who are loaded down with sins and are swayed by all kinds of evil desires, always learning but never able to come to a knowledge of the truth. . . . They are men of depraved minds, who, as far as the faith is concerned, are rejected. (2 Timothy 3:1–8)

For the flesh desires what is contrary to the Spirit, and the Spirit what is contrary to the flesh. They are in conflict with each other, so that you are not to do whatever you want. The acts of the flesh are obvious: sexual immorality, impurity and debauchery; idolatry and witchcraft; hatred, discord, jealousy, fits of rage, selfish ambition, dissensions, factions and envy; drunkenness, orgies, and the like. I warn you, as I did before, that those who live like this will not inherit the kingdom of God. (Galatians 5:17, 19–22)

Be alert and of sober mind. Your enemy the devil prowls around like a roaring lion looking for someone to devour. (1 Peter 5:8)

Watch out for false prophets. They come to you in sheep's clothing, but inwardly they are ferocious wolves. By their fruit you will recognize them. Do people pick grapes from thorn bushes, or figs from thistles? Likewise, every good tree bears good fruit, but a bad tree bears bad fruit. A good tree cannot bear bad fruit, and a bad tree cannot bear good fruit. Every tree that does not bear good fruit is cut down and thrown into the fire. Thus, by their fruit you will recognize them. (Matthew 7:15–20)

And because they thought it was worthless to embrace the true knowledge of God, God gave them over to a worthless mind-set, to break all rules of proper conduct. Their sinful lives became full of every kind of evil, wicked schemes, greed, and cruelty. Their hearts overflowed with jealous cravings, and with conflict and strife, which drove them into hateful arguments and murder. They are deceitful liars full of hostility. They are gossips who love to spread malicious slander. With inflated egos they hurl hateful insults at God, yet they are nothing more than arrogant boasters. They are rebels against their parents and totally immoral. They are senseless, faithless, ruthless, heartless, and completely merciless. Although they are fully aware of God's laws and proper order, and knowing that those who do all of these things deserve to die, yet they still go headlong into darkness, encouraging others to do the same and applauding them when they do! (Romans 1:28–32 TPT)

Make a tree good and its fruit will be good, or make a tree bad and its fruit will be bad, for a tree is recognized by its fruit. You brood of vipers, how can you who are evil say anything good? For the mouth speaks what the heart is full of. A good man brings good things out of the good stored up in him, and an evil man brings evil things out of the evil stored up in him. But I tell you that everyone will have to give account on the day of judgment for every empty word they have spoken. For by your words you will be acquitted, and by your words you will be condemned. (Matthew 12:33–37)

Jesus said to them, "If God were your Father, you would love me, for I have come here from God. I have not come on my own; God sent me. Why is my language not clear to you? Because you are unable to hear what I say. You belong to your father, the devil, and you want to carry out your father's desires. He was a murderer from the beginning, not holding to the truth, for there is no truth in him. When he lies, he speaks his native language, for he is a liar and the father of lies." (John 8:42–44)

Many will be purified, made spotless and refined, but the wicked will continue to be wicked. None of the wicked will understand, but those who are wise will understand. (Daniel 12:10)

Not a word from their mouth can be trusted; their hard is filled with malice. Their throat is an open grave; with their tongues they tell lies. (Psalm 5:9)

Whoever is pregnant with evil conceives trouble and gives birth to disillusionment. Whoever digs a hole and scoops it out falls into the pit they have made. The trouble they cause recoils on them; their violence comes down on their own heads. (Psalm 7:14–16)

In his arrogance the wicked man hunts down the weak, who are caught in the schemes he devises. He boasts about the cravings of his heart; he blesses the greedy and reviles the Lord. In his pride the wicked does not seek him; in all his thoughts there is no room for God. His ways are always prosperous; your laws are rejected by him; he sneers at all his enemies. He says to himself, "Nothing will ever shake me." He swears, "No one will ever do me harm." His mouth is full of lies and threats; trouble and evil are under his tongue. He lies in wait near the villages; from ambush he murders the innocent. His eyes watch in secret for his victims; like a lion in cover he lies in wait. He lies in wait to catch the helpless; he catches the helpless and drags them off in his net. His victims are crushed, they collapse; they fall under his strength. He says to himself, "God will never notice; he covers his face and never sees." (Psalm 10:2–11)

Do not drag me away with the wicked, with those who do evil, who speak cordially with their neighbors but harbor malice in their hearts. (Psalm 28:3)

Ruthless witnesses come forward; they question me on things I know nothing about. They repay me evil for good and leave me like one bereaved. Yet when they were ill, I put on sackcloth and humbled myself with fasting. When my prayers returned to me unanswered, I went about mourning as though for my friend or brother. I bowed my head in grief as though weeping for my mother. But when I stumbled, they gathered in glee; assailants gathered against me without my knowledge. They slandered me without ceasing. Like the ungodly they maliciously mocked; they gnashed their teeth at me. . . . They do not speak peaceably, but devise false accusations against those who live quietly in the land. (Psalm 35:11–16, 20)

I have a message from God in my heart concerning the sinfulness of the wicked: There is no fear of God before their eyes. In their own eyes they flatter themselves too much to detect or hate their sin. The words of their mouths are wicked and deceitful; they fail to act wisely or do good. Even on their beds they plot evil; they commit themselves to a sinful course and do not reject what is wrong. (Psalm 36:1–4)

The wicked draw the sword and bend the bow to bring down the poor and needy, to slay those whose ways are upright. . . . The wicked borrow and do not repay, but the righteous give generously. (Psalm 37:14, 21)

When one of them comes to see me, he speaks falsely, while his heart gathers slander; then he goes out and spreads it around. (Psalm 41:6)

Day and night they prowl about [the walls of their home]; malice and abuse are within it. Destructive forces are at work in [the home]. Threats and lies never leave [it]. . . . If an enemy were insulting me, I could endure it; if a foe were rising against me, I could hide. But it is you, a man like myself, my companion, my close friend, with whom I once enjoyed sweet fellowship at the house of God, as we walked about among the worshipers. (Psalm 55:10–14)

Do you rulers indeed speak justly? Do you judge people with equity? No, in your heart you devise injustice, and your hands mete out violence on the earth. Even from birth the wicked go astray; from the womb they are wayward, spreading lies. Their venom is like the venom of a snake, like that of a cobra that has stopped its ears, that will not heed the tune of the charmer, however skillful the enchanter may be. (Psalm 58:1–5)

Pride is their necklace, they clothe themselves with violence. From their callous hearts comes iniquity; their evil imaginations have no limits. They scoff, and speak with malice; with arrogance they threaten oppression. Their mouths lay claim to heaven, and their tongues take possession of the earth. Therefore their people turn to them and drink up waters in abundance. They say, "How would God know? Does the Most High know anything?" This what the wicked are like—always free of care, they go on amassing wealth. (Psalm 73:6–12)

Whoever corrects a mocker invites insults; whoever rebukes the wicked incurs abuse. (Proverbs 9:7)

But when grace is shown to the wicked, they do not learn righteousness; even in a land of uprightness they go on doing evil and do not regard the majesty of the Lord. (Isaiah 26:10)

Can an Ethiopian change his skin or a leopard its spots? Neither can you do good who are accustomed to doing evil. (Jeremiah 13:23)

Pride and arrogance are the root of the abuser's evil (2 Chronicles 16:16; 32:25; Psalm 10:4; 31:18; 59:12; 73:6; 101:5; Proverbs 3:34; 11:12; 13:10; 14:3; 15:25; 16:5; 21:24; Isaiah 2:11, 17; 13:11; 37:23; Daniel 5:20; Hosea 13:6; Amos 6:8; Obadiah 1:3; Romans 12:6; 1 Corinthians 13:4; 2 Timothy 3:1–7; James 4:6; 1 Peter 5:5; 1 John 2:16).

When we read these passages, we understand that God is speaking to us, the wife or partner of an abuser, about our own situation. He is confirming what modern day psychologists know about the dark characteristics and lifelong traits of narcissists, sociopaths, psychopaths, and other abusers. He is describing our situation and giving us His wisdom and directions to deal with abuse in our own lives.

CHAPTER 3

The Three Phases of a Romantic Abusive Relationship

Unlike healthy relationships, in which the behavior of the partners remains constant over time, an abusive relationship has three distinct phases in which the behavior of the abuser changes drastically over time. Of course, his character remains the same—he is always manipulative, deceitful, unempathetic, and without conscience or remorse. However, like a chameleon, he changes his behavior to achieve his goals at the time.

In healthy relationships, we move somewhat slowly in the initial phases of meeting someone. If we are intentional about choosing a mate who is a good fit for us emotionally, spiritually, physically, and intellectually and who has common goals and values in life, we may even have a written list of qualities we seek in a lifelong partner. Alongside these we may identify qualities we will not tolerate in a potential partner, and thus are a no-go when considering a relationship. We keep our list of qualities close to the vest, and when we start along the path of a potential relationship, we move with caution. We don't go from 0 to 100 on the intimacy scale right away. Rather, we reveal ourselves in stages, making sure we feel completely safe prior to sharing at another level. For example, on a first date we may discuss facts and current events, such as our job or where we attended college, a current movie or a good restaurant, the latest playoff standings, and other similar less personal subjects. If that goes well, the other person shares equally, and if there are no red flags, we might progress within a couple of weeks to sharing opinions, such as what we think about the things we previously shared. If that goes well, the other person shares equally, and if there are no red flags, we might progress in a few weeks to sharing our hopes and dreams about the future.

As we share and find that each level of intimacy is shared by the other person and we perceive no signs that would cause us to proceed with extreme caution, we slowly get to know each other. This is the gist of developing any new friendship, romantic or otherwise. As we reveal ourselves to each other, we can each assess whether the person across the table meets our criteria for someone we want in our life. Our list may include dependability, kindness, humility, and a sense of humor. However, we don't tell the other person that—rather, we let him reveal himself and we assess whether he has these qualities. Much like conducting a job interview, we don't tell the applicant the test answers we are looking for. Rather, we seek an applicant who portrays the unique qualities we need, while keeping those qualities to ourselves.

On the other hand, if we find during this process that a potential new friend is unable to share appropriately on a given level of intimacy, or if he signals that he is toxic, dangerous, or not a good fit, we can then determine we no longer want to continue exploring the relationship. For example, if a couple is on their first date (and thus, the lowest level of intimacy in their conversation) discussing current events and he wants to know her deepest, darkest secrets (a level of intimacy one would only discuss with a dear, trusted friend or sister) or pressures her to have sex (a level of intimacy one would only consider with a trusted, intimate life partner), these are huge red flags suggesting a dangerous person. Likewise, if he starts bragging about his pedigree and how his education from a prestigious school, stellar personality, and exceptional experience entitle him to a higher position than he currently has, these are red flags that indicate he is arrogant and prideful, not humble and thankful. Similarly, if he blames his ex-wives for all the problems in his former marriages, calls them crazy bitches, takes no responsibility for the breakdown of the marriages, and explains how he got even with them, these are indications he is not kind, but rather vindictive and dangerous.

Idealization Phase

In romantic relationships with an abuser, the initial phase is called the *idealization phase* or *love-bombing phase*. In this phase, the SNAP, like a predator, has identified his target victim, and his goal is to make her fall in love with him and become completely emotionally and financially dependent upon him. He has no intention of falling in love with her or becoming emotionally attached; however, he knows he must appear so. Therefore, an abuser moves quickly to secure his prey. From the initial meeting when he chooses his victim, the abuser is very charming, charismatic, romantic, and attentive. He quickly moves from being a relative stranger to asking the most personal, intimate details of her life, her hopes, and her dreams. Within days, he will tell her she is wonderful, the most interesting woman he has ever met, incredibly exciting, extremely talented, the most beautiful woman he has ever known, unbelievably intelligent, and that they share many things in common. He will tell her, with very little information and in an incredibly short period of time, he wants to spend every waking moment with her and that she is his soul mate.

The deception starts early. He likely won't share much about himself, but he is a master at extracting information from her that he will file away and use against her when convenient. If he is married or in another relationship, he will likely fail to mention that, or will claim he is divorced or in the process of divorcing. He may claim he filed for divorce or left a relationship because his former wife abandoned him or had mental health issues, when in fact, she filed for divorce because of his infidelity or abuse. He knows she will likely not look up the court records, and she will likely not talk to his former wife or friends to fact-check his story. She is much too trusting for that. He knows that playing the victim card, portraying himself as the poor abandoned husband who did nothing wrong and was betrayed by a horrible woman, will cause her to pity him and endear him to her even more.

With all this profuse flattery, and because she is naturally trusting with few strong boundaries, she reveals the intimate details of her life and her heart even more. With each bit of information he extracts, he mirrors her to quickly get her emotionally bonded to him. If she shares that family is important to her, he effuses that family is central to his very being. If she shares that she loves cooking, the theater, and travel, he claims that those are his favorite things too. If she shares that she loves children, he claims that he adores them. And so on, and so on. Within weeks, she is convinced she is in love with the most wonderful, kind, considerate, romantic man on the planet, and that he is in love with her. She is sure they have much in common and that she has finally met a man who understands her and appreciates her.

Despite her reluctance, he quickly moves to have sex with her to establish a claim on her body, not just her mind. He instinctively knows that by having sex she will form an attachment to him. He also knows that to a woman, having sex is being vulnerable to her partner physically, emotionally, and spiritually. That is precisely where he wants her—vulnerable. He may even suggest they move in together, buy a house together, or get married. She is swept off her feet with his expressions of love and a future together. Her body becomes awash with the love hormones of dopamine, norepinephrine, estrogen, testosterone, vasopressin, and oxytocin. She is euphoric. She feels like she is floating, the world is wonderful, she can barely eat or sleep, and she can't think of anything else but him.

But on his end, the abuser is merely manipulating his prey and doing everything he can to ensure that his partner forms strong emotional and financial attachments to him. He is incapable of love, but he is doing his best to pretend he is in love and to mimic what he knows are the proper things to say and do when a man loves a woman. At least, that is what he has seen other men do, and although he does not feel an attachment, he knows he must act like he does—at least until he has set the hook and she is completely emotionally and financially attached to him.

Devaluation Phase

In healthy romantic relationships, once a couple has decided they want to spend their lives together (and perhaps raise a family, buy a home, start a business, or however they envision their lives together), they will often want to make their commitment to each other official and celebrate their decision with a wedding. In healthy relationships, a wedding is a celebration of two people who love each other, are committed to each other for life, and want the best for each other, their families, and their children to come.

However, in romantic relationships with an abuser, once the SNAP has ensured that his victim is emotionally dependent on him, he will want to seal the deal to make sure her emotional and financial dependence is complete. Once he has control over her, it will be difficult for her to leave his clutches. He will suggest an event—usually a wedding, moving in together, giving up her job, becoming business partners, buying a house with both names on the title, having a child, etc.—to ensure that she is financially and emotionally tied to him and that he is in control both financially and emotionally. The event will also ensure that disentangling herself from him will be an expensive, gut-wrenching, and emotionally and financially difficult process involving costly lawyers. Of course, she will not be able to afford legal services once he has control of the finances. The difficulty in removing herself from her abuser will ensure that she remains under his control as long as possible, and he knows that. For example, if they marry and she gives up her job, she will incur substantial legal fees if she files for divorce, yet she has no access to funds, and lawyers typically require a retainer of $2,500 to $5,000. This is a huge deterrent to divorce. If they have a child together, she will be financially tied to him, will have limited mobility to move away, and will need to cater to his demands for at least the next eighteen years. If they have a business or a house together, she must follow his orders or risk severe consequences. Separating themselves will require legal agreements and significant legal fees.

Oftentimes the abuser ensures financial control first. He asks her to quit her job under the ruse that his income is plenty for both to live on or so she can stay home and raise the children. Once he is in financial control and she is tied to him financially, the way is paved for emotional and other types of abuse. Almost immediately after the abuser has secured his position in which his partner is emotionally and financially dependent upon him, he will methodically engage in abuse that escalates over time.

The goal of the abuser during the second stage is to devalue and diminish his partner. He does so to feed his fragile ego, make himself look better, and gain and maintain control over her. The basis of these goals is an intentional effort to destroy her spirit so there is nothing left of her. Only *his* goals, wishes, hopes, dreams, and opinions matter. She is essentially subsumed into him. In achieving his goals, a SNAP generally employs the tactics of all forms of abuse, which we discuss later in this book. However, the easiest form of abuse to achieve is emotional and verbal abuse. These come naturally to an abuser.

Most women in abusive marriages report the abuse started immediately after the wedding. Once the predator captures his prey, he starts to devour it. The difference between the adoring, affectionate, and romantic boyfriend up until the wedding day and the cruel, abusive, uncaring husband after the wedding day is overwhelming and alarming to most brides. The kind Dr. Jekyll turned evil Mr. Hyde personality shift is marked and perplexing. Many brides wonder, *What just happened here? Who are you and what have you done with Mr. Wonderful?*

Given the tremendous change in attitude and behavior a woman sees in her husband, a woman wonders who her husband really is. Most spend years, if not decades, hoping to get back to the state of euphoric bliss they experienced prior to the wedding. She wants very much to believe her true husband is the one she was dating, not the one who showed up after the wedding. She will do nearly anything to get him back: she will try to please him, give up her career if he asks, have children if he wants, perform humiliating sex acts if he demands, make their home immaculate and inviting, or undergo plastic surgery if he says her breasts are too small or her nose is too crooked. Nothing, however, will please him. Nothing will bring back what to her was a blissful, loving time of courtship, but what to him was a time of deceit, manipulation, and flattery to get her to fall for him. That phase of their lives is gone forever, never to return. Many women do not realize for many years that the person they were dating does not even exist. It was all merely an act put on by an abuser who targeted her for his next prize and was trying to gain power and control over her. And he did.

Discard Phase

Relationships may end because a party's goals change. Each determines they have different views of how they want their lives to look. Even when a relationship ends, healthy people still care for each other, wish each other the best, and maintain a friendship, albeit not as close as it once was.

However, every relationship with an abuser ends badly—very badly. Regardless of its length, whether they have children together, or how much the victim has sacrificed for the abuser, the abuser will discard his partner with as little empathy as discarding yesterday's newspaper, and he will try to destroy her. The abuser immediately moves on to his next victim, usually one he has been grooming during the marriage, and the cycle repeats with a new woman. He doesn't give a second thought to the utter emotional, physical, sexual, spiritual, and financial destruction he has caused his wife.

When a marriage to an abuser comes to a crashing end, a woman often feels guilty, believing that, despite her Herculean efforts, she could have done something else that would have saved their marriage. However, there is nothing she could have done differently that would have saved their relationship. It was doomed from the start, as are all relationships with abusers. Lasting friendships are built on honesty, trust, and wanting what is best for one another. However, an abusive relationship is built on the abuser's deceit. Both parties distrust each other, and the abuser wants only what he thinks is best for himself without any concern about the well-being of his wife.

A woman also often makes the mistake of believing that because they have had a long marriage, because she is the mother of his children, because she supported him through medical school, or because she took care of his elderly mother, he will be gracious and kind to her in the divorce. Nothing could be further from the truth. During the discard phase, the SNAP will be vindictive, uncaring, deceitful, malicious, and out to get the most money possible in a divorce agreement. Her years of caring for him, his elderly parents, and his children mean absolutely nothing to him. In his view, she was brought on to serve him and he was entitled to her services; he made all the money, and it should all be his; he owes her nothing.

Linda Martinez-Lewi, a licensed marriage and family therapist and author of *Freeing Yourself from the Narcissist in Your Life*, put it best:

> Relationships with narcissists always end badly. They often culminate in financial ruin, emotional devastation, physical illness, even death. They can terminate as precipitously as they started or span over many decades. Their length is dependent on how useful you are to the narcissist and how much psychological abuse you can tolerate. In some cases, the partner of a narcissist has become too ill psychologically or physically to withstand the association any longer. The narcissist effortlessly replaces those who are worn and tired with a fresh face, a bright-eyed adoring disciple.[38]

---

[38] Linda Martinez-Lewi, *Freeing Yourself from the Narcissist in Your Life* (New York: Penguin Group, 2008), 160. See also Andrea Schneider, "Idealize, Devalue, Discard: The Dizzying Cycle of Narcissism," *Good Therapy*, https://www.goodtherapy.org/blog/idealize-devalue-discard-the-dizzying-cycle-of-narcissism-0325154; Rhonda Freeman, "Relationship Cycle of Individuals with Psychopathy and Narcissistic Personality Disorder—Idealize, Devalue, Discard," *Neuroinstincts*, https://neuroinstincts.com/idealize-devalue-discard/; and Dale Archer, "The Danger of Manipulative Love-Bombing in a Relationship," *Psychology Today*, https://www.psychologytoday.com/us/blog/reading-between-the-headlines/201703/the-danger-manipulative-love-bombing-in-relationship.

Chapter 4

The Cycle of Abuse within a Relationship

In addition to the three macro phases of idealization, devaluation, and discard, micro cycles of abuse in the devaluation phase repeat themselves. These are designed to keep a woman in an abusive relationship or marriage. Abuse rarely occurs 24/7—if this were so, most women would leave. Rather, abuse occurs in cycles interspersed with good behavior that keeps a woman hoping the good behavior will continue and the abuse will cease. These cycles may repeat every few hours, days, weeks, or months. They may be consistent or inconsistent, but abuse always repeats itself. Once an abuser has crossed the line of abuse the first time, and his partner stays, he will do it again.

Acute-Explosion Phase

The first phase of the abuse cycle is an acute explosion or act of abuse. This may consist of a verbally and emotionally abusive explosion (e.g., "You f***king bitch!" "You are a brainless whore!"), a physical explosion (e.g., hitting, shoving, throwing an object, using a weapon), a sexual explosion (e.g., forcible sex, rape), a financial explosion (e.g., a transfer of assets without her permission, threats to withhold money or sell assets if she doesn't acquiesce to his demands, refusal to pay bills), or a spiritual explosion (e.g., "You must submit to me—I am your husband!" "If you were a Christian wife, you would have sex with me any time I need. The Bible says your body is mine!").

The victim reacts in one of three ways: fight, flight, or freeze. These responses are automatic brain responses to perceived threats. Our brains unconsciously assess the situation, the strength of our enemy, our ability to fight or flee, and the possible outcomes. In a split second, we make an unconscious decision to fight physically or verbally, to flee, or we are paralyzed by fear and do nothing. While the automatic functions of our brain take over, our cognitive brain function is put on hold. This defensive mechanism helps us respond to danger. However, it also explains why a woman being abused is confused about what to do and has a difficult time properly thinking through her situation and determining a logical course of action. As a result, a victim's reaction may include arguing, fighting back, running away, leaving the conversation, trying to reason with her abuser, moving out, trying to calm her partner down, calling the police, protecting herself and others, or sitting numbly in a corner.

The Cycle of Abuse within a Relationship

Honeymoon Phase

The second phase of the abuse cycle is the honeymoon phase. After the abuser calms down, he will assess the destruction he has caused and try to get his wife or partner to stay or come back to the relationship. During this phase, he is on good behavior as he goes into full-on damage control and tries to make amends. He will do or say nearly anything to work his way out of the hole he has dug. Although he is insincere, he may apologize and make promises he does not intend to keep. He will assure her he will never treat her that way again and will declare his love for her. He will play the victim. "I feel like I've lost my best friend," wrote one abuser in an attempt to gain his wife's sympathy when she left after one of his many abusive explosions. He will likely employ the assistance of friends and family to convince her to give him another chance. If she files legal proceedings against him, he will try to convince her to drop them with excuses: "I can't support you and the kids if I am in jail." "The order of protection will ruin my career and keep me from getting the job I applied for." "The kids need a father, and you are keeping me away from them if you go ahead with the restraining order."

The victim will usually respond with hope. She wants her marriage to work. She wants to keep her family together, and she wants to believe her abuser. So she forgives him, sets up a marriage counseling appointment, and agrees to either stay or return to the relationship. She believes him when he promises to change and apologizes for his behavior. Deep down, however, she has her doubts as to his sincerity. She falls for the pity play and drops the legal proceedings against him. She may even make plans for a trip together. She feels hopeful and happy and in control of the relationship since her abuser is being so accommodating and eager to please her.

Tension-Building Phase

The good behavior of the abuser during the honeymoon phase is short-lived. After all, he was putting on an act to get his wife back to the abusive marriage, and he can only act for a limited time. SNAPs are unwilling to change permanently and are unable to learn from their prior bad behavior. Either they simply don't care, they miscalculate the damage they do and the effort it takes to repair it, or both. At some point, the SNAP's true nature returns. During the tension-building phase, the abuser withdraws the feigned affection and remorse he showed during the honeymoon phase. His acting skills accomplished what they were meant to do—convince her to stay or return to him—and now he can return to his true abusive character. The tension-building phase is marked by the abuser's moodiness, grumpiness, negativity, irritability, nitpicking, criticisms, complaints, fault finding, insults, name-calling, and yelling. Anything or nothing seems to set him off.

The victim feels like she is walking on eggshells. She responds to his mood changes by trying to calm him, being subservient, and attending to his demands. She may try to reason with him, to no avail. She isolates herself from him to avoid anything that may cause an outburst. She withdraws from her support networks to avoid criticism. She tries to keep the children quiet to keep him from erupting in anger.

The abuser is like a bubbling volcano waiting to explode. At some point, perhaps within hours, but certainly within days or weeks or months, the boiling volcano explodes with another act of acute abuse, and the cycle repeats itself.

The Game

Abuse always repeats itself and always escalates over time. For the abuser, it's a game to see how far he can go and still have his victim stay in the relationship. He usually starts with crossing the line at a relatively low level of abuse or inconsideration, and if she stays, he gradually increases the level of abuse. Once an abuser has crossed a victim's boundary, he plays the "makeup game" of the honeymoon phase and waits to see if his victim will stay. If she stays, he knows she will endure that level of abuse, and he ups the game the next time, and the next time, and the next, to see how much he can get away with and still have her come back to him. He intersperses the abuse with periods of good behavior and perhaps even an apology (the honeymoon phase). In this way, his victim gets used to the abuse and it becomes normalized, especially when the abuser tells her it is what every couple does. The periods of good behavior convince her that he knows how to act "nice" and that if she stays in the relationship long enough, he will eventually be on good behavior all the time.

For example, on his first test he may show up an hour late to a dinner date without calling. If, after he acts contritely, she still continues the relationship, for his next test he may show up an hour late without calling and may accuse her of being too pushy and demanding, especially since he is so important at work and has so much going on. If she continues the relationship after that, the next time he is late again without calling, he may call her a "bitch," "selfish," and "not understanding" of him when she complains. If she stays, the next time she brings up the fact that he is late and didn't call, he dumps her out of the car and leaves her miles from home. If she still stays, he may decide to show her he's the boss by coercing her into having sex, even if she objects. And if she is still around after that, he will show her he is in complete control of her by tying her to the bedposts and raping her.

This progression from inconsideration to verbal abuse to physical abuse to sexual abuse to sexual assault is much easier when the victim is financially dependent on an abuser. For this reason, many, if not most, abusers start with financial abuse. Many an abuser asks his newlywed wife to quit her job, puts her on an allowance, and gives her no access to marital funds so she is completely financially dependent on him. It is the perfect set-up for the escalation of abuse.

Sometime during the relationship, she gives up on her hope of Prince Charming and begs him to "just be nice." In the end, the damage is irreparable. She realizes the true nature of her abuser and that the relationship can no longer be salvaged. She must decide to either stay in the dizzying and dangerous cycle of escalating abuse—or leave.

CHAPTER 5

The World according to the Narcissist, Sociopath, Psychopath, and Other Abusers

For the healthy person of faith, our worldview is informed by our view of God, the Bible, our Judeo-Christian traditions and morals, our family of origin, our community, our society, social norms and mores, common sense, and God-given wisdom. However, the worldview of the narcissist, sociopath, psychopath, and other domestic abusers is informed primarily by Satan and his morals. It's not that the abuser doesn't know about God, Judeo-Christian morals, and social norms and traditions. He very much knows about them and understands that most people abide by them. However, in his mind, he is above the norms others subject themselves to. He works to exploit those who abide by Judeo-Christian values, societal laws, and social norms. An abuser is the emotional equivalent of a gun-toting predator who walks into a church that has a No Guns Allowed sign on the door. He has targeted the church because he knows that everyone inside the church will abide by the rules and will not carry a gun. He counts on their conscious effort to be kind and welcoming to others as he opens fire on those who are defenseless and weaker than he is. The only thing that will stop the predator is a force greater than him—that is, a skilled person with a gun. The predator has no internal controls, code of honor, or conscience to stop himself. It should come as no surprise that a background of domestic abuse is one of the common characteristics of mass shooters.

People

Healthy persons of faith believe that people are made in the image of God and that their lives are gifts to be cherished. They treat others with respect, kindness, and goodwill simply because all people have intrinsic value.

For the SNAP, however, people are objects to be used for their own selfish goals. People are a means to an end. Individuals are to be exploited for what they can do for the abuser. Regardless of the relationship, the primary goal for an abuser is to determine how others can most benefit the abuser and employ them in his service for as long as they are useful. When a person is no longer useful or needed, the relationship ends.

An abuser wants what he wants when he wants it. He wants to win, and that means another person must lose. Unlike healthy people, he doesn't worry about hurting someone's feelings or damaging a relationship as long as he gets what he wants. He does not react well to "no." If someone refuses to acquiesce to his demands or disagrees with his opinion, the abuser will explode in anger or rage and will engage in ad hominem personal verbal attacks, or worse, until he gets his way. Abusers are ruthless to others and will take advantage of a person or business deal whenever possible. Rather than offering a fair price, an abuser will attempt to low-ball if he believes the other side is desperate. As one coworker said of Tim, a corporate executive known for his ruthlessness, and later fired for his abuse of employees, "Why kick a man when he's down when he can run over him with a steamroller? That's Tim's way."

Abusers typically want to surround themselves with those who will make them look better by association and who will provide them with the perks and privileges of wealth and power, or at least of associating with the wealthy and powerful. Therefore, they like to hobnob with celebrities, the rich, the powerful, and, of course, good-looking women. Many abusers are themselves celebrities, and thus they associate only with those of their own kind while looking down on those they view as inferior.

For example, if a neighbor has season tickets to the local professional football team, the abuser will make sure he chats with the neighbor, hints that he loves NFL football, and invites the neighbor over for a drink once in a while to ensure he procures a few invitations to the games. When the neighbor sells his season tickets, the relationship ends. If a boss has a private jet he takes to play golf, serves on prestigious boards, and is a member at the coveted country club, the abuser will ensure he befriends his boss, supports all of his ideas, and takes his side in corporate decisions. In this way he will become part of the inner circle. He will be included in golf vacations on the private jet, invited to serve on boards where he will meet other wealthy and powerful corporate titans, and sponsored into the "in" social crowd at the country club. When the boss is fired or retires, the relationship fizzles because he is no longer useful to the abuser.

Male SNAPs view women as inferior. Women are primarily seen as sexual objects to be conquered—as necessary but expendable tagalongs to their husbands to whom the abuser must be polite. If they are unattractive, he considers them blobs to be ignored. They are not viewed as individuals with value. An abuser views an attractive woman as a challenge to see if he can get her to sleep with him. Few things are more intoxicating to an abuser than pretending to be charming and convincing a beautiful woman to allow him to enter her body. It is the ultimate power game. Once he has achieved that goal, he may or may not have any further relationship with her. There are always other beautiful women waiting to play the game. The abuser views the wives of friends, colleagues, or associates as merely accessories to their husbands. He must be polite to continue his relationship with her husband, but she has no worth on her own. She is merely tolerated or used for her services or connections. He makes little effort to get to know her or engage her in a genuine conversation. She is treated much like a potted plant—ignored unless she needs watering. If her husband dies or is fired, she is no longer useful to the abuser and contact ends abruptly. The abuser views unattractive women as completely useless. He either ridicules them or pays them no attention.

Abusers have no need for people who have less power or money than themselves. They view them as inferior and as having little value other than to serve them. People who serve in the service professions all qualify as inferior to the SNAP. Therefore, administrative assistants, customer service representatives, wait staff in restaurants, hostesses, concierges, teachers, social workers, case workers, nannies, housekeepers, people who work in nonprofit organizations, and those in similar positions are all looked down upon and subject to merciless verbal abuse by abusers.

Healthy people treat others with respect and allow for minor shortcomings or corporate errors over which a representative has no control. Healthy people also find a way to solve the issue at hand. Abusers take those opportunities to excoriate a human being they view as less than human.

Marriage

Healthy people view marriage as a lifelong, equal partnership between two people who celebrate and appreciate two different people with unique hopes, dreams, strengths, weaknesses, and opinions, and who believe they are better together than apart. Healthy people espouse God's purpose for marriage, which is to be an example of God's love for us; to provide love, support, encouragement, protection, provision, and companionship; and to raise children in the love of the Lord. In God's design, the husband has the primary responsibility to care for and be a godly example for his wife and family. Like the police, he has a duty "to serve and protect." A wife has the primary responsibility to respect her husband and love, nurture, support, encourage and be a godly example to him and their family. Of course, in healthy families these roles are not rigidly enforced but allow for individual strengths and gifts. Although the roles may be different in different families, the husband and wife are equally valued, and both parties defer to each other out of their love for Christ. The life a couple builds and the material wealth they create is viewed as a shared creation between equal partners. A healthy marriage involves a monogamous relationship in which sex is a sacred act of giving one's self in the most emotionally, spiritually, and physically intimate relationship.

The SNAP, however, plays the starring role, producer, director, and promotor of his life. He allows for no costars and no directors. He directs his life as he pleases, not God. "My Way" is his life's theme song, not "God's Way." Everyone else exists to support *him*. His primary goals in life are to amass *his* wealth, create *his* lifestyle, build *his* house, buy *his* material possessions, and enhance *his* career. A wife, therefore, is there to serve *him* along *his* way to success, to attend to *him* as *his* arm candy, and to raise *his* children. The abuser, therefore, attempts to choose and groom a woman who will act as an extension of himself. She must sacrifice any hopes or dreams she may have and adopt his as her own. She must, in effect, be subsumed into him. Her career, if he allows her to have one, will always be less important than his. The wealth and material possessions they amass will always be viewed by the abuser as his own, as will the business they have built together and the community they have surrounded themselves with. Even the children they create together will be perceived as his own.

The wife's contributions of full-time counselor, cook, maid, nurse, tutor, caregiver, chauffeur, room mother, teacher, interior designer, vacation planner, social planner, community volunteer, corporate spouse, and general manager of a household are not considered by the abuser as valuable because she didn't earn any money doing these activities (although it certainly would have cost tens of thousands of dollars per year if they were hired out). Women who give up a career to raise a family with an abuser, or work at his company or practice, are summarily dismissed for failing to earn money or having marketable skills regardless of whether it was a joint or forced decision.

Even if she did have a career outside the home, a wife's contributions are not appreciated if the abuser earns more. As Tim sneered to his wife, Charlotte, during divorce negotiations, her six-figure salary, which was spent supporting their family for fifteen years, was "negligible." On the other hand, if his wife earns more than he, the abuser is more than happy to take advantage of her earnings, live off her, and demand maintenance from her during a divorce. An abuser will be the first one to cry "poverty," play the victim, and try to take advantage of his wife's resources. Patrick, who had easily earned hundreds of thousands of dollars per year as a lawyer prior to getting fired from his law firm, was only too happy to put all his children from a previous marriage on his new wife's corporate health insurance. When their marriage ended after only a year due to his physical abuse, he demanded an upfront payment, alimony, and part of his wife's retirement savings.

For the abuser, marriage does not mean a sexually faithful relationship, at least not for him. Because the abuser uses people for his own selfish desires, they are seldom monogamous. He understands that the rest of the world believes marriage should be monogamous, and he understands that his wife thinks their marriage is exclusive. Thus, he understands that he must hide his multiple affairs and porn addiction. On the other hand, he expects complete sexual fidelity from his wife. Ironically, abusers universally accuse their wives of infidelity because they project what they are most guilty of doing themselves.

Many women in a long-term marriage to an abuser state that they "lost" themselves—they do not know who they are, their likes and dislikes, their own opinions, their own strengths and weaknesses, or whether they are good at anything at all. The abuser co-opts his wife into becoming an extension of himself. She is criticized and ridiculed for her individuality until her likes and dislikes become his. Her opinion is belittled until it agrees with his; her strengths and weaknesses are exploited for his selfish pursuits, and her talents and skills are disparaged until they are never again used. At that point, the wife has melted into nothingness and the abuser comes into complete control, just as he planned all along.

Money

In healthy people of faith, money is viewed as a blessing from God. It is a resource to be used to carry out God's purposes, provide for life's necessities, afford blessings to one's family and friends, and offer support for worthy charitable causes. Because believers view money as a gift from God, they view themselves as stewards of the money God has entrusted to them. They neither hoard nor squander it. Rather, they invest their money wisely and use it prudently. They live under their means so there is a provision for a rainy day. Whether they are wealthy or of more modest means, God's people have a spirit of generosity and give freely to bless others, knowing they can never out-give God. They know that in God's economy, He will bless them far more than they give. Healthy people do not measure a person's worth by the amount of money they make or by their net worth. Rather, people are valued regardless of their financial condition.

However, for SNAPs, money is viewed as an extension of themselves. Their primary goal in life is to make as much money as they can and enjoy all the privileges that come with it. Therefore, they think about money constantly. They are often workaholics; they measure the value of others by a financial yardstick, deriving their identity from their net worth, income, and career.

Because money is their identity and an extension of themselves, abusers do not share well. For an abuser, parting with money is like chopping off his left hand and giving it away. They are loath to do so. If they do "give" money to an individual, it is usually a family member, and it will likely be in the form of a loan or investment the abuser will use to wield power over that person. He will constantly remind the recipient of the loan or investment of his power over him. The abuser essentially owns the debtor.

Because abusers use people as objects and value money over nearly everything, they are also loath to honor contracts or any form of obligation, particularly if it requires money. Yet they are the first to cry foul and initiate legal action when they believe they have been wronged. SNAPs clog our courtrooms with lawsuits. They are either the defendant who violates a business contract, refuses to pay alimony or child support to a former spouse, or any number of other ways they attempt to escape legal obligations—or they are the plaintiff who is incessantly harassing a former spouse or bringing a frivolous lawsuit when others no longer want to do business or employ them because they are too difficult to work with.

Thus, an abuser is happy to brag about his wealth and even exaggerate and lie about his wealth when it suits him. For example, when he is attracting a new partner, attempting to get into the right country club, or trying to get a loan from a bank, he will gladly speak of his riches. However, that same abuser will claim poverty and even lie by understating his wealth when it suits him. At no time is this more pronounced than when the abuser is in the middle of a divorce. Regardless of how much wealth he has, whether he is a prince or a pauper, the abuser will lie and claim poverty to wriggle out of paying spousal alimony and child support. An abuser will enter into an agreement he has no intention of upholding, forcing a former spouse to go back to court time and time again to enforce alimony and child support payments. Indeed, some abusers take the vindictive approach of quitting their jobs just to avoid paying alimony and child support.

In a marriage, an abuser views all the money made and assets acquired during the marriage as his own. Indeed, the abuser values money above people and relationships, including his wife. Thus, if the abuser earns more than his wife, it is not uncommon for him to require an onerous prenuptial agreement shortly before a wedding giving him ownership of anything made during a marriage. In addition, hiding money or assets; lying about money or assets; allowing a wife no access to money or assets; putting all accounts, houses, cars, and businesses solely in the abuser's name; and requiring a spouse to beg for money, provide sexual services in exchange for living expenses, provide detailed receipts, and be put on a tight allowance is typical for abusers with a higher earnings capacity and more assets than his spouse.

On the other hand, an abuser who has foolishly depleted his assets, squandered his money, is too lazy to work, or has been fired from his job will target a wealthy, vulnerable woman so he can take advantage of her wealth. Thus, older abusers who have gone through a divorce (or two or three) and are no longer earning what they were in their younger years often target a wealthy widow for their next victim. In this situation, since she has the wealth the abuser is trying to exploit, an abuser is not likely to demand a prenuptial agreement.

Abusers often choose careers that lead to power, control, and money. A recent article revealed that psychopaths make up a disproportionate percentage of people in careers such as CEOs, surgeons, politicians and civil servants, lawyers, chefs, police, media personalities, journalists, and pastors.[39] It comes as no surprise that the people in these careers are overwhelmingly male.

Unlike healthy people, SNAPs have no generosity of spirit. They are usually squeaky tight with their money, even if they are worth millions. If they spend lavishly, it is usually on themselves, to make an impression, or to get something in return. They do not give to charities quietly; they demand acknowledgment. Depending on the size of the donation, this may include a recognition in the donor lists, a special donor dinner, tickets to games, VIP invitations to events with the president, a named building, or a foundation named after them.

As we discuss in chapter 9, financial abuse takes place in 99 percent of abusive relationships. Financial abuse is the result of the overwhelming love of money, which is universal among abusers. The Bible warns that greed—that is, the love of money—is the same as idolatry (Colossians 3:5). When we read of idolatry in the Old Testament where people worshiped a gold calf or other idols they made, we often scratch our heads and wonder how they could have done so. It seems so silly. But in modern times, we see people who value, to the point of worship, money and all the things it can buy: houses, cars, and other material goods, as well as prestige, sex, and

---

[39] Lindsay Dodgson, "Ten Professions with the Most Psychopaths," *Business Insider*, May 20, 2018, https://www.businessinsider.com/professions-with-the-most-psychopaths-2018-5).

power. These are also created by man, yet abusers worship them and not the Creator who gives them. It comes as no surprise that abusers are greedy idolaters.

When we value money over nearly everything else, we become prideful, devalue and demean others, and make self-serving decisions to hurt others. Paul warns his young friend Timothy not that *money* is the root of so much evil, but that the *love of money* is the root of all kinds of evil (1 Timothy 6:10). The truth of this warning is no more apparent than in the profusion of destruction that a money-loving abuser leaves in his wake.

Sex

For healthy persons of faith, sex is a joyous, life-giving, loving, gentle, sacred time of giving to each other and pleasing each other in the context of a monogamous, committed, emotionally and spiritually intimate, lifelong relationship. Even among Christians, couples who are not married engage in sex. Nevertheless, outside of marriage, healthy sexual relationships still retain the qualities of a joyous, life-giving, loving, gentle, and sacred time between two people who are monogamous and emotionally and spiritually intimate. Christian mental health experts generally view healthy sexual relations as those within the context of a monogamous, intimate relationship.

For the abuser, however, sex is simply a desire that must be satisfied, and he is not particular as to who satisfies him. He does not need emotional or spiritual intimacy, or even a relationship, to engage in sex. Indeed, because abusers are unable to connect with others on a deep level of intimacy, all their relationships are shallow and superficial, much like the abuser himself. For the abuser, sex is a time to take what he wants and satisfy himself. If his partner is under the weather, exhausted, suffering a migraine, on her way to a business meeting, getting the kids to soccer, grieving over the loss of a parent, working on a deadline, or engaged in any of the other life experiences healthy people would consider a good reason to postpone sex until both parties are in a better physical and emotional state, it doesn't matter. He wants sex when he wants it, and her physical or emotional state is no matter. He will hound her and follow her relentlessly until she acquiesces, or he will simply force himself upon her. Sex is often rough, unromantic, coerced, degrading, and dehumanizing.

As we discussed above, sexual infidelity in marriage and other supposedly monogamous relationships is common among abusers. Because of the abuser's incredible ability to lie and deceive, multiple affairs and prostitutes are often hidden from a wife for years. While he has no compunction to be faithful, he clearly feels he owns his wife and expects her to be faithful, even when he is not. Indeed, even if he has had affairs, if he thinks his wife is unfaithful, he will be enraged, hound her relentlessly to reveal the supposed lover, play the victim, slander her among family and friends, and often be physically abusive. He will often sexually assault her multiple times to let her know he controls her.

Abusers feel they own a person with whom they have had sex. That woman is expected to stay sexually faithful to him until he calls off the relationship, even if he has other relationships. For example, a mafia boss will often have a wife and a girlfriend. Both are expected to stay sexually faithful to him, even though both the wife and the girlfriend are aware of each other.

Abusers use sex, and especially rape, to let their wives know the abuser is in complete control. Nothing is as humiliating, dehumanizing, and degrading as being raped. Rape takes an act intended by God to be a sacred act of love and adulterates it into an act of violence and control over a vulnerable human. Only Satan, with his willing faithful follower, can do that. Among abusers, marital rape and sexual abuse is common, not just once, but as a regular occurrence.

Most women who have been married to abusers feel as if they have been treated as a prostitute. They do not

The World according to the Narcissist, Sociopath, Psychopath, and Other Abusers

feel valued or loved during sex; rather, they feel used and exploited. How far this is from God's perfect design of loving, joyous, life-giving, sweet and tender moments in the arms of one's beloved!

Children

Healthy people of faith welcome the arrival of a child, marveling and rejoicing at the gift of God's miracle of life. It is an occasion of grateful humility that the Lord of the universe has entrusted a little person to their care. Every child is a gift from God, endowed with unique attributes, talents, skills, and characteristics that set them apart as their own independent person in the image of God. As children grow, we nurture them, encourage them, teach them, and help them become independent so they can make their own wise decisions, choose a mate, and start a family of their own. Our job is to work ourselves out of a job.

For abusers, however, children are a different story. Abusers are usually equal-opportunity abusers. The people who will stoop low enough to hurt a woman will also hurt a child. All abusers are cowards. They prey on vulnerable people and animals to make themselves look better. Children are always in a position of weakness and defenselessness compared to an adult male abuser. Of course, picking on weaker people and animals makes abusers look better only in their own warped minds. Healthy people are repelled and disgusted by men abusing weaker and defenseless women, children, and animals.

Physically violent abusers view children with the same disdain in which they view their partners. For a woman with this type of abuser, pregnancy and the child-rearing years are filled with fear for the safety of her children. Physically violent abusers often beat their wives during pregnancy, causing miscarriage or damage to the child and the mother. When a child is born, the abuser has little to no regard for the child's safety or well-being. Rather than protecting the child, which is a natural response, they view the child as a bother and intentionally physically harm or neglect the child. Their harsh disciplinary measures go far beyond what is reasonable and necessary to discipline a child. They have a sense of ownership over the child, and they ascribe to the adage, "I brought you into this world, and I can take you out."

Some abusers, due to cultural and ethnic factors, value the children but not the mother, whom they view as a brood mare who exists only to give them children. These are often the cultures that value men over women and boys over girls. Therefore, the male children are catered to, spoiled, and brought up to be entitled misogynists like their fathers, while the girls are considered as less than, second class, curses rather than blessings, and are brought up to serve the males.

Some abusers view their children as extensions of themselves rather than as independent beings with their own hopes, dreams, likes, dislikes, skills, talents, and strengths. These abusers, often "white-collar abusers" who exert financial and psychological control rather than physical violence, want to relive their lives through their children. The children are paraded among family, friends, and business associates like shiny little trophies to be admired when they are young, and then sent off when the abuser is done showing them off. The children are forced to take up the sports or activities the abuser excelled in or wanted to excel in, attend the college the abuser attended or wanted to attend, and go into the family-owned business the abuser is in or wanted to be in. Rather than unconditional love, the affection of an abuser is doled out in small measures only when the children meet the expectations of the abuser, and it is withheld when they don't. For the abuser, love is based on performance. Often children feel like they never measure up, because the abuser's expectations are unrealistic. Even when the children are exemplary in their studies or performances, the abuser is loath to give encouragement or affection. Thus, rather than a healthy relationship in which love is given freely because the child is part of a family who unconditionally supports and loves each other, the children learn that love must be earned. These abusers often exert lifelong control over their children, especially when the adult children work in the family business controlled by the abuser. Not only is the child's financial and emotional future in the hands of the abuser, but his social and family networks revolve around the abuser as well.

Children of abusers face lifelong challenges. In order to thrive, children need to be raised in a loving, secure environment where they are loved unconditionally, taught morals, values, and life lessons with patience, and have a sense of belonging. Abusers are incapable of providing these conditions.

Chapter 6

Emotionally Healthy Relationships

MANY WOMEN HAVE BEEN in a dysfunctional relationship for so long that they no longer know what is healthy. Oftentimes women in abusive marriages have been with their husbands their entire adult lives and have no comparison to healthy relationships. Therefore, before we dive into the description of an emotionally abusive relationship and the tactics used by abusers, we start with the characteristics of an emotionally healthy relationship.

Healthy relationships are life-giving. Humans are made to be in relationship with each other. We are not created to be solitary individuals. Our relationships give meaning and richness to our lives. In healthy human relationships, people bless, enrich, encourage, teach, exhort, and help each other grow.

In this chapter we will explore different viewpoints of healthy marriage relationships. Fortunately, this is an area where the secular world of psychology and the biblical world of God's ordinances agree. This should come as no surprise since the study of the psyche is a study of how God made each of us. Each may use different words to describe the same thing, or look at the characteristics of healthy relationships from a different angle, but in the end, both the secular and biblical views agree that healthy relationships bring out the best in us and help us thrive. And that is the very definition of the abundant life!

Secular Viewpoints of Healthy Relationships

Hierarchy of Needs

Psychologist Abraham Maslow, in his famous hierarchy of needs, noted that humans have five basic needs that must be met for healthy human development.

At the most basic level lies physiological needs of human survival: food, air, water, clothing, and shelter. Once the basic physiological needs are met, physical safety needs take priority. People need to feel safe in their environments. War, natural disasters, intimate partner abuse, child abuse, a dangerous work or community environment, financial ruin, and life-threatening illness are just a few things that threaten feelings of safety. If a person's need for safety and security are not met, they may experience PTSD or transgenerational trauma, a phenomenon that occurs when the effects of trauma are transferred from one generation to the next.

Once safety needs are met, the need for love and belonging take over. Humans need to love and be loved. Each person needs to feel a sense of love, belonging, and acceptance with their social groups, including their intimate partner, family, friends, colleagues, religious organizations, professional organizations, community, etc. The smaller the social group, the stronger the need for love, belonging, and acceptance. Thus, the need for love, belonging, and acceptance is the strongest between intimate partners and among family members. The need for belonging is so strong that in some cases it overrides the safety and even physiological needs, as evidenced by children who cling to or side with an abusive parent, or spouses who stay with an abusive spouse.

Once these needs are met, the person focuses on the need for esteem. The need for esteem encompasses self-esteem, self-respect, self-confidence, competency and mastery of one's abilities, strength, independence, and freedom. These needs focus on the inner life of the individual—their view of themselves. Another related need is the need for respect, status, recognition, prestige, and attention. These needs focus on how others perceive the individual.

When all other needs are met, individuals can focus on the highest level of need, which, according to Maslow, is the need for self-actualization. This is the need to be the most one can be or accomplish, given the way one is wired. Using all your God-given gifts and talents to be all that God has designed you to be is self-actualization. For example, if an individual is, by design, created with a great deal of artistic talent, he may have a deep desire to become a painter, sculptor, or designer. On the other hand, if someone has a natural aptitude for math and computers, she may have a strong desire to become a computer designer. Self-actualization applies the army's slogan to all of us: Be All You Can Be.

Although the needs can be overlapping, in general, Maslow maintained that everyone must meet their most basic needs before fulfilling the next level of needs. For example, it's nearly impossible to achieve the need for love and belonging when one doesn't have enough food to survive. Unless there is another overriding force (for example, a deeply religious person willing to die for another), if a person doesn't have food to live, he will risk being rejected by others in his community and keep any food that is found for himself. Likewise, it is nearly impossible for an individual to have self-esteem, self-respect, and self-confidence without first feeling loved and accepted.

In healthy, intimate relationships, we help each other meet these needs out of our love for each other. Love, at its essence, is doing what is in the best interest of another. In traditional families, husbands take on the role of provider, protector, companion, lover, supporter, role model, and teacher to his children. He makes sure his family's physiological needs of food, air, water, clothing, and shelter are met. As his family's protector, he ensures that the physical, emotional, and financial safety needs are met. A healthy man is an emotionally mature man who accepts the responsibility of loving, supporting, accepting, and encouraging his wife and children. A healthy man has self-respect and self-confidence (not to be confused with pride or arrogance), is secure in his abilities, accepts his limitations, and has the respect of others. He helps those in his family gain these same characteristics through patient teaching and encouragement. A healthy man strives to be all he can be, but he balances his professional life with the needs of his family. A healthy man does not sacrifice his wife and family on the altar of money, prestige, fame, or glory. Rather, he sacrifices his own desires for the more important needs of his wife and family.

A healthy husband and father is the financial and emotional foundation for his family. He makes them feel safe, secure, loved, accepted, and cherished. His family knows he loves them, and because he does, he will do whatever is in their best interest, sacrificing his own interests if necessary to make sure their needs are met.

Levels of Intimacy

In the book *The Seven Levels of Intimacy*, author Matthew Kelly discusses the requirements for a truly intimate relationship. To know and be known is the greatest joy and the height of a healthy husband and wife relationship.

According to Kelly, the first level of intimacy is clichés, those trite sayings or pleasantries we might say to a grocery clerk in passing. "Hi, how are you?" "Fine and you?" "Fine, thanks. Have a good day." There is no intimacy in this first stage.

The second level of intimacy is an exchange of facts. When people talk about sports, the weather, the economy, or other impersonal facts, this exchange of information keeps people at a distance. There is not much intimacy here either.

The third level of intimacy is a free expression of opinions of both parties. Here we reveal a little something about ourselves. The key to going to the next level of intimacy is to accept others regardless of their opinion, and to have the maturity to agree to disagree without trying to win others to one's side or insulting them for not sharing one's opinion.

The fourth level of intimacy is sharing one's hopes and dreams with another, which again reveals a great deal about someone's inner thoughts and character. The key to intimacy at this level is accepting another's hopes and dreams and helping your partner achieve them. It is important for a successful relationship to have a common hope and dream—a common purpose two parties pursue together. Athletic teams work better when individuals work together for the success of the team. Similarly, a successful relationship may require individuals to sideline their personal desires, at least temporarily, for the success of the couple in achieving their common purpose.

The fifth level of intimacy is freely sharing feelings. The key to intimacy at this level, again, is acceptance and true listening, which gives others the courage to make themselves vulnerable enough to share their true feelings. Sharing met with criticism or judgment will quickly stop.

The sixth level of intimacy is sharing one's faults, fears, and failures with another—the act of being emotionally naked in front of our intimate partner. It involves confessing and accepting responsibility for our faults and failures, owning up to our limitations, admitting our fears and who we really are, and humbly asking for help. It also involves wanting to be the best version of ourselves. Once again, achieving this level of intimacy with a spouse requires accepting and forgiving ourselves and others.

Finally, the seventh and highest level of intimacy is mutually knowing and helping each other meet their legitimate physical, emotional, intellectual, and spiritual needs. Physical needs are the basic needs of food, water, air, shelter, safety, etc. Emotional needs include the need to love and be loved, to express one's opinions, to be listened to and taken seriously, to share one's opinions, to be accepted for the person one is, and emotional intimacy with one's partner. Intellectual needs include intellectual stimulation that engages and challenges. And spiritual needs include the need for silence, solitude, and reflection. On the other hand, illegitimate wants are self-centered, ego-based, ruthless, selfish desires.

Genuine relationships are characterized by give and take—not taking what you want, but helping each other become the best version of themselves. Relationships in which one or both parties take without giving or demand that their own selfish desires be satisfied at the expense of the other are doomed to failure and will never achieve true intimacy. Those who enter a relationship with the what's-in-it-for-me and grab-what-you-want philosophy ensure the relationship will not last.

Love, according to Kelly, is:

> A desire to see the person we love be and become all he or she is capable of being and becoming. Love is a willingness to lay down our personal plans, desires, and agenda for the good of the relationship. Love is delayed gratification, pleasure, and pain. Love is being able to live and thrive apart, but choosing to be together. You know you love somebody when you are willing to subordinate your personal plans, desires, and agenda to the good of the relationship. You know another person loves you when he or she is willing to subordinate his or her personal plans, desires, and agenda to the good of the relationship.[40]

Seven Principles of a Healthy Marriage

Dr. John Gottman has devoted his entire forty-plus-year career to understanding what makes a marriage work and the warning signs that a divorce is on the horizon. By observing how a couple responds to each other, he can predict a divorce with 94 percent accuracy![41] Conversely, he has identified seven principles essential to a healthy marriage in his best-selling book *The Seven Principles for Making Marriage Work*.[42]

First, emotionally healthy couples are familiar with the details of each other's life. They know each other. They try to know each other's likes and dislikes, hopes and dreams, fears and struggles, goals and worries, history and important dates, and beliefs and values. Whether it's her favorite perfume, his allergies to oysters, her current project at work, or his love of family genealogy—they each make substantial efforts to know the other and to make each other their priority. The biblical term for sexual love is to know the other—and knowing the other is the first principle of a healthy marriage.

Second, emotionally healthy couples are fond of and admire one another. They recognize the good qualities in each other, cherish each other, feel that each other is worthy of honor and respect, and they regularly affirm each other and those good qualities they see and treasure in each other. In line with the biblical principles for seeing others as gifts made in God's image (Genesis 1:27), focusing on that which is honorable and pure and lovely (Philippians 4:8), and encouraging each other (1 Thessalonians 5:11), Gottman's second principle is crucial in a thriving, lasting marriage.

Third, emotionally healthy couples turn their hearts toward each other. They intentionally engage in small interactions throughout the day. They verbally reach out for the other, hoping for a positive response, and they respond positively when the other reaches out. When a spouse responds positively, it establishes points of emotional connection, builds trust, fans passion, and makes for a more satisfying sex life, as the couple remains emotionally connected. In turning toward each other, each spouse is making deposits of goodwill in their love bank, which grows with each positive interaction. When difficult times arise, a large balance of goodwill in the love bank will more than offset the withdrawals. Conversely, when a spouse is ignored, rejected, or criticized when he or she reaches out, this leads to fewer attempts to reach out for fear of further rejection, and it eventually causes them to withdraw. Gottman found that with happily married couples, spouses responded positively to the other's "reach out" 86 percent of the time, while with couples who eventually divorced, spouses only responded to the

---

[40] Matthew Kelly, *The Seven Levels of Intimacy* (New York: Simon & Schuster, 2005) 222–223.
[41] Gottman, Katz, and Buehlman, "How a Couple Views Their Past Predicts Their Future: Predicting Divorce from an Oral History Interview," *Journal of Family Psychology* 5, no. 3 and 4 (March/June 1992): 295–318.
[42] John Gottman, *The Seven Principles for Making Marriage Work* (New York: Harmony Books, 2015).

other's "reach out" 33 percent of the time.[43] Turning our hearts toward each other mirrors the biblical concept of turning our hearts toward God and those we love.

Fourth, emotionally healthy couples share power. They engage in joint decision-making, view the other as a true partner, and treat each other with honor and respect. Gottman found that husbands had the most difficulty allowing their wives to influence their decisions, rather than the other way around. Men who insist on their own way leave their wives feeling dishonored and disrespected. These men don't offer honor and respect because they are too concerned about getting honor and respect—they don't respect their wife's opinion because they fear losing power. When a man is unwilling to share power with his wife, there is an 81 percent chance his marriage will self-destruct.[44] However, men who shared decisions were willing to learn things from their wives, allowed their wives to influence them, had happier relationships with their wives and children, and were less likely to divorce. Mutual honor and respect in marriage is not only an important part of the wedding vows to love, honor, and cherish, but it is also an essential biblical principle outlined by Paul (Ephesians 5:21–33).

Fifth, emotionally healthy couples seek to resolve solvable conflicts. They do this by engaging each other with respect and without accusing, blaming, criticizing, or having contempt. They will use a normal, softer tone of voice and neutral, noninflammatory words that address the conflict without attacking the other person. Working together, they will de-escalate the tension, soothe one another, and reach a compromise that respects the other's point of view and heals any emotional wounds.

Sixth, emotionally healthy couples avoid gridlock on opposing views. Gridlock happens when couples continue to have the same argument with no resolution, when the issue cannot be addressed with humor, empathy, or affection, when the issue becomes more divisive over time, and when compromise seems impossible without giving up important values, beliefs, or a sense of self. Overcoming gridlock is accomplished by digging below the surface conflict to discover the deep hopes, dreams, and even fears of each spouse, respectfully honoring and acknowledging each other's aspirations, and making it a goal of the marriage to help each other realize their dreams.

Finally, couples who have a deep connection with each other share a spiritual kinship evidenced by a profound sense of a shared meaning and purpose for their lives, their marriage, and their family. Couples who share heartfelt convictions create a family culture in which they (1) establish rituals and traditions that connect them to each other, (2) support each other's roles in the family unit, (3) have mutual goals and legacies they wish to leave, and (4) have shared values and beliefs, oftentimes religious values and beliefs, that are the cornerstone of their worldview and influence their decision-making and lifestyle.[45] This seventh principle is like the biblical view of the primary purpose of marriage, which is to serve each other and to serve others as an example to the world of God's love for us.

Biblical View of Healthy Relationships

The Bible outlines a healthy marriage with specific roles for both husbands and wives. God has created us, and the Bible is His operating manual for human relationships. Unsurprisingly, the biblical viewpoint aligns with the psychological viewpoints of a healthy marriage.

---

[43] Gottman, *Seven Principles*, 88.
[44] Gottman, *Seven Principles*, 116.
[45] Gottman, *Seven Principles*, 260–271.

God's Purpose for Marriage

According to biblical scholars, an earthly marriage is designed to reflect the unconditional love God has for us. A marriage was created to be a little slice of heaven—a miniature version of the love, encouragement, peace, and joy that reign in heaven. Although secondary purposes include companionship, protection, mutual help, and a healthy environment for raising children, the primary purpose is to be an example to the world of God's unending love.

God's Description of Love

God is love. Love is His nature. Love is necessary for a healthy marriage. Love is the foundation upon which a marriage is built. Sadly, *love* is so overused and misused that its meaning has become distorted. Thankfully, St. Paul gave us a description of love as it applies to human relationships and our relationship with God: "Love is patient, love is kind. It does not envy, it does not boast, it is not proud. It does not dishonor others, it is not self-seeking, it is not easily angered, it keeps no record of wrongs. Love does not delight in evil but rejoices with the truth. It always protects, always trusts, always hopes, always perseveres" (1 Corinthians 13:4–7). As is evident by this description, love is an action word. It's not a feeling, and it's not something that comes and goes. If you sum it up, love is always acting in the best interest of another. This is the litmus test of love: Wherever you find the words *love* or *it* in the above passage, replace it with the name of your spouse or intimate partner. Is the statement true? If it is true, then you have real, godly love—the kind of love God designed for us. If not, whatever you may have, it is not love.

St. Paul informs us that both men and women should be in mutual submission to each other out of our respect and love for Jesus (Ephesians 5:21). Submission doesn't mean we should be doormats, but rather we should give respectful deference, when possible and when it is not contrary to God's Word, to the reasonable needs and requests of others.

Emotional Health in the Fruit of the Spirit

Only two emotionally healthy and mature persons can create a marriage that fully carries out God's purposes for marriage. The Bible describes an emotionally healthy person, and these are the characteristics we need to aspire to and the characteristics we should look for in a spouse. These qualities of emotional health and maturity are found in the character of God. It is no wonder, then, that they are called the fruit of the Spirit. The more we are filled with God's Holy Spirit, the more our character becomes like God's. These qualities are the natural by-products of a close relationship with God. Conversely, those who don't have God's Spirit in them do not have these characteristics. You will not find these traits in a narcissist, sociopath, psychopath, or other domestic abusers.

"But the fruit of the Spirit is love, joy, peace, forbearance, kindness, goodness, faithfulness, gentleness and self-control . . ." (Galatians 5:22–23). An in-depth look at each of these character traits gives us a fuller view of emotional health.

Love has already been described in 1 Corinthians 13:4–7 and in the paragraphs above. Love is the very nature of God. God is love (1 John 4:8). An emotionally healthy and mature person loves God, others, and himself.

Joy that comes from the Lord is the gladness of heart that comes from knowing God, abiding in Christ, and being filled with the Holy Spirit. While happiness can be a temporary state of mind when we get what we want, joy is an underlying, ever-present rejoicing of the heart regardless of earthly circumstances because of God's goodness and unending kindness. The Bible tells us, "The joy of the Lord is [my] strength" (Nehemiah 8:10). Those who possess this supernatural joy draw strength because they know God is for them, with them, and at work in all things to bring about good. Joy is a natural product of thankfulness, and thankfulness is a natural product of humility. When we are humble—that is, when we personally know the awesomeness of an all-powerful, all-knowing, all-present, all-loving, and just God who loves us in spite of our sins—we are thankful He loves us and showers us with His blessings. When our hearts are overflowing with thankfulness, we can't help but praise God. And when we praise the Lord, God inhabits the praises of His people (Psalm 22:3). Through praise, God draws near to us and fills us with joy—and the Enemy can't stand it, so he runs away. It is nearly impossible to be overcome with fear and doubt, the favorite tools of the Enemy, when we praise God with joyful voices. In fact, researchers now confirm what the Bible has said for thousands of years: gratitude is the remedy for anxiety, stress, and depression because it releases the hormones dopamine and serotonin, the two crucial neurotransmitters responsible for our feel-good emotions of happiness, optimism, and joy.[46]

Prideful and entitled persons never experience true joy because nothing is ever good enough. It is hard to be thankful for something when one thinks they are entitled to it anyway. Such people are unhappy, complaining, unsatisfied, and lack joy. When one is truly thankful—that is, when one understands and appreciates that every good thing in our lives is a gift from a loving heavenly Father, one is filled with a lasting joy that comes only from God. The key to joy is humility, thankfulness, and praise. An emotionally healthy person is joyful, humble, and thankful and gives praise to God and others for his blessings.

Peace that comes from the Lord is not just an absence of conflict, but is a state of tranquility or quietness of spirit that transcends circumstances. It is a sense of wholeness, completeness, and confidence in God's goodness, even amid the storms of life. Paul tells us that God's peace in us transcends all human understanding (Philippians 4:7). Peace is a natural product of trust in God, and trust is a natural product of faith in God. Those who have peace have a trust in the Lord that comes from a deep faith. Regardless of the turbulence of this life, they know God is our shelter, defender, and shield. When our time in this world is done, He will call us home to heaven, which will be inexpressibly wonderful. We have an eternal viewpoint, so whether we are in this world or heading to the next, peace, trust, and faith keep our spirit calm. The key to peace is trust and faith in the Lord. An emotionally healthy and mature person is peaceful, trusts the Lord, and has placed his faith in God.

Forbearance, or patience, is the ability to delay gratification, to help others in their development, and to not get upset when things don't go our way. Patience comes from unselfishness, and unselfishness comes from seeing God's image in others. When we see God's image in others, we become other-focused, we are unselfish, and we don't get frustrated by the failures of others, but we celebrate their successes as they move closer on their journey to becoming more like God. We can wait on the Lord in His good timing to bring about His purposes, not ours. The key to patience is unselfishness and seeing God's image in others. An emotionally healthy and mature person is patient, unselfish, and sees God in others.

Kindness is the tender, benevolent attitude of the heart. Kindness is not just good manners; kindness is love in action. Kind people make a point to be observant of the needs of others and go out of their way to meet that need. The key to kindness is loving others like God loves us. An emotionally healthy and mature person is kind and loving.

---

[46] Madhuleena Roy Chowdhury, "The Neuroscience of Gratitude and How it Affects Anxiety and Grief," February 11, 2020, https://positivepsychology.com/neuroscience-of-gratitude/.

Goodness is the attitude of the heart reflected in virtue, uprightness, and holiness in word and deed. The Greek word is *agathosune*, meaning "uprightness of heart and life" for the benefit of others. Goodness is the opposite of evil. It rests on the notion of righteous character: doing the right thing even if no one is watching, living by a code of honor even if it means sacrifice, and demonstrating honesty and integrity even when others are deceitful and lying. It means being fair even when others are cheating, and working hard even if others are goofing off, and having a generosity of spirit, giving to the poor and needy. Goodness encompasses providing for one's family, visiting and encouraging the sick or downcast, volunteering, protecting others who are weaker, and keeping promises. Goodness is the essential character of God. The glory of God is His goodness. When Moses asked to see God's glory, God responded, "I will cause all of my goodness to pass in front of you, and I will proclaim my name, the Lord, in your presence" (Exodus 33:18–19). The key to a life of goodness is a close walk with God and a desire to be righteous like Him. An emotionally healthy and mature person is virtuous, upright, honest, fair, hard-working, generous, philanthropic, responsible, dependable, protective, trustworthy—and just plain good.

Faithfulness is steadfastness, constancy, and loyalty. Faithfulness is keeping true to what we have been entrusted. When we value or cherish something or someone, we honor that person or thing with our faithfulness. Faithfulness values God's calling on us; it recognizes that God is who He says He is, that He keeps His promises and that we should keep our promises to Him. In a relationship, faithfulness values and cherishes the other because they have placed their trust in us and our commitment to honor the relationship by keeping our promises. An emotionally healthy and mature person is faithful, steadfast, loyal, values the persons and things entrusted to his care, honors his commitments, and keeps his promises.

Gentleness is restraining our strength with tenderness, grace, and humility. Gentleness is the opposite of harshness, anger, pride, and bossiness. Gentleness does not mean weakness, being a doormat, or accepting sin or ill treatment by others. Rather, it is channeling our power with humility and self-restraint to help, encourage, and move others in the direction of God. Although God is all-powerful and can crush us like a bug, in His gentleness He woos us to Himself—tenderly singing over us, reminding us He delights in us, and seeing us through His eyes of love as if we are the fully perfected beings He designed us to be. He does not focus on our sinful failures. Likewise, human gentleness can be found in a 300-pound linebacker who tenderly cradles, sings to, delights in, and protects his daughter. He knows she will disobey at some point, and when (not if) she disobeys, he reminds her of his love and appeals to her higher nature, encouraging her that she can do better. The key to gentleness is setting pride aside and humbly using our strength to encourage others. An emotionally healthy and mature person is gentle, tender, humble, and uses his strength for good.

Finally, self-control is the ability to employ moderation and constraint and to say no to words, deeds, and thoughts that are not God-honoring. Self-control is necessary to stay the course when temptations, disappointments, and frustrations take us in directions incompatible with God's will and are destructive to us and others. Self-control develops perseverance, patience, and the ability to deny ourselves something the world tells us is exciting. Our actions and words are informed by our hearts, and our hearts are informed by our minds. Our minds, in turn, are informed by what we put in them—what we read, see, and experience. Thus, effective self-control includes controlling what we allow ourselves to see and experience, as well as our thoughts, attitudes, and actions. This is why Paul exhorts us to focus our thoughts on things that are true, honorable, right, pure, lovely, admirable, excellent, and worthy of praise (Philippians 4:8)—so we can be transformed by the renewing of our minds and not brought down by the ugliness and depravity of this world (Romans 12:2). When we allow only good things to come into our lives, our attitudes and actions reflect those good things. Abusers who are full of pride and a sense of entitlement are unable to exercise self-control because they believe they are entitled to do anything they want—even if it is destructive to themselves or others. Self-control puts a lid on outbursts of anger or the desire for revenge and gives us the ability to walk away from sinful temptations that could destroy us, our relationships, and our careers. Like goodness, self-control is a matter of character. An emotionally healthy and mature person controls himself, for the good of himself and others, in all situations.

The closer we draw to God, the more God's Spirit abides in us. The more God's Spirit abides in us, the more His Spirit transforms us into His image. The more His Spirit transforms us into His image, the more we see these qualities of God, the fruit of the Spirit, borne out in our lives. If we are having a problem with patience, the solution is not to count to ten or yell into a pillow. The solution is to spend more time with God, to humbly and earnestly seek Him, and to let His Spirit transform our heart. He promises that when we seek Him, He will be found.

A Husband's Calling

Both a husband and wife are called to be supportive of each other in love "out of reverence for Christ. (Ephesians 5:21). Husbands have a high calling. They have been entrusted with the leadership of their family, in that "the husband provides leadership for the wife, just as Christ provides leadership for his church, as the Savior and Reviver of the body" (Ephesians 5:23 TPT). Husbands are called to "love their wives, "just as Christ loved the church and gave himself up for her to make her holy, cleansing her by the washing with water through the word, and to present her to himself as a radiant church, without stain or wrinkle or any other blemish, but holy and blameless. . . . Husbands ought to love their wives as their own bodies. He who loves his wife loves himself. . . . Each one of you also must love his wife as he loves himself" (Ephesians 5:25–28, 33).

Christ loves the church sacrificially. He loved humankind so much that He offered Himself on a cross to bear our sins so we could be in relationship with God and spend eternity with Him. He does not condemn us for our faults and failings, but rather woos us and encourages us and loves us to Himself. He created us and delights in us. He sings songs over us, like a lover would sing a lullaby to his beloved. The Creator of the Universe humbled Himself and took on human form as a living example of God's nature among us. While on earth, He was not a tyrant demanding His own way, but rather led by being a servant. As the head of the church, Christ modeled servant leadership by loving on people, protecting people from evil, blessing others, demonstrating and teaching how we should act, and being their Savior. He doesn't say, "Do as I say, not as I do." Rather, He says, "Do as I do; be like Me. I am your role model." Christ doesn't sit by and watch us as we struggle, but He intercedes on our behalf in the courts of heaven. He is *for* us, not against us, in both the physical and the spiritual realms.

Secure in His love for us, we may come boldly to the very throne of God and carry on whatever work we are called to do here on earth. His love gives us the strength to do all things through Christ. He lovingly sees the best in us and encourages us. As He does, our spirits blossom and we become more lovely and loving. As we spend time with Him and allow His Spirit to mold us more like Him, our sinful selfish nature is replaced with the nature of His Spirit: love, joy, peace, patience, kindness, goodness, faithfulness, gentleness, self-control, humility, forgiveness, singing, and thankfulness (Galatians 5:22–23; Philippians 2:3–8; Colossians 3:12–17). When we are in relationship with God, He gives us His peace, restores our soul, and protects us. He comforts us and honors us. He goes to battle for us. He blesses us with goodness and love, and He lives with us and in us (Psalm 23). He gives us wisdom, prosperity, and good gifts when we follow His ways. We love Christ because He first loved us. He pursued us—some of us He pursued for years, even when we rejected Him, because He loved us and wanted to be in a loving relationship with us.

Christ is the role model for husbands. A husband is to love his wife and family so much that he is willing to sacrifice his life for them. He steps up to the plate and shoulders the burden when things go wrong. A loving husband does not condemn or criticize his family for their faults and failings, but he woos, encourages, and loves them to himself and each other. A husband delights in the wonderful ways his wife and children are uniquely and marvelously made. Imitating God's love for us, a husband sings songs over his wife and family, both with his voice and in his heart. A husband may be an executive or leader at work, but at home, he humbles himself and is a role model of a godly man to his wife and family. Whether at home, at work, or at organizations to which he gives his time, he is a servant leader willing to take on any task before asking others to join him. When a wife or child has a question about how to approach a thorny issue in life, they can always ask, "What would Dad do?"

A husband doesn't sit by and watch his wife or family struggle, but he intervenes on their behalf. He is always for his family; he will always act in his family's best interest. Because his wife and children are secure in his love, they can express themselves within the family with boldness and confidence and let their true selves be intimately known without fear of criticism or rejection. They also have the courage to go out into the world and try to achieve what they are called to do, knowing that whether they succeed or fail, their father will support them. Because a husband sees the best in his wife and children and affirms them, the spirits of his wife and children blossom, they become more loving and lovely, and they in turn see the best in others and affirm them. A husband and father's presence fills his home, and his good spirit rubs off on his wife and children. His influence is felt in his family for generations as he raises the fathers and mothers of his grandchildren. As his wife ages and his children mature, they learn by the example of a Holy Spirit-filled husband and father to exhibit love, joy, peace, patience, kindness, goodness, faithfulness, gentleness, self-control, and humility.

A husband makes a home a haven for his family. With him, his wife and children feel peaceful and their souls are healed and restored from the pressures of the outside world. A husband and father protects his family physically, emotionally, spiritually, and sexually. He comforts his wife and children and makes them feel secure. "I got this" is his motto as he shoulders the burdens of his family. He honors and praises his wife and children and defends his family. He blesses his wife and children with goodness and love, and his good spirit can be felt wherever he goes. With patient instruction, a husband and father gives godly wisdom for living. He is respected by his peers. He works hard and generously provides for his family. He shares his time, talents, and treasures with his local church and other noble causes and charities. He gives good gifts to his family and others.

His wife loves him because he first loved her. She captured his heart with her good spirit, her joy, and her ways. Even before she knew him well, he was taken with this unique, lovely creature. He pursued her and proved his love for her because he saw in her someone with whom he wanted to be in a loving relationship. Of course she loves him, because he proves his love for her every day by fulfilling his wedding vows to love, honor, and cherish her in his thoughts, words, and actions. She can be the CEO of the world with his love supporting her. His children love him also because he first loved them. They captured his heart the minute they were born, and from the second he laid eyes on them, he vowed he would always love and protect them. The best part of their day and his is when he walks through the front door and they wrap their arms around his legs and scream, "Daddy's home!" Of course they love him, because he proves his love for them every day. They can test their wings and fly because they are firmly rooted in his love. A husband and father is the savior of his family.

If you think that is a tall order, it is. But that is the biblical model for a husband and father. God gives this assignment of loving sacrificially to a husband because that is what a woman needs most: love. God designed women, and He knows they cannot function to their highest capacity without love. By their nature, women are often plagued with insecurities, and in this world where women are treated as sex objects, a wife needs to know she is loved for who she is, not for what she does or what she looks like. When a woman feels loved, she blossoms and then has the confidence to love those around her—her husband, her children, her parents, her coworkers—because she is not afraid of losing the love she so desperately needs. A woman needs the confidence that comes from the love and acceptance of her husband so she can be the best version of herself.

God's assignment for husbands and fathers is not merely a suggestion. In fact, there are severe consequences for husbands and fathers who mistreat their wives and families. God rejects the prayers of husbands who mistreat or are unfaithful to their wives, the very ones they should protect and treat with respect as coheirs of the gift of life (1 Peter 3:7; Isaiah 58:4; Malachi 2:13–14). The wise writer of Proverbs 30 states that an unloved woman who is married is one of the things under which the earth trembles (Proverbs 30:21–23). In fact, God is so adamant about His commands that husbands lead the way in being faithful and loving toward their wives and being the spiritual leader of the family that the Bible says God will not punish a wife who commits adultery if her husband has not been faithful to her (Hosea 4:12–14).

A Wife's Calling

Wives also have a high calling. God recognized after making man that it was not good for him to be alone, and so He made a companion for him—a wife. In Hebrew, it is an *ezer kenegdo*. For centuries, *ezer kenegdo* has been mistranslated as a "suitable helper" (NIV) or "help meet" (KJV), suggesting a lesser, weaker, needy, inferior assistant to serve a man. This misunderstood term has been used against women to give primary value and roles to men while devaluing women and assigning them a supporting role as second-class citizens. Nothing could be further from the truth. A more accurate translation from the Hebrew means "a strong corresponding equal." Far from meaning merely a helper, the Hebrew word *ezer* means a strong rescuer, mighty to save. *Ezer* is used throughout the Bible in a military context to refer to God's strength as Israel's warrior. *Kenegdo* has been mistranslated as meaning merely suitable, but it is more accurately translated as meaning a match, a corresponding yet opposite equal—as ying is to yang, as north is to south. God didn't create women to be wimps. God created His daughters to be strong warriors with His sons—companions and brothers and sisters in arms fighting shoulder to shoulder to bring God's kingdom to earth. She will be his strongest ally in pursuing God's purposes, and his first roadblock when he veers off course.[47]

Of course, wives are called to love their husbands, since loving others is what we are all called to do. In addition, wives are called to support their husband's leadership and to respect him. "For wives, this means being supportive to your husbands like you are tenderly devoted to our Lord. . . . In the same way the church is devoted to Christ, let the wives be devoted to their husbands in everything" (Ephesians 5:22, 24 TPT). Many translations state that the "wife must respect her husband" (Ephesians 5:33).

This deference to a husband's leadership has been a point of some contention. However, when a husband follows his calling to sacrificially love his wife as Christ loved the church, it is much easier for his wife to defer to him and respect him. This passage does not, however, give husbands license to act as tyrants, nor does it require

---

[47] "Ezer Kenegdo," God's Words to Women, http://www.godswordtowomen.org/ezerkenegdo.htm; Carolyn Custis James, "The Ezer-Kenegdo: Ezer Unleashed," Faith Gateway, March 20, 2015, https://www.faithgateway.com/ezer-unleashed/#.Xot8cHdFzop.

a wife to blindly follow a husband who is requiring her to do things contrary to God's commands. We are always to obey God above men. Therefore, this passage does not require a wife to violate God's standards just because her husband orders her to do so. A husband who loves his wife would not demand her to do these things in the first place. This passage also does not require a wife to stand idly by as she watches her husband abuse her or her children physically, verbally, emotionally, or spiritually. Such behavior is contrary to God's commands.

Like all people, wives are called to spend time with the Lord and allow His Holy Spirit to mold them into being more like Him so that their sinful, selfish nature is replaced with the nature of His Spirit: love, joy, peace, patience, kindness, goodness, faithfulness, gentleness, self-control, humility, forgiveness, singing, and thankfulness (Galatians 5:22–23; Philippians 2:3–8; Colossians 3:12–17).

Proverbs 31:10–31 gives us a description of a noble wife, as well as a healthy husband-and-wife relationship:

> A wife of noble character who can find?
>   She is worth far more than rubies.
> Her husband has full confidence in her
>   and lacks nothing of value.
> She brings him good, not harm,
>   all the days of her life.
> She selects wool and flax
>   and works with eager hands.
> She is like the merchant ships,
>   bringing her food from afar.
> She gets up while it is still night;
>   she provides food for her family
>   and portions for her female servants.
> She considers a field and buys it;
>   out of her earnings she plants a vineyard.
> She sets about her work vigorously;
>   her arms are strong for her tasks.
> She sees that her trading is profitable,
>   and her lamp does not go out at night.
> In her hand she holds the distaff
>   and grasps the spindle with her fingers.
> She opens her arms to the poor
>   and extends her hands to the needy.
> When it snows, she has no fear for her household;
>   for all of them are clothed in scarlet.
> She makes coverings for her bed;
>   she is clothed in fine linen and purple.
> Her husband is respected at the city gate,
>   where he takes his seat among the elders of the land.
> She makes linen garments and sells them,
>   and supplies the merchants with sashes.
> She is clothed with strength and dignity;

> she can laugh at the days to come.
> She speaks with wisdom,
> > and faithful instruction is on her tongue.
> She watches over the affairs of her household
> > and does not eat the bread of idleness.
> Her children arise and call her blessed;
> > her husband also, and he praises her:
> "Many women do noble things,
> > but you surpass them all."
> Charm is deceptive, and beauty is fleeting;
> > but a woman who fears the Lord is to be praised.
> Honor her for all that her hands have done,
> > and let her works bring her praise at the city gate.

This passage is informative as an example of a godly husband. We see that a wife of noble character is priceless. Her husband knows this and values her for her goodness. He is fully aware she is a blessing to him and their family because she brings good to the entire household. He has full confidence in her and her abilities. He does not try to oppress or control her; rather, he supports her abilities, her running of the household, and her business acumen. He generously praises her and blesses her in front of her children. He is respected in the community by the civic and community leaders, and is himself a leader in the community. Because he is respected by the leaders in the community, we understand he is emotionally mature and a man of wisdom.

Of course, the passage is also an example of a godly wife. From this passage we know she is a confident, strong, and capable woman who makes her own decisions and runs her affairs with strong business acumen. She is multi-talented, as evidenced by her ability to confidently buy real estate with her own earnings and run her own successful businesses. She is confident and has the confidence of her husband. She does good to her husband and her family; that is, she does what is in their best interests. In other words, she loves him and respects her husband and her family. She has a strong work ethic and works into the evening on her business and for her household. She provides tasty meals for her family and her entire household, including her employees. She has a generous spirit, as evidenced by her generosity to the poor. She plans for the inevitable rainy day, so when it comes, she doesn't worry. She looks forward to the future without dread. She makes her house a home with love, godly virtue, and beautiful furnishings. She wears dignified, elegant clothing, and her whole demeanor is one of strength, dignity, grace, and goodness. She speaks uplifting words of wisdom and encouragement, and she patiently guides others in the right path. She does not foolishly spread gossip or rumors, as she knows her purpose and lives her life intentionally for that purpose. Her children, her husband, and her community praise her and honor her and recognize the wonderful woman they have in their godly mother, wife, and leader in the community. She strives to be beautiful not only on the outside, but also, and more importantly, on the inside, where beauty doesn't fade with age.

Why does God command wives to respect their husbands? Because that is what a man needs most. He needs to know he has what it takes to conquer the world, to thrive in his chosen field, to make good decisions for himself and his family, to provide for his family, and to be a success in the world. Without the confidence a man gains from the respect of his wife, he cannot be the best version of himself. The henpecked husband whose wife criticizes him day in and day out for everything rarely amounts to anything because he lacks the one thing that would make him successful—confidence. A man needs the confidence that comes from the respect of his wife.

As a rite of passage into manhood, many African tribes require each young man to successfully undertake a dangerous feat. The confidence a young man gains after completing his mission is exactly what he needs to succeed in life. No matter what may come, he knows he's got what it takes to handle it. Not every man in the modern world gets a chance to triumph in a conquest to gain his confidence, but every married man needs the respect of his wife to give him the confidence he needs to do battle and thrive in a difficult world.

Summary

Emotionally healthy relationships enrich our lives. God designed us to bless each other by being in relationships. In healthy relationships, people help each other grow into the best version of themselves. Marriage was designed by our Creator to be an earthly version of the love, encouragement, peace, and joy that reigns in heaven by being an example to the world of God's unending love. Scripture's guidelines reveal what emotional health, true love inspired by God, and a healthy marriage look like. Healthy relationships truly are a little bit of heaven on earth.

Chapter 7

Emotional and Verbal Abuse

MANY PEOPLE BELIEVE DOMESTIC abuse is limited to the highly publicized accounts of physical abuse or sexual assault they see in the news. Victims often rationalize that because their partner has not been physically abusive, their relationship does not qualify as domestic abuse. Many women have naïvely told themselves, "At least he doesn't hit me, so it's not abuse"; or "He's just high maintenance and has a big personality"; or "He can be difficult, but he still loves me." However, physical abuse is only a part of what is considered abuse.

Abuse is a comprehensive set of behaviors and attitudes designed to gain and maintain power and control over others. Abusers are characterized by a lack of conscience, empathy, remorse, and repentance; they use others for their own selfish needs. They have an insatiable need for power and control, especially over their wife or intimate partner.

Emotional abuse is the starting point of all other abuses. Emotional abuse is present in all abusive situations. If a woman has experienced physical, sexual, financial, or spiritual abuse, you can be sure she experienced emotional abuse first. The purpose of all abuse is to destroy another's spirit—that inner soul that makes her a person. An abuser uses emotional and verbal abuse to emotionally destroy his spouse or intimate partner by humiliation, ostracism, cruelty, making her think she is crazy, and turning her family and friends against her. The scars from emotional and verbal abuse are internal. Although they cannot be seen, they are no less devastating than physical scars. Emotional and verbal abuse wounds the very spirit of a person. While physical and sexual wounds often heal, the wounds of the spirit take a long time to heal, if they ever do.

The Relationship with a Narcissist/Sociopath/Psychopath or Other Domestic Abuser

Unlike healthy marriages, a marriage with a SNAP is emotionally, spiritually, and physically devastating for the partner and the children. The SNAP attacks the very spirit of his partner in his attempts to control her. He also views his children as trophies to be controlled and manipulated. In comparison to the various views of healthy relationships described in the previous chapter, we look at the unhealthy relationship with a SNAP through those same lenses.

The SNAP Attacks Every Level of Need in the Hierarchy of Needs of His Spouse

The SNAP attacks every level of need in the hierarchy of needs. He attacks the physiological needs by withholding food, water, shelter, and health. This is done numerous ways. He may refuse to give her needed medical attention, water, and food. He may lock her in the basement or chain her to a bed. An abuser may literally force his partner out in the cold by abandoning her on the side of the road or locking her out of the house. He attacks the need for safety by constantly putting her in fear, threatening her, raging at her, intimidating her, and physically and sexually abusing her, which we discuss in other sections. He attacks her need for love and belonging by heaping emotional and verbal abuse on her, which we discuss in this section. He attacks her need for self-esteem, self-respect, self-confidence, competency and mastery in her abilities, strength, independence, and freedom by breaking down her spirit with emotional and verbal abuse. Finally, he attacks her need for self-actualization, because no woman can be all she is created to be without all her other needs being met.

The SNAP Is Incapable of Intimacy

The SNAP is incapable of true intimacy with his partner or anyone else. There is no chance of a SNAP reaching the higher levels of intimacy. SNAPs are often socially charming, even charismatic, in social settings like cocktail parties or the country club, but they stay on a superficial level of intimacy, using clichés and talking about impersonal events like sports, the economy, current events, the weather, or even personal events like their latest promotion or how well their children are doing in school. A SNAP will venture to the third level, the level of opinions, only by sharing his own opinion and expecting others to admire him and agree. He is not interested in knowing anyone else's opinion. If someone has a different or conflicting opinion, the SNAP will go on the attack and engage in ad hominem attacks against the person rather than engaging in a discussion about the merits of the subject matter. The SNAP's only goal is to win an argument, not to understand or accept the other person. And a personal attack is the quickest way to shut down most people, so the SNAP feels like he has scored a victory. For example, if the SNAP's spouse has a conflicting opinion of a heated matter like politics, rather than calmly discussing the pros and cons of a policy or candidate, the SNAP will engage in name-calling, and the conversation will immediately shut down.

The SNAP deals with the fourth and fifth levels of intimacy, sharing hopes, dreams, and feelings, in much the same way as the third. He is happy for others to hear his dreams and to know his feelings, but he does not care about theirs. He is only concerned about having others help him achieve his dreams. He gladly accepts other's praise and admiration of him, but becomes defensive and verbally abusive if they share any negative feelings. If she is sad or hurt, the SNAP will tell her she is too sensitive. If she disapproves of his disrespectful behavior, he will deny that anything he does is wrong. If she expresses moral outrage at his behavior, he will blame her for making him do it ("Why do you make me mad? You know you make me mad when you say that! Why do you make me hit you?"). If she becomes angry, he must stop her anger by becoming even more angry, raging, and threatening and putting her in her place ("Don't you dare do that! I will divorce you!").

The SNAP does not share his fears, failures, or faults, the sixth level of intimacy, because he does not believe he has any. However, he will be sure to point out yours. If a woman shares her fears, failures, or faults, the SNAP will always use it against her. For example, if a woman shares that her biggest concern is being a good mother and that she feels inadequate in this area, the SNAP will tuck that away. When he wants to destroy her, he will call her an unfit mother who can't do anything right. Likewise, if a woman shares her failings at work, the SNAP will attack her self-esteem by calling her a failure at her career. The SNAP will always use what is most important to his partner (being a good mother, her children, her career, her desire to be a good Christian/Jew/moral person) against her when he engages in his abuse.

The SNAP cannot reach the highest level of intimacy—meeting legitimate needs of his partner—because he has no concern for her legitimate needs. He is all-consumed with ensuring that his partner meets his illegitimate selfish, controlling, ego-based, ruthless desires.

> Charlotte: Tim was great at cocktail talk and clichés, but after twenty-one years of marriage, we never spoke of anything meaningful or heartfelt. Even after I had moved out and we went to a year of marriage counseling, all he could talk about was politics (he is a staunch Republican and huge Trump fan) and business news from Fox News, while I listened. After a one-sided conversation like that, he would try to convince me we had connected, and it was normal. "See, we can talk to each other!" he would say. I confirmed with his first wife of twenty-one years, a lovely woman, who said they also couldn't talk about anything of substance.

The SNAP Refuses to Practice Principles That Make a Marriage Successful

The SNAP is incapable of putting into practice even the first principle of a successful marriage, much less seven. The SNAP does not learn the details of his partner's life because he simply doesn't care. Although the SNAP will expect his partner and others to listen to his likes and dislikes, his day, his dreams, his stories, etc., he will seldom, if ever, ask his partner about her life.

> Charlotte: After two decades of marriage, Tim didn't know my favorite color, favorite pizza, favorite Christmas song, or much else about me. He was never interested and never asked. But he told me every time he saw the color blue (multiple times a week) that it was his favorite, he ordered pizza every Friday night with only his favorite ingredients, and I heard about twenty times each Christmas that his favorite Christmas song was "Little Drummer Boy."

Second, SNAPs do not recognize or affirm the good qualities in their spouses or others. They see people as tools to get their way and serve their purposes. So naturally, if the spouse of a SNAP has a good heart and volunteers her time with needy children, this doesn't help him, and he won't even see it, much less affirm her for her good works. It's much like asking a blind man to see and describe the colors of a rainbow—he can't even see them, much less describe them.

> Charlotte: During our year-long marriage counseling while we were separated, our counselor gave Tim some homework and said to point out good things that made me unique that he saw and admired in me. He didn't do it the first week, so she gave him the same homework assignment the next week. He was unable to give me one compliment. When I reported this to our counselor in our next session, he protested, "What do you mean? I told you to have a nice day!" That is something you say to a perfect stranger like the cashier at the grocery store. That was as intimate and connected as he could get.

Third, SNAPs will ignore or reject their partner when she verbally reaches out for connections. Eventually, the wife stops reaching out for connections since she knows the answer is no.

> Charlotte: When Tim was fired from his big corporate position and started a company working part time from home only two blocks from my office, I tried to reach out and ask him for lunch once a week. Except for his birthday, the answer was always no. Occasionally, I would ask for help on a household project, but the answer was always, "I'm going 180 miles an hour! I haven't sat down all day! I don't have time for this!" On our anniversary, I tried to get him to go to a special dinner in downtown Chicago. But except for celebrating our fifteenth anniversary, he whined about how bad the traffic was and refused to go. I just stopped trying to connect. He always found a reason to say no. Something else was always more important.

Fourth, SNAPs will not share power or decision-making. They live for all-encompassing power and control. They want complete control of the decision-making and the money—so much so that they often refuse to put their spouse's name on a bank account, investment account, or titles to the house or cars. A SNAP will seldom ask his wife's opinion or permission before making a major purchase or making a major business decision that will affect them both.

> Charlotte: Tim made sure even before the marriage that he would not share power or even ask my opinion. The prenuptial agreement presented to me the day before the wedding provided that every dollar he earned while we were married was his individual property (not marital property), that everything he bought was his individual property, and that he was under no obligation to consult with me or get my approval for anything. And that is how he lived. During marriage counseling, I asked him why everything had to be his way. He said he viewed marriage like he viewed a business: everyone can't weigh in with their opinions; someone must be the boss and make all the decisions—and that someone was him.

Fifth, SNAPs do not engage in conflict resolution. He will not apologize or admit he is wrong. Conflict resolution with a SNAP is nonexistent. Conflict resolution in healthy couples requires being respectful, listening, and understanding, with the goal of continuing in a healthy relationship as they arrive at solutions that are good for both people. But for the SNAP, the goal is winning at all costs. The SNAP does not care about being respectful, listening, or understanding the needs of others. He simply wants to win. If he feels boxed in a corner because his position is unreasonable or unsupportable, he will switch to using personal verbal attacks, name-calling, blaming, or denying or justifying his actions rather than focusing on the issue. Eventually, the spouse of a SNAP learns to avoid conflict and avoid the SNAP. He does not care if he hurts or emotionally destroys his partner in the process. In fact, hurting someone and putting them in their place will give him an emotional high. If he gets what he wants, he doesn't care that he has irretrievably harmed the relationship with his spouse because, after all, to a SNAP a spouse is expendable. He can always find another one who will do what he wants—at least until she is replaced.

> Charlotte: There was no point trying to resolve a conflict with Tim. All our conflicts arose because of his intentional cruelty, either to me or to others. He never admitted anything he did was wrong, he wouldn't apologize, and he refused to change. Nothing was ever resolved, even when our marriage was at stake. He had to win and be right, and in doing so, he lost our marriage.

Sixth, life with a SNAP is constant gridlock because issues do not get resolved and the couple either argues about the same issues or the spouse avoids the SNAP to keep the peace.

Seventh, a SNAP does not share a spiritual connection with his spouse, nor does he engage in actions to fulfill a higher, spiritual purpose. A SNAP's highest purpose (in his own mind) is generally to achieve fame, fortune, or both. He spends no time trying to determine God's calling on his life or how he can make the world a better place. If he wants to leave a legacy, it is generally a legacy of a business or a fortune to his children, from which his spouse is cut off.

> Charlotte: I had always hoped to share a spiritual connection with my spouse—reading the Bible and praying together, volunteering together, serving a higher purpose together. That never happened. Although I had Bible study and prayer time, joined a small group Bible study, and volunteered, Tim was not interested. When Tim was fired in 2000, he had plenty of money so that he would never have to work again. I had hoped that he would volunteer on nonprofit boards so that he could share his wealth of financial and business experience with organizations that help others. He would have none of it. Instead, he poured millions of dollars into a business with his oldest son from a prior marriage that never got off the ground and eventually folded after a dozen or so years. Although Tim attended church and a couples Bible study after 2000, he viewed it as a social club rather than a place to become more like God or do good works.

The Harbingers of the End of a Marriage

Marriage expert Dr. John Gottman has identified predictors by which he can forecast with 94 percent accuracy whether a couple will divorce.[48] He puts couples in a "Love Laboratory" and asks them to resolve a conflict. Gottman then observes the couple, looking for the indicators of a toxic relationship—criticism, contempt, defensiveness, and stonewalling—which he identifies as the Four Horsemen of the Apocalypse—a reference to imagery in the book of Revelation in the Bible which signals the end times or apocalypse. These four negative interactions signal the end of a marriage with 82 percent accuracy.[49] When combined with other divorce predictors, the divorce predictability rate jumps to over 90 percent. Once they come out of the "love-bombing" dating stage and into the devaluation stage that occurs shortly after a marriage, SNAPs exhibit all these toxic behaviors and attitudes in abundance.

Criticism is usually the first of the Four Horsemen to appear. With criticism, the critical spouse expresses negativity about the other's character and personality rather than addressing an issue. For example, instead of addressing the fact that the vacuuming is not done, criticism attacks the person, often with "always" or "never" lines like "You're always so lazy," "You never follow through," or "What's wrong with you?"

When criticism becomes a regular habit, contempt is usually close behind. Contempt is a sense of superiority and condescension evidenced by sarcasm, sneering, name-calling, eye-rolling, mockery, hostile humor, cynicism, criticism, dressing down, mocking, an unwillingness to problem-solve, belligerence, threats, provocation, taunts, and other forms that convey disrespect, disgust, and disdain. The person with contempt has no interest in resolving problems. Rather, he is merely interested in insulting his partner for his own perverse pleasure. He

---

[48] Michael Fulwiler, "Announcement: The Research," February 11, 2013, https://www.gottman.com/blog/announcement-the-research/.
[49] Gottman, *Seven Principles*, 45.

may even throw in taunts, threats, provocations, and belligerence just for fun: "So, what are you going to do about it? Sue me?"

Defensiveness is a way of justifying his actions and blaming a partner for his own bad behavior. It often involves poor excuses, justification, and attempts to mitigate the abuser's reprehensible, unreasonable actions. For example, rather than admitting something was abusive and hurtful, the abuser will find an excuse and claim that his actions were "not that bad" or that his spouse was responsible for making him angry.

Stonewalling, which is engaged in more often by men than women, involves disengaging from a conversation. It involves avoiding eye contact, giving someone the silent treatment, and putting up other emotional roadblocks to the partner.

In addition to the Four Horsemen, another predictor of divorce is the inability (or refusal) to de-escalate tension when attempting to resolve a conflict. Abusers are unable to take a break when emotions get high. Finally, divorce is nearly certain when one or both of the partners are so overwhelmed by negative emotions toward the other that they rewrite history by recasting good memories in a negative light, fabricating facts rather than remembering what actually occurred, and ascribing ulterior motives to their spouse rather than viewing their actions as done with the best intentions. When an abuser rewrites history and believes his own lies, the end is imminent.

> Charlotte: Near the end of our marriage, our family was sitting in the family room on Thanksgiving and remembering ridiculous family moments. I was walking on eggshells and made a point not to say anything for fear of Tim taking even benign comments the wrong way. Danny made a playful comment remembering when Tim decided to clean out the garage and had all the contents of the garage on the driveway an hour before we were to host a big surprise birthday party for the kids' godmother. Two weeks later, Tim did not include me in a family brunch with Santa with our kids, his older kids, and his grandchildren. He said it was because I had made a mean-spirited insult at Thanksgiving about the garage cleaning and the party. He had convinced himself that I had intentionally insulted him, when, in fact, one of the kids was good-naturedly recalling a well-remembered family story.

The SNAP Refuses to Honor God's Design for Marriage

Marriage is God's masterpiece. God has a beautiful design for marriage that gives the couple, their children, and those around them what they need to lead abundant lives. However, all SNAPs refuse to honor God's design for marriage and pridefully replace it with their own design that ultimately ends in failure and destruction. Rather than viewing marriage with the purpose of serving God, each other, and those around them, a SNAP views a marriage as one more way others should serve his needs and aspirations. In contrast to the biblical perspective of viewing his spouse as a gift from God to be treasured and loved, he views his wife as an object to be used for his selfish purposes. Instead of seeing his role as a protector of his wife and family, he is abusive, manipulative, and harmful. As opposed to providing for his family, he makes sure he is financially well off even if his wife and children are not. Rather than viewing children as a gift of God to be trained up in the Lord, a SNAP will view them either as a nuisance or as trophies to be on display and controlled. Instead of seeing his role as a servant leader of his family, he acts as a tyrant. All relationships with a SNAP will end badly, and marriage is no exception.

The SNAP Is Emotionally Destructive

Galatians 5 not only describes emotional and spiritual health, as outlined in the fruit of the Spirit, but it also describes emotional destructiveness, as outlined by the acts of the flesh. These acts and attitudes of emotional destruction describe the SNAP. We will have an in-depth look at what the Bible describes in generalities in the pages to come.

"The acts of the flesh are obvious: sexual immorality, impurity and debauchery; idolatry and witchcraft; hatred, discord, jealousy, fits of rage, selfish ambition, dissensions, factions and envy; drunkenness, orgies, and the like. I warn you, as I did before, that those who live like this will not inherit the kingdom of God" (Galatians 5:19–21).

Emotionally and Verbally Abusive Tactics

The SNAP systematically destroys his partner emotionally and spiritually by employing several abusive tactics. These tactics are predictable and universally used by abusers. Many women are surprised to discover from other victims or counselors that their abuser uses the exact same words that another woman's abuser uses. Most abusers employ the same or similar verbal and nonverbal tactics because they have the same dysfunctional reasoning and thought processes. One might think all abusers go to the same Abuser University to learn abusive and controlling strategies.

While healthy people get a good feeling inside from doing good, being kind to others, and being in relationships with loved ones, abusers get an emotional buzz from being cruel, hurting, and controlling others. They enjoy the power they feel. While healthy people have a conscience that prohibits them from being intentionally cruel, abusers lack a conscience and therefore have no internal limitations on their cruelty. People with Cluster B personality disorder have no impulse control. The only limitations on an abuser are limitations imposed by someone bigger, stronger, more powerful, or with more authority. Abusers will never be influenced by guilt or a sense of responsibility to be decent to others, and thus appeals to their sense of morality is futile, as they have no sense of morality or conscience.

Healthy people tend to be kind, and other healthy people recognize kindness extended to them and reciprocate in turn. However, abusers mistake kindness for weakness, and they do not reciprocate. In fact, an abuser will attack the person who extends the kindness and will even criticize the kindness. When an abuser is extended a kindness, in his mind he identifies that person as "sucker!" For example, when an abuser engages in criminal actions, a woman will often extend grace and seek counseling with her abuser instead of seeking an order of protection or pressing criminal charges. In response, the abuser will never appreciate her grace nor reciprocate the kindness extended. Instead, he will later say, "I didn't do anything. If it was that bad, you should have gotten an order of protection." With abusers in mind, Jesus warned us not to throw pearls to swine lest they trample the pearls and turn to attack us (Matthew 7:6).

Once a woman identifies these tactics, she can be assured her partner is, in fact, abusive and that she is in an unhealthy relationship. Once a woman recognizes that she is in an abusive relationship and accepts the fact that abusers do not change and that abuse escalates over time, she has the confidence she needs to develop a plan to escape her bondage and reclaim her life.

We will look at nonverbal abuse tactics first, and then verbal abuse tactics.

Nonverbal Abuse Tactics

Dr. Jekyll / Mr. Hyde Double Personality

One of the most universal characteristics of narcissists, sociopaths, and psychopaths is their Dr. Jekyll/Mr. Hyde double personality. SNAPs deeply want to be perceived by others, especially those who are powerful and wealthy and those who have been targeted as their next romantic partner, as someone who is powerful, wealthy, successful, charismatic, charming, and an upstanding, honorable citizen within their community. If they are part of a religious community, they want to be perceived as a "good" Jew, Catholic, Protestant, Christian, Muslim, etc. In order to be perceived as such in front of people the SNAP wants to impress, he will put on a show, pretending to be someone with these characteristics—"a false persona" as mental health professionals call it. The SNAP can turn on this show as quickly and easily as someone turns on a light switch.

However, when a SNAP is with people whose opinion he doesn't care about, he reverts to his selfish, abusive, self-serving personality. Generally, these people include spouses, underlings, ex-wives, ex-girlfriends (those whom they view as inferior) and children—when the SNAP isn't trying to rally the troops and turn them against their mother. The SNAP can turn on this dark side as quickly and easily as he turns on his show for those he wants to impress.

The SNAP's victim falls in love with the charismatic, successful, larger-than-life figure he pretends to be. Unfortunately, that person does not exist. It is a false persona acted out with Oscar-worthy skills to win the girl. Or the job. Or the position. Once the SNAP has someone in his cross hairs, he will pursue her like a stealth lion pursues his prey until he overcomes her. This is the love-bombing stage of the relationship. It is, for the SNAP, a game to see if he can "get the girl." However, once the pursuit is over, once the SNAP has won the game and captured his target, once she is emotionally committed and within the emotional clutches of the SNAP, the true personality is revealed. He cannot pretend that he is someone else forever. The victim will try to understand this sudden change of personality and will oftentimes deny or try to justify the changes. Most victims continue to believe that the person they fell in love with will eventually return—if only she were nicer to him, if only she gave more time or energy or money to him, if only she were more understanding and forgiving of his shortcomings, if only she were a better Christian or Jew or Muslim, if only she were more submissive to him, if only she read some more marriage books. Sadly, it can be decades before a victim realizes that the Prince Charming she fell in love with never existed, and that the true person is the self-absorbed, abusive ogre with whom she is now stuck.

The following axiom is useful whenever a woman is wondering who the real person is: Evil people will often pretend to be good, but good people will never pretend to be evil.

The classic novella *The Strange Case of Dr. Jekyll and Mr. Hyde*, by Robert Louis Stevenson, reflects what victims of SNAPs find so frustrating. In one body is contained two completely different personalities—one the upstanding Dr. Jekyll, and the other the evil Mr. Hyde. Those who only know the upright Dr. Jekyll have no idea that this same person can, in fact, be quite evil. Even when the friends of Dr. Jekyll are confronted with the facts, they refuse to believe such incongruity. When a victim tells her pastor, rabbi, or friends what she has experienced, they simply do not believe her. They have only seen charming Dr. Jekyll, while she has seen Dr. Jekyll turn into Mr. Hyde behind closed doors.

This dual personality, one being decidedly evil and another appearing outwardly upright, is what the Bible calls being "double-minded." It is the very definition of hypocrisy—one who acts righteous in front of others to impress them, but whose heart is far from God. James, the brother of Jesus, understood the nature of SNAPs and put his finger precisely on point. James warns us that people who are double-minded are unstable, like waves blown and tossed by the wind, and they should not expect to receive anything from God (James 1:6–8). James calls those who are double-minded "adulterous people." He warns them that they cannot be a friend to both God and evil, and he informs them that God is not answering their prayers. James enlightens them that they (not their victims) are causing the quarrels that inevitably arise when dealing with them, and he calls them to put aside their pride—the underlying reason for their evil—and humble themselves. Finally, he rebukes them to resist Satan, who is behind this battle between good and evil.

> What causes fights and quarrels among you? Don't they come from your desires that battle within you? You desire but do not have, so you kill. You covet but you cannot get what you want, so you quarrel and fight. You do not have because you do not ask God. When you ask, you do not receive, because you ask with wrong motives, that you may spend what you get on your pleasures. You adulterous people, don't you know that friendship with the world means enmity against God? Therefore, anyone who chooses to be a friend of the world becomes an enemy of God. Or do you think Scripture says without reason that he jealously longs for the spirit he has caused to dwell in us? But he gives us more grace. That is why Scripture says: "God opposes the proud but shows favor to the humble." Submit yourselves, then, to God. Resist the devil, and he will flee from you. Come near to God and he will come near to you. Wash your hands, you sinners, and purify your hearts, you double-minded. Grieve, mourn and wail. Change your laughter to mourning and your joy to gloom. Humble yourselves before the Lord, and he will lift you up." (James 4:1–10)

Jesus was also on point in identifying SNAPs. Unsurprisingly, the SNAPs that He identified were leaders—the larger-than-life characters that SNAPs like to portray themselves as. While many people mistakenly believe that Jesus was wimpy, wishy-washy, and never said anything "unkind" about others, Jesus spoke truth and called out the SNAPs of His day. He wasn't afraid to call *evil* evil, even if it appeared in a religious leader. By His example, we also should not be afraid to call evil what it is and identify those who are evil, even if they sit in the pew next to us. God is not afraid to speak the truth, and neither should we be.

> Woe to you, teachers of the law and Pharisees, you hypocrites! You give a tenth of your spices—mint, dill and cumin. But you have neglected the more important matters of the law—justice, mercy and faithfulness. You should have practiced the latter, without neglecting the former. . . . Woe to you, teachers of the law and Pharisees, you hypocrites! You are like whitewashed tombs, which look beautiful on the outside but on the inside are full of the bones of the dead and everything unclean. In the same way, on the outside you appear to people as righteous but on the inside you are full of hypocrisy and wickedness. . . . You snakes! You brood of vipers! How will you escape being condemned to hell? (Matthew 23:23, 27–28, 33)

Jesus correctly pointed out that the same person cannot, with integrity, be double-minded. He cannot serve both God and Satan. He cannot stand with one foot in God's camp and the other in the devil's camp. He must decide. "No one can serve two masters. Either you will hate the one and love the other, or you will be devoted to the one and despise the other. You cannot serve both God and money" (Matthew 6:24).

David was no stranger to SNAPs. Nearly half of the Psalms contain David's heartfelt cries to God to rescue him from these evil people and to bring justice upon them. The most notable SNAP was King Saul, who, after befriending David, became intent on killing him. In Psalm 28, David describes the double-minded SNAP who talks cordially with others—he engages in small talk with the church crowd, can carry on a cocktail-hour conversation about his Mercedes or important job or his latest accomplishment; he is a social and political animal that weaves in and out of high society circles with ease—but has evil in his heart. David cries out to God for justice:

> Do not drag me away with the wicked,
> > with those who do evil,
> who speak cordially with their neighbors
> > but harbor malice in their hearts.
> Repay them for their deeds
> > and for their evil work;
> repay them for what their hands have done
> > and bring back on them what they deserve. (Psalm 28:3–4)

David knew that being with double-minded SNAPs was incompatible with following God. When a SNAP infiltrates someone's life, that person cannot follow God completely. Because the SNAP causes so much disruption and takes so much energy to deal with, God gets pushed to the sidelines. Having a SNAP in one's inner circle is like inviting a tornado to enter your life. One must always deal with the tornado, which demands attention and threatens death and destruction, before addressing anything else. It is impossible to wholeheartedly do God's will when there's a SNAP in your life, because he is working as hard as he can to do Satan's will. David understood this dynamic and was intent on staying far away from them so they would not drag him away from the God he loved:

> I hate double-minded people,
> > but I love your law.
> You are my refuge and my shield;
> > I have put my hope in your word.
> Away from me, you evildoers,
> > that I may keep the commands of my God! (Psalm 119:113–115)

Perhaps the best and most concise biblical definition of the double-minded SNAP comes from Paul in a warning to his young friend and colleague Timothy. He warns that these SNAPs will be abusive and evil on the inside, but they will have a "form of godliness" on the outside. This form of godliness may look good to others—they may attend church so others think they are "good Christians." They may be philanthropic when their name is on the donor list; they may do good deeds when people are watching—but inside they reject God and His power in their lives. The SNAP reigns as the lord of his life; he has not surrendered to God. They target gullible women who are unable to discern the evil hiding inside the outer shell of godliness. The SNAPs pretend to learn about God, and may even attend Bible study, but they never truly know God. They are perpetual liars and oppose the truth, especially when the truth reveals who they really are.

Knowing how evil will destroy everything it touches, Paul warns Timothy and everyone in the church to have nothing to do with them. Note that Paul doesn't say, "Have nothing to do with them, except for their poor wives, who must live the rest of their miserable lives in a brutal, abusive marriage to an evil man who will destroy her and her children and her grandchildren." Rather, Paul tells us all—including wives, girlfriends, children, grandchildren, church leaders, and the church—to have nothing to do with SNAPs. They are truly so destructive that Paul gives a blanket order to stay away from these evil people who pretend to be Christians:

> There will be terrible times in the last days. People will be lovers of themselves, lovers of money, boastful, proud, abusive, disobedient to their parents, ungrateful, unholy, without love, unforgiving, slanderous, without self-control, brutal, not lovers of the good, treacherous, rash, conceited, lovers of pleasure rather than lovers of God—having a form of godliness but denying its power. Have nothing to do with such people. They are the kind who worm their way into homes and gain control over gullible women, who are loaded down with sins and are swayed by all kinds of evil desires, always learning but never able to come to a knowledge of the truth. Just as Jannes and Jambres opposed Moses, so also these teachers oppose the truth. They are men of depraved minds, who, as far as the faith is concerned, are rejected. (2 Timothy 3:1–8)

Silent Treatment

In using the silent treatment, the abuser refuses to talk, text, email, or otherwise communicate with his partner. A SNAP makes frequent use of the silent treatment to attack his partner's need for love and belonging by excluding her from relationship with him, and often from the rest of the family, usually as a punishment for some perceived offense. The noncommunication can last for hours, days, or weeks. The SNAP has no intention of understanding the difference in opinion that may have given rise to his behavior, nor does he have any intention of keeping a relationship with his partner. To the contrary, the silent treatment cuts off communication and relationship with his partner, usually in retaliation for something the partner said or did. This tactic leaves the partner feeling unloved, excluded, and desperate (i.e., willing to do anything) to be back in relationship and communication with the abuser.

The silent treatment is a form of stonewalling, one of Gottman's indicators of the end of a marriage. Other forms of stonewalling include monosyllabic grunts (rather than words and conversation), changing the subject (rather than discussing an area of conflict), and physical separation (leaving home). The silent treatment and other forms of stonewalling convey disapproval, icy distance, separation, disconnection, or smugness.

> Charlotte: Whenever Tim wanted to punish me, he would give me the silent treatment. It could last for a few days or a few weeks. In 2011, I was interviewing for the presidency at a Christian organization. The organization wanted to interview spouses as well, but Tim soon started to sabotage and take over the whole process, and he childishly insisted, "I'm important! They want to interview me!" He threatened to boycott the interview, and I went without him. He pouted and gave me the silent treatment for days. Of course, my hopes at the presidency were dashed.

Leaving the Home

Many abusers will simply leave the home for a time without any information as to their whereabouts or communication with their partner. This form of abuse takes the silent treatment to an even higher level of emotional abuse. An abuser may leave for days, weeks, months, or even years before returning. Upon his return, he will often blame his partner for forcing him to leave.

> Ellen: In 2013, Rod left the house for four months and didn't tell me where he was going, when he

was coming back, or even if he was coming back. He just showed up again one day with no explanation. After I filed for divorce, I found photos on our computer of a woman and a little girl opening a present from Rod. The girl looked to be an age that she could have been conceived around the time Rod had been gone.

Traveling and Other Appointments without Notice

A SNAP may leave for a planned business trip, vacation, or other scheduled event, but fail to inform his partner until the actual departure or after his departure. In healthy relationships, partners will generally collaborate on schedules prior to putting events on the calendar, and certainly prior to out-of-town travel, to ensure that the other partner is able to take care of children and other commitments while one of them is gone. At the very least, if a person does not have control over when he must travel, a healthy individual will inform his partner with as much lead time as possible concerning the travel plans or other commitments. Only in cases of emergency will a healthy person travel out of town without informing his partner. However, the SNAP is so self-absorbed that he feels it is unnecessary to inform his partner that he will be out of town or otherwise engaged. After all, his world revolves around him, and spouses are simply expendable with no right to receive information of his whereabouts.

> Charlotte: Oftentimes I would find that Tim was going on a week-long business trip the morning of the trip—not because he had the courtesy to tell me, but because he woke up at 4:00 a.m. to pack. I felt like a piece of furniture—not important enough to him to be kept in the loop on his plans (that obviously affected the children and me) and ignored most of the time unless he needed a place to sit.

Abandonment

In a blatant show of "I'm in control and don't you forget it," the SNAP may abandon his partner miles from home while he drives off in a huff. To add to the terror and humiliation, it will likely be in a bad neighborhood and in the middle of the night. She is then left to devise a plan to get to safety, although she may have been dumped without a cell phone and without money.

Abandonment can also happen while on a boat, plane, train, or other form of transportation. Abandonment can happen near home or while on vacation, in a foreign country, or anywhere the abuser chooses to rage and wants to strike terror in his partner to show her who's boss.

Regardless of the situation, the SNAP will blame his behavior on his spouse and take no responsibility.

Social Isolation

People are designed to be in community. Women especially define themselves by their relationships as a mother, wife, daughter, sister, friend, sister-in-law, colleague, and professional. They derive meaning, emotional support, and strength from these relationships, as well as their concept of what is normal and healthy, a sense of personal and professional competency, and shared wisdom for dealing with the trials of life. Most women have a high need for relationships and community with others.

Abusers often isolate their partners from these important relationships to eliminate the partner's emotional strength and convince her that his emotional abuse is normal and acceptable. Abusers know that they have more control over one person who is isolated and who doubts her own perceptions than a person who has her entire network backing her. Isolation inevitably leads to depression, loneliness, low self-worth, and feeling that no one cares, especially as the abuse escalates and the victim has nowhere to turn. Our enemies use isolation in POW prisons as a form of torture to break the spirit of prisoners.

Isolation can include refusing to let the spouse have her own car or cell phone, prohibiting her from talking on the phone, or going through phone records and making her explain each call. Isolation includes refusing to let her see friends and family, complaining about spending time with others so that she eventually stops trying to see them, and making time with relatives and friends so uncomfortable or embarrassing that they no longer want to spend time together. He may forbid his spouse from visiting her friends and family without him, but may also refuse to visit. He may start arguments and belittle and criticize her social network when he is with them. After a while, his wife simply gives up trying to see them because it is easier to not see them and "keep the peace" than to have World War Three erupt just to spend time with them. Further, an abuser often spreads malicious rumors about his spouse to his friends and family so that they ostracize her.

Many abusers refuse to allow their wives to work outside the home, further isolating them and ensuring their financial dependence. Abusers know that if they can get their spouse isolated with no financial support, she is much easier to be control and dominate.

If his spouse is vulnerable due to a health condition, an abuser may not give her the cards and letters that friends and well-wishers have been sending her. He may delete the emails and texts that have been sent giving her good wishes. He may also prevent her from answering the phone, and may not pass along phone messages. This makes her believe no one cares about her.

In severe abuse cases, isolation can include kidnapping such as locking the spouse in a closet, room, basement, or other confined area with no means of escape.

After a victim leaves her abuser (or after the abuser leaves his victim), it can be almost guaranteed that the abuser will engage in a concerted smear campaign spreading false and malicious rumors designed to ostracize her from her support group. In nearly every case, the abuser will claim to be the innocent victim, that the real victim is crazy or abusive or has some other highly negative trait, and will often claim that the victim engaged in an extramarital affair. If the victim left the abuser, he will claim to have been abandoned. However, if the abuser left the victim, he will claim she is the problem. In every case, the abuser is attempting to rally the troops to support him and to emotionally destroy his victim by leaving her utterly alone.

Because abusers have no internal sense of worth formed by a faith as a child of God, they derive their sense of worth from the worship, praise, and support of those around them. Thus, they must gather their supporters around them to make them feel justified for their behaviors, even if that means lying to their supporters. Once they gather support, they will use anything others may say (or simply make it up) against the victim to prove to the victim that others disapprove of her.

Social isolation is an effective tactic. Many people who are undiscerning as to the tactics of SNAPs believe the SNAP. Women often state that the most devastating part of leaving an abusive marriage is having the so-called friends blindly support the abuser after a smear campaign rather than considering her character and asking for the truth. Some women feel so alone that they commit suicide rather than fight the battle with the abuser and his supporters. In these cases, the abuser and his supporters will always blame the victim, claiming that she was mentally unstable, rather than accepting any responsibility for making the situation so intolerable that the victim sought death over dealing with the abuser's mental torture.

Ellen: Shortly after we were married, I underwent a mastectomy and chemo treatments. People sent me texts, emails, letters, and cards, but my husband never gave them to me. I felt that no one cared about me. Later, when friends asked why I never responded, I finally realized he had intentionally kept them from me.

Sally: My sister-in-law was married to my ex-husband's brother. They are both abusive. He never let her go anywhere with anyone. She managed to get out to see me once, only because I was "family" and considered "safe." I took her shopping. I had to hide a bag of chocolates for her because he would not let her buy any. She took a few pieces and was afraid to bring the bag to her house. She had to account for every penny she spent. The control was out of this world. She had three little kids. She tried to escape, but couldn't. She committed suicide. The whole family then claimed that she was unstable, using the suicide as proof.

Sahira: My husband owned a kiosk at a mall just a few minutes from our house. He left with the one car we owned every day, which sat in the mall parking lot for ten hours, rather than letting me drive him to work so I could have the car during the day for me and our three small children. He came home every day and checked my texts, emails, and phone calls to see who I was communicating with and demanded an explanation. When I escaped, I had to walk to the nearest fire station with our children and was put in touch with the local domestic violence shelter.

Refusing to Help

Asking an abuser for help on everyday matters is a waste of time. Such matters are entirely beneath them. While healthy households ask for and receive help on routine matters such as taking out the trash, running an errand, preparing for dinner guests, cleaning the dishes, or making a bed, abusers simply refuse to help others in routine chores, even when specifically asked. They are always too busy on things they perceive as more important than helping their spouse or children. However, abusers expect others to drop everything and help them at a moment's notice. Since abusers look down on others, the abuser will always take the supervising role while letting others do the real work. They will even brag that they "specialize in supervision" so as not to be dragged into the heavy lifting.

Charlotte: For my entire marriage, whenever I asked Tim for the slightest help, I always got the same answer: "I haven't sat down all day! I'm going 180 miles an hour! I don't have time!" I stopped asking for any help and became very self-reliant. But when there was inevitable work to be done, he refused to help and bragged that he would "supervise" us. "I specialize in supervision," he would laugh as the rest of the family did the work that was needed, which included anything from cleaning the gutters to preparing Christmas dinner and cleaning the house for twenty-five guests. Whenever he wanted assistance with a task, we had to drop everything and do it, and then he stood back and supervised.

Flurry of Activity with No Accomplishment

In order to feel they are important and draw attention to themselves, SNAPs often seem like a flurry of activity, when very little actually gets accomplished. They swoop in at the last minute, after all the hard work is done, and take credit as the "leader" who supervised and orchestrated the project. They run here and there like a whirling dervish, but accomplish little other than causing a commotion.

> Charlotte: Whenever there was a hard deadline to meet, such as catching a plane, Tim would put himself into a frenzy in the hours leading up to his leaving. He would talk to himself, bark orders, and yell at everyone to serve him so that he could leave on time. (It didn't seem to matter that when we left as a family, it was our vacation, too, and that we had prepared in advance to avoid the last-minute insanity.) This was mostly because he refused to prepare the night before. Even when he had, he confused activity with accomplishment—which was something he always accused others of. One year we missed our plane, and several times we got to the airport by the skin of our teeth. His frenzied antics became so insane over the years that I finally told him a week in advance of our leaving on vacation that if he was going to act that way, he would be going on vacation by himself and I would stay home. It just wasn't worth it. Amazingly, we were able to calmly leave and catch a plane without his "look at me" antics.

Sabotage

SNAPs must always be the center of attention. If they are not the center of attention, they will find a way to sabotage an event to serve their personal interest, provoke a conflict, or draw attention to themselves. Not only will an abuser flat-out refuse to help his spouse, but he will sabotage his spouse's efforts that involve him and depend upon him for success. If a SNAP needs his spouse for his success, for example, to accompany him to his office holiday party or to entertain his colleagues from work, he expects her to cooperate and play the role of the supporting corporate wife. However, if a SNAP's spouse needs his cooperation for her success, for example, to accompany her to her office party or to entertain twenty-five guests for Christmas dinner, she can expect no help. In fact, she can expect her abuser to sabotage the event because he is not the center of attention and the event does not benefit him or his career. For example, if the couple is attending one of her work, charity, or social events, she can expect her SNAP to deliberately sabotage the event by being late, pouting about having to go, being rude to her colleagues, getting drunk, making inappropriate remarks, insulting other guests, or even refusing to attend at the last minute. If she is entertaining at home, she can expect her abuser to make a mess that she must clean up before guests arrive, work on other projects that have nothing to do with the immediate need of preparing for guests, and be snobbish and insulting to her guests, whom he views as beneath him.

> Charlotte: Tim was a master at sabotaging plans that were not his own ideas and in which he was not the center of attention. Part of the interview process for a position I applied for with a Christian university required the candidate to bring his or her spouse. They wanted input from the spouse and wanted to see if the spouse would be a good fit and be supportive. Tim wanted the interview to be all about him. He announced that he would drive to the interview using his GPS, which had been wrong in the past. He refused to let me print off Google maps as a hard copy back-up to his unpredictable and sometimes inaccurate GPS. He became arrogant and belligerent. I respectfully said that I was the candidate they were interviewing, and that they would be asking him questions about me to make sure there was a good fit with the leadership needs of a Christian university. He threatened to sabotage the interview by refusing to come. He didn't talk to me for three days, and I went to the interview alone. Obviously, a Christian university wants leadership in which both the

president and the spouse are committed Christians who live out Christian values and have put aside all arrogance and ego. I was not invited back.

Tim sabotaged any plans in which he was not the center of attention. We hosted a surprise fiftieth birthday party at our home for our children's godmother with seventy-five guests. It was all hands on deck to pull off the surprise. But an hour before the guests were to arrive, Tim decided it was the day he would clean out the garage. Not only was he not helping with the party preparation, but he had the entire contents of the garage outside on the driveway. It was like a little kid acting out: because he wasn't the center of attention, he would ruin it for the person who was. Every holiday, instead of helping with preparations for guests, he would instead change the lightbulbs in the closets in the basement or fiddle with the Christmas lights outside. (His first wife said the same thing. He has not changed in fifty years!) I finally came to expect that he was no help, but when he intentionally made extra work, it was infuriating.

Dirk: Rhonda both sabotaged my career and complained that I was not moving up the corporate ladder fast enough. Whenever I had a work function, such as a dinner or party that professionals were invited to, she ran two hours late, and when we finally showed up, she complained that we had missed cocktail hour and appetizers and that we were not at the table with the VIPs (because there was no assigned seating and we had to grab whatever table was available). In one case, we were so late that dinner was finished and the tables were being cleared. I couldn't encourage her to be on time, because she exploded in anger. I couldn't leave to be on time and meet her there when she came, because she exploded in anger. Other times, she would decide at the last minute she didn't want to go, so I would have to call and make an excuse for us not attending. The excuse always had to be my fault, not hers. One time, I fibbed and told my boss that I was allergic to strawberries and that I had eaten strawberries and was having an allergic reaction. I felt like an idiot.

Unreasonable Demands

SNAPs impose unreasonable demands and over-the-top perfectionism. They set standards and then change them so that no one can possibly meet them. The SNAP cannot even meet his own standards, yet he demands that others do. By setting impossible standards, the SNAP feels entitled to criticize and harass with impunity. He uses this ploy at work as well as in the home.

Jane: Lew made us wash the paper plates and plastic silverware. And he made the kids memorize Bible verses and stand up straight before everyone and recite them without flinching and without mistake. If they messed up, they had to repeat it.

Charlotte: Tim made our nannies do things to serve his increasing perfectionism and unreasonable demands. In one instance, he had a certain kind of hard-to-find pen that he liked. Rather than simply purchasing it online, he made one nanny run to all the office supply stores in the area in search of his pen. When she brought back the wrong kind, he made her go return them. He forced one nanny to clean the grout on the sunroom floor on her hands and knees with a toothbrush. I had no idea that he was doing such things. When I finally left the marriage, one of our nannies congratulated me and told me some of the things he had done. I was so embarrassed. I called every former nanny and apologized for his horrible behavior.

Emotional and Verbal Abuse

Impossible to Please

One of the hallmarks of a SNAP is that they are intentionally impossible to please. Regardless of how much their partner or children or employees attempt to please them, they will find fault, even when their demands are being complied with. For example, if their partner is in a good mood, the SNAP will attack them for being happy: "What are you so happy about?" If the SNAP's partner is sad, the SNAP will go on the attack again: "You're always such a downer!" In Matthew 11, Jesus spoke of this abusive tactic: "What shall I say about this nation? These people are like children playing, who say to their little friends, 'We played wedding and you weren't happy, so we played funeral but you weren't sad.' For John the Baptist doesn't even drink wine and often goes without food, and you say, 'He's crazy.' And I, the Messiah, feast and drink, and you complain that I am 'a glutton and a drinking man, and hang around with the worst sort of sinners!' But brilliant men like you can justify your every inconsistency!" (Matthew 11:16–19 TLB).

> Hilary: Stan would demand things, and then when I did them, complain that I did them. For example, when we broke up, he called, emailed, and texted unceasingly. I asked him to stop harassing me and tried to limit his constant harassment. He then demanded that I return his cell phone. When I did, he accused me of cutting him out of his son's life.

> Charlotte: During the marriage, Tim found something to complain about with everything I did. For example, I could go grocery shopping and get nine things that he liked and one thing that others liked, and he would complain about the one thing that he didn't like. He was nitpicky to a point of insanity. For example, he had a display frame of golf balls on his wall that was about an inch deep. The manufacturer had not varnished the one-inch-deep sides of the display case because they were unable to be seen behind the frame. Yet he demanded that I finish it. After we separated, there was absolutely nothing I could do that he didn't attack me for. I went into hiding for two years. During one of those years we were in counseling together; in the other he dragged out the divorce. When I went to pick up my clothes and the few personal things that I was allowed to take out of our home, he followed me around the house yelling at me, "Why didn't you get your stuff out three years ago?" Even though three years before, I had been living there. He accused me of stealing white cereal bowls and an old knife, which I had mistaken for mine because his looked exactly like the ones my parents gave me and had a retail value of ten dollars. He had threatened hundreds of times to divorce me, but when I filed for divorce, he was livid. He said if the abuse was so bad, I should have gotten an order of protection or left ten years ago. When I did, he claimed that I was just being vindictive.

Creating Conflict and Drama

SNAPs love to be the center of attention. They also get bored with the everyday, quiet lives that most people lead. Emotionally healthy people enjoy feelings of contentment and satisfaction through the close, intimate relationships that come from spending harmonious time with friends and family. However, because the SNAP is incapable of intimacy, spending time doing day-to-day things with friends and family, especially if someone else is the center of attention, is dull for them. Therefore, SNAPs create conflict, drama, and do whatever they can to turn the attention to themselves to alleviate their boredom. They thrive on perpetuating calculated chaos to sustain their need for entertainment and self-gratification.

Dirk: Rhonda seemed to get some satisfaction from making trips to see my family as miserable as she possibly could. My parents and sisters are the gentlest, kindest people. But she went out of her way to make everyone feel uncomfortable. My parents visited only once during the entire ten years we lived in Alaska because she made them feel so unwelcome. Rhonda would take anything anyone said, even a compliment, and twist it around, claiming that they were attacking her. One year, my mother bought leather jackets for my four sisters and my wife for Christmas. Mama wanted to get a picture of everyone in their new jackets, but Rhonda refused. She finally begrudgingly put it on for a picture, but afterward, I caught hell for my family "attacking" her. It was always something insane like that.

Disrupting Holidays, Birthdays, and Other Special Occasions

Holidays, birthday celebrations, and special occasions are prime opportunities for the SNAP to create conflict and drama. On these occasions, the focus is not on the SNAP, and the SNAP will do whatever he can to place the focus back on himself. But the drama of milestone occasions with a SNAP pales in comparison to the drama after a relationship with a SNAP has ended, because the SNAP will vindictively attempt to ruin these for a former spouse.

Ellen: When we were married, Rod never gave me a card or present or even acknowledged my birthday, our anniversary, or Christmas. One year my fifteen-year-old son, who is a classical pianist, won tickets to a concert on my birthday and invited me to go. I asked Rod weeks in advance if he would take us since I was recovering from cancer and was too weak to drive. He said he probably could, but he would not commit. The day of the concert, I asked him again if he would drive us since he wasn't doing anything. He waited until it was time to leave before he said he wouldn't take us. His cruelty brought me to tears.

Charlotte: Once a year, on our anniversary, I asked to go to Chicago for a romantic dinner. Except for one year, he flat-out refused, complaining that the traffic from Lake Forest to Chicago was too much hassle. However, if one of his wealthy friends asked him to be their guest at a professional sports event or a party where he could rub elbows with other wealthy and/or famous people in Chicago, he moved heaven and earth to go.

Our divorce agreement called for us to be cooperative in our co-parenting and for our children to spend time with each parent during that parent's birthday. It also specified the holidays and vacations the children would spend with each parent. However, as any parent with a SNAP knows, there is no cooperation or co-parenting with a SNAP. Tim ignored the divorce agreement and wreaked havoc on holidays, birthdays, and special occasions. In 2015, he had all three of my children on vacation with him and his girlfriend on my birthday. He constantly took our kids on vacations and on the holidays when I was supposed to have them. In 2016, our daughter graduated from college and our son graduated from high school and turned eighteen, so I suggested to Tim that we host a graduation-eighteenth birthday party, as we had done for our children in the past. (As a normal, mature adult, when my firstborn from my first marriage graduated from high school and college, I included his dad and his dad's family and guests in all his graduation celebrations.) Tim lied and told me that the kids didn't want a graduation-birthday party. Then, without telling me, he and his girlfriend hosted a party for them and invited all my friends who were important in their lives, including their godmother and her family, a friend who is like a second mom, and others. He refused to include me in the most important moment in their lives. It was painful and intentionally cruel and vindictive.

Three years later when my daughter graduated from law school and her brother turned twenty-one, I wanted to celebrate and host a party for them. Instead of going through Tim, I planned it with the kids. I made sure that they knew Tim, his new wife, and their stepsiblings and half siblings were invited so that the kids could see how mature adults handle these situations. I even offered to plan it around their schedules. I heard nothing, and Tim, his new wife, and the half siblings and stepsiblings refused to attend.

Stalking and Surveillance

In healthy relationships, people respect each other's personal space and privacy. People in healthy relationships act in each other's best interest, trust each other to act in each other's best interest, and do not feel the need to track every detail of the other's life.

A SNAP needs to control his partner and everything around them. SNAPs keep power and control over others by, among other things, intimidation, deception, or both. A SNAP is also often jealous and suspicious that his partner is seeing another man, even when there is no logical reason for his suspicions. They often project their own infidelities onto their partner, assuming that she would cheat on him because, if he was in the same situation, he would cheat on her. Because of his need for control, a SNAP will often stalk or surveil his partner.

Stalking shows a lack of trust and is designed to intimidate and bring fear to the victim. Stalking may include following a victim to her work or as she goes on errands, hacking into her personal devices or accounts, opening her mail or other private documents, rummaging through files or other personal places without her permission, calling her friends to get information on her, following her around her own house, and videotaping or recording her. It can also include using hidden recording devices, drones or other surveillance devices, following her or having her followed, and even hiring private investigators. All these violate personal space and privacy, regardless of whether the SNAP is married to the victim, and are illegal in most, if not all, states. The abuser will often use such tactics to intimidate, terrorize, and cause emotional distress.

Stalking generally leads to increased violence. Stalking appears to be the strongest indicator that the abuser will perpetrate other forms of physical violence. Studies indicate that 81 percent of women who were stalked by a current or former partner reported that they were also physically assaulted by that partner, and 31 percent reported that they were also sexually assaulted by that partner.[50]

> Hilary: When I became pregnant, Stan's need for control escalated. He became insanely jealous. Without my knowledge, he put a GPS tracking device on the car I used, and he put recording devices that looked like pens into my purse and in the car. He said he wanted to know where I was and who I was with when he wasn't around. He acted like he owned me. After I moved out, I installed a home security system with a camera because I was afraid for my safety. Without my knowledge, he logged in using my password and email to spy on me every day. He drove around my apartment and stalked me. He called the apartment manager and asked questions about me. He often called to let me know that he knew where I was and that he was watching me. He was also physically and sexually abusive.

---

[50] M. M. Carney and J. R. Barner, "Prevalence of Partner Abuse: Rates of Emotional Abuse and Control," *Partner Abuse, 3*(3), (2012): 286–335, https://doi.org/10.1891/1946-6560.3.3.286).

Sahira: Every day when he came home from work, Nadeem demanded to look at my texts, phone calls, and emails that I had made that day. He falsely accused me of having an affair, and for the next month, he incessantly demanded that I give him my phone records so he could go back for months and see who I had called. He wouldn't stop. Since I didn't have access to a car, because he took the one car we had to work which was just a mile way, I walked to the nearest fire station with my children and asked for help to get away. They got me in touch with a local domestic violence shelter, and I finally had the courage to leave and get an order of protection. Even with the order of protection, he sent hundreds of texts and called nonstop.

Charlotte: Tim falsely accused me of having an affair. After that, I caught him trying to hack into my cell phone. He showed up at my office numerous times when I was at lunch and rifled through my documents and tried to hack into my work email. I even found an invoice for a forensic computer specialist whom he had hired to hack into my work computer and phone. Thankfully, because I worked as an attorney at a large Chicago law firm, the firm had installed strong firewalls to protect from hackers. He had to show me he was in charge, so he raped me every morning before the kids left for school and every night after they went to bed, until the day I left. And he tied my hands and feet to the four corners of his four-poster bed and left me for hours. There is nothing quite as humiliating and degrading.

Cyberstalking

Younger SNAPs will cyberstalk their victims through social media, GPS on their cell phones, electronic cell phone recordings and surveillance, smart homes, and the like. The SNAP will often tell his victim that he is monitoring her. The victims feel as if their every move is being watched, and they eventually shut down and are afraid to do, say, or post anything lest it might bring a reaction.

Madison: My ex-boyfriend would call me in the middle of the night and say, "I saw you posting on Facebook. Why aren't you sleeping? You told me you would be sleeping!" I became too afraid to post or do anything.

Natalie: My ex-boyfriend had a GPS app on my phone to know where I was all the time.

Sahira: I got a note from my soon-to-be ex-husband with the names of my friends whom he didn't even know. I was suspicious, and a quick Google search told me how easy it is to record someone else's phone. So I downloaded an app on my phone and found out that he was recording my phone calls from his phone through an app that he had downloaded on his phone. I immediately went to the police.

Inability to Have or Respect Boundaries

SNAPs are unable to recognize boundaries. They are incapable of recognizing that people are human beings separate and apart from the SNAP who are entitled to their own opinions, ideas, privacy, space, career, successes, property, money, and life. SNAPs view their intimate partners as extensions of themselves who must disappear and melt into the SNAP. To a SNAP, "What's mine is mine and what's yours is mine." Thus, they see no distinction between their spouse's property and their own. It's all his. He does not respect that his spouse is a separate entity entitled to use her own assets, think her own thoughts, and have her own privacy.

He will happily use her inherited money (which is personal to her, not marital property) for his own uses. He will throw out her treasured possessions because he doesn't care about them. He views all the assets they have amassed during their married life as his. (This viewpoint becomes readily apparent when the divorce inevitably occurs and he argues that she should get nothing because he made it all and it's all his.)

He expects her to share his opinions on politics and people and gets quite upset when she does not. Although she may be successful in her own right, he will diminish her success and contributions to the marriage as though they are negligible. If this doesn't happen during the marriage, it will certainly happen during the divorce.

When a SNAP targets a woman, she must subordinate her life to revolve around his. He will demand that she attend his events rather than hers, especially if there is a conflict. He will ensure that she starts attending his church or synagogue with him, and not hers. He will require that they spend time with his family and friends, not hers. When they spend time together or entertain, it will be at his home, not hers. When they travel, it will be to the places he wants to go on his time, not hers. If they get married, he will likely ask her to quit her work so that she will be completely dependent upon him. In the SNAP's viewpoint, and oftentimes in her viewpoint as well, she will cease to exist as a separate entity with her own opinions, ideas, privacy, space, and assets. Over time, the process of eliminating her sense of individual self in favor of being merely an extension of him will be complete.

> Hilary: Stan had a home in California and a business in Illinois. When we were together, we were constantly traveling between California and Illinois. I couldn't really get a career started or a job of my own since we were hopping between states every few weeks. Our whole life revolved around his schedule. I had nothing going on in my life. I knew nobody in California, where we were living. Eventually, my role evolved into being his cook and maid and sex toy.

> Charlotte: Tim wanted me to stop working under the ruse that I could stay home with the children we hoped to have and travel with him. It was a power play. Our life revolved around his work, his friends, his relatives, and whatever he wanted to do. The only influence I had was insisting that we go to church, which he had not done for more than twenty years, but had been raised Catholic. I noticed that when he started dating wife number three, while still married to me, he simply replaced me with her. They started going to his church and sitting in the same pew where we had sat; they hung out with his friends; she moved into his home—the home I had just left; she went on a family vacation with my children just a few weeks after the divorce was final. Just like his previous wives, she melted into his life.

Perfectionism

One way that SNAPs keep everyone around them unsettled, insecure, and lacking confidence in their abilities is to impose a standard of perfectionism that is ever-changing and impossible to meet. No matter how hard a spouse, child, or employee may try, she cannot please a SNAP. He will continue to nitpick on the smallest details, or require only a certain impossible-to-find item, or demand yet another reiteration of a draft of a document or financial analysis until the poor spouse, child, or employee feels completely worthless, even though she may be quite proficient.

> Ellen: Nothing my son or I ever did was "good enough" for Rod. He nitpicked everything, even when it was being done properly. He would tell my son, "Sit up straight!" when he was sitting up

straight. He would tell him, "Finish your dinner!" when he was still eating dinner. It was a constant barrage of orders to a standard of perfection that no one could achieve. We call one of these outrageous incidents "the potato incident." My son, who was about fourteen at the time, was cutting potatoes for dinner. Rod was relentless in his criticism of how he cut the potatoes. My son finally left the kitchen, but Rod wouldn't let him leave in peace. He ran after him and hurled a potato at him, narrowly missing his head, shattering a glass cabinet in the living room.

Push-Pull Relationship

In a push-pull relationship, one is always chasing while the other is aloof, and then vice versa. The relationship starts when the male SNAP pursuer relentlessly pursues his target to "get the girl" and get the love and worship he so desperately wants. He uses charm, attractiveness, romance, and love-bombing techniques to lure his target. The target at first is standoffish, not sure what to think about the sudden onslaught of his advances. However, eventually, the target tires of resisting the constant barrage of promises and romance, and she is won over by the SNAP, who she thinks is a charming prince. When she finally agrees to open her heart and invites emotional intimacy with him, he suddenly does an about-face and becomes emotionally aloof, leaving her wondering what happened to all the affection, romance, and professions of love. He is, deep down, afraid of the emotional intimacy that he has been pursuing and inviting. Once she accepts his advances and his offer of intimacy, his fear of emotional intimacy causes him to put up walls to protect himself from getting too close. She then becomes the pursuer, trying to win back her Prince Charming in the hope of reinventing the romance when he first pursued her. She is, deep down, afraid of abandonment. He has pursued her, and now, once she has accepted his advances, he emotionally checks out and abandons her—her biggest fear.

After some time of chasing him, she may tire of the chase—after all, she is a woman, and women are not supposed to chase men. She has her dignity. So she stops the pursuit, pulls away, and becomes aloof again.

Now that she is emotionally distant, the SNAP sees that she is no longer worshipping him. The cycle of pursuit and reconnection repeats until one of the couple decides to get off the emotional roller coaster.

> **Charlotte:** My first husband, Don, was only affectionate when he was chasing me for my affection. Once he captured my heart with his charms, he became aloof, uninterested, and calloused. This went on throughout our marriage. I was always hoping for the person I was dating to reappear, but it never happened until I acted disinterested. After we separated, we did this crazy dance for the next two years. He begged me to come back, and when I did, he acted as if he didn't care. After dragging out the divorce for more than two years, we both agreed to stop seeing the other people we were dating by then and to move back in together as a family. I was so excited to be back together. He came over on Friday, and we watched a family movie with our son (who was also happy that we were back together). But after the movie, he left, saying, "I just can't do it." He didn't want a divorce, but he couldn't be together either. That was it for me. I couldn't endure the emotional roller coaster any longer.

Changing the Rules so He Always Wins

SNAPs constantly change the house rules so they always win. However, the SNAP refuses to honor his own rules. As soon as the rest of the family abides by the very rules that the SNAP has established but he refuses to honor, he will change the rules so that only he can win. Constantly changing the rules puts everyone on eggshells for fear of offending the SNAP, and it gives the SNAP an excuse to berate them and keep them scared and under his control.

> Charlotte: Throughout our marriage, Tim was always changing the rules so he always won. The kids and I had a running joke: "Rule Number 1: Dad always wins. Rule Number 2: see Rule Number 1. Rules Number 3–10: see Rule Number 1." By way of example, one evening I made plans to have a glass of wine after work with the godmother of my children. She had moved out of town and was back visiting for a day or two. I had not seen her in months. I told Tim about our plans, and he berated me for making plans without checking with him first. He then established a "rule" that we had to check with the other before making any social commitment. It was ironic, because for twenty years he regularly made plans and even went on out-of-town trips without checking with me. And he had made a commitment that same night to go out as a couple with his friends. So while he was upset with me for making plans without consulting him, he had done the same thing. I canceled my plans to see my friend whom I had not seen in six months, and we went out with his friends for the second or third time that month. The very next weekend, he again committed us to go to a social event without consulting with me. When two close girlfriends asked me to visit them for a weekend, before making a commitment I consulted him to see which weekend would work best for him. Even though I followed his rule, he exploded in anger. There is simply no winning. The calendar was always a power struggle.

Baiting

Baiting is commonly used by a SNAP to make his victim look crazy in front of others. By doing or saying something horrible to her behind closed doors, he provokes an angry or emotional response and then claims to others that she is crazy or otherwise at fault. Baiting illustrates how evil and insidious narcissism, sociopathy, and psychopathy are.

To combat baiting, it is important for a woman to keep her composure in front of others, no matter what craziness the abuser thinks up when others are not looking. Abusers view tormenting others as a game to play, and they are quite good at it. Not giving in to baiting allows a woman to keep her cool under pressure so that others don't see her emotional response and so the abuser cannot accuse her of being crazy or unreasonable.

> Charlotte: I learned the hard way that Tim was baiting me. When no one else was looking, he would have women over to our home, call me names, insult me, threaten me, refuse to co-parent, drag out the divorce proceedings, lie, violate the parenting and divorce agreements, push and shove me, etc. But in front of the kids or others whom he wanted to impress, he was as cool as a cucumber. It was like turning a light switch on and off. So the kids saw me hurt and upset and blamed me for not being cordial. Tim was stellar at this game, and he knew it. One time, he told me he signed Morton up for college orientation at Ohio University, but hid the fact that it was also parent orientation. He signed up himself for parent orientation, and only gave Ohio University his information, not mine. Even though I had been asking for months about orientation, he had once again intentionally excluded me from Morton's life, in violation of the parenting agreement that required us to cooperate and share information with the other. I found this out when we were all at Morton's high school graduation dinner, and college orientation was only four days away. When Tim told me this, he just sat back with an evil grin on his face and gloated, knowing that once again he had cut me to

the core by cutting me out of Morton's life. I didn't want Morton to think I was not interested in his college since Tim had repeatedly told him that I had abandoned him. I canceled all my plans for the upcoming week and drove eight hours one way to Ohio University to make it to parent-student orientation, but I had to act the entire time like nothing bothered me and sit with Tim and smile.

Favoritism

A SNAP will show preferential treatment to one child, employee, or business associate to the exclusion of others. Although this person is the one from whom the SNAP wants the most loyalty, once the favored one is in the clutches of the SNAP, he or she will find it hard, if not impossible, to extract themselves from the SNAP.

Charlotte: Tim always showed favoritism to his oldest son, Chaz, and his oldest daughter, Kira, from his first marriage, rather than our children from his second marriage. One day in 2005 (the year that he estimated his own personal net worth at $20 million), out of the blue he told me that he had invested more than $2.5 million in his thirty-year-old son's company and was supporting him, which he did until the end of our marriage in 2014, and until his son was well into his mid-forties. I found out after the marriage that Tim had also bought his eldest son a Porsche, but never told me. Tim took over the business, and after fourteen years, it folded. Even if he had wanted to, his son was unable to leave the business because he was beholden to his dad. His fiancée expressed that she wished that he was out from under his dad's control, but he was stuck.

For his eldest daughter, Tim paid $80,000 for a lavish wedding and a $50,000 down payment for her first house. However, he refused to give our children even a small allowance. In our divorce agreement, he refused to pay for our daughter's law school, even though he obviously could afford it. When we were married, although he was supporting his eldest son from his first marriage, giving him around $7,000 a month, he refused to support his family from his second marriage—and paid only for childcare, which was around $2,400 a month. He made me spend my entire salary on supporting myself and our children. He refused to help me pay for law school (which was the same price as his daughter's wedding). I was living with a multimillionaire, but never had any money. I remember often thinking that I wished he would show me just a quarter of the affection he showed his older daughter. Even my kids knew who his favorites were and told me. My son said he felt guilty whenever he asked his dad to spot him a few dollars, and then he added, "but then I remember Chaz, and don't feel so guilty." My daughter is going into debt to pay for law school because her dad won't pay for it. When she was younger, she said, "We all know Kira's his favorite," and tried to earn his favor by buying him expensive gifts and going on several father-daughter vacations rather than with her college friends or me. It is sad to see how they try to earn his favor, when a dad's love and resources should be freely given to all his family, not just some.

Perpetually Late/Abuse of Time

Many SNAPs are perpetually late so that they can make an entrance when they arrive. They think that they are the most important person in the room and that others should cater to their schedule. As in all other aspects of life, SNAPs do not care that others have to wait for them. They are no respecters of time. They may arrive an hour late for a dinner event and be miffed that the food is gone, expecting others to jump through hoops to serve them separately. They may be annoyed that others have gone ahead without them. If a spouse leaves the house on time without the SNAP and lets the late SNAP arrive on their own time, there will be hell to pay.

Emotional and Verbal Abuse

Dirk: Rhonda always ran two hours late to any event so that she could make a grand entrance. But then she complained that we had missed cocktail hour and appetizers, and sometimes even dinner. She then expected me to cater to her and get her cocktails and appetizers and even dinner. It was a no-win situation.

Charlotte: Tim was perpetually late to everything, usually by an hour. He was even two hours late for the birth of our son Morton, whose birth had to be scheduled with the doctor because he was past due. Tim runs twenty minutes late each Sunday to Christ Church, then swaggers down the center aisle to make sure everyone sees him; then he sprawls out, arms outstretched in the first pew behind the pastors. He is so noticeable and predictable that numerous people have commented to me about it.

Controlling and Owning Their Partner

An abuser feels entitled to own and control his partner, and he will often tell her that. An abuser views his partner as an object to serve him rather than as a gift of God to treasure and love. The partner of an abuser often feels totally controlled and owned by her abuser. She feels helpless, trapped, enslaved, and hopeless.

Pouting

When a SNAP does not get his way, if he does not rage or badger, he will at the very least pout until he does. He has been using pouting as a tactic since he was a young child. It worked on his mother, and still works for him.

Hounding and Badgering the Victim

If a SNAP wants something, and pouting doesn't get it for him, he will resort to hounding and badgering until he gets his way. He will follow her around the house, bring up what he wants, call her incessantly, and demand his way. Most victims will comply just to get rid of him and keep the peace.

Charlotte: Tim wanted what he wanted when he wanted it. I was expected to drop everything and serve him or pay the price. If he wanted sex, he wanted it right now—whether I was leaving for work, running to a kid's soccer game, or had just buried my dad. If he didn't get it, he would follow me around the house harassing me for sex until I finally gave in. Then he would ignore me until the next time he wanted it. I was constantly late for work or late picking up the kids and just not able to get essential things done since I worked, had three kids, and was taking care of my elderly parents all by myself. If I wouldn't or couldn't service him within a half hour or so, he got out a porn movie and serviced himself. I tried to get him to agree to have sex at a mutually convenient time so that I could plan around it, but he refused, saying it was better to be spontaneous.

Manipulation

SNAPs use manipulation in all its forms to control their victim. The following tactics are forms of manipulation:

- using words or behaviors to make a victim act in accordance with the abuser's desires

- arranging circumstances so that the victim is forced to choose between two negative options with little choice but to act in accordance with the abuser's wishes

Manipulation can be subtle or overt. Subtle forms of manipulation may include:

- instilling fear in the victim's mind if they make a certain choice ("You don't know how dog-eat-dog the workplace is; if I were you, I would just be a stay-at-home-mom.")
- guilt ("After all I've done for you and have provided for this family, you want to follow some silly dream and get your college degree?")
- any verbal abuse that serves to get the victim to conform to the abuser's wishes

> Charlotte: Tim was a master manipulator. Unbeknown to me, he had always planned to have a prenuptial agreement that threw fairness to the wind and provided that every penny he ever made during the marriage, and everything he ever bought with every penny he ever made, was all his individual property. As soon as we were engaged, he secretly started planning the prenuptial agreement with his attorneys and tax advisors. He also asked me to quit my position as an executive at a small publishing company, purportedly so that I could travel with him and stay home with the children we hoped to have. Since I was in my twenties, I did not earn anywhere near what he did, and I had a five-year-old son from a previous abusive marriage. I signed the prenuptial agreement the day before the wedding, although I had a gut feeling I was putting myself in a vulnerable position. He knowingly put me in a no-win position—the invitations were out, everything was paid for, I had no savings, I had no job, I had a mortgage to pay, and I had a five-year-old to support who was now calling him "Dad." He played me like a fiddle and knew exactly what he was doing.

Feigned or Selective Forgetfulness

SNAPs use feigned forgetfulness to get out of things they don't want to do, squirm out of agreements they don't want to honor, or get away with things they shouldn't do without being held accountable. If a SNAP wants something to get done, he will move heaven and earth to get his way. But if he doesn't want to do something, feigned forgetting is a well-used tactic that diverts blame. If they state that they refuse to do something, they will be seen as a jerk. But who can be upset when someone merely forgets as opposed to intentionally refuses to follow through on a commitment?

> Charlotte: When I graduated from law school in 1999, I had amassed $80,000 in student loans. Even though we were married, Tim would not pay for it. But he said he would pay off my student loan if I would pay him back at $1,000 per month. I agreed to that. He asked me if I wanted to write him a monthly check or if he should reduce my household budget by $1,000 each month. I had a gut feeling I should write a monthly check and insist on a written agreement; after all, I had just graduated from law school. But another side of me said, "You should be able to trust your husband. Just have him take it out of your monthly household budget. It will be easier than you remembering to write a check each month." What a mistake! After eighty months, I told him that I had repaid the loan and asked him to add the $1,000 per month back into my household budget. With a straight face, he looked at me and said, "I don't remember that agreement." And he kept taking out $1,000 a month from my household budget until the end of the marriage. I borrowed $80,000 but paid back $160,000—I paid for law school twice!

Emotional and Verbal Abuse

Refusal to Honor Agreements and Court Orders

SNAPs are either unable or unwilling to honor their obligations regardless of the agreement. Whether it is oral, written, notarized, or a court order, an agreement means nothing to them. However, they are quick to enforce the obligations of others. They key is to avoid entering into agreements with a SNAP. However, if one must enter into an agreement with a SNAP, be sure that it is in writing, is witnessed by people you know, is notarized, and has severe repercussions for a breach of the agreement—which is inevitable. Severe repercussions should include provisions that the one who violates the agreement will pay the legal fees of the one who must enforce the agreement. For monetary payments, the agreement should include interest and an acceleration clause so that everything owed in the future is immediately due and payable in the event of a breach.

> Charlotte: In addition to my own experience, I have counseled numerous women escaping abusive marriages. Not one of the abusers, including my own, honored the divorce, parenting, or child custody agreement, the order of protection, or any business or financial agreements. In my case, Tim even refused to honor the prenuptial agreement and the nine-page post-nuptial agreement that we signed six years after the wedding. He claimed these agreements were unenforceable during the divorce. However, he was quick to file suit against anyone who had violated an agreement with him.

> Liz: I obtained an order of protection for me and my daughter against Charlie. After years of dragging me through the court system, Charlie would not agree to any settlement, and he continued to violate the order of protection. So we went to trial on the divorce and the order of protection violations. Then Charlie appealed the divorce ruling of the court. He refused to honor the court's orders until, at long last, the judge put him in jail for contempt of court.

> Sahira: When I had obtained an emergency order of protection for me and my children against Nadeem, he acted as if it didn't exist and contacted me on my phone more than 200 times! He drilled the kids for information about me and falsely accused me of infidelity in front of the kids, asking who I was seeing and who their new father was. When I received a plenary order of protection, he continued to contact me, my family, and my children in violation of the order of protection.

Withholding Emotional Intimacy

The essential hallmark of a healthy relationship with someone is sharing emotional intimacy. Sharing feelings, hopes, dreams, plans, concerns, celebrations, and opinions in an encouraging, supporting, loving atmosphere forges connection and intimacy. Because SNAPs don't care about anyone but themselves and view others as objects that serve a purpose, the SNAP is unable to share emotional intimacy. He doesn't value the relationship; he only values what he can get from the relationship.

The SNAP withholds emotional intimacy by ignoring his partner, refusing to engage, belittling, and withholding support and affection. For example, he may simply grunt when his spouse bounds in the door with good news, or he may turn on the television when she is trying to engage in conversation. He will withhold affection by refusing to say kind words or hold hands, by discouraging her hopes and dreams and plans, by criticizing her opinions, and by refusing to say, "I love you," except when he wants something from her.

> Charlotte: As the marriage wore on, the only time Tim would be sweet or touch me, like an affectionate touch on the shoulder, would be when he wanted sex. He complained that his first wife,

Pat, wasn't affectionate, but I realized that in both of his twenty-one-year marriages, he went from being kind and affectionate while dating to completely emotionally detached the longer the marriage went. Every night, instead of dinner with the family, he emotionally checked out, ate dinner while watching violent and sexually graphic TV, and then fell asleep on the couch by 9:30. I finally stopped asking him to be at family dinners, because he never wanted to. Then, of course, the kids would balk, and everyone would end up mindlessly watching violent TV shows. We never spoke of heart issues—like hopes and dreams and things of love. He only talked about politics, finance, and scheduling kids' events.

My first husband, Don, was emotionally distant—except when he was trying to win me back. He went for two years refusing to say, "I love you." That was hard to take, knowing that for the rest of my life, my own husband would never express love.

Acting as if Nothing Has Happened after an Abusive Episode

After an episode of abuse, many SNAPs will act as if nothing has happened, or they will shut down altogether. In healthy relationships, a couple will talk after a disagreement to understand the other person's perspective, to come to an understanding of what went wrong, and to be reconciled again to each other. However, in a relationship with an abuser, one abusive tactic is to simply ignore his abuse and pretend it never happened. The victim, distraught from the violent event, will usually not bring it up. Over time, victims have been trained that trying to discuss the abuser's bad behavior and encourage behavior conducive to a healthy relationship is met with denial, blame, justifications, and more abuse. Therefore, if the abuser pretends as if nothing has happened, so will the victim—which is precisely what the abuser wants.

> Charlotte: After the night that Tim dumped me out of his car in Chicago with no cell phone, money, credit cards, or winter coat in December, leaving me to find a way to get home, he pretended that nothing had happened. He didn't ask me if I was okay, how I got home, or any other thing that would have shown he cared in the least that the mother of his two young children was even alive.

> Ellen: After a major episode of hitting me or yelling at me, Rod would zone out and just lie on the bed or the floor, pretending to be asleep. One night, the abuse was overwhelming, and my son ran away. Rod wouldn't help me look for him; he just laid on the floor. I asked the neighbors to help me look, and they did. One came into the house to tell Rod to help look for his stepson, but he wouldn't budge. The police found my son the next morning on the doorsteps of the church—waiting to talk to his youth pastor.

The Godfather

SNAPs like to be in control. They want to control others, situations, relationships, communications, information, outcomes, etc. They want everything to go through them. They want everyone to go to them for approval. They are often bottlenecks because they can't possibly keep up with all that they require to go through them.

Even after a relationship with a SNAP is over, the SNAP will want to control all relationships that his people have with others and his former partner, and if possible, he will destroy any relationships other people have with his former partner. With respect to information, he wants everything to go through him so he can either keep it to himself or share it as it serves his purposes.

> Charlotte: When I fled our house, Tim made sure that I had no relationship with his people—which included his adult children from his first marriage, people he considered his friends, and his relatives. He spread awful false rumors about me, and they cut off all communications, even when I tried to tell them the truth. However, I noticed that when some people saw his true self and distanced themselves from him, he made sure they paid. He made himself the gatekeeper between his adult children and their friends who had tried to distance themselves from him. Essentially, he made it so uncomfortable that if these people wanted a relationship with his kids, they had to go through him. If they groveled enough for being out of touch or for being unable to attend an event they had been invited to, and if he approved, then he would talk to his older children and tell him the offending person was back in his good graces, and they could be friends again. Tim was not to be ignored or pushed aside, as he had made sure all his friends had done to me. He was very proud of his Italian heritage and spoke favorably about the mob in his hometown of southside Chicago, as if they were saints who saved families from the poverty of the Depression. His favorite movie series was *The Godfather*, and he fancied himself one.

Verbal Abuse Tactics

Criticism

Once the initial idealization phase (also called the love-bombing phase) is over, the devaluation phase begins, usually with the onset of a major event—a wedding, moving in together, combining finances, going into business together—in which the abuser's target is now financially and emotionally tied to the abuser. One of the first verbal abuses to occur in this phase is criticism. During the idealization or love-bombing phase, the abuser was generous with his compliments, which were lavished upon his victim to make her emotionally dependent upon him. However, during the devaluation phase, compliments dry up and the abuser dishes out constant criticism—even on things he had formerly complimented his victim on. Nothing his spouse or partner does is good enough for his impossible standards, which are constantly changing to ensure that no one will ever meet them. The criticism a SNAP delivers is not helpful or constructive, nor is it done in a kind way that would help his partner. Rather, a SNAP delivers brutal criticism that attacks the very personhood and character of the partner.

The SNAP will often use phrases like "you never . . ." or "you always . . ." or "why can't you . . . ?" or "you are the type of person who . . ." Unlike healthy relationships in which a person builds up and encourages those around him, these generalizations are intended to attack another person while making the abuser feel better about himself by putting another person down.

The spouse or partner is completely taken by surprise, is incredibly hurt, and is left wondering where the knight in shining armor went who had been so affirming of her. Typically, the spouse will try to logically deduce what she has done that is causing the criticism, and resolves to be nicer/prettier/skinnier/smarter/faster/a better hostess/a better wife/a better cook/etc. so that the criticism will stop and the loving affirmations will return. What she does not yet realize is that she has done nothing to deserve this barrage of criticism. She so wants to believe that the loving person she was dating was the real character of her husband and that this critical man who has appeared post-wedding (or other major event) is not his true character. She does not recognize that the mask has come off and that what she is experiencing now is the real person, that his behavior in the idealization phase was insincere and served merely to hook his next victim. It may be years before she finally acknowledges that she was duped by a narcissist/sociopath/psychopath and that she fell in love with someone who never existed.

Criticism is one of the signs that a marriage is in dire danger of divorce, even though it may be years or decades before it occurs.

> Ellen: Rod was constantly criticizing and nitpicking everything my son and I did. It was a continual stream of criticism, and he blew up at every little thing. It never ended. He did it in front of our friends. One of them finally told him to stop it, but then it only got worse when he left.

> Dirk: Rhonda criticized everything I did and who I was. She even criticized how I walked and how I breathed. She wanted me to be the next president of the company, so she criticized that I wasn't a hotshot executive yet, even when I had just started. Nothing was ever good enough for her.

Contempt

A SNAP will always show contempt to his spouse or partner, because abusers do not value others. Others are simply a means to an end. SNAPs use people like healthy people use kitchen appliances. When she is no longer useful, the SNAP will toss her out with as much empathy as we would toss out an old toaster that no longer works, and he will replace her with a new one.

According to Gottman, the clearest indicator that a couple will divorce is the contempt one spouse has for the other. Contempt—an attitude of superiority, disrespect, condescension, and disdain—is the opposite of admiration, respect, and appreciation. Contempt is evident when an abuser attacks a spouse's sense of self-worth with the intention of insulting or psychologically abusing her. The most obvious and direct form of contempt is verbal, consisting of name-calling and insults. A less obvious and less direct verbal form of contempt is the use of biting humor, sarcasm, and mocking. Body language that indicates contempt includes sneering, rolling eyes, looking at someone with eyes half-closed or squinted, looking at someone out of the corner of the eyes, asymmetrical curling of the upper lip, a one-sided smirk, wrinkling the nose with disgust, raising the chin in a superior position, crossing arms, hands holding the face or chin in an unapproving manner, or turning the torso away.

Gaslighting

Gaslighting is a tactic that abusers use to make their victim question themselves and reality. The term *gaslighting* comes from a 1938 stage play called *Gas Light*, in which a husband attempts to drive his wife crazy by dimming the lights in their home (which were powered by gas), then denies that the lights change when the wife asks him about them.

Victims of gaslighting question their own feelings, instincts, and sanity, thus ceding power and control to their partner. Gaslighting, which usually occurs gradually over time, breaks down a victim's ability to trust her own perceptions and beliefs. It is perhaps one of the most insidious manipulative tactics because it distorts and erodes a woman's sense of reality. It eats away at a woman's ability to trust herself, and it inevitably disables her from feeling justified in calling out abuse and mistreatment.

When an abuser gaslights, he may deny saying something that he said or did. He may trivialize his partner's feelings by accusing his victim of being too sensitive or overreacting to something horrible that he did to upset her. He may deny having made an agreement with his spouse. He may question her memory concerning something she know happened, or conversely, he may claim to have forgotten something he promised and then claim his spouse is crazy or making things up. After doing something horrible that would upset a normal person, he may act like nothing happened, or he may claim to have said or done something when he did not do anything at all. The goal of all these tactics is to make his partner question her sense of reality by lying about what really happened, pretending something did or didn't happen, and questioning a healthy reaction to a clear act of abuse.

Most women who are being gaslighted feel like they want to record every conversation and play it back to their abuser to show what he really said or did. It is a good idea to record conversations, or at least journal daily, so that she can ground herself in reality, not in the distorted view of a malignant abuser. However, playing a recorded conversation back to the abuser may invite further abuse. In addition, recording a conversation without permission may be illegal in some states. However, with the advent of cell phone cameras and videos, many states now permit videos and accept them as evidence.

Gaslighting usually occurs over time. During the early stages of gaslighting, a woman is typically in disbelief. She thinks her abuser's behavior is strange and an anomaly. Most women have not even heard of "gaslighting" and do not recognize it. During the second stage of gaslighting, a woman may feel defensive. Her spouse has continued to deny things that have obviously happened, claims to have done things that obviously did not happen, or accuses her of being too sensitive to things that she has a right to be upset about. The woman then tries to defend herself against her husband's false claims. She doesn't understand how they can see things so differently—when, in fact, he is simply making up things to make her question her sanity.

During the final stage of gaslighting, a woman sinks into depression. She lacks hope and joy; she questions her sanity, second-guesses herself constantly, and wonders if she really is the problem he claims she is. She wonders if she is too sensitive, as he charges. She wonders if his behavior is really that bad since he tells her it's normal. She avoids conversations with him. She leads a separate life from her spouse so as not to depend on him or his promises that are later denied. She stops asking for his help with anything because the answer is always no, or he will agree to help and then claim he never agreed. She avoids family and friends so she doesn't have to explain things, and she lies and makes excuses to them for his behavior. She feels like she can't do anything right; she is not happy, but she can't put her finger on why. She starts to lie to her spouse to avoid his put-downs and twisted reality, and she wonders where the self-confident, fun-loving, kind person that she once was has gone.

> Charlotte: On occasion, I would approach Tim immediately after he had said something cruel and ask why he said it. He would always deny saying it—even though it had just happened seconds before. It was insane. I felt like I needed a recording device that was turned on all the time to have hard evidence of what he said so that he couldn't deny it. I finally just gave up. He was going to do or say whatever he was going to, regardless of how hurtful it was.

Projection

In another attempt to make his spouse question her reality and simultaneously avoid any accountability for his own flaws, a SNAP will project his distorted view of the world upon her and accuse her of the horrible things that he is most guilty of. SNAPs are unable to admit to any shortcomings of their own. One sure sign of toxicity is when a person is chronically unwilling to see his or her own shortcomings, using everything in their power to avoid being held accountable for them. Projection is a defense mechanism used to displace responsibility of one's negative behavior and traits by attributing them to someone else. It is important to realize this is a tactic, and that a SNAP is describing himself, not the person to whom he is speaking. When a woman leaves her abuser, the most common accusation from the abuser is that she left because of infidelity—when, in fact, it is the abuser who has been unfaithful.

The philandering SNAP will falsely accuse his wife of having an affair. The SNAP who is hiding assets falsely accuses his spouse of hiding assets. The lying SNAP falsely accuses his partner of lying. The haughty SNAP who abuses others will label someone else an "arrogant jerk" or worse if they disagree with him.

> Charlotte: Tim admitted to me that he had had multiple affairs over a dozen years when married to his first wife. So of course, he falsely accused me of divorcing him because I had an affair. He abandoned me in Chicago one snowy night, so he falsely accused me of abandoning him when I left. Unsurprisingly, he also claimed his first wife abandoned him and that he had to go on business trips to great places all alone because she wouldn't go with him. I endured his abuse for years. When I walked in on Tim and Didi romantically involved in our family room, after he had been telling me that I was the most important person in his life and that he wanted to make our marriage work, I finally recognized his projection tactic of accusing me of an affair. When I finally left, he was vindictive and cruel. He sat in the first pew at church to make himself appear saintly, yet he called me the devil and a hypocrite.

> Sahira: I know Nadeem was seeing a girlfriend when he went on vacation by himself for two weeks to our home county. Yet he accused me of an affair and demanded that I hand over my phone to him every night so he could see my texts, phone calls, and emails. I finally left with my young three children and got an order of protection when he hounded me for weeks, falsely accusing me of an affair. Even though he accused me of affairs, Nadeem got remarried in Pakistan 40 days after our divorce was final.

> Lori: When I finally left my fifteen-year marriage because of his never-ending verbal and emotional abuse, Ted accused me of leaving because I was having an affair. There was no affair. I just wanted to get away from the abuse.

Name-Calling

One of the more obvious and sophomoric tactics used to show contempt is name-calling. A SNAP uses name-calling in a variety of settings.

When someone disagrees with the SNAP or challenges his opinion, he resorts to name-calling. The SNAP cannot tolerate his opinion being wrong or questioned; different opinions or questions are perceived as a threat to their superiority. In their world, only they can ever be right, and anyone who dares to say otherwise creates a narcissistic injury that results in narcissistic rage. While some mental health professionals claim that narcissistic rage results from low self-esteem (causing the SNAP to constantly put others down to cover up his lack of confidence), others assert that the cause is a high sense of entitlement and a false sense of superiority. The lowest of the low resort to narcissistic rage in the form of name-calling when they can't think of a more sophisticated way to manipulate someone's opinion or micromanage their emotions. Name-calling is a quick and easy way for a SNAP to put down his wife and degrade and insult her intelligence, appearance, or behavior while invalidating her right to be a separate person with a right to her own opinion. Keep in mind that to a SNAP, a wife is merely an extension of himself with no right as a separate entity worthy of respect, her own perspective, her own gifts and talents, or her own money.

SNAPs also use name-calling to criticize a spouse's beliefs, opinions, and insights. A wife's well-researched perspective or informed opinion suddenly becomes silly or idiotic in the hands of a malignant narcissist or sociopath who feels threatened by it and cannot make a respectful, convincing rebuttal. Rather than target an argument, they target the person and seek to undermine their credibility and intelligence in any way possible. This is referred to in debate tactics as an *argumentum ad hominem*, or *ad hominem* for short. It is a logical fallacy in which an argument is rebutted by attacking the character, motive, or other attribute of the other person. It is an attack on the person rather than on the substance of the argument.

A SNAP may resort to name-calling because it excites him sexually while at the same time degrades and dehumanizes her. To a SNAP, a woman, whether a wife or a mistress or a one-night stand, is simply someone to satisfy his sexual needs. SNAPs usually demonstrate no sweetness and tenderness in the bedroom that would show a wife or lover she is valued for her wonderful qualities both inside and outside the bedroom. In line with the degrading and dehumanizing sexual abuse that almost always comes with a SNAP, abusers use degrading, dehumanizing language in the bedroom, rather than tender expressions of genuine love.

> Charlotte: Tim was never tender and sweet in the bedroom. I never once received a tender kiss on the forehead with an "I love you." When he wanted to get himself excited sexually, he would say, "I want to f*ck you." He had to have porn on to get excited. He only called me "c*nt" or "p*ssy" in the bedroom—never "sweetheart" or "darling" or anything endearing. I always felt like a prostitute.

Finally, a SNAP will resort to name-calling for no reason whatsoever other than to hurt and humiliate his spouse. She can be doing absolutely nothing, and the SNAP will call her a horrible name. Usually, the SNAP will find something that is important to his wife and insult her with names to increase the painfulness of the name-calling.

> Ellen: Soon after the wedding, Rod started calling me horrible things: "beast," "poisonous viper," "ugly," "not even human," "crazy," "brainless," "stupid," "pig," "worthless," "good for nothing." He had been so kind before the wedding; he said he was a Christian. But he turned so cruel afterward.

> Charlotte: My first husband, Don, called me names constantly after we were married. "Stupid b*tch" or "f*cking b*tch" was something he said fifteen to twenty times every day for most of our marriage. One time he even called me that as we were sitting in church listening to a sermon. I tried very hard to be a kind, generous, loving person. I kept thinking throughout our marriage that maybe if I was just nicer, Don would be nicer to me in return. It never happened. I worked hard to graduate summa cum laude from college, so being called "stupid b*tch" for no reason was very painful.
>
> My second husband, Tim, resorted to calling me names during and after the divorce. He knew that my faith and my children were very important to me, so he specifically attacked those areas. He called me "pharisee," "hypocrite," "the devil," "martyr," "asshole," and a "horrible Christian" to attack my faith. And he called me an "unfit mother" and "a mother who abandoned her children" to attack my motherhood and love of my children.

As with other forms of verbal abuse, it's important to end any interaction that consists of name-calling and to communicate that you won't tolerate it. It is also important not to believe the lies they project. Realize that SNAPs resort to name-calling because they are incapable of having an intelligent exchange of ideas and, quite frankly, are simply abusers who are uninterested in a healthy relationship.

Insults

Like name-calling, insults attack a person's core. Insults are condescending remarks that undermine another's self-worth. They are not accurate depictions of a person. Healthy people encourage and build up their partners and those around them, while abusers tear them down.

> Charlotte: It was impossible to keep nannies for very long, especially after Tim was fired and began working from home. He barked orders all day. Some stayed for only a few weeks. Tim ordered one poor lady to clean the sunroom floor with a toothbrush. When she protested, he said "If you were smart, you would just do it." When she told him that she felt used and manipulated, he would tell her that she didn't feel that way. She had just graduated with a master's degree in counseling, and she left a note telling why she left and the things he had done. It was embarrassing to me, especially since I served on the board of the Christian university she attended.

> Ellen: I had a double mastectomy followed by chemo just five days after our wedding. Within a short time, Rod was hurling painful insults: "Chemo destroyed your brain." "You have no memory." "You've lost your mind." "Something is wrong with your brain." He wasn't at all like the sweet person I knew when we were dating.

Threats

SNAPs employ threats as a tactic used effectively by other terrorists to control their victims. Make no mistake—SNAPs are terrorists and they control and manipulate their victims by, among other things, intimidation and fear. One of the best ways to instill intimidation and fear is to make threats, especially if a victim knows her abuser can carry through with them. The typical threat sound like this: "If you _____, I will _____." The SNAP is attempting to stop his victim from doing what a normal person would do under the circumstances (leaving, exposing his bad behavior, expressing an emotion, etc.) by threatening to do something that would be disastrous to her. It is an effective technique to get their way.

Abusers use so many "standard" threats so often that one might think there is a website for sharing them among abusers. Sadly, abusers think alike and arrive at these threats all by themselves. Here are just a few:

"If you leave, I will kill you."

"If you leave, I will kill myself."

"If you leave, you will never see the kids again."

"If you leave, you will never get a dime."

"If you leave, I will tell everyone you are crazy. You will have no friends, no family, no church, and no money. You will be a bag lady and live on the street."

"If you tell [the police/your mother/your father] that I hit you, I will lie and say it never happened."

"Don't ask me to take care of it. If you don't do it yourself, I will kill the [dog/cat/rabbit]."

Emotional and Verbal Abuse

Dirk: Rhonda threatened to divorce me constantly over ridiculous things. One day I accidentally spilled a beer and it got on one of our dogs. She threatened to divorce me because I had showed disrespect to our family because I wasn't being more careful. Another day, I was grilling a pork chop. I touched the pork chop with my finger to see if it was done, licked my finger, and touched it again after a few minutes. She threatened to divorce me for contaminating the pork chop.

Hilary: While we were calmly watching television after the birth of our son, Stan told me, "If it doesn't work out between us, if you don't make me happy, I'm going to hire someone for $100,000 and get rid of you." After that initial death threat, he threatened multiple times to hire a hit man if I didn't please him.

Linda: My husband heads one of the departments at a major medical center in Chicago. I helped him get through medical school, and we've been married for forty-three years. He always threatens that if I ever leave him, he will tell all our friends and relatives that I'm crazy, and that I need psychological help, and he tells me that I won't get a dime. So I stay.

Charlotte: Tim's threats started even before the wedding. The day before the wedding, he handed me a prenuptial agreement that was so one-sided it was financial suicide for me. I asked to postpone the wedding or even just live together, knowing this prenuptial agreement was a horrible way to start a marriage. His raging response: "If you don't sign this, I will never see you again!" I signed it on the day before the wedding, my birthday, and hoped for the best.

I was devastated and depressed at his cruelty. As I was crying uncontrollably in the lawyer's office, he was completely unfazed and was joking with his attorneys. After the wedding, he was not the kind person he had been before. He immediately changed into something cruel I had never seen before. He angrily threatened to divorce me at least once or twice a week for the entire first year. "I want a happy, chipper wife! If you don't get chipper, I will divorce you!"

He owned two vacation homes and a large house in Lake Forest. He refused to rent out the vacation homes when we weren't using them to defray the costs, but if we didn't use the vacation homes as often as he thought we should to make the costs worthwhile, he would threaten to sell them. He finally did sell his home in Naples, Florida, after he was fired. But he continued to threaten to sell the home in Lake Geneva as "incentive" to make us go there. He even threatened to sell our primary home in Lake Forest, claiming it was too big and too expensive. When I started looking for other smaller homes, he stopped his threats.

He became a porn addict and made sexual demands that were abusive, degrading, and dehumanizing. When I objected, he made it clear that he was entitled to me or anyone else he wanted, and threatened to have affairs: "I can have sex with anyone I want, anytime I want, anywhere I want, anyhow I want!" He had already gloated that he had multiple affairs for a decade when he was married to his first wife, and he had quite a reputation, so I knew that he meant it. And that is exactly what he did. In retaliation for me pointing out his abuses and asking him to go to counseling, he forced me to have sex every morning after the kids left for school and every night for months. When I fled the house and refused to be raped twice a day every day, he finally agreed to go to counseling. While in counseling, he continued his porn addiction. While the kids and I were using his computer to do a college search, I discovered that six of his ten most popular websites were porn sites. Even though he told me that I was the most important person in his life, I walked in on him and Didi making out in our family room when I came home unannounced one evening.

Sahira: When I left and got an order of protection, Nadeem threatened to kill himself if I filed for divorce. He didn't—it was just another way to control me. His mother even called my brother, who is her nephew, and threatened to burn down my father's business and his house. My father is her own brother.

Ellen: When we were dating, Rod told me he had a job and was a US citizen. Shortly after the wedding, I learned that Rod had been in this country illegally for more than ten years and was unemployed. He wouldn't go to work. He constantly threatened to kill me, even when I was sick with chemo treatments: "You're going to die if you don't do what I tell you! Give me money and get me a green card!" he threatened constantly. I finally realized, after eight years, that he had married me right before my cancer treatment in the hope that he would get a green card and I would die so he could inherit my home and my assets.

Kerry: Within four months of being married, the emotional abuse started. He started threatening divorce on a regular basis to manipulate me. He would tell me that he had women at the house when I was away on business trips. He constantly criticized my job the way I looked.

Blame-Shifting

Rather than accept responsibility for his bad behavior or poor decision-making, a SNAP will blame the victim, blame others, or blame circumstances. In his own deluded way of thinking that has little to do with reality, he is always right and always perfect. Therefore, someone or something else must be to blame. Always. For example, a SNAP will become enraged and hit his wife, and then blame her: "You know you make me mad when dinner is late. Why do you make me do this? Why don't you just make dinner on time and you won't have to be hit." It is a waste of time to attempt to point out to a SNAP how he caused his own actions or course of events.

Charlotte: Tim never took responsibility for any of his bad behavior or the results of his bad behavior. Nor could he say, "I was wrong. I am sorry for being [fill in the blank of cruel behavior]." For example, in 2000, when he was fired from his high-paying position as chief operating officer for being verbally abusive to employees and creating a hostile work environment, he blamed the board of directors for firing him and the CFO, who later became president, for conspiring with the board. He called them traitors and Judas and claimed that they couldn't run the company without him. He never once took responsibility or acknowledged that his own poor treatment of his employees caused his demise. He had been with the company for more than twenty-five years, but his abusive behavior escalated with his increase in power and salary. They had to protect their employees. To cover up the fact that he was fired, he told everyone that he had retired.

It was the same when I filed for divorce. He was abusive and I needed to get away. He blamed me for leaving, even though I bent over backward to try to make the marriage work and went to counseling for more than a year. After the divorce, when I stopped by his house to get my mail, he called me names and insulted me, grabbed my shoulders, shook me, and shoved me out the door. He blamed me for making him mad and making him do it.

False Accusations

Along the lines of blaming, projection, and lies, a SNAP will use false accusations to emotionally abuse his victim, often accusing her of something that he is guilty of. This puts the victim on the defensive, trying to prove that something that didn't happen actually didn't happen. It is quite difficult to prove a negative. For example, an abuser may falsely accuse his wife of having an affair to cover up the fact that he, in fact, is having an affair. She is left trying to prove that she actually did not have an affair that never happened. Or he may accuse her of losing something that he misplaced himself, and she must somehow prove she did not lose his missing item.

Raging

Raging, a tactic to keep others in line through intimidation, is a go-to reflex for SNAPs. Raging includes loud and violent verbal, emotional, and physical explosions designed to threaten the safety and security of the victim and violate personal boundaries. They are completely out of proportion to a perceived dispute or occurrence. A victim experiencing the rage of her abuser will justifiably feel afraid and violated. To stop her abuser's raging, she will retreat and comply—the precise reason an abuser rages.

> Charlotte: Tim flew into rages about nothing. He turned on me or someone else in an instant. Tim and his oldest son, Chaz, owned a company together. I have heard him rage on the telephone for an hour lambasting and excoriating his own adult son about something he did that Tim disagreed with. An admission of guilt or apology is never enough to appease him. Tim must go on until the other person is completely demoralized. On several occasions when a car rental agency or hotel did not have a car or hotel room available, Tim raged at the poor service representative, calling them names and having a temper tantrum in the hotel lobby. None of that did anything to produce a car or hotel room, of course. When I would point out that it was not the fault of the service personnel, he would yell, "Yes, it is her fault for working for such a bad company!" He was completely illogical. There was no calming him down. He was like an uncontrollable two-year-old in an adult body. It was always very embarrassing for all of us.
>
> One day he called me at work, and I answered him on speaker phone to hear him yelling, "You f*cking c*nt!" I asked him what was wrong (and quickly picked up the phone so the rest of my office would not be subjected to his profanities). He was driving in our small, quiet town of Lake Forest, Illinois, and explained that the woman in front of him was too slow. Rage was his only emotion when even little things didn't go his way.

Intentional Cruelty Followed by Blaming the Victim for Feeling Hurt

SNAPs are well known for victimizing the victim. A SNAP will often purposely inflict emotional distress on his victim, who then naturally feels hurt, terrorized, and traumatized by his cruelty. Normal reactions to intentional cruelty include crying, hiding, and shutting down. The SNAP will then revictimize her by intentionally inflicting further cruelty because she is crying, hiding, or shutting down. He may call her a baby, claim that she is too sensitive, insult her, call her weak, threaten to leave, demand that she snap out of it, or any number of intentional acts of cruelty when she is especially vulnerable. Unlike healthy people who feel good when they help others, SNAPs are sadistic in that they enjoy hurting people, and they get a power buzz knowing they can keep hurting someone who is defenseless.

> Charlotte: When Tim waited until the night before our wedding, my birthday, to foist a prenuptial agreement on me, stating he would never see me again if I wouldn't sign it, I was devastated. This was no way to start a marriage. I cried uncontrollably at the signing meeting, while he just laughed

and joked with his attorneys. My soul and spirit were wounded. His actions told me loud and clear that he didn't love me and that his promises to "love, honor, and cherish" were empty. I wasn't my normal bubbly self after that. I lost my zest for life. Within two weeks of the wedding, he went on attack and yelled at me, saying that he wanted a "happy and chipper" wife and that if I wasn't, he would divorce me. He yelled at me and said this several times a week for the first year. I finally left, because I would rather be single than suffer his intentional cruelty for the crime of being sad as a result of his intentional cruelty. He begged me to come back, and he was nice for a while—until the children were born. But every time that he would intentionally hurt me and I was crying in a fetal position in bed, he would then rage and yell at me and intentionally hurt me again for being hurt. It was sadistic; he enjoyed hurting me, and he enjoyed the power rush that he got knowing that he could do anything he wanted. I could never get mad at him for hurting me, because then his rage would be even worse. There was nowhere to go to escape, unless I left. And that's what I eventually did.

Public Verbal Flogging of Service Workers

Because they think of themselves as superior to those below them (and that is nearly everyone), SNAPs treat service workers with abuse and disrespect. Whether over the phone or in person, SNAPs shout, rage, name-call, insult, and criticize service workers who are attempting to help them.

> Charlotte: I stopped going out to dinner with Tim the night he spent twenty minutes telling off a waiter and a restaurant manager for the unforgiveable crime of being out of his favorite Bombay gin on a Monday evening. After he finished insulting the waiter for ten minutes, he demanded to see the owner or manager and repeated the process. It was completely and utterly abusive of service workers, who did not deserve it. But this was typical of his treatment both in person and over the phone. After that, with very few exceptions, I only agreed to go to dinner with him at his country club because he was on good behavior when other members were watching.
>
> Whenever a car rental place ran out of cars or a hotel made a mistake with a reservation, he verbally abused the poor representative in front of everyone, calling them names. One time he discovered his hotel did not have a room available because he failed to confirm his reservation. He called the hotel desk clerk an idiot and yelled for twenty minutes into his cell phone at his friend who worked for the hotel company and did Tim a favor by reserving him a room at a discounted rate. He caused such a disturbance in the hotel lobby that the hotel desk clerk called the police. I quickly called another hotel a mile away and booked a room for the night. Problem solved. But Tim would rather abuse people than just solve a problem. None of his raging made a car or a hotel room magically appear when there was none to be had. Our children were often with us when he verbally abused service people, and he set a horrible example for them. If he is on the phone with the bank, the insurance company, the cable company, etc., he yells and calls them names. It's just not right to treat people like that, no matter who you are.

Child Abuse

Verbal abuse of the SNAP's intimate partner and verbal abuse of a child often go hand in hand. Research indicates that when intimate partner abuse is present, child abuse is present in approximately 40 to 70 percent of those households.[51] Whatever abusive techniques the abuser uses on his intimate partner are often also used on the children. Even when an abuser does not direct his verbal and emotional abuse at children, the fact that children are witnesses to his abusive actions and attitudes is itself abusive and detrimental to children. Studies show that children of abusers are more likely to grow up to be abusers themselves or partners of abusers.[52] Nearly 70 percent of abusive fathers in court-ordered visitation threaten to kill the mother, kidnap the children, or physically hurt the children.[53]

A unique form of child abuse, when an abuser colludes with the children and they all turn against the mother, is called *parental alienation*. This is especially devastating for the mother, as her entire universe of people she loves has cruelly turned against her. Parental alienation is described more fully below.

Employee Abuse

SNAPs are equal-opportunity abusers. In addition to being abusive to intimate partners, children, and service workers, SNAPs are also abusive to employees, whom they view as inferior. They tend to sexually harass the female employees and often have multiple office affairs. SNAPs instinctively know a sexual bond is created when two people have sex, and thus they will often sleep with multiple women at the office to make allies. However, SNAPs are generally well-behaved toward their bosses, those in power, and those with whom they want to curry favor. They are aware of the hierarchy of power in organizations and choose who they abuse and who they stroke carefully. However, in many cases, over time, it becomes clear that the SNAP creates a hostile, abusive, and fearful environment that makes it difficult for employees to perform at their best, and that causes many good employees to leave the company. While SNAPs tend to rise quickly in organizations because they strive for leadership positions and tend to exude confidence, SNAPs are often fired for being abusive or sexually harassing to their employees.

> Roberta: Dan worked for a large accounting firm. But for the last ten years of our marriage, he would get fired from one firm and then move on to the next. He was so condescending to his employees that he was constantly being let go.
>
> Cathy: After more than two decades of working for a family-owned company, John was fired for being verbally abusive to a young lady who worked there. Unbeknown to him, she also was a friend of the owner.
>
> Charlotte: Tim was with a large holding company for more than twenty-five years. He was the chief operating officer and reported directly to the CEO. He was always pleasant to the owners, the CEO, and the board members. But he was abusive and condescending to others whom he viewed as inferior. His boss, a narcissist worth $100 million, called all the ordinary people "the great unwashed." Tim admitted to me that he had numerous affairs with women at the office. He even gloated about them. He said his most recent affair had been with "Julie, in accounting." He usually hired secretaries who were pretty. In 2000, he was finally fired for being so abusive. But instead of

---

[51] "Children and Domestic Violence Facts," National Coalition Against Domestic Violence, https://www.uua.org/sites/live-new.uua.org/files/documents/ncadv/dv_children.pdf.
[52] "Children and Domestic Violence Facts," National Coalition Against Domestic Violence.
[53] "Children and Domestic Violence Facts," National Coalition Against Domestic Violence.

looking at his own behavior, he blamed the board and his replacement (who had reported to him) for being disloyal and betraying him.

Elder and Disabled Abuse

Real men use their strength to protect the weaker and less powerful and those they love. They will even take on people who are stronger and more powerful in their efforts to protect those who need protection. But all abusers are cowards. Cowards oppress and abuse those weaker and less powerful than they are, including the elderly and their own parents. Abusers view others as objects to serve them, and since the elderly and disabled no longer serve the abuser's purpose, they are no longer of value. The elderly and disabled are treated with contempt, scorn, and worse.

> Charlotte: Tim's elderly mother came to live with us when she was in declining health. I helped her get dressed, gave her showers, took her to dialysis and doctor appointments, and generally tried to keep her spirits up. She often fell, and we were going to various doctors to try to figure out what the problem was. We eventually discovered that a vertebra was pressing on her spinal cord and she needed a spinal operation. But Tim had no patience or empathy for her. When she fell, Tim yelled at her to get up. It was horrible how he treated his own mom. She adored him, but he had complete contempt for her.

> Hilary: Stan lost his driver's license because of his drinking, so he made his frail eighty-five-year-old, ninety-pound mother on oxygen drive him around. She broke her arm when he took her to a bar. When he visited his son, he wouldn't play with him, but he brought his mom and directed her to care for him while he posed for pictures. He even dragged her to our court appearances, with her oxygen tank, to garner sympathy from the judge.

Cruelty to Animals

A sure sign of a SNAP is his cruelty to animals. Because abusers are cowards, their victims are weaker and less powerful than they are. Therefore, they choose women, children, employees who report to them, and innocent animals. Cruelty to animals, especially family pets, is particularly emotionally abusive to the human members of his family.

> Liz: In addition to being abusive to his family, my husband was abusive to our pets. One day he kicked the cat, who had done nothing. The cat was never able to walk without limping after that.

Pathological Lying and Rewriting History

A pathological liar is a person who habitually lies to serve their own needs, to the detriment of others. All SNAPs are liars because they live to get their own way and simply do not care about who they hurt along the way. SNAPs lie to their girlfriends, wives, children, parents, lawyers, judges, and even to their pastors and rabbis. If money or their well-kept image is at stake, they will certainly lie without batting an eye. They will deny any allegations of abuse, regardless of how heinous they are, even when there is evidence to prove it or whether they have previously admitted to it. During divorce proceedings, a SNAP will most assuredly lie to hide his income or assets from his wife, accuse her of being an unfit mother, and falsely portray himself as the doting, caring father, when up until the time of divorce he had no time for his family. Abusers lie so often that I often tell clients, "You can tell when your husband is lying because his lips are moving."

The best lies start with a grain of truth. To make themselves look better, cover up bad behavior, and put the blame on someone else, a SNAP will rewrite history based partly on just enough truth to be believable, fabricating a version that is not reality. "Rewriting history" is a kind way that some describe the actions of an abuser. In other words, they habitually lie.

> Dirk: Amy lied about nearly everything throughout our marriage. After losing weight, she had multiple affairs that she denied, but later admitted to. After we separated, to be vindictive, Amy texted a friend of mine and threatened to tell her husband that we were dating unless she paid Amy $15,000. So she was also an extortionist. My friend refused to be extorted and didn't pay. Amy called her husband and made up a story that we were dating. Unbeknown to Amy, my friend was married to an abuser, who then made life a living hell for her. Amy denied calling him, but it was clear from phone records that she did. What amazing destruction two abusers can do when they join forces!

> Charlotte: During our marriage, a lot of things happened that never made sense. So I did some research on the public records and in the files kept at our home. I found that in 1990, Tim, while still married to his first wife, Pat, bought a lot in Lake Forest for $365,000 to build a house on. So that Pat could not trace his ownership of the lot, he bought it through shell companies and a land trust. For the same reason, he convinced his employer and best friend, Bill, to loan him the money to buy the lot and build the house, and then forgive the loan after a few years as part of an executive compensation package. When Tim was asked, under oath, about the land purchase in a deposition during his first divorce, he denied knowing who the beneficiary of the trust was (himself), saying that the company bought it as an investment. When Tim married me, he gave me a prenuptial agreement in which he falsely inflated his net assets by millions of dollars. When we came to the end of our marriage, he gave the banks one financial statement to get a loan, but gave me a falsified one showing that he was worth millions less than what he told the banks. He then argued in court that his own prenuptial agreement was unenforceable and claimed I should get nothing because, based on his falsified financial statements, he was worth less at the end of the marriage than at the beginning. I wonder what lies he has told to Didi, Wife Number 3.

Fraud and Deception

A dominant characteristic of the SNAP romantic relationship is the SNAP's fraud and deception. No sane woman would sign up for a marriage of abuse, cruelty, and lies. It is only because the SNAP masquerades as a wonderful, caring, soul mate that a woman gets entangled with one of these broken individuals. Almost no woman is expecting to date a sociopath, psychopath, or narcissist. However, few are discerning enough to know the signs of these emotional predators. Thus, a woman is swept off her feet by the attention, compliments, professions of love, claims of being a soul mate, romance, and his insistence that he is single and available, when he is actually married or engaged. And because the fraud and deception worked so well to get a woman to say, "I do," the SNAP will continue his fraud and deception throughout the marriage.

Ellen: After dating Rod for more than a year, I found out I had breast cancer and needed an immediate mastectomy and chemo. He claimed that we should get married right away, even before the surgery, because otherwise he couldn't and wouldn't take care of me. I was scared, so I agreed to the wedding five days before surgery. I quickly found out after we were married that he married me because he wanted my money, needed a green card, and planned that I would die and leave everything to him.

Ordering

In healthy relationships, people ask others to do something for them. This basic mark of respect for the other person acknowledges their boundaries and recognizes that others have a choice in what they do. Even if the person who is being requested to do something has little choice in the matter, such as an employee answering to a supervisor, it is a mark of good manners and respect to ask rather than order that something be done. However, a SNAP will likely order his spouse, children, and employees to do his bidding. An order is a mark of disrespect and does not acknowledge the other person as a separate and distinct person with boundaries and choices.

Bragging about Crimes and Things to Be Ashamed Of

Because they lack a moral compass, a SNAP will often brag about things that others would be ashamed of. In their deviant minds, they do this to impress others with their ability to control people or situations. However, if the SNAP suffers legal or social consequences, he will be quick to backpedal and deny any involvement.

Hilary: Stan bragged that he had committed crimes but was never convicted. He boasted that he got out of a battery conviction when he beat up someone at Midway Airport. He bragged about raping a woman in Wisconsin but was never brought up on charges, and he claimed he paid a cop $1,000 to get out of a drunk-driving ticket because he would have lost his license. After we split, he continued to be physically and verbally aggressive, and he stalked me so that I had to move five times. I made Freedom of Information Act (FOIA) requests to several police departments and found that he had, in fact, been arrested for all these crimes, yet in each case managed to escape conviction. I even spoke to the woman he raped and discovered that he befriended her and her husband while at a resort, drugged her drink, and then raped her while she was unconscious. She was shocked that the police did not bring charges because they couldn't recover enough evidence after he moved out of his hotel room. She said that he had bragged to her husband about crazy sex parties at his house in Malibu, which, in fact, were true, but the story was so outrageous that they didn't believe him. His driver's license was eventually revoked due to his multiple drunk-driving tickets.

Charlotte: Tim bragged about all sorts of things that most people would be ashamed of, thinking he would impress others with his tough guy persona—unless, of course, it meant that there were consequences. He boasted that during his time in the Coast Guard he was responsible for the ship's records and distributing paychecks, and that when one of the men on the ship didn't like him and gave him a hard time, Tim took his paycheck, ripped it up, and disposed of it in the toilet to destroy the evidence. When the man asked him about his paycheck, Tim lied and told him it never came in, but said he would look into it. After this happened for three paycheck periods, Tim had made his point, the man left him alone, and his paychecks magically appeared again. Stealing federal property is a crime, but Tim was smart enough to destroy all evidence and never get caught.

He had a reputation at work for womanizing. He bragged whenever he had insulted someone, put someone down, or was able to make someone look bad in front of others. He loved being right and showing someone else they were wrong in front of others, or having the last word if someone offended him. He was a businessman, and he bragged that after he had negotiated a deal, he would still make another million dollars in the drafting of the agreement.

Exaggerating Their Own Accomplishments, Achievements, and Contributions

SNAPs live to impress others. Because their sense of self-esteem is outward focused—that is, it depends on what others think of them, they are constantly trying to make themselves look more favorable to others, particularly the powerful and wealthy, by exaggerating their accomplishments, achievements, and contributions to success. They will, however, distance themselves from any failures, which they readily blame on others. This exaggeration is a large part of the false persona that they put out for the world to see. They feel threatened by the accomplishments of others, and therefore find ways to minimize others while exaggerating their own importance.

For example, in the workplace, the SNAP may claim to have been the leader of a team at work that developed a successful new product, when in fact he played a minor role. He may claim to have made the winning argument in a legal brief, when another lawyer came up with the argument and the SNAP merely included it. At home, the SNAP will take credit for everything from the success of the family vacation to a child's school project rather than giving credit to the responsible party.

Healthy individuals have a quiet, inward-focused confidence that doesn't depend on what others think of them. They have a sense of self and identity that is not wrapped up in the opinions of others. They affirm others and give credit to others for good ideas, contributions, achievements, and accomplishments without feeling threatened.

Trivializing the Accomplishments, Achievements, and Contributions of Others

In healthy relationships, we celebrate each other's accomplishments, achievements, and contributions, even if they are small. A raise or promotion at work, a house project accomplished, a piece of art completed, a piece of writing published, or a successful dinner party are all causes for celebration and praise. However, a SNAP will trivialize the accomplishments of others while boasting of his own. Again, the SNAP feels threatened by others and foolishly thinks that by minimalizing others, he elevates himself.

> Dirk: There was never any affirmation or satisfaction with my accomplishments. I lived in a constant state of belittlement. I had been promoted several times, but each time, instead of congratulating me, Rhonda told me, "It's easy to look like you are soaring like an eagle when you fly with a bunch of turkeys." When I did house projects and remodeled our home myself, she minimized it, said everyone's house looked like that, and wanted to know the next project I was going to do for her.

> Charlotte: In my first marriage, to Don, I shared at one point that my professional goal was to be the CFO of a company. He just laughed at me like I was entirely too stupid to ever achieve that. I became CFO of a publishing company at the ripe old age of twenty-eight.
>
> Early in my second marriage, at the end of each year, I wrote a year-end poem for each of the children and one for our family. I put it on a large piece of watercolor paper and created a water-

color to go with the poem. The kids loved having their very own work of literary art. I would recite it while we were on Christmas vacation in Florida. One time, Tim just told me to be quiet because he was busy watching yet another violent movie on TV (his favorite thing to do). I still remember the movie he was watching—*Gladiator*. His words stung, and I never wrote another family poem. But I later became a published author and a lawyer.

As long as we were married, he was happy to have me support myself and our children, but after he was fired for being abusive to his employees and we were divorcing, he shrugged off my six-figure salary and contributions as a mother and called them negligible.

Crazy Talking in Circles

Unless one wholeheartedly agrees with him and offers praise and admiration, most attempts to resolve issues with an abuser can be classified as crazy talk. In a healthy relationship, parties carry on a conversation to understand each other. They may not agree or share the same opinion, but they will come to an understanding of the other person's position.

Anyone who has been in a relationship with a SNAP has a difficult time describing their conversations with the SNAP. They are unproductive, anything but problem-solving, filled with the abuser's projections and false accusations, and consist of the SNAP blaming the victim, even though whatever problems arise are due to the abuser's bad behavior. These conversations and attempts by the victim to resolve problems are exhausting. They can only be described as nonsensical crazy talking in circles.

The abuser has no interest in understanding another person. His goal in every conversation is simply winning. Most often, the other person will simply get exhausted trying to explain her position and give up. Even if he is dead wrong and claims that the sky is purple, the abuser will engage in illogical arguments, circular logic, no logic, false assumptions, distractions, contradictions, false accusations, personal attacks, changing subjects, or lies—anything but attempting to understand and come to some logical agreement of the matter at issue. If he can't win, he will still engage in crazy talking simply to harass his victim.

Once a relationship with an abuser is over, counselors universally recommend that victims have no contact with the abuser. Not only is this directive necessary to heal from an abusive relationship, but any attempt to contact an abuser to resolve conflicts results in talking in circles and resolves nothing. However, parents who share custody of minor children are often forced to communicate. In these situations, crazy talking in circles is almost a guarantee. Oftentimes, the victims are continuously going to court to simply enforce an existing agreement or court order that the abuser refuses to honor.

Because the conversations are impossible to describe, below are some actual situations and verbatim conversations between abusers who refuse to honor their parenting agreements and their former partners who are attempting to resolve the problems created by the abusers:

September 15, 2015. Background: Charlotte received an email from Tim, her former husband, informing her that he will be out of town for a week and that he has arranged for their son to spend the week with a friend rather than Charlotte, with whom he shares custody. Although the parenting agreement calls for 50/50 custody, Tim has claimed custody of Morton 100 percent of the time, and Morton has spent only one night in the past year with his mother. The parenting agreement states that the parent who will be out of town will contact the other parent and allow them "right of first refusal" to have custody of the child for the time that the traveling parent is out of town.

Emotional and Verbal Abuse

Charlotte: I just received your email that you are going out of town and that Morton is going to Chris's house for the week. As you know, that is a violation of the divorce agreement, in that we agreed that if one of us is out of town, that person would contact the other, and if they are available, the other would have custody.

Tim: It's not a violation of anything. I just told Morton I would be out of town and he said he wanted to go to Chris's house, so I said okay.

Charlotte: Exactly. The agreement states that you should have contacted me first, as the parent, not Morton, the child, and let me have the option to have custody while you are gone.

Tim: I told Morton I was out of town. He wants to go to Chris's house. That's all I did.

Charlotte: Again, the agreement states that you should contact me first and have Morton stay with his mother, not pawn him off on a friend. The reason we have that provision in the agreement in the first place is because in the past you went out of town for a week or had an extended hospital stay, and you didn't tell me, and you sent Morton to stay with friends or your cousin instead of letting him stay with me, his own mother.

Tim: You are always bringing things up from the past! That's in the past. That's why I hate talking to you. You should focus on the spirit of the law, not the letter of the law. Maybe he has good reasons he doesn't want to stay with you.

Charlotte: I'm sure he does—because you have told him that I abandoned him.

Tim: Well, you did abandon him, and all of us.

Charlotte: In fact, as I have told you and the pastors and the counselors, I finally left the house because you forced me to have sex in front of my own children when we were on vacation in Italy—that is a crime in the state of Illinois—and forced me to have sex multiple times a day for months up until the day I left—that's a crime too. I didn't abandon anyone. I didn't want to drag the kids out of the only home they knew to a woman's shelter while we tried to work out our differences and go to counseling.

Tim [yelling]: Bullshit. If you were so abused, you should have filed a restraining order. You were having an affair. You are a hypocrite and a liar. You claim to be a Christian, but everyone says you can talk the talk, but you don't walk the walk. You are a pharisee, a hypocrite, and a liar.

Charlotte: I was trying to work things out with us. That's why I didn't file a restraining order—I was trying to be nice—and I went to counseling for an entire year until I realized you weren't sorry for anything. Who says those things? Do you have any names?

Tim [yelling]: Everyone at church says those things. Everyone says that about you. Your friends say that about you. And all the kids are mad at you. You always bring up the past. You are always so negative. That's why I hate talking to you [slams down the phone].

January 31, 2015. Background: Their son Morton is wrestling in a high school wrestling meet that his father, Tim, is attending. Morton is injured in a match, the EMTs are called, and the EMTs believe Morton's arm has been broken. Morton's mother, Charlotte, is running ten minutes late, and when she arrives she finds Morton on his back on the mat surrounded by the EMTs, a host of onlookers, and Tim. An ambulance is about ready to whisk Morton away to the nearest hospital. Tim did not call Charlotte to inform her of Morton's injury and ignores Charlotte when she arrives. Charlotte talks to an EMT to find out what happened before Morton is taken to the hospital.

Charlotte: Tim, it would have been nice if you had texted or called me to let me know about Morton.

Tim [yelling]: You are not my concern! I don't care about you. I don't care what you think. I don't care what you feel.

Charlotte: Well, that is true. I agree that you don't care about me.

Tim [yelling]: You are the devil! You are a hypocrite! Don't ever talk to me again! [He storms away in a huff.]

At the hospital, when Morton, Tim, and Charlotte are all in the same small emergency room together, Tim acts as though nothing happened and asks Charlotte questions. She must talk to him to answer, against what he has just demanded, and he demands that she make a follow-up doctor appointment for Morton.

November 2015. Background: The joint parenting agreement required each parent to consult the other prior to making out-of-town travel plans and provide the other parent as quickly as possible with flight, hotel, accommodation, and phone information while out of town. Because of past instances of Tim forcing Charlotte to have sex with him in front of the children while in the same hotel room, the joint parenting agreement prohibits either parent from having sex, watching porn, or drinking excessively in the presence of the children. Charlotte was told by one of the children that their father was taking them and his girlfriend, Didi, on vacation to California, but Tim had neither told Charlotte that they were going on vacation nor provided travel information. Charlotte requested by email travel information and confirmation that he had obtained separate hotel rooms for the children so they would not have to experience watching their father and his girlfriend have sex in front of them. Tim refused to provide travel information, stating that he was not required to. Charlotte quoted the section of the joint parenting agreement that required him to provide travel information. After he still refused, she contacted her attorneys, who then contacted Tim's attorneys, who finally complied with the request. While sitting in a doctor's office for Morton a few days later, this conversation took place:

Steely silence.

Charlotte: It would be much easier if you would just comply with the agreement.

Tim: I did. Even my attorneys said your request was ridiculous.

Charlotte: I don't really care what your attorneys say. You should give me your travel information. I'm their mother.

Tim: I don't really care what you say.

Charlotte: I would love to have a truce. Can we have a truce?

Tim [yelling]: You aren't capable of a truce. You are the most self-righteous hypocrite I have ever met. [He gets up and moves away to the other side of the room in a huff.]

December 6, 2016. Background: Charlotte texted Morton to arrange spring break 2017. Tim had Morton for spring break 2016, and pursuant to the parenting agreement, parents were to alternate years. Since the divorce in 2014, despite the fact that the parenting agreement calls for 50/50 custody, Tim has agreed to let Morton stay overnight at Charlotte's house only 2 nights in the last two years. Morton replied he was going to Utah with Dad. Charlotte called to discuss with Tim.

Charlotte: I texted Morton today. He said he's going on spring break with you, but as you know, this is my year. You had him last year for spring break.

Tim: No, you had him last year.

Charlotte: You had him in 2016. I had him in 2015. It's my year.

Tim: Well, Morton called me and asked to go to Utah with some of his friends.

Charlotte: You and I should be discussing this first. We are the parents. Our agreement requires us to consult with each other first. And that's what normal parents do—consult with each other about their kids.

Tim: Well, Morton asked me to go.

Charlotte: I understand that. You are missing my point. You and I agreed to consult with each other; that's what parents do.

Tim: I'm just trying to make him happy.

Charlotte: The point is we should coordinate and agree first, which you have never done. I do each time I have a vacation with the kids. Like last summer, I asked you first, and even rearranged our trip around your and Didi's trip to Greece. I would like the same courtesy. That is what our parenting agreement says. You took Kristen on the last four spring breaks; you see the kids all the time. I would like some time with them.

Tim [escalating]: Yes, I do see them all the time—because you left us! I can't coordinate with you because you weren't here! You abandoned us. I don't stop them from seeing you.

Charlotte: You know very well why I left.

Tim [yelling]: I'm not going to go there! The past is the past! You abandoned us!

Charlotte: I would like to go with Kristen for spring break, then, and with Morton the following year.

Tim [yelling]: Kristen and I already talked about her going with me on spring break. And you'll have to talk to Morton yourself.

It continues in circles.

March 2017. Background: Stan earns well over $400,000 per year and has a long history of drug and alcohol abuse, DUI, revoked driver's license, rape, battery, and sex parties. Hilary has been a stay-at-home mother. After their separation, the parenting agreement provides a flexible visitation schedule and requires Stan to provide Hilary with a monthly visitation schedule prior to the beginning of the month. It also requires him to undergo drug and alcohol testing. He continuously refuses to follow the parenting agreement. Instead, he contacts her a day in advance, demands that she drive an hour to him so that he can see his infant child, makes threats when she cannot drop everything and do so, refuses to take drug and alcohol tests, and threatens to cut her off financially.

Stan: This is going to go on for eighteen to twenty-one years. You're going to lose.

Hilary: Lose what?

Stan: I'm going to make sure of it. Everything this time. My money gets me things, okay? Once you get bombarded with certified letters and lawyer stuff, anybody is going to say, "That guy can't be drunk every day or on drugs or whatever. He does certified letters to her every day. He's like a businessperson sitting in a desk all day." Believe me, bring it. You're going to see a whole new chapter of this. The things your mother went through with your dad is nothing compared to what I am going to bring, okay?

Hilary: Okay. Well that sounds like a threat, Stan.

Stan: It could be. I'm saying my family is going to have a discussion with your parents. And if your parents want to call the police, that's fine. Bring it. The police will be at the house all the time anyway from now on. This has been coming a long time. I've been warning you. Believe me—when I'm really quiet, that's when you need to worry. The court will say, "You're not allowing Aaron to see his father." You're not co-parenting, my dear. You are the problem. You are not co-parenting. The court will see it my way.

Hilary: Stan, when you act like a crazy person, you're not nice to be around.

Stan: It's not being crazy. If I raise my voice eloquently, that's not crazy.

Hilary: You have no reason to raise your voice.

Stan: I'm a f*cking winner! I have nothing to fear from you anymore. You got nothing on me, and the more you do this—try and threaten me and shit—I will come down on you!

Hilary: I'm not threatening you.

Stan: I will come down on you. Believe it. Because I got nothing to worry about. I hate when someone threatens me with a gun that has no bullet in it. I'm going to come down on you now. F*ck you. You have nothing. I've been through that before with Janet, and we settled just fine. They won't do shit for you.

Hilary: Okay, Stan, well I've literally never been treated this way.

Stan: Janet tried the same thing on me years ago. Believe me, I've been through this. You will owe me money. I'll pull up. You know there's nothing.

Hilary: You're just hurting Aaron, and that's what bothers me.

Stan: Look, you're going to lose. Look, I want to see my son. I'm a winner and I'm going to win. You're easy to win on. I'm going to win over this. I've won a lot of other things, believe me. We are going to your family's house.

Hilary: You can't just show up unannounced.

Stan: You know what I think we are going to do? We are going to show up late one Saturday night to see your mom when she's good and drunk. With the cops, okay?

Hilary: You're not going to show up unannounced.

Stan: No, we are going to show up when we want.

Hilary: Okay, Stan, I don't even know what you want me to say at this point. This is just going in circles. I'm really trying to give you the benefit of the doubt.

Stan: Don't mess with me. You know what you used to say? Don't mess with crazy, get it? You're going to get it now, all right?

Hilary: Don't mess with crazy?

Stan: Don't mess with me! (laughing) You should be a lot nicer to me.

Hilary: It's in Aaron's best interest to be in a safe environment.

Stan: Yea, my mother has something to say to you too. Would you like to talk to her?

Hilary: No, this is not her child, and this is not of her concern.

Stan: I feel like you should talk to her.

Hilary: I don't need to speak with her because I have no idea what type of ideas you've put into her head.

Stan: She listens to our phone conversations.

Hilary: Okay. Then does she realize how much stuff you've made up and how difficult you've made life for me and Aaron?

Stan: She thinks it's terrible that you don't let her see her child.

Hilary: I never said that.

Stan: Tell her right now. When is she going to see Aaron?

Hilary: I don't know. When you and I can work through things and talk in a civil manner.

Stan: F*ck you! F*ck you! We are done! I'm not very generous when I don't see my child!

Hilary: But you understand the impact of your decision?

Stan: You're going to be on welfare. He's going to be on welfare. Or you have to go get a waitress job or something. Waitressing job.

Hilary: But you're not understanding the point here.

Stan: The point is money. Power and money. If you don't give me power, you get no money. Got it?

> Hilary: This isn't a game, Stan.
>
> Stan: This is about satisfaction. I don't work and slave for nothing. You don't take my money for nothing. You wanna call that blackmail? You wanna call that extortion? I will call what you're doing extortion before you can ever say anything to me.

Discounting, Denying, and Criticizing the Feelings of Others

People in healthy relationships experience a wide range of emotions, just as those around them do. It is natural to feel hurt when belittled, angry when we experience injustice, sad when we are disappointed, and grief when we lose something or someone dear to us. However, a SNAP will often tell their spouse or partner that the emotions they are feeling are not reliable or accurate or that they are not entitled to feel the way they do. A SNAP wants everyone to be happy and worship him, and anything less is unacceptable, even when the SNAP caused the feelings.

> Charlotte: Regardless of his latest cruelty, Tim always required me to be happy, as if his latest insult or cruelty should have no effect on me. Throughout the marriage, whenever I was anything but happy and worshipping him, he raged at me and accused me of being "too sensitive" if I was hurt and crying, or "trying to start a fight" if I confronted him about his abusive behavior. It was a no-win situation. By the end, I just tried to avoid feeling anything.

Telling Others What They Are Thinking or Feeling

Many SNAPs will tell others what the SNAP thinks they are thinking or feeling. This tactic is yet another form of insult and abuse. This ploy might include the abuser saying, "You think you're so smart!" or "You think you're the queen of this house!"

> Charlotte: We had several lovely young Christian women who were nannies to the children when I was working. Inevitably, they left, sometimes after only a few weeks, due to Tim's cruelty. One nanny, who had just received her master's degree in counseling, took the time to write me a letter to let me know what had happened. Although she tried to talk to him, he kept making her feel worthless. On the day he made her clean the floor on her hands and knees with a toothbrush, she told him she felt disrespected. He denied her feelings, saying, "You don't feel hurt; you're too stupid to feel hurt. Just clean the floor, why don't you!"

Abuse and Criticism Disguised as a Joke

A favorite strategy of some abusers is verbal abuse and criticism in the form of a joke. When the victim understandably feels hurt, the abuser will brush it off as a joke. He will then accuse her of being unable to take a joke, not having a sense of humor, not being funny, always being such a stick-in-the-mud, taking things too seriously, being too sensitive, being too serious, etc.

> Charlotte: Tim would constantly make crude jokes in front of our children, his older adult children, and guests, complaining that he didn't get enough sex (even though we had sex at least once a week). At every gathering, he would make some inappropriate sexual remark and then laugh. "Hope springs eternal!" It wasn't funny; it made everyone feel uncomfortable, and it humiliated me.

Withholding Information and Keeping Secrets

A rather insidious practice SNAPS use is withholding information from their partner, coworker, or employee. This approach makes others look bad, miss important meetings, make uninformed decisions, constantly seek out the SNAP for more information, depend on the SNAP to go forward, or otherwise ensure that the SNAP is in power and control. Knowledge is power, and SNAPs make sure they are in the know while keeping others in the dark. SNAPs have many secrets, most of which would reflect poorly on them if they got out.

In the workplace, a SNAP may play this game by not informing a team member that an important meeting has been rescheduled. When his team member misses the meeting, it will reflect poorly on the missing team member, while the SNAP who attended the meeting will appear to be a star. When the SNAP is confronted about it, he may respond, "Oh, didn't you get the email I sent?" even though the victim's name was not included on the distribution list. This will be dismissed by the SNAP as an oversight, something that slipped through the cracks, or a technical glitch.

In a marriage relationship, this can be applied in a variety of ways. When dating, the SNAP will not disclose that he is married to someone else, nor will he inform his wife that he is dating someone else. The SNAP will not reveal why his last relationship ended. All relationships with a SNAP end badly, and the SNAP will always blame the former spouse or girlfriend for the breakup rather than exposing the truth that he was to blame. The SNAP may even withhold information from his girlfriend, fiancée, or wife that he has children from a previous marriage or children out of wedlock.

During the engagement and marriage, when his partner or wife has a right to know his and their financial condition, the SNAP will invariably withhold financial information. He will keep her in the dark about their financial condition, whether the mortgage has been paid, his income, expenses, and assets, whether he has been supporting a girlfriend or an illegitimate child—the list is endless. The SNAP may use a trust to purchase real estate to keep from being found as the owner. The SNAP will withhold tax information until the last minute when he needs her signature to file the tax returns, or perhaps he will simply forge her signature. Both actions are another form of financial abuse. After a separation or divorce, the SNAP will keep information about the children's activities from her to exclude her from their lives and make his spouse look bad in front of the children. This is a form of parental alienation. He will withhold information about his income and assets to keep from paying the proper amount for property distribution, maintenance (also called alimony), and child support.

> Donna: During our thirty-plus-year marriage, Len had a child out of wedlock whom I didn't find out about until years later.

> Ellen: I had no idea what Rod did for work, where he went all day from 8:00 a.m. to 11:00 p.m., who he spoke with, or what he was doing on the computer all day and through all hours of the night. Whenever he logged into his computer, he would shield his password so I couldn't see what he was typing. We didn't share bank accounts, so I had no idea what money he made or if he made money—or if he was even working. After I filed for divorce, I went through his computer and discovered that he had a girlfriend and child in the Czech Republic.

Playing the Pity Card and False Accusations

Healthy people with a properly calibrated moral compass take responsibility for their bad behavior and accept the consequences of their actions. We hear many a country singer lamenting the loss of a girlfriend or wife, admitting that he is alone due to his own selfishness and failure to "treat her right." However, SNAPs will never take responsibility for their own abusive behavior that drives others away. According to Dr. Martha Stout, author of *The Sociopath Next Door*, a sure sign that a person is dealing with a sociopath (or psychopath or narcissist) is that they play the pity card when they are about to be cornered. "Crocodile tears at will are a sociopathic trademark."[54]

For example, when a SNAP is subjected to an order of protection or put in jail because of his abuse, his first response will be to evoke pity from family and friends and blame his predicament on his wife or partner who sought legal protection. Unfortunately, instead of being horrified at the abuser's behavior that forced the victim to obtain a restraining order, the friends and family of the abuser usually blame the victim for trying to protect herself and continue to support the abuser.

This blame-the-victim behavior is akin to blaming the *New York Times* for publishing a story about a criminal rather than being outraged at the criminal's behavior. However, blaming the victim is common among the friends and family of abusers, and it is as revealing regarding their moral compass as is it about the abuser's.

> Liz: When I finally obtained a plenary order of protection against Charlie, he used the children as pawns, saying to his mother and family, "Look at my poor son Johnny. My wife is taking my son away from his father!" When he was put in jail, he blamed me: "I can't believe she did this to me! How can I survive in here?" I moved from California, where my entire family lived, and went to Chicago to be with Charlie when we were married twenty-eight years ago. So his family was very dear to me. But he turned his entire family against me, and it was devastating to see the people I loved turn on me because they believed his lies. It took years, and catching Charlie in his own lies, before they realized that he was the problem, not me.

> Hilary: Stan refused to follow the parenting agreement for visitation, which was very flexible. Instead, he just demanded to see our son whenever he felt like it. I tried to accommodate him as much as I could. But if I couldn't drop everything and drive our son to see him (he refused to pick him up at our house), he played the pity card, falsely claiming that I was the reason he couldn't see his son and that I was cutting him out of his life: "You are terrible to do this. You obviously don't want me to see my son. I can't believe you are making me wait until Sunday to see my son! You are a criminal! You don't want me to see my son until he is eighteen?"

> Charlotte: Tim was verbally and physically abusive for years, even after we were divorced. The abuse occurred every time we spoke on the phone or saw each other in person when no one else was present. I finally got an order of protection against him. Instead of taking the responsibility for his abusive behavior, he falsely claimed to my children, "Your mother is just being vindictive because I'm seeing someone else and we're getting married. She wants to ruin the wedding." After I obtained a permanent protective order, I forwarded it to the leadership at Christ Church, who continued to let Tim worship there and even married him to his next victim, Didi, in the church. I didn't receive any response except from a pastor, who said it was "sad" that a church had to be mentioned in an order of protection and recommended that the church seek legal counsel. Not one pastor reached out to me expressing outrage at Tim's abusive behavior that continued for five years after I fled my home. And why would they? By continuing to let him worship and marrying him in church, they were giving full approval to his abusive behavior and adulterous affair that led to the end of our marriage and the beginning of his next one.

---

[54] Martha Stout, *The Sociopath Next Door* (New York: Harmony Books, 2005), 91.

Smear and Slander Campaign

When a victim finally leaves her abuser, the first order of business for the SNAP will be to call as many family, friends, pastors, and church members as he can, feign devastation, and claim that his wife abandoned him for no reason. During this pity play, he will also lie and falsely accuse his wife of breaking up the marriage. The most common lie a SNAP will concoct is that she left because she was having an affair, (even though in most cases the SNAP is having or has had an affair). He may claim his spouse or partner is mentally unstable, or some other some other false accusation to deflect the blame from his own bad behavior that has made living with him impossible. If she takes her children with her, he will falsely accuse her of kidnapping. If she doesn't, he will accuse her of abandoning them.

After years of bullying, the abuser inevitably turns into a sniveling, pitiful victim putting on a performance worthy of an Oscar. But if you are observant, when the abuser thinks no one is watching, you will also see a slight smirk on his face when he sees that his trick is working.

Sahira: When I left and moved into a local domestic violence shelter because of Nadeem's abuse, he immediately went on a pity party to get our families, friends, and me to feel sorry for him, make me feel guilty for leaving, and return to him. He said he was depressed and was hospitalized and was taking medication for his depression. He said he would commit suicide if I didn't come back and give up my order of protection and divorce proceedings. Both our families put enormous pressure and guilt on me to return to the marriage, so I moved into the domestic violence shelter. He never backed up his claims with hospital records or copies of prescriptions, and he never committed suicide. It was just another tactic to get me to come back.

Charlotte: The final straw in our marriage was when Tim inflicted the ultimate humiliation and degradation by raping me for months and then raping me in front of our children while we were all in the same hotel room on a family vacation in Italy. I fled, went into hiding, and sent him a lengthy email spelling out exactly why I had left, encouraging him to seek counseling. I didn't tell anyone where I was because I suspected that he would try to call my friends and find out where I was, under the ruse of concern for me. I didn't want to put my friends or children in the middle or have them lie for me about my whereabouts. The very day I left, he went on a phone-calling and smear campaign worthy of the Jerry McGuire movie claiming that I had abandoned him and had left him because I had an affair. Of course, he left out the fact that he was abusive and that his own prenuptial agreement required me to vacate his house in the event of a marital breakdown. It worked with a few people. Some "friends" who had been in our Bible study group that I had led believed him hook, line, and sinker. They didn't even call to see if his outlandish claims were true. They cut off all ties and continued to spread his rumors in our church and community. Even when I defended myself and told them what had happened, giving them written proof of his lies, they continued to support him. It was painful because I had considered them friends, even considering one whom I was close to be a spiritual mentor. I finally realized that they shared Tim's depraved moral compass.

Minimizing and Trivializing His Abuse

SNAPs and their minions will attempt to downplay, minimize, or trivialize their abuse—if they admit to it at all. They will try to convince the victim that the SNAP's behavior is normal, that everyone goes through a rough patch, that true love hangs in there when it's tough, that things aren't that bad, that every couple has their differences, etc. SNAPs believe they are always right and try to project an image of perfection to the world.

Admitting that their actions are abusive would be recognizing that they are not perfect or right. It would be admitting defeat. Since the goal of all SNAPs is to win at all costs, they are unwilling to admit to the abusive nature of their actions.

From a spiritual perspective, the SNAP's pride gets in the way. He simply cannot humble himself, admit he is wrong, and recognize that he needs to change his ways. Yet these are the very actions required if there is any possible hope of reconciling with his spouse. Sadly, even when the SNAP knows that he will lose his marriage and everything else he values, he will not humble himself, admit he is wrong, or make efforts to make it right. Throughout the Bible, God warns that pride is from the Enemy and leads to destruction, admonishing us to humbly seek God and walk in His ways. Satan is behind the SNAP's refusal to humble himself, resulting in self-destruction and the destruction of others. The SNAP doesn't even realize he is a tool of Satan and that after he has finished destroying his wife and family, his employees, his finances, and his career, he will destroy himself.

> Charlotte: Tim would never admit that his behavior was abusive. When I sent him a fifteen-page letter outlining the abuse, he said, "It's not that bad. If it was that bad, you would have left ten years ago." Then his abuse escalated, and I did leave. Even after I had fled, gone into hiding, and warned him that a divorce was on the way if we could not work things out with a counselor, he was so full of pride that he would not admit he was abusive. He would not admit that anything he had done was "that bad." He sauntered into the counselor's office, sprawled out on the couch with his arms spread out and his legs splayed, confident that nothing was wrong. He spent half of our session just talking about his social life rather than the real problems we needed to address. When I point-blank asked him how he justified abandoning me in the middle of a December night in Chicago, he only admitted, "Well, maybe it was inconsiderate and maybe it was rude." As to raping me every day, twice a day, and then raping me in front of my teenage children, he said that I consented. That a Christian mother would agree to have sex in front of her children, which is not only severely detrimental to their well-being but is also a felony, is ludicrous. It just shows to what lengths a sociopath will go to claim they are right.

> Julie: Our counselor told Ted, a litigator at a large Chicago law firm, that he needed about $100,000 in counseling or he would be quickly looking at a divorce. Compared to the cost of a divorce, the $100,000 was a drop in the bucket and was far less than attorney's fees would be. Nonetheless, Ted would not admit he did anything wrong, and he refused to go to counseling. The divorce cost him millions of dollars. I guess it was worth it to him to be right.

Twisted Definition of Love

A SNAP will skew the definition of love and require sacrificial love from others, claiming that putting up with his abuse is what unconditional love is all about. At the same time, he puts no requirements on himself to love.

Comparing Himself Favorably to Even Worse Abuse

When confronted by the victim concerning his abuse, a SNAP will also try to compare his actions to even more heinous acts or to others whom he views as worse. Their justification typically starts with self-righteous indignation along these lines, "Well, at least I didn't . . . [insert a more despicable act]."

Denise: I found out during our marriage that my husband, who was a church worship leader with me, had fondled our teenage daughter's breasts. When I confronted him, he retorted, "Well, at least I didn't rape her!"

Charlotte: When I confronted Tim on his numerous acts and years of infidelity, even though he claimed to be a Christian, he responded, "Well, at least I stayed married!" His idea of marriage and the Christian concept of marriage are incompatible.

No One Else Will Want You

All humans have a need to be loved and accepted, not for what they do, but simply for who they are. Abusers attack the very soul of their victims when they claim their victims are unlovable.

To simultaneously emotionally devastate their victim, keep them from leaving, and keep them under their control, a SNAP may claim that no one else will want his victim. He will charge that no one will ever love her and that she is unworthy of being loved. The SNAP will often tell his victim that she is lucky that he has tolerated her and that she has anyone at all.

Dirk: Rhonda would start an argument, then threaten to divorce me if I didn't do what she wanted. Then she would say that if she divorced me, no one else would want me and I would be completely alone. After fifteen years, I realized it was better off to be alone than to be with an abuser.

Charlotte: Don often told me that there was a better chance of being hijacked on an airplane than for a woman over thirty to get married. Then he would tell me how lucky I was that he stayed with me since he could have anyone he wanted.

Guilt

An abuser will attempt to use guilt to make others do what he wants. He can be quite persuasive, especially when others have a strong sense of responsibility and conscience. The abuser has none of these qualities, but he knows that others do. So, while appealing to an abuser's conscience or trying to persuade him to do the right thing is seldom successful, unless there's something in it for him, an abuser knows that others will cave if he uses guilt and can convince them they are not a good person if they don't go along with his plans.

Hilary: Stan refused to honor our parenting agreement, and he never gave the notice we agreed upon for scheduling visitation time. He seldom even wanted to see our child, but when he did want to see him, he demanded to see him the next day. And I was supposed to move heaven and earth to cancel my plans. He expected me to drive our child more than an hour to him, bring diapers and supplies because he never had any, wait for him to finish visitation, and drive our child back (even though he was required to come pick him up at my house). When I couldn't do this, Stan would try to make me feel guilty that he couldn't see his son, that I was stopping him from seeing him, and that he had rights to see him, that I was a criminal and "horrible" for refusing to let him see our child. He was relentless. I usually gave in, and life was out of control because I could never plan anything. This went on for a year until I finally hired an attorney who understood domestic abuse and explained the tactics he was using.

Sahira: When I left, Nadeem immediately went on a pity party to make me feel guilty for leaving and to try to get me to return to him. He said he would commit suicide if I didn't come back. He obviously didn't miss me that much. He remarried forty days after our divorce.

Dirk: After I left Amy, who had been having affairs with multiple men for years, she went to great lengths to make me feel guilty for leaving. She told me that she was diagnosed with cancer, was undergoing chemotherapy, and was down to ninety-eight pounds. However, friends who had recently seen her reported that she looked just fine. If she was really that sick, I wanted to help. But since she was a pathological liar, I suspected this was just another lie. To get to the bottom of it, I told her that I had called the church, explained to them that she had cancer and was undergoing chemo, and that they had organized a group of women to bring meals over to her for the next several weeks (as they often do when someone needs extra help). I didn't actually call the church; it was a test to see her reaction—which would confirm if she was, in fact, undergoing chemo. She was livid with me, yelled at me for telling others about her cancer, and said that she didn't need any help. Her reaction confirmed she was lying (again).

Attacking Criticism No Matter What

While the SNAP criticizes constantly during the relationship, it rises to a new level of attacking when the romantic relationship is over. SNAPs see the world in black and white: people are either an ally or an enemy who must be crushed. Once a SNAP ends a relationship, the former spouse is now considered an enemy who must be destroyed. The victim now has no redeeming qualities and can do nothing right in the eyes of the SNAP. The SNAP will criticize his victim for leaving and will criticize her for not leaving earlier. He will denounce her for exposing the truth of his abuse, and then claim that if it was "that bad," she should have left earlier. He may demand that they go to counseling for a period, and then castigate her for wasting his time when she leaves, although he shows no long-term change. She may decide to leave after she learns of his infidelities, and yet he will chide her for not trying to work on their relationship.

Charlotte: Tim claimed that he divorced his first wife because they grew apart and she abandoned him because she refused to travel with him. So I was confused when Tim shared with me when we were dating that he was upset that she didn't fight for their marriage. Unbeknown to me, when we started dating he had not yet filed for divorce or was even separated, as he had claimed. For twenty-five years I was under this mistaken belief, until I spoke to Pat after I filed for divorce. She informed me that she filed for divorce because of his infidelity. So it is almost unbelievable that Tim had a dozen years of affairs with various women, made plans to marry me while he was still married to Pat, was upset that Pat didn't fight for him and their marriage, and that he shared that with me—the person he claimed to want to marry. That is crazy thinking.

Triangulation

SNAPs are masters at triangulation—a manipulation tactic in which the abuser pits people against each other by telling each untruths about the other—setting up a triangle of lies. The effect is to turn people against each other in the competition for the SNAP's affection. For example, the SNAP will tell one of his children something about her mother that will turn mother and child against each other. The blame, rightly directed to the abuser, is directed to another instead.

While a SNAP is ending a romantic relationship, he will almost always be grooming a replacement for his partner, who is waiting in the wings. Once she makes her appearance, which is barely after his wife's side of the bed is cold, the SNAP will brag about how wonderful the replacement is or how well-connected her family is, and he will genuinely expect his wife to be happy for them. Otherwise the SNAP will accuse her of being bitter, vindictive, jealous, or catty.

What the wife may not realize is that the SNAP was likely dishonest about his marital status, telling his new interest that he was single, separated, or divorced—just like he told her when they first started dating. At some point, when the hurt and bitterness subsides many wives pity the other woman because they realize that she is just like the wife was years ago: naïve, trusting, believing the SNAP's claims that the former lover was crazy or had committed some unpardonable marital sin, and believing that the SNAP was single and available.

When otherwise amicable partners divorce, they exchange contact information and communicate regarding shared parenting responsibilities. When one of the partners is a SNAP, however, he keeps his former and current wives separated as much as possible to prevent their comparing notes and his inevitable lies that he has told to each of them.

> Brenda: I didn't realize until after our fifteen-year marriage broke down that Bill had been married to someone else when we started dating. He told me he was divorced, but he wasn't. He was also abusive toward her and broke her nose, but he claimed it was an accident.

> John: My dad left my mother and married another woman when I was an infant. He never wanted a relationship with my sister and me, which was painful. After forty-five years, he shot his wife, and then himself. After he died, his family realized that he had been telling lies his entire life to family members about other family members to ensure that we had no relationship with each other. He also lied to his wife about finances, keeping one set of books and bank statements that he showed her, and another of the actual finances. While it was painful having no relationship with my biological father, I came to realize that it was God's protection over me so that my father would have little influence on me. I chose to be a pastor, and I'm sure that I would not be the person I am now if my biological father had raised me.

> Charlotte: When we started dating, Tim claimed that he was going through a divorce and that he had been separated and had not been intimate with his wife for more than nine months. We met at work, and since it was a small office, he asked me to look for a job at another company, claiming that his divorce would be over in six months at the most. Among other things, he claimed that his wife never went on trips with him and that he was lonely because she had essentially abandoned him. I was so naïve that I fell for it. A year after I left the company, he still hadn't introduced me to his friends or children, so I asked him why. He said he was still married and living together and had not actually filed for divorce. I broke off our relationship, but within a few weeks he told me that he had filed for divorce, and he begged me to get back together. I found out at the end of our marriage, after talking to his first wife, Pat, and confirming with the public court files, that, in fact, Pat had filed for divorce after she discovered his numerous affairs. She also claimed that she always went on trips with him, except near the end of the marriage after she found out about his affairs. So, after Tim and I were in counseling and he claimed he loved me, it should have been no surprise when I came home one day to find him and Didi (who eventually became wife number three) making out on my family-room couch. Just like with his first marriage, he claimed that I abandoned him. I'm

sure the lies he told Didi about me were as creative as the lies he told me about Pat. When we were with our children and we had to spend time together, Tim bragged about Didi and her brother, that he is a well-known marathoner in New Jersey who had been interviewed by the *Wall Street Journal*. When I didn't gush over her, he called me catty. Since the day I walked in on them making out in my home when we were married, he has never introduced Didi to me, and he has tried to make sure that we don't attend anything, like gatherings for the children, together.

Slander and Parental Alienation

SNAPs come in at least two categories. One category includes those who abuse their children in addition to abusing the mother of their children. A high correlation exists between spousal abuse and child abuse. Although studies vary, it is estimated that in 40 to 70 percent of households in which intimate partner abuse exists, child abuse also exists. When the child is a victim of abuse, it is more likely that the child will side with the nonabusive parent against the abusive parent. The abusive parent has alienated the child against himself by his abusive actions.

However, another category includes SNAPs who view their children as trophies and heirs of their kingdom, but treat their children's mother as a brood mare. I call this second category the Henry VIII SNAPs. King Henry VIII was king of England from 1509 to 1547. He is a fine example of a narcissistic sociopath with ultimate power and wealth. He was known as an attractive, educated, accomplished, and charismatic ruler, and his court was the center of scholarly and artistic innovation along with glamorous excess. He had six wives: two he divorced (or more accurately, had his marriages to them annulled), two he executed, one died shortly after childbirth, and one outlived him. Not only did Henry execute wives whom he felt betrayed him, but he executed numerous governmental and church leaders who did not agree with his ideas. Henry desperately wanted male heirs, but he abused, murdered, divorced, maligned, repeatedly cheated on, and falsely accused his six wives (and mothers of his children) of adultery and treason.

During a marriage, and especially in the early years when child-rearing is labor intensive, a SNAP may be supportive of his wife, if for no other reason than that he won't be stuck with childcare duties if she leaves. However, when children reach their teen years and the SNAP is having affairs and considering leaving, the SNAP will attempt to alienate his children against their mother. He may insult her, call her names, degrade her, tell them not to talk to her, give her the silent treatment and tell them to do the same, or tell them she is worthless and doesn't do anything. Especially if she has not worked outside the home or if she has a lower-paying job, he may tell them that she never contributed to the family.

After a separation, the Henry VIII abuser will, without fail, attempt to alienate his children from their mother. The abuser will tell lies to his children about their mother or stepmother, while the mother typically tries to take the high road and refrain from telling her children about their father's abuse.

The following are the more typical things a SNAP says to his children to turn them against their mother:

- "She's leaving. It's her fault. If it wasn't for her, we would have more money and we could have a new car/a vacation/money for school/a new house/etc. She's the reason we don't have any money."
- "She took all the funds in your college savings account."
- "She took all the funds in our joint account."
- "I have to pay her because of the divorce, so you don't have any money now."

- "She abandoned you."
- "She left because she's having an affair."

Why do abusers do this? After a separation, everything is now a competition to the SNAP, who must win and dominate at all costs. He must gather the troops for battle against his soon-to-be ex-wife, whom he perceives now as his enemy. The troops he gathers on his side against her will be his children, his family, friends, church, and even her family. They are all just pawns in his efforts to destroy her, even though all she typically wants is to be free from daily abuse. He doesn't care that it is emotionally damaging to his children to turn them against their mother with lies and false accusations. He just cares that he destroys her. And he knows that, above all, a mother's heart and love is for her children. There is nothing on earth that will destroy her more than if her children turn on the mother who loves them. He does so intentionally and gloats with evil pleasure when they side with him.

Often people wonder how children can turn against their own mother and not see the lies that the father is fabricating in a shameless attempt to alienate his children. The answers are multiple. First, because the abuse was not directed at the children but at the mother, the children will not want to distance themselves from the abuser the same as they would if the children had been the target of abuse. It seems to be a truism of human behavior that if a person is not personally a target, that person will continue their relationship with the abuser, regardless of whether the abuser intentionally hurt someone else.

For example, a few years ago the worship leader at our church was found to be stealing thousands of dollars from the church through false expense reports. The amount of money he embezzled was so large that it constituted a felony. The elders decided not to report him to the police, but required him to return the money and go through a program designed to restore him to the congregation. He showed little remorse, failed to follow through with the restoration program, and generally had the same arrogant, self-serving attitude as he had prior to being caught. Many of the congregation cut off ties with him, determining that they did not want to be associated with someone who was so morally deficient but who portrayed himself as a godly man. Yet some continued to support him. It is doubtful that if he had stolen thousands of dollars from their personal pockets and shown no remorse they would have continued their friendship.

Second, older children are savvy enough to know that their father holds the power and the money. They have just witnessed their father excommunicate their mother from all family functions, cut off her funds, and speak horrible things about her to her children, friends, and family. They have also seen their mother move to a small apartment, barely able to make ends meet, while their father has taken over the family home, possibly with his girlfriend. Therefore, for survival's sake, they side with the parent who holds the power, money, social relationships, and family home. They do not want their father to treat them the same way they see him treat their mother, and they are afraid that if they show her kindness or favoritism, he will also eliminate them from his life. This is human nature. For example, some Europeans in World War II sided with Hitler or befriended his SS troops. It is highly unlikely that they thought of Hitler and his troops as kind, gentle people they wanted to befriend. Rather, they sided with him out of fear of being annihilated.

Third, in accordance with Maslow's hierarchy of needs, children desperately need to feel that they belong and are loved. This is a deep-seated need. Children need to feel that they are part of a family unit and that the people in their family are good people. We all want to believe that the people we associate with—family, friends, work associates, professional organizations, church or synagogue membership, charities, political groups, etc.—are generally good and decent people. When we associate with good and decent people, we are assumed to also be a good and decent person. In our patriarchal society, a father is generally seen as the head of a family unit, and thus the children desperately need a relationship with their father and need to think that he is a good and decent person. Children want to believe that what their father says is true. They do not want to believe that their father would lie to them. Even when a mother defends herself and tells the truth about their father's abuse, children will often disbelieve the mother's true account of abuse and believe the father's lies, especially in a patriarchal family.

Fourth, cognitive dissonance plays a large role. Humans strive for internal consistency. We try to ensure that our actions are consistent with our beliefs, that our beliefs are consistent with the facts, and that our beliefs are consistent across the board. In psychology, cognitive dissonance is the mental discomfort that arises when one's actions are inconsistent with one's beliefs, when new information is inconsistent with our existing beliefs, or when we hold contradictory beliefs at the same time. Confronted with cognitive dissonance, we attempt to reduce the dissonance and to reason ourselves into consistency, especially when the matter is important to us.

For example, if a person elects to be a vegetarian because he is ethically opposed to eating animals, but then eats a steak, he must somehow reduce the cognitive dissonance that arises from acting in a way that is inconsistent with his beliefs. First, he can change his beliefs to align with his behavior, and therefore elect to not be ethically opposed to eating animals. Second, he can change his behavior to align with his beliefs, and therefore stop eating the steak. Third, he can justify his behavior by modifying his beliefs, and therefore allowing himself to cheat occasionally because "it's not that bad." Or he can deny or ignore any information that conflicts with his existing beliefs, and therefore he may refuse to believe that steak is not on a vegetarian menu, or he may choose to believe that perhaps the cow would have died anyway.

A child desperately wants to believe that his father is a good, honest, kind protector of his family. As a child, he needs to belong to this family of which the father is the head. When his mother defends herself and explains that she left because of his abuse, the child is put in a position of cognitive dissonance. He believes his father is good, but he has just heard information that his father is, in fact, an abusive monster. These two opposing things cause cognitive dissonance, which the child then tries to resolve.

If the child accepts the fact that his father is abusive, he must discard his belief that his father is basically good and acknowledge that his father is evil. And because the child belongs to the family of which his father is the head, he must then shed his belief that he belongs to a good family and realize that he is in an abusive family, and therefore he is not good. This will cause his entire world to collapse, and therefore the child cannot accept that his father is abusive.

If the child justifies the information concerning his father's abuse, the child may conclude that there have been extenuating circumstances that would justify his father's actions. For example, perhaps the child can tell himself that his father was simply intoxicated or mentally unstable and didn't mean to abuse his mother. Therefore, the child can blame alcohol or a mental condition for his father's abusive behavior instead of his father. Or perhaps the child reasons that the abuse wasn't that bad, especially if the mother did not go into graphic detail. With either justification, the child can still believe that his father is basically good and that the child belongs to a decent family. This resolves the cognitive dissonance, and the child therefore will side with his father.

Finally, if the child simply refuses to believe, denies, or ignores the facts concerning his father's abuse, the child can still believe that his father is basically good and that the child belongs to a family that is basically good. Refusing to believe that his father is abusive resolves the child's cognitive dissonance, and the child therefore will side with his father.

Thus, in most cases with preteens, teenagers, and adult children, a child will align with the father if the child himself was not physically abused. It may take years for a child to be in a healthy relationship with his mother again. This often occurs when the child is on the receiving end of his father's abuse that was formerly reserved only for his mother and the child finally recognizes that his mother had valid grounds to leave the marriage.

Lori: Tim owned his own CPA firm. When we divorced after fifteen years of marriage, Tim told the children the divorce was my fault, that they couldn't go on vacation because he had to pay me due to the divorce, and he falsely accused me of having an affair. He stopped paying the mortgage on the house, which went into foreclosure. He blamed that on me. The children sided with him, lived with him, and shut me out of their lives. It was painful and lonely. I became depressed and had to take prescription antidepressants. After five years, he ran for office and demanded that my daughter help with his campaign efforts. She quit her job and quit college to assist in his campaign (which failed). When he became controlling and abusive to my daughter during the campaign, she finally saw what I had been dealing with and moved in with her aunt—a neutral place.

Jennie: Armen started to alienate our children from me when they were teenagers at a time when he was seeing several other women and coming home at four in the morning. When we were sitting around the dinner table, he would insult me with contempt in front of them: "Look at your mother. She is useless and good for nothing. She's a horrible excuse for a mother." When Armen took one of my sons with him to his homeland, Jordan, for a month vacation, my son came back almost as verbally abusive as his father. During the divorce, Armen falsely told them I had taken their college funds and other money. He was a wealthy physician, and since I worked as his office manager, I had no income after we separated. He refused to make house payments or to pay the real estate taxes or other household bills. When the court sided with me after I produced detailed bank statements, I had to send the court order to my children to defend myself. Even though I tried not to speak ill of their father, I had to clear my name from his intentionally destructive and false allegations. Nevertheless, they all sided with their father. It was incredibly painful, especially when they all went to Florida to be with their father and his girlfriend for Christmas while we were still married.

Robin: My husband told my children that since he made the money and I just stayed home, he made the rules, and I had no say-so in anything. Then he took all the funds from our joint account and put them in his account without my name on it. He cut me completely off from any funds and told me I had to ask for grocery money and for any other household expenses. But he invited my eighteen-year-old son to be on his account and to decide whether I should be allowed to have any money.

Charlotte: Although during our marriage we successfully co-parented, after I filed for divorce, Tim cut me out of the lives of my children. He even refused my request for a weekly ten-minute phone conference to discuss their activities. He told the children that I abandoned them and acted as if I never existed. After the divorce, even though the parenting agreement required us to share equal time with the children and gave the other parent right of first refusal when one was out of town, he told my children that they never had to spend any time with me. Although we had a close relationship before the divorce, and my daughter had asked me to get a divorce, my children spent a total of three days in my house in the two years after the divorce was final and until my youngest turned eighteen. I know I could have gone to court to enforce the parenting agreement, but the year I fled, three teenagers committed suicide in our town by jumping in front of a train. One of the teenagers came from divorced parents with such a destructive relationship that they held separate funerals for the child. It was widely thought that their toxic family life was responsible for his wanting to commit suicide. I never wanted that to happen, so I did not bring any legal action to enforce the parenting agreement. In the Bible account of the women who were arguing before Solomon about the baby, the true mother who loved her child was willing to let the other one raise the child rather than split the baby in half. Like the true mother who loved her child, I did not want to put my teenage children in the middle of a custody battle with a vindictive father who was just using them as pawns to hurt me.

When I finally became engaged to a wonderful, godly man, in order to further destroy my relationship with them, Tim told them that I left because I had an affair. After that, my daughter refused to talk to me for two years. I kept trying to co-parent with him, but anyone who has an abuser as a former spouse will tell you that co-parenting is impossible.

Slander and Social Alienation

In much the same way that an abuser alienates a victim's children from their mother, in every instance a SNAP will try to alienate her friends, his family, and even hers. While he may have had high praise for his spouse during the marriage, ensuring that he would also be highly regarded, that will immediately change when his victim leaves. When a romantic relationship is over, the abuser will rush to get his story out first, accusing his victim of everything from abuse to infidelity to cover up his own abuse and to engender pity. A pathological liar, he is very effective in getting people to believe him. In the meantime, the real victim is usually taking the high road and not talking about the abuse. She may even be in a domestic abuse shelter or taking refuge at the home of a friend or family member. Once the victim learns of the false rumors, the damage has already been done.

Friends, family, and even church friends and pastors often side with the abuser rather than the victim for many of the same reasons the children do.

First, unless the abuse happens directly to that person or to their own daughter, most people simply don't care that much if another person gets abused. Only those who have a strong moral compass, who are protective of those they care about, and who have decided to take a stand against evil will cut off a relationship with an abuser when they discover his true nature. Thus, it is a rare person who defies their family, circle of friends, church associations, or business relationship to support the innocent victim rather than the abuser.

Second, people often side with the person with money and power. If there is something in it for them, most people don't care if the character of the people they associate with is evil. Churches will usually support large donors, even if they are abusers. Church members and others will usually support and continue to do business with abusers with whom they have a business relationship. Others enjoy the star status of being associated with the wealthy and famous, even if they have a reputation for cruelty.

Third, we all have a need to belong. We all want to believe that the people we associate with are generally good and decent people. We do this because associating with good and decent people means we are a good and decent person. By and large, people do not want to believe the facts about the abuse. People will side with the abuser because they don't want to believe that the person they know is really a monster. To do otherwise would mean that they themselves are not good and decent people, because good and decent people don't associate with monsters. This would upset their social gatherings, divide their church or synagogue, or be a detriment to their income. It is easier to ignore the truth.

Finally, cognitive dissonance will force others to do one of four things: (1) Accept as fact the allegations of abuse. They must change their long-held belief that their friend, relative, or business associate is good, and recognize that he is, in fact, evil. This rarely happens because it is too much of a mental leap, even in the face of facts. (2) Attribute the abuse to alcohol or mental impairment and thus regard it as a one-time incident or as excusable. (3) Ignore or refuse to believe the wife's story and side with the abuser. (4) In the face of the abuser's claims of regret and seeking forgiveness, religious persons can claim that they forgive him. In this way, they can side with the abuser without feeling guilty. In their self-righteousness, they often criticize the victim for not forgiving her abuser and demand that she stop saying un-Christian things about him. The Catholic Church's response to decades of child abuse provides a classic example: the Church and its members silenced the victims to cover up the abuse, blaming the victims for exposing the truth and demanding accountability. Abusers are masters at playing church leaders and members by feigning apologies without any change of heart. Indeed, the abuse intensifies after a divorce is filed, while the abuser cries crocodile tears to his pastor.

Ironically, if others don't perceive the abuse as that bad, they will blame the victim for leaving and being unforgiving, and they will side with the abuser. However, if the reported abuse is horrific, it will be perceived as too outlandish to be believable about someone they know. Things like that happen only in the evening news or on TV shows, they reason. Thus, many people will side with the abuser. Either way—whether the abuse is not bad enough or whether the abuse is heinous—most people side with the abuser rather than the victim.

Most abuses go unreported to the police. The majority of women attempt to change the abuser's behavior with pleading or counseling because they are afraid of the retaliation they will endure if they report his actions to the police or try to obtain an order of protection from the court. However, even when the abuser has an order of protection against him or has been arrested or found guilty of criminal charges, his family and friends will often blame the victim for trying to protect herself. Reporting him to the authorities is viewed as betrayal rather than clear-eyed acknowledgment of the abuser's true character. Church-going abusers will often reach out to their pastors for a letter of recommendation or to serve as a character witness at hearings for orders of protection and criminal proceedings. SNAPs always do their best to look good in church, while keeping their abusive actions well hidden. An abuser is by nature a Dr. Jekyll/Mr. Hyde personality. When a pastor supports the abuser, stating that he is a long-standing church member or a dependable volunteer, it is incredibly painful to the real victim who is trying to protect herself from further abuse. Church support of an abuser furthers abuse and victimizes the victim by someone with moral authority who should be standing on the side of good, not evil.

In all cases of spousal abuse, people will support an abuser for one of three reasons. First, they are intimidated by the abuser and fear what the abuser may do to them. Second, they are deceived by the abuser and believe his inevitable lies and deception. Third, if they are neither intimidated nor deceived, then they share the same deficient moral compass of the abuser and simply do not have the moral fortitude to stand for good against evil. Whatever the reason, the majority of people will side with the abuser rather than the victim.

> Charlotte: When I fled my home in 2012, I did so with only an overnight bag and went into hiding for two years. I didn't tell any friends where I was because I wanted to protect them and myself. I knew Tim would ask them where I was, and I didn't want them to be put in a position of lying to protect me or to let my whereabouts slip out. And like most women, I did not tell anyone of the abuse that was going on behind closed doors. When he received my email that I had left, Tim immediately called all my girlfriends, demanded to know where I was, and accused me of leaving because of infidelity. He called the busybodies in church and claimed that I left because of infidelity.

They, in turn, quickly spread rumors throughout the community and cut off all contact with me. This was especially painful when the people in my own Bible study shunned me and didn't even check with me to see if his accusations were true. I had considered one older woman to be a spiritual mentor and had gone to her from time to time for advice on children. Even though she had not spoken to me since I left in 2012, I received the following scathing email when I announced through a blog in December of 2015 that I was resigning from the law firm where I worked because I felt the Lord's calling to start my own law firm to help women escape abusive relationships and to volunteer with a local domestic violence shelter. In the email, she attacked me as a mother, my volunteer work for Christian organizations, and my career. She inferred that I had lied about the abuse. She did not acknowledge Tim's abuse or false accusations of infidelity to my own children and to the community; she passed off his rape and abuse, for which he was completely unrepentant, as if it were another ordinary sin; and she misinterpreted the Bible (which calls for the offender to seek forgiveness and reconciliation from the victim, not the other way around—which would be dangerous in instances of abuse and rape). Clearly, the language in her email indicated that she had been brainwashed by Tim's lies and thought I was the one who lacked credibility.

It finally became clear to me that she sided with my abuser, not because she was intimidated by him (he held no power over her, although he was a wealthy client of her husband, who was a successful money manager) or was deceived by him (she knew exactly what he had done), but because she was just like him.

> *Charlotte—I have just read your Inspiration message and I do not find it to be inspirational at all. I have read your divorce decree—a multi-page epistle—your book, your most recent Christmas letter, and this current message. If your life had been as bad as you portrayed in your divorce decree, why did you stick it out for twenty years? The marriage turned into a sad situation, but you could not have stayed in it for the sake of your two youngest children as you were hardly ever home—law school, law clerk with a respected judge, a full-time job at a law firm, teaching at Trinity nite school and on the Trinity board. You continue to mention in your writings you suffered domestic and sexual abuse—it is not Christmas nor Inspirational material. You have been out of that relationship for years—mentally long before you moved out. You are continuing to cast negative aspersions about your former spouse—and God is holding you accountable for CONTINUING to do this. Your past ex-husband has moved on and does not represent you to your two children and Danny in an unfavorable lite. You need to stop continuing to do so—it is not a godly thing to do.*
>
> *Please read Romans 7:11–25 and accept that challenge. None of us are sin-free—we all sin and only need to ask God for forgiveness—read Matthew 5:21–24 where Scripture speaks about our attitudes and how they can break our relationship with a holy God. Verse 23 mentions that if you are at the altar—meaning in today's life it would be taking communion—be reconciled to someone where there is a grudge before you can take communion. In your case I would say that you will not reconcile, but you need to turn your attitudes and words around and drop the continuing hostile comments about your former unhappy situation before taking communion on a regular basis. God is holding you accountable for continuing to spread your bad, unforgiving attitudes to others re: your second husband this many years later. You no longer need to explain why you took your counseling training.*
>
> *You APPEAR to have moved on—but you have NOT moved on.*
>
> *Judy (K ****)*
>
> *Sent from my iPhone*

Overcoming the Narcissist, Sociopath, Psychopath, and other Domestic Abusers

Refusing to Cooperate on Scheduling and Other Household Events

SNAPs must always be in control and will make simple exercises complicated by refusing to cooperate. They will obfuscate the facts, stonewall, obstruct progress, or use other tactics to frustrate the smooth running of a household. Simple tasks, such as committing to events and putting them on a joint calendar, can be extremely frustrating for the wife of an abuser. For example, if an event or trip is the abuser's idea and he wants his wife to attend, he will put it on the calendar and order her to attend. If he doesn't want her to attend, he will not consult with her and she will often not find out until right before the event, which leaves her scrambling with childcare and other household duties. But if the wife tries to consult with the abuser concerning an event or trip, he will sabotage her attempts at cooperation.

> Hilary: I tried to cooperate with Stan surrounding the birth of our son and visitation after our relationship ended. But he wouldn't even cooperate enough to pick out a name, much less put his name on the birth certificate as the father. Because of his strange fear of numerology (the study of how letters, when coded into numbers, can determine one's future), he refused to even give our son a last name—instead demanding a single name that would give him a destiny of strength and power based on numerology. Scheduling visitation was a nightmare. Stan ignored the advance notice that our parenting agreement required. Instead, he demanded that I meet him on a day's notice, then he would cancel at the last minute. If I couldn't agree to his demands, he blamed me and falsely accused me of trying to keep him and his mother away from our son.

> Charlotte: For our entire marriage, and after our divorce, scheduling anything that wasn't Tim's own idea was a nightmare. The calendar was just another way of him exercising control. When he left on trips, he didn't check with me or even let me know until the day he left. He scheduled fishing and hunting trips over holidays. He was more than two hours late for the scheduled birth of our son Morton, which had been on the calendar for weeks. Without checking with me, he scheduled a golf vacation with his cousins the day I graduated from law school, and then yelled at me because my graduation interfered with his trip. When I tried to check with him to schedule anything, he stonewalled, refused to commit, delayed, or yelled at me for trying to schedule something. He said, "I don't have my calendar with me right now," "I'll have to get back to you," or "I don't know. I have to see how such-and-such is." Then he wouldn't follow up or get back to me. It took me six weeks just to schedule a time to pick up the dog!

Cruel and Unreasonable Demands

The SNAP must be the center of attention, even when his spouse is sick, is rushed to the hospital, is recovering from surgery, or is giving birth to a child. Because SNAPs have no empathy, they simply don't care how their spouse feels emotionally or physically.

> Dirk: Rhonda refused to let me go to bed at night if she wasn't ready to go to bed, even when I was sick and had the flu. I literally had to stay up and keep her company, even when I had a fever and was throwing up, until she said it was time to go to bed.

> Charlotte: The day I brought Morton home after he was born was Father's Day. I was sore and could barely walk. But Tim insisted on hosting a Father's Day party for himself with his mother, older

kids, and other family members. He expected me to entertain them. When I spoke to his first wife, she told me that he made her host a Christmas party when her daughter Kira was only two weeks old. When my dad died and I was grieving after the funeral, Tim demanded sex. When Kira was in her thirties, she developed brain cancer and needed surgery. She and her husband, Jim, invited Tim to go with them to a doctor's appointment in Chicago. On the way back from the surgeon, Tim insisted they stop by some deli on the South Side to get his favorite Italian sausage. Nobody mattered to Tim except Tim. It was always about him.

Imposing Household Rules

A SNAP will impose household rules that apply to others, but not to himself. If he is caught violating his own rule, he will change the rules so he always wins. The family rules in a SNAP's home go like this: Rule Number 1: SNAP always wins. Rule Number 2: See Rule Number 1.

> Charlotte: Tim had a zillion rules that he imposed, and none of them were made by a collaborative process with other family members. I usually wanted us to have family dinners around the table so that we could catch up on each other's day. Studies show numerous benefits for families who share mealtimes. But Tim always wanted to eat dinner in front of the TV. Ironically, he complained that in his first marriage they didn't have family dinners, which I later found was because he was either working late or having one of his many affairs. Everyone was supposed to pick up their own dishes and put them in the sink. Tim, who expected to be waited on, almost never cleaned up his own dishes. At the end of the night, I would take in whatever dishes were left on the coffee table, put them in the dishwasher, and clean up the kitchen. Once or twice, Tim picked up a few dishes and went into a rage claiming that he always had to clean up the dishes for everyone. So I started an experiment and put on the calendar all the nights that I picked up his dishes and all the nights he picked up any dishes. At the end of the month, it was clear that I had picked up his dishes twenty-eight times that month. He had not followed his own rules. When I pointed out this fact, he flew into a rage. After that, I just shut up and picked up his dishes and everything else. It was just easier than trying to reason with him.
>
> When we were first married, Tim imposed the rule that we had to go to bed at the same time. He refused to let me go to bed until he was ready to go to bed, and when he wanted to go to bed, I was not allowed to stay up. He wanted to be in charge of bedtime, and we had to go together. But it wasn't long into the marriage before he fell asleep watching TV on the couch every night and finally came to bed around 3:00 a.m. Again, he violated his own rule.
>
> At one point, because of his constant criticism of all of us, I drew up a family contract that stated that people would be kind and respectful and honoring of each other. Everyone signed it, but Tim violated it within days. It was a complete waste of time.

Demanding, Then Blaming for Complying with the Demand—"No-Win" Situations

A SNAP will constantly demand that his victims comply with his demand, and then blame them when they do. SNAPs put their victims in no-win situations, where no matter what actions she takes, he will criticize, blame, and falsely accuse her.

> Hilary: After Stan and I broke up, he was livid. He demanded that I return a cell phone that he had given me to use. But when I returned it, he blamed me and accused me of cutting off com-

munication and not letting him talk to our son. He insisted that the court's parenting judgment was the only effective court order and that I had to comply with it, yet he never complied with it. Under the court order, he was required to give me seven days advance notice before the beginning of each month to set up visitation for the month. He never once complied, but he sent daily emails harassing me that I was not allowing him to see his son. I offered numerous dates and times, but he said none of those worked for him. He was unrelenting in his harassment through emails, texts, and phone calls.

Calculated Abuse

One can never believe an abuser when he pretends to be remorseful. If he did think his actions were wrong and abusive, he would not have committed them. Rather, he acted abusively for the express purpose of harming his victim. He calculated both his actions and their results. He intended that his actions would so harm his victim that she would be intimidated and stay, not leave. You see, each abuser makes an internal assessment as to how much abuse is enough to keep someone intimidated and under his power and control, but not enough to leave. The abuse must be bad, but not bad enough for her to leave. There is a fine line, a threshold, that the abuser is always determining as he plans his abuse. As he violates boundary after boundary, and his victim still tolerates it, the abuse escalates to a new level. However, if a victim leaves, the abuser must conclude that he miscalculated her reaction. This time, his abuse was enough to make her leave, and he must scramble to get her back.

> Charlotte: After I left, rather than apologizing or being the least bit remorseful, he justified his actions. "It's not that bad. If it was that bad, you would have left ten years ago." He didn't view marriage as a relationship in which each person blessed each other, but rather one in which he could abuse me as long as it wasn't bad enough to make me leave. After that letter, he didn't see a counselor, and he escalated the abuse to include raping me every day, twice a day, for the next two months. I finally fled with only an overnight bag in early April. I concluded that in ten years, in 2022, I didn't want to hear him say again, "It wasn't that bad. If it was that bad, you should have left ten years ago."

False Claims of Mistakes or Accident

A feigned apology or a claim that "mistakes were made" is not an apology or admission of wrongdoing. It is a non-apology. A mistake is when a person intended a good action, but because he does not have an accurate knowledge of the facts, he unintentionally does something wrong.

An abuser does not mistakenly lie, steal, cheat, hit, deceive, slander, rape, or otherwise abuse his victim. He knows exactly what he is doing, and he does so intentionally.

For example, a person who is grocery shopping and intending to pay for a candy bar at the checkout line, but doesn't see it under the bag of potatoes, may mistakenly leave the store without paying for it. An honest person will go back in the store when they discover the oversight and make it right. However, when an abuser borrows money and doesn't return it, or requires his wife to hand over her paycheck to him even though he is a multimillionaire, or sells his wife's property and pockets the money, that is intentionally stealing.

When someone incorrectly adds the numbers in a column, she makes a mistake. When she discovers her mistake, she corrects it and informs others who may have relied on her numbers. However, when an abuser falsifies financial statements to hide assets in a divorce or falsifies financial statements to magnify assets in a prenuptial agreement, he is intentionally defrauding and stealing from his spouse.

An honest person may mistake his son coming in past curfew for an intruder, tackle him, and inflict bodily harm. Realizing his mistake, he will apologize, tend to his physical needs, and be careful never to do that again. When an abuser hits his victim, he does so with the full knowledge of who she is and repeats it when he wants. That is physical abuse.

Likewise, an abuser may claim an incident was an accident. Accidents occur when a person intends something for good, but something unforeseen and unintentional happens instead. An abuser's actions are intentional, not accidental.

If a man walks by a woman, loses his balance, and unintentionally falls into her, causing her to hit a wall, that constitutes an accident. A healthy, loving person will help her up, apologize, and do his best to ensure it won't happen again. However, when an abuser intentionally slams his wife into a wall, it constitutes physical abuse.

> Charlotte: After I fled our home, Tim finally agreed to see a counselor, but only to try to get me to return to the abusive marriage. After a year, he refused to continue the counseling, saying he was wasting his time if he couldn't get me to come back. He feigned apologies, wrote letters claiming he was praying for us, and vaguely admitted in the most general of terms, "Mistakes were made." But he would not admit that any of his individual actions were wrong.

Monopolize Conversations

Because SNAPs believe they are the smartest, most interesting people in the room, they monopolize conversations, steer them only to topics that they want to talk about, and make themselves out as experts to appear superior to others. They cannot simply let a conversation take its own course—the conversation might run out of their control and it may turn to topics that the SNAP knows little about. So to keep things under his control, the SNAP must manage all conversations in which he is involved.

Using Opinions of Others

Healthy people rely on their internal moral compass, guided by their faith in God, to determine right and wrong. They live by a code of honor. They believe it is more important to be able to look themselves in the mirror every morning knowing they have done the right thing than to be concerned about what others think. Even more important is their ability to bow before their God and be able to tell Him they have done the right thing rather than rely on others' opinions. However, the SNAP, who has no moral compass or code of honor, lives to impress others. Throwing God's favor to the wind, he seeks the favor of others—especially the wealthy and powerful and his next sexual target.

Because the SNAP values the opinions of others, he assumes his victim will also be swayed by others opinions and uses them or their purported opinions to intimidate, coerce, or guilt his partner. He may claim that no one likes her, that she has no friends, that her friends tell him she is horrible, that her counselor thinks she's crazy, that their marriage therapist says she's bipolar, etc. If she is a person of faith, he will likely claim that the church is upset with her, that she is an awful Christian/Catholic/Jew/Muslim for leaving him, that she doesn't walk the walk, that the church leaders say she is sinning, etc. If she values her children (and all mothers do), he will likely claim that her children hate her, that they don't want to be with her, that they want to live with him, etc. If she values her extended family, he will use them to coerce her.

> Sahira: After I left, Nadeem contacted all his family, my family, and our extended families and friends. He falsely told them I was having an affair and that I was wrong to leave. I was inundated with calls, texts, and emails from cousins, parents, in-laws, and his friends repeating his false accusations and trying to coerce me to go back to the marriage. Some even brought in their opinion that Allah would not be happy with me. It became so overwhelming that I and my children moved out of my parents' house and into the domestic violence shelter because he even had my parents convinced that I should go back to his abuse. Over time, my parents were able to see his manipulation and abuse, and I was able to move back in with them.

> Charlotte: After I left, Tim told me I had no friends, that my church friends all say that "you talk the talk, but you don't walk the walk," and that I needed psychological help. When I asked who said those things, he wouldn't say. Fortunately, there were many people who saw through him. He said my children hated me because I abandoned them. But my daughter had asked me to get a divorce because he was being verbally abusive to her. He said that his physician (who is also my physician) and the psychologist whom we were seeing told him that he wasn't a narcissist. But when I spoke to each of them, just as I had suspected, they each said they had never said that. In fact, the psychologist, who quickly caught on that he was a narcissist, confirmed that he was "way up there on the narcissist scale." And my physician had referred women in domestic abuse situations to me because of my work with victims of domestic abuse.

Inability or Unwillingness to Affirm or Appreciate Good Attributes in Others

SNAPs only see others for how they can be useful to the SNAP, and they discard people when they no longer benefit or serve their uses. Like a person who throws out an old pair of holey socks, he doesn't shed tears for the socks or consider their years of faithful service. He simply throws them out and gets new ones.

A SNAP does not value or affirm the wonderful qualities of his spouse or family. The SNAP is so self-centered and self-directed that he barely notices his greatest blessings—his wife and children—much less their inner qualities. It is nearly impossible for him to offer an affirmation or sincere compliment.

The SNAP looks for a partner with attributes that he can exploit. Typically, the wife of a SNAP embodies such qualities as kindness, patience, forgiveness, graciousness, generosity, mercy, goodness, a moral compass, self-control, integrity, selflessness, inner and outer beauty, cheerfulness, loyalty, faithfulness, gentleness, dependability, conscientiousness, hospitality, and empathy. Because the SNAP has none of these qualities, having a wife with these characteristics makes him look better. He clearly would not seek out someone like himself, as he needs someone who will take his abuse and not call it that. However, he never admits that this is why he pursued her. In time, rather than admiring her qualities, he becomes contemptuous of them and her.

Universally, the women I counsel who are escaping domestic abuse have amazing qualities and strong religious beliefs. They are artists, composers, CEOs, homemakers, entrepreneurs, and administrative wonders. They are wonderful women. Unfortunately, their spouses take advantage of these attributes, refuse to affirm them, and do not treat them as the treasures that they are. These amazing women have no idea how fantastic they really are.

When they finally can get away from their abusers and heal, they flourish and return to the fun-loving, cheerful, confident person they were before the abuser left a trail of destruction.

Ad Hominem Attacks

In the world of logic, cases are won on the merits of an argument. That is, given two opposing viewpoints on an issue, the argument with the most compelling and pertinent points to the matter should prevail. For example, legislators might want to know whether physicians should have a license to practice medicine. One could argue that physicians should be held to a high standard of care because people's lives and health are at stake. A license would restrict those who are unqualified from practicing medicine; therefore, physicians need a license to practice medicine. In response, one could argue that people should have the freedom to engage in whatever career they want, and that such a license would severely limit those who want to practice medicine, and therefore individuals should not need a license to practice medicine. Of these two arguments, the former is more compelling, and thus, every state in the union requires a physician to have a license to practice medicine.

However, when SNAPs argue, they often engage in ad hominem attacks on those who oppose their viewpoint. Ad hominem attacks do not argue the merits of a position, but rather denigrate the person making the argument. For example, in the above argument concerning licensing physicians, in response to the first argument, an ad hominem attack might be, "You stupid, ugly b*tch. What planet did you come from? You're a loser. Everyone thinks you're an idiot. You're not a doctor. How do you know? You're not smart enough to be a doctor anyway. I was a plumber and now I'm a legislator. Everyone should be able to do what they want." Note that the argument does not argue whether physicians should need a license to practice medicine, but attacks the appearance, character, intelligence, credentials, and success of the person making the argument in an attempt to shut them down. Then the opponent goes on to use his own personal, but unrelated and inapplicable, experience to argue his position. Ad hominem attacks often work, as the other person is shocked by the argument and put in the position of defending themselves or arguing why the other person's experience is inapplicable.

Infidelity

Although this is also included under sexual abuse, infidelity, like all physical and sexual abuse, is also a form of emotional abuse. When a couple pledges their sexual fidelity to each other in marriage, the breach is also emotionally abusive. Sexual fidelity leaves the other party feeling hurt, abandoned, violated, and betrayed. In healthy marriages, spouses do not consider sexual infidelity because it would ruin the intimacy they share and, among other things, it would be crushing to the spouse. In addition to the physical sexual act, infidelity includes pornography, going to strip clubs, engaging in oral sex outside of marriage, as well as sexual intimacy in all its forms with someone who is not one's spouse. SNAPs are notorious for their sexual promiscuity.

Other Forms of Sexual Abuse

The goal of sexual abuse is emotional abuse. Due to its intimate nature, sexual abuse is one of the most destructive forms of emotional abuse. It is nearly impossible to separate one's body and emotions. A personal attack on someone's body attacks their soul and spirit as well. Healthy marriage relationships include loving, tender sexual relationships. Sexual relationships that degrade, demean, and dehumanize are abusive and are intended to hurt the soul and spirit.

Series of Emotional Abuse When the Victim Attempts to Leave

Feigned Apologies and Crocodile Tears

Eventually, a spouse has no choice but to leave her SNAP. If, however, the abuser believes that he has a chance of persuading her to return, he will typically first try his best to draw her back into the abusive relationship. This persuasion will take the form of apologies, promises to change and to go to counseling, professions of love, claims that he wants to make her happy, and perhaps even an admission that mistakes were made. He will be on his best behavior during this phase, perhaps even bringing flowers or chocolates. He may even shed a few tears.

An abuser who says these things is not sincere, but is merely trying to lure his victim back into the relationship. It is, after all, easier to get her to return than to go out and find a new victim. That would require significant time, effort, and money to go through all the wining and dining and love-bombing required to lure in a new victim.

Abusers use insincere apologies and promise change when they have no intention of change, because they work. Victims usually fall for these false apologies and crocodile tears, at least a few times. Women want to believe that the apologies and promises are sincere. Women want to believe that the man they fell in love with still exists and has not been replaced by a monster. Women want so much to believe that the man who was so affectionate and romantic is the "real" husband, and that the stranger who showed up after the wedding is an aberration and will certainly disappear once the "real" husband understands how much she is trying to make the relationship work. Women desperately do not want to believe that the man they fell in love with was just a predator putting on an act to catch his prey, and that she is the prey. On average, a woman will return to her abusive partner seven times before she finally leaves for good.[55] That is how much a woman will try to make a relationship work. Women, by nature, want to be in lifelong relationships with their mate and father of their children, and they will do nearly anything to make that relationship work.

Inability to Repent and Permanently Change for the Good

Feigned apologies and promises to change are not indicative of true repentance, but are mere expressions of sorrow by the abuser that he was caught. True repentance means that (1) the abuser admits that what he did was wrong; (2) the abuser takes full responsibility and blame for his actions; (3) the abuser admits to others that what he did was wrong; (4) the abuser has a change of heart and is now committed to doing what is right; (5) the abuser makes every effort to make things right to put the victim back in the place she was before the abuse (i.e., if he took money, he repays it with interest; if he broke something, he replaces it; if he damaged a relationship, he works to repair it; if he lied about her to others, he admits it to her and others and tells them the truth; if he lied to her, he tells the truth; etc.); and (6) the abuser has a permanent change in attitude and behavior so that, on a consistent basis, he exhibits healthy attitudes and behaviors.

As every victim eventually discovers, SNAPs are not capable of true repentance. All abusers, and therefore all SNAPs, are pathological. The definition of pathology, as set forth by world-renowned author and psychotherapist Sandra Brown, is "the inability to sustain positive change, grow to any meaningful depth, or develop insight about how one's behavior affects others."[56]

---

[55] National Domestic Violence Hotline, "50 Obstacles to Leaving: 1–10," https://www.thehotline.org/2013/06/10/50-obstacles-to-leaving-1-10/.

[56] Sandra Brown, "How Pathological Is 'Too' Pathological?," *Psychology Today*, May 2012, https://www.psychologytoday.com/za/blog/pathological-relationships/201205/how-pathological-is-too-pathological.

Emotional and Verbal Abuse

The false apologies and insincere promises to change are part of the cycle of abuse called the honeymoon phase. This phase includes apologies and good behavior that occur after a major emotionally, sexually, or physically abusive event. Despite their promises to change, abusers are unable and unwilling to sustain positive change. After a victim returns to her abuser, the abuser will eventually return to his abusive behavior when he is confident that she is emotionally and financially dependent upon him again. He may even be able to keep up the good behavior for months, or perhaps years, but the abusive behavior will return.

Enlisting Supporters

The abuser may resort to enlisting supporters to help him woo his spouse back. Such individuals will believe his insincere expressions of regret. Along with the abuser, they will try to make the victim feel guilty for leaving. They will say things like "Everyone makes mistakes," "You need to forgive and move on," "Think about the kids," and "I know he has changed." Fellow believers may say things like "No sin is greater than another," "We all have sinned," and "You need to forgive and reconcile because God hates divorce." They will quote Scripture out of context and guilt the woman of faith into returning to her abuser. We will discuss what Scripture says about abuse, divorce, and the role of a husband to his wife in a future chapter. For the purposes of this section, know that no theologically sound interpretation of Scripture requires a woman to return to an abusive husband.

Playing the Victim and the Pity Card

If the false apologies don't work, the SNAP will play the pity card and pretend to be the victim to get his partner back. Although a SNAP has been a bully and abuser to his spouse for years, once she leaves he will morph into a sniveling, pathetic wretch claiming that *he* was the one abused, *he* was the one she pursued and tricked into a relationship, *he* was the one who fell in love with someone who didn't love him back, and *he* is the one left all alone because she is leaving for selfish reasons. In addition, he will usually throw in that she is having an affair, because that is what he would do. All this whimpering is done solely for the purpose of gaining her pity and guilting her into returning. A victim may leave in anger over her abuser's persistent bullying, but it will be harder to leave someone they pity. Notice that the SNAP will cunningly manipulate his partner so that the focus is all on him, poor little thing. He completely ignores the fact that for the last several years he has been an abusive bully who never loved her in the first place and that she has every right to leave. Ironically, as soon as the SNAP says these things out loud, he will start believing his own lies and will repeat them to everyone who will listen, gathering pity as he goes.

Again, it is wise to remember that the sure sign of a sociopath is when he plays the pity card. Healthy people do not abuse others in the first place. But if they happen to get out of line and their partner leaves, a healthy person will own his cruelty, accept responsibility for his actions, and live with the consequences. Only cowards pick on others who are weaker than they are and expect pity when they incur the natural consequences of their actions.

Demands to Forgive and Forget, the Past is the Past

When feigned apologies and promises of change fail to get his victim to return, an abuser's tactics will become more aggressive. Once the "poor me" tactics fail, the abuser will demand that his victim forgive him and forget the abuse because the abuse was in the past. He may charge his victim with not living up to her religious beliefs if she does not forgive him and return to him. He may recite out-of-context Scripture to reinforce his demands for forgiveness and reconciliation. The abuser is no more repentant or godly than he was when he committed the abuse. He simply has determined that the nice-guy and poor-me tactics have failed to convince his victim to return and that he needs more persuasive tactics to guilt his victim into doing what he wants.

Victims often fall for this because they confuse forgiveness with forgetting and reconciliation. Victims do not realize, or perhaps do not want to admit, that past behavior is a strong indicator of future behavior. And victims get confused by the abuser's perverted argument about erasing the past. At any certain point, our lives consist entirely of things that have passed. The abuser's insistence that his victim forget the past is just another ruse to absolve himself of guilt.

Forgiveness cannot be demanded. When a person has intentionally and repeatedly wronged someone and shows no remorse, they have no right to demand forgiveness. Repentant persons know they do not deserve forgiveness for their wrongdoing. They will humbly admit their guilt and ask the victim what they can do to make things right. They will not demand anything from their victim, especially not forgiveness. The one who demands forgiveness is not repentant.

Forgiveness is largely misunderstood. Abusers always demand a perverted perception of forgiveness, telling the victim that forgiveness means forgetting the abuser's unrepentant bad behavior and reconciling. When the bad behavior inevitably repeats itself, the abuser again demands that the victim forgive and forget because that behavior is now in the past too. This pattern of abuse and demands continues without end because, logically speaking, all behavior is in the past. Even things that happened thirty seconds ago are now past, and the abuser, in his depraved mind, will continue to demand forgiveness to erase his abuse from the mind of the victim and make her stay.

Properly understood, forgiveness does not excuse bad behavior, expect the victim to pretend it didn't happen, or pronounce bad behavior acceptable. Forgiveness does not require the forgiver to forget about the abuse or to reconcile with the abuser. Neither does forgiveness require the victim to trust her abuser. Forgiveness does not require the victim to forego legal means of protection, stay in an abusive relationship, forego prosecution of a crime, or receive less than she is entitled to monetarily in a divorce settlement or in a contract. Forgiveness does not demand silence about the abuse or promises not to expose the truth.

Forgiveness merely means that the victim gives up the right for revenge, leaving that up to God. With forgiveness, the victim does not repay evil with evil. Forgiveness is not for the abuser, who doesn't care whether he is forgiven, just like he doesn't care if he has hurt his victim. Forgiveness is for the victim. God realized when He made humans that when we harbor hate and unforgiveness, we nurse a cancer inside us that grows into bitterness and eats us alive from the inside. Like hate, unforgiveness destroys our soul with bitterness that then seeps into everything we do. So He asks us to release that desire for revenge, trusting that He will hold each one of us accountable for our actions when the time is right—either in this world or the next. Forgiveness is a choice. Because abusers either want to own their victims or destroy them, the abuse will continue even after a woman leaves. Forgiveness, therefore, is a very long process. Healing and forgiveness will be discussed more fully in a later chapter.

A victim can choose to forgive her abuser; however, she would be foolish to ever trust her abuser again. A victim can choose to forgive her abuser but should still insist that reconciliation is not an option. A victim can choose to forgive her abuser, and, when she is ready, she should still insist on a divorce, still demand to be paid the amount she is entitled to by law, and still demand the amount of child support her children are entitled to by law. A victim can choose to forgive her abuser yet still report his abuse to the police, cooperate with law enforcement to prosecute his crimes, and obtain an order of protection. A victim can choose to forgive her abuser but still insist that he never contact her again. A victim can forgive her abuser and still do the right thing by telling the truth about the abuse.

Justifying His Abuse

When an abuser's feigned apologies, attempts to curry pity, or demands for forgiveness fail to persuade his victim to return to him, he will move on to more hostile tactics. He generally switches from playing the nice guy to more argumentative tactics when he feels that his chances of persuading his victim to return are diminishing. He will attempt to justify his bad behavior and attack her perception that he was in the wrong. He will justify his abusive actions with fabricated reasons, motives, and circumstances.

On the other hand, in circumstances in which a victim has not yet left, an abuser may simply start with aggressive tactics, such as justifying his abuse, when a victim confronts him with his bad behavior. After all, if he can convince her that *she* is wrong and that his behavior is justified, then she will continue to stay under his power and control.

> **Charlotte:** I spent more than a year in both pastoral and psychological counseling with Tim, hoping that he would change and that we could save our marriage. He needed to address his most heinous actions—rape and abandonment. After a year, he still would not address these issues. I knew that if he could not admit that these atrocious acts were wrong, he could never admit that the other less brutal (but more frequent) acts were wrong or change his ways. In April of 2013, when I said I could not be married to a man who was not repentant of these horrible actions and I had filed for a divorce, rather than admitting wrongdoing, he switched tactics from his false apologies and claimed that I had consented to having sex in front of the kids, and that I had consented to sex each and every day from January to April the prior year. I told him that neither I, nor any mother, would ever agree to having sex in front of their children. And I reminded him that he grabbed my shoulders and shook me and would not let me get away for three months—and that is not agreeing to sex. As for dumping me out of his car thirty-five miles from home, he again switched tactics from feigned apologies and first claimed that he opened the door for me and asked me to get back in. I responded that no, he did not. I had hoped that was what he would do, but he took off in his Mercedes so fast that his tires squealed. When that lie didn't work, then he claimed that he went to look for me. Again, I reminded him that he was nowhere to be found and that he went directly home and pounded on the nanny's door demanding to know where I was—and then he went to bed. Our nanny had relayed to me the whole terrifying evening from her perspective. When I finally came home around 5:00 a.m., he was there.

Denying the Abuse

After the abuser is unable to convince his victim to return and is feeling that he has little chance to win her back, the SNAP will turn hostile. Although he attempted to act like a nice guy with feigned apologies, playing the pity card, and false promises of change when he thought he had a fairly good chance of getting his victim to return, once he is convinced that she has left for good, the abuser will turn hostile and aggressive to further abuse and destroy his victim. If an abuser can't own and control his victim, he wants to destroy her.

When he turns hostile, the SNAP will no longer admit to his abusive actions or even try to justify them. At this point, he denies that they ever happened. This will always be the abuser's position in a divorce situation, an order of protection situation, or a criminal trial when he is accused publicly of his wrongdoing. SNAPs desperately want others to think they are decent, upstanding citizens as they infiltrate our communities, businesses, churches, and synagogues. Thus, when their abuse is held out to public scrutiny, they will always deny it, even though they may have readily admitted to it or even bragged about it to their victim or in counseling.

Projection: Accusing His Victim of Wrongdoing

As the SNAP considers various tactics to destroy his victim when she leaves, the clever SNAP will turn the tables and falsely accuse the victim of wrongdoing or other abuse. He may accuse her of abusing him, lying, having an affair, abandoning him, wasting marital funds, stealing, being a bad mother, incompetence, or any other thing that will make her look like the one responsible for the divorce instead of him. He will often accuse her of the very things that he is guilty of.

> Sally: My husband, who is over six feet tall and well over 200 pounds, was physically abusive and even broke down a door. At one point when my husband was attacking me, I tried to defend myself and ended up scratching him. He went to court and obtained an order of protection against me, and because he had a scratch on his face, he was very convincing. After that, whenever he attacked me, the police would not come to my aid because they said I was the abuser. He even shoved me out of a moving car, but I could get no one to help, and I could not obtain an order of protection against him.

Using the Kindness of His Victim against Her

In the ultimate act of abuse, the SNAP will taunt his victim for her kindness and use it against her. SNAPs are predators and will target a victim for the very characteristics he lacks and looks for in others. They know that someone with these characteristics will be easily bamboozled by their feigned professions of love and romance and that it will take her years (or at least until it's too late) until they figure out who her abuser really is underneath the mask.

Healthy people appreciate kindness and respond in kind. SNAPs look at the kindness that a person extends to them and thinks, "Sucker! I got you again! What an idiot!"

In the Sermon on the Mount, Jesus warned us about this particular tactic of evil people: "Don't give holy things to depraved men. Don't give pearls to swine! They will trample the pearls and turn and attack you" (Matthew 7:6 TLB). Jesus warns us not to extend kindness (i.e., "holy things" and "pearls") to abusers ("depraved men" and "swine"). If we do, the results are predictable. Jesus tells us that when good people are kind to abusers, they will not appreciate the kindness—"they will trample the pearls" and will use it against us—"and turn and attack you."

This is most evident when the victim seeks a divorce or an order of protection or prosecutes their crime. A healthy woman will usually seek to save a marriage before automatically seeking a divorce or restraining order. She will first approach her husband with reasonable requests to stop the unhealthy and destructive behavior and instead engage in healthy, life-building behavior. She will read books and conduct research to unlock the secrets to build a mutually beneficial marriage. She will try positive reinforcement as outlined in the Bible and will practice everything her counseling and books tell her to do to try and change his destructive behavior. If that doesn't work, she will participate in marital counseling or will see a pastor. As a last resort, she may seek church discipline. In effect, a healthy woman follows the steps set forth in Matthew 18:15–17 to resolve the marriage conflict. Only when all else fails will she seek legal solutions, such as a protective order or divorce.

However, her abuser will use her kindness and patience against her, claiming, "If it was so bad, why didn't you leave a long time ago? If it was so bad, why didn't you get a restraining order?" Many judges will not grant an order of protection if there has been a significant amount of time between the abuse and the time a victim seeks the order of protection. Thus, even the legal system uses a victim's kindness and forbearance against her. If there is money in their joint account, the abuser will clear it out when she leaves. If she suggests a fair and equitable division of assets and joint parenting arrangement, the abuser will whittle it away so that it is completely unequitable and in his favor.

> Charlotte: During our marriage, I constantly read Christian books on how to have a better marriage. And I read the Bible every day to be a better person and wife. I now know that marriage books do not address the abusive marriage, but I didn't know it at the time. We all know that most people don't respond to nagging and criticism. And Philippians 4:5 and 8 (TLB) tells us, "Let everyone see that you are unselfish and considerate in all you do. . . . Fix your thoughts on what is true and good and right. Think about things that are pure and lovely, and dwell on the fine, good things in others. Think about all you can praise God for and be glad about." My direct approach of asking him to "just be nice" or confronting his abusive behavior was received with explosive raging and excoriating yelling. So instead of nagging, I would try to appeal to what I hoped was his higher nature, focus on the positive things he was doing, and encourage him to do good things that were healthy for our marriage and our family. When things got out of control, I would write a letter. I wrote several of them over the course of our marriage—and they never made a difference in his behavior. Near the end of our marriage, I wrote a fifteen-page letter asking for real change and that he attend counseling. He responded with even more abuse. When I finally left, he accused me of lying and never telling him I was unhappy with our marriage. Of course, for twenty years I had asked him to be respectful and nice, but he never heard it. I told him that nagging never works, and I tried to focus on the positive, as we are told in Philippians, but he just yelled and continued to accuse me of lying. He even claimed, "Well, maybe if you had nagged more, we wouldn't be here right now!"
>
> During counseling, he admitted to the abuse (although he didn't characterize it as abuse) and even said "mistakes were made." But of course, he was not sincere in his feigned apologies. After he refused to continue with counseling, he later threw it up in my face every time we talked, "If it was so bad, you should have got a restraining order! You left! You abandoned us! You had an affair! You're a liar! You're an asshole! Etc., etc., etc." There is really nothing you can do to make an abuser change to be kinder and more respectful. If you are kind, they use it against you and attack you; if you confront them, they attack you. It's a no-win situation.

Demonization

Once the SNAP figures out that his sweet talk and false apologies will no longer work to get his victim back into his web, he will demonize the victim. In the SNAP's mind, there are three kinds of people: nothings, supporters, and enemies. Nothings are people who don't matter—they are below his radar because they aren't wealthy, powerful, or celebrity enough. Supporters are those who worship and serve the SNAP. Everyone else is an enemy. Enemies are to be destroyed. A small disagreement or difference of opinion can immediately, like the flip of a light switch, turn a supporter into an enemy. The wife who leaves is definitely an enemy.

The leaving wife must be destroyed, and all traces of her must be destroyed as well. All photographs that include her will be immediately taken down, and all gifts from her will be thrown out—unless they were expensive, in which case the SNAP gloats that he "wins" after all. All memories of her are twisted and darkened; all feelings will immediately turn to hatred. The SNAP can be likened to one of the famous SNAPs in the Bible—King Nebuchadnezzar of Babylon. His story is told in the book of Daniel. He declared that everyone, including his most trusted advisors, must fall down and worship a gold statue of him, and that if they did, things would go well for them. But if they did not worship him, he would kill them and throw them into a fiery furnace.

> Charlotte: When I finally left, Tim immediately went from "I love you. You are the most important person in my life. You are an angel. Thank you for introducing me to God and bringing me closer to Him. Come back to me. I've changed." to "You are the devil. You're not a Christian. You talk the talk, but you don't walk the walk. You are a hypocrite and a liar. Even your friends say that about you. You have no friends. I don't care about you. I don't care about what you think. I don't care about what you feel." When I reached out for a truce, he yelled, "You're not capable of a truce! You're the most self-righteous hypocrite I have ever met!" At first, he said he would like to reconcile, even if we got divorced. But when I tried to reach out and reconcile, he said, "I've moved on."
>
> He fabricated memories that had no basis in reality and accused me of all sorts of false things—projecting his own characteristics onto me. For example, when we began dating he was a successful businessman and had pursued me. He targeted me, wined and dined me, told me he had been separated from his wife for nine months (a lie), and then claimed he had filed for divorce (another lie). He even gloated about all the affairs that he had had during his first marriage that went undetected. But after I filed for divorce, he claimed that he was the poor victim who had been targeted all those years ago: "You pursued me! You went after me!" The lack of reality and delusion was stunning.

Frivolous Litigation

During and after the divorce, the SNAP will engage in frivolous and costly litigation to be vindictive and destroy his former spouse. Even when a judge recommends a course of action or terms of a marital settlement, an abuser will plow ahead with his demands, completely unaware of how skewed and out of touch with reality his thinking is. Even when being reasonable could save thousands or even hundreds of thousands of dollars, the SNAP would rather pay lawyers to thwart such plans than do the right thing.

Once agreements are finally reached or a judge has rendered a verdict in a trial, because the SNAP has been unwilling to reach a settlement, the SNAP is unwilling and/or unable to honor his obligations under any agreement or verdict. Whether it applies to child support, custody, parenting decisions, maintenance, or anything else, a SNAP will flat-out refuse to honor his obligations under any agreement. Former spouses of SNAPs are constantly in a position of having to take their SNAP to court to enforce an agreement. However, if a former wife breaches an agreement even slightly, e.g., brings the children back fifteen minutes late from a visit due to a traffic jam, the SNAP is the first one to run to court claiming a violation of an agreement. Anyone who has a child with a SNAP can be almost guaranteed numerous trips to the courthouse until the child has completed college.

Liz: After hearing reports from the guardian ad litem assigned to our learning-disabled daughter and the psychological evaluations of both of us, the judge "highly recommended" a marital settlement agreement and parenting agreement, which Charlie refused. He fired his attorneys and dragged us through a week-long trial representing himself. We had to interrupt the trial several times because he had violated the order of protection and was required to appear in another courtroom. On the days he was responsible for our daughter, he simply didn't arrange to have her picked up from school, and we had to stop the trial so that he could either pick her up or I quickly made arrangements. At the end of the trial, the judge made her ruling, and he appealed, causing even further emotional trauma and costing even more money. Charlie violated the ruling and emptied the retirement account, and he was put in jail for contempt of court. How is it that a man who calls himself a Christian can act this way?

CHAPTER 8

Physical Abuse

WHILE MANY ABUSERS EMPLOY physical abuse to maintain power and control over their partner, not all physical abuse is overt. Some forms of physical abuse do not leave bruises, scars, or loss of life or limb, thus leaving others wondering if they've experienced physical abuse at all. Physical abuse is any form of intentional physical action against another that is offensive, degrading, humiliating, painful, coercive, or impairs movement or escape. Physical abuse occurs in approximately 98 percent of abusive relationships.[57]

Healthy Relationships

A healthy person respects the physical boundaries of another, recognizing that others have the right to safety, privacy, and protection of their own bodies. The healthy person recognizes that others have the right to peaceably move about as they wish, determine their own future, and not take orders from their intimate partner. A healthy person has a natural tendency to care for, nurture, and protect family members, as well as friends, and to act in their best interest. When a family member or friend is sick or injured, they respond with compassion, empathy, and appropriate expressions of help and concern. Fitting attention for a spouse or child normally includes emotional as well as physical support, such as sympathy, cleaning up after vomiting or bowel movements, taking the spouse to the doctor or emergency room in a timely manner, talking with the physicians and nurses, advocating for the patient, and staying with the sick or injured person while in the hospital. It would also include doing things for the sick or injured that they cannot do for themselves.

A healthy person also cares about the physical interest and health of coworkers, neighbors, members of his church or synagogue, and those in his community. Appropriate responses might include calling, sending a card, taking over meals, offering to do errands, or similar helpful behavior.

A healthy adult male understands that he is the stronger of the sexes, and he uses his physical strength to protect and defend his family. This may take a variety of forms. If there is danger from an intruder in his home or an assailant while walking down the street, he uses his strength to protect them, even at risk to himself. He keeps his family in safe neighborhoods and in the company of safe people and avoids dangerous neighborhoods

---

[57] Adams, "Measuring the Effects of Domestic Violence on Women's Financial Well-Being."

and dangerous people. If there is danger from a wild animal, tornado, car accident, drowning, or other force of nature, he again uses his strength to protect his family, even at risk to himself.

A healthy husband and father protects his family from physical danger by keeping a home in good repair. He puts age-appropriate boundaries in place for his children such as curfew, rules about no drinking, smoking, or drugs, limits on driving, and limits on friends and activities. As protector of his children, he gives the young men who want to date his daughter "the talk" about how to treat her with respect and what will happen if they don't. He instills in his daughter and son how precious they are and how they must expect respect from, as well as treat with respect, those they choose as friends and those they choose to date so they can set healthy boundaries.

A healthy person recognizes that he does not have the right to physically make any other adult do what he demands. He may request or ask that another do what he wishes, but he recognizes that he does not have a right to physically force, coerce, or threaten them to do something. A healthy person never intentionally physically hits, slaps, kicks, grabs, restrains, shakes, runs into, slams into, burns, cuts, throws, throws something at, or uses any kind of weapon (gun, knife, bat, etc.) or anything that can be used as a weapon (fireplace poker, stick, rock, letter opener, etc.) against another person except in self-defense from an assailant.

Overall, a healthy person recognizes that by physically taking care of those around him, he also takes care of himself. Making sure his wife and children are physically healthy also benefits him. For a husband and father, a healthy family means less stress for him, fewer medical bills, and generally a better quality of life. Sick or injured family members take a toll on others. The medical bills and restrictions on normal activities create stress. If his wife leaves the marriage or dies, this causes enormous emotional, financial, and physical upheaval and distress for himself, as well as the rest of the family. Therefore, the healthy individual knows that by acting in the best physical interest of others, he also acts in his own best interest. Paul summed this up by stating, "husbands ought to love their wives as their own bodies. He who loves his wife loves himself" (Ephesians 5:28).

Physical Abuse with a SNAP

Contrast this with the SNAP. He views others as a means to his own selfish needs without regard to theirs. He sees his role not as a protector or nurturer of his family, but as a tyrannical despot with total dominion over his wife and children, who exist to serve him. Like a tyrannical despot, he uses physical strength and power to inflict pain, humiliation, and terror to keep his subjects under control and loyal to him.

And unlike the healthy person, the SNAP does not recognize that by acting in the best physical interest of others, he also acts in his own best interest. Nor does he recognize the corollary to that principle: that by physically hurting those around him, he also hurts himself. He will therefore physically abuse his romantic partner to gain power and control over her, seemingly uncaring that his actions will cause her to eventually leave the relationship (or be killed), which only hurts him.

Punching, Hitting with an Object, Slapping

One of the most recognized forms of abuse is physically punching or slapping a woman. Most people recognize this as abuse. It is also a crime in every state. A woman subjected to this form of physical abuse is in danger and should have a safety plan for herself and her children to protect themselves from her husband or partner. She must remove herself and her children from an unsafe environment. In addition, she may choose to file a restraining order, which requires her partner to keep his distance from her and the children. In many states, the local courthouse offers a special courtroom dealing with domestic violence where victims can get assistance in filing restraining orders. Emergency restraining orders should be filed as quickly as possible following a violent incident—within a day or two. The victim can appear before the judge the same day without notice to the abuser. Emergency restraining orders typically last for two or three weeks, at which time the victim will want to appear in court and request a long-term restraining order. Depending on the state, long-term restraining orders can be in effect for up to two years. They require the abuser to be served notice by the local sheriff and to appear in court before the judge grants the order. Regardless of whether a victim obtains a restraining order, she needs to be vigilant. A restraining order is merely a piece of paper, and many women who have obtained restraining orders have been killed by their abusers. Restraining orders are discussed in more detail in chapter 25.

After a physically violent episode, a SNAP may feign an apology to his wife or partner, and perhaps promise to change. The so-called apology generally does not take responsibility for the intentional crime, but rather is couched in terms such as "mistakes were made" or "I didn't mean to." In any event, the apology is only meant to keep the victim in the relationship. It does not mean he is truly repentant. The so-called change will be short-lived, as once a punch is thrown, others are sure to follow. More likely, the SNAP blames his partner with remarks like, "You made me do it. You know that makes me mad," or "If you would just behave and not make me mad, that wouldn't happen."

The wife then makes every attempt to behave and please her husband to avoid future violence, but the SNAP will change the rules to keep her off-balance and walking on eggshells. One week he is angry about dinner being cold, but the next week he is angry because she made social plans without consulting him, even though he makes plans all the time without asking her and expects her to drop her schedule to fit in with his. The following week he is angry because dinner is too hot. One rule is always true: the SNAP is always right and the center of the universe.

However, violence is never acceptable. An abuser's lack of self-control or bad temper, regardless of his partner's behavior, is never an excuse to hurt someone.

Some people mistakenly recognize only punching or slapping as abuse. Many SNAPs are too intelligent to have their bruised and bandaged wife walking around their community. Therefore, they choose physical abuse that does not leave evidence, that is not as blatantly recognized as abuse, and that they can plausibly deny being their fault.

> Ellen: Five days after we got married, I underwent a double mastectomy and then underwent chemotherapy treatment for a year. I remained weakened and in pain for the rest of the marriage. But throughout our marriage, Rod punched me in the chest and threw me against walls.

Shoving, Grabbing, Holding, Twisting, Shaking, Hair Pulling, Pinching

A SNAP does not usually start with punching and slapping his wife. He starts in less obvious ways and crosses boundary after boundary, escalating the abuse over years. He tells her it's okay, until even punching, slapping, and using weapons are acceptable forms of punishment or control. Gateway forms of physical abuse may include shoving, grabbing, holding, twisting, shaking, pulling hair, or pinching. At first, the SNAP may claim these behaviors are accidents or he may claim he is just being playful and then criticize his partner for not being more fun when she requests that he stop. However, as the abuse continues, it undoubtedly escalates. The SNAP will lose his temper and shove his spouse across the room, into the wall, or out the door. The SNAP may grab her shoulders and shake her as he yells at her or calls her names. To inflict pain, he may grab her wrists and twist them, or grab her breasts and squeeze them. He may hold her shoulders and refuse to let go until she tells him what he wants to hear. He may hold her so that she cannot escape from him as he makes demands upon her.

Kerry: The first time Patrick physically abused me, I had just picked him up from The Bar at the DeerPath Inn in Lake Forest, and he was upset that I had not picked him up sooner. I was just walking back to the car to get my purse, and he came up from behind me and pushed me down on the driveway. When I hit the pavement, I scraped my knees, my wedding ring, and my face, but the biggest bruise was to my heart. Who is this man? My home was supposed to be my safe place. When I confronted him a couple days later, he said that I must have pushed him first for him to have done that. He dismissed the entire event. How could he not feel bad that he did this to his wife? Why did he not apologize? When I finally left, it was because he grabbed my head and slammed it into a table. I needed stitches. When Patrick saw my bruises and what he had done to me, he said that I deserved everything that had happened to me and that I could look in the mirror and thank myself for it. I told him I was going to call the police. For months after I left our home, I regretted telling him that I was going to call the police that night. I thought that maybe if I hadn't, things would have been different. He would have apologized. He would have realized he was hurting me. He would have changed. I later realized that that statement saved my life.

Charlotte: My first husband would grab my breasts and squeeze them until they hurt and grab my wrists and twist them until I begged him to stop. He shoved me into walls, and then claimed that it was accidental.

When my second husband thought I was being unfaithful, he grabbed my shoulders, shook me, and yelled in my face, "Tell me you love me! Tell me you won't leave me!" Two and a half years after I left, and over six months after our divorce was final, I went to the house to pick up my mail. He started to put some of my personal belongings into a box with his girlfriend's name and address on it. Since he had been sleeping with her while we were married, I didn't want to have to look at her name and be reminded of his infidelity. So I asked him to put my things in a grocery bag instead. No one else was in the house, so he flew into a rage, grabbed my shoulders, shook me, and shoved me out the front door. After that, I made sure that I was never around him without other people in the room.

Burning

A SNAP may also burn his wife, which may take place in the kitchen with boiling water, by a stove, by a fireplace, with a hot curling iron, with a cigarette or cigarette lighter, or any number of ways. This type of abuse is especially terrifying and leaves scars, which are a daily reminder of his power, control, and cruelty.

Strangling, Choking, Scratching, Biting, and Spitting

A SNAP may resort to strangling, choking, or scratching his victim. A SNAP may bite his victim and even cut through the skin, requiring medical attention. Or, in further efforts to show his contempt and disdain, he may spit on his victim—an action that humiliates and degrades her.

Sally: In addition to other acts of physical violence, Ernie spit on me when he became angry.

Stairs

Stairs are especially tempting for the SNAP. Not only do they multiply the pain and injury of his shoving her down the stairs, but he can also claim plausible deniability: "She lost her balance." It's easy for an abuser to accidentally shove his wife and then claim that she lost her balance and fell.

> Dirk: Most of Rhonda's abuse was emotional, but one day, when I was off my guard, she simply kicked me in the stomach and shoved me down the stairs.

Denying Medical Care

Denying or delaying medical care is an insidious form of abuse. A SNAP may refuse or delay taking his wife or partner for medical treatment when she clearly needs it and cannot transport herself. Regardless of whether his partner has fainted, experiences unexplained pain, has been in an accident, is in labor, or has some other condition requiring immediate medical attention, the SNAP will either ignore her condition or try to minimize the pain by telling her it's all in her head. As a delaying tactic, he may engage in other activities that are more important to him, or he might refuse altogether to take her to the emergency room. It is simply too inconvenient for him to be bothered, and it keeps his victim completely dependent on him.

The SNAP will also not want to be bothered with attending to his wife. Even in an emergency, the SNAP will view his partner's medical needs as a major inconvenience to his schedule. He may chastise her for her poor planning, as if she had anything to do with the medical emergency or when the baby decided to arrive, or he might just leave to do other things that he had on his to-do list. Helping her go to the bathroom, change bandages, clean up after vomiting, drive to chemo treatments, or other things a healthy person would do for an ill wife will not happen with a SNAP.

A SNAP will also refuse to refill or administer medications for an ailing wife or partner. Or he may demand that she take a smaller dosage than the one prescribed by a physician so that the medication will last longer. He may also simply refuse to make a doctor's appointment for an ailing partner who is too ill to make the appointment herself. He may claim that he is trying hard to get in to see the doctor, and then claim the doctor is too busy to see her.

A SNAP can be so evil as to yell at and berate the poor woman who is physically unable to perform her normal duties. This may be true of a wife, partner, or even his elderly mother. Truly, there is no depth to which a SNAP will not stoop to express his displeasure at a woman who inconveniences him because of her medical condition. In his perception, she is no longer useful to him, and thus is easily discarded.

> Ellen: After my mastectomy and chemo treatment, Rod did not support my treatment. When I needed X-rays or other treatment, he would twist the Bible and say, "We are married, so we are one flesh, we are one body, and if you get an X-ray it's like me getting an X-ray. You need to get my approval before you get an X-ray. I don't want an X-ray!" He wouldn't support my treatments and wouldn't help, even though he wouldn't work either. My son, who was only ten years old at the time, was homeschooled and he became my caretaker. He dropped behind a year in school.

> Charlotte: Any time I needed to be rushed to the emergency room, rather than taking me to the ER, Tim would put me in the back of his car and go on shopping errands for hours while I writhed in pain. When my water broke and I went into labor, he invited friends over for a two-hour cocktail

party. When we finally left, even though we lived only ten minutes from the hospital, it took two hours to get there for the births of both our children because he had to stop by Blockbuster videos to shop for videos, and he had to stop by Brown's Chicken because, as he said, "Well, you aren't going to cook for me tonight." He even went shopping at the high-end audio-video store to get a new video recorder and look at flat screen TVs.

When I had painful bouts of diverticulitis and was throwing up because of the constant stress, he put me in the back of the car and went to look at tiles and marbles for a spec house he was building. After a few hours, he dropped me off at the ER and then went on shopping. I ended up staying in the hospital for days. When his elderly mother fell due to a vertebrae pushing against her spinal column, he had no pity. He just yelled at her to get up. It was heartbreaking. She had to get back surgery, but he had no empathy at all.

Liz: Charlie hated doctors, and he wouldn't let me or our four children go to doctors. When I was in labor and begging him to take me to the hospital, he refused to take me to the hospital. I was forced to give birth to one of our children at home.

Denying Basic Needs

If a woman is unable to care for her basic needs due to illness or injury, a SNAP may deprive her of these basic needs. He may refuse to bring her food or feed her if she needs assistance. He may refuse to help her bathe. Even if a woman is not ill or injured, many SNAPs do not let their partners have adequate sleep so that they are constantly sleep deprived and unable to concentrate or focus.

Abandonment

Abandonment is a favorite form of physical abuse that leaves no bruises or scars. Abandonment occurs when an abuser leaves his victim in an unsafe situation, such as dumping her out of a vehicle, boat, or train, or leaving her while far away from home. For the SNAP, it has the added benefit of putting his victim in harm's way and letting someone or something else directly inflict the harm, while he assuages any guilt and tells himself that he really didn't do anything wrong. It is terrorizing for the victim, which is another bonus for the SNAP.

Charlotte: The most terrifying night of my life occurred on December 7, 2002, when the law firm that I worked for in Chicago hosted a holiday party. One of our guests had entirely too much to drink and couldn't even walk, much less drive. As the most junior associate, I was asked by our managing partner to drive our drunk guest home. Tim, my husband, drove behind us. After I had dropped off our inebriated guest, I got into Tim's car. He was livid. I had never seen him so angry. I guess the inconvenience of me saving someone's life and complying with the request from my managing partner was just too much for his self-importance to take. He started yelling and raging out of control. I had never seen him so mad. I was terrified that he would hit me. At the next stoplight, I hopped out of the car, hoping that he would come to his senses, apologize, ask me to get back in the car, and drive home in peace. Instead, he took off so fast that his tires squealed, and he never came back. It was two-thirty in the morning in Chicago, twenty degrees, with snow on the ground, in a gang-infested neighborhood, and I had only an evening gown on with no coat, no cell phone, no money, no credit cards, no nothing. I didn't know what to do, but I knew that no matter what I did, Tim would blame it on me, like he always did. I started walking north because Northwestern

University was north of me, and I assumed somewhere near campus would be an all-night diner that would let me use their phone. I ran into a 24/7 Blockbuster Video and asked to use their phone and a phone book. I dialed a cab, but my fingers were so cold that I could barely dial. The cab took me home to Lake Forest, thirty-five miles away, and I arrived about 5:00 a.m. I crawled in bed with my four-year-old son, Morton, wondering what I should do and wondering what his life would be like without a mother if something had gone horribly wrong that night. I knew that Tim would quickly replace me without a second thought or any remorse, since I always felt replaceable. I found out from our nanny that Tim had driven home, banged on her door in the middle of the night, and angrily yelled, "Where is my wife?"—as if he didn't know that he had dumped me in Chicago and left. Tim never asked how I was, never apologized, and just continued like nothing had happened.

I never again went anywhere with him without my cell phone and my wallet. Twelve years later, in 2014, when we were in marriage counseling, I brought up the incident. He never apologized. The most he would say was that it was "inconsiderate." He was so full of pride that he would not apologize, even when our marriage was on the line. When I finally made it clear that I was not returning to my abusive marriage, he lied and claimed that he'd asked me back in the car. When I pointed out that he didn't, he changed his lie and claimed he went back for me. When I pointed out that he didn't, because he was there when I came home and our nanny confirmed that he had come home, he raged at me again. He was never remorseful or apologetic. To cover up his abuse, he lied again and told everyone that I left him for another man.

Physical Restraint

A SNAP may physically restrain his wife or partner by refusing to let her leave or enter the premises. He may take away her car keys, lock her in a room or the basement, or stand in front of the door so she cannot exit. If she does make it to the car, he may block her entry to the car or stand in front of the car when she attempts to leave, or he may physically restrain her.

Conversely, a SNAP may refuse to allow his wife or partner to enter her home. He may lock her out or abandon her miles from home (see above on "Abandonment").

Dirk: When she was raging, Rhonda locked the door and refused to let me in the house. I was forced to sleep in the car.

Hilary: We lived in Stan's house. He was a binge drinker who would drink and use drugs for three days straight. During these times, he would often lock me out of the house, and I had to sleep in the car, even when I was pregnant, even in the winter.

Charlotte: When we were separated but going through counseling, I went to the house two or three times a week for family dinners and to do homework with the kids. One night while searching for colleges on Tim's laptop around the kitchen table, I accidentally hit a button that showed me that of Tim's top ten websites, six were porn sites. His porn addiction and sexual abuse was the final nail in the coffin that led to me separating. I was so upset that I got up to leave, but Tim stood in front of my car door and refused to let me leave for more than thirty minutes.

Physical Abuse

Placing a Victim in Harm's Way and Blaming Others

An abuser may put his victim in harm's way or engage in risky behavior of his own doing, and then blame the foreseeable damage on a "freak accident." Or he will deflect and blame someone else's wrongdoing. The blame in such cases lies squarely on the abuser. However, because he did not personally inflict the harm but only instigated the actions that inflicted the harm, the abuser will declare innocence of any wrongdoing and try to convince his victim of the same.

> Charlotte: Tim owned a Streblow mahogany boat that he drove on Lake Geneva, Wisconsin. He drove it with complete disregard for other people on the lake. We would usually go out early in the morning when it was calm before other power boats got on the lake. At that time, there were usually several people sitting in bass boats fishing calmly by the shore of the lake. For no reason, Tim would zip by them within ten to fifteen feet, leaving a huge wake and rocking their boats. We got a lot of unfriendly gestures and yelling in response, and deservedly so. When I told him how incredibly rude it was, he didn't care. "This lake is for power boaters, not fishermen," was his self-serving response. It was so embarrassing.
>
> On July 4, 2010, Tim took our son Morton and his friend Mike on the inner tube behind the boat and drove entirely too fast trying to flip them off the tube as he made a circle. He did flip them off. They flew off so hard that Mike's teeth landed in Morton's behind, and his teeth were pushed up into his gums from the impact. Mike was screaming, they were both bleeding, and Morton had a big open gash in his rear. They were both rushed to the emergency room. Morton received stitches in his rump, and Mike had to undergo orthodontic surgery to pull his teeth down from his gums. Tim just blamed it on a freak accident. He took no responsibility whatsoever for driving too fast and trying to make them fly off the inner tube.

Accidents

A SNAP has a unique ability to devise ways to harm his partner, yet claim it was an innocent mistake. This can take any number of forms. He may "accidentally" turn on the disposal while her hand is in the disposal trying to dislodge something from it. Likewise, he may drop her from a playground teeter-totter, causing a broken tailbone when she lands. He may "accidentally" shove her into the wall or down the stairs as he brushes past her in the hallway, or not turn off a piece of machinery or equipment, pretending he doesn't hear her cries. He may "accidentally" drop or forget something while they do house projects, causing a ladder to fall out from under her, or electrocution, or some other injury, or he may drive a car, boat, or motorcycle too fast for conditions, causing injury to her and then claim it was a "freak accident." There is truly no end to what can be claimed as an "accident" when a SNAP is involved.

Throwing Objects and Hitting Objects

In a blatant (and usually successful) attempt to intimidate his wife or partner, a SNAP will throw or threaten to throw objects at her, throw objects and break them against a wall, or hit an object. The SNAP will use anything that is handy—a lamp, glass, bottle, book, can of food, barbells—anything that has weight and mass and can cause injury. The result is often a terrified, shaking, and/or injured wife.

As with throwing objects, hitting objects is designed to intimidate a SNAP's wife or partner. The most frequent targets of his hitting are a door or a wall.

> Sally: Ernie was physically violent and often broke doors and hit walls when he raged. He's over six feet tall and weighs more than 200 pounds. His dad and brother are the same way. Our court-appointed psychiatric evaluator diagnosed him as completely untruthful and with antisocial personality disorder. He's a sociopath. He's also an active member of the men's group at church. The men at church told him that when he argues with me, he should grab my wrists and hold me down.

Weapons

Guns, knives, bats, martial art equipment, and other weapons are the ultimate weapons of domestic terrorism in the hands of a SNAP. Threatening his wife or partner with a weapon is a tactic the SNAP uses to keep her submissive before he uses it on her. He may threaten to kill her if she leaves, or he may sleep with weapons by his bed or under his pillow so that she cannot sneak out while he is sleeping. A person who threatens to use a weapon or who has used a weapon in the past against his wife or partner is extremely dangerous, and the situation must be treated with extreme caution. A woman is much more likely to be killed when she leaves an abusive relationship than if she stays in the relationship.[58] Thus, if a woman chooses to leave, she should take her children with her, and she must ensure that neither she nor her children can be found by the abuser. This often means that the woman needs to go to her local domestic abuse shelter—usually located in undisclosed locations. She should immediately obtain a protective order against her abuser. Even with a protective order, a woman is at great risk and should use extreme caution. Police often do not take threats of domestic violence seriously, and they cannot provide round-the-clock protection. To protect herself and her children, she may wish to take gun safety classes and/or hire security protection if her abuser has access to weapons.

Leaving Her in Harm's Way

Although a healthy husband understands that one of his roles is to physically protect his wife and family, a SNAP sees no such duty. In fact, he believes that his wife's role is to protect him because he is the most important person in the family. If his wife or family is in danger, and saving them would endanger himself, he will save himself instead of them.

> Charlotte: On a trip to the Bahamas, Tim, my teenage son, and I were snorkeling with friends and their children. A ten-foot shark swam underneath us. Tim immediately started yelling "Shark!" to the people on the boat. Saving himself, he quickly swam to the boat and got out of the water onto the boat, leaving me, my son, and all the other children in the water with the shark. That is telling of a person's character.

Child Abuse

The correlation between intimate partner abuse and child abuse is difficult to substantiate. Likewise, statistics determining the exact percentage of homes in which both child and partner abuse is present are difficult to locate. However, studies show that up to 70 percent of the time when intimate partner abuse is present, child

---

[58] Martin Daly and Margo Wilson, "Evolutionary Social Psychology and Family Homicide," *Science* 242, (October 28, 1988): 519–524. According to the Domestic Violence Intervention Program, women are as much as 70 times more likely to be killed within the two weeks after they leave than at any other time in the relationship. Jennifer O'Neill, "Domestic Violence Statistics: The Horrific Reality," *Good Housekeeping*, February 24, 2016, https://www.goodhousekeeping.com/life/relationships/a37005/statistics-about-domestic-violence/.

abuse is also. The SNAP uses similar tactics on his children that he does on his intimate partner and others. However, even if the child only witnesses abuse rather than is a victim herself, the abuse has a destructive effect on the child.

Animal Cruelty

SNAPs are evil cowards who bully and abuse people and animals who are physically weaker than they are and who depend on them. Exercising power and control over their victims makes them feel superior. Therefore, the likely targets are animals as well as humans whom he perceives as inferior. SNAPs will kick the dog, throw a kitten against a wall, throw out the family hamster, or step on the family lizard to show the animal and the family that they are in charge. Sometimes they do this in a fit of rage, while other times they will plan the attack when no one is watching.

They may even claim to have done so accidentally. While normal people keep a watchful eye out for smaller pets to avoid harm, a SNAP shows reckless disregard for smaller animals, and therefore can claim with plausible deniability that they stepped on (and killed) the beloved pet by accident. He will then blame the poor pet for being "in the way," saying "It should have known better."

Woodland creatures who live in the family yard are also targets. If a bird lives in a bush or tree that the SNAP plans on trimming or cutting down, he will do so regardless of the nest of eggs or babies that live there. Likewise for bunnies, squirrels, raccoons, or other creatures. Because of their lack of empathy or conscience, SNAPs often shoot or torture animals just for fun. While normal, healthy people may hunt, because they have a conscience they try to honor the animal by eating the meat and, at the very least, giving it a death with dignity and the least amount of pain. Not so for the SNAP, unless, of course, a good shot gives them bragging rights.

> Liz: Charlie was cruel and abusive to our cat, in addition to us. He kicked her down the stairs, and she always walked with a limp after that.

> Charlotte: We had a robin who had built a nest in a bush on our patio and had her babies. One day, Tim decided to have the landscapers trim all the trees and shrubs, and even though I asked him not to touch the bush with our robins, he made them trim that one too. The robin never came back. Any small animal that was a child's pet, from a hamster to a lizard, was either thrown out or killed.

CHAPTER 9

Financial Abuse

ONE OF THE LESSER recognized methods a SNAP uses to abuse his partners and others is financial abuse. Many people do not even know this is a form of abuse. It occurs when one person in a position of trust takes advantage of the other to their detriment. Financial abuse occurs in 99 percent of abusive relationships.[59]

Healthy Relationships

A healthy person views money as a resource—a tool for obtaining the necessities and extras in life: food, clothing, shelter, education, vacations, etc. A person with a healthy view of money cherishes people and uses money to bless those he loves, gives to those in need, meets the obligations into which he has entered, and pays a fair price in a transaction. Money is seen as disposable, but people and relationships are not. A healthy person understands boundaries—he knows what money or possessions are his and what money or possessions are someone else's. A healthy person does not measure his or others' worth based on money. Money is separate and apart from a person, and people have intrinsic value whether they are wealthy or not. A healthy person does not base his friendships or other close relationships on whether someone has money, but on their character.

A healthy person views marriage as a partnership to bless each other, raise children, and do good works together, regardless of who brings home the paycheck. It is an ancient Judeo-Christian tradition that the husband is responsible for providing for his wife and family. Providing for his family is part of a husband and father's job as the protector of his family. And while in these modern times women have more options to work outside the home, in the vast majority of homes, the husband is the primary breadwinner while the wife often puts her career on hold or takes a less demanding job to take on the responsibilities of maintaining the house and raising children. Thus, in healthy marriages, the money and assets a couple have acquired during their marriage are jointly earned and jointly owned, and both spouses have equal access to funds. While both are accountable to the other, they do so in a position of trust, such that one does not need to report every penny that has been spent. They

---

[59] Adrienne Adams, "Measuring the Effects of Domestic Violence on Women's Financial Well-Being," University of Wisconsin Center for Financial Security Research Brief, 2011-5.6.

make financial decisions in the best interest of their family with transparency and honesty. Both spouses have equal value and worth and equal say, independent of one's paycheck.

A person with a proper moral compass will act fairly in all circumstances, whether business or personal, fulfill his agreements, and not take advantage of another person. With those in which he is in a position of trust—i.e., a spouse, a family member, or a business associate—he will be transparent, fair, and generous.

A healthy person understands that he is just passing through this world and that he is merely a steward of the money with which God has entrusted him. Indeed, a person of faith believes that this world and everything in it is God's, and that the money with which he has been entrusted is God's. Therefore, he has a generous spirit and, to the best of his ability, uses his money to bless his family, give to those in need, and be a blessing to the community. He knows that he cannot take money with him to the next life and that relationships are the only thing he will take with him to heaven.

A healthy person also is wise with the money entrusted to him. Although he is generous, he is not frivolous. He does not waste his money on things that do not matter. Depending on his economic situation, he may indulge in a luxury now and again, but he does not waste large sums of money on foolish schemes or lavish items that he cannot afford. If a large purchase or investment is to be made, the wise man does a good amount of investigation prior to purchasing or investing, and he solicits the advice of his wife and other people whose wisdom he values. The wise man knows that if he wants to go forward, but his wife is feeling adamantly against it, there is usually a good reason for her reticence. The person of faith will take the decision to the Lord in prayer and ask for the guidance of the Holy Spirit. In the end, the decision is a joint decision that both he and his wife have agreed on.

The Narcissist/Sociopath/Psychopath and Finances

The SNAP, on the other hand, has an unhealthy view of money and possessions, both of which lead to his ultimate goals: power and control. According to the Center for Financial Security, financial abuse is present in nearly every abusive relationship. Unlike a healthy person, a SNAP cherishes money and uses people to get more for himself. In his world, money is his goal and people are disposable. He feels entitled to acquire money at the expense of others. He often demands complete control of the family finances. Because he is naturally untrusting of others, when marrying, he automatically assumes it will end in divorce. In a self-fulfilling prophecy, he sets the marriage up for failure with financial and other forms of abuse, and then ensures that all financial arrangements and transactions are for his sole benefit, not both spouses. Inevitably, the divorce eventually occurs. Financial abuse includes planned, deliberate acts designed to keep the partner in the abusive relationship and to keep her from breaking free. It is one of the primary reasons that women stay in abusive marriages and relationships. Remember, no relationship with a SNAP ever ends well—and that is especially true when it comes to finances.

What follows are some of the more popular tactics of financial abuse.

Using Other People's Money

SNAPs embrace the term "OPM" or "Other People's Money" because they use OPM to get more for themselves. If a SNAP can get other people to pay for something he wants, or if he can weasel out of something he is obligated to pay for, he will do so without a hint of guilt. In fact, he will gloat and brag about it. Because money is such a big part of a narcissist's mindset, and thoughts of money take up so much of their waking hours, they often are drawn to high-power, high-salary careers, like businessmen, lawyers, Wall Street, doctors, and entertainment. Even those who are not drawn to high-powered jobs will find others to leach off to get what they want.

Allowing His Wife No Access to Family Funds

In nearly every relationship with a SNAP, the SNAP has cut off his wife or partner from all sources of funds. The SNAP has refused to add her name to checking accounts or any other accounts into which he may deposit what he earns. In his view, everything he earns and everything he buys with everything he earns is his. His marriage is not a fifty-fifty partnership. He is the breadwinner; therefore, he is the boss. If he puts her name on the accounts, to him it would mean that she owns half and is entitled to half of his earnings and assets. And he will never agree to that. He may allow her to have her own account to deposit what she earns, but he will not deposit his paycheck into her account, although he may give her an allowance from time to time.

> Jane: From the earliest days of our thirty-year marriage, I had no access to marital funds. Lew had me stop working to raise and homeschool our children, but would not put my name on any accounts. I opened my own account and started to work part time to feed my family. It made him so mad that I was able to have my own money.

> Robin: I worked before we were married, but because my husband made more than $100,000 a year, we decided that I would stay home to raise the kids. But after a while, he opened an account in only his name and transferred all the funds to his account. I had no money even for groceries.

Forcing His Wife to Hand Over Her Paycheck

Even if the SNAP earns significantly more than his wife, he will often force her to hand over her paycheck to him or deposit it in his account.

> Jamie: Even though my first husband made more than $1 million a month and I was just a secretary, he made me give him my paycheck, and he put it in his account. I had to ask him any time I needed my own money. He was a complete control freak.

Making His Wife Ask for Money

Nothing makes a SNAP feel more in control financially than to make his wife ask, or sometimes beg, for money. And since his wife has no access to funds, the wife of a SNAP must always ask for money.

> Sally: My sister-in-law, who married my husband's brother, was not allowed to buy anything without his permission. We went out shopping one day, and we had to sneak out. She asked me to buy a bag of Hershey's kisses because her husband would not let her buy any—and she needed to have a little chocolate. When I told her to take the bag with her, she said she couldn't because she couldn't let him know that she had been out shopping or that she had chocolate. She was under his complete control. She had three little ones, but she eventually committed suicide because she saw no way out.

Financial Abuse

Putting His Wife on an Allowance

SNAPs will often put their wife on an impossibly small allowance for monthly household expenses or insist that the spouse come to them and beg for money prior to shopping for everything from necessities to extras. The allowance is set so low that it could not possibly cover normal household expenses, therefore setting the wife up for failure to keep within the budget and giving the SNAP a reason to justify withholding money. The SNAP will refuse to give money when asked or will interrogate her so that she is afraid to ask for money, and then he will berate his wife for failing to keep beer and food in the refrigerator and for the shabby way she and the children are dressed.

> Charlotte: Before we dated, Tim informed me that his wife had a bigger allowance than my yearly salary. I should have known better. After we were married, he put me on an allowance even less than that of Wife Number 1 that only paid for childcare.

Requiring Expense Reports and Receipts

If the wife needs something that is not in her budget, she must plead her case and get permission to make a purchase. Then she must either (1) submit an expense report with receipts after she makes the purchase, hoping the SNAP will keep his promise to reimburse her, or (2) ask for the money prior to making the purchase and submit the receipt and any change.

If the SNAP ever pays for anything that is in the general category of something that his wife's allowance should cover, the SNAP will charge back the wife for the expenditure, regardless of how small, much like a business expense account.

These arrangements meet the SNAP's sense of entitlement and need for power and control over his wife.

> Jeannie: Milton would only let me have so much for groceries that couldn't possibly feed our family, and then he would require me to give him the receipts. I would cash in the coupons and keep the money so that I could have a little extra for the kids and me, and so Milton wouldn't find out.

> Robin: If I needed money for anything, I had to ask for it and come back with a receipt and change in my hand to give to him.

> Charlotte: I had to provide an expense report for extra things (like home furnishings or trips) that were not covered by my monthly household allowance. But if a bill ever came to the house that Tim attributed to me (like a thirty dollar insurance co-payment or a five dollar parking ticket), he charged me. It's hard to believe someone making seven figures a year would charge his wife for a parking ticket, but that is his mindset.

Controlling Her Job and Earnings

Because SNAPs want control over their spouse so that she remains financially dependent, they will often not allow or strongly discourage the wife from working outside the home. Many SNAPs own their own business or work at a family business because they have a hard time with authority and have greater flexibility working on their own or with their own family business. If the wife is allowed to work outside the home, many SNAPs will want their wife to work in his family business at little to no pay. If she does work outside his family business, oftentimes the SNAP will sabotage her efforts so that she must either quit, work part time, or take a low-level position. If the wife has potential income-earning property that she owned individually prior to her marriage (such as a house or condo that she could rent), the SNAP will often force her to sell the property so that she does not have her own independent income and does not have a fallback position in the event she needs a home when hers becomes unsafe. Alternatively, the SNAP may require her to retitle her individual property as a joint asset. When she does this legally, she effectively gives the SNAP half of her asset as a gift. In a divorce, the assets titled jointly will be treated as marital property and will be divided between parties. They will not be treated as her individual property that she would otherwise be solely entitled to.

On the other hand, if he wants her to contribute financially, he may force her to work outside the home. He will either take control of the money she earns by requiring her to deposit it into his bank account to which she has no access, or he will force her to spend it on living expenses (such as food, clothes, school fees for the children, taxes, house repairs, etc.) while he saves his earnings in his account. If she works outside the home, you can be sure that her position doesn't interfere with his lifestyle or cause him to make any adjustments to his life. She will still have all her household and child-rearing responsibilities, as well as her job responsibilities. The SNAP will not offer to take on additional household or child-rearing duties.

> Sahira: I wanted to work and help our family since we were living near poverty and on government assistance, but Nadeem did not let me. He said I could work in his business, which was failing, but he never paid me.

> Charlotte: Before our wedding, Tim asked me to quit my job as an executive of a small publishing company and become a stay-at-home mom under the fraudulent ruse that I could travel with him and raise our children, and that we didn't need my income. After he foisted the prenuptial agreement on me, he went from kind to cruel after the wedding, put me on an allowance, and wouldn't establish any joint accounts. It was clear that I needed to have my own money and my own nest egg. So I went to law school, graduated third in my class, and worked part time for a law firm. But then he forced me to pay for all the personal household expenses with my new income, and he paid only for childcare. I was never able to build a nest egg. At the end of our marriage, my assets were nearly zero, while his were more than $10 million.

Holding Assets in the SNAP's Name

Titled assets, such as the home, vehicles, life insurance policies, and other assets, will usually be titled in the sole name of the SNAP. If the abuser has no prenuptial agreement, most assets purchased during the marriage are considered marital assets, which will be divided between the spouses during a divorce. However, the abuser will title the assets in his name because he feels entitled to the assets, believes that all the assets are his, and because it gives him a sense of power over his wife.

> Charlotte: Absolutely every asset was titled in Tim's name. Three houses, four cars, two motorcycles, one boat, all the insurance policies (both his and mine), every investment account, every checking and savings account—it was all in his name. He gave me a motorcycle for my birthday one year, and then sold it for $20,000 without telling me and pocketed the money. He bought a "mom" car for me to drive the children in, and "gave" me his old hand-me-down car to drive. But he titled all the cars in his name, and of course, in the divorce, he claimed that all four cars were his. During the

divorce, I came across letters between him and his attorneys who drafted the prenuptial agreement specifying that he intended to never have anything held jointly during the entire marriage—and he never did.

Holding Assets in a Trust

Titled assets will often be titled in a trust over which the SNAP has control and is the beneficiary. He uses this financially sophisticated method to hide assets from his wife since trusts are not public documents and can be used to conceal the identity of the owner. If not hidden from her outright, a SNAP will often use the ruse of estate planning or tax planning to justify excluding his wife from the title.

> Charlotte: Tim purchased property to build a house while he was married to his first wife. He used a land trust and shell companies to hold the title so that he could hide it from her during the divorce that he planned so that when she checked the county property records, his name would not appear. When he was questioned about it during his divorce, he lied under oath in a deposition and claimed that he did not know the beneficiary of the trust—which, of course, was him. When the real estate broker found out that he did a runaround, he sued Tim for fraud and for bilking him out of his real estate commission. Tim eventually paid. My own husband had this lawsuit when we were married, and I had no idea. I found all this out during and after the divorce.

Obtaining Credit Cards and Loans in His Wife's Name

While a SNAP will try to ensure that all assets are titled in his name, he will also ensure that as many of the credit cards, utilities, expense accounts, and loans as possible are in the wife's name. He will also, without her knowledge or permission, take out credit cards and loans in his wife's name and use the money. In this way, he can keep her financially hostage. He can (and will) increase debt without her knowledge, refuse to pay bills and loans that are in her name, and ruin her credit rating.

> Jane: Lew used my social security number and my name to get loans and credit cards in my name and took the money. When we got divorced, I had all this debt in my name, and had no idea. My credit was ruined.

Charity—Only When It Makes Him Look Good

Because he wants others to think of him as a great guy, a SNAP may give to a charity, but he will make sure that others know about it, and he will only give if it benefits him. When it fails to make him look good in front of others, the charity is dropped.

> Charlotte: Tim gave to his college, but only when it named a room after him. Our church went through a building campaign, and we hosted a meeting in our home to help raise money. Tim pledged $30,000, but when the pastor changed the Sunday morning format, Tim did not like it and canceled his giving. When we were married, he supported AIDS orphans in Nigeria, a church ministry that I was very passionate about. But as soon as I left, Tim stopped supporting the AIDS orphans. He only gave when others could see it and he could look good.

Money Is an Extension of Himself

A SNAP sees money as an extension of himself, much like others would view their left arm. His measurement of his success and others' is money and possessions. He thinks about money constantly—how to make it, how to make more, how to hide it, how to invest it, and how much he has. Therefore, he wants to make as much money as he possibly can, regardless of the means. And once he makes the money, he wants to keep as much as he possibly can. He only wants to associate with "friends" who make him look good by association, and since he values money and power, he only wants to be associated with others who have money and power. If you ask a wealthy abuser how his friend, the executive of some company, is doing, the SNAP will respond with how much money the acquaintance earned this year, how much money he made in the latest initial public stock offering of a company, how much his new house is worth, how he was just quoted in the *Wall Street Journal*, etc. He will not even mention his children, wife, or health.

> Hilary: Stan was consumed with money and status and winning and using his money to control me. He wrote me texts stating that his "children *are* where they live in their environment. Lake Forest, Glencoe, Highland Park, Wilmette," etc. He was worried that with me driving in his Mercedes in "poor cheap areas" like Hawthorn Woods, Inverness, and Kildeer (all of which are lovely, but not as affluent as Lake Forest and the North Shore of Chicago), his "son could get kidnapped." He yelled at me and threatened me. "My money gets me things. I'm a f*cking winner! The point is money. Power and money. If you don't give me power, you get no money. Got it?"

> Charlotte: Tim was obsessed with money. He made a personal financial statement at least once a year to show himself how much his net worth was. He thought and talked about his money constantly. He told me early in the marriage that his goal was to be worth $20 million. And he achieved it. His personal financial statement that he prepared for 2005 shows that he had a net worth of $22 million. But regardless of his wealth, he was not generous. He refused to give me more than $2,400 a month to help with household expenses and childcare for six of us. He gave very little to charity. Tim had very few true friends, but he had several business acquaintances. He complained about the traffic and the hassle and refused to go to dinner or an event with me that required going into the city of Chicago from the suburbs. But if one of his wealthy acquaintances invited him, he was super excited to be included in the rich crowd, especially if there were celebrities there. He would then talk endlessly about the celebrities he met. One of these business acquaintances, John, went on to become a CEO of a large company and then made tens of millions of dollars. Any time I ever asked him how John was doing, Tim told me how much money he was making that year, how much he made from the most recent IPO, etc. He never shared how his kids or wife were doing because he just didn't care. It was all about the money.

Always a "Win-Lose" in Business Transactions

SNAPs will not be fair or transparent in transactions, nor will they honor their commitments unless there are severe penalties that can and will be enforced by someone in authority, e.g., a judge in a court of law. Rather than viewing business transactions as a win-win opportunity benefiting both parties, SNAPs always have to win and make someone else lose. Therefore, they will always try to put the other side in a position without leverage, and then take advantage of the other side's lack of leverage. Even after an agreement has been struck, they will try to weasel out of it.

Hilary: During our child support and parenting negotiations, Stan was completely irrational. He wouldn't agree to anything. He eventually stopped paying, and I was forced to hire lawyers. Whenever I tried to come to some agreement on child support and visitation, he reminded me that to him it was all about winning, all about not paying me anything, not about doing what was best for our kids. "This is going to go on for eighteen to twenty-one years. You're going to lose. I'm going to make sure of it. I'm a f*cking winner. You're going to lose. I'm a winner and I'm going to win. You're easy to win on. I'm going to win over this. I've won a lot of other things, believe me. You're going to be on welfare. He's going to be on welfare. You have to go get a waitressing job. You need to go wait on tables."

Charlotte: Tim fancied himself a shrewd businessman. Whether it was for a multi-million-dollar deal or buying a car for one of his kids, he nickeled and dimed everyone to death, but complained when others did the same to him. When he saw that someone was in a difficult situation and had little leverage to negotiate, he took advantage of the situation. As one of his former employees said of him, "Why kick a man when he's down when he can run over him with a steamroller? That's Tim's way." A banker who found out we were divorced unloaded several stories of their negotiations. After a deal had been struck, Tim always wanted more. He would brag that he could make a million dollars by simply drafting an agreement after a deal was already agreed to. At closing, he would demand even the $150 fees, which he could well afford, be waived on a million-dollar loan. It was a game to him to see how much he would get at closing.

Treating His Marriage as an Employer-Employee Arrangement

A SNAP will always view his marriage as a relationship in which his wife serves him and meets his needs. Like a sun around which all other lesser planets orbit, the SNAP views himself as the primary person in the family around whom all the other family members must circle. It is an employer-employee relationship, or a master-domestic servant relationship, not an equal partnership. As the employer in the relationship, the SNAP feels that he is entitled to all the money, power, and decision-making. He views their possessions acquired during the marriage as all belonging to him. If the wife works outside the home, he views her paycheck as something he owns. He views the wife, the employee in the relationship, as existing to serve his needs, increase his net worth, and take care of his home and his children. Although he calls her a wife because that gives him an air of respectability in civilized society, make no mistake, she is treated as an employee at best, or more typically, as a personal prostitute and domestic servant.

Charlotte: Even our marriage was a negotiation for Tim. He had been planning a prenuptial agreement for months with his attorneys. To ensure that I would sign his one-sided agreement, he made sure I had no leverage by sweetly telling me to quit my job as a small publishing house executive so that I could travel with him and so that I could be with the children whom we hoped to have, and also because we wouldn't need the money I was making. It was a fraud. After I had resigned, hired my replacement, and sent out the wedding invitations, and after my five-year-old son started calling him "Dad," he foisted his prenuptial agreement on me and said he would never see me again if I didn't sign it. We signed it on my birthday, the day before the wedding. It was essentially an employment agreement and preplanned divorce. It provided that everything he earned and everything he bought was his individual property, not marital property. He did not have to consult me for anything; he had no responsibility for my son, whom he had known since he was twelve months old. It further provided that when the marriage ended, I was required to move out of his house and, "immediately" after I moved out, he was required to pay a lump sum so that I could purchase another house for myself and the children, and he was required to pay a sum for every year we were married. I was crying so uncontrollably that my attorney took me out of the room while Tim joked and laughed with his attorneys, completely unconcerned about the distress he was putting on me and our relationship.

He ran our marriage according to the agreement—everything he made was his individual property, not marital property; he made every decision and never consulted me. My name was never on any account. I had no access to what most couples called marital funds. We had no joint assets whatsoever. All the cars and houses were titled in his name. My name wasn't even on the phone account—so I could never even have access to phone records. I later found a letter between his attorneys that he planned to never have any joint assets. He only paid for childcare. I was required to pay for all household expenses—such as groceries, clothes, meals out, school fees, haircuts, health care insurance, and medical expenses for a family of five and a live-in nanny—out of my part-time salary. I had to submit a monthly expense report for reimbursement for large household expenses like furnishing the house (because neither of us came to the marriage with any furnishings)—and he would often take months to reimburse me. If he paid for something he thought was attributable to me, even if it was a five dollar parking ticket or a thirty dollar insurance co-pay, he gave me a monthly expense report and demanded immediate payment. We even signed a nine-page postnuptial agreement to reaffirm the prenuptial agreement.

During our year of counseling when we were separated, I asked him why he always had to make all the decisions and why everything always had to be his way. He responded that no one can run a business with everyone making the decisions; only one person can make all the decisions, and that one person was him. As I had felt all along, he confirmed that he viewed our marriage like a business in which he was the CEO and owner, and I was just an expendable low-level employee with no rights or input.

Keeping Financial Secrets and Lies

A married SNAP will always keep financial secrets from his wife. "After all, it is really my own money, not hers," they tell themselves. "If it wasn't for me, she would have nothing." Wealthy and sophisticated SNAPs will have secret offshore accounts and complicated financial structures that make it difficult to find where they have hidden their assets. SNAPs often insist on having separate accounts and do not put their wife's name on the husband's account to ensure she cannot have access to his money.

A SNAP will use a land trust to hold real estate that he wants to keep hidden from his wife. He will use other forms of trusts or privately owned companies to hold other assets he wants to keep hidden from his wife.

A SNAP who keeps financial secrets will inevitably lie to keep those secrets from his wife. He will give her falsified financial statements or account statements; he will lie about the assets he holds. If discovered, he will lie and state that an asset is for an investment or estate planning or financial planning, when in fact it is being held solely for his benefit, not for the benefit of both spouses.

> Jennie: Armen was a doctor. After he retired, he planned to make large transfers of funds into trusts in the names of the children to reduce our marital estate. When the marital estate was small and there was next to nothing for me, he planned to divorce me. When I heard of his plan, he had

already started making large transfers, and I had little choice but to divorce him before there was nothing left.

Charlotte: Near the end of our marriage, I dug through some files in the basement and public real estate records. What he had been hiding for over twenty years was shocking. I discovered that in 1990, while married to Pat, his first wife, Tim bought a $365,000 property in Lake Forest through a land trust so that the public records would not show that he owned it. He convinced the privately owned company at which he worked as a chief operating officer to give him the loan to buy it so there would be no record of a loan or any money transfer in his bank accounts. He did both transactions so that the asset would be completely secret from her. I also discovered that during their divorce, he lied under oath in a deposition claiming that he did not know who the beneficiary of the trust was that owned the property and surmising that the trust bought it as an "investment." In fact, he was the beneficiary of the trust and he bought the property to build his home, which he later listed for $2.5 million. I found out years after our divorce that, while we were married, Tim's real estate agent sued him for fraud because he bought the property through the land trust and wouldn't pay the realtor's commission. Tim eventually paid, but dragged the realtor through three years of litigation. In 2011, near the end of our marriage, he transferred his house from the land trust to a trust solely in his name, also without my knowledge. He waited for twenty years to transfer it, so the entire time it was hidden from his first wife and from me.

Since he lied to his first wife with whom he had two children, I knew that he would also lie to me. I also discovered that he had fraudulently inflated his financial statements that he had given me with his 1992 prenuptial by millions of dollars. His purported net worth in the statements that he gave me was at least $3 million more than the net worth in his own statements. So it was no surprise when I discovered that he fraudulently deflated his financial statements that he gave me during the divorce by millions of dollars. I found a net worth statement with "Given to Charlotte" handwritten on the front of it that was approximately $2.5 million less than the statements he gave to the bank. He wrote "Given to Charlotte" on the one he gave to me so he wouldn't mix them up with the one he'd given to the bank, and vice versa. So his claimed net worth at the beginning of the marriage was equal to his claimed net worth at the end of the marriage, according to his falsified financial statements. During the divorce he claimed that his own prenuptial agreement was unenforceable and that we should instead follow Illinois divorce law. He further argued that since his net worth at the end of the marriage was approximately the same as his net worth at the beginning of the marriage, and that since he had acquired zero assets during our marriage, I was entitled to half of zero. I was fortunate to be a CPA and an attorney to see through his lies and schemes that he had been preparing for more than twenty years.

Sole Decision Maker, Risky Investments, and Extravagant Purchases

SNAPs not only keep financial secrets from their wives, but they do not consult with them on large expenditures or investments. A SNAP views his money as "his" money and views their marital money as "his" money, and therefore his wife is not entitled to an opinion in how he spends it. He adheres to a "father knows best" mentality, even with spouses of the same age and education level. Because of their enormous ego, pride, and sense of entitlement, SNAPs often go deep into debt on flashy purchases or squander a great deal of money on risky deals and investments without consulting their wives. Their wives are blindsided with the news of a bankruptcy or the loss of millions after it is too late to recover financially.

> Charlotte: Tim's prenuptial agreement stated that he did not need to consult with me about finances or anything else. He entered business transactions without consulting me, and many times, without even informing me. He sold a vacation home, and even sold my motorcycle that he had given me as a birthday present without getting my approval, and then pocketed the money. One day around 2005, he couldn't sleep. When I asked why, he informed me that he had given $2.5 million to his thirty-five-year-old son to help get his second company started. He had also given him more than $30,000 to get his first company started, which quickly failed, and he was giving him about $85,000 a year to support him and his family while his company got started. He ended up supporting him throughout the rest of our marriage and beyond—even though he would only give me an allowance of $28,000 a year to support our family of three children, two adults, and a live-in nanny. Now he claims he cannot pay the required maintenance and division of assets payments because he is too poor—yet he travels the world on luxurious vacations, lives in a six-thousand-square-foot house in Lake Forest, and spends a million dollars a year.

Supporting the First Family While Ignoring the Needs of the Second or Third

Multiple marriages are common among SNAPs. Therefore, many have children from their first wife and from their second and successive wives. Many SNAPs will treat the children of the first wife with favor, while treating the children of the second or successive wives as second class. The older children receive more assets in the will and trusts than the younger ones; the older children receive more expensive gifts. The older children may even be supported well into middle age while the younger children's mother is on an allowance so small that it is impossible to meet all their needs.

On the other hand, some SNAPs ascribe to the "love the one you're with" mentality. They favor their current family and tend to ignore children from previous marriages or relationships. Because the SNAP lacks empathy and is uncaring about how his children perceive the special treatment he gives to some children and not others, and how this negatively affects them, he plays favorites.

> Charlotte: Tim favored his kids from his first marriage over those from our marriage, his second out of three marriages (so far). He gave his eldest son from his first marriage a Georgetown University education, $30,000 or so to start his first company, a Porsche, $2.5 million to start his second company, and approximately $85,000 a year until his son married the president of a film company in 2015. He hosted a wedding for his eldest daughter from his first marriage that cost $80,000—as much as my law school education—and gave her a $50,000 loan for her first home. He promised our youngest, Morton, an allowance of $100 a month during junior high school, but refused to pay him, so I did. He paid only a fraction for our daughter Kristen's law school, even though he could well afford to pay more. She is going to help people with disabilities, a field that makes very little money, yet she was forced to take out large student loans. Danny told me one time, "I feel guilty asking him for any money, but then I remember how much he gives Chaz." And Kristen reminded me that "We all know Dad's favorite is Kira [his oldest daughter]." He included Chaz and Kira in his estate planning for millions of dollars, but he didn't provide for any of the rest of the kids in his will.

FINANCIAL ABUSE

Controlling and Stingy toward Others, While Extravagant for Himself

SNAPs are loath to spend money on their families, even for the basics. They are even less willing to spend money on extras unless there is an element of show to it that makes the SNAP feel important, like private lessons for a star athlete whom the father can brag about to his circle of admirers. They have an unrealistically low expectation of the cost of normal household expenses. At the same time, they are happy to spend money on themselves for designer clothes, shoes, and jewelry, and adult toys such as guns, boats, motorcycles, jet skis, fitness equipment, ATVs, golf memberships, vacation homes, travel, and even private jets.

It is not unusual for the wife and children of a SNAP to purchase their clothes at thrift shops and garage sales while the SNAP shops at Neiman Marcus and travels first class. The spouse, who is often not working or is only working part time, is usually on a strict "allowance" that does not fully cover household expenses, and she frequently has no access to funds except what the SNAP gives her. Even though married, the typical SNAP does not have his wife on his bank or investment accounts. Thus, she must get by on her scant household funds and buy clothes, shoes, and sports equipment for growing children at resale shops and garage sales to give her children a normal life. She often clips coupons at the grocery store and is constantly looking for ways to save, even when living with a millionaire.

Adding to the craziness, some wives are forced to ask for money every time they shop. They then must go through an interrogation process with the SNAP as to why the money is needed and must report back with any change and the itemized bill. This again is a tool to humiliate and control the wife. Many SNAPs will rage at being asked for money and will go into a long tirade about how hard they work, how they are not appreciated, and how the wife is wasting his money. This, of course, makes the spouse reluctant to ask for money. However, to keep the wife in a constant state of fear, the SNAP will also rage when he finds there is no food in the house, no toilet paper to use, and the children have holes in their shoes. It is a no-win situation for the wife, which is exactly what the SNAP wants.

> Tina: Steve was all about the money and his get-rich-quick schemes, like being a millionaire by selling Amway products. He had an MBA from the University of Southern California and a good job with IBM in our early years of marriage, but his attitude got him fired. He bounced around for many years without a steady job, and I ended up buying the clothes for myself and my four kids from thrift stores and garage sales. He demanded to know where I spent every penny, but he would buy himself extravagant toys like ATVs and expensive racing bikes for his bicycle races. When I did buy something new, he made me return it. When my good friend came to visit for a few days and took my children and me to Disneyland and SeaWorld paying for us out of her own pocket, he handed her a $200 invoice and expected her to pay for the groceries that she ate. He finally got a job selling insurance and found that he was good at selling—so good that he became the top producer. After he started making money, he left me for a coworker and got remarried in a lavish wedding on the Queen Mary. But he eventually got fired from that job too. I now sleep on the floor of a one-bedroom apartment so my girls can have the bedroom when they are with me, and he kept the house.

Manipulating Spouse and Her Money

Oftentimes, a SNAP will offer to do something that appears to be beneficial to his romantic partner in order to appear magnanimous. Be careful! SNAPs never do anything out of pure altruism. If an abuser appears to do something nice for his romantic partner, there is always something in it for the SNAP to the detriment of his partner, which the partner doesn't know about—at least not before it's too late. SNAPs are planners, schemers, manipulators, and deceivers. While the romantic partner may go along with the offer thinking it is a gesture of generosity, she will eventually put the pieces of the puzzle together and find out she has been duped into yet another scheme that puts money in the pocket of the SNAP and takes it out of hers. A SNAP's seemingly kind offer is always a trojan horse.

> Ellen: I divorced my second husband of twenty-three years because he was unfaithful. He had received a large settlement because he had started a successful company. Afterward, when I met Rod, he was so charming and sweet that I thought my dreams had come true. He told me he was working a union job and that he was a US citizen, but it was all a lie. I was diagnosed with cancer and had to undergo a double mastectomy. Rod claimed that he could not help me unless we got married, and I was so scared. So I agreed to get married, and five days later I underwent a double mastectomy and then chemo for a year. I was wheelchair-bound for a year. During the entire marriage, he refused to work and demanded money and that I sponsor him for a green card. He refused to even pay for gas for the car, and he demanded that I add him to my bank accounts and put my house in both our names. It was near the end of our eight-year marriage that his true reason for marrying me—to get my money and gain US citizenship, not to help me with my cancer treatments—finally became clear.

Refusing to Fulfill Commitments and Agreements

The SNAP is unwilling to keep any commitment, agreement, or obligation, particularly ones involving the outlay of money at a future date. Just as in their business deals, in which they will only fulfill their obligations if there is a huge penalty enforceable by either a larger business entity that is not afraid to flex its muscles and enforce an agreement, or by a court of law, a SNAP will only fulfill his obligations to his spouse if there is a huge enforceable penalty. Otherwise, all arrangements, agreements, and commitments between a SNAP and his wife, written or otherwise, will be breached by the SNAP. The SNAP will even go so far as to claim that he never agreed to the arrangement or doesn't remember doing so.

> Liz: Repeatedly during and after the divorce, Charlie refused to pay court-ordered payments, even though he inherited more than $1 million from his mother. Finally, the judge put him in jail. It was crazy.

> Julie: Within months of our divorce, I was back in court trying to get child support that had been ordered the previous year. Within the first year, I had at least twelve court appearances.

> Sherrie: Our divorce agreement required me to give a quit claim deed to my ex-husband and required him to refinance the house and take my name off the mortgage. I was always the only one with a steady job, so the mortgage note was in my name alone. Of course, I complied with our agreement, but he never did. So here we are twelve years later with him refusing the pay the mortgage and living in the house for free for two years, the bank foreclosing on the house, and me with my credit being dragged through the mud.

Charlotte: Tim was always the first to get indignant and file a lawsuit whenever someone else breached a contract; however, he refused to honor any agreement with me, written or otherwise. During the marriage, he refused to honor any of our financial agreements, except when it was beneficial to him.

During the divorce, he claimed his own prenuptial agreement was unenforceable and refused to honor it. Even after the divorce was final, he refused to honor the parenting agreement or the divorce agreement. He refused to make payments on time, and he kept custody of the children 100 percent of the time rather than the fifty-fifty agreement. He refused to let me take or even make copies of precious family photos, keeping them hostage until I finally went to court to get them and an order of protection three years later.

After four years, he completely stopped paying maintenance and property settlement payments, claiming poverty. After the divorce, he listed his house for $1 million over the market value, inflated his financial statements, went to the banks and got hundreds of thousands of dollars of loans on his falsified financial statements, spent all the money, and then claimed he had nothing left for me, just as he had planned all along. We are still in court.

Protecting His Money in Marriage and Prenuptial Agreements

Marriage presents a unique opportunity for the SNAP to sink in his claws and exercise complete control over his romantic target. He has used the idealization phase of their relationship to flatter and convince his target that he cares about her. He's chosen her because she possesses all the qualities he lacks. Next to her, he will look better than he really is. Many a woman, after finally divorcing her SNAP, is approached by discerning people, each with their own unflattering story of the SNAP, and each saying something like, "We have always adored you, but we never liked him and could never understand why you were with him. But since we knew you had such a good character, and because you married him, we assumed he must have some good character that you saw in him that we were missing."

Having convinced his target he loves her, they prepare to marry. As the wedding day approaches, the SNAP realizes that in the event of a divorce, she will be entitled to half of his money. Because he views everything he earns, and everything she earns, as his, he must devise a scheme to ensure that he will keep all his money in a divorce. An onerous prenuptial agreement is the perfect way to do that. However, if the bride has an escape route, she might refuse to sign his prenuptial agreement and call off the wedding—which would be very embarrassing to the SNAP. So he must devise a way to stack the leverage so much in his favor that the bride will sign the prenuptial agreement, regardless of how one-sided it is, and marry him. How can he do that? By keeping the prenuptial agreement a secret until the very end, sending out the wedding invitations, and convincing the bride she should resign from her job so that she can plan the wedding, decorate their new home, stay home with the children who will come, and travel the world with the SNAP as they live happily ever after. Who wouldn't love that? And then the day before the wedding, he will insist she sign his unconscionable prenuptial agreement or there will be no wedding. She will be incredibly hurt and betrayed, but, with her back against the wall, she will sign it, and it's a price he is willing to pay to protect his money.

Keep in mind, however, that when the inevitable divorce arrives, even the prenuptial agreement that the SNAP insisted on will now be breached by the SNAP, if it is in his favor to do so, claiming that it is unenforceable, unconscionable, against public policy, or any number of legal arguments to drag his soon-to-be-ex-wife through expensive litigation rather than fulfill the obligations under the very agreement he demanded.

Charlotte: Tim demanded that I sign a prenuptial and postnuptial agreement that would pay me a set amount according to a formula based on the number of years married in the event of a divorce. But during the divorce, he claimed his own agreements were unenforceable, and he tried to argue that I should get nothing. He made this argument because he had falsified his financial statements that he gave me both at the beginning and end of the marriage, and according to the fraudulent financial statements, his net worth was the same at the beginning of the marriage as at the end. So because he fraudulently claimed he had made zero dollars over twenty-one years (even though he was making millions of dollars a year and had a net worth of $22 million at one time), I should get half of zero.

Valuing Money or Addictions over Wife and Family

SNAPs are incapable of truly loving someone else—that is, acting in someone else's best interest. Likewise, they are incapable of true intimacy and of valuing their spouse as a separate and distinct being made in the image of God with wonderful gifts, talents, and attributes all her own. Spouses are replaceable and expendable to SNAPs. Because a SNAP views his spouse only as "useful" to achieve his purposes, one is as good as another. They are interchangeable and disposable. A SNAP might attempt to keep a spouse from divorcing and offer some feigned apologies, not because he loves her, but because he doesn't want to pay her in a divorce or make the effort of finding a replacement. However, once the wife has decided to leave, the wife will be replaced immediately (if he doesn't already have a replacement or two that he has already been seeing), without a second thought.

Many abusers also abuse alcohol or drugs. Before too long, a wife of a SNAP will discover that her husband values his money or his drugs or alcohol more than her and their family. SNAPS are unwilling to give up these addictions, even to save a marriage. Oftentimes, women blame the drugs or alcohol for the abuse; however, abusers are abusive even without their drug of choice.

Kerry: Eight months into our marriage, Patrick's oldest son told me that I had been duped. He explained that his dad was an alcoholic and that he had hidden it from me until we got married. I went to Patrick's family to help me, hoping they would help with an intervention or that one of them could talk to him. No one would help me because they had all tried in the past and had given up on him. None of his friends would help me because they wanted their drinking buddy. "Patrick is so funny and fun to be around when he drinks," they told me.

Lydia: Chuck was a wine collector, and we had thousands of bottles of fine wine. He was also a functional alcoholic and abusive, even when he wasn't drunk. I told him that unless he addressed his drinking, I would seek a divorce. But he chose his drinking over me, and I filed to end a thirty-eight-year marriage.

Charlotte: I used the test that Jesus used on a wealthy young man to see if Tim valued me or his money more. After a year of counseling, during which he claimed to be sorry, we had not made any progress. The counselor said I needed to make him uncomfortable and see his reaction to know what was really going on inside of him. She said this in front of him, and he invited it. So I wrote him a letter asking for specific changes, like seeing a mentor, being more patient, and viewing us as a couple rather than just him in charge and me subservient, and I wrote that he should put his money where his mouth was. I offered to stay in the marriage if he would pay me what he would owe under his own prenuptial agreement if we got divorced. However, he refused to pay me anything. He refused because, if we got divorced, he was already planning to pay me nothing based on his fraudulent financial statements. I knew then that he valued his money more than me or his family. In fact, he didn't value me at all, since after I filed for divorce he told me, "I don't care about you. I don't care about what you think. I don't care about what you feel." I finally understood firsthand what Jesus meant when He said, "It's easier for a camel to go through the eye of a needle than for a rich man to get to heaven." It's an awful feeling when you know that someone you love loves his money more than you.

Borrowing without Repaying; Lending Leads to Indebtedness Forever

Money is all-important to the SNAP. It is an extension of himself. And because a SNAP has no conscience, empathy, or moral compass, he will lie, deceive, and swindle to get or keep money. He will borrow with no intention of repaying, he will enter contracts with no intention of fulfilling his obligation, and he will lie under oath and falsify financial statements. He will cheat on his taxes and even pay off another's debt under the ruse of a favor. In exchange, the debtor is now indebted to him and will never be able to get out from under it.

> Charlotte: Tim's son-in-law made the mistake of borrowing money from him to buy his home. Whenever they got together, Tim held it over his head and reminded him about it. His son-in-law was so happy when he finally paid it off and got free. Tim's son asked him to help fund a start-up company. Tim paid in millions, and what started as a loan turned into ownership of the company. The company never got off the ground, but Chaz could never quit. He was in too deep. His father owned him. Tim called him daily, for hours at a time, to talk about business or berate him for mistakes.

Falsifying Taxes

A SNAP will often falsify tax records, claiming additional reductions or business expenses that are, in fact, personal deductible expenses. At the very least, since he has all the information necessary to complete tax forms and he wants to keep secrets from his wife, he will complete the tax forms without the spouse's input and expect her to sign at the last minute and ask no questions. If the wife is uncomfortable and suggests they file separate tax returns, the SNAP will balk because the tax rate is lower for married filing joint returns than for married filing separate returns.

> Jane: Lew worked at his family's business and was able put through personal expenses to reduce taxes each year. He showed me the tax returns on the day of the deadline and told me to sign them or else. I had no idea what he put in there.

> Sahira: Nadeem wanted to buy a house, and he falsely increased his income for two years on his income taxes so that when the bank asked him for his tax returns, he could qualify for a mortgage. But after he got the loan, he claimed that personal expenses, including rent, utilities, and restaurants, were business expenses to reduce his income and his taxes.

> Hilary: Stan's family owned and managed real estate, so he put everything imaginable through as a business expense, even though it was a personal expense. His hook-up website stated that he made

$300,000–$400,000 per year, and his cash income was far more, but his tax returns reported only $60,000.

Claiming Poverty to Not Pay Child Support and Maintenance

Regardless of the SNAP's financial situation, he views his wealth as all his and all for his benefit, not for his wife or children, and certainly not for his ex-wife and children. Thus, whether the SNAP is a millionaire or a gas station attendant, he will brag about his wealth and assets during a marriage or relationship, but during a divorce or separation, he will claim poverty to avoid paying maintenance and child support and fairly dividing the property.

> Sahira: Nadeem owned a small shop in a kiosk in a mall. He has his master's degree in computer science, but chose to not use his degree, which would have afforded us a nice lifestyle. During the divorce, he reduced the salary he paid himself (as the only employee) to only $800 a month—or $9,600 per year. That amounted to about half of minimum wage, and it was far below the poverty line—all so he could avoid paying child support and maintenance.

> Jane: Since Lew worked in the family business, during the divorce he manipulated his income to avoid paying child support and maintenance.

> Hilary: While we were together, Stan paid me about $5,000 a month to support me and our child. But when we separated, he claimed he only made $5,000 a month and dropped our support to either nothing or $1,000 a month, depending upon how he felt.

> Charlotte: Tim made more than $1 million a year the year before we were married. But the divorce agreement he had with his first wife (that I found years later) only provided for $1,000 a month to support his daughter. So it was no surprise when he refused to pay any child support whatsoever when we divorced.

Refusal to Pay Child Support and Maintenance

Even when an abuser has the means to support his children and pay maintenance, he will often refuse to do so. Oftentimes, the only thing that will provide enough incentive to pay is a court imposing fines, legal fees, or incarceration for refusing to follow court orders. Without a court order, it is nearly impossible to get an abuser to pay anything.

> Hilary: Even though we agreed on court orders for child support, attorney's fees, and psychological evaluation fees, Stan refused to pay as soon as the order was entered. We went back to court several times to enforce the order, and the court found him in contempt. I had to take my children out of their learning center, move out of my house, move back in with my parents, and go on government aid because he tried to financially strangle me and refused to pay what he had agreed to in court.

> Charlotte: Tim was constantly late on his maintenance and payments for our property settlement. He finally refused to make payments altogether, claiming poverty and threatening bankruptcy. I had to take him back to court to enforce the agreement. His moves after the divorce were brilliant.

He married a wealthy widow, provided inflated financial statements to the banks, borrowed hundreds of thousands of dollars on fraudulent financial statements using his houses as collateral, spent all the money, and claimed he had nothing to pay me with. He can now live off his third wife for the rest of his life, knowing that a court won't go after her money. Brilliant.

Sahira: I moved into a domestic violence shelter with our three children, and then moved back in with my parents. Even though Nadeem took international trips, one as long as forty-one days, he refused to pay any child support until we got a court order. Then he kept trying to reduce the child support, claiming he made less than the poverty line. I had three little mouths to feed—yet he didn't care if his own children and their mother starved.

Paying Child Support to Maintain Power

SNAPs rarely pay anything just because it's the right thing to do, but if they do, they will extract a high price. If a SNAP pays child support without a court order, he is doing so to maintain power and control over the mother and child. He will demand to see the child on a moment's notice and make unreasonable demands, then threaten to withdraw all support if the mother doesn't meet his demands. For the SNAP, it's like pulling the strings on a puppet, and they love the game.

Hilary: Before we got the lawyers involved, Stan would pay child support, but it was sporadic, and he refused to follow our parenting agreement. Instead of giving me a monthly visitation schedule as we had agreed, he just called or texted and demanded to see our child on demand. If I was busy with something I couldn't reschedule, he exploded and called me names, and then he complained that he wasn't allowed to see his son. He demanded that I drive more than an hour to drop off our son, then insisted I wait for an hour or so while he played with him and got bored. Then I drove an hour back. He refused to come pick him up. He berated me constantly, saying, "My money gets me things." Since he paid child support, he thought he owned me. During one of his crazy-talking-in-circles incidents, in which I was trying to persuade him to pay child support, he said, "The point is money. Power and money. If you don't give me power, you don't get no money. Got it?"

Using the Court System to Financially Drain the Spouse

SNAPs use the court system to inflict further financial and emotional abuse on their leaving spouse or partner. Emotionally healthy individuals settle matters in reasonable periods of time, respond in a timely manner to requests, follow well-established laws and court orders, and try to avoid expending unnecessary legal fees. SNAPs, on the other hand, will drag matters out to force the leaving spouse or partner to pay additional legal fees and incur additional fees himself. He would rather give his money to lawyers than to his soon-to-be ex-wife, and he often succeeds in doing so. SNAPs will take unreasonable and unsupportable positions, file motions that are not based on facts or the law, lie, refuse to settle and refuse to follow well-established laws or court orders. They tend to hire attorneys who have a similar moral compass, and they play the victim to the judges, who often miss the mass manipulation of the court system. A divorce from an abuser takes significantly longer and costs significantly more than a divorce from a nonabuser.

Liz: During our divorce, Charlie went through four attorneys. He either fired them or they quit. After the fourth one, he represented himself, even though he could well afford an attorney since he had just inherited more than a million dollars from his mother. The judge highly recommended a parenting agreement and marital settlement agreement, which he refused to agree to. So he forced us to go to a week-long trial. During the trial, we had to stop so that he could attend a hearing in the criminal courtroom for violating an order of protection. He dragged the divorce on for more than two years, and we went through more than $100,000 in legal fees. When the divorce was finally over, he appealed and dragged it on for another two years.

Hilary: Stan refused all proposed parenting agreements and child support agreements. We weren't married, so there was no property to divide or maintenance to figure out. He could well afford to support the children since he made more than $300,000 a year and I was a stay-at-home mother. But he dragged the litigation on for over two years. I had two newborn babies, and I was forced to leave my apartment and go on public aid. It was humiliating and awful.

Charlotte: Our divorce could have been over in a few weeks since we had a prenuptial agreement with an easy-to-calculate formula. But he dragged it on for more than a year, after we had already been separated for a year. In the meantime, I was running out of money and in hiding because he had been stalking me and raping me before I left. I was so distraught that I couldn't concentrate, and I drastically cut my hours at work.

Leeching Off His Wife

Abusers will do anything for personal gain, including finding a wealthy or career-minded woman to support them. Because of their extreme arrogance, abusers are often fired from their jobs. If an abuser feels that his career is in jeopardy or he is fired, he will often claim that he has retired or resigned to save face, and then happily live off his wife's earnings. He may even claim maintenance in a divorce, even though he can earn quite a bit more than his wife.

Kerry: When I married Patrick, he was a partner in a successful law firm in downtown Chicago and earned more than $500,000 a year. About four months into the marriage, he came home from work and said that he had left his job and did not want to practice law anymore. After that, he claimed he was looking for a new job, but I found out that he was sleeping till 11:00 a.m., going out for lunch, and never looking for a job. In the summer he would take my boat that I had purchased before we were married out all afternoon. I was working to support Patrick and his four children, whom he had put on my company health-care plan. After all of the verbal, emotional, and physical abuse he inflicted, when I filed for divorce after only fourteen months of marriage, he wanted spousal support during the divorce and maintenance after the divorce. To make everything even harder, I had left my home with only the clothes that could fit in my car. He would not let me have anything else out of our home that was mine unless I paid him $20,000. He tried to turn my family and friends against me, he tried to access my bank account, my investments, and my retirement account that I had before we married, and he tried to sabotage my job. I was a shell of a person trying to keep it all together. He fought me in court for the car, which was in my name, but then left it at the dealership with a huge maintenance bill. It was all about him trying to have control over me.

Financial Abuse

A Word from the Word about Money

Scripture teaches us that how a person handles money is a direct reflection of his character. A SNAP's attitude toward and values concerning money are the opposite of the values of Scripture.

Throughout the Old Testament, the Bible warns that once a person, particularly one in leadership, achieves success and money, he often becomes prideful. Pride is the root of abuse.

More than one hundred times, Proverbs discusses money and greed. These verses are directly applicable to SNAPs. Indeed, it is quite likely that the proverbs were written to describe the writer's observations of SNAPs and their money. For example:

> Greed brings grief to the whole family, but those who hate bribes will live. (Proverbs 15:27 NLT)

> Don't rob the poor just because you can, or exploit the needy in court. For the Lord is their defender. He will ruin anyone who ruins them. (Proverbs 22:22–23 NLT)

> There is treasure in the house of the godly, but the earnings of the wicked bring trouble. (Proverbs 15:6 NLT)

Jesus had more to say about money than any other subject. In the Sermon on the Mount, Jesus instructed His followers to treasure the eternal things that God treasures—people, relationships, love, joy, peace, and serving God and others—not money or possessions that will pass away.

> Do not store up for yourselves treasures on earth, where moths and vermin destroy, and where thieves break in and steal. But store up for yourselves treasures in heaven, where moths and vermin do not destroy, and where thieves do not break in and steal. For where your treasure is, there your heart will be also. (Matthew 6:19–21)

Jesus warns us that whatever we treasure—money or people—and where we keep our treasure—earth or heaven—is where our heart will be. Those who value money instead of people, as SNAPs do, will always act in their nature, and will not please God or make it to heaven. Their hearts and their loyalty are attached to their money, not to their families, spouses, or others.

Jesus clearly states that one cannot love both God and money. They are opposites:

> "No servant can serve two masters. Either you will hate the one and love the other, or you will be devoted to the one and despise the other. You cannot serve both God and money." The Pharisees, who loved money, heard all this and were sneering at Jesus. He said to them, "You are the ones who justify yourselves in the eyes of others, but God knows your hearts. What people highly value is detestable in God's sight." (Luke 16:13–15)

A person who loves money, as SNAPs do, does not love God or walk in His ways. He is an enemy of God and all that God stands for.

Jesus calls greed evil: "What comes out of a person is what defiles them. For it is from within, out of a person's heart, that evil thoughts come—sexual immorality, theft, murder, adultery, greed, malice, deceit, lewdness, envy, slander, arrogance and folly. All these evils come from inside and defile a person" (Mark 7:20–23).

Jesus knew how to get to the heart of the matter. To determine whether a person loved Him and was committed to Him, as he professed, Jesus asked a rich young man to part with his money and follow Him. The result should not surprise any of us:

> As Jesus was starting out on his way to Jerusalem, a man came running up to him, knelt down, and asked, "Good Teacher, what must I do to inherit eternal life?"
>
> "Why do you call me good?" Jesus asked. "Only God is truly good. But to answer your question, you know the commandments: 'You must not murder. You must not commit adultery. You must not steal. You must not testify falsely. You must not cheat anyone. Honor your father and mother.'"
>
> "Teacher," the man replied, "I've obeyed all these commandments since I was young."
>
> Looking at the man, Jesus felt genuine love for him. "There is still one thing you haven't done," he told him. "Go and sell all your possessions and give the money to the poor, and you will have treasure in heaven. Then come, follow me."
>
> At this the man's face fell, and he went away sad, for he had many possessions.
>
> Jesus looked around and said to his disciples, "How hard it is for the rich to enter the Kingdom of God!" This amazed them.
>
> But Jesus said again, "Dear children, it is very hard to enter the Kingdom of God. In fact, it is easier for a camel to go through the eye of a needle than for a rich person to enter the Kingdom of God!" (Mark 10:17–25 NLT)

Jesus's example is instructive. If a woman wants to know whether her spouse or boyfriend or fiancé truly loves her, she can ask him to show it by parting with his money. If he loves her, he will do so gladly, and will consider it a bargain. If he balks, he likely loves his money more than his partner.

God is so adamant about greed—that is, the love of money—that He calls it "idolatry." God equates the love of money with worshipping other gods instead of Him. It is a sin to be taken seriously. Scripture is also clear that a person who worships money over God is not one of God's people and will not enter the kingdom of God (heaven):

> For of this you can be sure: No immoral, impure or greedy person—such a person is an idolater—has any inheritance in the kingdom of Christ and of God. (Ephesians 5:5)

> Put to death, therefore, whatever belongs to your earthly nature: sexual immorality, impurity, lust, evil desires and greed, which is idolatry. (Colossians 3:5)

Chapter 10

Sexual Abuse

One of the most destructive forms of abuse is sexual abuse. Sexual abuse assaults the victim's soul as well as their body. An act that should be good, loving, and life-giving between two people who love each other is perverted into an act that is hateful, degrading, dehumanizing, and evil. Sexual abuse and rape have for centuries been used to destroy and humiliate women in war, in sex trafficking, and in homes, businesses, and governments.

Sex in Healthy Relationships

In a healthy marriage relationship, a man and a woman express love for each other through a variety of ways. They affirm one another through words that encourage and build the other up. They perform acts of service such as vacuuming or taking out the trash without being asked, giving thoughtful gifts, physical touch such as hugs or backrubs, and spending quality time together. One of the unique ways that a husband and wife express love for each other is also sexual intimacy. In a healthy relationship, sexual intimacy is reserved only for the couple, not with anyone else. While some affectionate expressions can be shared with others outside the couple—an encouraging word or small gift, for example—sexual intimacy is uniquely designed for a mature couple to express love within their relationship. In healthy marriages, sexual intimacy is a way for a couple to bless each other emotionally, physically, and sexually. A healthy sexual relationship requires mutual vulnerability, openness, generosity, respect, and most importantly, love for the other. There is no place for selfishness, contempt, immediate selfish gratification, or objectification in a loving, sexual relationship.

In a healthy relationship, neither partner demands sex, but respectfully and lovingly makes a request for sexual intimacy when the time is appropriate. "If it's not good for both, it's not good for either" is a good maxim to follow. Each partner is respectful of the other's time, emotional and physical state, and circumstances when requesting sexual relations. If one person is on the way out the door for an important interview for which they must prepare, it is not loving to demand sex. Nor is it loving to demand sex if one person is emotionally upset or distracted, physically ill, or if the dog just died.

In healthy relationships, a husband and wife enjoy sexual intimacy frequently (the national average is 66.3 times each year)[60] and in ways that both enjoy. If both husband and wife enjoy a sexual act, there is no reason to stop. However, if one is uncomfortable with a sexual request, it should be avoided. Clearly, if a wife is requesting that the husband stop an action, or objects to an action, or states that an action is painful, or is crying or in distress, the concerned husband immediately stops and comforts his wife.

Sex with the Narcissist/Sociopath/Psychopath

Like everything else in life, the SNAP uses sex for his personal gain to the detriment of others. Because the SNAP has no empathy and no conscience, he is incapable of the emotional intimacy needed for true sexual intimacy. To a SNAP, a sexual partner is something to be used and taken for his own sexual gratification whenever and wherever and with whomever he chooses. He does not view sex as a way to connect spiritually and emotionally with his wife or significant other. Rather than an act of love and a way to bless her and make her feel valued and loved, the sex act satisfies the SNAP's sexual urges. Women who are sexually inexperienced or who have religious beliefs that teach they must submit sexually to their husband often do not recognize sexual abuse.[61] Below we will look at some of the more common forms of sexual abuse.

Although sexual abuse is prevalent in nearly every abusive relationship, this form of abuse is particularly devastating for women. Rape, perhaps the most egregious form of sexual abuse, occurs in 68 percent of abusive relationships, and 80 percent of women who are raped by their partner or husband are raped multiple times.[62] Approximately half the victims of marital rape are also forced by their husband to submit to anal sex.[63] Partner or marital rape understandably causes significant mental and physical health issues in the victims, including more PTSD symptoms, pregnancies, sexually transmitted diseases, alcohol and substance use, and attempted suicides. Women of faith are more likely to accept sexual abuse and marital rape because they fear their husbands will divorce them or have affairs, or that they will be labeled a sinner.[64] Wives rarely report marital rape to the police. To add to the tragedy, almost 90 percent of the children of partner or marital rape victims see their mother being raped, which causes severe mental and physical health problems in the traumatized children.[65]

Sexual Infidelity

Even though almost every marriage vow includes a promise of sexual fidelity to one's partner, SNAPs feel no moral obligation of sexual fidelity, whether married or not. A SNAP looks upon a potential sexual partner as a conquest, something to be won over and conquered. The idealization phase of any romantic relationship with a SNAP involves over-the-top gestures of romance, "love-bombing," to win over his target. Because SNAPs must always win at everything they attempt, the target has little chance for resistance or escape as his efforts increase

---

[60] Tom W. Smith, "American Sexual Behavior: Trends, Socio-Demographic Differences and Risk Behavior," (National Opinion Research Center, University of Chicago, GSS Topical Report No. 25, March 2006), 65, https://www.norc.org/PDFs/Publications/AmericanSexualBehavior2006.pdf.
[61] "21 Amazing Spousal Rape Statistics," Health Research Funding, https://healthresearchfunding.org/21-spousal-rape-statistics/.
[62] Lauren Taylor and Nicole Gaskin-Laniyan, "Sexual Assault in Abusive Relationships," NIJ Journal, Issue 256, Jan. 2007, https://nij.ojp.gov/topics/articles/sexual-assault-abusive-relationships.
[63] "21 Amazing Spousal Rape Statistics," Health Research Funding.
[64] "21 Amazing Spousal Rape Statistics," Health Research Funding.
[65] "Sexual Assault in Abusive Relationships," NIJ Journal, Issue 256

until he wins her over. However, much like a hunter will hunt for sport and display his trophies, once a woman is conquered, a SNAP will put the trophy on the shelf—the beginning of the devaluation phase.

If the SNAP is married, he will keep his wife following the adage, "It's cheaper to keep her," while he pursues others in the same way he pursued her. The wife, who is often unaware of his philandering, will be left wondering why the romance is suddenly gone, what she did to cause it, and how to get the romance back. In fact, she did nothing to cause it, and there is little she can do to get it back. It is simply the way SNAPs work. Once they have won, they get bored with their prize, need more entertainment, and are on to the next conquest. If she makes hints that she may be leaving the relationship due to his affairs, he may make what appear to be Herculean efforts to win her back. A SNAP hates to lose, and a wife dumping him would clearly be perceived as a loss. However, if he does succeed and she remains in the relationship, these efforts will be short-lived once he feels comfortable that she is under his control again. On the other hand, if she threatens to leave, he may react by dumping his wife since he will already have a replacement waiting in the wings. Either way, he will blame the divorce on his wife, assassinate her character to friends and family, play the poor abandoned victim, and usually win in the court of public opinion.

Demanding Sex in Exchange for Money

Some abusers use their financial control over their wife to demand sex as a condition for giving them money for both necessities and extras.

> Darci: My husband was a pastor. You would think that he would have a healthy idea about sex. But since I stayed home as the pastor's wife, he had all the control over our finances. Any time I wanted to get groceries or fill up the car with gas, I would have to perform sexual acts for him to give me grocery or gas money. It was so humiliating.

Aggressive Sex

Rather than the tender and sweet sexual intimacy that occurs when a husband and wife truly adore and value the other, SNAPs demand sex when they want and approach it aggressively and roughly, almost like a wrestling match. To them, sexual conquest gives them the sense of power and control over another human being that they crave. It is even more powerful when they can force the other person to have sex after they have yelled at them or verbally abused them, because it reinforces that they are in complete control of the other person, even when they are mean and degrading. Unlike healthy couples, it is normal for a SNAP to yell at their spouse and then demand sex, or to have sex and then yell at them because they didn't finish the laundry.

Sex with a SNAP is often rough, cruel, and degrading to the female partner. It can often result in tearing and bleeding in the vaginal area, bite marks and bruising, bleeding from the cervix, or other injuries.

> Charlotte: Sex was never tender and sweet. I felt like an animal being attacked or a personal prostitute for Tim. We would have sex, and within minutes he was yelling at me because he wanted me to do something—do the laundry, put a suitcase back, make dinner, etc. He never called me endearing names like *sweetheart* or *darling*—he only called me c**t or p***y and then pounced. Many times, it was so rough that I was bleeding, but I was too afraid to tell him.

Sexual Deviancy

Almost all SNAPs practice sexual deviancy, some to the point of criminality. Sexual deviancy is a mental disorder with an obsession for socially proscribed practices characterized by recurrent sexual urges, sexually arousing fantasies or behavior involving use of a nonhuman subject, or the suffering or humiliation of oneself or one's partner, children, or other nonconsenting parties.[66] A SNAP may practice multiple forms of sexual deviancy and force his partner to do the same, despite her protests. If she objects, the SNAP will force her to comply, hound her relentlessly until she complies, or threaten her with divorce, affairs, or anything else that he knows will destroy her to make her comply.

> Linda: My church-going husband had affairs and saw prostitutes for our entire thirty-year marriage. I had no idea. He kept it well hidden. This, coupled with all the other abuses, was the final straw.

> Joan: In 2016, my husband seemed to go crazy. He bought and sold five cars, he bought numerous cells phone thinking that he was being recorded, he worked all day and drove an Uber all night, and he took heroin in front of the kids. And then I found out he saw prostitutes too. When I left with the kids, he threatened suicide. Oh, and did I mention he goes to church?

> Charlotte: Tim needed crazier and crazier things to get aroused. I dreaded sex, but he became enraged when I protested. He demanded anal sex, which was excruciatingly painful and damaging. He got the family dog involved by holding me down, putting peanut butter on my genitals, and forcing the dog to lick it off. Whenever he demanded oral sex, he refused to take a shower just to humiliate me, and I ended up with dried urine and dried feces in my mouth. I literally had to wash my mouth out with soap.

Risky Sex

Those without conscience, which describes all SNAPs, seem to be inherently bored with life because they lack the love and emotional attachments that make life meaningful for healthy humans with a conscience. Accordingly, SNAPs engage in risky behavior of all types to entertain themselves and alleviate their boredom. In the sexual realm, SNAPs engage in risky sex—or at least sex that is risky for their partners. Risky sex might include unprotected sex with multiple partners, sex in public places where he might get caught, or even sex in one's own home at times or places where one might get caught by another member of the household, such as a party, right before company is due to arrive, or outside on the patio. As the SNAP becomes accustomed to or bored with the risky sex, his need for excitement drives him to engage in riskier and riskier behaviors.

---

[66] *DSM-5*, 685–705. Sexual deviancy includes bestiality (sexual arousal by having sex with an animal or watching a partner have sex with an animal); exhibitionism (exposing the genitals or an act of sex to an nonconsenting person to achieve sexual excitement); fetishism (sexual arousal using an inanimate object, or using the object to assist in masturbation); sexual masochism (sexual arousal caused by humiliation or pain to oneself); sexual sadism (sexual arousal caused by humiliation or pain inflicted on one's partner); frotteurism (sexual arousal by rubbing one's genitals against another without their consent); voyeurism (sexual arousal by watching other nonconsenting people undress or engage in sex); urolagnia (sexual arousal by urinating or watching someone else urinate); coprophilia (sexual arousal from feces and defecation); obscene phone calls (engaging in sexually explicit phone conversations without consent and masturbating); sexting (sending photographs of one's genitals by texts or emails); and pedophilia (sex with children). Although not listed in the *DSM-5*, sexual deviancy includes sex with multiple partners, sex with prostitutes, pornography addiction, and other sexual behavior that is considered outside the boundaries of normal, healthy sexual behavior.

Charlotte: I guess it was more exciting to Tim if it was risky sex. He would demand sex outside on the patio or the deck where we might get caught. We did get caught on occasion—how embarrassing. One time, on a fly-fishing trip with a guide, he demanded sex right there on the side of the river. At least he went behind a boulder, but really—how utterly humiliating. He thought it was great.

Pornography

Heavy pornography usage and addiction is so universal among SNAPs that it deserves its own mention. While not all pornography users are SNAPs, it is safe to say that all male SNAPs are avid pornography users. While some experts do not consider pornography an official form of sexual deviancy, it nevertheless is extremely damaging to a healthy, emotionally and sexually intimate marriage or relationship. With pornography, the viewer has sex with the object of the film or photograph in his mind and masturbates until he has reached an orgasm with her. The porn star is simply an object to satisfy his sexual urges. And because SNAPs are incapable of emotionally and sexually intimate relationships, sex is not seen as something that requires intimacy to be performed. For the SNAP, the sex act is separate from any emotional intimacy. It does not even require a partner—a pornographic movie or photograph will do fine.

However, research shows heavy pornography use destroys a healthy romantic relationship.[67] In traditional relationships, sex is a physical manifestation of the love, kindness, and emotional intimacy a couple shares. The couple enjoys physical intimacy and accepts the other's physical imperfections because of their emotional intimacy and their shared love and acceptance of each other's imperfections. However, when a person is involved with pornography, the brain is chemically rewired, forming strong neuronal pathways[68] so that normal physical intimate relationships are no longer exciting or satisfying, and the pornography user needs more deviant behavior to arouse him.[69] As time goes on, the pornography user needs more and more deviancy to bring him to climax, and thus the sexual deviancy demanded by the SNAP escalates to bizarre and sometimes dangerous levels.[70]

Ironically, pornography addiction and the masturbation that goes with it often lead to erectile dysfunction. Pornography-induced erectile dysfunction (PIED) is common among even young men in their twenties. Behavioral addiction research shows that heavy pornography users numb the brain's normal response to pleasure by overriding the natural limits of human libido with intense stimulation.[71] The intense stimulation of frequent masturbation and internet erotica causes the brain to become desensitized to the neurochemical dopamine, which is produced by the body by things that are rewarding (including sex and watching pornography), novel (such as various forms of sexual deviancy), surprising (such as unusual sexual acts found in pornography), and even anxiety-producing (for example, watching pornography or having illicit sex in a forbidden place with the potential of being caught). Dopamine is the culprit behind motivation, wanting, and all addictions, as it drives the search for rewards. Dopamine causes sexual arousal, which in turn activates a male's erection through a

---

[67] "How Porn Kills Love," Fight the New Drug, May 4, 2017, https://fightthenewdrug.org/how-porn-kills-love/.
[68] "How Porn Changes the Brain," Fight the New Drug, August 23, 2017, https://fightthenewdrug.org/how-porn-changes-the-brain/.
[69] "Why Consuming Porn Is an Escalating Behavior," Fight the New Drug, August 23, 2017, https://fightthenewdrug.org/why-consuming-porn-is-an-escalating-behavior/.
[70] "How Porn Affects Sexual Tastes," Fight the New Drug, August 23, 2017, https://fightthenewdrug.org/how-porn-affects-sexual-tastes/.
[71] Marnia Robinson, "Porn-Induced Sexual Dysfunction Is a Growing Problem," *Psychology Today*, July 11, 2011, www.drjudithreisman.com/archives/2011/10/porn-induced_se.html.

steady stream of nerve impulses sent to the genitalia. Too much dopamine, driven by pornography addiction, decreases the brain's ability to respond to normal levels of dopamine (i.e., desensitization) that occur in normal sexual relations. Unlike the *Playboy* readers of old, today's internet pornography addicts can view sex videos of sexual acts in multiple screens 24/7, fast forward or rewind to the most erotic portions, have live sex-chats, view deviant sexual acts, and watch escalating, extremely dangerous, and anxiety-producing sexual images, causing the constant release of ever-increasing amounts of dopamine. Normal sexual encounters with real women, producing normal levels of dopamine, are unable to arouse the habitual pornography user. Thus, the man needs increasing levels of dopamine, and therefore increasing levels of pornography, deviant sexual behavior, and illicit sexual encounters, to get an arousal.

As a result, SNAPs will often prefer pornography and masturbation to sex with their partner. They may demand their partners watch pornography with them while they masturbate, demand escalating deviant sexual behavior often mimicking the deviant or violent sexual acts seen in internet pornography, and demand multiple sexual partners. Again, for the SNAP, the goal of sex is not to show love or to enhance intimacy since the SNAP is incapable of intimacy. The goal of sex for the SNAP is simply their own gratification. Period.

Even more frightening is the fact that the majority of pornography shows physical and verbal violence against women, who were either neutral to the abuse or responded with pleasure. This has a profound effect on the men who watch porn, as these violent acts become normalized for them. Consumers of porn are more likely to have attitudes that support aggression against women and girls, are more likely to use verbal coercion, drugs, and alcohol to coerce people into sex, and are more likely to commit violent assault.[72] Porn shapes the way that men see women and has turned the bodies of women and girls into commodities to be used, not gifts made in the image of God to be treasured. As one psychotherapist has observed, ten years into her practice, she had not treated one case of sexual violence that had not involved pornography.[73]

Pornography has a profoundly detrimental effect on a marriage or committed relationship. Marriage experts Drs. John and Julie Gottman put it clearly: "Pornography poses a serious threat to couple intimacy and relationship harmony."[74] The SNAP's wife or partner feels unworthy, unloved, dirty, humiliated, degraded, dehumanized, and used. She feels that way because her abuser has treated her that way.

For porn-induced erectile dysfunction, even prescription drugs such as Viagra and Cialis may be ineffective. Sexual-enhancement drugs work by inhibiting the breakdown of cGMP,[75] a blood vessel dilator that is the on/off switch for engorgement and erection in the penis. The more cGMP, the longer the erection. By inhibiting the natural breakdown of cGMP, thus allowing it to accumulate in the penis, the drugs allow for an erection and increase its duration. Sexual enhancement drugs work well in men when normal sexual arousal causes a normal increase in dopamine levels, but, because of age, erectile dysfunction is caused by cardiovascular conditions or diabetes. However, for men with pornography-induced erectile dysfunction, the problem is not the blood ves-

---

[72] "How Consuming Porn Can Lead to Violence," Fight the New Drug, www.fightthenewdrug.org.
[73] Dr. Mary Anne Layden, director of Sexual Trauma and Psychopathology Program at University of Pennsylvania; Jonathon Van Maren, "Feminism's Self-Defeating About-Face on Porn," January 25, 2015, https://www.lifesitenews.com/blogs/fighting-porn-isnt-anti-sex-its-profoundly-pro-sex-and-pro-woman.
[74] John and Julie Gottman, "An Open Letter on Porn," April 5, 2016, https://www.gottman.com/blog/an-open-letter-on-porn/.
[75] (cyclic guanosine monophosphate)

sels and nerves in the penis, but the inability for normal sexual arousal because of the desensitization to normal dopamine levels.[76]

> Charlotte: Tim started using porn when our daughter Kristen was born. He quickly became addicted. When porn became available on the internet, he watched it regularly. One day I was looking up something for a college search on his computer and accidentally pushed a button that showed his top ten websites. Six of them were porn. It got to a point where he needed porn to get aroused or have sex. The girls in the porn movies were younger than his own daughters; it was disgusting. Finally, he preferred porn and masturbating to me.

Sex Videos and Illicit Photographs

To complete the humiliation, some abusers insist on taking videos and photographs of their sex and sexual abuse. This is far more prevalent since the advent of digital cameras and cell phones because abusers no longer need to take film to the local drugstore to develop it.

> Charlotte: In the early 2000s, after the invention of digital cameras and videos, Tim decided he wanted to be his own director in porn movies. I was forced to do all sorts of humiliating things and smile for the camera when doing it. He even took pictures of his own abuse and rape of me, when he tied me with belts to the corners of his four-poster bed and left me for hours, penetrating me whenever he wanted and then leaving again. He took literally hundreds of pictures and videos. It was the ultimate in human degradation.

No Physical Affection Except for Sex

After the initial love-bombing and luring-in phase, many SNAPs will show little or no physical affection except when they want sex. In normal relationships, partners show nonsexual physical affection with hugs, a tender kiss on the forehead, a touch on the shoulder or back, backrubs, foot-rubs, holding hands, snuggling on the couch, cuddling or "spooning" while in bed, etc. These are all physical forms of saying, "I love you. I care about you. I value you."

Humans need physical touch for our well-being. Renowned psychologist Virginia Satir stated, "We need four hugs a day for survival. We need eight hugs a day for maintenance. We need twelve hugs a day for growth."[77] Many of us remember the psychological experiment included in our Psychology 101 textbooks of a group of infant orphans who were given food and clean diapers but were not held or spoken to. The scientists were forced to cut short the experiment because the babies died without human affection.

SNAPs deprive their partner, and often their children, of the physical affection needed to survive and thrive. Because they are hypersexual, they view all physical touch as sexual or foreplay. Tender touches that convey, "I love you. I care about you. I value you" are nonexistent because SNAPs don't love, care about, or value their partners. A SNAP will only engage in these acts when they want sex and need to warm up their partner.

---

[76] Robinson, "Porn-Induced Sexual Dysfunction Is a Growing Problem," 2011.
[77] Virginia Satir and Erica Cirino, "What Are the Benefits of Hugging?" *Healthline*, April 10, 2018, https://www.healthline.com/health/hugging-benefits#5.

> Charlotte: In our marriage, there were never any tender kisses on my forehead or sweet touches just to say, "I care about you." My attempts at nonsexual touching were rebuffed. Near the end, I received no physical touch at all unless he wanted sex. Of course, having no affection was the same thing that he had complained about regarding his first wife. I suspect that he has a twenty- to twenty-five-year shelf life in a relationship before people just want out. His first wife left after knowing him twenty-five years, his employer fired him after twenty-five years, and his second wife left after twenty-five years. The pattern is consistent and predictable.

Shaming His Partner

In addition to making his partner perform degrading, dehumanizing, and humiliating sexual acts for his sexual gratification, a SNAP will use shame and humiliation to verbally belittle his partner before, during, and after sex. He might shame her for her inability to have an orgasm, her inability to please him, her physical flaws, her sexual history, etc. If she shares with her SNAP that she has had no or few sexual partners, he will often claim that no one wanted her and that she is unable to perform. If she shares with her SNAP that she has had sexual partners before him, he will often throw that in her face and call her a whore or slut. If she shares with her SNAP that she was sexually abused as a child or in previous relationships, he will instill great fear in her and claim that she is incapable of pleasing him because she is flawed.

> Tina: Steve shamed me because of my childhood sexual abuse. I could not achieve orgasm, and he was as mean and selfish inside as outside the bedroom. When we got a divorce, he told everyone about my childhood trauma and that the divorce was my fault because I could not sexually please him.

> Linda: Paul always criticized me that my breasts were too small, that my behind was too big, that I wasn't thin enough, etc. After thirty years of that, I still have a hard time thinking of myself as worthy of any romantic relationship.

Shaming His Partner in Front of Others

Not only does the SNAP verbally shame his partner to her face, but he shames her in front of others. Oftentimes this comes in the form of humor or a joke where his partner is the butt of the joke. This is humiliating to the partner, and clearly not honoring. When she protests, he attacks her as being too sensitive, saying, "It was only a joke." For example, he may claim that he "doesn't get any" or "Hope springs eternal" or "Maybe I'll get lucky tonight" to show he is not receiving enough sex. Given that SNAPs are hypersexual, they never have enough sex. He may shame her about her physical sexual attributes—for example, that her bottom is flat or her breasts aren't big enough. In the mind of the SNAP, when he puts others down, he elevates himself. Usually, the unfortunate partner and those hearing these jokes have no idea how to respond to these public attacks, and an awkward silence follows such inappropriate remarks. However, even others' stunned reactions do not stop the SNAP from repeating them as his favorite type of humor.

> Charlotte: Tim would always joke in front of others that he didn't get enough sex, saying things like, "Hope springs eternal." He even joked in front of the kids and other adults. It was embarrassing. No one laughed; there was only awkward silence. No one knew what to do. He just kept doing it.

Sexual Abuse

Demanding Sex at Inconvenient Times

To prove to himself and his partner that he is in complete control and that he does not value his partner, a SNAP will use sex to derail his partner at the most inconvenient times for her. For example, he may demand sex when she is leaving for work, headed to a job interview, taking the kids to a soccer game, or trying to get small children under control. He may demand sex after a distressing major life event such as the death of a parent, the hospitalization of the family dog, or a fire that destroys the family house. He may demand sex when she has been distraught and crying over the loss of a friend or has just been fired from her job.

Rather than agreeing to a time that is mutually convenient, he will claim that sex should be spontaneous and unplanned, which always means: "I want sex when I want it, and I don't care about your obligations because I don't really care about you. I will demand it when it's least convenient for you or when you are emotionally distressed because it gives me a sense of power and control."

> Charlotte: It must have given Tim a sense of power to demand sex when it was inconvenient for me or when I was going through an emotionally or physically difficult time. Since he was fired in 2000, he had plenty of time on his hands. He demanded sex when I was on the way out the door for work in the morning or when I was running around doing errands on weekends for the kids. We had an enormous house fire in 1996, and we had to move out. He was out of the country when it happened, but when he came back, he demanded sex right then and there. It didn't matter that I was the sole caretaker for my elderly parents who then passed. He had no respect for me or the emotional state I was in. He refused to plan a time for sex that was convenient for both of us; he just demanded it whenever the mood hit him.

Sex on Demand

Because sex is only for the SNAPs gratification, not his partner's, a SNAP will generally demand sex when he wants it and refuse to have sex when his partner requests it. When the partner of a SNAP makes a reasonable request for sex or to reserve a mutually convenient time for sexual intimacy in advance, the SNAP will come up with any number of reasons why he cannot: "I'm getting the car washed." "The playoffs are on TV." "I'm having dinner with an associate" (the fourth time that month). "It's too late." "It's too early."

The message the SNAP sends to his partner when he refuses to grant her request for sexual intimacy is, "I, and I alone, determine when we have sex. It is for my gratification, not yours. I don't care about your needs. All these things are more important than you."

Pouting, Brooding, and Threats

When the partner of a SNAP objects to sex or deviant sexual acts when he demands it, there are consequences. The SNAP will often hound his partner like a dog, following her around the house until she acquiesces to his demands. He will often brood, pout, or become distant and hostile until she agrees to sex. Sometimes he will get aggressive and rage until she submits to his demands. He may accuse her of infidelity or not loving him. He may grab her shoulders, wrists, or arms and not let go until she tells him what he wants to hear. He may threaten to have affairs or see a prostitute since she is not doing her wifely duty to him.

Most partners eventually acquiesce to the SNAP's demands just to keep the peace. He will then claim that she agreed to sex. It doesn't really matter to the SNAP how his partner feels as long as his sexual desires are met. Intimacy or emotional connection is not his goal; power, control, and sexual gratification are.

> Charlotte: If I didn't immediately comply with his demands for sex whenever he wanted it, Tim would hound me relentlessly and follow me around the house until I finally gave in and serviced him. And if I objected that the sex was humiliating or unkind, he would yell and threaten, "I can have sex with anyone I want, any time I want, anywhere I want, anyhow I want!" He absolutely felt like he owned me or anyone else he wanted sex with. And, of course, he did have sex with anyone he wanted. He had even bragged about his affairs in his first marriage, and I walked in on him and his girlfriend making out in our family room during our marriage. Given the hundreds of times he had threatened divorce and threatened affairs, the message was clear: have sex when and where and how I demand it, or I am going to have sex with others and divorce you.

Sex as a Weapon

When he is angry or when he feels that he is losing control over his partner, the SNAP uses sex, in many cases rape, to terrify, humiliate, control, and force his partner into submission. The behavior is similar to the way soldiers rape women when they invade another country—terrifying, humiliating, and forcing them into submission. To add to the humiliation and helplessness, soldiers have even been known to rape women in front of their husbands or fathers as they look on helplessly. Because healthy husbands and fathers generally feel a need to protect their wives and daughters, this type of rape is especially cruel and harmful to both the woman and her family, and it causes lifelong psychological damage to the entire family. If a baby is born because of the rape, the baby is a lifelong reminder of the violation.

Likewise, the most vile SNAP will rape his partner in front of her children as they look on helplessly. This constitutes the felony of child sexual exploitation in most states, and by law it must be reported to the Department of Children and Family Services or an equivalent state agency, and also to local police for prosecution. If the victim confronts him with his criminal behavior, he will use the normal tactics to deflect any responsibility. He may deny it ever happened, claim that she consented to have sex in front of her children, minimize the nature of the abuse, attempt to justify his actions, or simply blame it on his partner.

> Maria: My husband Carlos raped me every single day of our marriage, despite the fact that he attended a Catholic church. One day, I refused. Later, when I took a shower, he dragged me out of the shower by my hair and raped me right on the bathroom floor. My seven-year-old son walked in on us. He could tell my humiliation, and he laid a towel over me and left. My husband just kept going. I have nowhere to go, I don't work, and in my culture, divorce is not accepted. He still rapes me every day. I don't even fight it anymore. We are still married.

> Charlotte: In January of 2012, I gave Tim a long letter outlining the many abuses over our nineteen-year marriage and asked him to get counseling. He dismissed the abuses, refused to get counseling, and accused me of having an affair. To show me he was in charge, he raped me every morning after the kids went to school and every night after dinner. I stopped fighting—rape twice a day, every day, was just a given. He also stalked me, came to my work office when I wasn't there, tried to go through my papers, phone, and emails, and followed me wherever I went, even when I was at the house. He forced me to have sex when we were on a ski vacation in Jackson Hole and all our kids

were in the same hotel room on the other side of the suite—they yelled, threw a pillow, and told him to stop it. When we were on spring break in Italy in March of 2012, he forced me to have sex when our teenage kids were awake in the bed right next to us in the hotel room and were begging him to stop. One time he grabbed my arm, and I wrestled free and ran down the hotel hallway to where the kids were with some friends. I hoped that he wouldn't follow me and drag me back when so many people were watching. I could not endure the humiliation anymore. When we got back home after vacation, I got an apartment, left with only an overnight bag, and went into hiding. He, of course, lied and told everyone I abandoned him and left because I was having an affair.

Sex and the Female SNAP

Although most SNAPs are men, a small minority are women who, like men, use sex to control their partners. A female SNAP uses her sexuality to lure her partner in to the relationship. She dresses provocatively and promises unending, mind-blowing sex when they officially become "a couple," only to withhold it later after she has secured the relationship with marriage or some other commitment by her partner.

After she has enticed him to a committed relationship, the female SNAP will quickly shift from frequent and intense sexual encounters with her partner to demanding that he be good enough to earn her affections. Sex for a female SNAP is an obligation or a favor. As an obligation, it becomes an infrequent chore that she reluctantly provides in exchange for good behavior. Alternatively, as a favor, if she does agree to have sex with her partner, her attitude is one of "You owe me whatever I want because I let you have sex with me."

Another tactic used by a female SNAP is shaming her partner's normal sexual desires and bodily functions, as well as his sexual performance. When her partner expresses a desire to have sex, she will shame him with comments along the lines of "You're a pervert" or "All you want is sex," or "You're a sex addict." Yet if her partner says he is not in the mood for sex (especially after being ridiculed repeatedly for wanting sex), she will accuse him of infidelity, not loving her, or being unable to perform. When her partner has normal and healthy bodily functions, such as emissions when being aroused, she may shame him and accuse him of premature ejaculation. Likewise, she may shame him, claiming he is unable to satisfy her and is utterly inept in the bedroom.

Just to keep her partner insecure and in the relationship, she may on occasion sprinkle her normal disdain and refusal to have sex with hypersexuality and a sexual performance that a porn star would envy. This keeps her partner in the relationship for just a bit longer, hoping that perhaps she is capable of the intimate, healthy sexual relationship that he longs for. However, like a male SNAP, a female SNAP is incapable of a vulnerable, trustworthy, intimate, empathetic, respectful relationship, which is the hallmark of a healthy sexual relationship.

Thus, a female SNAP primarily uses her sexuality to lure partners into a relationship. Then once her partner has committed to her, she withholds sex, uses sex as consideration in a transaction, shames her partner, and intersperses hypersexuality.

> Dirk: My first wife constantly criticized and belittled me sexually, as well as in every other area of life. Even on our wedding night, I was humiliated. We had a loveless, sexless marriage for years. It wasn't until I married my current wife that I was able to heal from the shame that I had felt for so many years from my first wife's constant criticism. With my current wife, I have a wonderful, loving, tender love life—the love life that I had always dreamed of, and the life that I had always dreamed of. I finally realized that all that criticism and belittling was a lie that I had believed, and another aspect of her overall abuse.

Chapter 11

Spiritual Abuse

SPIRITUAL BELIEFS ARE AT the core of healthy individuals. They are imbedded within us, and it is difficult to separate the rest of ourselves from our spiritual beliefs. Our spiritual beliefs inform our values and attitudes, which in turn inform our behaviors. In the Judeo-Christian tradition, spiritual beliefs rest in an Almighty God who is both loving and just, who is good and hates evil, and who commands His followers to do the same. We humans are made in His image and therefore have inestimable value because we are loved by Him. Because we are made in His image, we should show honor and respect to one another. God commands us to love Him, walk in His ways, and to love others as we love ourselves.

Spiritual Life in Healthy Relationships

Love is a word that is tossed around casually. We love pizza, we love summer days, we love our children, we love our spouse, and we love our dog. Paul, the apostle and author of about half the New Testament, describes love so that we all may know what real love looks like. This passage is read at many weddings:

> If I speak in the tongues of men or of angels, but do not have love, I am only a resounding gong or a clanging cymbal. If I have the gift of prophecy and can fathom all mysteries and all knowledge, and if I have a faith that can move mountains, but do not have love, I am nothing. If I give all I possess to the poor and give over my body to hardship that I may boast, but do not have love, I gain nothing.
>
> Love is patient, love is kind. It does not envy, it does not boast, it is not proud. It does not dishonor others, it is not self-seeking, it is not easily angered, it keeps no record of wrongs. Love does not delight in evil but rejoices with the truth. It always protects, always trusts, always hopes, always perseveres. Love never fails. (1 Corinthians 13:1–8)

Love always acts in the best interest of the one who is loved. We know we are loved if we can substitute our partner's name for the word *love* in the above verses 4–8, and it is true. Likewise, if we cannot say this about our partner, it is a clear indication that, regardless of whether he uses the word *love*, it is not love.

relationship that is unlike any other and must be kept pure and holy. Paul gives husbands a high calling to love their wives with the same sacrificial love with which Jesus loved us. Jesus loved us first, even though we were sinners, and He pursues our hearts. It because of His love, when we accept His love and turn our hearts to Him, we are forgiven and made radiant. We are transformed by His unconditional love and become more like Him—able to love Him and others—not because of a set of rules, but because we love Him and His love lives in our hearts. Jesus went through torture and death for us because of His love for us, and God calls husbands to show the same kind of sacrificial love to their wives.

In courtship, a man's heart is captivated by a woman. Perhaps it is the joy of life she has, the easy way she has with others, the kindness she shows to those around her, the goodness that is in her heart, or the laughter she brings to every situation. People are attracted to one another for a myriad of reasons. In courtship, a suitor finds that he admires a woman for her wonderful qualities, and he decides he wants to spend his life with this amazing person, if he is lucky enough for her to say yes. Typically, a man loves a woman before she loves him—and he seeks her and pursues her heart. She is won over by his love for her. And when a husband loves his wife, even though she is not perfect, his love transforms her and she becomes radiant in his love—and therefore better able to love him back, even though he is not perfect. In return, she is kind to him not because she is following a set of rules, but because his love has captured her heart and she loves him in response. God calls this giving and receiving of transformational love one of His great mysteries, and Paul explains it beautifully in Ephesians 5:25–33:

> Husbands, love your wives, just as Christ loved the church and gave himself up for her to make her holy, cleansing her by the washing with water through the word, and to present her to himself as a radiant church, without stain or wrinkle or any other blemish, but holy and blameless. In this same way, husbands ought to love their wives as their own bodies. He who loves his wife loves himself. After all, no one ever hated their own body, but they feed and care for their body, just as Christ does the church—for we are members of his body. "For this reason a man will leave his father and mother and be united to his wife, and the two will become one flesh." This is a profound mystery—but I am talking about Christ and the church. However, each one of you also must love his wife as he loves himself, and the wife must respect her husband.

The side effect of ennobling his wife and children is a benefit for the husband as well. His whole family is stronger and healthier when he reaches out to them in love.

Paul also describes the nature of God, and our nature if God's Holy Spirit lives in us and leads us:

> But the fruit of the Spirit is love, joy, peace, forbearance, kindness, goodness, faithfulness, gentleness and self-control. Against such things there is no law. Those who belong to Christ Jesus have crucified the flesh with its passions and desires. Since we live by the Spirit, let us keep in step with the Spirit. Let us not become conceited, provoking and envying each other. (Galatians 5:22–26)

Humility and thankfulness are key characteristics of someone who walks in the Holy Spirit:

> Do nothing out of selfish ambition or vain conceit. Rather, in humility value others above yourselves, not looking to your own interests but each of you to the interests of the others. In your relationships with one another, have the same mindset as Christ Jesus. Who, being in very nature God, did not consider equality with God something to be used to his own advantage; rather, he

made himself nothing by taking the very nature of a servant, being made in human likeness. And being found in appearance as a man, he humbled himself by becoming obedient to death—even death on a cross! (Philippians 2:3–8)

Where the conscience is involved, modern psychology is in step with age-old theology: human attachments lead to love, and love leads us to act kindly and in the best interests of others, which, as it turns out, is also in our best interest. In a healthy person, the conscience urges them to do the right and honest thing toward others in general because we are attached by our shared humanness. Our conscience compels us to be particularly kind and generous to those closest to us—our spouses and family—because we are spiritually attached to them, and because of that attachment, we have undertaken an obligation to act in their best interest—that is, to love them. Quite simply, our conscience arises from our human attachments and love for one another.

As imperfect human beings, we will never treat others with perfect love and kindness. However, our conscience alerts us when we hurt someone. We feel bad and empathize with their hurt. When a healthy person hurts another unintentionally with a misplaced word or revealed secret, or even intentionally with a cutting remark or the taking of money that is not his, the offender damages the relationship with the one he has offended. He has wounded her spirit, and he has destroyed her trust in him to act in her best interest and in the best interest of their relationship.

Assuming that the offense is not a serious one, to recover the relationship, heal her spirit, and win back her trust, he must (1) admit his offense to her and any others he might have harmed, (2) apologize for the harm that he has caused without making excuses, blaming others, or justifying his actions, (3) turn away (that is, repent) from such harmful behavior and not repeat it, and (4) do all in his power to make things right. Only after he has done this consistently for a prolonged period does he have any standing to ask for her forgiveness. And only then can he hope for a restored relationship. For most smaller offenses, relationships are restored and forgiveness is offered and gratefully received.

For example, if he has damaged her monetarily, he must admit to his wrong actions, apologize, refrain from repeating this or similar actions, and repay all that she has lost as quickly as he can. If he has revealed a secret and caused a rift in another relationship that she has, he must try to repair the damage.

However, if the offense is serious or is a repeated intentional offense, the wounded party may need to establish healthy boundaries prior to restoring a relationship or trusting her partner again. If the offense is particularly egregious, such as an affair or abuse, this is a grave breach of trust and of the covenant of marriage. The wronged party may wish to consider whether she wants to restore the relationship—which she has no obligation to restore. If she does want to continue the relationship, the offender will need to show by extended good behavior and a changed heart that he is worthy of her trust again.

Spiritual Life in SNAP Relationships

"All disorders involve spiritual problems, because the human being and the wounding of the human being are essentially spiritual in nature."[78]

One of the defining characteristics of abusers—those people with Cluster B personality disorders of narcissism, sociopathy, and psychopathy—is their lack of conscience. They lack human attachments and the healthy

---

[78] John Firman and Ann Gila, *Psychosynthesis: A Psychology of the Spirit* (Albany, NY: State University of New York Press, 2002), 169.

sense of obligation to do the right thing. Therefore, they are unable to act kindly in the best interests of others except when doing so directly benefits themselves. Sadly, because they lack a conscience, they lack the ability to love with the sacrificial love required for healthy human relationships.

A SNAP may use the words "I love you" when speaking to his spouse or lover, but it is not the selfless love that Paul describes in 1 Corinthians 13 or Ephesians 5. Further, most SNAPs are adept at using language they think will get them what they want without meaning it. They understand that women want to hear the "L-word," and so SNAPs use it to lure them into emotional and then financial dependence upon them. It is telling that the first phase of any SNAP romantic relationship is called *love-bombing*. However, looking at the SNAP's abusive actions during the second phase of a SNAP romantic relationship, the devaluation stage, should leave no question that a SNAP's actions do not match up with the SNAP's professions of love. The SNAP's all-out maliciousness during the third and final discard phase of a romantic relationship leave no doubt that the SNAP is devoid of love or even a conscience.

SNAPs do not value others except for how useful they can be to serve the selfish needs of the SNAP. Therefore, their attachments are at best shallow and self-serving. Their attachments, if they can be called that, are more aptly called *arrangements*. They are similar in character to an attachment one would give to a helpful kitchen appliance. As long as the appliance is functioning to their liking, it will be kept with minimal maintenance. Likewise, when people are useful, they will be managed and maintained if it can be done with minimal effort. When a person is no longer useful to the SNAP, they are tossed aside like an old blender. The SNAP feels no obligation to treat a discarded, inoperative blender with any kindness. Similarly, he feels no obligation to treat a discarded spouse with any kindness. They are both useless to him, regardless of their years of service, and they will both be quickly replaced with a newer, more useful model.

SNAPs are incapable of grasping the notion that being kind and acting in the best interests of their spouse is also acting in their own best interests. They do not seem to grasp the idea that in strengthening and exalting their spouse, they are also strengthening and honoring their children, themselves, and their entire family. In their twisted view, the way to happiness is to attain their own selfish desires—power, control, wealth, a high-powered career, influence, social standing, a large home, expensive cars, etc.—regardless of the relational cost to others. They malignantly think that in order to strengthen and lift themselves up, they must put others down—in particular, their spouse. But in doing so, it hurts not only their spouse, but their children and themselves as well. After years of suffering under his tyranny, a wife often chooses to leave the relationship for her own sanity and self-preservation. Likewise, in the business world, SNAPs often have a meteoric rise to the top, but they inevitably come crashing down as years of emotional abuse, sexual harassment, and tyrannical behavior force them out.

Unlike healthy individuals with a well-developed conscience, the SNAP feels no remorse, regret, or repentance when he wounds others. He has no attachment to them, and he feels no pain or empathy when they are wounded. He inflicts spiritual abuse—that is, an attack on another's spirit—with impunity.

Spiritual Abuse

Spiritual abuse occurs when a husband misuses spiritual authority to control his wife. In abusive relationships, it occurs whenever her faith or spirituality is important to the victim. The SNAP who claims to know the Scriptures may use them to inflict further abuse on his spouse to keep her subjugated to his power and continue in the abusive relationship. No doubt, he will take Scripture out of context and will adulterate the actual meaning of Scripture—which in no place condones or allows for abuse. We will look at some of the more common tactics of spiritual abuse and the SNAPs twisted and perverted use of Scripture in the Judeo-Christian culture to keep his partner under his power and control. We will also unpack the truth about what Scripture says.

Claims that He is the "Head of the Household" and His Wife and Children Must Obey

Often a SNAP will claim that God has appointed him the head of the household. He will pervert the Scripture as a reason to rule with an iron fist, demand that his wife and children obey him, and act as an authoritarian tyrant. He will claim that the following biblical passages support his skewed interpretation of Scripture:

> But I would have you know, that the head of every man is Christ; and the head of the woman is the man; and the head of Christ is God. (1 Corinthians 11:3 KJV)

> For the husband is the head of the wife, even as Christ is the head of the church: and he is the saviour of the body. Therefore as the church is subject unto Christ, so let the wives be to their own husbands in everything. (Ephesians 5:23–24 KJV)

> Children, obey your parents in the Lord, for this is right. (Ephesians 6:1)

> Honour thy father and thy mother: that thy days may be long upon the land which the LORD thy God giveth thee. (Exodus 20:12 KJV)

While the SNAP claims that he is the head of his wife and household (thus justifying his abuse), he completely ignores the fact that these same Scriptures hold him to the standard of Christ. Scripture calls a husband to be the Christ figure in his home, with humble, compassionate, healing, giving, patient, kind, forgiving, wise, protective, extravagant, self-sacrificing love to his wife and children. Scripture calls him to put the best interests of his family above his own, just as Christ did for us.

For example, in the same passage in Ephesians, Paul commands:

> Husbands, love your wives, just as Christ loved the church and gave himself up for her to make her holy, cleansing her by the washing with water through the word, and to present her to himself as a radiant church, without stain or wrinkle or any other blemish, but holy and blameless. In this same way, husbands ought to love their wives as their own bodies. He who loves his wife loves himself. After all, no one ever hated their own body, but they feed and care for their body, just as Christ does the church—for we are members of his body. . . . However, each one of you also must love his wife as he loves himself, and the wife must respect her husband. (Ephesians 5:25–30, 33)

Christ was never arrogant, boastful, proud, self-serving, mean-spirited, impatient, unkind, demanding, or abusive in any way. Rather, He was the standard of love to which husbands are called. Christ is nothing like the SNAP, who demands obedience, respect, and loyalty from his family and retaliates in vicious vindictiveness when his demands are not met. Christ loved us so much that He humbled Himself and came down from heaven as a human baby. In His ministry, He healed the sick, raised the dead, cast out demons, gave hope to the hopeless, taught us to love God and love each other, died a sacrificial death on a cross for us, and always gives us the choice to follow Him or not. Because of Christ's love and encouragement, we blossom and flourish into being the person that God intended us to be—a radiant reflection of His glory. It is the same with a husband and wife. A husband's Christlike love and encouragement enables his wife to blossom and flourish into the woman that God intended her to be. She reflects God's glory because of the love of her husband. Their marriage blesses one another, their family, and all who come in contact with them.

Christ came with the legitimate authority of His heavenly Father, yet He was not a tyrant. Conversely, a SNAP is a tyrant and abuser; thus, his self-proclaimed authority is illegitimate. We are not required to obey illegitimate authority that stands in opposition to Christ's authority.

Furthermore, we are called to obey God, not man. When there is a conflict between human demands and God's demands, we are always to choose God's mandates over man's. A typical SNAP will make demands that are against God's specific commands. For example, a SNAP may demand that his wife sign a fraudulent tax form, lie for him, verbally or physically hurt a child because of some perceived slight, or demand illicit sex. Nowhere does Scripture require a wife to obey commands that are contrary to God's.

Claims That the Wife Must Submit to Him and His Every Whim

A SNAP will point to Scriptures to claim that his wife must submit to him, saying this allows him to be a tyrant. As we pointed out above, the SNAP's argument is a perversion of Scripture. The SNAP will typically point to Ephesians 5:22 and 24 to support his claim: "Wives, submit yourselves to your own husbands as you do to the Lord.... Now as the church submits to Christ, so also wives should submit to their husbands in everything."

The SNAP will conveniently omit the previous sentence that begins the discussion of marriage: "Submit to one another out of reverence for Christ" (Ephesians 5:21). He will also leave out Ephesians 5:25–30 and 33 that require him to act Christlike out of love and sacrifice himself for his wife.

Properly interpreted, *submit to* does not mean to act as a doormat, obey mindlessly, or accept abuse. Properly interpreted, *submit* means "defer to." Thus, for marital harmony, both husbands and wives should, in kindness and respect, defer to the reasonable, legitimate needs and requests of others. This is simply common sense. Always demanding our selfish ways rather than both parties deferring to the other leads to a breakdown in relationship.

> Jane: Lew was a fundamentalist, self-proclaimed Christian. He made me homeschool the kids, we couldn't watch TV or movies, he isolated us from others, he forced me to quit my job, and he demanded that I always submit to him sexually and otherwise. It was like a military camp, not a home.

Claims That the Wife Must Satisfy His Sexual Desires Whenever He Wants

A SNAP will point to Scripture to support his claim that his wife must satisfy his sexual desires whenever he wants. He will claim that this gives him permission to demand sex, to the point of rape, regardless of the emotional or physical needs of his wife. This may go on day after day and year after year. The wife is nothing more than a sex slave, held prisoner in her own home, often with no way out. The most egregious cases are like sex trafficking, where a woman is forced to perform sexual acts at knifepoint or gunpoint and has no prospects of escape. A wife is often precluded from leaving because she has children, has been threatened with death or great bodily harm to her or her children, has no access to resources, and has no support group.

Contrary to the claims of the SNAP, the Scriptures never give permission for a man to force himself sexually on his wife or anyone else. The act of physical love should be like all other acts of love—characterized by kindness, patience, not demanding its own way, not selfish, respectful, deferring to the other's needs, compassionate, and caring (see 1 Corinthians 13:4–7). Physical love as contemplated by Scripture is an act of giving, never demanding.

Claims That the Partner Must Forgive and Forget Past Abuses

A SNAP will point to Scripture to support his claim that his partner must "forgive and forget" his abuse. He will then accuse her of being un-Christian or a bad Jew if she doesn't forgive him, forget about the abuse, and return for more abuse. This is, once again, a perversion of the Scriptures.

The SNAP may demand that she forgive him seventy times seven times by quoting Jesus when one of His disciples asked Him how many times he must forgive someone: "Then Peter came to him and asked, 'Sir, how often should I forgive a brother who sins against me? Seven times?' 'No!' Jesus replied, 'seventy times seven!'" (Matthew 18:21–22 TLB). Some translations say seventy-seven times. However, in his efforts to garner forgiveness for something for which he has no regret and in order to get things back to normal (i.e., abusive) with his partner, the SNAP takes this passage out of context.

"Forgiveness" and "repentance" are two of the most misunderstood words in the English language, not to mention in the Scriptures. According to Scripture, God forgives our wrongdoing when we genuinely repent and turn our hearts to Him. God also wants us to forgive others if they genuinely repent of their sins. The verses in Matthew 18 are part of a larger passage discussing repentance and forgiveness among believers.

Jesus said, "If a brother sins against you, go to him privately and confront him with his fault. If he listens and confesses it, you have won back a brother. But if not, then take one or two others with you and go back to him again, proving everything you say by these witnesses. If he still refuses to listen, then take your case to the church, and if the church's verdict favors you, but he won't accept it, then the church should excommunicate him" (Matthew 18:15–17 TLB).

The gospel of Luke recites a similar command and summarizes the passage found in Matthew: "If your brother or sister sins against you, rebuke them; *and if they repent,* forgive them. Even if they sin against you seven times in a day and seven times come back to you saying 'I repent,' you must forgive them" (Luke 17:3–4, emphasis added).

In other words, if a husband sins against his wife, she should rebuke him privately and respectfully. If he truly repents, then she should forgive him. Otherwise, she should go back with one or two others who rebuke him, such as a pastor who understands domestic abuse or a domestic abuse counselor. If the husband truly repents, then she should forgive him. Otherwise, she should approach the church leaders, who should rebuke him. If he truly repents, she should forgive him. Otherwise, the church should excommunicate him.

The emotionally and spiritually healthy husband will repent even before his wife rebukes him for his bad behavior, or at the very least, he will repent when she rebukes him. Unhealthy husbands will repent only after third parties point out that he was in the wrong (thereby discounting his wife's opinion and her hurt feelings). However, abusers rarely repent. They may fake an apology and be on good behavior for a time, but someone with narcissistic personality disorder, sociopathy, or psychopathy is incapable of true repentance. As we've noted previously, they lack a conscience and empathy, which means they don't care if they hurt someone, even if that someone is their spouse. They lack the Holy Spirit, who convicts us of wrongdoing so our hearts turn back to God. Abusers are controlled by Satan and are his evil minions—scheming, deceiving, and doing his bidding. Abusers do not truly repent or truly turn to God.

Abusers can also be found among the clergy. Even they cannot repent or turn to God. They are imposters, using their positions of leadership in the church or synagogue to carry out their own selfish purposes. Like the Pharisees, they are poisonous snakes. Jesus called them out, correctly described their evil hearts, giving rise to evil words and actions, and warned them that they would be accountable to God for their words and actions: "You brood of vipers, how can you who are evil say anything good? For the mouth speaks what the heart is full of. A good man brings good things out of the good stored up in him, and an evil man brings evil things out of the evil stored up in him. But I tell you that everyone will have to give account on the day of judgment for every empty word they have spoken. For by your words you will be acquitted, and by your words you will be condemned" (Matthew 12:34–37).

The word *repent* is mentioned throughout the Old and New Testaments. In the Old Testament Hebrew, two words convey the concept of repentance. The first word, *nahum*, means to lament, to grieve. This word describes the emotions that are aroused when motivated to take a different course of action. The second word, *shub*, expresses a radical change of mind toward sin and implies a conscious moral separation from sin and a decision to forsake it and agree with God. In the New Testament Greek, two words are used that parallel the Hebrew usage. The first word, *metameloma*, means to have feeling or care, concern or regret, that is akin to remorse. The second word, *metanoeo*, means to have another mind, which describes that radical change whereby a sinner turns from the idols of sin and self to God. Putting these together, repentance is the informing and changing of the mind stirring and directing the emotions and attitudes to urge the required change, along with the action of the yielded will in turning away from sin and to God.

In practical terms, in the situation of a husband committing a wrong against his wife, true repentance requires multiple steps. First, repentance involves the husband admitting to his wife and to others that what he did was a serious wrongdoing against God and others. A non-apology apology is not enough (see chapter 7 for "Feigned Apologies and Crocodile Tears"), nor is admitting wrongdoing only to his wife, but refusing to admit his wrongdoing to others. If he refuses to admit his wrongdoing to others, he is engaging in a cover-up. He is hedging his bets so that if he and his wife divorce, he can later spread lies and slander that it was her fault and not his.

Second, repentance involves putting her back in the same position she was in prior to the wrongdoing. For example, if he lied to her, he must tell the truth and put her in a position that she would be in if he had told the truth. If he took her money, he should pay her back plus some. If he has lied about her and her relationships have suffered as a result, he should do everything in his power to restore those relationships and tell the truth.

Third, repentance involves taking responsibility for his actions, not blaming others or circumstances for his abuse. Frustrating things happen that we cannot control, but each person always has the ability and the responsibility to control their response.

Fourth, repentance involves offering sincere regret to her, not just for his wrong behavior, but also for hurting her.

Finally, repentance involves changing his heart and attitude away from wrong and toward God and his wife and ensuring it doesn't happen again.

True repentance results in permanent change, not simply in temporary good behavior until his true nature reemerges. To ensure that someone's purported "repentance" is real, the victim should require each of the above steps and expect his changed behavior and attitude to continue for at least twelve months before accepting that the wrongdoer has truly repented. SNAPs are incapable of true repentance; their pride simply won't let them.

Furthermore, forgiveness does not mean that the victim must forget the wrong, pretend that everything is all right, reconcile with her abuser, or have any type of relationship with the abuser. Forgiveness does not mean that she shouldn't divorce her abuser. Forgiveness does not mean that the victim allows the abuser to escape the law or wriggle out of legal and moral obligations. Forgiveness does not mean that a victim shouldn't testify in a civil or criminal trial against her abuser. Forgiveness does not mean that a victim allows her abuser to keep all the marital assets and forego alimony and child support payments in a divorce. Forgiveness does not mean that the victim should not hold the abuser accountable.

Forgiveness, from a biblical perspective, is giving up one's right for revenge, knowing that God will bring the wrongdoer to justice. In Deuteronomy 32:35–36 God says this of evil: "It is mine to avenge; I will repay. . . . The Lord will vindicate his people." Jesus tells us that "everyone will have to give account on the day of judgment for every empty word they have spoken" (Matthew 12:36). The writer of Romans tells us that "each of us will give an account of ourselves to God" (Romans 14:12). Forgiveness is being free from malice in your dealings with the wrongdoer. Those who believe Scripture know that God will hold everyone accountable for their actions and attitudes and that justice will be done—whether it is in this world or the next. Scripture calls people to leave revenge to God.

Forgiveness is for the benefit of those forgiving, not for the benefit of those who have committed a wrong. Often people who commit wrongs are not repentant. That is certainly the case with abusers. Even so, forgiveness—leaving revenge to God and freeing oneself from malice and hatred toward the abuser—is a benefit to the victim. Otherwise, like a cancer, unforgiveness festers and grows and spreads throughout one's body and mind, making her miserable and negatively affecting everything she does. Victims who hold on to anger and unforgiveness allow evil to have power over them, and they can be overcome with bitterness. Righteous anger at injustice that spurns one on toward doing good deeds and confronting evil is a good thing. Even Jesus had righteous anger. But anger that is caused by conceit or hatred will eat a person up inside and consume them.

American author and spiritual mentor Marianne Williamson put it succinctly: "Unforgiveness is like drinking a poison yourself, and waiting for the other person to die."[79]

That's why Paul tells believers in Ephesians: "'In your anger do not sin': Do not let the sun go down while you are still angry, and do not give the devil a foothold. . . . Be kind and compassionate to one another, forgiving each other, just as in Christ God forgave you" (Ephesians 4:26–27, 32). We also see in Scripture that Christ only forgave those who repented from evil and turned toward God. Therefore, we, too, are called to forgive those who repent.

Abusers make forgiveness difficult because they do so much damage, and because if they cannot own their victim, they go to great lengths to destroy her. Thus, forgiveness is an ongoing process for most victims—a process that can only be done in conjunction with the work of the Holy Spirit.

> Charlotte: Whenever I attempted to deal with our issues, Tim would yell, "The past is the past. You can't dwell on the past!"—even if the instance of abuse was just three minutes old. Of course, since everything was in the past, Tim would never deal with it. He didn't apologize; he just expected the past abuses to be erased from my memory.

---

[79] Marianne Williamson Quotes (n.d.), BrainyQuote.com, retrieved March 18, 2020, https://www.brainyquote.com/quotes/marianne_williamson_635346.

SPIRITUAL ABUSE

Claims That God has Forgiven Him for All Past, Current, and Future Actions

A SNAP may twist Scripture to support his claim that he has been forgiven by God for all his past abuses and that God has forgotten his sins. He may quote Psalm 103:12: "as far as the east is from the west, so far has he removed our transgressions from us." Or he may quote Hebrews 8:12: "For I will forgive their wickedness and will remember their sins no more," or Hebrews 10:17: "Their sins and lawless acts I will remember no more," both of which quote Jeremiah 31:34. He may pervert Scripture to justify his continued wrongdoing, perhaps even claiming that Jesus died once for all our sins, and therefore, all his past, present, and future sins are forgiven if he claims to be a Christian. In support of this argument, he may quote Hebrews 10:14: "For by one sacrifice he has made perfect forever those who are being made holy." He will then use this as a license to keep abusing, because, after all, he reasons that God will forgive him. This reasoning is, again, a perversion of Scripture.

Contrary to what abusers would have their victims believe, Scripture tells us that God only forgives or pardons those who repent and turn to Him. This is found in both the Old and New Testaments. In the Old Testament, the author of Chronicles writes: "If my people, who are called by my name, will humble themselves and pray and seek my face and turn from their wicked ways, then I will hear from heaven, and I will forgive their sin and will heal their land" (2 Chronicles 7:14). And the prophet Isaiah writes: "Seek the Lord while he may be found; call on him while he is near. Let the wicked forsake their ways and the unrighteous their thoughts. Let them turn to the Lord, and he will have mercy on them, and to our God, for he will freely pardon" (Isaiah 55:6–7).

Scripture also tells us that those who do not repent of their evil ways and do not turn toward God are not forgiven by God. "If we deliberately keep on sinning after we have received the knowledge of the truth, no sacrifice for sins is left, but only a fearful expectation of judgment and of raging fire that will consume the enemies of God" (Hebrews 10:26–27). Jesus said, "But unless you repent, you too will all perish" (Luke 13:3). Peter repeated the message of Jesus: "Repent and be baptized, every one of you, in the name of Jesus Christ for the forgiveness of your sins. And you will receive the gift of the Holy Spirit" (Acts 2:38).

Indeed, people who deliberately and repeatedly continue to sin without repentance are called "children of the devil." The disciple John wrote:

> No one who lives in [Jesus] keeps on sinning. No one who continues to sin has either seen him or known him. Dear children, do not let anyone lead you astray. The one who does what is right is righteous, just as he is righteous. The one who does what is sinful is of the devil, because the devil has been sinning from the beginning. The reason the Son of God appeared was to destroy the devil's work. No one who is born of God will continue to sin, because God's seed remains in them; they cannot go on sinning, because they have been born of God. This is how we know who the children of God are and who the children of the devil are: Anyone who does not do what is right is not God's child, nor is anyone who does not love their brother and sister. (1 John 3:6–10)

Of course, this does not mean that only those who are perfect and sinless are called children of God—otherwise, no one would qualify. But it does mean that those who have God's Holy Spirit in them will not choose evil as a habit or lifestyle, nor will they behave in ways that are unloving or unkind to others. This is because God's very nature is not evil, but good. And God requires that we love Him and that we love others. Jesus said, "'Love the Lord your God with all your heart and with all your soul and with all your mind.' This is the first and greatest commandment. ³⁹ And the second is like it: 'Love your neighbor as yourself'" (Matthew 22:37–39). John repeated it: "Dear friends, let us love one another, for love comes from God. Everyone who loves has been born of God and knows God. Whoever does not love does not know God, because God is love" (1 John 4:7–8).

However, those who continue to choose evil and intentionally harm their brother or sister as a regular habit or lifestyle are children of the devil and have the devil's spirit in them. The devil's very nature is evil, not good, and he cannot act otherwise, nor can his people act otherwise. People who continue to choose to be cruel to others, which is the very definition of an abuser, are controlled by Satan, not God.

Further, the Bible stands in stark contrast to an abuser's claim that because they are "saved by grace," they are entitled to keeping sinning since it will all be forgiven. "So what do we do now? Throw ourselves into lives of sin because we are cloaked in grace and don't have to answer to the law? Absolutely not!" (Romans 6:15 VOICE). In other words, grace is no license to sin.

As we discussed above, abusers do not repent or truly turn to God. They continue in their evil cruelty. Therefore, God does not forgive them.

> Charlotte: Tim heard from one of our pastors during our separation that God had forgiven all his sins, even when there was no sign of repentance. It was sloppy theology and what Dietrich Bonhoeffer called "cheap grace." So Tim threw that in my face, demanded forgiveness from me, and demanded that I go back to the marriage. The problem, of course, was that he was completely unrepentant. I am pretty sure that God requires repentance for forgiveness. Even if I did forgive him, I certainly required repentance before I would reconcile. He was never truly repentant, as evidenced by his vindictiveness after I would not go back to an abusive marriage.

Claims That He Should Suffer No Consequences

Along the same lines as the claim that God has forgiven him and that his spouse should forgive him, the SNAP will claim that, because of that forgiveness, he should have no consequences for his bad behavior. Again, this is a perversion of Scripture.

Scripture tells us that while God forgives those who truly repent, those who sin will still suffer the consequences of their wrongdoing, and God still remembers. By way of example, King David used his absolute power to take another man's wife, Bathsheba, for his own pleasure. To be clear, Bathsheba, as a woman and subject to the king, had no say in the matter and was an innocent victim. David then tried to cover up his sexual assault and the resulting pregnancy by having Uriah murdered in battle. Although God forgave King David because David confessed his sin and repented, he still paid dearly for his transgression. The baby who was born as a result of David and Bathsheba's adulterous relationship died (2 Samuel 12:18), one son murdered another son for raping his sister, and then he rebelled against David, took over his kingdom, and slept with his concubines. In addition, all this was written down in Scripture for us all to read 3,000 years later. Suffice to say, sin has serious consequences to both the wrongdoer and innocent parties. God remembers, and people remember, even if the sin is forgiven.

Claims That Divorce Is Not an Option Because God Hates Divorce and It Is a Sin

Many a SNAP may quote the Bible and claim that his victim cannot morally divorce him because God hates divorce and divorce is a sin. To support his claim, the SNAP may quote Malachi 2:16 NLT: "'For I hate divorce!' says the LORD, the God of Israel." The SNAP may also quote the words of Jesus: "I tell you that anyone who divorces his wife, except for sexual immorality, and marries another woman commits adultery" (Matthew 19:9). He may quote Paul: "A wife must not separate from her husband. But if she does, she must remain unmarried or else be reconciled to her husband. And a husband must not divorce his wife. To the rest I say this (I, not the Lord): If any brother has a wife who is not a believer and she is willing to live with him, he must not divorce her. And if a woman has a husband who is not a believer and he is willing to live with her, she must not divorce him" (1 Corinthians 7:10–13).

God, indeed, hates divorce, but not for the reasons the abuser sets forth. God hates divorce because divorce is the result of unrepentant, irreparable sin by a spouse who has made a vow to love, honor, and cherish another spouse. God hates divorce because it permanently damages the spouses, children, grandchildren, and generations to come. God hates divorce because a marriage, first and foremost, is designed to show the world what His love for us looks like, and a marriage resulting in divorce does not reflect that. God hates divorce because He wants us to live in loving, peaceful, joyful homes, and a marriage ending in divorce has not been loving, peaceful, or joyful for quite some time. You see, the divorce is not the sin. The abuse leading to divorce is the sin. For more discussion on divorce, see chapter 34: "What Does the Bible Really Say about Divorce?"

Claims That Everyone Sins and She Should Not Expect Perfection

The SNAP will often claim that everyone sins, including his victim, and that she should not expect perfection from him. The SNAP will quote Romans 3:23 in support of his argument that everyone sins: "For all have sinned and fall short of the glory of God."

While it is true that everyone has committed sin, those whom God calls righteous and are filled with His Holy Spirit do not make a habit of sinning, because God's Spirit leads them to do good, not evil.

> If you are constantly doing what is good, it is because you *are* good, even as he is. But if you keep on sinning, it shows that you belong to Satan, who since he first began to sin has kept steadily at it. But the Son of God came to destroy these works of the devil. The person who has been born into God's family does not make a practice of sinning because now God's life is in him; so he can't keep on sinning, for this new life has been born into him and controls him—he has been *born again.* So now we can tell who is a child of God and who belongs to Satan. Whoever is living a life of sin and doesn't love his brother shows that he is not in God's family; for the message to us from the beginning has been that we should love one another. (1 John 3:7–11 TLB)

Claims That His Sins Are No Worse than Hers Since All Sins Are Equal

The SNAP will often claim that all sins are equal, because if a person commits one sin, they are equally guilty before God. The SNAP will quote James 2:10 in support of his twisted perspective that all sins are created equal: "For whoever keeps the whole law and yet stumbles at just one point is guilty of breaking all of it." The abuser will try to convince his victim that his cruelty and abuse are no worse than her occasional swear word or lack of tithing.

Contrary to the claims of the abuser, there are degrees of sin. While Scripture states that any sin will separate us from a relationship with God (James 2:10), as Eve found out when she ate from the tree that God had expressly commanded them not to eat from, Scripture also clearly shows that some sins are worse than others. Common sense says some sins, such as murder, stealing, violence, emotional cruelty, or fraud generate more harmful consequences for ourselves and others. These more egregious sins also bring more displeasure to God and a serious disruption in our relationship with Him. They also have more serious punishments than other sins.

For example, when Jesus stood before Pontius Pilate, He said, "The one who handed me over to you has the greater sin" (John 19:11 NLT). In a vision, God told Ezekiel to observe the pagan idol that was at the gate of the altar of the temple and the "utterly detestable things" that Israel was doing. Yet plainly stating that some sin is greater than others, God warned Ezekiel that he "will see things that are even more detestable" (Ezekiel 8:6). Jesus warned the religious leaders of the day: "Woe to you, teachers of the law and Pharisees, you hypocrites! You give a tenth of your spices—mint, dill and cumin. But you have neglected the more important matters of the law—justice, mercy and faithfulness" (Matthew 23:23). Clearly, Jesus believed that justice, mercy, and faithfulness were more important than tithing. In the Old Testament, God imposed more serious penalties for more serious sins. For example, if someone obtained property by stealing, fraud, extortion, or deception, he was required to make full restitution plus 20 percent to the owner and make an offering (Leviticus 6:1–5). However, if someone killed another person, he was to be put to death (Numbers 35:30–31). The Old Testament also distinguished unintentional sins, which carried a less severe penalty (Leviticus 4 and 5; Numbers 15:22–28), from intentional sins committed with arrogance and disdain for God's commandments. These called for excommunication from the people of Israel (Numbers 15:30–31).

In the Old Testament, God also makes it a point to say that He puts a vastly higher importance on His people showing loving-kindness and knowing Him as their God than He does on their offerings and sacrifices (Hosea 6:6). God doesn't want our sacrifices and offerings; He wants a broken and repentant heart (Psalm 51:16–17). Rather than offerings, attending temple, and going to religious functions, God wanted His people to "stop doing wrong. Learn to do right; seek justice. Defend the oppressed. Take up the cause of the fatherless; plead the case of the widow" (Isaiah 1:11–17).

In the New Testament, the importance of loving God and others remained paramount. When Jesus was asked what the most important commandment was, He answered, "'Love the Lord your God with all your heart and with all your soul and with all your mind.' This is the first and greatest commandment. And the second is like it: 'Love your neighbor as yourself'" (Matthew 22:36–39). In doing so, He elevated these two commandments, from Deuteronomy 6:5 and Leviticus 19:18, as being more important than any others. Thus, sinning by breaking these commandments is more serious than other sins.

In other words, God doesn't want people to simply sit in church pews pretending to be religious, participate in religious holidays like Christmas and Easter without knowing Him, or make large donations pretending to be pious. More than anything, He wants us to know and love Him as Lord and follow His ways. God calls His followers to be kind to others, to do justice, and to help women and children who are vulnerable. The role of a father in the Old Testament and in current times is to love his wife and children, provide for them, and protect them. When a father and husband is gone, his love, provision, and protection are gone too. Children who have an abusive father are essentially in an even worse position than fatherless orphans because their father is abusing them, not loving, providing for, or protecting them. A wife who has an abusive husband is essentially worse off than a widow because her husband is not fulfilling his God-ordained obligations to her and their family. Yet abusers will attend church and make large donations while continuing to abuse the oppressed, orphans, and widows.

The emotional, physical, sexual, financial, and spiritual abuse that an abuser imposes on his victim are intentional, deliberate, malicious, serious sins. These sins, and the eternal punishment for those who carry them out, are spelled out in several places in the New Testament. The following passage in 2 Timothy is perhaps the best biblical description of SNAPs. The Bible instructs us to have nothing to do with them:

> But mark this: There will be terrible times in the last days. People will be lovers of themselves, lovers of money, boastful, proud, abusive, disobedient to their parents, ungrateful, unholy, without love, unforgiving, slanderous, without self-control, brutal, not lovers of the good, treacherous, rash, conceited, lovers of pleasure rather than lovers of God—having a form of godliness but denying its power. Have nothing to do with such people. They are the kind who worm their way into homes and gain control over gullible women, who are loaded down with sins and are swayed by all kinds of evil desires, always learning but never able to come to a knowledge of the truth. . . . They are men of depraved minds, who, as far as the faith is concerned, are rejected. (2 Timothy 3:1–8)

Paul's letter to the church in Galatia also has a good description of evil people: "The acts of the flesh [evil] are obvious: sexual immorality, impurity and debauchery; idolatry and witchcraft; hatred, discord, jealousy, fits of rage, selfish ambition, dissensions, factions and envy; drunkenness, orgies, and the like. I warn you, as I did before, that those who live like this will not inherit the kingdom of God" (Galatians 5:19–21).

In Paul's letter to the church in Corinth, he addressed a situation in the church where one person in the congregation was sleeping with his father's wife. He instructed individuals to have nothing to do with them, and for church leaders to expel them from the congregation, until they genuinely repented. In similar situations, when a person is defiantly and openly engaging in continuous serious sin, such as domestic abuse, with no repentance, the modern-day church is required to do the same. Individuals, including the wife, should have nothing to do with him, and church leaders should excommunicate the person from the congregation until he repents. Unfortunately, most churches don't have the courage to do so. Paul instructs: "But now I am writing to you that you must not associate with anyone who claims to be a brother or sister but is sexually immoral or greedy, an idolater or slanderer, a drunkard or swindler. Do not even eat with such people" (1 Corinthians 5:11).

Even Paul knew that there was little chance that a person with this hardness of heart would ever repent. However, Paul also knew that if there was any hope of repentance or redemption, it would only occur if the abuser suffered serious consequences and was isolated from his community to do some serious soul-searching. This acknowledgment of the extreme unlikelihood of repentance is reflected in Paul's comment: "Cast out this man from the fellowship of the church and into Satan's hands, to punish him, *in the hope that his soul will be saved when our Lord Jesus Christ returns*" (1 Corinthians 5:5 TLB; emphasis added).

Claims That His Wife Should Not Judge Him

Due to their self-serving, faulty understanding of Scripture, SNAPs often claim that no one should judge them, regardless of how bad their behavior is. They base this demand on Matthew 7:1: "Do not judge, or you too will be judged." According to the religious abuser, he should have no standard of behavior, words, or attitudes. His partner should accept him as he is, because to do otherwise would be un-Christian. This is not what Scripture requires.

The SNAP's claims would have the rest of the world throw out all the rest of Scripture, which clearly does have standards and requires those who call themselves followers of Christ (Christians) or followers of God (Jews) to abide by those standards. Scripture further requires churches and synagogues to require their members to abide by the same standards.

The Old Testament clearly imposed judgment for purging evil people from the community to keep their evil from infecting others. Entire chapters discuss serious sin and the requirement to remove it from Israel's midst. See Deuteronomy 13, 17, 19, and 21:18–21.

The New Testament ushered in a period of grace, and so did away with the animal sacrifice system and death sentences for sinners. Yet it still requires Christians to live by godly standards, the most important of which is to love God and love others (Matthew 22:37–39). SNAPs are incapable of doing either. In 1 Corinthians 5, 2 Timothy 3, and Matthew 18:15–17, Scripture clearly instructs Christian believers to have nothing to do with people who claim to be believers yet continue their blatant, intentional, unrepentant sin. Church leaders should excommunicate them and remove them from their midst, and others should "not even eat with such people" (1 Corinthians 5:11; Matthew 18:17).

As for judging, Paul states:

> When I wrote to you before I said not to mix with evil people. But when I said that I wasn't talking about unbelievers who live in sexual sin or are greedy cheats and thieves and idol worshipers. For you can't live in this world without being with people like that. What I meant was that you are not to keep company with anyone who claims to be a brother Christian but indulges in sexual sins, or is greedy, or is a swindler, or worships idols, or is a drunkard, or abusive. Don't even eat lunch with such a person. It isn't our job to judge outsiders. But it certainly is our job to judge and deal strongly with those who are members of the church and who are sinning in these ways. God alone is the Judge of those on the outside. But you yourselves must deal with this man and put him out of your church. (1 Corinthians 5:9–13 TLB)

Not only should a victim judge an abuser by scriptural standards, but she should also follow what Scripture tells believers to do with wicked, evil, unrepentant people: have nothing to do with him. The Bible made no exceptions for wives and children, who would have the most to lose by being forced to stay with an abusive person.

Thankfully, Scripture does not say: "Have nothing to do with wicked, evil people who refuse to repent, except for spouses who must stay and be physically, verbally, spiritually, and sexually beaten and abused by Satan until they either are beaten or raped to death or die a slow, painful spiritual death so that they are like lifeless bodies with no hope and no future. That is what God wants for the wife of evil, wicked people controlled by Satan. But for everyone else on the planet, God wants an abundant life full of joy and purpose and filled with His Spirit to do His good works that He created them to do. The prayer 'your kingdom come, your will be done, on earth as it is in heaven' only applies to those people who are not married to one of Satan's minions. Those trusting, gentle souls who were deceived and lied to and married a child of the devil must stay under Satan's bondage forever. But everyone else, you should have nothing to do with them." This is not what Scripture tells us! But it is what abusers, pastors, and others tell us when they claim a woman cannot leave her abusive husband.

Scriptures clearly give permission, indeed require, that people have nothing to do with evil people, even if they are a spouse.

Claims He Is Ethical and Values Family and Integrity

SNAPs think so highly of themselves that they are delusional and out of touch with reality. Nothing displays this delusional characteristic more than when a SNAP claims to be ethical and honest and to value family, church, kindness, and humbleness, yet acts just the opposite. The SNAP lures people in with his talk of morals and family values, but eventually the dichotomy between what he says and what he does becomes apparent to the wife, business partner, or anyone else he has lured in. His claims are so far removed from his actual practice that it causes severe cognitive dissonance with his victims, yet the abuser has no qualms about the obvious lack of reality in his perfect perception of himself.

The biblical answer to the SNAP is found in 1 John 4:20–21: "Whoever claims to love God yet hates a brother or sister is a liar. For whoever does not love their brother and sister, whom they have seen, cannot love God, whom they have not seen. And he has given us this command: Anyone who loves God must also love their brother and sister."

Claims That Unconditional Love Requires His Wife to Accept His Abuse

A SNAP will often claim to his abused spouse, "If you really loved me, you would stay with me. That's what true love does. Unconditional love stays."

In this flawed logic, the SNAP blames the spouse for not enduring his abuse. He does not realize that true, unconditional love neither abuses others nor accepts abuse. Abuse destroys a relationship. When one spouse abuses the other, he breaks the marital covenant to love, honor, and cherish the other, to act in the best interest of the other, and to protect the other. Contrary to what the SNAP would have his wife believe, a marriage covenant, like God's covenants, is conditional upon the other party keeping his covenant.

God loved His people Israel, but His promises to bless them were conditioned on their hearts being turned to Him. When they turned away from God, God turned away from them. Deuteronomy 28 outlines the blessings for obedient hearts and the curses for hearts that turn away from God. The entire Old Testament tells the story of a people who turned from God and suffered the consequences. God withdrew His blessings, and they reaped what they had sown.

The New Testament promises eternal blessings for those whose hearts are with God and eternal fire and judgment for those whose hearts do not repent and turn to God. We can easily spot these people:

> The one who does what is right is righteous, just as he is righteous. The one who does what is sinful is of the devil, because the devil has been sinning from the beginning. The reason the Son of God appeared was to destroy the devil's work. No one who is born of God will continue to sin, because God's seed remains in them; they cannot go on sinning, because they have been born of God. This is how we know who the children of God are and who the children of the devil are: Anyone who does not do what is right is not God's child, nor is anyone who does not love their brother and sister. . . . We know that we have passed from death to life, because we love each other. Anyone who does not love remains in death. Anyone who hates a brother or sister is a murderer, and you know that no murderer has eternal life residing in him. (1 John 3:7–10, 14–15)

When an abuser continuously violates his marriage covenant with repeated unrepentant abuse, he shows that he does not love, honor, or cherish his wife. He does not protect his wife or provide for her. He has turned his heart against his wife. This is not a marriage. The abuser has violated the marriage covenant, and the victim is under no requirement to stay. While Scripture admonishes her to not repay evil for evil, the proper course of action is to remove herself from a relationship that is no longer a marriage, but is an opportunity for the abuser to inflict more evil. Scripture tells us to love another as we love ourselves, which implies that we must love ourselves. In this case, the loving thing for the wife to do to remove herself from evil, heal, and live the abundant life God desires for her.

Claims That He Has Changed or Can Change with Time and Spiritual Counseling

When the SNAP feels that his victim is on the verge of leaving, or perhaps has already left but the SNAP thinks he might have a chance at luring her back, he will often claim that he has had an epiphany, a "come to Jesus" moment, or some other spiritual awakening so dramatic that he has changed, repented, and will from now on be her ideal husband. This is immediately followed up by begging her to stay or return. Alternatively, if his victim doesn't believe him and continues to leave, he may claim that he can change and be the man she needs if he only got some spiritual, psychological, sex addiction, Alcoholics Anonymous, anger management, or other form of counseling. Again, this is followed up by begging her to stay or return.

While counseling can work for the normal transgressions that typical marriages and people go through, counseling is nearly wholly ineffective for SNAPs and domestic abusers. Counseling is only effective for people who want to change, and SNAPs see no reason to change. Narcissistic personality disorder, sociopathy, and psychopathy (forms of antisocial personality disorder) are permanent personality disorders that are essentially untreatable and incurable.

The abuser is a pathological creature. According to Sandra Brown, one of the preeminent experts in the area of pathological relationships, pathology means that (1) the person is unable to sustain positive change, (2) is unable to learn from past consequences, and (3) does not appreciate the negative consequences of his behavior on others.[80]

For the domestic abuser, this means that while he can put on a good show for a short time (at least long enough to get his wife to come back), he will eventually return to his true nature. It also means that regardless of the past consequences of his abusive behavior, which may include divorce, being fired from his job, alienation from former friends, severe relationship problems, etc., he will continue his abusive behavior. Consequences have virtually no effect on SNAPs. They will never look in the mirror and see themselves as the reason for difficulties in all their past relationships, employment, or business partner breakups. They will always place blame on someone or something else.

Finally, it means that the domestic abuser simply doesn't care how his actions and attitudes affect those around him. He willingly sacrifices relationships on the altar of ego and selfishness. As long as he wins and gets what he wants, he really doesn't care how it affects his family, wife, employer, employees, or friends—that is, until they leave. He wants them around to serve him, but he has no interest in nurturing relationships and making sure the people around him get what they need in a relationship.

Unfortunately, most victims and pastors treat the SNAP like a normal person, erroneously thinking, "If only he had some counseling, he will see what he is doing wrong and how destructive he has been to the relationship. When he recognizes that, he will surely change and all will be well." This is a fantasy. Counseling only works on people who have a conscience and the capacity to change. As noted earlier, on average, a woman in an abusive relationship leaves her partner seven times before she finally realizes that he is incapable of change.

From a spiritual perspective, God can only work on hearts that are capable of turning to Him. Regardless

---

[80] Sandra Brown, "Chronic Personality Problems in Problem Relationships," *Psychology Today*, December 11, 2009.

of whether the abuser is a pastor or a slick Wall Street banker, with rare exceptions, the heart of a SNAP is so hardened that it cannot turn to God.

Attacking His Spouse's Kindness and Grace

Healthy women want their relationships to last, and they invest heavily in their relationships and marriages. They don't typically blow up a marriage because of one episode, an unhealthy trait, or even several unhealthy behaviors. Healthy women practice patience and extend grace in the hope that their husbands will return that grace and grow into an emotionally mature, safe person with whom they can have a loving, healthy marriage.

Unfortunately, women who are with a SNAP will not have their kindness repaid. In fact, their kindness will be returned with evil. Their kindness will be mocked, used against them, and in most instances, be their downfall. In addition, instead of recognizing her acts of kindness for his own good, the SNAP will twist and manipulate her kindnesses and label them as evil, malicious, or vindictive. He will then call her names like "Satan," "the devil," "Jezebel," "witch," or some other name that attributes wickedness to her. Of course, this is incredibly painful for the woman of faith, who is trying exceedingly hard to be kind, patient, and gracious in the face of an evil creature.

Jesus warned us of people like this in His Sermon on the Mount: "Don't give holy things to depraved men. Don't give pearls to swine! They will trample the pearls and turn and attack you" (Matthew 7:6 TLB). Jesus knew that certain people—depraved people such as SNAPs—would trample the kindness of good people and then turn and attack them for their kindness. His advice was to establish healthy boundaries and not extend kindness to these people. Save it for decent people. Jesus echoes the wisdom of Isaiah hundreds of years earlier: "When grace is shown to the wicked, they do not learn righteousness" (Isaiah 26:10). King David laments the SNAPs in his life: "They repay me evil for good, and hatred for my friendship" (Psalm 109:5). He expresses the wounding of his heart: "They repay me evil for good and leave me like one bereaved" (Psalm 35:12).

Jesus was no stranger to those who attributed His acts of kindness inspired by the Holy Spirit as wicked and as acts of Satan. When driving out demons, Jesus was accused by the Pharisees of driving them out by the power of Satan. Because their accusations attributed goodness from the Holy Spirit as evil from the devil, Jesus said they were engaging in the one unforgivable sin: blasphemy against the Holy Spirit (Matthew 12:25–31; Mark 3:20–30; Luke 12:10).

The sad truth about SNAPs who do such things is that they are eternally doomed. Their hearts are so hard they are incapable of repenting. The apostle John tells us we should pray for believers who sin so that they may be reconciled to God: "If you see any brother or sister commit a sin that does not lead to death, you should pray and God will give them life" (1 John 5:16). But he specifically excludes prayers for those who commit the one unpardonable sin of attributing the goodness of the Holy Spirit to the evil acts of Satan: "There is a sin that leads to death. I am not saying that you should pray about that" (1 John 5:16). If someone is so wicked that he labels as evil what is good, it is a hopeless case. He will not change, he will not repent, and he will never be forgiven by God; don't bother to pray.

> Charlotte: I pored over the Scriptures when I left, trying to find answers. Reading the Bible through the lens of domestic abuse makes certain passages jump off the page. When Jesus warned us not to throw pearls to swine because the swine will trample the pearls and attack you, I was thankful that Jesus was adamant about setting boundaries with toxic people and explaining what happens if

we don't. Every time I had gone out of my way to be kind to Tim, it was not appreciated and then was used against me. After I had stayed in an abusive marriage hoping for his heart to change, Tim mocked me. After years of focusing on the positive and refraining from nagging, he accused me of lying and said, "Maybe if you had nagged, we wouldn't be here right now." After I didn't go to the police immediately or seek an order of protection, he retorted, "If it was so bad, you should have gotten a restraining order." I eventually had to get a restraining order because, even years after the divorce, he simply wouldn't stop the abuse.

Claims That the Wife Is a Horrible Christian or Jew

If misquoting Scripture doesn't work to keep his wife submissive and under his control, the SNAP will charge her with being a poor representative of her religious beliefs.

We know these vague accusations are from Satan, who is the great accuser and stands before God accusing his followers day and night (Revelation 12:10). Satan's accusations are vague and unspecific and are meant to destroy our spirit and shame our entire being. He wants us to be so beaten down that we are incapable of joy and doing good works.

The Holy Spirit never accuses, never destroys our spirit, and never shames us. Why would He? He loves us. He wants the best for us. He wants us to be in fellowship with God and each other, and He wants us to be Godlike in character. If we have sin in our life, the Holy Spirit will gently and lovingly inform us of the specific sin. The Spirit will then work in our hearts to bring us to repentance so we can continue in righteousness. The Holy Spirit works like a skillful cancer surgeon removing a dangerous tumor. He does a laparoscopic surgical strike to remove only the cancer, while leaving the healthy tissue intact. The Holy Spirit affirms us, loves us, sings over us, delights in us, and lets us know that we are wondrously and wonderfully made in God's image. And then He refines us so that we are more like God. On the other hand, Satan's accusations are nebulous and vague and attack our very soul and being. They are the attacks of the abuser.

CHAPTER 12

Other Annoying Attitudes and Behaviors

In addition to the traits identified in the previous chapters, several other traits are also common to abusers. While these traits may not rise to the level of abuse, they are clearly not traits to admire or ascribe to.

First in Line

SNAPs think only of themselves, and therefore they want to be first in line, willing to push others out of the way to get there. They think of themselves as superior to others, believing that they should not have to wait in line like inferior people do.

> Charlotte: Tim always had to be first in everything—especially the first on an airplane, even though we all landed at the same time. He always wanted VIP status at every event and premier status on planes so he could board first. And when he did, he stood in the aisle blocking everyone behind him while he slowly got himself organized and all his reading material out, completely oblivious to the fact that he was blocking a long line of other people trying to board. One time, he just left me at the airport bar because it was so important to him to board first. I finished my drink at the bar, and, remarkably, arrived at our destination at the same time he did.

First-Class or VIP Seating

SNAPs love the special attention of first-class or VIP seating—it feeds their already enlarged ego. If a SNAP has a seat upgrade to first class and his partner or family doesn't, he has absolutely no problem leaving his partner with the kids in coach class while he spends the flight in first class. If he can get a ride on a private jet, he will have no problem leaving his partner to take the family in coach.

> Charlotte: Tim would always get a ride in first class or on a private jet if he could. One year, he took the company jet and left me with three children, ages two, five, and twelve, and his eighty-year-old mother. We flew from Chicago to Florida, with a plane change in Atlanta. I lost the two-year-old

at the Atlanta airport because I was busy getting Tim's wheelchair-bound mother something to eat. Some nice person rescued our toddler from the ascending escalator, where he had fallen, and took the return elevator and brought him back. I was a wreck. It never even fazed Tim that his child was lost in the busiest airport in the world. He just wanted his private jet.

Encroach on Your Personal Space

SNAPs have no boundaries. What's theirs is theirs and what's yours is theirs. That includes your personal space. When the SNAP and his partner sit together in a plane, for example, the SNAP will take over his partner's tray table and personal space as his own. When the SNAP is finished with dinner, he will push his plate aside into someone else's space who is still eating. When the SNAP has a project, he will skew his papers or articles over someone else's space and take over the space. Those who push back and claim their space will receive an angry explosion from the SNAP.

Head of the Table

SNAPs seek out for themselves what they perceive to be the most important place. When dining, they will seek the head of the table, rather than the sides, to feed their ego and show others they are more important.

> Charlotte: No matter where it was—at a formal dining table, at the kitchen table, at a restaurant, or just outside on the patio—Tim always had to sit at the head of the table and would explode in anger if one of the kids or I tried to sit there. Sometimes one of us would sit at the end just to watch him explode—it was utterly predictable.

Loud Talking

Because SNAPs think they are superior to others, they talk louder so that others will think their conversations are more important, and because they simply don't care that they are being obnoxious to others. They not only talk loudly in the house, but also at the office and on a train, plane, or other place where people are normally respectful and quiet. They have no problem talking loudly on the phone about their multi-million-dollar deal with others sitting quietly around them.

Controlling a Conversation

A SNAP always wants to be in control, and controlling a conversation is just one way he controls others. He controls the subject matter, which is always something he thinks he has some expertise on, something from his own experience that he thinks will make him look superior, or something on which he has a strong opinion—like politics or religion. It's nearly a monologue, but he might allow others to pipe in short snippets to affirm him before he cuts them off and continues. If they disagree with his opinion, he will cut them off, talk more loudly, tell them they are unintelligent for thinking that way, and continue. It can go on for hours.

Talking about Themselves

A SNAP loves to talk about himself—after all, he is the most brilliant person he knows! Who wouldn't love to hear about him? He will, of course, only talk about those things that he thinks make him look superior to others, like his newest car, boat, business deal, or extravagant vacation. Because SNAPs are shallow and have no emotional depth, much less moral depth, their conversations about themselves will be equally shallow and superficial. Don't expect to engage a SNAP in a heartfelt discussion of the purpose of life, how he is instilling good values in his children, or how he healed after the heartbreak of losing his mother to cancer. The short answers to those would be that the purpose of life is to have the most toys, his kids got a private education, and she's dead and he's fine.

Finishing Your Sentences

The SNAP is not really interested in what you have to say. While you are talking, he is busy thinking about what he is going to say next. And to hurry you along, he will finish your sentences.

Shows No Interest in You

Most people show their interest in others by asking how they are, what is new with their children, how their project is coming along, etc. Everyone with any conscience always asks how someone is healing if there has been a serious illness or injury. However, as a corollary to the previous characteristic that SNAPs talk about themselves, they also show no interest in you, your thoughts, your dreams, or your recovery from your recent major surgery. They simply don't care about you, which is why they don't ask.

> Charlotte: Tim's daughter Kira had brain cancer in 2010 and needed radiation and surgery. His daughter and her husband, Jim, invited Tim to attend a doctor visit with them in downtown Chicago to discuss options. It was at least an hour drive. She was distraught. After the doctor visit, Tim insisted that they take a detour and stop by his favorite store in Little Italy to pick up some Italian sausage that he liked. He had no awareness of the extreme mental distress that Kira was in, being only focused on himself.

Their Rich/Powerful/Famous "Friends"

SNAPs feel superior to the "little people," and therefore do not want to be associated with them lest others might think they are likewise inferior. SNAPs try to make themselves feel important by associating with people who have money, power, and celebrity status. Even though the associations may be superficial, it feeds a SNAP's ego when he can say he talked to so-and-so at a gala or other function. The fact that they talked or were at the same event bolsters the SNAP's internal voice that says, "You must be just as important; you were at the same event."

Likewise, SNAPs love to impress others with the fact that they know rich, powerful, or famous "friends" because they think it makes them more important when they have these types of friends. The person may not even be a friend, but merely an acquaintance the SNAP met at a cocktail party, or a friend of a friend. Nonetheless, the SNAP will claim the rich, powerful, or famous person as his own "friend" and tell others how wealthy, how powerful, and how famous he is.

Difficulties with Commitment

Another indication of the SNAP's controlling personality is that they only want to make plans or attend things that are their ideas or that revolve around them. They especially want to attend events if they are invited as a guest of someone who is wealthy, powerful, or famous, as this feeds their overinflated ego. However, a spouse does not qualify as someone important enough to go out of their way for. SNAPs will demand that their wife commit to an event if they are making plans for something that interests them, and will either not commit or back out at the last minute if their wife is making plans for something that interests her.

> Charlotte: If Tim was invited by his wealth management advisor or a wealthy friend to dinner or a professional hockey game with spouses in the city, he would gladly accept the invitation, make plans without consulting me, and expect me to drop everything I might have had on my calendar to attend with him. On the other hand, if I asked Tim to have a special night out in the city for our anniversary, he would be unable to commit to a date, whine over what an inconvenience it was to go all the way into Chicago from the suburbs, and try to back out with lame excuses. I finally quit trying to ask him to celebrate our anniversary at all. The last anniversary we spent together, our nineteenth, he didn't even bother to get me a card.

> Ellen: My son got tickets for a concert for my birthday. I was too sick to drive, and my son wasn't old enough to have his license, so we asked my husband, Rod, to take us. After some time, he finally agreed, but then backed out on the day of the concert just to be mean. He didn't want to go, but he didn't want us to go either.

Plans without Consulting Partner

SNAPs are so focused on themselves that they will make travel arrangements for days or weeks at a time without consulting with their spouse. They view themselves as the center of the universe and have no common courtesy to announce their out-of-town plans, much less consult others or coordinate schedules.

> Charlotte: For years, Tim went on business trips without telling me first. There was no notice, no asking how I'll do with three little children in the house, no consulting with me, and no mention on the calendar. He had it planned for months, but I was just a tagalong, just a wife. I had no right to know.

The Runaround

SNAPs are the masters of the evasive answer. They want to be in control and will move heaven and earth when they want something to be done. But when an idea is not theirs, or they may be caught in a lie, or they just don't want to do something, they will give the runaround to avoid doing something they don't want to do or to sidestep revealing something they don't want you to know. You will likely hear the following from a SNAP: "Well, to be honest with you, I haven't really thought about it." "I will need to get back to you." "I have to check into it." "I need to check my calendar to see when I'm free." "To be honest, I'm not sure." "My computer died and I lost the information." "My cell phone wasn't working, so I couldn't get back to you." "I was out of town; sorry I couldn't call."

Secrets and Evasion

SNAPs have a lot to hide, and they try to keep their awful secrets from partners and others. They have bank accounts and safe deposit boxes that their spouses don't know about or have no access to. Records of their lies, depositions with falsehoods told under oath to previous spouses, documents of being fired for abuse, lawsuits and criminal records, and falsified financial statements and the like are hidden in secret places.

Bad Teachers and Trainers

SNAPs don't see others as separate individuals with hopes and dreams and the need for kindness. So they make the worst teachers because they simply don't care about their students, whether those students are their own children or pupils in a classroom. Those who do teach in classrooms often do so strictly for the money or for the prestige, not because they love young people. Teaching will be a means to an end for a SNAP university professor who is known for his research or for a SNAP teacher's assistant who just needs the money to get through graduate school.

Taking Credit for What Others Do

The SNAP has no guilt over taking credit for the work of others or for the brilliant ideas of others. He has no conscience, and therefore, no guilt.

Ridicules Others for the Same Things He Does

In a corollary to projection, SNAPs ridicule others for the same things they do. For example, a SNAP may call someone a jerk or incompetent when, of course, they themselves are being a jerk or incompetent.

Hates to Do Real Work and Gets Others to Do It for Him

SNAPs feel that they are above real work that requires someone to humble themselves, roll up their sleeves, and get dirty. Physical work such as cleaning, car or home repairs, yard work, dishes, laundry, taking care of others, and serving others is abhorrent to the SNAP. He views himself as superior to people who do these menial tasks. He will, therefore, fill his time with what he views as more important tasks, getting others to do those tasks he feels are beneath him. Although a SNAP may like to entertain to show off his house, his children, his possessions, and his trophy wife, don't expect him to lift a finger to help in the real work of cooking, serving, cleaning up, or making guests feel comfortable. He will be too busy showing off his collection and drinking cocktails to be of any real help.

Supervises So He Doesn't Have to Work

Closely related to the characteristic above, the SNAP will not only get others to do real work for him, but he will simply refuse to help and will brag that he is good at supervising—i.e., telling others what to do so he can continue to be in control.

> Charlotte: Tim brags, even to this day, that he is great at supervising to get out of doing anything that would require work around the house, which he is loath to do. Although he bragged about having an MBA, he claimed he could not turn on the washing machine. He gloated that he ran a billion-dollar company, but claimed he could not stir a pot of pasta sauce. He bragged that ten thousand people reported to him, but purported to not know how to set a table. So he just barked orders.

Sarcastic Responses

An abuser is often the King of Sarcasm. It deflects and attacks others all at the same time.

Non-Responses

Abusers feel that they are above needing to inform anyone of their business, although they feel entitled to know everything about others. To the simple question a wife may ask of, "Where are you going?" the abuser may respond, "You don't need to know" or "Why do you need to know?"

To the reasonable question a wife may ask of, "How much was the new car?" the abuser may retort, "Does it matter?" "I can spend what I want," "I'm a grown man. You don't need to check up on me," or "As much as it needed."

Misrepresenting Communications

Claiming ignorance that they were not informed or that they were incorrectly informed is a common occurrence when the SNAP wants to deflect blame from his failure to fulfill his obligations. He will never admit that he failed; he will find a way to look innocent and blame others.

Withholding Important Information and Blaming Others

When other people are working for or doing favors for the SNAP, he will purposefully withhold important information that they need to make informed decisions or do their work properly. After he sabotages their ability to do a good job, he will then turn around and blame them for not doing it properly.

Only Volunteers or Does Charity Work to Get the Spotlight

SNAPs like to be thought of as morally superior and upstanding to cover their inward depravity. They also love the attention of the spotlight. So there are few things that the SNAP likes better and that will raise his standing in the community more than public charity. You will not find a SNAP behind the scenes doing dishes, helping up chairs, or cleaning up after a charity event. No, the SNAP demands the spotlight so everyone can see him in a positive light. He will be the usher at church who greets with a smile, he will be the emcee at the fund-raising event, and he will be the one who starts a foundation (with his own name) and makes his wife do the background work while he gets the glory and accolades as a generous and upstanding member of the community.

Appears Religious to Camouflage Bad Behavior

As evil as they are, one might wonder why a SNAP would set foot in a church, synagogue, or other house of worship. Unlike healthy people, SNAPs do not attend a church or synagogue to get to know God, to become more like God, or to serve others. SNAPs might appreciate the educational, historical, or intellectual aspect of religious teaching, but they have no interest in developing or living out a genuine faith. In fact, they disdain biblical characteristics and the fruit of the Spirit as weak. Rather, they embrace what Christians call the desires of a sinful or evil nature: sexual immorality, impurity, lustful pleasures, idolatry, greed, sorcery, hostility, quarreling, jealousy, outbursts of anger, selfish ambition, dissension, division, envy, drunkenness, wild parties, and other similar characteristics (Galatians 5:19–21).

To hide these less-than-desirable traits, they attend a church or synagogue as a camouflage and to appear respectable to others. A woman whose husband attends church or synagogue has the false hope that somewhere deep down inside, his better nature is being awakened. If she just stays in the marriage a little longer, surely the weekly messages will melt his heart of stone and he will be transformed into the man of God that she always hoped for. Nothing could be further from the truth, as the evil of abuse always progresses from bad to worse.

After the SNAP has discarded his spouse and destroyed his family, churches and synagogues are target-rich environments for his next target. A SNAP preys on women of faith because he knows they are, in general, trusting and unsuspecting of his nature. Likewise, if a SNAP attends a church or synagogue, a woman will, in general, let her guard down, assume that he embraces the values of that church or synagogue, and let him into her life without ever suspecting that he is a narcissist, sociopath, psychopath, or other abuser.

A SNAP may also view church or synagogue as a social club. In many communities, the church or synagogue serves the important role of building communities and relationships for people with common ethnic, family, geographic, or religious backgrounds. Attendance is viewed as a near requirement for inclusion in the community. In other places, churches and synagogues are gathering places for social activities.

> Kit: My husband and I met at Wheaton College. I thought I had found a wonderful Christian young man who would love me and be a role model for our children. We attended church together, and he became financially successful. Little did I know that he would be controlling, abusive, and have affairs throughout our thirty-plus-year marriage. He used the church as a cover-up to look good.

> Charlotte: Tim always claimed to be a good Catholic and an altar boy when he was young, but when I met him, he had not attended church for twenty years. However, finding a church family was important to me. When we moved to Lake Forest and he discovered that Christ Church had numerous people who were also members of his country club, it became an extension of his social club and a place to see and be seen. It was also a good cover-up for his abuses. I am sure that his church attendance made him look better in the eyes of his girlfriend, who later became Wife Number 3, even though they were dating while we were married. Tim loves to brag to others how he is involved in various church activities. I laughed when I heard that he claimed he went on a mission trip with the church. In fact, it was merely a vacation to Turkey with other church members. A mission trip would require actual humble service to others, which he is incapable of.

Boasting about Accomplishments and Assets

SNAPs derive self-worth by inflating themselves and putting others down. Therefore, inappropriate boasting about themselves, their accomplishments, assets, businesses, or practices, as well as the accomplishments of their children, the wealth of their "friends," or similar things, makes them feel more important, even though it is in poor taste.

Bragging about Things Others Think Are Rude, Unethical, or Inappropriate

While people of good character are ashamed of their acts that may have been rude, unethical, or inappropriate, a SNAP will brag about them.

Charlotte: Tim gloated about things that would make others hang their heads in shame. Years of affairs, using trusts and shell companies to hide assets from his first wife during their divorce, flushing his fellow shipmate's paychecks down the toilet until he complied with his demands and lying about it when he was in the coast guard, insulting people when he felt offended, putting people in their place when they disagreed with him, and berating service people when things did not go his way all made him feel superior when he bragged about his shameful behavior. He was so proud of himself that he told these stories bursting at the seams.

Hilary: Stan boasted to me about how he had gotten away with assaulting a police officer and even raping a woman at a hotel after he slipped a roofie in her drink. He was proud of how he had gotten away with these horrible crimes without prosecution.

Easily Bored

Healthy people find joy and excitement through their relationships with others—together we celebrate the happy moments in our life and the lives around us, and we hold together in the struggles. Humans are made for relationships and community. Sharing such times usually gives us a little boost caused by the increase in dopamine, serotonin, endorphins, and oxytocin. The ups, the downs, and the dramas of regular life are usually more than enough excitement for healthy people. But the SNAP has no intimate emotional connections because he has no conscience. He may have a family, acquaintances, or coworkers, but to him they are merely objects to serve him. So while most of us look forward to connecting with friends and family at gatherings that make up the fabric of our lives, a SNAP is easily bored, unless he is the center of attention, because he doesn't really care about the people around him.

Risky Activities

Because the SNAP is easily bored, he engages in risky activity to add excitement to his life. The mere fact that something is forbidden or illegal makes it risky and more desirable for the SNAP. The possibility of getting caught makes it even more attractive. This also applies to the sex life of SNAPs, who habitually engage in risky sexual activity. Pornography, sexual deviancy, and affairs are standard fare for SNAPs. Gambling and spending large amounts of money on risky investments are financial risks that SNAPs typically engage in. Other potentially dangerous physical activities that SNAPs undertake include hang gliding and racing motorcycles or sports cars.

Hilary: Stan was constantly looking for the next thrill. He owned places in Illinois and California. He threw money at hotels and girls like it was going out of style. He participated in orgies in California, did illegal drugs, abused alcohol, drove fancy cars, raped a woman, lied on his tax returns, made illegal recordings, illegally put a GPS on my car—you name it. And he always seemed to get away with it.

Forgetting People/Remembering Objects

SNAPs don't care about people. They view others as servants to get what they want. People are strictly utilitarian. SNAPs thrive on collecting experiences like a great vacation or attending a unique sports event. And they flourish on collecting material goods like cars, boats, houses, and money. They even get a thrill from collecting names of famous, wealthy, or powerful people whom they have met so that they can name-drop. But ask a SNAP who they attended an important life event with, and they have no idea. They didn't care in the first place.

> Charlotte: I value people and I have kept in touch with most of my elementary, high school, and college friends. I love to hear us all retell stories of times past. When my own kids went to prom, I dropped a text to my old prom date, and we had a good laugh. So when I asked Tim who he went to prom with, I was surprised to hear that he had no recollection of his date, but he remembered his car. Typical.

Charming When around People They Want to Impress, but Poor Manners around Others

To feed their own egos, SNAPs want to hang around people whom they think will make them look better by association—people who have wealth, power, and influence. It makes a SNAP feel wealthier and more powerful and influential to rub elbows with these movers and shakers. Likewise, to make them look better morally, SNAPs also want to hang around people whom others know are good and decent people, but only if they are also people of influence. For example, a SNAP will be happy to spend time with a pastor, rabbi, religious university president, or the founder of a well-known nonprofit organization because not only are these people viewed as morally upright, but they are also influential leaders. However, a SNAP will not waste his time with a good and decent person of humble means. And when he hangs out with the people he wants to impress, the SNAP will be charming and on his best behavior.

On the other hand, SNAPs don't care about people they view as inferior. One of the ways they show their disdain for people they view as "lesser than" is to ignore common courtesies and manners.

> Charlotte: Tim turned on the charm with celebrities, owners of NFL franchises, and wealthy businessmen, but he refused to do even the most common courtesies and have manners with people he did not value. For example, he never helped me with heavy luggage, even though he knew I had a painful back due to scoliosis. When we all took a trip to California in 2011 for a wedding, he refused to help anyone with luggage. He got on the shuttle bus taking us to our rental car before anyone else, put his luggage up, garnered the best seat in the back of the bus, stretched out his arms on the top of the seats, and just watched as the children and I struggled with our heavy luggage. I had to help the kids with their fifty-pound bags. Tim didn't bat an eye or offer to help. During the holidays, he insulted the extended family of our children's godparents by refusing to serve them the expensive wine, telling them that they would not appreciate it. He always chewed and talked with his mouth full of food when he was with me or others he viewed as inferior, but used good manners when he was with wealthy and powerful people.

Eager to Accept Invitations from Rich/Famous/Powerful People, but Loath to Accept Invitations from Regular People and Spouses

Because SNAPs need to constantly feed their egos to make themselves feel superior to others, they jump on invitations from the wealthy, powerful, or famous.

Because SNAPs fear that being associated with "regular" people whom they view as inferior will bring down their stature, they will usually decline invitations from people who lack the wealth and influence they aspire to. If social rules require an acceptance, they will accept the invitation, but they will let others know they are lowering themselves by their own good graces to spend time with them.

> Charlotte: When we were invited by the adult children of our children's godparents to attend their destination weddings in the Bahamas in 2003 and in California in 2011, Tim complained for months ahead of time about the cost and inconvenience to attend the weddings. He continued his complaining throughout the trips, even though they were fabulous times to be together and celebrate with close friends and family. Yet when he was in the love-bombing phase of a relationship with his new girlfriend, he gushed to me about attending her brother's wedding in New York, telling me several times that her brother was famous for his running and had been featured on the front page of the *Wall Street Journal*.
>
> In the early phase of our relationship, he would drive into Chicago where I worked, and we had lunch once a week and dinner in the city all the time. I did not realize at the time that, starting with the wedding, we had moved into the devaluation phase, and he was showing me in word and deed that he did not value me. He wouldn't take me out to lunch or dinner locally, much less in Chicago, even though he clearly could afford it and had the time since he wasn't working after he was fired in 2000. One day when we were at his country club and I had taken the kids swimming, some friends asked us if we wanted to join them for a bite on the nearby patio. Tim refused, so we sat down at a table with them, talked, and watched them eat. How awkward! Then he made me go grocery shopping and make dinner for him at home.
>
> However, whenever one of his wealthy or powerful friends asked him to go to dinner or to a party in Chicago in the middle of the week—a time when it could easily take ninety minutes in traffic—he would readily accept it and gush for weeks about the other wealthy or famous people he talked with.

Arrogant

A person's heart and attitude determine his actions and speech. Goodness naturally pours out from a good and humble heart. SNAPs view themselves as superior; therefore, they cannot help but be arrogant in their speech and actions. Their arrogance comes to light in a variety of ways, some more subtle than others. While you cannot always explain exactly how they made you feel inferior, the message is clear: "I am better than you, and you don't matter to me."

Ad Hominem Attacks

SNAPs think their opinions are superior to others and do not take suggestions or opposing opinions well. When discussing an issue, if his position is questioned, the SNAP will likely resort to an ad hominem attack—an attack of the person or his character—rather than addressing the merits of the issue. An ad hominem attack can take many forms, including an insult of the person ("I'm not going to listen to you. You're fat and ugly!"), accusing the person of the same thing ("You're no better—you do the same thing!"), or telling them that everyone is against them ("Nobody likes you anyway!"). Even if the setting is small talk at a cocktail party, when the SNAP is backed into a corner with an indefensible position, expect an ad hominem attack.

Other Annoying Attitudes and Behaviors

Changing the Subject

To skirt an issue when they have been caught in an obvious lie, the SNAP will change the subject or leave, claiming they have no time or must get to another appointment, or some other excuse.

Repeating Themselves

The SNAP thinks others are idiots. The SNAP will always assume they are the smartest one in the room. Therefore, to get his ideas, instructions, or opinions across to the nitwits whom he is surrounded by, he repeats himself several times. Most of us get something the first time it is said, and certainly by the second time it has been said. By the fifth or sixth time something is repeated, it is plain annoying.

Explaining Jokes That Others Already Get

As a corollary to repeating themselves, because the SNAP assumes everyone is an idiot, he will explain his own jokes, thinking that others are not smart enough to get them.

Must Win an Argument—Even in Social Settings

SNAPs have one goal when they have a disagreement: winning. A SNAP does not care about keeping a relationship, finding the right answer, arriving at a workable solution, understanding another person's viewpoint, empathizing with other's struggles, reducing future disagreements, learning, accepting responsibility, or any of the other goals that healthy people have when confronting different opinions. SNAPs simply want to win at all costs—and if a relationship is destroyed, the SNAP is willing to pay that price as long as he can win.

Belittle Waitstaff and Service Staff

A SNAP's sense of superiority is heightened toward people in service positions. He views them as particularly inferior, useful only as tools to assist the SNAP in getting what he wants. The SNAP does not see them as individuals with hopes, dreams, feelings, or other human characteristics. Rather, he views them as appliances that he can take out when he wants something done, put away when he doesn't, swear at when they don't work correctly, and discard and replace when they no longer give him the results he needs.

> Charlotte: After several embarrassing incidents when he berated waitstaff, I quit going out to dinner with him. The only time he could behave himself was when he was at his own country club and he didn't want to look like a jerk in front of everyone. Thank goodness, they had a policy of members treating the waitstaff with respect. He regularly insulted hotel and rental car customer service attendants when things were not to his liking, calling them idiots and other names, and making a loud scene. It was always embarrassing to go on vacation with him. I still use the same bank that he does, and I hear of his verbal abuse from the bank tellers.

Attention Seeking

SNAPs like to be the center of attention, and they dress to bring attention to themselves. The more people comment, the more they will wear the outfit that draws attention.

> Charlotte: Tim loved to wear flamboyant clothes because so many people commented on them. For example, he bought an $800 beaver-felt cowboy hat on a ski trip and had it hand-delivered to him at a restaurant in front of our party of twenty and the entire restaurant. People still remind me of his bright red jacket that he wears at Christmas. He had several pairs of custom-made cowboy boots, a fringed deerskin jacket, and a fluffy full-length fur coat. He dressed cowboy style even though he didn't ride horses, and he wore loud gold and diamond jewelry in an ultra-traditional town where the norm was understated preppy. He was quite a sight.

In the same way they dress for attention, SNAPs will drive cars and boats that draw attention to themselves and make them feel more attractive. Because of their overly active sex drive, they equate driving a sports car with sex appeal, regardless of age. A large part of their identity is driving an ostentatious car.

> Charlotte: Every car that Tim chose for himself was expensive and luxurious: Mercedes-Benz, BMW, Jaguar. His cars were always new. The cars that he chose for me were mom cars: Jeep, Lincoln, GMC SUVs. Except for one, he chose my cars without any input from me, and he always titled them in his name. He had a red Jaguar sports car that he loved because everyone commented on how beautiful it was. When he saw a sports car that he thought was good looking, he would get excited and say, "That's raw sex!" He was always quick to point out to others that he drove a mahogany custom-built boat, even though he had trouble maneuvering it—so much so that he crashed it once and had several close calls—and it was a poor choice for family water activities like water skiing.

> Hilary: Stan was all about the image. He insisted that his son live in the affluent suburbs and that we drive a Mercedes.

SNAPs want to be noticed for their homes as well as for their clothes and cars. A SNAP's home, with its fine furnishings and collection of unique things, is designed for the guest to "ooh and aah" over. A SNAP does not always have class, so unless his partner has good taste, a SNAP's home can run the risk of looking like expensive trash because the main goal is to impress others with his success.

> Hilary: When we were determining where to live, I received this unbelievable text from Stan that outlined just how materialistic his thinking was about where he lived and where he wanted his child to live: "My children *are* where they live in their environment . . . 1. Lake Forest 2. Glencoe 3. Highland Park 4. Wilmette 5. Barrington Hills 6. North Barrington. . . ." He unabashedly equates money and a fancy home with value as a person.

Unapologetically Uses People

SNAPs view all people—family, friends, business acquaintances, even strangers—as tools to serve their needs. When meeting a new person, they automatically size up how that person can be useful to them—whether for good tickets to a special event, an introduction for a lucrative business opportunity, free services or products of some sort, or some other self-serving purpose. They keep in touch occasionally to make sure someone on the other end will pick up the phone when they need something. As one young SNAP in the making said, "It's always good to have a friend with IT skills at your disposal."

Other Annoying Attitudes and Behaviors

"Spin Doctors"—Truth Twisting, Excuses, and Cover-Ups for Poor Behavior or Failure

SNAPs are the kings of spin. They will never admit failure, defeat, or wrongdoing to themselves or others. So their spins sometimes take on mental gymnastics to absolve themselves of appearing less than perfect. When you listen closely, it becomes clear that a SNAP is so out of touch with reality that he is delusional.

> Charlotte: Tim could never admit that he did something wrong. For example, even small things, like missing a highway exit because he wasn't paying attention, were blamed on nonexistent things: "The truck was blocking the sign." "The sign didn't give me time to turn off." In truth, he was on the phone and missed the exit.
>
> One day he got lost going home from work. He had a horrible sense of direction. Rather than admitting he was on the wrong street, he called up the nanny and yelled at her: "Where have you moved the house?" That is a whole new level of delusional—that he would blame someone for moving a house rather than admit he wasn't paying attention and went down the wrong street.
>
> He was fired in 2000 because he was so verbally abusive to his employees. In something that seemed like a scene from a Hollywood movie, the board of directors of his company flew in on Monday, June 5, 2000, and he was fired and escorted out that day. He was the chief operating officer and executive vice president, made more than a million dollars a year, and had worked there more than twenty-five years. Normally, if a board wants someone who has had decades of service to retire, they will bring up the conversation years in advance, start a succession plan, choose a retirement date, and send them on with good wishes. There was none of that. Before the press release got out, Tim started calling his people and said that he had "retired." He blamed the board and accused the new president of being a traitor. In his irrational mind, he never accepted any responsibility that he had created an environment of hostility and fear that made it impossible for people to function.
>
> In an amazing display of self-delusion, on April 19, 2013, when I told him that I could not remain married to a man who raped me in front of my children and raped me every day, twice a day, for three months and would not admit to wrongdoing, he claimed that I had agreed to it all. Having sex in front of children constitutes the felony of child sexual exploitation in Illinois (but I couldn't prosecute because it happened in Italy). No sane mother in the world would ever consent to that, nor did I consent to have sex multiple times a day every day. He literally grabbed my shoulders or wrists and wouldn't let go until I capitulated, but he had to blame someone other than himself.
>
> When I reported Tim to DCFS (Department of Children and Family Services), he lied to the investigator and claimed that I had a long-term mental illness, that I abandoned my family, that he filed for divorce because of my abandonment, that I had an affair and remarried within six months of the divorce, that he had never sexually abused me, and that he had never abused me in any way. DCFS never even interviewed me.

The Non-Apology Apology

A SNAP will only apologize if he will gain something from it. He will not apologize or admit to any wrongdoing only to admit guilt. If he does apologize, it will not be a true apology. True repentance requires admitting that what he did was intentional and wrong—confessing that he is truly regretful and acknowledging that he caused pain or loss to another person. A person who sincerely apologizes makes every attempt to make things right by repaying a debt, paying for a loss, repairing a relationship, or reversing the effects of their actions. A heartfelt apology is accompanied by a change of heart and attitude, ensuring that the harmful behavior won't be repeated. A SNAP is not capable of true repentance, but if he wants something badly enough, he might eke out the non-apology apology.

The non-apology apology consists of a weak utterance that, when closely examined, puts the blame of his wrongdoing back on the victim. Rather than admitting he has hurt someone, the SNAP will say something like, "I'm sorry that you feel that way." "I'm sorry that you can't forgive me." "I'm sorry that you don't want to make things work." "I'm sorry, but you do the same things to me." The SNAP may even state the all-inclusive, vague non-apology of "Mistakes were made," which doesn't admit that his actions were intentional, but merely an accident.

The non-apology apology is so prevalent among politicians, many who may be labeled SNAPs, that it has its own Wikipedia page.

> Charlotte: Like all SNAPs, Tim could not admit wrongdoing or apologize. For example, when my daughter was filling out a high school form that required her to put down her weight, he saw it and said something like, "Oh, my gosh! That's a lot!" She was in tears and went running to her room. I told him he needed to apologize, but all her sixty-nine-year-old father could muster to his crying fourteen-year-old daughter was, "I'm sorry, but you hurt my feelings sometimes too!"
>
> On July 4, 2010, Tim was driving his boat way too fast with two boys being pulled in an inner tube and Tim trying to fly them off. He whipped them around a curve, and they both launched into the air. They had a midair collision, requiring a trip to the emergency room, stitches for one boy and surgery for the other. Tim never admitted that his foolishness and reckless driving caused the collision. Instead, he called it a "freak accident."
>
> After I left our house and we went through a year of pastoral and psychological counseling, Tim still could not bring himself to admit the intentional things he had done to destroy our relationship. The pastor suggested that he go through my letter line by line and apologize for each of the abuses and make amends. Although Tim agreed that everything I had put in my letter was true, he wouldn't do it. He just said, "Mistakes were made." That's not an apology. I finally filed for divorce after a yearlong separation. Seeing that his "apologies" weren't working as he had planned to lure me back, he immediately changed his tune, blamed all his abusive behavior on me, and blamed me for leaving the marriage.

Not every behavior or attitude of a SNAP is abusive, but his entire demeanor clearly shows that he is the most important person in his life, and he expects that he fills the same role in everyone else's life too.

CHAPTER 13

The Other Woman (and There's Always Another Woman)

Christian women are often surprised when, as their attorney or counselor, I tell them that their abusive, narcissistic, so-called Christian husband has another woman on the side. A quick look through his laptop computer typically confirms this. We should not be surprised. A narcissist, sociopath, psychopath, or other domestic abuser is simply acting in line with his character.

You see, SNAPS have similar characteristics. When comparing notes, women in support groups often discover that their husbands do or say the exact same things as other husbands do. Once you know what you are dealing with, SNAPs are predictable.

Among other things, they lack empathy, a conscience, or remorse, they are incapable of accepting responsibility for their deceit and manipulation, they rage, and they have a sense of entitlement and grandiosity. SNAPs are users. They exploit people, regardless of their relationship, for their own selfish gratification. Sexual promiscuity is one of the Hare diagnostic features for sociopaths and psychopaths. While a man filled with the Holy Spirit will view his wife as a treasured gift and consider lovemaking a time of giving and sharing, a SNAP simply sees women as a means to an end and views sex as a time of taking what he wants, when he wants, and how he wants.

When we feel hungry and need to eat, we might like to go to our favorite local restaurant for a juicy steak. However, if that restaurant is closed or we are out of town, we are still hungry, and to satisfy that hunger, nearly anything will do. We don't feel remorseful or guilty or a sense of betrayal about going to McDonald's or Chipotle instead of our favorite restaurant. We're just hungry. An abuser views sex in much the same way. He's hungry, and if his favorite gal is unavailable or he is out of town, he is still hungry for sex, and nearly anything will do. Because he lacks the deep emotional and spiritual attachment to his spouse that healthy couples have, and because he does not view sex as a God-designed way to make spouses feel loved and cherished, he feels no sense of remorse or guilt for getting his needs met elsewhere. But due to social norms that still value monogamy and view infidelity as grounds for divorce, he will usually try to keep his sexual escapades hidden.

A SNAP uses the word *love* to entice a woman he views as useful. He "hooks" her emotionally and financially so she will fall for him and possibly marry an abuser. He may view her as arm candy or someone who can advance his career or take care of his house and his kids. In the meantime, he'll make his fortune and ensure that she gives him whatever resources and prestige he needs to meet his goals. Abusive relationships repeat the cycle of love-bombing, devaluating, and discarding with each new target.

The SNAP will have a woman waiting in the wings with whom he has already embarked on a new cycle of love-bombing while he completes a cycle of devaluation or discarding with his previous partner. Most women who have married an abuser unwittingly start as "the other woman." Many Christian women find, to their surprise and sometimes years later, that they were the other woman while their husband was married to another. This discovery is often made during the throes of a divorce, when she has separated from the toxicity and has excavated the truth. Things that were unexplainable before start fitting together like the pieces of a puzzle. This fraud often goes undetected for years due to yet another trait of abusers—pathological lying—in which an abuser tells his unsuspecting girlfriend that he is single or divorced, his wife left him for no reason, his wife had mental issues, his wife had an affair, all his exes are crazy, etc., etc., when in fact he is very much married to a lovely woman very much like her.

> Charlotte: The night I met the other woman, I came home unannounced to switch cars before going to our youngest son's wrestling match. I found my husband and my replacement making out in front of the roaring fireplace in our family room, drinking Chardonnay wine from our glasses. (I knew he was interested in her because he would only drink red wine.) She was attractive and well-dressed, with the look of a well-to-do North Shore real estate agent. A BMW was parked in our driveway. A nauseous feeling came over me that I cannot describe. How could he say I was the most important person in his life and that he wanted to make our marriage work when he obviously didn't care about me? How could he be so lovey-dovey to her when he could not say a single nice thing to his wife and the mother of his children? It was awkward, so Tim got up off the couch and walked over, introduced Didi with a big smile, and gushed about how wonderful she was to have gone to the pharmacy to get him some medications because he wasn't feeling well. I couldn't even get a thank you for all I had done for him, but now he was bragging to his wife about his obviously longtime girlfriend. I felt I was in a soap opera.
>
> A few weeks later, I had lunch with Pat, his first wife, to get a reality check. Was it me, or had he always been abusive? When we had first started dating, Tim had told me that he had been separated from his wife for nine months, and later he told me he had filed for divorce because she had essentially abandoned him and refused to go on trips or social events with him. He had at one point admitted to me that he had had a number of affairs over the years when married to his first wife, but I had naïvely assumed that since he started going to church with me and he professed to be a Christian, those days were behind him.
>
> Pat was a lovely woman and had been gracious to me. She had offered to go to lunch, so I took her up on it. When Pat and I compared notes, we discovered that our mutual husband had not changed much in his forty-two years of collective marriage, including his pathological lying. She shared that she had never refused to go anywhere with him, and his claims of abandonment were false. I shared that I had recently discovered that in 1990 he had purchased the home he now lives in while he was married to her, but had carefully hid it in a land trust and got a personal loan from Bill, a wealthy friend, to keep it hidden during their divorce. But the bombshell came when Pat informed me that she, not Tim, had filed for divorce because of his infidelity. Not for the affairs with the women whom he had kept carefully hidden over the years, but with me! I had been the

other woman! His claim that he was separated when we met and that he had divorced her because she had abandoned him were false. The reality sunk in that I had believed his lies for twenty-five years. How foolish and naïve I had been! I could do nothing but apologize profusely and thank the Lord that I was escaping from a man who has never cared about any of his wives, including the one who would come after me.

Later, I discovered through reading a transcript of his interview with DCFS that Tim lied and told others (and very likely Didi) that he divorced me because I had abandoned him, had a mental illness for many years, and had an affair.

The pieces of the puzzle started coming together. Tim was repeating a page out of the Abuser's Playbook that he and all abusers know so well: (1) Abuse the wife so she can't leave. (2) If you miscalculate and she leaves, then start a slander campaign. (3) Play the victim. (4) Claim your wife abandoned you. (5) Claim you divorced your wife for her abandonment. (6) Falsely accuse her of infidelity, mental illness, and abuse to keep others from knowing about your own infidelities, narcissism/sociopathy/psychopathy, and atrocities (a useful tactic known as projection). (7) Go to church to appear respectable and where naïve folks will believe you, support you, and give you cheap grace instead of hold you accountable. (8) Turn the unsuspicious other woman into your next wife before she figures all this out.

A woman in a marriage with an abuser often feels replaceable, expendable, and disposable because—well, because to an abuser, she is. Both his words and deeds have told her so repeatedly. And when she has been defrauded by her own husband, the one she should be able to trust, to discover that she was the other woman or has been replaced by the other woman, she often feels guilty and foolish and dirty.

Dear reader, if you have been in an abusive relationship, I want to talk directly to your wounded heart. Daughter of the heavenly Father, princess of the King of Kings, beloved of the Lord of Lords, you are not replaceable, expendable, or disposable. You are not guilty, foolish, or dirty. Reject those lies that are straight from the mouth of the Enemy, the Father of Lies. Replace them with God's truth: you are fearfully and wonderfully made; you were planned by Papa God before the beginning of the world; you were designed in the workshop of heaven to be like no one else. There is no one like you on the planet. God loves you. He delights in you. He sings songs over you. He is with you, He is for you, and He upholds you with His strong right hand. He will fight your battle for you. He will rescue you, and He has amazing plans for you. He designed you to be in healthy, loving, life-giving relationships with those who love Him and cherish you, not with an abuser who can do neither.

Chapter 14

Confronting the Abuser and Conflict Resolution

Conflicts eventually arise in all relationships. How couples handle them largely determines how happy the parties are and how long the relationship will last. In healthy relationships, each person seeks to understand the other. Each party will listen to come to an understanding of the other's position. Successful resolution of conflict requires each party to be respectful, open, and avoid defensive language and behavior. Each must honestly try to understand the other's perspective and sincerely attempt to do what is best for each other and for the relationship. In healthy relationships, each person will adjust for the other out of love and respect. For example, if a husband must get up early for work, his wife may ask him to get ready quietly so that she can sleep in another hour because she has been up all night with a sick child. The wise husband who wants to maintain harmony in his marriage will acquiesce to his wife's request out of love and respect. The thoughtful husband will not have to be asked to be quiet, because he already recognizes that his wife has been up and needs her sleep.

In healthy relationships, neither party will intentionally try to hurt the other because what hurts his partner and the relationship also hurts him. The healthy person recognizes that the couple's interests are intertwined. If a husband continually hurts his wife, which in turn damages the relationship, the wife may emotionally or physically leave the relationship, which in turn hurts the husband emotionally and/or financially.

Conflicts will certainly emerge in a relationship with a SNAP because of his extreme selfishness and repeated abuses. However, when a SNAP is asked to be more respectful or kind, or when the SNAP is confronted for his bad behavior, no matter how gently or kindly the request is presented, his goal is never conflict resolution, understanding his partner, or forging a better relationship. While healthy people acknowledge that they have imperfections and can still go on with their lives, the SNAP cannot admit that he is less than perfect. When confronted, his goal is to win at all costs. Because he doesn't care about the feelings of others or his relationships with others, they are the first casualties. Even when the outcome means that the abuser is headed for divorce, which will certainly cost him financially, the abuser will refuse to resolve conflict. There is never a conflict resolution with an abuser. Eventually, the victim learns to simply be quiet, not ask for anything, not ask to be treated with respect, and not bring up any bad behavior. Life with an abuser eventually becomes two separate lives—with the victim walking on eggshells trying to appease the unappeasable.

Confronting the Abuser and Conflict Resolution

A small movement may sometimes be achieved if the victim presents the situation to the abuser in such a way as to not confront him with his bad behavior. She may present his behavior in a way that strokes his ego and praises him, or as something advantageous to him. She may even attempt to inject humor. For example, SNAPs are well known for their sexual appetite and complete disregard for their partners' feelings, as long as their own sexual appetite is satiated. This often results in the SNAP demanding sex late at night after a long, busy day when the wife is exhausted. The fact that his wife has just buried her mother after a long illness, during which time she was the caretaker, will make no difference to the SNAP. The wife may be able to delay sex until the next morning so she can get a decent night's sleep by praising the SNAP and telling him what an amazing lover he is, letting him know that they will have more time for sex and she will perform better if he can wait until morning after their houseful of relatives leave. The SNAP will likely ignore her and demand sex anyway, but it is worth a shot.

SNAPs will often act as if nothing happened after they have just behaved atrociously. It seems that if they pretend nothing happened, then the victim will pretend nothing happened, and will perhaps even question themselves if it really did happen. Things will just go along like nothing happened, which is precisely what the SNAP wants.

Confronting a SNAP will certainly invite further abuse. The Bible warns, "Whoever corrects a mocker [i.e., the proud and arrogant] invites insults; whoever rebukes the wicked incurs abuse. Do not rebuke mockers or they will hate you" (Proverbs 9:7–8). Any woman who has ever lived with a SNAP knows this to be true.

Because SNAPs will exacerbate the abuse when confronted, many women choose to ignore it, walk away, or go along to get along until it escalates to a point that is unsafe or unbearable.

Below are some of the tactics and emotional abuses used by SNAPs when the victim confronts her abuser.

Rage

A common reaction is full-blown rage. Rage is a SNAP's typical reaction when he perceives even the slightest suggestion that he is less than perfect or is not being worshiped properly. While healthy people are not thrilled about being called out on their bad behavior, the SNAP goes from calm to rage as quickly as the flip of a switch. The raging intimidates and silences the other person, which is precisely what the abuser wants. If the partner reacts with anger, the abuser will up the ante and rage even more. Because the abuser must win at all costs, he will continue to escalate his rage until the other person backs down, and the abuser will smugly perceive he has won.

Denying the Abuse

Even if the victim has just heard or witnessed the abuse within the last few seconds, the SNAP may deny it. Denying reality is a form of gaslighting, intended to make the victim question her sanity and whether things really happened. The abuses that the SNAP carries out are often so beyond the pale that most healthy people have trouble wrapping their heads around what just happened. The SNAP has learned that simply denying his bad behavior or words can make the victim believe it never happened—because she usually wants to deny that it happened too. If she can pretend it never happened, then she can pretend that everything is still okay and is not the crazy reality she's experiencing.

Minimalizing the Abuse

If the SNAP doesn't outright deny the abuse, he may attempt to minimize or trivialize it. "It wasn't that bad." "You're making a big thing out of nothing." "You always blow things out of proportion." These are all common ways an abuser will try to make light of his abuse.

Claiming She Consented

An abuser may falsely claim that his victim consented to his actions, so she has no reason to complain. To an abuser, everything that happens has been agreed to by his victim—even if it was done because of his blackmail, fraud, coercion, distress, intimidation, bullying, or raging.

Blaming Others

An abuser will oftentimes blame his bad behavior on the victim or someone or something else. He will never take responsibility for his poor behavior. For example, he may claim, "Well, if you didn't make me so mad, I wouldn't hit you. You know when you do that, it makes me mad. You shouldn't do that to me." Or he might blame something else: "I couldn't get the payment in on time because the teller at the damn bank wouldn't cash the check." When blaming something or someone else, the abuser will ignore the fact that the bank wouldn't cash the check because he waited until the last minute to deposit it.

Justifying His Actions

When an abuser is confronted with his bad behavior, he will often try to justify completely unjustifiable actions. This is often couched in a statement that she should be thankful he didn't do something worse, or he is not as bad as so-and-so. Although it may be logical to his disordered mind, there is simply no reasonable explanation.

> Denise: After my teenage daughter confided in me that my husband had fondled her breasts, I confronted him. His response: "Well, at least I didn't rape her."

Attacking Her Verbally and Physically

When confronted with his bad behavior, an abuser will undoubtedly verbally attack his victim using a variety of tactics including projection, name-calling, insults, and gaslighting.

When an abuser has very little self-control, he may also physically attack his victim when confronted with his own bad behavior. Physical attacks may include spitting, shaking, shoving, hitting, pushing down stairs, throwing objects, or even using a weapon against her.

Threats

An abuser will often lash out and threaten those who confront him to get them to comply with his demands and keep silent. Threats of divorce are common, as are threats to sell the house, ghost her by vanishing and ensuring that his wife is stuck with all the bills and raising the kids, or tell everyone that his wife is having an affair and that she is crazy so they will align with the abuser. Abusers use money to control others, so they will threaten to refuse to pay for things that they have already agreed to pay for, or things that their spouse has already put on her credit card and will not be able to pay off without help. For children, this can be devastating. A father will threaten to not pay for college if the child doesn't comply with his unreasonable demands. Prior to marriage, the abuser will refuse to marry his fiancée if she doesn't comply with his demands, such as a one-sided prenuptial agreement. This, of course, is a screaming red flag to run the other way, but she may have already given up her job or moved or had his child, and she so very much wants the relationship to work.

Playing the Victim

An abuser will play the victim when confronted and when his partner has emotionally cut him off or left. If the abuser still feels he can control his partner, he will use one of the other tactics to silence her and shut her down. But if he feels that she has distanced herself emotionally and/or physically, he will play the pity card, claiming to feel alone and abandoned to garner sympathy and to get her to come back to his tangled web. It usually works.

> Charlotte: During one of the times that I needed some space and spent a day or two in a hotel to get away from my abusive husband, I came back to the house to pack some things and saw a pitiful note from Tim on my bathroom mirror: "I feel like I have lost my best friend." Of course, I then felt sorry for him and came back, just as he had planned.

Defensiveness

A SNAP will be defensive when approached by his partner. His goal is never to come to an understanding and move forward together. His goal is to win and blame someone or something else so that he can retain his perfect image of himself.

The Non-Apology Apology

If the SNAP apologizes at all, it will not be a real apology. He will admit next to nothing and will place the blame back on the victim or somewhere else.

CHAPTER 15

Counseling and Marriage Books

IN A TYPICAL RELATIONSHIP, women tend to be deeply invested. They want to preserve their marriages and will often buy books on marriage to improve their relationship with their husband. They will propose marriage counseling for the two of them in the hope that he will recognize the damage he is doing to their relationship and will make the changes necessary for a healthy, vibrant relationship. When books and counseling fail, women married to SNAPs become discouraged and lose hope. They are emotionally, spiritually, and often physically wounded, and they usually suffer PTSD from living under a constant toxic environment.

Every marriage book should have on its front page a huge warning in bold letters: **THIS DOES NOT APPLY IF YOU ARE IN AN ABUSIVE RELATIONSHIP WITH A NARCISSIST, SOCIOPATH, PSYCHOPATH, OR OTHER ABUSER. IF YOU ARE IN ONE OF THESE RELATIONSHIPS, NOTHING IN THIS BOOK WILL HELP YOU.**

Marriage books like *The 5 Love Languages, Men Are from Mars, Women Are from Venus, The Marriage You've Always Wanted, The Power of a Praying Wife,* and thousands more are based on the premise that the marriage consists of two generally good-hearted, semi-healthy humans who want the best for each other and for their marriage. That is the only way a marriage can work, and that is an assumption most marriage books make.

Selfishness and lack of empathy, like all characteristics, are on a sliding scale for most people. Marriage counseling may be effective for some couples when these and other unhealthy traits are at the lower end of scale. However, conventional marital advice does not apply when one partner has no conscience and no empathy, takes delight in hurting people, is vindictive, and has a split personality.

A competent marriage counselor knows that marriage counseling is contraindicated for abusive marriages and that narcissistic personality disorder and antisocial personality disorder are incurable, permanent personality disorders that do not respond well to treatment.[81] Expecting a SNAP to change with counseling is akin to expect-

---

[81] Lindsay Dodgson, "How Psychopaths and Sociopaths Deceive and Trick Their Therapists," *Business Insider*, August 8, 2017, https://www.businessinsider.com/psychopathy-treatment-2017-8?r=UK; Lindsay Dodgson, "Psychopaths Cannot Be Cured—Here's Why," *Business Insider*, March 4, 2018, https://www.businessinsider.com/psychopaths-cannot-be-cured-heres-why-2018-2; Yvette Brazier, "Living with Someone with NPD," *Medical News Today*, January 2, 2018, https://www.medicalnewstoday.com/articles/9741.

ing someone who has a severe permanent intellectual disability to change with counseling. It will not happen. Most SNAPs are undiagnosed, but even if they are diagnosed, they are permanently cruel.

That is not to say that having a personality disorder excuses the abuser's actions. They always have a choice in how they treat people. Unlike other diagnoses that may cause unintended behavior, a diagnosis of narcissistic personality disorder, sociopathy, or psychopathy is based on the intentional, cruel, sadistic behavior toward others. For example, someone diagnosed with cerebral palsy will act differently from healthy individuals because his condition causes unintentional movements that are largely out of his control. Conversely, diagnosis of a Cluster B personality disorder is based on observations of intentional behaviors: lack of empathy and conscience, grandiose fantasies, and outlandish arrogance. An abuser cannot use the excuse that he has a personality disorder and therefore is not responsible for his actions, because he chooses his behavior and he can act perfectly acceptable when he wants to impress someone or he wants something from them. And just as quickly as he switches a light on, he can change those pleasant actions to cruelty aimed at his victim. This Dr. Jekyll/Mr. Hyde double personality is prevalent in abusers.

Most SNAPs will refuse to attend counseling, preferring to throw away years or even decades of a marriage rather than discuss how they played a part in its breakdown and how they must change in order to stay in the marriage. This, of course, is the opposite attitude of healthy individuals, who are willing to accept responsibility, admit fault, and make reasonable changes to keep a marriage and family intact. A SNAP's refusal to seek help also demonstrates their self-destructive nature. They are so proud and so insistent on being right that they will engage in behaviors that are harmful to themselves (such as divorce), just to avoid having to admit that they are imperfect.

Those SNAPs who agree to attend counseling do so with only one purpose in mind: to get their victim to return to the abusive relationship and make her feel like any problems are her fault. Many SNAPs are such good liars and manipulators that they will deceive an inexperienced counselor into thinking that the fault lies with the victim. This is, obviously, even more harmful to a victim, who is now being told by her counselor and her abuser that she is in the wrong. Therefore, great care must be taken to choose a counselor who has experience in domestic abuse, narcissistic personality disorder, and antisocial personality disorder. A local domestic violence shelter should be able to direct you to an appropriate counselor. In addition, having a preliminary interview prior to engaging in counseling and asking how much experience the counselor has with Cluster B personality disorders and domestic abuse will give the victim an idea of whether she needs to look elsewhere.

The gold standard for treating a SNAP requires two psychologists (with PhDs), both with ten years of experience treating SNAPs in the room at the same time, so that when one is tripped up by the crazy talk of the SNAP, the other can move in and keep the conversation on track. Even if progress can be made, it takes months, if not years, and is miniscule. However, the gold standard is rarely, if ever, followed. It is cost-prohibitive for most, and it is very difficult to find even one psychologist with a specialty in SNAP, much less two psychologists with specialties in SNAP who will practice together.

The abuser may admit his deeds in counseling, and he may even cry and feign an apology, but these are crocodile tears and insincere apologies intended to manipulate the wife to return to the abusive relationship. Even in counseling, most victims are afraid to confront an abuser. So the abuser attempts to be on good behavior in the hope of getting the victim to return to what will be an even more abusive relationship. However, if the victim pushes back by making the abuser uncomfortable, confronting him, denying his request, or refusing to return to the relationship, the true nature of the abuser will surface. The apologies will evaporate, and the lies, accusations, denials, justifications, and rage will reappear. The abuser will refuse to attend any more counseling sessions if he sees no hope of his victim returning, even if the counseling sessions would be helpful to manage the divorce process for the sake of the children, or would make him a more understanding father. Once the counseling sessions end, the relationship will deteriorate quickly.

The most a victim can expect from counseling with her abuser is confirmation that she is doing the proper thing when she decides to leave. At some point in counseling, the victim will come to the realization that the SNAP does not, in fact, love her or care about her or their marriage. Although she will go into counseling hoping that the Holy Spirit will work on the hard heart of her husband, she will eventually find out that his heart is too hard. He is too proud to humble himself and make the changes necessary for a healthy relationship. He will never love her the way Ephesians 5 describes a husband's self-sacrificing love for his wife. There is no hope that this marriage will fulfill the purpose of marriage of being a blessing to each other and to others. She will reluctantly discover that her husband uses the word *love* merely to keep her in an abusive relationship, and that his behavior has nothing to do with love, but is rather the conduct of a self-centered, cruel monster who takes delight in hurting her and others to feel superior. She will come to the painful realization that he will never view her as a treasure, a true partner, and a unique and beautiful gift from God with wonderful qualities—including a caring nature, a forgiving spirit, and a desire to invest in relationships and people. She will finally realize that he views her as an object that can be used for his purposes until it no longer works, and then it will be discarded and replaced.

In much the same way that a doctor will do all he can do to save a dying patient before the patient is pronounced dead, a healthy woman will do all she can do to save a marriage before declaring it over. Although counseling will not save her marriage, there is some comfort in a woman knowing that she has done all she can do.

CHAPTER 16

Why Do They Do What They Do?

THIS IS THE AGE-OLD question—what makes narcissists, sociopaths, psychopaths, and other abusers do what they do? We don't have all the answers, but we do have a few.

Abuse Is Learned Behavior

First, we know that a great deal of abuse is learned behavior. Research shows that individuals with secondary psychopathy (i.e., those who are emotionally reactive, dysregulated, and anxious) generally come from a severely dysfunctional family of origin that also had abuse, trauma, and other environmental factors.[82] They learned from an abusive dad (or mother) how to abuse others. We also know that they know how to be on good behavior, because they can do so when they want something. For example, a SNAP may act politely to a boss or person of influence, even though behind closed doors the SNAP chooses to be abusive to a spouse. The SNAP knows that to get what he wants or to garner favor with a person of influence or authority, he needs to act appropriately to them. The SNAP also knows that he can act abusively to his spouse because he has the power over her, and he knows that she will tolerate his behavior.

Abusers also learn good behavior because they have figured out it will get them what they want, not because it comes naturally or because they are altruistic. A SNAP will love-bomb his new love interest in an effort to win her over, knowing that most women will not fall for an abuser if he reveals his abusive nature. However, even in the love-bombing phase, he is already planning on setting the hook so he can switch to abusive behavior when she is emotionally, financially, and sexually dependent upon him.

When a woman sees her abusive spouse wining and dining another woman, she is often distraught and wonders why he can't be that nice to her anymore. The fact is abusers seem to have a shelf life. They can only be on good behavior for a limited period before they implode and their true selves appear. Once an abuser has moved on to the devaluation or discard stage of a romantic relationship, he cannot go back to the love-bombing

---

[82] B.M. Hicks, M.D. Carlson, D.M. Blonigen, C.J. Patrick, W.G. Iacono, & M. Mgue, "Psychopathic Personality Traits and Environmental Contexts: Differential Correlates, Gender Differences, and Genetic Mediation." Personality disorders, (2012) 3(3), 209–227. https://www.ncbi.nlm.nih.gov/pmc/articles/PMC3387315/

stage with the same woman. The other woman, who is also a victim, will eventually see this. It would behoove a woman to realize that the abuser doesn't love the next woman any more or less than he loved her. In fact, he doesn't love anyone. She is just next, and he is doing what predators do to get her into his lair.

The Biological Component

Second, some abuse is biological. Research correlates primary psychopathy, i.e., psychopaths who are unemotional, emotionally under-reactive, lack anxiety, and have high narcissism, with a genetic foundation and biological predisposition.[83] Nonetheless, abusers still know right from wrong and acceptable from unacceptable behavior. This is clear because whenever they are accused of unacceptable behavior, their first reaction is to deny, minimize, or justify. I would venture to say that there has never been a rapist who has not denied the accusations of rape when it came to light before a judge, jury, employer, or pastor.

Some may feel that a diagnosis of narcissism, sociopathy, or psychopathy is an excuse for their behavior; however, we must be careful not to think that way. Regardless of our genetic tendencies or upbringing, we each are required to choose to behave in appropriate and healthy ways. Diagnoses of one or more dangerous personality disorders are not excuses for harming others. Permitting some to have no standards of behavior and have no accountability would wreak havoc on society.

The Spiritual Side of Abuse

Third, and perhaps most important, is the spiritual component of abuse. In the same way we recognize Spirit-filled individuals by their godly speech and conduct, we also recognize those who are under Satan's influence. Abusers have chosen to reject God and follow Satan. Secular psychologists and psychiatrists speak in nonspiritual terms when they describe SNAPs, using terms such as "unhealthy" and causing "trauma," "abuse," and "betrayal." But for those of us who see the world from a spiritual perspective, we must call an abuser's actions and abuse what it is: evil. No sugarcoating, no minimizing, no excuses.

A person filled with the Holy Spirit produces the fruit of the Spirit: love, joy, peace, patience, kindness, goodness, faithfulness, gentleness, self-control, humility, and unselfishness. They are not jealous, not self-seeking or attention seeking, slow to anger, slow to take offense, and don't keep grudges. Spirit-filled people are truthful, protective of loved ones, trusting in God's promises and His goodness, discerning, persevering, grateful, generous, and hopeful. They have an accurate idea of God, see the best in others, want the best for others, support others, respect others and themselves, and act in the best interest of others (Galatians 5:22–23; 1 Corinthians 13:4–7). We know that people who have these characteristics are God's people because they act in obedience to Him, in accordance with God's good character. "If you are constantly doing what is good, it is because you *are* good, even as [Jesus] is. . . . The person who has been born into God's family does not make a practice of sinning because now God's life is in him; so he can't keep on sinning, for this new life has been born into him and controls him—he has been born again" (1 John 3:7, 9 TLB).

---

[83] Hicks, Carlson, et al., 2012; R.D. Hare and C.S. Neumann, "Psychopathy as a Clinical and Empirical Construct." Annual Review of Clinical Psychology, April 2008, Col. 4:2-7-246. https://www.annualreviews.org/doi/full/10.1146/annurev.clinpsy.3.022806.091452?url_ver=Z39.88-2003&rfr_id=ori%3Arid%3Acrossref.org&rfr_dat=cr_pub++-0pubmed;
E. Viding, J.R. Blair, T.E. Moffitt, R. Plomin, "Evidence for Substantial Genetic Risk for Psychopathy in 7-year-olds." J. Child Psychol Psychiatry 2005 June: 46(6):592-7. https://pubmed.ncbi.nlm.nih.gov/15877765/.

On the other hand, a person filled with the evil of Satan's spirit demonstrates an unrepentant lifestyle filled with these characteristics: sexual immorality, lustful thoughts, pornography, greed, hatred, resentment and jealousy, raging, temper tantrums, angry quarrels, selfishness, arrogance, haughtiness, enviousness, and murder. They engage in uncontrolled addictions, wild parties, impurity, debauchery, drunkenness, divisiveness, senseless arguments, lying, discord, selfish ambition, orgies, and the like. They value and chase after money and material things while rejecting God, they manipulate and abuse others, and they think only of themselves (Galatians 5:19–21). Scripture tells us that someone who lives this lifestyle will not enter the kingdom of God. We know that people who have these characteristics are Satan's people because they act in accordance with Satan's evil character—and the fruit of their life shows it. "But if you keep on sinning, it shows that you belong to Satan, who since he first began to sin has kept steadily at it. But the Son of God came to destroy the works of the devil. . . . So now we can tell who is a child of God and who belongs to Satan. Whoever is living a life of sin and doesn't love his brother shows that he is not in God's family; for the message to us from the beginning has been that we should love one another" (1 John 3:8, 10–11 TLB).

One might think that nearly everyone has done something on the naughty list that disqualifies them as a child of God. But Scripture is clear that those who are God's children have the Holy Spirit in them, convicting them of sin and bringing them to their knees in repentance. Their lives are not characterized by the sins Paul identifies in Galatians 5. That is, they do not have a lifestyle of sin.

Lest we fall into the trap of excusing the SNAP under the fallacy of "the devil made me do it" reasoning, rest assured that abusers have made a conscious choice to reject God and follow the Enemy. Satan is the underlying force behind evil, but following Satan's ways is always a deliberate decision of the person who refuses God and joins the Enemy's team.

To discern God-followers from those enslaved to the Enemy, look at the fruit of their lives, which reveals their hearts. Jesus warns that evil people often come disguised as good people, and He cautions us to stay away from them because they will destroy us.

> Beware of false teachers who come disguised as harmless sheep, but are wolves and will tear you apart. You can detect them by the way they act, just as you can identify a tree by its fruit. You need never confuse grapevines with thorn bushes or figs with thistles. Different kinds of fruit trees can quickly be identified by examining their fruit. A variety that produces delicious fruit never produces an inedible kind. And a tree producing an inedible kind can't produce what is good. So the trees having the inedible fruit are chopped down and thrown on the fire. Yes, the way to identify a tree or a person is by the kind of fruit produced. (Matthew 7:15–20 TLB)

In nearly every case, the SNAP not only destroys his family, but in the process destroys himself. In many situations, a SNAP will implode physically due to a combination of abuses and addictions, including illegal drugs, prescription drugs, alcohol, pornography, sex, prostitutes, cigarettes, gaming, etc. These, in turn, lead to severe health disorders such as heart conditions, liver disease, sexually transmitted diseases, cancer, etc. The SNAP's arrogance, raging, selfish ambition, manipulation, hatred, and all his other antisocial behaviors often lead to his financial and social implosion as well. In nearly every divorce litigation involving a SNAP, he refuses to settle a case simply to inflict further financial and emotional distress on the departing spouse. In the process, the SNAP incurs huge legal fees, which is not only detrimental to the soon-to-be-ex-wife, but also to him and his children. The legal professionals call these "high conflict divorces," and every high conflict divorce involves a SNAP.

Almost every victim of a SNAP asks herself, "Why does he do that? Why is he hurting me and the kids? Why does he do things that hurt himself too?" Understanding that SNAPs behave in evil ways because their hearts have been taken over by Satan is, perhaps, the best answer. Rational people do not destroy their families and then destroy themselves; rather, they seek to bless those around them. However, we know that Satan's mission statement is to "steal, kill, and destroy." And once Satan is finished using the SNAP to destroy his family, Satan will destroy him too. Unfortunately, the SNAP has no idea that he is being used as Satan's tool.

Almost every victim of a SNAP also asks herself, "Will he ever change?" Just as we cannot change the good nature of God, who is both loving and just, we cannot change the wicked nature of Satan, who is evil. We cannot change the nature of people who are sold out for God and filled with His Spirit, and we cannot change the nature of people who are sold out for the devil.

Part II

Removing the Narcissist/Sociopath/Psychopath/ Domestic Abuser from Your Life

The first "R" of the "3 Rs" of an abusive relationship is recognizing the abuse and the abuser. The second "R" of the "3 Rs" is removing oneself from the abuse and the abuser. This must be done with forethought, strategy, and as safely as possible. No one escapes an abuser unscathed. Conflict and turmoil abound because abusers will have it no other way. In part 2, we help a woman remove herself from her abuser with as few emotional, financial, spiritual, physical, and sexual blows as possible. It's important to remember during this time to keep moving and not return to the abuser. Life will eventually get better if she leaves, and it will undoubtedly get worse if she stays.

Chapter 17

Why Does She Stay?

Many women stay in abusive relationships for years. Critics, detractors, and those who don't understand domestic abuse often ask, "Why didn't she leave?" The abuser may taunt, "It's not that bad. If it was that bad, you would have left years ago." The abuser's minions may mockingly say, "If it was so bad, why did you stay so long?"

Women stay in abusive relationships for several reasons. These are the top ten reasons:

- Lack of finances. Financial abuse exists in 99 percent of abusive relationships, leaving the wife with no access to funds.[84] To safely leave, she needs money for rent, including a security deposit, utilities, phones, food for herself and her children, car payments, gas, insurance, and all the other necessities of life. She needs money to buy new furniture and start a whole new life. She needs money to hire a divorce lawyer, typically requiring a $5,000 retainer. Lack of finances is the most significant reason why women don't leave.
- Hope that Prince Charming reappears. Her husband was not always this way, and she keeps hoping the person she thought she fell in love with will reappear. She doesn't realize she was love-bombed and the person she fell in love with does not exist.
- She does not recognize the cycle of violence. The abuser perpetrates an act of abuse, the victim tries to separate herself, and the abuser apologizes, even begs her stay, and promises to change. For a time, the abuser will be on good behavior, but eventually, the abusive behavior will return, and the whole process repeats itself. During the good times, it gives her hope that he can change. Women in such relationships don't understand that the cycle will continue until they permanently leave or are seriously injured.
- Her faith prohibits separation or divorce. Many people, including pastors in the Christian faith, misunderstand the Scriptures and believe that the only reason for divorce is adultery or desertion by a nonbeliever. Even though this is not an accurate interpretation of Scripture, it is a widely held belief.

---

[84] Dara Richardson-Heron, "Here's the Number One Reason Victims of Domestic Violence Stay," HuffPost, July 14, 2016, https://www.huffingtonpost.com/dr-dara-richardsonheron/economic-empowerment-is-c_b_7792540.html.

As a result, most sources the believing woman consults encourage her to stay in the marriage and offer techniques to resurrect her marriage. Pastors, especially those in churches with a highly patriarchal tradition, give similar advice. But almost every Christian book and pastor gives advice on normal marriage issues for normal people. They do not address narcissistic personality disorder, sociopathy, or psychopathy, and they don't address abuse. The advice in most Christian books or coming from pastors is not applicable to abusers. We discuss biblical divorce in cases of abuse in chapter 34.

- Most women with children do not want to break up their family. Women overwhelmingly define themselves by their relationships. For most women, and all women of faith, protecting her children and keeping her family together is her highest priority. She knows that the family is the foundation of healthy children. She also knows that divorce has a devastating effect on children. She understands that her husband is not perfect, but she is struggling with whether it is worse to (a) stay in the marriage so that her children at least have a father at home and she can protect the children and be a positive influence, or (b) leave the marriage, likely becoming impoverished and being forced by a court to send her children to their abusive father's house 50 percent of the time, or perhaps losing custody all together.

- Denial. No woman wants to believe that what she is experiencing is really abuse. Women in middle- to upper-class communities frequently deny that their experience is abuse. The abuser has told her for years, "This is normal." If she lives in a beautiful home, belongs to a church family, is well educated and has healthy children, she probably doesn't even recognize the signs of abuse. She may admit that her husband is high maintenance, has a big personality, and may even be controlling, but acknowledging abuse requires her to decide whether to stay or leave. It can be easier to just get a good night's sleep and hope things look better in the morning. After all, her husband will act like nothing has happened, and it is simply easier to deny that anything is terribly, terribly wrong than to blow up her life and leave him.

- Threats. The abuser has threatened, among other things, to kill her or the family pet, hurt the children, or cut her off from family and friends. She's been a victim of his physical abuse and realizes these are not idle threats. Whether the abuser is a construction worker or a physician who leads a hospital, he will vindictively attempt to destroy her with all the tools at his disposal. An abuser who is a respected professional will appear credible when he slanders his wife, an abuser who is a financial professional will know how to leave his wife penniless, an abuser who is a pastor will be able to turn his entire church and family against his wife, and an abuser who is a dirty cop will know how to kill his wife without a trace. While every divorce is difficult, a divorce from an abuser is likely the most difficult experience any woman will ever go through.

- Life change. A marriage is unlike any other relationship. One's entire financial, social, emotional, familial, and spiritual well-being is tied up with a spouse. Leaving a spouse, especially an abusive one, means a huge loss on many levels, and it is not a decision to be taken lightly. A woman who leaves an abuser must leave her old life behind and start an entirely new one. Friends and family will side with the abuser because he has slandered her, denied any abuse, and has played the victim; her pastor will likely side with the abuser as he naïvely believes the abuser's feigned apologies and newfound religion; her church will become an unsafe place because the pastor will likely not impose any church discipline; and the abuser will lie and hide his finances so that she will be punished financially.

- Biological impact of trauma. When a woman is physically intimate, her body makes the hormone oxytocin, which forms a strong emotional bond to the person she is intimate with, even if he is toxic.

Why Does She Stay?

Oxytocin, also known as "cuddle hormone," is the superglue God uses to bond couples through the ups and downs of marriage. But in abusive relationships, Satan uses it to emotionally bond a woman to her abuser. When her abusive husband says or does unkind things, she is emotionally distressed because the person to whom she is bonded is attacking her and trying to destroy her spirit. When a woman attempts to leave, she often feels so emotionally distraught that she returns, even though she knows they have an unhealthy relationship. One of the keys for a woman to successfully separate is to break the emotional trauma bond with her abuser. She needs to realize that the abuser will not change and the abuse will escalate. She needs to see herself as a beloved daughter of God. Oxytocin stays in a woman's body for at least six months; therefore, she needs to separate from her abuser for at least that long to break the emotional bond.

- Her children are threatened. When a woman finally leaves, it is usually because the abuse has escalated and is now directed toward the children. A mother often assumes that she can withstand the blows and stand between the abuser and the children. However, once the abuse is directed at her children and she realizes that she can no longer protect them, the mama bear comes out. She takes action to protect them and leaves. Many women who are very nurturing are willing to protect others more than they protect themselves. Even if they are unwilling or unable to recognize the abuse directed at them, they recognize the abuse toward their children. Although for years she may have known that she needed to leave her abuser, sometimes it takes abuse affecting someone she loves and protects more than herself to make her act. This is God's wake-up call to get out.

Kerry: I finally left our home on January 6, 2018. You might be wondering why I did not leave sooner. No one goes into a marriage thinking that this could happen to them or thinking they will have to leave their husband or wife. I stayed because I hoped that he would realize that he was hurting me and apologize. I stayed because I hoped that he would change and that this would never happen again. Where was the man that I dated and fell in love with? Where was the love of my life?

Chapter 18

Realize that He Will Never Change and She Is Not the Problem

Women often stay in abusive relationships because they hold on to the hopeful fantasy that their husbands can and will change. However, once a woman realizes that her husband is either a narcissist, sociopath, or psychopath and has an incurable personality disorder, it gives her permission to leave.

SNAPs can change their behavior for a short time to achieve a self-centered purpose. However, SNAPs will always return to their own nature. Mental health professionals agree that SNAPs are incurable and don't respond well to treatment because they don't want to be cured. While others with mental illness who see mental health professionals often seek help because they realize they need it, SNAPs see nothing wrong with exploiting or abusing people for their own purposes. They are untreatable because they don't want to be changed. Only people who want to change can change.

From a spiritual perspective, a SNAP has such a hardened heart that he is not capable of repentance. While God is capable of redeeming anyone, it requires a humble heart willing to confess his wrongdoing and turn his heart away from evil and toward God. Scripture is clear that evil people reject God, deceive others, and harden their hearts to a point where it is impossible for them to hear the Holy Spirit. God leaves them to themselves as they become more and more deceived and more and more evil (Romans 1).

Almost every woman in an abusive relationship feels that his abuse is her fault and that she has done something to bring on the abuse. However, she needs to realize that there is nothing she did or did not do that brought on the abuse. And there is nothing that she can or cannot do that will change him.

Her SNAP would have been abusive to his wife whether that wife was her or anyone else. As a predator, he chose someone with all the wonderful characteristics that he lacks—kindness, concern, generosity, and loyalty, among others. He chose women with the same characteristics before her, and after she leaves, he will choose women with those characteristics as his next victim. And he will abuse them all.

Although she may feel guilty for having chosen such a horrible person to be her husband and the father of her children, given the information that she knew at the time, she could not have known that the person wooing

Realize that He Will Never Change and She Is Not the Problem

her was a narcissist, sociopath, or psychopath. Every woman hopes to marry a prince; no one expects to marry an abuser. Even female psychologists, therapists, and other mental health professionals have been fooled by these professional liars and deceivers. Abusers are experts in deceit. The only characteristic she lacks is discernment between good and evil, which is a quality she must develop to avoid similar mistakes in judgment in the future.

Charlotte: One of the hardest moments of my life was realizing that Tim had never loved me, that my entire marriage was a sham, and that the life I had built with him for over twenty years was a fraud. At that time, it all came crashing down on me that he had lied to me (and his other wives), that I had believed his lies for twenty-five years, that he was not remorseful or repentant for all his abuse, that he was simply mean and evil, and that no matter what I did, he would not change and our marriage would never get better. The scales fell from my eyes, and I saw that people I had considered friends were just his minions and that the church I had called home supported him, despite giving them a mountain of evidence confirming his abuse, including photographs, documents, and his own admissions. Until then, I had held out hope that the Holy Spirit would miraculously soften his heart. That realization was brutal, but life changing. It was the revelation I needed to leave, stop looking back and wallowing in my grief, and make a new life for myself. I didn't know how many years I had left on this earth, but I knew that I didn't want to spend it with someone like that, and I knew that I didn't want friends or a church that supported someone like that.

Chapter 19

What to Expect from the Abuser if She Stays in the Relationship

If a woman chooses to stay in an abusive relationship, she can expect more of the same. Abusers are predictable. The abuse will continue and escalate as the abuser's personality disorder intensifies. A common misconception is that abuse reduces in intensity over time due to age and reduction in testosterone levels. The fact is that abuse will escalate as long as the abuser is alive.

Financial abuse will intensify. He will hide assets from his wife, divert assets to hidden accounts, and reduce her access to funds. If he is sophisticated financially, he will use trusts, private companies, and complicated financial instruments to hide assets that he controls. He may choose to divorce her after he has successfully transferred most of his assets out of his name so that she will have few financial resources after the divorce.

Emotional and verbal abuse will intensify. His remarks will become more cutting, crueler, and more frequent. They will become more painful for her. His power and control will become complete.

Physical abuse will intensify. "Accidental" bumps will turn into intentional shoves, which will turn into punching, which will turn into choking, which will turn into more. Far too many women are killed or maimed.

Sexual abuse will intensify. What started as pornography and affairs will turn into "rough sex," which will turn into coerced sex, which will turn into rape.

Spiritual abuse will intensify. As she questions why she is staying with an abuser who obviously does not love her, he will try harder to keep her in the relationship. He will increasingly tell her that she should submit to him, that she must have sex with him, that she must stay in the marriage, that God hates divorce, and that it is un-Christian to leave.

She will die a slow emotional and spiritual death. All humans are made to love and be loved. With long-term abuse, humans shrivel and die inside. They may survive physically, but they become shells. She will develop PTSD, depression, anxiety, headaches, insomnia, heart issues, and gastro-intestinal issues, among other things. Far too many women commit suicide because they see no way out and they are hopeless.

Chapter 20

What to Expect from the Abuser if She Leaves the Relationship

ONCE A WOMAN DECIDES to leave a relationship, a predictable series of events ensues. Abusers are, as we've noted previously, predictable creatures. Knowing what to expect, a victim of abuse can prepare for what's to come.

He Maintains Power and Control at All Costs

During the relationship, the abuser rejects her attempts to get him to see how hurtful and destructive his behaviors and actions are. Unable to accept any criticism or acknowledge any imperfections in himself, the abuser's primary goal is to maintain power and control and to win at all costs. He is not interested in reconciliation or relationships. He will sacrifice a relationship to win an argument. He remains in control and rules with an iron fist. Therefore, when a wife who is seriously considering leaving pleads with the abuser to change or attend counseling as one last-ditch effort before she leaves, the abuser will likely dismiss her pleas, just as he has done before.

When the Abuser Senses She Might Leave—He Escalates Abuse

However, once an abuser senses that his wife might leave, he will generally escalate the level of abuse to keep her under control. The escalation of abuse may include stalking, constantly calling or texting to know her whereabouts, putting a GPS tracker on her car (which is illegal in most states), increased physical threats or acts of abuse, increased verbal abuse, accusations of affairs, hiding money, opening separate accounts to which she has no access, refusing to financially support her, and other ways that he exerts even more control over her. The abuser may also use forced sex and rape to show her he is in control, because there is virtually no act more humiliating and showing a victim that the abuser is in control and has power over her. Rape has been used to subject women for millennia, and is, unfortunately, a well-known abuse tactic used against women in everything from warfare to gangs to the workplace to marriage. Again, his primary goal is to maintain power and control and to win at all costs, and he uses the same tried and true methods that have worked before.

When She Separates—He Puts on an Act to Win Her Back

Once a wife leaves the home, separates, obtains an order of protection, or similar action of separation short of filing for divorce, the abuser may realize that he has lost some control, but generally believes that he can convince her to return to the abusive relationship. Often, the separation will come as a complete surprise to the abuser, who believes that he is so wonderful and so powerful that no one would ever leave him, and if she did, it must be because she is having an affair.

The abuser often shifts into damage-control mode to keep her from filing for divorce and to persuade her to return to the abusive relationship. He may offer an apology, but it won't be sincere. He may cry, but they will be crocodile tears. Martha Stout, PhD, states:

> Crocodile tears at will are a sociopathic trademark. . . . Crocodile tears from the remorseless are especially likely when a conscience-bound person gets a little too close to confronting a sociopath with the truth. A sociopath who is about to be cornered by another person will turn suddenly into a piteous weeping figure whom no one, in good conscience, could continue to pressure. Or the opposite: Sometimes a cornered sociopath will adopt a posture of righteous indignation and anger in an attempt to scare off [his] accuser.[85]

He may acquiesce to counseling, but only to get her to come back. In fact, in counseling he will learn all the professional terms for his abuse and will likely try to convince his counselor that *he* is the victim of abuse, blaming the breakdown of the marriage entirely on his wife. During this time he may be on his best behavior, claim that he has "found God," and start attending church or synagogue. He may enlist the help of a pastor or church friends to get her back, and he may start quoting Bible verses. He may claim to have repented and demand that his wife "forgive and forget," because, he will claim, that's what good Christian women do. He may try to "date" his wife again so that he can show her how he has changed and win her back. The actions are a ploy to get her back. And if she does, the abuse will eventually return, and the abuse will escalate. Whatever his actions may be, his heart has not changed.

During this time, the SNAP will hedge his bets. While he is feigning apologies to his wife to win her back, he is, no doubt, "gathering the troops" and making his case in the event she doesn't come back. He will contact his family, his friends, pastors, and her family, her friends, and often even her clients and coworkers, playing the victim and claiming that she has abandoned him, that she is having an affair, that she has lost her mind, and that he, being magnanimous, would take her back to save their family if she would just come back.

At this point, his primary goal shifts to preventing divorce so that he can continue to keep all his money. He recognizes that divorce is expensive and that the courts will force him to divide his assets with his wife, and he may also be required to pay alimony and/or child support. He views all their assets as belonging to him, not something acquired jointly through the partnership of marriage. SNAPs view their money as an extension of themselves; therefore, asking a narcissist to part with his money is akin to asking him to part with his left arm. He will fight ferociously to keep his money—even if that means putting on a temporary act of repentance to get his wife back.

---

[85] Martha Stout, *The Sociopath Next Door* (New York: Random House, 2005), 91.

Filing for Divorce or Permanent Separation—the Risk of Homicide

The decision to file for divorce or separate permanently ushers in a very volatile and dangerous time. Homicide is the number one cause of death among African American women ages fifteen to forty-five, and the seventh leading cause of death among US women overall. Women are killed by their intimate partners more than any other type of perpetrator, with approximately 40 to 50 percent of homicides committed by a woman's intimate partner. Eighty percent of homicides were preceded by the physical abuse of a woman by her intimate partner or spouse. Other significant risk factors include the abuser's unemployment and access to firearms, having a child in the home who is the victim's but not the abuser's biological child, prior threats with a weapon, and prior threats to kill.[86]

A woman is nine times more likely to be killed by a highly controlling, abusive intimate partner after she leaves than if she stays.[87] If a woman leaves a relationship for another partner or because of her abuser's jealousy, she is five times more likely to be killed by the abusive intimate partner.[88] A woman is forty-one times more likely to be killed if her abuser has made prior threats with a weapon.[89]

First Steps

Therefore, when a woman leaves her abuser, it is critical to not confront him personally with her decision to leave. Instead, she needs to leave when he is not present, take her children with her, and go to a safe location where he cannot find her. She can either leave a note or send a text or email message later when she has arrived at a safe place. She needs to be vigilant about her safety, including avoiding places where her abuser may be or where her car may be recognized and followed. She must not disclose her whereabouts to her abuser or to anyone who might disclose her whereabouts to her abuser. An abuser may persuade friends and family to disclose her location under the ruse that he is concerned for her safety. Therefore, best practice calls for keeping the location secret, with the exception of informing law enforcement along with her reason for leaving. If she has a location finder on her phone or car to which the abuser has access and can track her, she needs to discard the phone and take the car to a mechanic to remove the GPS system.

Filing for Divorce or Permanent Separation—Seven Guaranteed Acts of Abuse

A woman filing for divorce or separating from her spouse can expect a series of actions. Remember, the abusive personality is highly predictable. The victim has experienced the abuser's cycle of violence and abuse for several years, giving her some clues as to his moves when he realizes she is serious about leaving.

The Abuser Will Become Vindictive

Everything now becomes a competition to the abuser. He wants to win at all costs and punish his spouse for leaving. He has no interest in playing nice, being reasonable, or being cordial for the sake of the children. He wants to appear like the good guy, so he will continue to smile and be charming to those he wants on his side:

---

[86] Jacquelyn C. Campbell, et al., "Risk Factors for Femicide in Abusive Relationships: Results from a Multisite Case Control Study," *American Journal of Public Health* 93, no. 7 (July 2003):1089–1097, https://www.ncbi.nlm.nih.gov/pmc/articles/PMC1447915/.
[87] Campbell, "Risk Factors," 1090.
[88] Campbell, "Risk Factors," 1091.
[89] Campbell, "Risk Factors," 1091.

pastors, church leaders, mutual friends, family members, children, his employer, and people with money and power. But while they are not looking, in ways they cannot see, he will spend the rest of his life trying to destroy the spouse in every conceivable way.

Until this time, when his wife left and filed for divorce, the abuser restrained his abuse. He played the game of controlling and abusing her, while taking care not to cross the line that would make her leave. After all, without a wife he has no one to serve him and no one to abuse. However, now that he has crossed the line and she has left, there is no reason for any restraint. He will pull out all the stops. Like the childhood game of pitching pennies against a wall, his game was to hurl the pennies (abuse) as close as he could to the wall (her decision to leave) without hitting the wall. Now that he has lost the game, he will throw his abuse as hard as he pleases.

Most women make the mistake of believing that the SNAP will play fair because he feels guilty for having destroyed his family, because he claims to be a Christian, or because he has some inner conviction to treat her decently due to the years of being together. She may feel he will behave himself during the divorce process because they have children together, because she worked to put him through medical or law school, because she cared for his elderly parents, because she worked for no pay to start his business, or for some other sacrifice that she has made for him. This is a huge mistake. Because he has no conscience, the SNAP feels absolutely no guilt and no conviction to be decent. He rewrites history, casting himself as the poor victim who did nothing wrong, and casting his wife as the evil Jezebel committing the ultimate sin of leaving him. The beautiful children they have together were her idea; she tricked him into getting pregnant. She was a gold digger and lowly secretary who wanted to marry a doctor. She pursued him and convinced him to marry beneath himself, and he did because he pitied her; his parents never liked her. She should be grateful he gave her a job with no pay at his company because she has no skills, etc. The more he ruminates on these self-deceptive lies and the more he says them out loud to himself and others, the more they become truth to him. At some point, he believes them, and they justify his vindictiveness.

The Abuser Will Play the Victim

Emotionally mature people take responsibility for their bad behavior and its consequences. Abusers play the pity card. They pretend they are the victim. "Poor me. My wife left me, and I never did anything wrong," is their mantra. According to Martha Stout, the most universal, reliable sign that a person is dealing with a sociopath is the pity play: "The combination of consistently bad or egregiously inadequate behavior with frequent plays for your pity is as close to a warning mark on a conscienceless person's forehead as you will ever be given."[90]

The abuser's prevailing theme is "My wife left me for another man." False accusations of infidelity are nearly universal among abusers. They project their own infidelity onto their spouse. As long as others do not know of his sexual dalliances, he will always play this card. But even if others are aware, he will justify his affairs and still falsely accuse her. Uncontrolled jealousy and suspicions of infidelity during and after the marriage are universal themes for abusers.

Even when their behavior is so violent and inexcusable by legal standards that they end up with an order of protection against them or in jail, the SNAP will play the pity card. The SNAP will phone his blood family and blame his wife for calling the police, for exposing him, for being vindictive, etc. He will try to elicit pity from others so his wife will drop criminal charges or dismiss an order of protection: "Poor Johnny, he won't get to see his daddy because his daddy's in jail. And you put him there. He will grow up without a father. *You* are keeping

---

[90] Stout, *The Sociopath Next Door*, 91.

him from seeing his father. *You* are the criminal!" Rather than admonishing the abuser for his bad behavior, the family will usually pressure the wife to drop the charges, voluntarily dismiss the order of protection, and stop the divorce proceedings. If the abuser has involved the children in his pity play (which he usually does), the children pressure their mother as well.

Some abusers take the pity play to extraordinary levels, claiming depression or threatening some self-destructive behavior if the victim doesn't return. When the bully-turned-victim feigns depression and distress at his imploding marriage, he is, in fact, manipulating others to gain the sympathy of supporters. Sometimes the abuser will even threaten to end his own life in a last-ditch attempt to gain pity (and therefore control) over his wife and his supporters. He may even check himself into a psychiatric hospital or make a half-hearted attempt of suicide to make his story more believable. His supporters will redouble their efforts to get the wife to return so that the abuser won't take his life. Supporters may blame the wife, claiming that his death will be her fault if he dies. Alas, the abuser who threatens does not actually go through with the suicide—it is merely another ploy.

Many women make the mistake of falling for the pity play. We naturally do not want to hurt others. When we pity someone, our defenses are down, and we tend to give them anything and believe anything. The abuser knows this. She also doesn't want her entire family and children turned against her. She feels completely betrayed, as she should, that her family and children have supported the abuser, despite his lies and violence, rather than supporting her as she exposes the truth. However, if she drops the criminal charges, he will certainly be even more vindictive the next time. If she voluntarily dismisses the order of protection, he will continue his abusive behavior—although he will try harder to be more clandestine so as not to get caught. If she stops the divorce proceedings, she will walk back into a living hell. Most women who have left abusive marriages have tried to do so many times before, and many of them have started prior divorce proceedings but were convinced by the abuser's pity play to return to the marriage. On average, a woman returns to her abuser seven times before leaving for good.

The Abuser Will Immediately Lie and Start a Smear Campaign

This campaign will take place at their church, with his family, her family, his friends, her friends, his colleagues, her colleagues, his clients, her clients, and the community. He will falsely accuse his wife of everything from adultery to insanity and from lying about the abuse to kidnapping if she takes the children with her, or abandonment if she doesn't. Psychologists call this social isolation, and it is designed to remove her support network. Abusers know that one of the best ways to hurt a Christian woman is by turning her church, her family, and her friends against her. He wants to win at all costs, and he will lay claim to her support network as his territory and force the victim out.

The abuser knows that the best and most believable lies start with a grain of truth. With the combination of playing the poor abandoned victim and using believable lies, the abuser systematically turns the victim's support network against her. He will work the phone, arrange lunch dates, take them out for dinner, and use each opportunity to slander and tell lies about his wife until her support network comes around to his side.

In cases of domestic abuse, as in all cases of evil, the church is obligated, as the moral authority, to support the victim and stand against evil. If church leaders do not support the victim, the abuser will turn everyone in the victim's life against her and force the victim out of her community.

The victim usually takes the high ground. Whether out of shame or decency, she usually doesn't share details of the abuse or the divorce with others. However, at some point, she may feel the need to defend herself against the lies and slander. When she does expose the truth about the years of abuse, it usually falls upon deaf ears. The damage caused by her abuser's lies and slander is already complete, and her former supporters no longer believe or support her. In fact, after years of silence and hiding the abuse, when the victim finally exposes the abuse, family and friends will side with the abuser and rebuke the victim for discussing the truth, rather than admonishing the abuser for his reprehensible conduct. It is as illogical and unreasonable as readers of the *Chicago Tribune* rebuking the newspaper for reporting the truth about a criminal's behavior, rather than being outraged at the criminal behavior reported and demanding justice. For the wife, it is another gut-punching betrayal.

The Abuser Will Engage in Parental Alienation

Using a variety of techniques, the abuser will try to turn the victim's children against her in much the same way that he obliterated her support network. Psychologists call this technique *parental alienation*. Healthy adults promote good relationships between their children and the other non-abusive parent, but an abuser engages in alienation. He knows that nothing will hurt a mother like children turning against her. While they were together, they may have cooperated in raising the children, or he may have left most of the responsibility to his wife. However, when a divorce is upon him, parenting becomes a competition. He wants to win, and he uses the kids as pawns in his game to destroy his ex.

The tactics that abusers use to alienate children against their mother can be summarized in five general categories.

- Poisonous messages. The first category of tactics used in parental alienation is poisonous messages to the children that their mother is unloving, unsafe, unavailable, and has some moral deficiency. For example, he will lie to her children and falsely accuse their mother of affairs, abandoning them, destroying their family, being insane, stealing their college money, being the reason why they don't have any money, being the cause of their inability to afford vacations, being worthless, wrongly seeking an order of protection, and the like. This technique destroys children emotionally. They often become convinced that their mother is a horrible, stealing, lying philanderer who cares so little for them that she broke up their family. The alienation often lasts throughout their childhood and into adulthood. It is entirely devastating for the mother, whose heart aches for her children who often cut her out of their lives.

    Cathy: The narcissist in my house was my mother. She told my sister and me that our dad left to play professional baseball and abandoned our family. She had five husbands who came in and out of our lives. I didn't find out until I was nearly sixty years old and reconnected with my biological father that my dad had left his baseball career when my mom became pregnant so that he could marry her and raise our family. But she left him for another guy, pushed my dad out of our lives, and told us that he was a horrible person who left us. I had believed her lies my whole life. I am so grateful to have a relationship with my father now, but how I missed a loving father all those years.

- Disrupting and limiting contact and communication. In addition to verbal attacks on the mother of his children, the second general category includes nonverbal ways to disrupt and limit contact and communication between the child and her mother, thus wreaking havoc on their relationship. Holidays, birthdays, and special occasions become a playground for further abuse. During the marriage, holidays

What to Expect from the Abuser if She Leaves the Relationship

were always stressful because the abuser tried to be the center of attention and shanghaied every event that was not about him. In the aftermath of a divorce, the holiday becomes a competition for time spent with the kids, an opportunity to make the mother look bad in front of her kids, or the perfect occasion to thwart her plans. The SNAP will breach agreements regarding parenting time. For example, if the SNAP and his wife agreed for the kids to spend Christmas Eve with him and Christmas Day with her, he will spend all Christmas Eve with the children and drop them off Christmas afternoon at their mother's house so they have little time with her. He will plan a trip with his children during their mother's birthday, a day that almost all divorce agreements prescribe for the children to be with their mother, so that she spends the day alone. If she asks the SNAP to cohost a graduation party for the children, he will decline and say they aren't interested, and then plan it himself without inviting her.

During nonholidays, the abuser will limit or even eliminate communication with the mother when the child is with the abuser, and will reduce or even eliminate visitation time with the mother. He will refuse to deliver mail from the mother to the child received at his house (and likely add that she must not care, if she didn't bother to write). He will ignore unwritten or even written parenting agreements or court orders, tell his children they do not have to or should not spend time with her, make them feel guilty that he will be all alone without them, or use some other form of manipulation so they will stay with him during her parenting time.

A common form of manipulation is the absence of appropriate house rules in the abuser's home designed to make the children want to stay at his house rather than their mother's. Children, particularly older children, naturally gravitate toward environments that are less restrictive. So when the abuser places few restrictions on his teenage children, while Mom enforces a strict set of house rules, the teens tend to spend more time with Dad—just as he planned. Abusers often do not require their children to complete homework, household chores, or other responsibilities. Abusers with older children commonly allow underage drinking, illegal drugs, parties, and sleepovers with friends of the opposite sex. Frequently, abusers will blame others for the shortcomings of their children. For example, when a child receives a poor grade, the abuser will blame the teacher for being too hard, not the student for failing to turn in his homework or study for a test. Blaming others is a tactic that the abuser has used his whole life, and now he encourages a similar lack of accountability in his own children.

Older children also naturally gravitate toward the parent with power and money who showers them with expensive clothes, vacations, gifts, concert tickets, a large house with a pool, and other toys. Therefore, using money and power is another ploy by well-to-do abusers to gain favor with children.

- Erase and replace mom. Third, in a move domestic violence professionals call "erase and replace," the SNAP will attempt to erase all indications that the children ever had the victim as a mother, replacing her with a new woman. All evidence of her existence (photos, letters, knickknacks, cards, crafts she has made, etc.) will be wiped from the house. The abuser will not speak of her nor consult her on matters both parents typically confer on. The abuser will act as if she never existed. During the marriage, the abuser may have established bank accounts or college accounts for the benefit of the children in his name only. Now the children must ask him for money and are completely dependent upon his good graces. In the meantime, he will quickly find a new romantic partner (oftentimes, one with whom he was already in a relationship during the marriage and who was "waiting in the wings") and move swiftly to solidify the new relationship (often while the abuser is still married to the mother of the children). Many times, he will move in with the new girlfriend, who becomes a wife shortly after the divorce. The abuser will often refer to the new woman as "Mom" in front of the kids and require them to call her "Mom." He addresses their mother by her first name and may require them to do the same. The victim has been erased from the lives of her children and replaced with the next one.

- Undermining the mother's authority. Fourth, in a related category, the abuser will undermine the authority of the mother. He will do this overtly by telling his children that she doesn't matter, her opinion doesn't count, they don't need to get her permission, etc. Or he will do this covertly by simply pushing her out of their lives, refusing to consult with her on matters that involve the children, and using many "erase and replace" tactics. He will put himself on school and medical forms as the sole parent without her information. He alone will have the discussions with the children regarding academic classes, extracurricular activities, vacation plans, and college choices. She will very much feel like she is on the outside looking in and that the abuser has hijacked her life and her children from her.

- Betraying trust. Fifth, another category of tactics SNAPs use is encouraging the children to betray their mother's trust. The children are expected to spy on the mother and report back to the abuser, or are asked to keep secrets from the mother. An abuser often wants to know what his ex is doing, how much money she is making, who she is dating, and what friends she is seeing. Financial or dating information is useful to the abuser because he wants to find ways to reduce his child support and/or or eliminate alimony, which generally stops when the victim cohabitates or gets remarried. Information on social connections helps him determine whose side people are on and whether he needs to redouble his efforts at social isolation. On the other hand, he does not want his ex to know how much money he is making, whether he just got a new job, that he bought a new home, and that he is living with or marrying the girlfriend he was dating while they were married.

An abuser will continue his parental alienation regardless of the ages of the children. Adult children will also be targets of the abuser's efforts to turn them against their mother, and the abuser will share far too many details with them. The abuser will also target grandchildren. Once the abuser has his adult children on his side, he will also succeed in alienating the grandchildren from their grandmother.

Stepchildren of the victim—that is, the abuser's children with a former partner—will also be targeted for alienation and will almost invariably side with their father. He has groomed them to be like him, and they might view the stepmother as simply another person to be used. She is now no longer useful. In many instances, the abuser has groomed them to be financially dependent upon him. The abuser will view any continuing friendship with her as a breach of their loyalty to him. Therefore, their loyalties will be with him, regardless of the horrible acts he has committed.

For all these reasons, co-parenting with an abuser once a divorce has been filed is impossible. The abuser will not cooperate. The nonabusive parent must then engage in what is commonly known as "parallel parenting," in which she makes independent decisions for the children when they are with her, and the other parent makes decisions for the children when they are with him.

What to Expect from the Abuser if She Leaves the Relationship

The Abuser Will Hide Assets and Lie about His Financial Condition

Regardless of his finances—multimillionaire or pauper—during a divorce the abuser will claim he has no income or assets to keep it from his former spouse and children in his efforts to avoid marital division of assets, alimony or maintenance, and child support.

As he has done throughout the marriage, the abuser will continue to hide assets that he does not want the leaving spouse to know about. If he has not already done so, the abuser will open bank and investment accounts in his name only and start depositing his paycheck in these accounts so his wife has no funds. For the accounts that are in both names, he will drain the account and put the funds in an account solely in his name. If he wants to purchase new assets for himself, he will do it in such a way so that his leaving spouse will not know. For example, he may hide the title of a car, boat, or motorcycle from his spouse and park the vehicle in a friend's garage.

Many abusers own their own businesses or work for their family's business. This is often the case because they do not like authority and they cannot work well with others in a large corporate setting. Many, in fact, have been fired for being abusive to fellow employees or breaking other rules that they feel do not apply to them. Owning their own business allows them to be the absolute ruler of their kingdom with no accountability. It also provides the ultimate flexibility for taking time off, seeing paramours during work time, using company funds as their own personal banking account, expensing personal expenses through the company, and reducing reported personal income for tax and other purposes. In doing so, they will falsely manipulate income statements and tax returns to appear nearly penniless. Although in years past he may have bragged about how much money he has or how he uses his money to bully others or gain privilege, during a divorce he will suddenly claim to be a pauper.

Many abusers have been known to quit their jobs to avoid paying maintenance and child support. They may work again at some point, but will quit as soon as his ex-wife discovers his new employment and files a petition for child support. Many educated abusers take a job far below their ability in order to avoid financial obligations.

Abusers with means such as family trusts and businesses may enlist the help of parents or siblings to hide or divert assets. Abusers may enter fraudulent transactions to drain their wealth and divert it to their parents, siblings, family business, or trusts to reduce their financial obligations to their spouse and children. After the divorce, they will reverse the transactions to regain the assets. For example, an abuser may sell his interest in a family business to a sibling for no money up front and a ten-year payback, which reduces the assets available to divide with his spouse and reduces income for maintenance and child support. Any payments the abuser receives at the end of the payback period and after the children are grown are no longer eligible for child support. A parent who gifted the abuser and his spouse money to purchase a home may now call the gift a loan, demand payment, and file a lawsuit.

The Abuser Will Abuse the Legal System

An abuser will lie to exhaust her financially and emotionally and to get custody of the children. Abusers who abuse the legal system to gain advantage over their leaving spouses are deceitful, lie under oath, falsely deny the parentage of children, file frivolous motions, and put up frivolous opposition to reasonable requests or motions. They refuse to follow court orders, drag litigation on for months, refuse to enter into any reasonable settlement, and make demands based on neither law or fact. They are labeled "high conflict divorces" by the legal profession, when, in fact, the conflict arises from one unreasonable side: the abuser.

People generally hire lawyers and other professionals who share their values and ethics. Thus, the lawyers abusers tend to hire are complicit in abusing the legal system. Abusers will also lie or twist the truth to their attorneys, who may at first believe their client. A professional attorney with a strong moral character will either attempt to persuade his client to act reasonably or withdraw from representation once he discovers the abuses and lies of his client.

Wealthy abusers cause unique problems. The wealthier they are, the more money they can pay their lawyers, and the worse the abuse. Poorer abusers, at some point in the litigation, can no longer afford to pay lawyers for wasting the court's time, so either proceed *pro se* (representing themselves) or their lawyer will withdraw, thereby forcing the abuser to find new legal counsel. However, wealthy abusers who can pay their attorneys handsomely can and often will drag out litigation for years, file appeals, and continue dragging their ex-spouses back to court for post-divorce decree matters such as child support payments and visitation arrangements, disputes over holidays, and monetary disagreements. They continue to prove that they are more concerned about their money than the people in their lives.

Abusers Who Are Church Attenders Will Hang Out in Church

For abusers, it's all about the image they want to portray to others. When an abuser recognizes that a spouse will no longer believe the false promises and has left for good, he feels he is in competition for the children, family, friends, and their support network. Abusers will suddenly be regular attenders and volunteers in recognizable positions to look good to the pastors, congregants, their kids, and of course, the next woman. The "volunteer" work will be in high profile positions that everyone can see—an usher, a greeter, a speaker, a reader, the head of a committee, etc. It will not be in a humble behind-the-scenes position such as cleaning up after an event, helping the janitor, making cupcakes for a bake sale, etc. The abuser wants to look like the good guy, and he wants his wife to look like the divorcing, philandering hypocrite that has the nerve to call herself a Christian. The abuser will claim the church as *his* territory. He will make it unsafe for her to attend. She will feel like she is running into her rapist every Sunday, who glad-hands everyone with a smile on his face. He will likely give her that little satisfied smirk when he sees her that conveys to her he knows he is acting as a hypocrite and getting away with it, and there's nothing she can do about it. She knows exactly what he is doing, but the pastor, family, friends, and church won't. If the church leaders refuse to carry out church discipline and remove him from the congregation, she will eventually stop attending church and may lose faith altogether. She has been betrayed by her husband, her pastor, and her church family. God has not betrayed her, but those who are supposed to represent His love to her have. Therefore, she will feel that God has betrayed her as well.

Chapter 21

What to Expect from Family and Friends When She Leaves

Many women who are victims of domestic or sexual abuse mistakenly believe that family and friends will provide comfort and support when she exposes her husband's abuse and asks for their emotional support. Unfortunately, what typically happens is that the family and friends support the abuser or don't want to get involved. Relatives and friends of the abuser will, in almost every case, be the abuser's strongest allies, even if they are also related to or friends with the victim. Former friends or family members shun the leaving spouse, blame her for breaking up the family, or worse. This reaction of apathy or opposition is incredibly painful to the victim. Many women report that the most painful part of leaving an abuser is the indifference or outright betrayal of those she has loved, sacrificed for, and supported for many years. It is uncommon, perhaps even rare, for a woman to be believed and supported when she comes forth and exposes the truth about an abuser.

Many abusers will send or encourage their supporters to further inflict emotional abuse and isolation upon the leaving spouse. These minions of evil taunt the victim and engage in victim-blaming—that is, they blame the victim for the abuse, accusing her of exaggerating the truth or of outright lying. Domestic abuse professionals often refer to these cronies as "flying monkeys," after the winged creatures in the movie *Wizard of Oz* that were sent by the Wicked Witch of the East to torment Dorothy and her kind friends. The flying monkeys will blame the victim for leaving and then blame her for not leaving earlier, with sneering comments such as, "If it was so bad, why did you stay so long?" They will silence her and shame her for exposing the truth, claiming that it is un-Christian to say unkind things about her husband. While not using the word *cover-up*, that is precisely what they are demanding. The more severe the abuse, the louder the demands to be silent. If the abuse is relatively mild, they will dismiss it as something not worthy of a divorce. But if the abuse is horrific, they will view it as unbelievable and call her a liar. While this defies reason for most people with a moral compass, it is almost universally the case. They will tell her that she needs to reconcile and seek forgiveness from her abuser. They will attack her—especially those persons and activities most valuable to a woman of faith. It's a painful sting to a woman who has tried to hold together her family, faith, and career while living with domestic abuse.

Blaming and Shaming for Speaking the Truth/Blaming and Shaming for Being Silent

The reaction from former friends and family who support the abuser often fall into two categories: (1) blaming and shaming the victim for speaking the truth, and (2) blaming and shaming the victim for her silence. The general argument goes something like this: If the abuse was as bad as she claims, she should have left and reported it to the police years ago. And if the abuse was as bad as she claims, the abuser would be in jail. And since she didn't complain then, it must not have been as bad as she claims, so she's lying or exaggerating, and she should not be complaining now.

Of course, the logic of this argument breaks down because no matter when the victim speaks up, naysayers will still support the abuser. In fact, if it is early in the relationship when the victim exposes the truth, the naysayers will accuse her of giving up and not trying hard enough. If she has been in a long term relationship, she is labeled a liar because she has been silent for so long, and, if what she said were true, she would have said something a long time ago. The victim in an abusive relationship is seldom supported. We, as a society, simply don't want to believe these accusations about people whom we know.

We saw this phenomenon firsthand with the Harvey Weinstein case. It took nearly eighty women to share their own personal experiences of sexual harassment and assault before anyone took their allegations seriously. The women who first spoke up were dismissed and accused of lying. Of course, a wife does not usually have eighty other victims to support her. It is only her. And no one wants to believe her.

Why Do People Support the Abusers?

If the shoe was on the other foot—that is, if her friend or family member shared a story of abuse with the victim—it would seem unimaginable to the victim to support an abuser. After all, spouses of SNAPs are often extremely loyal, kind, and compassionate, and they have a spirit of justice to stand for what is right. However, delving into the psychology of those who support the abuser reveals why supporting an abuser is a common reaction. Overall, people support an abuser for one of three reasons: they are deceived by the abuser, they are intimidated by the abuser, or they share the same depraved moral compass as the abuser.

Deception

As noted in the previous chapter, the abuser will always start a smear and parental alienation campaign against the victim. The victim, on the other hand, has suffered in silence for years and has told no one of the abuse. Even when she leaves, victims often take the high road and refuse to disclose details of the abuse. The abuser, being an expert liar, includes a grain of truth to make his lies more believable. Most people naïvely believe what others tell them, particularly when they know the other person and when that person is in a position of leadership or authority, like many men. This is true even when they know there is a substantial likelihood that the other person is not telling the truth. Human nature simply wants to believe that we tell the truth and that others tell the truth.[91] Humans have a fundamental need for trust—particularly in those we call family, friends, and fellow church members. And so they believe the lies of the abuser—that his wife left because of an affair, that she suffers from a mental illness, that she took the family fortune, that she abandoned him, etc., and they side with the poor deserted husband.

---

[91] Wray Herbert, "Why Do We Assume People Are Telling Us the Truth?" *Washington Post*, September 6, 2019, https://www.washingtonpost.com/outlook/why-do-we-assume-people-are-telling-us-the-truth/2019/09/06/c51641fc-bf59-11e9-a5c6-1e74f7ec4a93_story.html.

WHAT TO EXPECT FROM FAMILY AND FRIENDS WHEN SHE LEAVES

Intimidation

The abuser intimidates the children and forces them into the middle of an adult dispute. Older children witness the power shift. Although they may not be able to name it, they acknowledge that the abuser has erased and replaced their mother, cut her off financially, and slandered her. Acceptance and belonging are fundamental for children. They want a relationship with their father, even if he has treated their mother cruelly. Sometimes this need runs so deep that they want a relationship with their father even if he has abused them. Children may be threatened by the abuser, or at least hold a valid fear that if they align with their mother, he will treat them as he has treated her and erase them from his life, cut them off financially, and slander them as well. Children also know that in most cases, no matter what happens, their mother will love them and care for them. Therefore, unless they themselves have been victims of physical or sexual abuse, older children will often align with their father out of fear and for their own survival.

Others are also intimidated by the abuser. They may be cut off from relationships with the rest of the family if they don't align with the abuser. Abusers act very much like a Mafia godfather of a family. Everyone must go through and pay homage to the abuser to be able to have any associations with the family. To act otherwise would be an act of disloyalty. Business associates may be threatened or intimidated by financial manipulation or destruction unless they align with the abuser.

Intimidation may even come through the abuser's threats of suicide. Many times, the abuser feigns depression and distress at his imploding marriage, and thereby gains the sympathy of his supporters. And sometimes, the abuser will even threaten to end his own life in his last-ditch attempt to gain pity (and therefore control) over his leaving wife and his supporters. He may even check himself into a psychiatric hospital or make a half-hearted attempt at suicide to make his story more believable. His supporters will redouble their efforts to get the wife to return so that the abuser won't take his life. Alas, the abuser does not actually go through with the suicide; it is merely another ploy.

Depraved Moral Compass

If supporters of the abuser are not deceived by the abuser and are not intimidated by the abuser, then they support the abuser because their moral compass aligns with his. They may be narcissists, sociopaths, or psychopaths themselves, or they may just not care enough to stand on the side of what is morally right. When a victim exposes the truth of an abuser, people are caught in the middle of cognitive dissonance, which they desperately need to resolve. Recall that after physical needs are met, acceptance and being part of a group are strong needs on Maslow's hierarchy of needs. At times, they may even outweigh the physiological needs. It's especially important to feel part of a family, social group, or church that shares our moral values. Therefore, we need to feel that we have a good, upright family member, friend, or fellow church member. In our minds, that means we are good too. What would associating with thieves, liars, convicts, and rapists say about us?

Therefore, when a victim exposes the truth that someone's family member or friend has abused his partner, that person experiences cognitive dissonance: they find it impossible to hold two opposite ideas in their head at the same time. Our human brains cannot simultaneously believe that someone is both good and a monster. The adult child of the abuser says to himself, "Dad cannot be both the good father that I want to think he is and the person who raped my stepmom." The church member says to himself, "My fellow parishioner cannot be both the morally good and friendly person who volunteers as a leader at church and the person who gave his wife a black eye." The friend says, "My good ol' beer-drinking, golf-playing buddy cannot be the same person who dumped his wife out of the car thirty-five miles from home in the middle of the night." Our minds work overtime to resolve the tension of cognitive dissonance so that only one cohesive notion remains. Because we need to feel that our family member or friend is morally good, it is much easier to attack the idea that he did horrible things. We tell ourselves that she's exaggerating, she did something to provoke him, she deserved it, or she's flat-out lying about the abuse. In this way, we can dismiss the idea that he is an abuser, still telling ourselves that our family member or friend is morally good; therefore, we can still tell ourselves that we are morally good. We do nothing, continue our relationship with the abuser, and life goes on as we continue to feel good about ourselves and the people we associate with.

The closer we are to the abuser, the stronger we feel we must align with him and defend him. We feel very strongly about defending our father, but not nearly as strongly about defending a distant uncle or stranger. This may explain one reason why the older children of powerful and wealthy narcissists align with and so vigorously defend their father, even when he has had numerous public affairs with other women when married to their mother, and even when she has stated publicly that he raped her during their marriage. The wealthy narcissist also has made his children millionaires in their own right, which they obviously do not want to risk losing by aligning with their mother.

It is much harder to resolve the cognitive dissonance in the other direction. If we believe that our family member or friend is guilty of abusive actions and attitudes, we must then dismiss the notion that he is morally good. We must accept that we belong to a morally corrupt family, social group, or church, and that means we must decide whether to disassociate with the abuser or maintain a relationship with him. Disassociating lets the world know we disagree with his actions and that our moral values are not his moral values; continuing a relationship with the abuser gives notice that we agree with his actions and are morally just like him. Resolving cognitive dissonance by dismissing the victim requires little or no action. Disassociating with an abuser is far more difficult because abusers often hold positions of leadership and power and have money. Anyone who disassociates themselves from an abuser and takes a moral stand for the right will pay a steep price. Most people do not have the moral fortitude to make that stand. Therefore, it's simply easier to align with the abuser and tell ourselves the victim is lying or exaggerating or did something to deserve it.

CHAPTER 22

What to Expect from Children of the Abuser When She Leaves

Women with children in abusive relationships face a difficult decision: stay with the abuser to protect her children from the abuse and be a good influence in their lives, or leave the abuser, knowing that there will be negative emotional and financial consequences to her children. Either way, there are significant severe negative consequences to the abused spouse and her children. Many women try to stay in a marriage as long as they can in the hope of providing a stable home. They finally leave when the abuse is directed toward the children, or when she can no longer protect them.

Once a mother leaves, she can be assured the abuser will apply the parental alienation tactics described in detail in chapter 20. Children who have been the target of his physical or sexual abuse usually side with their mother when she leaves, as she is their protector and provides stability. However, when the abuse is directed primarily toward the mother, the children's alliances often change based on their age and what lies and disparaging comments the father has spread about their mother. Younger children usually side with their mother because of her role as protector and the strong bonds they share. However, older children—teenagers and adults—often side with their abusive father and engage in emotionally and sometimes physically destructive actions against their mother when she leaves an abuser.

When a woman finally leaves and exposes the truth about the domestic abuse that she has been living with, she will often expect that those she loves who are closest to her will understand and be sympathetic, comfort and console her, and support her. This, sadly, is rarely the case. Why do otherwise normal children side with an abuser? As with everything regarding a personality disorder, the answer is complicated. The twentieth-century psychologist Richard Maslow observed that people's basic needs must be met on one level before meeting the needs of the next level. As more fully discussed in chapter 6, these basic needs are physiological survival needs, safety needs, love and belonging, esteem, and self-actualization.

Children need to belong to a family, and they desperately want the approval of their father. They want to believe that their father is a decent individual. They often perceive that their father is a good father and husband, even if he abuses their mother. Most mothers will bend over backward to portray the father as a decent human by hiding the abuse, protecting the children, and making excuses when they see the abuse. The children's positive perception of their father is skewed by the mother's own actions. Mothers who are abused usually do not leave a relationship until the abuse is also directed at her children.

When a mother finally leaves an abusive relationship, she is in a difficult position. This is especially true if only the mother has been the target of abuse and the children have not been subjected to severe physical, emotional, or physical abuse. The abuser will use parental alienation tactics to turn the children against their mother. These tactics include lying about their mother by alleging infidelity, abandonment, kidnapping, stealing, and a host of other falsehoods to make him appear the victim and the mother at fault. He will also assault her character as a liar, thief, cheater, money-grubber, and hypocrite. He will violate parenting agreements, disparage the other parent, and encourage the children to spend time with him while ignoring the mother.

Abusers commonly use a tactic called *baiting*. In baiting, the abuser uses subversive parental alienation tactics against the other parent designed to provoke and stir up anger in the other parent in the hope that the other parent will explode in front of the children or others. While the other parent reacts with normal frustration or anger, the abusive parent remains calm, claims to have no knowledge of the matter, and tells the children something like, "See, I told you your mom is crazy. Look what she's doing. I have no idea what she's talking about. You need to be careful around her. Why don't you spend this weekend with me instead of her?"

If the mother takes the high road and does not respond to the allegations, it appears she has left a marriage for no reason other than the reasons set forth by the abuser, and they blame her for doing so. In their limited and rather selfish perspective, it is the mother disrupting their lives for no good reason, not the father. Oftentimes, women need to physically flee the marital home because it is no longer safe. Abusers rarely give up control of the marital home without a court order, and it is usually the wife who must leave for her safety and sanity. However, for children, the house is an important part of the family unit. The children need to belong to a family unit, and if a mother leaves, she will be blamed for doing so, and the children will side with the portion of the family unit left behind—the abusive father.

On the other hand, if the mother exposes the truth of the abuse, the good perception the children desperately want to have of their father is smacked against the reality that he, in fact, has done bad things to someone he should love. And they very much hope he will not do it to them. Discovering the truth of his character conflicts with their perception that he is good, creating cognitive dissonance. This is such an uncomfortable, stressful mental state that people will do nearly anything to relieve it.

In most cases, older children desperately want to continue to believe that their father is still good. They will resolve the dissonance by discounting or dismissing the reports of abuse. In this way, they can continue with the false sense of security that their father is good, and they can maintain their relationship with the more powerful and wealthier parent. Children often align with the abusive father to survive. Older and adult children know their father controls the money and has the power in the relationship. They have also seen the father discard the mother, erase her memory, and replace her with the next woman. They desperately do not want to be treated in the same way, so they dare not cross their father or align with the mother. Many abusers threaten to cut off their children if they align with or visit their mother. Many abusers send the children to spy on the mother and report back. The children are caught in a no-win situation. Most children recognize that the nonabusive mother is the "safe" parent who will love them through the turbulence, even if they align with the abusive parent or do not spend time with her. They recognize that the abusive parent is not safe and will withdraw love, money, and family support if they align with or spend time with the nonabusive parent. Therefore, children may align with the father for a time, but as they grow older and become more emotionally, financially, and physically independent, they often gravitate back to their mother.

In many cases, the abusive father who, during the marriage, was absent or neglectful, suddenly demands to be an active part of his children's lives upon the filing of a divorce. These are the "divorce-activated dads." They really don't care about the children, but when a divorce is imminent, they view the control and affection of the children as a competition with the mother. In these cases, the children are often so starved for their father's affection that they play into his hand and succumb to his pressure to spend time with him instead of their mother.

Discounting or dismissing the mother's account of abuse comes in a variety of forms. Below are just a few of the ways that older and adult children of abusers disregard the reports of abuse so they can continue to align with the abuse:

1. They don't believe the truth told by the mother.
2. They tell the mother to be silent so they don't have to hear the truth.
3. They tell the mother the past is the past; move on.
4. They are in denial, claiming that neither the mother nor the father are truthful.
5. They mitigate the severity of the abuse.
6. They fabricate a new history that blames the mother for the divorce—often projecting the very abuse the father did to them onto the mother.
7. They accept the truth of what the mother says, and they have to deal with how to relate to a father who is capable of great evil and may use it on them, so they align with the father anyway to avoid being treated the same way.

Divorce in abusive marriages shifts all the family relationships. The children, who viewed Mother and Father as a single unit during the marriage, now must figure out how to communicate with them individually, knowing their parents are now adversaries. In the past, the children may have assumed that if they told Mom something, she would tell Dad. That is no longer the case. In the past, the parents may have consulted with each other regarding a child's requests and activities; now they don't, and the child gets conflicting messages. During the marriage, the parents and children worked together on important decisions like college and sports; now these issues are battlefields. Just as the parents are navigating a new relationship, the children are also learning to maneuver new relationships. They learn not to talk to one parent about the other, to refrain from sharing emotions that might upset a parent, and to discuss matters with each parent individually rather than assume a united front by the parents.

Emotionally mature children may accept the truth that their father can be abusive, yet may still try to have a relationship with both parents while imposing healthy boundaries. As children mature and become more independent, most will want a relationship of some sort with both parents. However, they will also recognize that some distance and healthy boundaries are necessary to keep from being manipulated by the abusive parent. It is incumbent on the nonabusive spouse to help her children set healthy boundaries to keep them from being used by the abusive parent as well as by others who would use or manipulate them. Of course, that requires that the nonabusive spouse work on establishing healthy boundaries for herself, as the lack of healthy boundaries is one major factor in becoming a targeted victim of a SNAP.

It is in the best interest of the family for the nonabusive parent to handle the shifting relationships and bad behavior of the abusive parent with maturity, calmness, and perseverance. Children do not want to hear or be put in the middle of the disagreement between parents. A mother must carefully steer a course for herself and her children, and in doing so, she must walk a fine line.

Assuming the abuser is not abusive to the child, the mother should understand that a child desperately desires a relationship with his father. Even though that relationship may never be the ideal father-child relationship, the mother should encourage it to be as healthy as possible for the benefit of the child. Abusers often take one of two opposite approaches to their children: either they recuse themselves from their lives and lead a single life with no responsibilities, or they attempt to take over and shove the other parent out of their children's lives. If the abuser is absent, the mother must accept that he is unwilling or unable to be a loving full-time father. She can, however, encourage a relationship more akin to a benevolent uncle who visits occasionally—which is better than no relationship at all. An abuser who attempts to erase the other parent from the lives of his children is engaging in severe parental alienation tactics, which are discussed in the next chapter.

Women often do not know whether they should take the high road and not discuss the abuse or the reasons they left, or share appropriately with their children the true nature of their former husband. On the one hand, the children need to know that his behavior is not healthy or normal. If she discounts, denies, or excuses his bad behavior, the children will learn that such behavior is normal and expected. It will teach them either to emulate it in their own lives (and thereby become abusers themselves), or that living with a person with these tactics is normal (and thereby become a partner of an abuser). Research tells us that a boy who sees his mother abused is ten times more likely to abuse women partners as an adult, and a girl who sees her father abusing her mother is more than six times more likely to be the victim of sexual abuse.[92] The children must be given the tools to protect themselves from the abuser and his manipulations. And if the child is in danger, the mother's first priority must be protection.

On the other hand, children do not need to know every detail of the abuse against their mother. The mother must be careful not to treat her children as a friend, a therapist, or a surrogate spouse. She still needs to be their mother, and she needs professional domestic abuse counseling to heal and to share her story. Unloading on the children is not appropriate.

Children who are being manipulated by their father often come back to their mother carrying false accusations told to them by their father. "Dad said you . . ." These are not questions; they are statements. Often the best response is something along the lines of: "Honey, I am not going to say anything untrue or slanderous about your father. The issues we have are between us. If you have a direct question, I will answer you and tell you the truth and provide documentation and witnesses if you need evidence. You can ask these witnesses questions too. I have given them my permission to talk to you. But be prepared—it will not be pretty. So if you want to hear the rest of the story, you can ask me a direct question, but I will not respond to your father's allegations."

---

[92] "Effects of Domestic Violence on Children," Office of Women's Health, US Department of Health and Human Services, https://www.womenshealth.gov/relationships-and-safety/domestic-violence/effects-domestic-violence-children#8; L. Vargas, et al., "Domestic Violence and Children," in G. R. Wals and R. K. Yep, eds., *VISTAS: Compelling Perspective on Counseling* (Alexandria, Virginia: American Counseling Association, 2005), 67–69.

Chapter 23

Dealing with Parental Alienation and the Inevitable Harm to Children

WHEN AN ABUSER'S CAMPAIGN to denigrate the mother of his children and alienate from her is successful, the children are brainwashed. Despite a long history of a good relationship with their mother, the children will turn against their mother without justification and will be convinced they are happier and better off without her in their lives. Professionals call this phenomenon parental alienation syndrome, or PAS. It results from the combination of a programming parent's indoctrinations and the child's own contributions to accept the vilification of the rejected parent.[93] Many consider parental alienation in itself child abuse because it causes severe short- and long-term psychological harm. In addition, it severs the all-important parent-child relationship for no reason other than an abusive parent's hatred. The alienation can be mild, moderate, or severe. Severe parental alienation occurs when the child refuses any contact with the rejected parent and develops an unhealthy alliance with the abusive parent based on the distorted beliefs about the rejected parent.

The Inevitable Harm to Children

Short-term negative effects of parental alienation include self-hatred, guilt, distortion of reality, and general emotional and psychological problems.[94] Long-term negative effects in adult children include low self-esteem, self-hatred, depression, drug and alcohol abuse, lack of trust, alienation from their own children, divorce, and various other psychological and relationship issues.[95] Low self-esteem and self-hatred appear in approximately two-thirds of adult children as a result of three primary reasons.[96] First, the children feel the rejected "bad" parent

---

[93] L. Gottlieb, *The Parental Alienation Syndrome: A Family Therapy and Collaborative Systems Approach to Amelioration* (Springfield, Illinois: Charles C. Thomas Pub. Ltd., 2012), 4.

[94] K. Waldron & D. Joanis, "Understanding and Collaboratively Treating Parental Alienation Syndrome," *American Journal of Family Law*, no. 10 (1996), 121–133.

[95] A. J. Baker, "The Long-Term Effects of Parental Alienation on Adult Children: A Qualitative Research Study," *American Journal of Family Therapy*, no. 33 (2005), 289–302.

[96] Baker, "The Long-Term Effects of Parental Alienation," 293–296.

was part of them, both genetically and relationally, and therefore they must also be bad. They also feel that the rejection directed toward the rejected parent is directed toward them as well, especially if they looked like the rejected parent.

Second, the children feel unloved because the alienating parent told the children that the rejected parent did not love or want them, and she abandoned them. Alienating parents will stop at nothing to make the rejected parent look bad. Alienating parents will even return letters, refuse to forward phone calls, and stop all contact that the rejected parent attempts with the children to make the rejected parent look bad. But these subversive tactics have devastating effects on the children. The children then assume that they are unlovable and unworthy of love because all they have heard from the alienating parent is that the rejected parent does not love them and has no contact with them. Third, after realizing the lies and manipulation of the alienating parent, the children feel guilt, shame, and self-loathing for betraying and being horrible to the rejected parent.

Seventy percent of children alienated from a parent experience depression, primarily as a result of early emotions of feeling unloved by the rejected parent, the extended physical separation between that parent and the child, and the inability of the child to discuss or grieve the loss of the rejected parent.[97] About one-third of children turn to drugs and alcohol, usually during late adolescence or early adulthood, to escape the feelings of pain and loss of the rejected/targeted parent, low self-esteem, self-hatred, and the conflict with the alienating parent.[98]

Nearly half of alienated children struggle to trust themselves and others.[99] Women who were alienated from their fathers believe that no one can love them because, after all, if a father doesn't love them, who can? Some will repeat the past and create unhealthy conflict in relationships to see how much a man can take before he eventually leaves, like their father, which then reaffirms to them that men are untrustworthy. This impulse to repeat the past, even if it is painful, is called *repetition compulsion*. Lack of trust also arises because they doubted their own perceptions when the alienating parent said the other parent was bad, dangerous, or in some way worthy of fear and contempt. This conflict between their perception and what they were told to believe leads them to doubt their ability to trust themselves and others. Even worse, once a child realizes they have been lied to and manipulated by the alienating parent, they become even more doubtful about whom to trust. If a parent is supposed to be trustworthy and has only lied about a child's most important relationship, who can ever be trusted?

In a tragic repetition of the pattern, approximately half of adult children who are alienated from one parent will also be alienated from their own children.[100] In some cases, a narcissistic parent will alienate a child from the other parent, and the child grows up to marry a narcissistic partner, who then alienates the adult child from his own children during a divorce.[101] Sadly, family patterns often repeat themselves in the next generation, with children of abusers growing up to be abusers themselves, or marrying an abuser.

Children who are alienated from one parent have statistically higher than average divorce rates. Approximately two-thirds of the marriages of adults who suffered parental alienation as a child end in divorce.[102] Many marriages fail because of the inability to trust a partner or be intimate, and also because of struggles with depression and drug and alcohol abuse. Many adult children unknowingly marry a person very much like the alienating parent—a narcissist, sociopath, or psychopath who is extremely self-centered and controlling and lacks empathy.

---

[97] Baker, "The Long-Term Effects of Parental Alienation," 296–297.
[98] Baker, "The Long-Term Effects of Parental Alienation," 297–298.
[99] Baker, "The Long-Term Effects of Parental Alienation," 298–299.
[100] Baker, "The Long-Term Effects of Parental Alienation," 299–300.
[101] Baker, "The Long-Term Effects of Parental Alienation," 299–300.
[102] Baker, "The Long-Term Effects of Parental Alienation," 299–300.

Adults who suffered through parental alienation as a child often experience other negative impacts, including a lack of identity, sense of belonging, and roots. These individuals often choose not to have children to avoid being rejected by them, have low achievement in their lives, and experience bitterness over lost time with the rejected parent.[103]

Fortunately, many children who have been alienated by a parent realize at some point that the alienating parent has lied and manipulated them into rejecting a parent who is kind and loving and who loves them. Many children restore the relationship with the rejected/targeted parent. The tactics of the alienating parent sometimes backfire, and the child becomes angry at the alienator for the years of lies, manipulation, and separation from a parent who loved them.

Manifestations of Parental Alienation

The process of alienating children from a parent is a process of brainwashing.[104] The alienating parent recounts to the child the horrible things the rejected parent has done, and threatens, either directly or by implication, that he will reject the child for not aligning with the alienating parent so that the child eventually succumbs to the alienating parent's distorted view. Psychologists identify eight indications of parental alienation, which are described below. Note that these characteristics are also observed in the alienating parent. The first two symptoms are required and sufficient in themselves, along with two of the other six symptoms, to make a diagnosis of parental alienation syndrome, while the remainder are additional evidence.[105]

Campaign of Denigration against the Rejected/Targeted Parent[106]

At the orchestration of the alienating parent, the alienated child who once had a good and loving relationship with both parents now rejects one parent and is manipulated by the other to believe the rejected parent is worthless, selfish, unloving, malicious, wicked, undeserving, lying, dangerous, etc. The alienated child and the alienating parent will then exhibit denigrative behaviors and attitudes toward the rejected/targeted parent, such as the following:

- Refusing or shunning visits without justifiable reason.
- Behaving miserably, disrespectfully, or abusively when they are together.
- Refusing to inform, include, consult, or collaborate regarding important aspects of a child's life, such as medical and educational information or decisions, or social events; informing the rejected parent that she is not entitled to the information, nor is she entitled to be included in the decision making process.
- Refusing to inform or include the rejected parent regarding normal family events such as parent-teacher conferences, medical appointments, birthday celebrations, religious celebrations, funerals, graduations, etc.

---

[103] Baker, "The Long-Term Effects of Parental Alienation," 301.
[104] Gottlieb, *Parental Alienation*, 4.
[105] D. Lorandes, W. Bernet, S.R. Sauber, Parental Alienation: The Handbook for Mental Health and Legal Professionals, (Springfield, Illinois: Charles C. Thomas Pub. Ltd., 2013), 17. It should be noted that parental alienation syndrome is not included in the DSM-5 and there is some disagreement among professionals regarding parental alienation as a syndrome.
[106] Gottlieb, *Parental Alienation*, 23–56.

- Belittling, criticizing, and deprecating the rejected parent.
- Removing photographs and memorabilia of the rejected parent.
- Refusing to communicate with the rejected parent by telephone, texting, video chatting, emailing, direct talking, etc.
- Verbally or physically abusing or refusing to acknowledge the rejected.
- Defying the supervision and authority of the rejected parent.
- Refusing or returning gifts, cards, letters, vacation invitations, guidance, counsel, and offers of help from the rejected parent.
- Making false allegations of child abuse or domestic violence purportedly done by the rejected parent.
- Amnesia and denial of a loving and supportive relationship with the rejected parent prior to the onset of the alienation.
- Refusing to contact or visit the rejected parent on important days, such as her birthday, Mother's Day, holidays, or other special occasions.
- Refusing to contact or visit the rejected parent when she is sick, hospitalized, having surgery, has had a serious accident, recovering, or has other serious health-related matters.
- Making the rejected parent feel unwelcome and unwanted in their lives.

Weak, Frivolous, and Absurd Rationalizations for Deprecation of the Rejected Parent[107]

Children with parental alienation syndrome distort and revise history to such a degree that the rejected parent is remembered and portrayed in the worst possible light. The alienated child claims a laundry list of perceived grievances and vague accusations they claim were inflicted by the rejected parent. The child may state that the rejected parent is annoying, embarrassing, lying, or even abusive, but will be unable to cite specific instances to support the claims. However, following the false accusations of the abusive parent, they will revise history and fabricate ludicrous and exaggerated accusations to justify their claims.

Black-and-White Views of Rejected Parent as Evil and Alienating Parent as Worshiped[108]

Children with PAS unequivocally view the targeted parent as evil with a laundry list of deficits. With utter disdain, they appear to suffer amnesia and forget the many ways in which the rejected parent has loved and supported the child and continues to do so. On the other hand, the alienating parent is worshiped and revered, even when others would objectively view the alienator as a person with reprehensible attitudes and behaviors.

Claims of Independent Thinking[109]

Children with PAS claim their strong negative opinions of the rejected parent are their own independent views uninfluenced by the alienating parent. They will also claim responsibility for their cruel actions to the rejected parent and claim that the alienating parent did not encourage them. The children do not seem to realize that the alienating parent has influenced and encouraged their attitudes and behavior.

---

[107] Gottlieb, *Parental Alienation*, 57–76.
[108] Gottlieb, *Parental Alienation*, 77–82.
[109] Gottlieb, *Parental Alienation*, 83–86.

Dealing with Parental Alienation and the Inevitable Harm to Children

Cruelty Toward the Targeted/Rejected Parent with No Remorse[110]

Children who are alienated from a parent will treat the rejected parent with intentional cruelty, both verbally and physically, with surprisingly no guilt or remorse for the pain that they purposefully inflict.

Unwavering Support of the Alienating Parent[111]

Alienated children unwaveringly and without critical analysis align with the alienating parent against the rejected parent, particularly when disagreements arise between the parents. This occurs as a result of the alienating parent's triangulation, a term used by mental health professionals when the alienating parent manipulates the child into forming a coalition against the rejected parent. Like many of the tactics used by the abuser, triangulation is a destructive technique that requires the child to choose between two parents. It puts the child in the no-win position of being forced to sever his relationship with the rejected parent or incur the wrath and rejection of the alienating parent. The child will align with the alienating parent against the rejected parent with no regard for the facts, the credibility and high character of the rejected parent, and the questionable character of the alienating parent. The enmeshment with the alienating parent is sometimes so complete that the alienated child will reject any attempts by the rejected parent to defend themselves against the alienating parent's humiliating behavior and outright lies. The child views the rejected parent's attempts to defend themselves and speak the truth as an attack on not only the alienating parent, but on them as well.

Narratives and Language from the Alienating Parent[112]

Alienated children use (or "borrow") the language used by the alienating parent to describe the rejected parent. They will also adopt the alienating parent's fabricated narrative about the demise of the relationship, placing the blame on the rejected parent. Children will use sophisticated words far above their cognitive skills and vocabulary level that have been indoctrinated by the alienating parent. Children will fabricate stories that have been repeated over and over by the alienating parent, sometimes claiming to know facts, even when they have no personal experience or knowledge.

Animosity to Extended Family of the Rejected/targeted Parent[113]

The vilification of the rejected parent often extends to her family of origin. Thus the grandparents, aunts, uncles, and cousins of the rejected parent, who may have had a loving relationship with the child prior to divorce, are now rejected without explanation or remorse. Attempts to communicate, visit, or have a relationship with the child are rejected, thereby expanding the circle of pain and wounding.

Principles for Dealing with Parental Alienation

Dealing with an abusive father who is intentionally alienating the children from their mother is like looking in on one's own family from outside and not being allowed to be part of one's own family. The rejected parent may want to take the high road and not say anything about the alienation, which gives the alienating parent free

---

[110] Gottlieb, *Parental Alienation*, 95–99.
[111] Gottlieb, *Parental Alienation*, 87–94.
[112] Gottlieb, *Parental Alienation*, 99–104.
[113] Gottlieb, *Parental Alienation*, 105–106.

rein to proceed unobstructed in his campaign to erase the mother from the lives of her children. If, however, the rejected parent says or does something to counteract the alienation, she must do so in a way that doesn't put the child in the middle. She must take care not to criticize her child or appear to be denigrating or criticizing the other parent, which will result in further alienation.

Strategies for dealing with parental alienation start with a few overarching principles. If you are a rejected parent, remember that the child is a victim of the brainwashing tactics of the alienating and abusive parent. Children are often in survival mode, just trying to figure out how to get through childhood and adolescence without incurring the wrath of the alienating parent. Even if the child is disrespectful, keep in mind he has been reprogrammed, and do not respond in kind. Another important principle to remember is that the alienating parent is baiting you—hoping that his bad behavior and malicious lies will provoke you to explode in front of the children or be in conflict with them. He can then say, "See, I told you your mother is crazy/stole your college funds/left because of an affair/doesn't care about you/has a bad temper, etc." Don't take the bait. Remain calm.

It is also important to pick your battles. Remember that the alienating parent is watching your every move and will exploit, criticize, and exaggerate everything you do. He may even call the police to make you look bad in front of your children and destroy your relationship. Therefore, you must be mindful, knowing that the children will be spying, reporting back, and complaining to the alienating parent that you are too strict or that punishments are too harsh. On the other hand, children need limits and structure. Whether they admit it or not, having limits gives them a sense of security and provides an out when their friends want them to participate in risky behavior. Be sure that your rules and punishments are reasonable and fair.

Because the child and alienating parent will be scrutinizing you, be sure to follow your parenting plan, continue to reach out to communicate with your child, attend every event, and arrive every time you are scheduled to be with your child, even if the alienating parent cancels your parenting time. You don't want to give the alienating parent any ammunition to say to the child, "See, I told you your mother doesn't care and abandoned you. She didn't even show up to your college visit."

Be sure to be aware of the developmental level and unique qualities of each child. A one-size-fits-all approach is not helpful. Children are unique individuals. The way you relate to one child may not work with another. Be alert to the abuser's specific qualities and his favorite tactics. In addition, be mindful of your natural responses so that you are not playing into his hand. For example, if a child sees that that you are fearful of him, it may reinforce the child's fear of him and cause further alignment with him. If a child observes you being contemptuous or critical of him, it may push the child to defend the alienating parent. Your goals should not be to exact revenge upon the alienating parent. Keep in mind that abusers are far more evil than you are smart, and they will find a way to make your efforts at revenge backfire and make you look bad in front of your children, further hurting your relationship with your child. Your goal should always be to have a strong, healthy relationship with your child, while not interfering with the alienating parent's relationship with the child.

Rejection is always painful, but it's especially painful for a woman when her child rejects her. Some women are so dependent upon their children's opinion for their self-image that they resort to groveling for their affection, even when the children are exhibiting to her the same abusive behaviors that their father has shown. It is important for every woman to know that her self-esteem and value do not depend on the opinion or acceptance of her children. The only opinion that counts should be God's. Particularly for older children who are choosing to copy the abusive tactics of their father, a wise woman releases her children physically, emotionally, and spiritually and entrusts them to God's care. God hears the fervent prayers of a righteous mother to turn the hearts of

Dealing with Parental Alienation and the Inevitable Harm to Children

her children to the Lord and to her. When the hearts of her children turn to the Lord, they will naturally turn to her as well. Releasing them to God's care will allow her to refrain from begging for their affection, set healthy boundaries when they are verbally or physically abusive, and welcome them back with open arms when they decide to act like respectful human beings again.

The story of the prodigal son resonates with the mother whose child has rejected her. Even as the father is rejected by his son, the father releases the son to go his own way and trusts God to take care of him. He continues to pray that the son's heart would turn back to both his heavenly Father and his earthly father. He continues to look to the horizon for his son, anticipating answered prayer. When the son discovers how cruel the world can be without the love and protection of a father, he returns home. The father joyously runs to see him and celebrate his return—no questions asked, no apology demanded. Just love and acceptance for two reconciled hearts. This is the model for mothers who are alienated from their children.

Of course, there are no guarantees. Some adult children adopt the same abusive characteristics of their father and become abusers themselves. If this is the case, it is truly heartbreaking. While a mother can love them from afar, it is not safe to continue a relationship with an adult abuser.

> Donna: My two adult sons have taken up the narcissistic, abusive characteristics of their father. One has fabricated history, slandered me, and accuses me of abuse and adultery, even though their father had a child out of wedlock when we were married and was abusive. My son refuses to have any relationship with me and won't even let me be involved in my grandchild's life. A counselor whom we have worked with tells me that he is the worst case of narcissistic personality disorder she has ever encountered and that I will never be able to have a relationship with him. My other son is not much better. I stayed to protect my boys, and they became just like my abuser. My mother's heart is broken.

Seek a trusted, experienced therapist upon whom you can release your frustrations and who can guide you through this difficult period. A support group with other parents who have also experienced domestic abuse that goes hand in hand with parental alienation is also strongly advisable. Also, seek out a supportive attorney who understands parental alienation, as some alienation strategies must be addressed by a court. Parental alienation escalates quickly and is difficult to correct. Therefore, it is important to seek professional help in a timely manner when signs of parental alienation arise. It is not realistic to expect friends and family to be trusted sources of advice or support. Well-meaning friends and others who have not had experience with SNAPs will simply not understand the dilemma you are in.

Specific Strategies for Dealing with Parental Alienation Tactics

Abusive parents use several parental alienation tactics to turn their children against the rejected parent. Below are some helpful suggestions from parental alienation expert Dr. Amy Baker to mitigate the damage to the children and your relationship when confronting these tactics.[114] Of course, there is no guarantee or magic bullet,

---

[114] Amy Baker and Paul Fine, "Beyond the High Road: Responding to 17 Parental Alienation Strategies without Compromising Your Morals or Harming Your Child," https://www.researchgate.net/publication/265450917_Beyond_the_High_Road_Responding_to_17_Parental_Alienation_Strategies_without_Compromising_Your_Morals_or_Harming_Your_Child. Dr. Baker is the author or co-author of eight books and more than sixty-five peer-reviewed articles on parental alienation, child welfare, parental involvement, early intervention, and attachment.

but the following strategies may alleviate the effects of alienation on children who are not already completely alienated.

Derogatory Comments by the Alienating Parent

Research studies indicate that derogatory comments by the alienating parent against the rejected parent is the most common parental alienation tactic. To the child, the accusations are believable, especially if the rejected parent has no opportunity to explain her side of the story. Keep in mind that most children want to believe a parent is telling the truth; therefore, children will give the parent with the first story the benefit of the doubt—and that parent is usually the abuser.

If the alienating parent makes derogatory statements in front of the child, take advantage of the opportunity to show the child that you are empathetic to the other parent, you want to amicably work out any differences, and there are two viewpoints by responding along these lines in front of the child: "I see you are upset. I'm sorry you feel that way. There are a few things between us that I'm upset about too. Let's go out for coffee and talk it over so that we can have a better relationship. That's the least we can do for Susie, whom we both love."

Some children will report to the rejected parent hurtful things that the alienating parent has said about her to the child. You may hear: "Daddy says you abandoned us," or "Daddy said you left us because you had an affair," or "Daddy says that you don't love us anymore," or "Daddy says you are crazy and have a mental illness." These are painful and awkward moments, but also good opportunities to interact, be empathetic with your child, and ask your child what she needs from you. Take the time to have a frank discussion, neutralize the derogatory comments, and show your child that she was not told the whole truth. Avoid badmouthing the other parent or criticizing the child. It is far better that your children talk about what they hear and ask questions than for them to shut down all communication with you because they believe the alienating parent.

The abuser knows that telling a child that the rejected parent doesn't love the child is one of the most destructive parental alienation tactics. You must remain calm and unflustered and listen to your child. You must also be empathic and provide a safe space for your child to ask difficult questions and still feel loved and heard. A response can be along the lines of, "That must have been very upsetting to hear. What was it like for you when Daddy said that?" Listening and understanding is key. You will want to assure your child, many times, with genuine warmth and affection, that he or she is very much loved. For example, you may wish to say something like, "I want you to know that I love you very much no matter what. Sometimes when parents divorce, kids think a parent doesn't love them anymore, or they hear that from someone else. I want you to know that you are my son/daughter and I cherish you and love you to the moon and back. Nothing, nothing, nothing will ever change that."

If a false accusation is involved, without getting into details, you will also wish to inform your child that she did not receive accurate information, without saying that the alienating parent is a liar: "Honey, you did not get accurate information. When parents can't get along, sometimes they must live in different houses. That doesn't mean I abandoned you or left for someone else. We both love you very much, and we both will always be your parents." If the children are older, you may want to add more age-appropriate information, such as, "You did not receive accurate facts. I'm sorry about that. I will not badmouth your father. However, if you want to know the other side of the story and you have specific questions you want to ask of me, I will answer them truthfully—even though the truth may be ugly. Otherwise, I am not going to talk about things that are between your father and me, or dad bash." If they follow up with specific questions, you can inform them of the truth (without unnecessary details), provide documentation to neutralize the false allegations (such as a cancelled check to disprove a false allegation that you refused to pay for college tuition), or refer them to an objective third party—such as a counselor or friend—if they feel they need more facts. Note that counselors are usually subject to the counselor-client privilege unless you and your spouse signed a release of information giving the counselor permission to speak with another person.

You should also encourage your child to think for themselves and consider your character before believing bad things said about you. The child may be wondering why their father is saying such negative things. A kind response that shows empathy for the other parent and does not criticize either the other parent or child might sound like this: "Sometimes when people are upset, they say things that they don't mean or aren't true. Remember when you told Billy 'I hate you!' when you were mad? You didn't mean it—but sometimes things slip out when people are upset that are painful to hear."

If an older or adult child has already eliminated the rejected parent from his life because of the derogatory comments of the abuser, you may wish to continue sending an unobtrusive text once a week or so to let him know you are thinking of him and love him. If you text too often, the child will likely view it as annoying. But if you text too infrequently, the child will likely think the alienating parent was right—Mom just doesn't care. You may also wish to reach out and let him know he received inaccurate information and that you would like to share the facts, if he's interested. Something along these lines may help open the lines of communication: "Honey, I believe that you have received inaccurate information about me. I love you and value our relationship. If you would like to know the truth of what happened, please reach out so we can talk about it."

For women, this break in a relationship with their child is gut-wrenching. A mother's heart yearns to be close to her child. This is a God-given desire. He wants us to be in relationship; that is how we are wired to thrive and develop into healthy adults. We are designed to love and be loved. When love is absent, especially from those closest to us, it is a great loss. However, God can change hearts. In fact, God is the only one who can change hearts. Prayer and fasting and asking the Lord to turn the hearts of your child to Him and to you is comforting and reassuring and changes hearts. This may take time. However, do not give up hope. At some point, many children realize the lies and attacks of the alienating parent and return to the rejected parent. Remember that God loves your children even more than you do. He is working in their hearts and behind the scenes to bring about restoration. And when restoration comes, remember to thank Him for changing hearts.

Limiting or Eliminating Contact with the Rejected Parent

Alienating, abusive parents seek to reduce, limit, or, if possible, eliminate contact between the child and the rejected parent altogether. The alienation may range from small infractions of time to all-out claims of complete custody with no time with the mother. The alienating parent may arrive early for pickups or drop the child off late for drop-offs. You may wish to remind the father, in front of the child, what time you agreed for pickups and drop-offs. If this continues, despite reminders, you may need to be more creative—such as taking the child out to an activity or a meal and arrive back just before pickup time (but not late!), or arrange to pick up the child from the other parent's home so that he is not late in a scheduled drop-off.

The alienating parent may make excuses for the child not visiting with the rejected parent during her parenting time or simply ignore the parenting plan. In this case, you will want to let the child know that you are trying to have contact, without assigning blame to the alienating parent: "I had planned to have dinner with you last week at our favorite restaurant. I'm sorry that Dad said you couldn't make it." For an older child, you may want to make plans directly with the child, not the parent.

Of course, you should attempt to resolve the scheduling matter amicably with the other parent, which is not likely to be effective. You should have a written trail of efforts to resolve the matter, such as emails or texts. If the above scenarios continue to happen, you will want to document the deviations from the parenting plan and let your attorney know. Your attorney should also inform the father's attorney of the continued breaches and demand adherence to the parenting plan. Sometimes a phone call with a stern demand to stick by the parenting plan, or incur further legal fees if you need to file a motion and go back to court, will be the incentive that an abuser needs to know that you mean business. Other times, a trip to the court may be necessary.

An extremely alienating parent may lie and tell the child that he was awarded full custody, that his mother has no rights to see him, that she has no authority, that he isn't required to see her if he doesn't want to, and/or that the alienating parent's plans with the child always take precedence over any plans the mother may have. If she attempts to enforce the parenting plan, the alienating parent will redouble his denigration to turn the child against her: "Your mother is taking me back to court again! That little money-grubber! She abandoned you and doesn't love you, she left us because she had an affair, and now she wants to see you. You don't ever have to see her!" Abusive parents seek full custody in court much more than nonabusive parents, and often get it. If they don't achieve full custody by court order in a parenting plan, they will essentially achieve it by ignoring the parenting plan. This extreme alienation tactic requires legal action to enforce the parenting plan. You will need to document every time the child does not spend his assigned parenting time with you. You will also need to inform your attorney about the parental alienation and parenting plan violations, ask the judge to enforce the parenting plan and direct the alienating parent to stop the derogatory remarks, and ensure that the child attends scheduled parenting time with the other parent.

Interfering with Communication between Child and Rejected Parent

Most children and parents want communication when they are apart, either by text, phone, email, social media, instant messaging, video chat, or old-fashioned cards and letters. Typically, alienating parents expect to have full access to their children when they are with the other parent, but insist on limited or no access to the child when the situation is reversed.

Consider creative approaches to counteract this tactic:

- Let the child know you have been trying to contact her without blaming the other parent. Mention that you tried to call, or ask if she received the card or letter you sent.
- Go shopping with the child and pick out some treats or cards that you can mail and that they can look forward to receiving when the child is with the other parent. Don't discuss this with the alienating parent. When you ship it or mail it, keep a receipt and tracking number. Ask the child if she received the package, and if not, you both can look up the tracking number together online to see that it was delivered. Your child will see that you sent the package. You can also set up an Amazon account so that your child can send you a link to what they need, and you can have it shipped directly to your child. You can then forward the shipping information to their cell phone. Refrain from telling your child that

his father is lying and keeping the cards and letters. Over time, the child will come to this conclusion on their own.

Of course, communication with the child while he is with the alienating parent should be reasonable. It is not reasonable to call every thirty minutes. How often would you like the child to communicate with the other parent when the child is with you? Your answer is the proper amount you should try to communicate with the child when he is with the other parent. Assuming there is no other issue or crisis going on, once a day for a brief conversation is probably adequate. If there is a crisis—a death in the family, school or friend issues, etc.—then more often to provide emotional support is appropriate. If you are helping with school homework for which the other parent is unable or unwilling to help, then a longer conversation may be needed.

Eliminating Photographs and Other Symbols of the Rejected Parent

Displaying photographs of the other parent and other symbols of their relationship, such as a special gift given to the child, are important to provide comfort and tangible evidence of the parent's love and presence in the child's life. However, universally, the alienating parent will remove all evidence of the rejected parent from the child's room and their home in his efforts to erase the other parent from the child's life. To combat this tactic, while you and your child are with the alienating parent, give the child a photo of you and the child or a family photo that includes you and ask the other parent to let the child display this in his room at his home. At the same time, ask for a photo of the child with the other parent and let the child and other parent know that you will keep it in the child's room at your house. Do the same thing for special gifts to the child from you and the alienating parent. If the alienating parent refuses to exchange photos or throws out the photos, the child will view this himself. If this strategy is unsuccessful, send digital pictures via text, email, or social media, or start a family website.

Withdrawing Love or Approval from the Child

Without expressly stating it, the alienating parent will withdraw his love, affection, or approval as emotional punishment for the child who shows positive feelings toward or spends time with the rejected parent. Although the slight is nonverbal, the child senses the rejection and will do nearly anything—including foregoing time with the rejected parent—to avoid his anger and disapproval. The child is caught in a trap.

In this case, without criticizing the alienating parent, point out the obvious and let the child know you are the safe parent who will never withdraw love or approval. You may say something along these lines: "You seem very worried about disappointing and angering Dad. I imagine it must be hard for you. I don't want to be the reason Dad is mad at you, and I don't want to put you in the middle. I love you to the moon—so just know that nothing you do will make me love you any less." This reassures the child of your love and expresses empathy for the difficult situation he has been put in.

Forcing the Child to Choose between Parents to Attend Events

Sometimes an alienating parent will force the child to choose which parent he wants to attend an event while excluding the other parent. The alienating parent and the child may keep the event a secret from the rejected parent or may even make the child call the rejected parent and request that she not attend. This is obviously hurtful to the rejected parent, who may inadvertently lash out at the child. Once again, the child is caught in the middle and is forced to be a messenger in a battle of loyalties—but remain calm.

Document every instance, and bring it up to the alienating parent in writing. The alienating parent will likely not change, and thus you may need to seek legal intervention. If legal steps are not taken, expect to be excluded from important events in your child's life, and because of the constant voice of the alienating parent telling him that you don't care, your child may come to believe you don't care about him anymore.

Forcing the Child to Reject the Rejected Parent

When both parents attend a child's event, the abusive, alienating parent may belittle, disparage, or shun the rejected parent and encourage the child to do the same. He may encourage the child to be rude to or ignore the rejected parent and to stand by or talk to only the alienating parent. Once the alienating parent has left, the child may be pleasant again to the rejected parent.

Some moms feel so rejected by the abusive parent and the child that they forego their children's events to avoid the humiliation and poor treatment. However, this only gives more power to the abuser and demonstrates that it's more important to avoid the other parent than to support your child at her event.

One strategy is to stand close to the alienating parent while leaving room for your child to stand between the two of you. After the alienating parent has left, you may be able to say something like, "Sometimes it must seem hard to choose where you want to stand or who you want to talk to. I know you like to talk to both of us. And as far as I'm concerned, you don't have to choose between us. I would like you to feel free to talk respectfully to both of us. Is there something I can do to make this easier for you? It's important that we all treat each other with respect. None of us feel good when any of us are treated rudely or disrespectfully." This lets the child know you understand he's been put in the middle, doesn't criticize the other parent or the child, and still lets the child know that respect is expected.

Forcing the Child to Spy on the Rejected Parent

An alienating parent may send the child on a mission to dig up whatever documents can be found on the rejected parent or whatever news the rejected parent may share with the child, and then report back to the alienating parent. The aim of this tactic is often to obtain financial information that would be instrumental in reducing child support payments (or increasing child support payments from the rejected parent), stalk the rejected parent, or use information about a new relationship against the rejected parent.

If a child is spying on you, she is forced to pledge loyalty to one parent at the expense of the other. It puts emotional and psychological distance, and even animosity, between you and the child. It is best to do what you can to protect the child from this destructive mission. Of course, you should never ask your child to spy on the other parent for you. You must also be mindful to not share anything with the child that you do not want to get back to the alienating parent. You will also want to put any documents that you do not want discovered in a locked filing cabinet. Arranging for a post office box is another way to keep prying eyes from seeing mail when you are not home.

If you happen upon a child rummaging through your private documents, you will want to address it with the child on the spot: "It appears that you are looking for something in my private papers. I'm wondering what you're looking for. Can I help you find something in particular?" This usually stops the spying, but it also means that you should be honest and proactive about financial matters that may affect child support payments. For example, if you have obtained a better paying job or a raise at work, you will want to contact your attorney so the child support payments reflect the additional funds. When you do so, feel free to share the good news with your child, and they will likely be relieved when they know that you have already informed the other parent. You might be able to share the news along these lines: "Hey, I've got good news! I let Dad know, and I want to share with you, too, that I just got a nice promotion at work. Let's go out for ice cream to celebrate." If the child has been looking in your papers, the next time you see the alienating parent, you will want to say something in front of the child in a light, nonaccusatory tone, along the lines of the following: "Johnny was looking for some information that he thought you might want. If you want to know about something, you can ask me directly. As you know, I received a promotion. For your records, here is a copy of my pay stub that I have already given to the attorneys."

If the new position doesn't involve a change in pay, and if you are not required to share with the other parent, you can say, "Hey, I've got good news! I want to share with you that I got a new job. It doesn't pay any more, but I'll be transferring to the local office, so I'll be closer to home and can see more of your games." If the child has been looking in your papers, the next time you see the alienating parent, you will want to say something in front of the child—again, in a light, nonaccusatory tone, along the lines of the following: "Johnny was looking for some information that he thought you might want. If you want to know about something, you can ask me directly. I got a new job, but the pay is the same, so I didn't mention it. For your records, here is a copy of my pay stub." This shows the child that you are being responsible and trying to get along.

Forcing the Child to Withhold Secrets from the Rejected Parent

Like spying, forcing a child to withhold secrets from a rejected parent is destructive to the child. It forms an unhealthy alliance between the child and the alienating parent, creating psychological distance and an "us versus her" mentality. If you find your child has been keeping secrets, you will want to discuss it with her directly. It may go along these lines: "I think you have known for a while that [insert secret here], but I just found out about it. That is like keeping a secret from me. For some things it's okay to have secrets, but for others it's not. Can you think of something that's okay to keep as a secret? [Wait for the child. Things like a crush on someone, or an imaginary friend, are examples.] Can you think of something that's not okay to keep as a secret? [Wait for the child. The matter you are discussing, planning something important, a school event, an important social event, an athletic event, etc., are examples.] Do you know why it wasn't okay to keep it a secret? [Wait for the child. Hurt feelings, missed events, inconveniencing someone else, and consequences are all examples.] I'm sorry you felt like you had to keep that a secret. What can I do to make you feel like you don't need to keep secrets in the future?" If the child shares that the other parent asked him to keep a secret, you might be able to say, "How can we brainstorm to see how we can help Daddy from asking you to keep secrets?"

The next time you see the alienating parent, in front of the child you might be able to say, "I understand that [whatever the secret was.] I would have liked to have attended that event for our child [or whatever the secret was]. Of course, I will keep you informed about things that relate to our child that you might like to attend, and I would hope that you would do the same for me." Again, a light and nonaccusatory tone will hopefully keep the reaction to a minimum, avoid putting the child in the middle, and let the child know that you are being responsible.

Referring to the Rejected Parent by First Name

Alienating parents sometimes start referring to the rejected parent by her first name to the children, instead of "Mom," as a way to devalue the other parent. The child may follow suit. On the other hand, sometimes a child goes through a phase to try it out on both parents. Be sure you know the source of this before assuming that the other parent has prompted this. When you are assured that the other parent has encouraged this, politely say to the alienating parent in front of the child, "Please refer to me as Mom in front of Johnny, and I will refer to you as Dad. It might be confusing for him to have us start calling each other by first names." It is also advisable to let your child know how special he is to you, that you will always be proud to let others know he is your child, and that only he can call you "Mom" and you are so proud of that.

Referring to a Stepparent as "Mom," and Encouraging the Child to Do So

Part of the abuser's erase and replace tactic is to refer to his new spouse as "Mom" in front of a child to eliminate the real mom from the child's life. Some alienating parents even require the child to refer to the new spouse as "Mom." You will need to address this with the alienating parent in front of the child, in a nonthreatening way, such as, "There must be some confusion or mix-up because the school nurse seems to think that [name of new spouse] is Johnny's mom. Let's be clear to the school, to Johnny, and to others who is who. And I will do the same." You will also want a discussion with your child: "I know you and [name of stepparent] are close, and it may be easier to call her 'Mom,' but for now I would like to be the only one you call 'Mom,' just like you and your siblings are the only ones I call my children. It eliminates confusion and reminds us of our special relationship. Maybe you and [name of stepparent] can come up with a special name that you can call her."

Withholding Important Information

Withholding information from the rejected parent, or not disclosing the name or even the existence of the rejected parent to teachers, schools, physicians, coaches, etc., is an effective tactic to erase the rejected parent from the child's life. When the rejected parent doesn't attend an important event that she is not aware of, the child likely thinks, "If Mom cared, she would have shown up." Other people may think, "Johnny's mom must not care about him; otherwise, she would come to see his games." This technique is effective for both parental alienation and social alienation.

This situation must be corrected. If you are the rejected parent, you will want to have routine contact with schools, teachers, coaches, physicians, youth pastors, etc., to ensure you are included in their contact information and have all the necessary information. Continue to be proactive in obtaining information directly from the source, and verify the information you receive from the alienating parent with the institutions and organizations. Some alienating parents are so malicious that they will give the other parent incorrect information and dates and then plan or attend an important event, such as graduation or college orientation, without the rejected parent.

Sometimes a rejected parent will be so hurt and angry at being excluded that she is hostile to the school or organization personnel when contacting them. You will want to avoid being hostile or accusatory; be calm. Explain there has been a divorce due to domestic abuse, and that if they notice anything about the child that causes them concern, they should contact you. If you have an order of protection, you will want to provide them with a copy. If you are attending a physician's or teacher's office with the child and the abusive parent, be sure to contact the nurse or attendant ahead of time, making sure that they are aware of the situation so that you are not left alone with the other parent in the office. You will want to wait outside the office if the physician or teacher takes the child out of the room for X-rays or other procedures so that you are not left alone with the abuser, who may take the opportunity to hurl insults and slurs at you when no one else is around.

If the alienating parent continues to deny access to information about important events in your child's life, consider contacting your lawyer. Most parenting agreements require parents to exchange information, keep the other informed, provide schools and physicians with parent information, and be nondisparaging and cooperative.

Changing the Child's Name

Another way that abusers erase the rejected/targeted parent from the child's life is to confer a different nickname or surname on him. Fathers may remove the mother's name if it is a hyphenated name, and mothers may use only their maiden name. Parenting agreements usually decree that the name of the child not be changed while the child is a minor. You will also want to remind schools and physicians of the child's correct name. You will want to gently correct the alienating parent and the child so that the attempted change in names won't be confusing for the child and others.

Fostering Dependency

Ordinarily, parents foster a healthy sense of independence, critical-thinking skills, and age-appropriate experiences independent of parents in their children. Alienating parents, however, foster financial and emotional dependency, thinking that mimics their own opinions, and experiences that continue the dependency on the alienating parent. For example, the alienating parent may remind the child how much college or vacation or their car costs, thereby reminding the child that she is financially dependent upon him. Or he may claim the other parent has abandoned the child, thereby fostering fear in the child and reinforcing the sense that the child would be all alone were it not for the alienating parent. Many alienating parents urge or require their older children to attend college nearby while living at home to have more influence and control over them. Alienating parents often pressure adult children to work for them in the family business, thereby exercising nearly complete control over the child and ensuring the child's financial dependence on the parent indefinitely. An unnecessary and inappropriate sense of dependence is akin to being in a cult in which the child is unable to survive without the approval and support of the parent. The alienating parent adores the child's worship and unbridled view that he is perfect, exceptional, and above reproach. He does not want the child to grow up to live an independent life, as that would require the parent to release control over the child.

If you see your child acting in this way, you will want to encourage the child to develop independent, critical-thinking skills that foster autonomy and self-sufficiency. Support a college age child to attend a school away from home, so that the alienating parent has less control and the child has the opportunity to develop independence. You may also want to encourage the child to get a job to earn his own money so he is not financially dependent upon the alienating parent. Encourage an adult child to become financially, emotionally, and physically independent from the alienating parent. For example, encourage him to obtain a conventional loan to purchase a house rather than borrow money from his father and thereby become beholden to him. Achieving adult independence may mean declining a job with the family business or relocating out of physical range of the abusive parent's control so the adult child can develop his own identity, set of friends, accomplishments, financial independence, and self-reliance.

Chapter 24

Co-parenting with an Abuser

THE NONABUSIVE PARENT MUST navigate a new relationship with her abuser once a divorce is filed. Although during the marriage there may have been some success at co-parenting, it is impossible to co-parent with an abuser after a divorce is filed. A woman may reach out and seek the abuser's cooperation in raising their children to adulthood. However, the abuser will be uncooperative and will actively sabotage and undermine her well-intended actions. He will be vindictive in his efforts to destroy her emotionally, financially, spiritually, and physically if possible—and he will use the children to do so.

Abusers usually go one of two ways: he will either drop out of his children's lives entirely or he will try to control every aspect of their lives to the exclusion of the mother. He will view time and activities with the children as a competition with his former spouse and will employ every trick he can to win. Abusers regularly ignore parenting agreements and divorce agreements, even if they are court orders or judgments.

Many times women are surprised at how low their former spouses will stoop to hurt them. There is, truly, no depth to which an abuser will not sink to inflict additional wounds on a leaving spouse. Abusers will engage in all the alienating techniques of the prior chapters. They generally refuse to impose reasonable house rules on the children, and they sabotage the attempts of the leaving spouse to impose age-appropriate rules and guidelines on the children.

Thus, the former wife of an abuser must engage in parallel parenting rather than co-parenting. In parallel parenting, the former wife manages her household and the children when they are with her by reasonable and appropriate rules and guidelines without seeking the input or cooperation of the abuser. When the children are in her custody, her rules apply and her decisions stand. However, when they are in the custody of the father, his rules and decisions apply. He will not seek the input or cooperation of their mother. Given the abuser's lack of appropriate rules and moral values, the former wife typically will work overtime in compensating for the abuser's shortcomings. For example, the abuser may impose no curfew for the children, allow teenage drinking in his house, and invite his girlfriends overnight while the children are with him. Unless there is a court order or parenting agreement that prohibits these, the wife will be unable to impose reasonable guidelines upon him. She can inform the police if there is underage drinking in the house or if the children are out after the town curfew, but that comes with its own set of legal repercussions to the children and the abuser, as well as further alienating the children from the mother and inviting further vindictiveness from the abuser. However, she can have reasonable guidelines while the children are in her custody, and, if questioned, she can explain why having the guidelines are in the best interest of her and her children.

Holidays, vacations, and special occasions will always present a problem with an abuser. Abusers delight in causing chaos at the holidays and disrupting schedules. An abuser generally cannot stand that a holiday puts the attention on something other than him. Therefore, he will sabotage holiday plans so that he is, once again, the center of attention. Being polite and trying to coordinate is likely to result in planning nothing at all. While a woman is trying to be considerate and waiting to plan around the abuser's schedule, the abuser will sabotage events and constantly change plans, and Mom is left not knowing how to plan Christmas Eve dinner. Generally, the best way to handle these days is to make a plan, announce it to the children, indicate that all are invited if they can make it, and go with it. Celebrations may not be on the exact day of the holiday, but the important point is to be together. Be grateful when they can make it, and fill the home with positivity and warmth. Welcoming them with open arms and not making them feel guilty if they can't make it or if they need to come late or leave early is the best way to calm everyone's jittery nerves and make the most of the time you do have together. Making holidays as joyful as possible and refraining from negativity will draw the children to their mother. At the age of eighteen, children can then choose where they want to be for the holidays.

Of course, if the abuser poses a danger to the child's mental, emotional, physical, or moral health, the mother ought to seek legal counsel for supervised visits and/or counseling for the abuser. Clearly, if an abuser is directly abusing the child, the mother will want to gather evidence and seek legal action immediately. Among other things, the mother will want to seek legal action if she is aware of the following occurring in the presence of the child: excessive drinking, watching pornography or other graphic materials, the unsupervised use of weapons, engaging in sex, or the use of illegal drugs or other illegal activities. If any of these are occurring, it is advisable to obtain evidence (which can be difficult) and report the actions to the police and the state department of children's services.

Chapter 25

Have a Safety Plan

We know that when a woman leaves, it is an especially dangerous time for her and her children. Abusers want control over their circumstances, people, and especially their spouse and children. To an abuser, a spouse's leaving is the ultimate insult, betrayal, and indication that the abuser has lost control of her and the situation. He will retaliate for this affront. Thus, a woman must be wise, cautious, and expect an abuser to be violent and out of control when she leaves. She can expect her abuser to stalk her and the people she cares about—especially anyone he suspects of aiding her escape or sheltering her.

Women fleeing an abusive relationship need a physical safety plan to ensure her and her children's safety while still living with the abuser, during her escape, and after she leaves. The following are some suggestions:

Physical Safety Plan While a Woman is Still Living with an Abuser

- Make an emergency escape plan.
- Know what windows, doors, stairwells, or fire escapes you will use to escape quickly and safely.
- If the abuser is escalating and getting violent, position yourself to get out quickly, and get near a phone to dial 911.
- Move to a space where there is less risk. Avoid arguments in the bathroom, garage, kitchen (where there are knives), basement, near weapons, or in rooms without access to an outside door.
- Use a code word with children so they can call 911 for help and/or run to a neighbor.
- Use your judgment and intuition to try to keep the abuser calm and protect yourself until you are out of danger.
- Turn on the fire alarm if necessary.
- Create a telephone list with numbers of local police, the local domestic violence crisis line, family members, counselors, and children's friends. Keep the list with you and your children.
- Arrange to stay with family, friends, or in a domestic violence shelter.
- Have an extra set of car keys in a location that only you know, so you can use them during an emergency escape.

- Ask your neighbors to call the police if they hear fighting or screaming in the house.
- Ask your neighbors if the children can run to their house in an emergency and use their phone, and teach the children to go there if necessary.
- Be aware if your car has a GPS tracker on it or whether the brakes are sound (an automotive repair shop can check for you). If your car has a GPS tracker on it, drop it off and use a cab or Uber.
- Turn off the phone so that you cannot be tracked. Know that your abuser can track your calls if the phone bill is addressed to him or it is in his name. Get a temporary prepaid (burner) phone that your abuser is not aware of, if necessary.

Teaching Children a Physical Safety Plan While a Woman Is Still Living with an Abuser

- Teach the emergency escape plan to your children, and practice it.
- Teach your children to let you know when someone is at the door before opening it.
- Teach your children how to use the telephone to call the police or 911 and what to say. Rehearse with your children what to say when they call for help. They should not use the phone in view of the abuser. Children should know their full name, address, and phone number and be able to give that information to the 911 operator. Arrange to let your children use the neighbor's phone if they cannot call from home or a cell phone.
- Create a code word with your children, neighbors, friends, and family so they know you are in danger and will call for help.
- Teach your children how to make a collect call to you or to the police if your partner takes the children.
- Teach your children how to escape from the trunk of a locked car, and practice. If a trunk cannot be unlocked from the inside, they should kick out the rear lights and wave their hands outside the car until someone calls for help.
- Teach children not to get in the middle of a fight between you and your abuser. Tell the children that the best thing they can do is to keep themselves safe and call 911.
- Teach children how to get to safety during a violent incident between you and your abuser. If the children are not a target, let them choose a room in the house to go to, lock the door, and dial 911. If they are a target, you all must leave the house immediately using your emergency escape plan.

Physical Safety Plan When Preparing to Leave

Women in abusive relationships frequently leave the home they are sharing with an abuser when they separate. Abusers are unresponsive to reasonable requests, are unwilling to change when confronted with their abusive behavior, and are unwilling to give up control of their home. Not only is it extremely intimidating to ask an abuser to leave the home, but he will simply refuse to do so in most cases. Often, the only option for the abused spouse is to leave the home and go to a safe place—either the home of a friend or relative, a domestic abuse shelter, or a separate apartment or home if she has the resources. Pets are a concern, as the abuser may turn to abusing the pet if it's left behind. The leaving spouse should always take the children to avoid further abuse and parental alienation. Personal items such as jewelry, clothes, and heirlooms should be taken if possible, as the abuser is likely to retaliate by destroying them. Taking furniture or household items that both the abuser and victim acquired together will likely anger the abuser even more; however, the abuser will be angry no matter what she does or doesn't take. Furniture and household items can always be replaced, and it is far more important to be safe than to insist on taking furniture or other personal items.

Because abusers are likely to turn violent when a spouse leaves, it is usually advisable to leave when the abuser is not present. She should allow for enough time to move without the threat of him returning early, so leaving when he is at work or gone for a weekend is optimal. She can either leave a note or send an email or text after arriving at a safe place—however, she must not disclose her new location. If a woman must leave due to increasing violence but she doesn't have the time to move household items, she should take several days of clothes for herself and her children and hide them in the trunk of the car—so she can escape quickly without the abuser seeing her pack—and then leave. If necessary, she can pick the children up from school and inform the school of the domestic abuse.

Planning an escape is important when leaving an abuser. The following are some safety strategies to consider when preparing to leave:

- Keep originals of important documents such as passports, birth certificates, marriage license, etc., at an off-site location such as a friend's house, your attorney's office, or a safe deposit box in your name only and to which no one else has access.
- Keep copies of important documents such as the mortgage, deed to the house, title on cars, car loans, health and life insurance, etc., at an offsite location.
- Keep an extra copy of keys at an offsite location.
- Open a post office box to continue receiving mail without having to go back to the house.
- Inform a trusted friend or family member of your intentions and whereabouts.
- Make arrangements with a family member, friend, apartment manager, or domestic abuse shelter for housing for yourself, your children, and your pets.
- Make arrangements with a storage facility for storing your personal items or furniture if you can.
- Make arrangements with movers or friends in advance if you plan to ask them to help you move or provide shelter.
- Immediately seek an Order of Protection. See below for more information on Orders of Protection.

Calling Police and Making Police Reports

Many women are afraid to call the police or file a police report—often for good reason. Her abuser often retaliates. And far too often, police are not sympathetic to victims of domestic abuse. However, involving the police will, at best, result in an arrest and conviction of criminal behavior, or, at least, indicate to the abuser that others are watching his behavior. Generally, the abusive behavior will subside when law enforcement becomes involved.

If the police are called during a physically violent incident, witness the incident, and/or see evidence of the violent incident (such as a black eye, bruising, cuts, etc.), they may be able to arrest and remove the abuser from the home. However, if police don't witness the incident or have no evidence, they will likely not be able to make an arrest on the spot. A woman can still file a police report, but the state's attorney will then determine whether to charge the abuser. To convict a person of battery, assault, domestic abuse, or any other crime, there must be enough evidence beyond a reasonable doubt to indicate he is guilty. That is a very high standard. In domestic abuse cases, evidence is often difficult to obtain because it happens behind closed doors. In most cases, there are no video or audio recordings or witnesses to provide adequate evidence for conviction. The abuser will deny the abuse, which puts the entire burden on the victim to produce sufficient evidence to convict. Therefore, collecting evidence of the abuse is important. Nearly every cell phone has a video recording device which can be used as evidence (audio only recordings may or may not be admissible evidence, depending upon the state laws regarding this). Texts, documents, video recordings, and all other types of evidence should be gathered if possible. Obviously, the abuser does not want recordings made of his abuse, so it must be done with extreme care and caution.

A woman can also alert the police to the domestic abuse and ask the police to make extra rounds near her home. When an abuser knows the police are watching him, it often gives her the protection she needs, and the violence may abate. If she is dropped off from his car, as many abusers do, calling the police is also advised. Although the police might not be able to make an arrest, they will be able to protect her, give her a ride home or to a safe location, file a police report, and have a stern talk with the abuser. A woman may also be able to work in concert with the police to glean enough evidence to make an arrest, such as wearing a recording device given to her by the police.

In general, it is advisable to inform the police of the domestic abuse. If there is no record of police reports, when a woman needs to file for an order of protection, gain custody of the children, or press charges for criminal behavior, the court will have no evidence that there has been a history of violence.

Order of Protection

An order of protection is a civil protection designed to stop and prevent violent and harassing behavior. Although laws vary by state, in general, an order of protection can be obtained by a victim who is living or has lived with an abuser, or is related to, is dating, or has been in a dating relationship with an abuser if there is physical or sexual abuse, stalking, or harassment. Because it is a civil remedy, the standard of evidence to obtain an order of protection in most states is the "propensity of the evidence"—that is, whether the judge believes that it is more likely than not that he was abusive. In some states, the standard is "clear and convincing evidence." Either standard is far more lenient than the "beyond a reasonable doubt" standard for criminal conviction. In fact, the civil order of protection was introduced because legislators recognized that so many women needed protection but were unable to bring criminal convictions against their abusers because of the onerous criminal standard of evidence. Unfortunately, many judges are unmoved by the pleas of a domestic abuse victim. It is truly remarkable what some judges expect victims to tolerate. Nonetheless, it is usually wise to attempt to obtain court-ordered protection.

The remedies offered by an order of protection are many. They include barring the abuser from physical contact (usually 500 feet away) with the victim, giving the victim exclusive use of the residence (thereby forcing the abuser out of the family home), prohibiting the abuser from any communications with the victim (including email, phone, text, social media, etc.), prohibiting the abuser from attempting to communicate with the victim through third parties (such as telling friends to relay a message), giving the victim exclusive possession of pets and other personal property, paying for the victim's rent if she is forced to leave the home, exclusive custody of the children, changing the phones to her name, and requiring the abuser to complete counseling, among other things. Orders of protection also can bar the abuser from being within 500 feet of the victim's home, school, place of employment, place of worship, or other places that the victim frequents. A victim will want to include as many protected places as possible on the order of protection. Minor children can and should be included in the order of protection.

Orders of protection generally come in two forms: an emergency order of protection (which lasts for up to three weeks and then expires) and a plenary order of protection (which can last up to two years). Under an emergency order of protection, the judge will usually set a hearing date three weeks out for the victim to obtain a plenary order of protection. The victim must come back to court and seek the plenary order of protection. If the victim does not seek the plenary order of protection or if the plenary order of protection is denied, the emergency order of protection will expire, leaving her unprotected.

A victim can obtain an emergency order of protection by completing an affidavit and petition in the domestic violence courtroom in the local county courthouse where she resides. An advance appointment or court date is not necessary in an emergency petition. The judge will hear the victim and, if the actions of the abuser qualify, will issue the order of protection on the spot. Notice to the abuser is not required for an emergency hearing; however, the abuser will be served notice of the emergency order by a sheriff, and he will receive notice of the plenary order of protection hearing, which he has a right to attend. Once an order of protection is granted, if a woman is still living at home, it is important for her not to alert the abuser until the sheriff serves the abuser with the order of protection and escorts him off the property. Otherwise, she will be in great danger as the abuser will retaliate for her taking legal action against him. Depending on the county, the sheriff may take hours or several days to serve the order of protection. She may wish to leave the house and visit friends or relatives while she waits for the sheriff to serve her abuser.

It is important to seek an emergency order of protection immediately or as soon as possible after a violent incident, preferably within 24 to 72 hours. Otherwise, the judge will not view the petition as an emergency or the incident as violent because the victim did not quickly seek to protect herself. When a woman of faith works patiently to resolve conflict by seeking marital or pastoral counseling rather than destroying a relationship by immediately seeking the assistance of the courts, the delay works against her. Also, it is important to seek an order of protection prior to filing a petition for divorce. If the order of protection is sought after a petition for divorce is filed, the judge may suspect the order of protection is being sought to gain an advantage in the divorce litigation rather than because of a genuine need for protection. In some courthouses, orders of protection are heard by a judge who hears only orders of protection. However, once a divorce is filed, the order of protection will often be combined with the divorce case and heard by one of the divorce judges, who may not be as sympathetic to the victim.

It is important to seek the plenary order of protection, which can extend the protection for up to two years. If the risk remains, the plenary order can be extended another two years. Oftentimes, the abuser will try to talk the victim out of seeking a plenary order of protection. The victim must disregard his lies and blatant attempts at manipulation and go forward with the hearing, seeking protection. If the abuser was serious about changing his ways, he would have done so long before she was forced to seek the protection of the courts. Further, if the abuser is communicating with the victim after an emergency order of protection has already been issued, this is in itself a violation of the emergency order of protection. Therefore, it is also important to inform the judge at the hearing for the plenary order of protection that the abuser has already violated the emergency order of protection, which is usually grounds for granting the plenary order of protection.

A violation of an order of protection is a criminal offense, enforceable by the police. Therefore, if an abuser violates an order of protection, the victim should immediately contact local law enforcement. They should arrest the violator if they see him in the act of violation or send a warrant for his arrest if there is evidence for the arrest (such as a photo taken of the violator within 500 feet of the victim). However, many police are not properly trained in orders of protection and therefore do not arrest a violator when they should. For example, some police are under the false impression that if the violator violates the order of protection in a public place, or a place that is not listed on the order of protection as a protected place, an arrest is not warranted. In fact, an arrest is warranted when the abuser comes within 500 feet (or the limit set in the order of protection) of the protected individual, regardless of where she may be. The onus is on the perpetrator to stay away from the victim, not on the victim to stay away from the perpetrator.

It is important to know that an order of protection is ultimately only a court order written on a piece of paper. Many women have been stalked, harmed, kidnapped, and even murdered while under an order of protection. Therefore, it is imperative that even with an order of protection, a woman is mindful of her surroundings, locks her doors, takes precautions, and otherwise protects herself.

Domestic Restraining Order

Another protection option for women is a domestic restraining order. This is an order issued by a judge in a family law courtroom, usually in connection with a divorce or other family law case. Usually the order will prohibit either party from communicating or physically contacting the other party. If an abuser has been emotionally abusive, but the actions are not severe enough to qualify for an order of protection, a restraining order may be possible.

Like an order of protection, a domestic restraining order can prohibit communication or physical contact. However, a restraining order differs from an order of protection in a few ways. First, the provisions of a restraining order can be mutual (that is, applying to both parties). Therefore, the onus is on both parties to stay away from the other. Second, it can last indefinitely rather than just two years. Because it can last indefinitely, it is advisable to include a restraining order provision in a divorce agreement with an abuser. That way, if an order of protection expires, the abuser is still prohibited from communicating with or contacting the victim. Third, violations of domestic restraining orders are not criminal violations and are not enforceable by the police. Therefore, if an abuser violates the restraining order, the victim must go before a judge to enforce the order. While orders of protection are included on police reports, restraining orders are not. Finally, domestic restraining orders issued during a divorce litigation generally expire when a divorce is finalized, while orders of protection extend until the expiration date set forth in the order of protection. Therefore, if a woman is relying on a restraining order for her protection during a pending divorce, she should include the provisions of the restraining order in the divorce agreement so that it continues.

Chapter 26

Have a Financial Plan

THE BIGGEST IMPEDIMENT TO leaving an abuser is often a woman's lack of finances. As more fully discussed in chapter 9, "Financial Abuse," in 99 percent of abuse cases, the abuser exerts financial abuse and assures his power and control over his partner by keeping her financially dependent upon him.[115] An abuser often has bank and investment accounts in his name only, so that his wife has no access. He may demand that she quit her job so that she is completely dependent upon him. If she works, he may demand that she deposit her paycheck into his account, or he may demand that she pay so many expenses that she has nothing left. He also threatens her that if she leaves him, he will ensure that she is a homeless bag lady and he will get custody of the children. This is not an idle threat, and abusers attempt to make good on that threat throughout the divorce process. When a divorce petition is filed, many, if not most, abusers will empty out the joint bank and investment accounts and deposit the funds into an account in their name only—thereby leaving the wife with no funds. An abuser will often ruin the credit score of his spouse by using her social security number and other information, forging her signature, taking out credit cards and loans in her name or in joint names, and then refusing to make payments. During the divorce, an abuser will hide assets, refuse to cooperate with discovery requests, and lie about assets and income.

Abusers don't play fair. Whether you have been married for twenty-five months or twenty-five years, the abuser views every penny earned during a marriage as his, and his goal in a divorce, as in all other areas of life, is for him to win and for you to lose. Because of the ongoing financial abuse, it is imperative for women to have a financial plan in place prior to leaving an abuser. The following are some important parts of a financial plan.

Make a Budget

It is essential to know how much your income and expenses are to become financially independent. Make a detailed monthly budget so that you will know how much you need to make and what you can afford. When you finally make your move, you will be prepared and have essential information about your finances, and that will reduce anxiety.

---

[115] Adrienne Adams, *Measuring the Effects of Domestic Violence on Women's Financial Well-Being*, (University of Wisconsin Center for Financial Security Research Brief, 2011), 5.6.

Post Office Box

One simple step is obtaining a post office box in your name only. You will need this to send mail and packages that your abuser should not see. You will want a post office box with a street address if a financial institution requires a street address to open an account. The post office box should preferably be in a different town from the town you live in so that mail is not inadvertently delivered to your home address by your town's post office.

The post office box offers additional safety precautions as well. If you move out, it is important that your abuser not discover your whereabouts. By using a post office box rather than a new physical home address, your abuser will be less likely to find you using public records or by the change of address notifications that are often sent to the old address.

Accounts

Open a bank account in your name only, preferably in a different bank from your joint account or other family accounts. Use the post office box or your work address for your contact information so that statements are not sent to the home address and so your abuser won't discover this. Ideally, you will want to stash away six to twelve months of expenses to live on while the divorce is ongoing. This may take several months to several years.

Independent Financial Income

Establish your own income that is not dependent upon your husband. Your monthly budget will tell you how much you need to make to be financially independent. Many women are employed by their husbands. For example, a pastor may have his wife work as the church secretary. A business owner may have his wife work as his bookkeeper. This puts the wife in a vulnerable position. As soon as a divorce petition is filed, the wife will likely be fired. In any event, no one wants to work with an abusive soon-to-be ex-husband.

Many women feel that they cannot work outside the home due to young children at home or a lack of higher education. If this is the case, explore part-time positions or working from home. Consider starting a home-based business. Numerous positions are flexible and can add to your income, ranging from an Uber driver to marketing research.

Education

Many women have foregone their education to marry and raise a family. As you prepare for life on your own, consider going back to school to get the degree, certification, or training you will need to support yourself and your family. Local community colleges provide vocational training, associate degrees, and general education requirements for bachelor's degrees at reasonable rates. While it may seem discouraging to know that it may take years to earn a degree, keep in mind that the years will go by anyway, and it is better to arrive at that future date with a degree than without one.

Almost every institution of higher education provides scholarships, grants, loans, and other financial aid. The listed tuition price is usually discounted with grants and scholarships.[116] A handful of colleges even offer free—yes, FREE—tuition. A Google search will reveal the requirements of these schools. Many colleges offer free tuition to employees and their children in addition to offering flexible hours and benefits, making a job at a college a very desirable position.

---

[116] See appendix for resources concerning scholarship information.

Housing

Housing is one of the biggest monthly expenses. If it is unsafe to stay in your home and you are unable to convince your abuser to leave, investigate affordable housing. Most women need to downsize their home during and after a divorce. However, downsizing to a cozy home that is more manageable in size is a blessing and should not be viewed as a negative. It is much better to live in a smaller home filled with peace and love than to live in a large home filled with abuse, strife, and division.

You may need to temporarily live with family or friends. While this may seem embarrassing as an adult, any shame or embarrassment is a lie from Satan. View the offer of housing from a family member or friend as a provision from the Lord in a time of need. Not only is such an offer a financial blessing, but it also provides a safe, loving, healthy environment for you and your children, which is particularly important for healing at this vulnerable time. It also allows you and your children to strengthen relationships with these important people.

Most counties in the United States have a domestic abuse organization that offers free counseling and services, and sometimes free or low-cost housing for women and children escaping domestic abuse. For example, in Lake County, Illinois, A Safe Place offers free group counseling, free individual counseling, free court-ordered supervised child custody exchanges, free court-ordered supervised visitation, free emergency shelter for ninety days, and free or greatly reduced long-term housing.[117] Even if your local domestic violence organization does not provide free housing, it may be able to direct you to organizations that do. Most counties in the United States also are home to churches and other parachurch organizations that provide free short-term housing for people in need. Again, the proper perspective of this housing is provision from the Lord when you need it.

You may need to move from your leased apartment or home. Several states, including Illinois, have passed laws that allow a person to terminate a lease without the normal penalties due to domestic abuse. You may need to move from the town in which your home is located, and your children may need to change schools. Several states have laws that require the former school system to provide free transportation to and from a new location if the move was due to domestic abuse.

Furnishings

Most abusers view all assets and household goods in the marital home as belonging solely to them. If your abuser insists on keeping the furniture, the china, and the crystal you acquired during the marriage, don't fret. Unless it has sentimental value, it's typically not worth fighting for. What your abuser likely doesn't know is that you can pick up beautiful home furnishings for pennies on the dollar by visiting thrift stores, estate sales, garage sales, flea markets, antique stores, and consignment shops. Most items can be found for 10 to 20 percent of the regular retail price, and it's refreshing to go on a treasure hunt and reuse, repurpose, and recycle items with a story behind them. Many counties and churches have ministries that offer home furnishings for free for people in need. For example, Love INC. (Love in the Name of Christ; www.loveinc.org) is a national organization with 134 affiliates that partners with local churches and organizations, including domestic violence organizations, in offering free furnishings to women escaping domestic abuse and restarting their lives.

In addition to the joy of furnishing your new home with things you have picked out yourself, perhaps for the first time, these items don't bring with them the difficult memories that furnishings from your marital home would. It's hard to sit at the same kitchen table in your new home without remembering the many times your

---

[117] www.asafeplaceforhelp.org.

abuser yelled at you across the table. It's especially important to get a new bedroom set to start a new life of rest and relaxation, while leaving behind memories of sexual abuse that may come with an old bedroom set.

For marital settlement purposes, assign a replacement retail value to the furnishings and take the cash value in lieu of the furnishings in the settlement. Let your abuser keep the old furnishings with all their bad memories. You will be able to furnish your new home with a fraction of the replacement retail value.

Maintenance and Child Support

If you have children who will live with you, you will likely be entitled to child support. Likewise, you may also be entitled to maintenance and an equitable division of marital assets. During a pending divorce, you may need to petition the court for temporary child support and maintenance. Each state has its own laws concerning the amount, duration, and conditions of child support, maintenance, and division of marital assets. It is advisable to consult legal counsel and your own state laws. However, abusers are well known to violate support orders and orders to divide assets. Therefore, ensuring your own financial independence without dependence upon an abuser is the best way to go forward.

Government Assistance and Nonprofits

While many women are loath to accept help from the government or nonprofits, assistance programs are designed for just such a time as this. Research government websites to know the requirements for food assistance, government sponsored health care, and other big ticket items. Check with local churches and other nonprofits to know the benefits that they can provide. These often include career counseling, clothes for interviews, car maintenance, counseling, food pantries, shelter, medical services, and childcare. For example, the YWCA, a nationwide organization for women, offers, among other things, low-cost childcare through a network of childcare providers. Willow Creek Church, a megachurch in the Chicago suburbs, offers free or low-cost career counseling, job fairs, low-cost clothes, a free grocery store, mental health counseling, dentist services, and vehicle repair and replacement. Almost every junior college offers free or low-cost dental hygiene services and other services to allow their students enrolled in these professions to practice. Many cosmetology schools offer free haircuts. It is important to know your options and to take advantage of these if you need to. Once you get back on your feet, you can pay it forward and help someone else.

Chapter 27

Have a Legal Plan

DEVELOP A LEGAL PLAN and prepare to implement it. Resolving most entanglements with SNAPs requires legal solutions. The abuser specializes in creating legal entanglements that are difficult to extract yourself from. While it may be relatively easy to get involved with the abuser, he will purposely make it very difficult to remove yourself from his web of entrapments. Below are some important factors to consider.

Seek the Protection of the Legal System

Some Christian women are afraid to use the protections of the courts and legal system. Perhaps their abuser or pastor has tried to dissuade them, citing 1 Corinthians 6:1–8 as support for enduring further abuse without seeking protection. This is a skewed interpretation of Scripture, primarily for their own selfish reasons to allow the abuse to continue. In 1 Corinthians 6:1–8, Paul reprimands Christians taking other Christians to court for their pettiness, lack of eternal perspective, inability to resolve conflicts in a peaceful, Christlike manner, and lack of unity of spirit. He says they discredit the church. However, we must view this passage in light of the entire Bible.

We know God is a God of justice and mercy. In Micah 6:8, the Lord asks a question and then answers it: "And what does the Lord require of you? To act justly and to love mercy and to walk humbly with your God."

In the Old Testament, laws were clearly delineated, and a system of judges was in place to enforce the law, ensure justice, and to protect the innocent from the wicked. Laws were established regarding, among other things, contracts, real estate, negligence and other torts, damage to property, marriage, divorce, sexual assault, theft, battery, murder, and other crimes. Clearly, when severe, unrepentant sin was involved, the message was "expel the wicked person from among you" (Deuteronomy 13:5; 17:7; 19:19; 21:21; 22:21; 24:7). Paul cites the same principle in 1 Corinthians 5:13, when he commanded the church to excommunicate a so-called Christian from the church for the continuous, unrepentant sin of having sex with his father's wife.

In Romans 13:1–7, the writer explains that everyone should obey the laws and be subject to the governing authorities, who have been established by God. Clearly this passage infers that seeking protection of the laws is not only allowed, but encouraged.

Have a Legal Plan

In Matthew 18, Jesus provides principles for resolving conflict between two believers. First, the victimized believer should approach the perpetrator privately. If the perpetrator does not listen, the victim should approach the perpetrator with one or two others. If the perpetrator refuses to listen to the group, then the victim should take it to the church. If the perpetrator refuses to listen to the church, the church should treat him as an unbeliever and excommunicate him from the church. Thus, if a perpetrator is treated as an unbeliever, he would not be considered a Christian for purposes of applying the passage from 1 Corinthians 6:1–8. Further, it is highly questionable whether anyone who continues to abuse his wife without repentance is a true Christian.

These passages taken together suggest that Christians should use the court and legal systems sparingly, not for petty matters, but to bring protection and justice to resolve gross injustice inflicted by unreasonable, wicked people, such as abusers.

Police Reports

Recall that calling the police and filing a police report can be a huge protection when dealing with abuse. Police should be called immediately so they can obtain evidence and make an arrest if possible. Unfortunately, police are not always understanding of domestic abuse and do not always arrest the abuser. When this happens and the abuser is let back into the home, it can be terrifying for the victim, who may have nowhere safe to go. Even if an arrest is made, it is the decision of the state prosecutor to determine whether to bring criminal charges against the abuser. If charges are not brought, the abuser may retaliate with any number of tactics—many of which are criminal in nature.

Order of Protection and Domestic Restraining Order

We've noted previously that the order of protection is one of the best defenses against an abuser. However, it is merely a piece of paper. Every victim of abuse should exercise caution when she has an order of protection, as this is an indication that the abuser is clearly capable of severe physical and mental abuse.

As explained in chapter 25, if an order of protection cannot be obtained, a domestic restraining order is a civil protection that can be ordered during a divorce proceeding. The order typically expires at the end of the divorce proceedings. Thus, the provisions in the restraining order that protect the victim should be included in the marital settlement agreement. Check with an experienced divorce attorney who is familiar with domestic abuse when looking into orders of protection and restraining orders.

Safe Housing

Many states have enacted safe homes laws that allow the victim of abuse to terminate a lease early without penalties if she is in a domestic abuse situation. The laws also require a landlord to change the locks upon request by a tenant if she is a victim of domestic abuse. Check the laws of your own state or contact an attorney. Many communities also have legal clinics that provide free legal counseling for landlord and tenant matters.

School Busing

Many states require that the school continue to offer free school bus transportation to children whose parents have moved due to domestic violence. An attorney should be able to advise you of your rights.

Divorce

Marriage to an abuser is not a marriage at all. None of God's purposes for marriage can be accomplished in an abusive marriage. Because abusers refuse to change, divorce is often the only viable option to escape abuse. For a more complete discussion of the biblical view of divorce from an abusive marriage, see chapter 34.

Many wives of abusers would like a family court to pronounce their abuser "guilty" of being a bad, mean, abusive philanderer. Family court will never be able to give the victim of abuse this satisfaction. A criminal court might—if the prosecutors can prove a crime beyond a reasonable doubt. Some women expect a family law judge to provide them with additional funds due to their husband's affairs, general nastiness, and abuse. However, courts in many states are prohibited from making financial allocations based on the marital misconduct of an abuser. For many reasons, it is important for a woman who is divorcing an abuser to heal and have the confidence to walk away from an evil man. If she wasn't sure before, the divorce process will leave no doubt that her abuser is evil, vindictive, and has never cared for her or her well-being.

Divorcing an abuser takes patience, shrewdness, and an expectation that the abuser will lie, hide assets, falsify financial information, alienate the children from the other parent, refuse to be reasonable, drag out the litigation, and engage in extreme emotional and financial abuse. One should also assume that the abuser will refuse to honor any parenting or divorce agreements that are made. It is advisable to retain an experienced attorney who understands domestic abuse and the characteristics of abusers, along with having a strong understanding of the law.

The Divorce Process

A divorce is usually initiated by a petition for divorce or petition for marital dissolution. The entire process, from filing the petition to a final judgment of divorce, can take up to two years. Between 70 and 80 percent of divorce petitions are filed by wives.[118] The petitioner is often the wife leaving the abuser, because abusers typically do not want the cost of divorcing. They do not want to give up the power and control or want the hassle of replacing one spouse with another. They are not as unhappy with the relationship as their victim is.

The reason for the divorce must be set forth in the petition, which initiates the process. A growing number of states have eliminated the traditional grounds for divorce of physical or mental cruelty, abandonment, or adultery—the very things of which abusers are most guilty. As a result, many states simply allow only "irreconcilable differences" as the grounds for divorce, and do not allow for financial allocations based on marital wrongdoing. These are known as "no-fault divorce" states.

After the county sheriff has served the petition to the other spouse, a response to the petition is typically required within thirty days, although a judge will often grant an extension to allow the respondent time to retain legal counsel. After both a petition and response are filed, a period of discovery follows. During this time, financial and other information is exchanged through discovery requests, requests for documents, interrogatories, subpoenas to third parties, and depositions. Information concerning the children and each parent is also gathered at this time, particularly in the event a *guardian ad litem*, child representative, or psychiatric evaluation is ordered by the court. Abusers typically are uncooperative in providing information as they continue to think

---

[118] Douglas LaBier, "Women Initiate Divorce Much More Than Men, Here's Why," *Psychology Today*, August 28, 2015, https://www.psychologytoday.com/us/blog/the-new-resilience/201508/women-initiate-divorce-much-more-men-heres-why. See also "Why Women File 80 Percent of Divorces," Divorcesource.com, January 20, 2016, https://www.divorcesource.com/blog/why-women-file-80-percent-of-divorces/.

they are above the law and do not need to respond to discovery requests. Therefore, it is always advisable to gather as much information as possible prior to leaving the relationship.

While the divorce is in process, the abuser typically cuts off all financial support. If the couple has a joint account, he will often open up a separate individual account, move all the money into his individual account, and deposit any paychecks into the new individual account to which his wife no access. When this occurs, the spouse can request the court to order the abuser to pay temporary maintenance and child support for the duration of the litigation until a final marital settlement and parenting agreement establishes more permanent obligations of maintenance and child support.

If the parties can settle, they enter into a divorce agreement, also known as a marital settlement agreement. Roughly 95 percent of cases settle. If the parties are unable to settle, the parties will go to a trial, and the judge will decide the case. It is safe to assume that if a trial is held, at least one party or one lawyer is being unreasonable. Often this is the abuser and/or his lawyer, as people tend to hire attorneys like themselves. It is also safe to assume that if a trial is held, at least one party or one lawyer is an abuser. Trials are time-consuming and expensive in terms of legal fees, the court's time, and emotional distress. Judges far prefer parties to settle cases than to go to trial, and they will even offer recommendations to legal counsel on how to settle the case in pretrial conferences.

Divorce Agreements

A divorce agreement settles the couple's finances prior to a judge granting the divorce. To the courts, a divorce is merely a financial division of assets (called property division) and, depending on the length of the marriage and circumstances, an allowance going forward for the lesser-earning spouse, also called maintenance, alimony, or spousal support.

The marital settlement agreement needs to be drafted with the assumption that the abuser will breach the agreement. Accordingly, the agreement should have teeth to enforce the obligations, penalties for breach of the agreement, and remedies for the victim to seek when the inevitable breach occurs. Marital settlement agreements should have as many of the following provisions as possible.

Contact and Communications

An order of protection will eventually expire, and a domestic restraining order typically expires with the finalization of the divorce. Whether a woman has an order of protection at the time a divorce is final, a domestic restraining order, or neither, a victim of domestic abuse will want the provisions of a restraining order included in the marital settlement agreement. Thus, the marital settlement agreement should include provisions that prohibit the abuser from coming within a certain number of feet (usually 300 or 500) of the victim. The agreement should also prohibit the abuser from contacting or communicating with the victim in any form. Because abusers will try harassment through any mode, the agreement should specify that communications via phone, email, mail, text, social media, through third parties, through the children, and any other form of communication is prohibited. Any required communications (such as communications to fulfill the obligations of the marital settlement agreement) should be limited to communications between the parties' legal counsel. These provisions are typically mutual. Carve outs can be made so that both parties can be in closer proximity when they are both attending events for the children. However, even during these events, communications should be limited, nonviolent, and nonharassing. Carve outs can also be made when co-parenting is involved, but communications should be strictly limited to matters necessary for co-parenting the children to avoid continued verbal and emotional abuse. (See the recommendations for communications under parenting agreements below.)

Deadlines

Abusers are notorious for not honoring agreements, trying to circumvent obligations, refusing to do things in a timely manner, blaming everything and everyone except themselves for failure to comply, and overall being irresponsible when it comes to their obligations. All obligations that they are required to perform in the marital settlement agreement should have a deadline by which time they must be performed, or they will never get done. For example, if monthly payments are to be paid, ensure that they must be received (not just paid) on a certain day of the month (usually the first day). If he is obligated to reimburse the spouse for additional expenses relating to the child, such as extracurricular activities, childcare, or medical expenses, make sure the agreement requires him to pay within a certain number of days (fifteen is reasonable) from receiving notice and a copy of the invoice. If he is required to obtain life insurance to ensure payments or health insurance for the children or move out of the house, make sure there is a deadline certain by which time these obligations must be met. When he fails to meet his obligations (and he will), the wife will then be able to point to a certain deadline of the agreement that he failed to comply with if she must take him to court to enforce the agreement.

Details

For the same reason, the marital settlement agreement must include specific details as to how the parties are to fulfill their obligations. Do not assume that a current practice will continue after the divorce is final. For example, if a woman needs a child support payment by the beginning of each month, she will want to provide in the agreement that the funds shall be transferred by electronic funds transfer on the 28th day of each prior month. Otherwise, it is likely the abuser will put a check in the snail mail on or after the beginning of the month, which will arrive several days after it is needed.

Assurances for Payment

While responsible people ensure obligations are paid on a timely basis, abusers, by their nature, are irresponsible. Procedures need to be put in place to ensure a greater likelihood of getting paid in a timely manner. For example, most states have systems in place that will garnish wages and send a check to the custodial parent for maintenance and child support. This becomes problematic when the abuser is fired or is unemployed, as many of them are. Therefore, it is preferable to directly debit the abuser's bank account if this is an option for your state's system. The forms initiating these types of payment are available in the local courts and should be completed at the time of the judgment of dissolution.

Some states provide that the maintenance, child support, and property payments can be assured through the purchase or continuation of life insurance on the life of the payor (the abuser) with the recipient (the victim) as the beneficiary. These laws often require the payor to pay for the life insurance premiums. Even if your state doesn't have this in its statute, it is advisable to include a provision for life insurance in a marital settlement agreement. Proof of payment of premiums should be required every year. However, it may be well worth it for a woman to simply purchase the insurance policy on her former husband herself and make the life insurance payments to ensure compliance and payment in the event of the abuser's death.

Remedies for Nonpayment and Noncompliance

One characteristic of abusers is their inability to abide by agreements. Therefore, any marital settlement agreement must have remedies with teeth for the nonpayment and noncompliance that is certain to come. The remedies need to be triggered when the abuser defaults with as little court intervention (and additional legal fees) as possible.

The remedies in notes and mortgages from banks and mortgage companies are instructive. For example, when the abuser defaults on maintenance, property division, or child support payments, the marital settlement agreement should provide for interest on the unpaid portion after written notice is given. Typically, the payor is given a few days (five or ten business days) to cure the default prior to more severe remedies. Most mortgage notes include an acceleration clause that causes all the outstanding amounts to be immediately due and payable. It is advisable to include an acceleration clause in the marital settlement agreement if the default remains uncured (that is, outstanding and unpaid) for sixty to ninety days.

Another remedy includes the option for the wife to return to court to automatically adjust garnishment from wages to ensure payments. A further remedy includes an automatic wire transfer from the abuser's bank account to the wife's bank account. If the abuser continues his refusal to make payments, another remedy may include a lien on the abuser's home or other real property owned by the abuser.

A marital agreement often requires the parties to do more than make payments. These obligations may include deeding the marital home to the other party, signing the title of a vehicle to the other party, obtaining or maintaining insurance, splitting the retirement accounts, providing for separate phone accounts, and other matters. In the event the abuser refuses to comply with these obligations, a woman has the ability to return to court to enforce the agreement. She can also file a Petition for Rule to Show Cause, which, if granted, gives the court the ability to put the abuser in jail until he complies with the marital settlement agreement.

The marital settlement agreement should include a provision requiring the abuser to pay for legal fees incurred by the former wife arising from any breach of the marital settlement agreement.

Division of Property

One aspect of divorce is dividing the property accumulated during a marriage. The value of property amassed during a marriage can be significant. In most states, absent a prenuptial agreement, all property acquired by either spouse during the marriage is deemed marital property, regardless of how it is deeded or titled. Exceptions include property that is inherited, acquired prior to the marriage, gifted, or the result of a personal injury settlement—all of which are deemed individual property. Abusers generally believe all property acquired during a marriage belongs to them, and they often threaten that in case of divorce, she will get nothing. Despite the abuser's attempts to intimidate her and make her back down, most courts will not let this occur.

Property division is nontaxable for both parties. Whatever a wife or husband may receive from an allocation of property is not considered income and is not taxable by the federal or state governments.

A wife of an abuser will generally want to be free of all financial entanglements with her abuser. Thus, in most cases, a payment of cash is the most desirable asset to be awarded. In some cases, however, the best option for a wife is to keep a house purchased during the marriage for a lower-than-fair market value or one with a small mortgage.

The abuser, on the other hand, will generally want to be in control of any payments and will want to keep his wife entangled so that any payments to her are contingent upon a certain event he controls. For example, an abuser will generally want to make any payments to his wife contingent upon the sale of the marital home. He will argue that the sale of the marital home should be contingent upon the sale price that he sets (which will be too high and unattainable for buyers), the real estate agent whom he will choose (his buddy who lives in another town, doesn't know the market, and hasn't sold a home in years), his availability to show the home (which will be seldom), and his conditions (which will be unreachable for any buyer). If he has no incentive to sell the home, he will make every effort to ensure that it doesn't sell. In effect, he will hold the house hostage so he doesn't have to pay his former wife. This ensures she will not get paid for many years, or until she goes back to court and obtains a court order to set a reasonable selling price and conditions. To avoid this situation, the agreement should establish a reasonable fair market value for the home (established by licensed real estate appraisers), and the wife should be awarded a cash property settlement to be paid upon a certain date based on the established fair market value, regardless of whether the marital home sells. If this is not possible due to a lack of finances, and the marital home must be sold, the agreement should provide that two licensed real estate appraisers establish the selling price (taking an average of their appraisals), that one of the top three (based on actual recent sales) real estate agents in the town the home is located will be the listing agent, that both parties will follow the recommendations of the real estate agent regarding editing, cleaning, maintenance and showing, that any offer within a certain percentage (six percent is reasonable) will be accepted, and other reasonable requirements to ensure that the house is actually sold. If the house does not sell within sixty days of listing, the agreement should require that the listing price be reduced by a certain amount (specify either a dollar amount or percentage of the listing price) every thirty days until it sells. If he refuses to comply, the wife will need to return to court to enforce the agreement.

Other tangible property divisions are usually less emotionally charged and have less value. Typically, each spouse keeps their own clothes, jewelry, items given to them as gifts or inheritance, items they brought with them into the marriage, the car they normally drive, and personal items. Home furnishings can be more problematic, as they are typically acquired together over the course of a marriage. Abusers will usually want to keep all the furniture, paintings, rugs, and other home furnishings simply to be vindictive. Because narcissists think so highly of themselves, they usually also think these items are far more valuable than they are and will expend huge amounts of time and energy (and legal fees) to hold on to these items. The smart wife will not fight over these matters, but rather assign a value to the home furnishings based on the replacement value (not resale value), let the abuser keep the furnishings, and take her share in cash rather than tangible goods. If the items were purchased new and the invoice is still available, this value can be used. The abuser, in his smugness, will think he has won. She can then go to nice consignment shops, thrift stores, estate sales, garage sales, eBay, Craigslist, and the like and purchase beautiful gently used home furnishings of the same or even better quality for literally pennies on the dollar for her new home, with plenty left over. (See "Creating a New Home" in chapter 45 for more tips.)

A trusted legal counsel will be needed to properly divide investment accounts, IRAs, pensions, and other retirement accounts. These require certain legal instruments to effectuate the division of property.

Maintenance Payment

Maintenance is the support of a former spouse by the higher-earning spouse for a certain period of time, depending upon the length of the marriage and other factors, including income, education, and health of the lesser-earning spouse. In the past, maintenance has typically been paid by a former husband to a former wife based on biblical principles that a husband should provide for his wife, as well as the fact that many women gave up careers to raise a family. However, in present times, gender makes little difference, and if the wife is the higher-earning spouse, the husband will often try to collect maintenance from her. For our purposes and examples, we will presume that the former husband is obligated to pay maintenance to the former wife.

In some situations, the payment is based upon a percentage of the larger wage earner's income less a percentage of the smaller wage earner's income. For example, in Illinois, the statutory formula for most households in 2020 is 33.33 percent of the larger wage earner's net income less 25 percent of the smaller wage earner's net income, as long as the amount plus the payee's net income does not exceed 40 percent of the combined net income of the couple.[119]

This approach has pros and cons. If the wages significantly vary from year to year and the paying party refuses to adjust payments accordingly, it requires the parties to go back into court frequently to recalculate the maintenance amount, which can incur significant legal expenses. It also requires the parties to exchange financial information on a yearly basis. But because most abusers try to hide their income, whatever financial information a woman receives from her former husband is usually falsified and lower than his actual income. If the abuser loses his job, the former wife suffers a loss in maintenance. On the other hand, if the former spouse suddenly has a significant increase in income, the former wife will benefit accordingly, but only if he is truthful about his additional income.

In other situations, a flat maintenance rate based upon existing incomes is appropriate. Many women want financial security and prefer a steady income rather than worry about how much their former spouse makes in the future. If this is the case, the marital settlement agreement should include a provision that the maintenance amount cannot be changed regardless of circumstances, including increase in income, unemployment, disability, etc., and cannot be changed by the court except by written agreement of both parties.

In certain situations, such as the disability of the lesser-earning spouse, the maintenance will vary from the statutory norm.

How long maintenance payments must be paid may also be based largely upon a formula, which is determined by the length of the marriage. Maintenance payments for short-lived marriages will be shorter than for longer-term marriages. Marriages of twenty to twenty-five years or more may require permanent maintenance, particularly when one spouse has given up a career to raise children and doesn't have work-force skills.

Until 2019, maintenance payments were included in taxable income by the receiver and were deductible from taxable income by the payor. However, for marriages that were dissolved on January 1, 2019, or later, maintenance is neither includable in taxable income to the receiver nor deductible from taxable income to the payor. Because laws can change, it is advisable to provide in the settlement agreement that maintenance payments are not included in taxable income for the recipient or deducted from taxable income for the payor.

Maintenance payments paid from a husband to a wife are typically terminated by the remarriage or cohabitation of the former wife, or the death or disability of the former husband. However, in some instances, such as when certain monies owed to the former wife by way of a contract or prenuptial agreement are titled "maintenance," the maintenance obligations should be paid regardless of the remarriage or cohabitation of the former wife. In instances where contract obligations are entitled "maintenance" or "property division" and must be paid regardless of circumstances, a provision should be included that payments are nonmodifiable for any reason, including remarriage, cohabitation, disability, lack of employment, inability to sell real estate, retirement, or the

---

[119] Illinois statute 750 ILCS 5/504.

death of either the abuser or the former wife, and any unpaid amounts remaining at death shall be a claim against the estate of the abuser, any trust for which the abuser is the grantor or beneficiary, or any ownership interest in businesses that the abuser may have.

Parenting Agreements

Divorce courts require parenting agreements to determine how much time a child will spend with each parent, how the child will be raised and spend their time, and how parents will make decisions concerning their children during and after the divorce. For parents who have never married, parenting agreements are generally sought when the parties separate. The difficulties of co-parenting have been previously detailed; therefore, parenting agreements with abusers should be carefully written to limit communications between former spouses or partners, limit the power and control of an abuser, and provide adequate protections for the children.

The parenting agreement will also spell out the dates and times for custody exchanges, holiday schedules, communications between parents, communications between parents and children when the children are with the other parent, vacation schedules, and how decisions are made concerning the education, religion, health, and extracurricular activities of the child. The parenting agreement must be drafted with the expectation that the abuser will not honor it. Thus, remedies must be available to the healthy parent to be able to move forward so she is not held hostage by an unresponsive, nonpaying, unreasonable abuser. Parenting agreements should include as many of the following provisions as possible.

Protection of the Children

An order of protection often protects the children as well as the parent who is a victim of domestic abuse. However, courts seem eager to have children spend time with both parents, even if one parent is abusive to the other parent or the child. If both the mother and the children are under an order of protection, the courts may wish to carve out time for the children to be with the father, usually with supervision.

If the healthy parent can show to the court by a preponderance of evidence that the abusive parent engaged or engages in conduct that seriously endangers a child's mental, moral, or physical health, or significantly impaired or impairs the child's emotional development, the court is required to enter orders necessary to protect the child. These orders can reduce or eliminate time with the abusive parent. They can also reduce or eliminate the decision-making abilities of the abusive parent. For example, a court order may prohibit overnight visits, prohibit the abuser from driving with the children, require supervised visits by either an agency or a family member, prohibit the abusive parent from drinking alcohol or taking nonprescription drugs during visits with the child, require a drug or alcohol treatment program, require counseling, or any number of other restrictions that are necessary for the child's safety.

The problem, of course, is proving to a judge that the abuser is harming the child. Unless the abuser has abandoned the family, most abusers demand their rights for time with and decision-making for the children, even if they have no interest in the children and even if they have been abusive. In the "he said, she said" controversy that ensues, many judges have a difficult time determining who to believe. At the request of one party, most family law courts will appoint a *guardian ad litem*, or GAL, to be the judge's eyes and ears to determine custody issues and parenting time. In some cases, the judge will appoint a child representative so that a child will have his own legal counsel to represent the child's legal rights. The child representatives are lawyers, and the GALs are often lawyers, who will interview the children, the parents, and perhaps even the counselors. They will also observe the parents with the children in order to make a recommendation as to custody, parenting time, parental decision-making, and any necessary restrictions. However, they are not counselors or psychologists. Abusers, therefore, will do a convincing Dr. Jekyll performance when they know they are being watched, and then turn back into the abusive Mr. Hyde behind closed doors.

At the request of one of the parties, the judge may also assign a court-appointed psychologist or psychiatrist to conduct a psychological evaluation of the parents to determine mental health issues, parental alienation issues, or other dangers that may impact the children negatively. Even if only one parent is suspected of having a mental health issue, a judge will likely order psychological evaluations of both parents to ensure there is no appearance of bias that may cause the abuser to file an appeal.

During these evaluations with GALs, child representatives, and mental health experts, abusers typically attempt to turn the tables and use projection to accuse the victim of the very things they themselves are most guilty of: parental alienation, abuse, mental illness, etc. Thus, a victim should be careful and know that she is under a microscope in these situations.

The good news is that the healthy parent and her legal counsel can share with the GAL, child representative, or court-appointed expert items that may not be admissible evidence in court—such as video tapes and recordings of the abuse. She can also share her concerns, specific instances of abuse or alienation, and any documentation that may be relevant, such as police reports, DCFS reports, school reports, counselor concerns, medical diagnosis of the child or the abuser, medical reports, and any other relevant matters. All these should be taken into consideration. The GAL, child representative, or expert will typically write a report with his or her findings and make recommendations to the judge concerning child custody, parental decision-making, safety precautions, and other child-related matters.

Communication

Communication should be limited to emails, preferably to an email system sponsored by the county court system that cannot be altered. Many courts use systems designed for such security and include apps that can be downloaded to a cell phone. Our Family Wizard and Talking Parents are two widely used applications. Texts or phone calls should be reserved for emergencies. Communications should also be limited to discussions concerning the children. Abusers will continue to be verbally abusive if allowed free communications concerning any subject. Keeping communications limited to emails and children will reduce the verbal abuse and provide evidence of written verbal abuse if you need to bring it to the court's attention.

Many parenting agreements include a nondisparagement clause that requires parents to refrain from saying anything uncomplimentary about their ex-spouse to the children. With an abuser, by the time a parenting agreement is drafted and signed, the abuser has already conducted a slander and smear campaign against his former spouse and is in the full swing of a parental alienation campaign. He will continue regardless of the parenting agreement. Thus, the nondisparagement clause is ineffective to protect the healthy parent and will be used against her by the abuser if she simply tells the truth. The better approach is to include a clause that simply requires the parents to be truthful and to refrain from name-calling and harassing language, or not include one at all. Any nondisparagement clause will be breached by the abuser and used against the healthy parent if she tries to explain the craziness of the abuser or attempts to help her children establish healthy boundaries when dealing with their abusive father.

Decision-Making

If possible, the healthy parent should have decision-making authority for the children. Abusers simply are incapable of co-parenting in healthy ways and will often veto things that are in the best interests of the children because of their own issues. For example, an abuser may prohibit the children from attending much-needed counseling because the abuser doesn't want his children to have the stigma of going to "a shrink." Or an abuser may prohibit a child from getting braces or getting therapy because he feels they are unneeded and too expensive. Abusers regularly prohibit children from attending extracurricular activities because they simply don't think those activities are important, they are too expensive, or it would require too much effort to take the child to practice or games.

If the abuser will not agree to give the healthy parent decision-making authority, the next best thing is to allow the healthy parent day-to-day decision-making for regular matters, reserving joint decision-making for extraordinary matters such as major medical or education concerns. Most abusers don't really want to concern themselves with the drudgery of the routine decisions, but they do want power and control over important things. So promoting this approach while giving them some say in more important decisions often makes parenting time go smoother. One can ask the abuser, "Do you really want the job of reviewing homework each night, picking out school lunches each day, making cookies each week for the class, carpooling every other day, and scheduling routine dentist appointments?" Defining daily responsibilities that will be handled by the healthy parent and clarifying the extraordinary matters that will be decided jointly will go a long way toward making most things in life smoother without the constant power play of the abuser. In the event that an abuser vetoes an important matter that the child needs, such as a medical treatment or counseling, the healthy parent can petition the court to allow for it, if necessary.

In the event an abuser insists on joint parenting and approving every decision, the parenting agreement should be written in such a way that provides for "necessary, advisable, or prudent" procedures, counseling, therapy, or medications for the children, while elective procedures will be jointly determined by the parents. Provision should also be made for payment in the event a procedure is not covered entirely by insurance. In this way, if a father refuses to approve or pay for a procedure, counseling, therapy, or medication for the child that the mother and her doctor determine is necessary, advisable, or prudent, the mother can provide the child with the needed treatment. Most emotionally healthy mothers will always want to do what is right for their children, while abusers tend to be obstructionists. If he chooses, the father can bring a motion in the court and attempt to prove to a judge that the treatment is not necessary, advisable, or prudent. This will likely be exceedingly difficult to do, particularly if the mother's decision to go forward with the treatment was supported by tests and physician's recommendations.

Deadlines

The parenting agreement needs to provide specific deadlines for responses to requests or payments. If the parent does not respond by the deadline, the request shall be deemed granted or the payment considered reasonable. For example, if a parent is requesting to take a child on vacation or is requesting reimbursement for childcare expenses, the agreement should provide that the other parent must respond with a clear answer or pay the expense if supported by documentation within a certain number of days. Further, the agreement should provide that if the other parent doesn't respond by the deadline, the request will be deemed granted and the opportunity to object will have expired. Abusers are notorious for being unreasonable, dragging their feet, and putting the more responsible parent in a difficult position by not responding. Spelling out the expectations and consequences for missed deadlines ensures that the healthy parent is not left in an untenable position of being held hostage by an unresponsive parent.

Details

The parenting agreement needs to provide the details—the who, what, when, where, and how—of the specific obligations of each parent. For example, when a child is on vacation with one parent, that parent should provide the other parent with flight information, the hotels or other accommodations, the phone number and address of the people they may be staying with, and a phone number to call in the event of an emergency. The agreement should include specific details of child exchanges, including the precise time and day of exchanges, whose house or other locations the exchanges will take place at, whether the exchanges are curbside (if you don't want him on your property) or at the front door, whether the children will have already been fed dinner prior to the exchange, etc. The agreement should include requirements that both parents will ensure that they will give a child any prescribed medications while the child is in their care. The agreement should include requirements that both parents will ensure that the child attends all sports practices and games or musical practices and performances for which the child has signed up while in their care. Because abusers generally think none of the rules apply to them and that they have no obligations to anyone, it is essential to include this basic information as a requirement of the parenting agreement.

Child Support

Like maintenance, child support payment amounts are usually set forth by statute in a formula that takes into account each parent's income. If at all possible, payments should be established through a state run garnishment system to ensure timely payments. Term life insurance on the abuser's life in the amount of all future payments plus college tuition is prudent to ensure payments in the event of the abuser's death. Child support payments typically vary, and each party can petition the court to modify child support in the event of a significant change in circumstance, such as a job loss or promotion of a parent, or additional needs of a child. Many parenting agreements require a set amount for child support, and additional payments for a parent's share of extra-curricular activities, health insurance, child care, etc. that must be paid within a certain number of days from when the responsible parent sends the invoice and requests payment for the other parent's share of expenses. Abusers are notorious for failing to pay these additional sums, leaving mothers holding the bag and paying the entire amount. Rather than this approach, it is advisable to estimate an annual budget for these additional expenses and simply add them on to the base child support payment. In this way, the mother avoids the hassle of sending over invoices that will never get paid, and has a bit more assurance that the basic child support will be paid, especially if going through a state run wage garnishing system. Of course, it is important to properly estimate these additional expenses.

College payments are also matters that must be contemplated in a parenting agreement. An abuser will claim poverty by the time a child goes to college, therefore, establishing each parent's obligations towards college is important to do up front, rather than waiting for the time the children are off to college. Typically, a parent's obligation to pay for college is limited to the in-state tuition, room, board, and fees at the state university of their home state, less any loans, grants, or scholarships that the child is able to obtain. Parents usually share college obligations in proportion to their respective incomes, assuming all other forms of financial resources are equal.

Like maintenance, if child support payments are not made, a mother has the option of enforcing payment by filing a petition for rule to show cause. If non-payment is found to be willful, the abuser can be found in contempt of court and may be incarcerated and forced to pay attorney's fees in addition to back child support.

Remedies

The parenting agreement needs to provide remedies in the agreement in the event the agreement is breached. For example, if the parenting agreement requires the noncustodial parent to pay half the day care expenses within fifteen days of being presented with an invoice and request for payment, and the payment is not made, there should be a remedy so that the custodial parent can get paid by going to court and automatically changing the wage garnishment form to include the additional payment. The remedies need to be swift, cost little or nothing to implement, and make the responsible, healthy parent whole as much as possible. A good approach is requiring the one who breaches the agreement to reimburse the innocent party for any legal fees incurred arising from the breach of the agreement. Again, drafting the parenting agreement with the assumption that the abuser will breach it is a good approach.

Post-Divorce Legal Needs

The victim of domestic abuse may feel like she can never get away from her abuser, because abusers are vindictive and expend tremendous mental, emotional, and physical energy scheming of ways to make the life of their former spouse miserable. If agreements are not complied with, the innocent spouse always has the option of going back to court to force compliance. In such instances, she should also request attorney's fees incurred as a result of the noncompliance. She can also file a petition for a rule to show cause, which can result in court-ordered jail time if the abuser continues nonpayment and his actions are proved to be willful and contumacious.

In the event that physical threats or abuse, stalking, or harassment continue, other legal protections are still available after a divorce. These include an order of protection, restraining order, and calling the police. Of course, if a woman finds herself in real physical danger, these protections may be inadequate, and she must consider other tactics to protect herself and her family, including going into hiding, changing jobs, changing her cell phone number, moving, moving to another state, closing down all social media accounts, blocking cells phones, and self-defense classes.

Of course, hiring competent legal counsel is always a good idea when divorcing an abuser. The information in this book provides generalities and should not be considered legal advice or a substitute for obtaining legal counsel.

CHAPTER 28

Have a Communication Plan

An abuser will have a well thought out public relations plan and narrative to make him look like an angel and an innocent victim of a mentally ill, unfaithful, morally bankrupt wife who has abandoned him in his moment of need. Immediately upon a separation, and oftentimes before, he will make every effort to be the first to share his story to everyone he can, as quickly as he can, to gain supporters. He will be on the phone with calls to everyone he knows and people he barely knows, including his wife's closest friends. It will remind you of the scene in the movie *Jerry McGuire* as the sports agents are busy working the phones to get clients the second Jerry announces he is leaving his firm. The abuser will tell his tale of woe with such conviction that most people will believe him and come to his support and defense. They will spread the slander, just as the abuser had planned, and will shun the wife, perhaps even making mean-spirited and hurtful comments about how "un-Christian" she is, even though she has made Herculean efforts to save her doomed marriage. Only those who are discerning and have dealt with abusive people will recognize the smear and slander campaign for what it is.

To combat the smear and slander campaign that is sure to come from the abuser, and to share information appropriately, a wife who plans to leave an abuser ought to craft a communication plan of her own.

Pastor and Church

First, *prior to leaving*, she should inform her pastor of the abuse and ask for his prayers and support. Although a pastor should be sympathetic to an abused wife, many are not, and will only focus on preserving a marriage, not ensuring the emotional, physical, or spiritual safety of the wife. If the pastor is supportive, there is a good chance the church leaders will also be supportive. In this case, she may want to inform some of the church leaders and ask for their prayers and support. In this way, the church family will be informed of the situation and will be more likely to provide support and comfort to her when the inevitable separation occurs and when the abuser starts making calls pretending to be the victim. On the other hand, if the pastor is not sympathetic or supportive, there is little chance the rest of the church leaders will be, as the pastor typically sets the spiritual tone of the church. Although a church should be safe for victims of domestic violence, they often are not, and a woman should exercise a great deal of caution before putting her trust in church leaders.

Safe People

Prior to leaving, the wife may also wish to share the abuse with safe people—family members and friends who know her, love her, and have her back. She can ask for their prayers and support and inform them that the abuser will likely call with a sob story when she leaves. When the abuser attempts to bring these people on to his team, they know the phone call is coming and should not be swayed.

Employer

Abusers commonly cause disruptions and sometimes violence at a woman's place of employment. A woman should also inform her employer of the situation before she leaves so that precautions can be made to protect her and the entire workforce. For example, the employer may want to lock the doors and certainly will not want to allow the abuser on the premises or into a building after a woman leaves an abusive situation. The employer will want to provide extra security measures as the woman goes to and from her car into the workplace.

Parents and Siblings

A woman should generally let her parents and siblings know of the abuse prior to her leaving if they fall into the category of safe people. A strong father and honorable brothers might be able to alleviate some of the abuse by having a straightforward conversation with the abuser and a promise of justice for their daughter and sister if the abuse continues.

His Parents and Siblings

Parents and siblings of the abuser are a different matter. Regardless of how heinous an abuser's behavior is, his parents and siblings will likely support him. After all, he and his siblings most likely learned abusive behavior from one or both of his parents. Even if his parents are wonderful people and he is an anomaly in his family of origin, he is their son, and they will likely take his side. Nonetheless, if they are kind people, a woman might consider sharing the specifics of the abuse while she is still in the marriage and let them know she has been doing all she can to keep the marriage together despite his abuse. A good father might even be able to influence his abusive son into better behavior, at least temporarily. When the separation occurs, the parents may remain civil and still want some relationship with their former daughter-in-law, even if only for the sake of the grandchildren. If they are not understanding or kind, they are unlikely to support their son's victim regardless of how much they learn about his abuse. If this is the case, it is best to keep them at a distance.

Children

Knowing what and how much to share with children and stepchildren is, perhaps, the most difficult aspect of divorce to navigate. Regardless of their age, oversharing is difficult for the child and will often backfire for older children, resulting in the child supporting the abuser rather than the victim. On the other hand, not sharing anything may give the impression that the mother left the marriage for no reason and is likely to make a child question whether she will also leave the child. Further, making excuses for abusive behavior is likely to confuse the child as to what is acceptable behavior for themselves and others.

While there is no formula for what should or shouldn't be said to children, there are a few important principles to keep in mind during the difficult process of leaving an abuser and an ensuing divorce. In most instances, after a few years, relations and communications with children return to normal. But during the separation and divorce, relations and communications can be strained, and the mother should be intentional in her communications.

Young children know that half of them is from their father and half is from their mother. In their view, when one parent tells them the other is horrible and worthless, they will likely view themselves in the same way since half of them consists of that person.

Children may believe that if a mother divorces a father, she might divorce or leave them too, that they caused the problems, or that they will never see their father again. A mother should reassure young children that she will always love them, will always be their mother, will always be supportive of them, and will never leave them. She should also reassure them that they did nothing to cause the problems and that the problems would have arisen even without the children. Assuming the father remains in their lives and he is not abusive to them, she should assure them that he will always be their father and that both parents love them. If a father has chosen to have no contact with the child or he is abusive to the child, the mother must reassure the child that she loves her and never will abandon her or be abusive. The mother must also assure the child that the father's decision is not right and that his decision to leave or be abusive has nothing to do with the child, but rather is because of the father's own issues.

Children should not be involved in, be given a play-by-play, or be used as pawns in the parents' divorce battles. It is emotionally distressing for them to be put in the middle of two people they care about.

Children will not always be as supportive of the mother as she may expect. Teenagers and older children can be particularly mean, say hurtful things, shun the mother, and may even join in abusing the mother in ways that they have learned by watching their father. A wise woman will seek emotional support from counselors, friends, or others, but not her children.

Most mothers try to hide their abuse from their children and protect their children from direct abuse. Therefore, a divorce may come as a surprise and shock to the children. They will want answers as to why their world is crashing. A wise woman will refrain from divulging all the sordid details, and she will also refrain from saying nothing. She will tailor her explanations to be age-appropriate, and she will be sensitive to whether her child is also a victim of abuse.

For a younger child, possible communication may look like the following: "Daddy and I have some differences and we cannot live together anymore. I am very sorry about this. We both love you very much, and you will always have both of us in your life."

For an older child, possible communications may look like this: "Your father and I have some serious differences of opinion in how we should treat each other. I am no longer willing to be treated the way that he treats me, which is very disrespectful. He is not valuing me as a person made in the image of God, and he is not valuing me as his wife, to whom he had promised to love, honor, and cherish. I am very sorry this relationship has ended. We both love you very much, and you will always have both of us in your life. I am not going to tell you the whole long story of our relationship and why it ended. Suffice it to say, I have some very strong reasons to end our marriage. I will answer your questions; however, be aware that my answers will be honest with no sugarcoating."

Older children will often get a laundry list of lies from their father and his distorted view of reality in an effort to place all the blame for the divorce on their mother and make himself look good. Children see their father as an authority figure and want to believe he is telling the truth. Therefore, they may believe his lies and confront their mother with them. It is natural for her to be defensive and want to lash out at the false accusations. However, this is usually a mistake. Not only is the abuser baiting her and hoping for her explosive reaction, but now his children are as well. The wise woman will keep her composure, stay calm, put her shoulders back, and with an air of confidence say something close to the following: "I am not going to dignify that with a response. If you want to know the rest of the story, then feel free to ask me a direct question and I will give you an honest and direct answer. Or, if you want to check the facts yourself, just ask the [psychologist/pastor/counselor] we saw. Here's their number—you can call them yourself. Now let's get back to dinner, shall we?" Often, that will stop the conversation in its tracks. It tells the child she did not get all or even most of the facts, it doesn't call her or her dad a liar, it doesn't lose control or bad-mouth the dad, it offers facts if the child wants to go further and ask a specific question of the mother, and it even opens the doors to objective third party professionals if the child wants to double-check the facts. All of this will give the impression that the father is not being entirely truthful and is hiding something that would impugn his character if the child found out. The child will likely never follow up with the mother or the professionals, but if she does, she has been put on notice that the truth will be ugly.

Older children will often side with the abuser for various reasons.[120] They see how the abuser treats their mother and fear similar abandonment or abuse if they side with their mother. Sometimes the father threatens that if they see their mother, he will have nothing to do with them. Other times, the father will buy a lavish gift like a new car and allow the child to drive it anywhere but to see the mother. Many times, the father uses money to manipulate the children and buy their affection with expensive gifts. He will often plan a vacation or other event at the same time the mother has planned an event, making the child choose between the two, with the obvious underlying threat that the child must choose to be with the father or suffer the ramifications. He will demand their allegiance by threatening to cut off funds, college tuition payments, payments for important athletic events, and the like. The abuser will also use his smear and slander campaign against their mother to alienate the children from their mother. The wise mother will recognize the abuser's tactics as gamesmanship designed to cause her further emotional distress. She knows they won't last forever and that the children will eventually see through them. She stays the course and doesn't let the abuser rattle her.

Children will often be hardest on their mother, even when they have asked her to divorce their father. Their lives are also in upheaval and their emotions are running wild, swinging from anger to depression to uncertainty to fear. The mother must be the adult in the room and remain calm. Children are often unpleasant to the mother because she is the safe parent. They know they can dump their feelings on her and she will love them anyway. They do not unload on the unsafe parent, who will immediately retaliate and rage due to what he perceives as disrespectful behavior.

Children might bring up old hurts from the past that they perceive were inflicted upon them by their mother. If this is the case, a mother should listen carefully and apologize for any hurts that she either intentionally or unintentionally inflicted. This is not the time to defend one's position or point out how wrong the child is and how right the mom is. It is a time for reconciliation and mending hearts. If the child was unintentionally hurt by a misunderstanding, the mom might say, "Oh, honey, I am so sorry that what I said hurt you. I didn't mean it that way at all. I was talking about _____, not you. I am sorry you thought I was talking about you, and I am so sorry that you were hurt and have been carrying that all these years. I love you and I value our relationship, and I want us to get back to us." If the mom was at fault, she might say, "Darling, I am so sorry I hurt your

---

[120] This is more fully discussed in chapters 7, 22, and 23.

feelings. I was wrong. I see that now. I don't have an excuse. I hope I have matured into a better person since then. What can I do to make it up to you? I value you and I value our relationship, and I want us to get back to us. I love you."

Overall, this is a time when a mother should love on a child because they both need it. During an abusive marriage, there is not nearly enough love and encouragement to go around. People often fall into the habit of nitpicking and putting others down because that is what the abuser does. But during a separation and divorce, a mom should institute new ways of relating to her children that speak life, love, blessings, positivity, and encouragement into them. The trajectory of their relationship and their lives will change as they replace negativity with positivity.

The child who has been the victim of abuse may have been secretly hoping his mother would leave his father, or he may have openly asked her to leave. If this is the case, the mother will want to acknowledge that abuse is never right and that they both have been victims of abuse. She may explain that she had stayed because she had hoped her abuser would change and that they would be a loving family. Now she realizes he won't change, and it is time for her and her children to remove themselves from the abuser.

Generally, it is advisable to simply not discuss the abuser. A wise mom doesn't ask her children questions about their father or to spy on their father. The abuser is already using the children in that capacity, and the mother can be assured that anything she shares with her children will be shared with their father. Therefore, a wise woman will say very little about herself because it will all get back to her abuser and it will be used against her. Her conversations should revolve around the children and what they are doing or other nonpersonal matters such as thoughts on a movie, book, church activities, or current events. If the children are recalling a family story or humorous event involving their father, it is best to let them bring up the ridiculous thing that their father did. If the mother brings it up, it could be construed as dad bashing.

The need for a father or father figure is high on Maslow's hierarchy of needs (see chapter 6). Even if a father has abused a child or her mother, the child wants a relationship of some sort with her father. Every child longs for the redemption of a loving relationship with her father, and that longing runs throughout her entire life. There is always a father-shaped hole in the heart of a person without a loving father in his or her life. When an abuser who has shunned a relationship with his child finally dies, the child, even as an adult, suffers not only the loss of a father, but also the loss of a relationship that can never be restored.

Therefore, if it is not dangerous for the child, the wise mother will encourage a healthy relationship between the father and child because it is good for the child. However, because an abuser is, by definition, unhealthy, the wise mother will teach a child about setting healthy boundaries with the father and be frank about the limitations without painting him as horrible or worthless. To avoid any accusation of parental alienation and to encourage the child to think on her own, she will want to ask plenty of questions rather than make only statements. For example, if a child has a father who tries to manipulate him with money, the wise mother will teach her child to recognize the signs of manipulation and how to establish a healthy boundary. When the father dangles money or a trip or an expensive gift in front of the child in exchange for something, the mother can ask the child, "Why do you think Dad is offering you a car in exchange for living with him?" or "Why do you think Dad is offering you a trip to Greece on the same week that we had planned a trip to see Grandma and Grandpa?"

If the father loses his temper easily, she will teach the child that losing one's temper is not emotionally mature, even when an adult does so, and will suggest that the child remove himself from the situation until the father calms down. After an incident, the mother can ask the child, "What happened to provoke his anger? Do you think his anger was reasonable or unreasonable under the circumstances? Do you know that two of the gifts of the Holy Spirit are patience and self-control? The Holy Spirit gives us these gifts so we don't hurt others in our lives, and because you have the Holy Spirit, you can do things differently now and when you become a dad. Do you know that if we have the Holy Spirit we all have the ability to control our responses and our emotions if we want to?"

If the father fails to show for visitation, she must tell the child that it is not because of anything she did or didn't do, but it is due to the issues that the father has. It is also good to have a backup plan with an activity the child enjoys when the father doesn't show. After the father doesn't show, the mother might say, "I'm sorry that Dad didn't show today. I know you are disappointed, and so am I. Did you know that one of the fruits of the Holy Spirit is faithfulness? Faithfulness helps us keep our responsibilities to others, which is very important. I can't excuse Dad's behavior, but I do know that you can be different and be responsible, and I promise that I will always try to keep my promises to you. Now let's go get some ice cream." And she will continue to encourage the father to see the child as much as possible. A wise mom will let the child know that the child is not to blame when someone else behaves badly. She will teach her child appropriate healthy behavior so the generational patterns of abuse will stop with her. She will also encourage family counseling with the father and children so they can learn healthier ways to relate to each other.

Of course, if the father is so abusive that a relationship with a child would be dangerous, then the mother must do all she can to persuade the courts that the father is a serious danger to the physical, emotional, or moral health of the child, and she should seek a restriction on visitation, such as supervised visitation or even no visitation, depending upon the abuse.

Stepchildren

Stepchildren will generally side with their biological parent unless that parent abandons them or abuses them directly. Children of remarried abusers have already seen their father go through a divorce with their own mother, and perhaps others, and quickly move on to the next woman. Unlike children from relatively healthy parents who often form strong attachments and bonds of love with a stepparent, when an abuser with older children remarries, his children are often less attached to the stepmother, even though the stepmother may love them very much. Like their father, they may view the stepmother as expendable, temporary, or someone who can be used for their own purposes while she is married to their father. And, like their father, they may simply discard their stepmother when her marriage to their father is over. Nonetheless, a stepmother who wants a continued relationship with her stepchildren should reach out and try to continue the relationship.

In the end, however, it will take both sides to continue a relationship. If a stepchild does not want a relationship, the stepmother has little choice but to let him or her go and grieve the loss of yet another relationship that the abuser has destroyed. Sometimes this also means letting go of grandchildren who are dear to the step-grandmother. While some states have grandparent visitation laws that allow grandparent visitation, the standard to establish visitation is high. Courts have ruled that parents have the constitutional right to decide who to let their children associate with, and a grandparent who wants visitation against the wishes of a parent will have to overcome a constitutional burden in the courts. Oftentimes, Christmas and birthday cards are the most that many stepmothers and step-grandmothers can expect.

Have a Communication Plan

Charlotte: I had kept quiet through the entire divorce, even while Tim spread lies about me to everyone, including our children and his adult children from his previous marriage. After the divorce was final, an elder and director at my church suggested that I should tell the truth, because my silence was being perceived as admission. They had never received training in domestic abuse—it was bad advice. I loved my stepchildren and step-grandchildren. I had hoped that they would not cut me out of their lives, especially since I was the victim of their father's abuse and had tried so hard to make the marriage work. I wrote each of my stepchildren a letter, explained the abuse that led to the divorce, and included some supporting documents so they would not think I was lying. I had hoped we could continue some kind of relationship. I was sorely mistaken. Tim's damage had already been done. The oldest stepchild, Chaz, forty-three at the time, refused to talk with me ever again, even though I had provided hundreds of thousands of dollars of free legal services to his company and his fiancée. He also left my law firm with unpaid bills of thousands of dollars. The youngest stepchild, Kira, thirty-nine at the time, returned the letter unread with a nasty note: "I can think of nothing more inappropriate. No interest in seeing any of this. This is between you and my dad. How dare you get us all involved. If you ever wanted your side to be heard, I can think of a million appropriate ways to do so. This is definitely not it. . . You can't do it . . . by sending all of this 'garbage' to us. How very disrespectful." I don't know what those other "million appropriate ways" to tell them are that she had in mind—they refuse to talk to me, text, or meet me. It was clear that no matter how heinous their father's abuse was, they were going to support him and discard me, just like he did. I have never seen either of them, or my step-grandchildren, again. Everything about breaking free of Tim's abuse has been one huge heartbreak after another.

Supporters of the Abuser

Some people will always support the abuser. The fact that they know he is abusive will likely not affect their support. These are people whom Jesus was referring to when He told the disciples, "If anyone will not welcome you or listen to your words, leave that home or town and shake the dust off your feet" (Matthew 10:14). Those who are unsympathetic, unsupportive, or unbelieving of a Christian wife who is seeking help with an abusive husband have shown their true allegiance—not to Christ, but to Satan. She does not need those people in her life, and she should "shake their dust from her feet" and not look back. She may have considered them friends, but if they are unwilling to support her against an abusive husband, they are not friends, but are merely acquaintances. A true friend will have her best interest in mind and will want what is best for her. She may have even considered that person her pastor or spiritual mentor. Those who give lip service to Christianity but are not led by the Holy Spirit will not want to get involved. They will continue to socialize or attend Bible study with the abuser, will continue to do business with him, or will actively support the abuser.

Keep in mind the three kinds of people who support an abuser: (1) those who are intimidated by the abuser (the wife and children are usually in this category because they are the most vulnerable to the harm he inflicts); (2) those who are deceived by the abuser (due to the Dr. Jekyll/Mr. Hyde double personality that abusers have, many people can be in this category until they know the truth of the abuse); and (3) those who have the same moral compass as the abuser. If a person who supports an abuser is not intimidated or deceived by the abuser even when he or she knows the facts of the abuse, then that person shares the same depraved moral compass as the abuser.

Some women may mistakenly think supporters of abusers are supporting him because they have been deceived and don't know all the facts. These women believe that once these supporters know all the facts of the abuse, they will surely drop their support of the abuser. And thus, these women share information concerning the abuse—sometimes even photographs of the abuse, or actual documents providing hard evidence of lies—in hope of changing the minds of abuse supporters. However, this approach rarely works, and often backfires.

Again, the example of Jesus is instructive. He never begged and pleaded with the hypocrites, Pharisees, and other evil people to come over to His side. They knew of His miracles, signs, wonders, and teachings as much as those who became His followers, yet they still rejected Him. He didn't do more miracles just for them so they would believe Him. Quite the contrary, He rightfully assessed that they rejected Him because they were sons of Satan, the father of lies (John 8:42–44), hypocrites, wicked, snakes, and a brood of vipers (Matthew 23:33). He did not let their opinion of Him affect His self-worth or purpose on earth one bit. The only opinion that counted to Him was God's. The only purpose that counted to Him was God's. In the same way, the only opinion a woman should care about is God's. The only purpose she should care about is God's. Knowing that she is doing God's will and has God's approval is incredibly freeing, and she is no longer bound by the chains of others' opinions.

Jesus wisely instructed His followers, "Do not throw your pearls to pigs. If you do, they may trample them under their feet, and turn and tear you to pieces" (Matthew 7:6). A wise woman doesn't waste her precious time or emotional energy speaking with an abuser or his supporters. They will trample her kindness and truthfulness, and turn against her, thereby revictimizing the victim.

The reality that people she once trusted will support an abuser rather than the victim will likely be a blow and a loss to the wife who is leaving an abuser. Not only has she lost her marriage and her husband, but she has also lost relationships with people she once thought were friends, spiritual mentors, her church family, and even family members. The pain of losing someone she once held dear is an undeniable reality to many who divorce an abuser. Many Christian women report that the betrayal of friends and church members is worse than their abuser's betrayal. After all, over the years, she expected the abuser to betray her, but she didn't expect friends and family to betray her. However, knowing that someone does not have her best interest in mind allows the wife to let go of that person, grieve the betrayal and loss, and go forward with spiritual maturity and new eyes of discernment.

> Charlotte: Based on the advice of an elder and a director who helped me through the divorce process and advised me that my silence was being perceived as an admission of guilt, I wrote to less than a handful of people at church who were supporters of Tim and let them know the truth of why I left. Rather than having the courage to stop the rumors themselves by going to the source—my ex-husband and his minions—my pastors and church leaders left me to defend myself. It was horrible advice, and the letter was not well-received. One person returned the letter unread. Others called the elder complaining about the letter. Two years later, these same people appeared with Tim as "character witnesses" during a meeting with the senior pastor when Tim petitioned the pastor to get remarried in the church. The senior pastor originally refused, but later caved to pressure and let him remarry victim #3 in church with his blessing. However, when I requested a meeting with the senior pastor to show him photographs of the abuse that Tim himself took, and documents supporting the order of protection, he refused to see me or respond. For years, I had served as a deacon, a Sunday School teacher, a mission leader, and even served as the church's pro bono legal counsel.

I had also served on the Board of Regents of a Christian university. Clearly, one would think that I at least had some professional credibility. Yet, I was completely shut out while the pastors, church leaders, and Tim's minions embraced my abuser. It was a complete betrayal of everything Christ stands for. It was clear that their moral compass was as depraved as Tim's. I had considered them friends. Obviously, I was as mistaken about their character as I was about Tim's.

The Abuser

Generally, there should be no contact or communication with the abuser, if possible. If this is not possible because of minor children, communication should be extremely limited. An order of protection usually includes a no contact order. If communication is necessary, it can be done through attorneys. When children are involved, the parties can communicate through court-approved email applications like Our Family Wizard or Talking Parents.

Abusers will take every opportunity to harass their leaving spouse, accuse her of outrageous things, and bait her to respond with something that they can take to the court. All communication is designed to inflict emotional distress on her. Wise women remain calm and do not respond to the craziness. They simply dig out the nugget of information that relates to a child and matter-of-factly respond if necessary. For example, if Johnny needs to be picked up from school because it is the abuser's day to pick him up, the abuser might write that he will pick up Johnny at three o'clock and drop him off with his mother at seven, but the rest of the email may be filled with insults, false accusations, and name-calling. While anyone would want to defend themselves against such attacks, the wise thing to is simply confirm the pertinent information of drop-off and pickup times. Continued harassment should be brought to her attorney's attention, as it may qualify for an order of protection or a reprimand by the judge.

Many abusers will use communication devices to spy on the divorcing wife. These tracking devices and recordings are misdemeanors or felonies in most states and should be reported to the police as a criminal matter with as much evidence as possible.

Most abusers will also try to use the children as spies on their mother. Children don't typically understand that they are being used as spies, and they don't want to lie to their parents, so they often answer openly. The best approach for a woman to take with children is to say as little as possible about herself if she doesn't want her abuser to know.

Chapter 29

Have a Spiritual and Emotional Support Plan

Every woman leaving an abusive husband or partner needs emotional support to survive the spiritual and emotional warfare that the abuser will bring on her. While a woman is in a relationship with an abuser, the abuser may use a modicum of restraint. But after a woman has left and the abuser knows she won't return, he will unleash his abuse with a viciousness and vindictiveness never seen before. A woman often mistakenly thinks that because they have been married for so long, or because he is the mother of their children, or because she has taken care of his ailing and elderly parents, or because she has sacrificed so much for him to achieve success, he will remain civil and fair during the separation and divorce process. She will, however, be surprised at just how low he can stoop. Every day is a new realization of the depth of his depravity. Eventually, she realizes there is simply no depth to which he will not stoop to inflict as much emotional abuse as he can on the spouse whom he believes has abandoned him for no reason.

Divorce is emotionally difficult, but a divorce from an abuser will be the most traumatic and difficult experience most women will ever go through. If she makes emotional and spiritual healing her number one priority, she will come out of the process stronger and wiser, closer to God, and with a boldness and confidence that nothing will be able to shake. She will be forged in the fire, stronger than steel, and able to stand against anything.

Many women in abusive relationships and marriages have been isolated by their abuser. She may feel all alone on this divorce journey. Without a strong emotional support network, a woman is likely to return to the abuser, become depressed, and be crushed under the abuser's nonstop emotional attacks.

A woman leaving an abuser will need emotional support from people who understand both the tactics of abusers and their effects. Most importantly, she will need support from people who can love her through the process and speak truth into her to replace the abuser's lies.

Visualize the emotional support network as a series of concentric circles, with the woman in the middle. The inner circle is comprised of safe people—those she trusts, knows intimately, and with whom she can share her heart. In the next circle will be a less intimate, but still safe group of people with whom she can share her story. In the farthest circles are people who are not safe, whom she should not trust, and who are not worthy of hearing her story or her heart.

Have a Spiritual and Emotional Support Plan

Domestic Abuse Professionals

Counseling from professionals who understand domestic abuse is essential. A woman leaving an abusive marriage must seek individual counseling as well as the group counseling available in support groups. Seek out the counselors or counseling services that specialize in counseling victims of domestic abuse. Domestic abuse is a specialty among therapists and counselors. A kind, wise, skilled domestic abuse therapist is invaluable for validation and healing after leaving the abuser. Conversely, advice from one who is not knowledgeable about domestic abuse will cause further pain.

Domestic Abuse Organizations

Connect with the local domestic abuse organization. Nearly every county in every state has a domestic abuse organization that provides support services to victims of domestic abuse. The range of services vary from county to county and organization to organization. Some provide only counseling and therapy services, while others may provide wrap-around services such as emergency housing, long-term housing, food, financial and career counseling, childcare, connections to other social service agencies such as those providing immigration or legal services, and connections to government services such as food stamps.

Support Group

The local domestic abuse shelter is likely to have a support group. Group therapy is helpful because a woman can talk to others who understand her situation and can share things that have worked for them. Lifelong friendships often develop out of support groups. Facebook also has a number of domestic abuse support groups where members can ask for advice, emotional support, prayers, and the like. Although a Facebook group is not the same as person-to-person contact, it is a good way to glean advice and hear experiences of many others who understand domestic abuse.

Family

Seek out compassionate family members. Parents and siblings are often supportive. Unfortunately, many family members may not be sympathetic or safe. They may not believe her, they may want her to stay married, they may side with the abuser, or they may see nothing wrong with his actions. Some may be too busy, they may be aloof and uninterested, they may not realize or care how emotionally painful a divorce from an abuser can be, or they may be unwilling or unable to give emotional support. Some may even be abusers, manipulators, narcissists, sociopaths, or psychopaths themselves. On the other hand, they may be overly involved, overly interested, and expect her to share things that she is not comfortable sharing. Some may be busybodies and unable to keep to themselves those things said in confidence.

A woman will need to establish healthy emotional boundaries to protect herself from those who are not emotionally safe for her. She must avoid those who are not emotionally safe and refrain from sharing details with them. To avoid feeling victimized again, she should not expect their support.

Most family members will not be familiar with narcissistic personality disorder, sociopathy, psychopathy, and domestic abuse, and thus they may not be helpful in helping her understand the abuser, his tactics, or the damaging effects of abuse on her. However, they can provide love and support. Family members are not therapists, however. They may give unhelpful or even dangerous advice, and they will likely tire of listening to her tales of her abuser's bad behavior. So, a wise woman will cherish them as family, but save most of her story for her therapist.

Friends

Safe, compassionate friends ought to be part of a woman's support system. As with her family, she will need to be discerning as to who is safe and who is not, and she will need to set healthy boundaries. Given the smear and slander campaign that abusers are certain to employ, a woman must be careful to sort out the minions of the abuser from true friends.[121] True, safe friends will be compassionate and believing. Unsafe people will be judgmental, self-righteous, unbelieving, rumor spreaders, and/or supporters of the abuser. This is an excellent time to remove anyone who is unsafe from the list of so-called friends. Those who are not safe are not deserving of hearing her story.

Like family, even safe friends are not therapists. Unloading every detail about the abuse and ongoing divorce for years will likely lead to bad advice and dampen a friendship. A discerning woman will enjoy time with friends who can lift her spirits, and save the unloading for her therapist.

Children

Children should not be expected to provide support during this time. They have been put in a most difficult position. They may have been told details regarding abuse and divorce they do not understand or believe and yet still love their father despite his abusive ways. Their family is being pulled apart and their emotional tanks are empty. They cannot give what they do not have.

For all these reasons, a wise woman will provide emotional support for her children, reassure them of her love, and not expect emotional support from them.[122] She will also recognize that she cannot give to her children what she doesn't have. She needs to be whole and healed so that she can provide wholeness and healing to her children. Therefore, she needs to make healing her top priority.

Bible Study Group

She may find a Bible study for women who are healing from abuse, but these are rare. A group of empathetic, Holy Spirit-filled women who can support and pray for each other is a wonderful place to find healing. However, if they have not experienced domestic abuse, they may not understand the dynamics of abuse. A wise woman will not use a Bible study group as therapy, but as a place of mutual support.

Pastors

A woman will often go first to a pastor for emotional and spiritual support. If the pastor is supportive, this is wonderful. However, very few pastors have any training in domestic abuse or in dealing with narcissists, sociopaths, or psychopaths.

A pastor's reasons for being unsupportive may mimic family members' reasoning. If the abuser attends the same church or is a generous donor, a pastor may have a difficult time being supportive of the victim. In the same way a woman must discern which friends and family members are safe, she must determine whether her

---

[121] See previous sections on those who support abusers in chapters 7, 21, and 28.
[122] See sections involving children in chapters 28 and 46.

pastor and church are safe. If the pastor does not make the church a safe place physically and emotionally for the victim, he supports the abuser. In particular, if the pastor does not prohibit the abuser from attending services so that the victim can worship safely and without fear, and if the pastor refuses to stop the smear and slander campaign that the abuser and his cronies have instituted, he has shown that he supports the abuser. Thus, the victim will want to consider attending another church that has a sympathetic, Holy Spirit-led, biblical attitude toward protecting victims of domestic abuse. Jesus's words to us to wipe the dust off our feet hold true even for churches who are not led by the Holy Spirit and who refuse to make the church a refuge for sheep rather than a protector of wolves.[123]

---

[123] See chapter 35 for ways in which the church can support the victim and hold the abuser accountable.

Chapter 30

The Spiritual Battle

The woman being abused by or escaping from an abusive husband often assumes that the battle is between her and her husband. This is a mistake. A much larger battle is going on—an unseen battle is being waged in the spiritual realm for her and her children, and, yes, even her husband. Satan has his sights set on families. He knows that a family committed to God—and a strong woman committed to God—is one of his biggest threats. A woman who fulfills her God-designed purpose puts a big dent in Satan's plans. The ripple effect of a woman on fire for the Lord is nothing short of devastating to Satan. She will turn all she touches—her family and friends, people in her place of worship and employment—into God's warriors. The Lord may even call her to start her own company or nonprofit that will affect hundreds, if not thousands, for the Lord. She is a threat to Satan, and he knows it, so he devises ways to destroy her and her children, using her husband. And when he is done using her husband, Satan will destroy her husband too.

Satan's Original Attack

Satan has launched his attack on women from the very beginning. We know from God's Word that Satan was once an angel who led a revolt against God. God banished him from heaven, along with his followers, and sent him to earth (Isaiah 14:12–15). In Scripture, he is called the "prince of this world" (John 14:30), "prince of the power of the air" (Ephesians 2:2 KJV), "ruler of the darkness of this world" (Ephesians 6:12 KJV), and "god of this age" (2 Corinthians 4:4). The earth is a battle zone into which humankind was placed. Our job was to "be fruitful and increase in number; fill the earth and subdue it" (Genesis 1:28). God's assignment to Adam and Eve was to be productive, have children, and fill the earth, and with those God-loving children, bring the earth under God's submission. Sadly, Adam and Eve failed in this assignment. God gave them the ability to choose God or Satan, just like He gives us that choice today. They chose to rebel against God, and humankind has been in a state of rebellion ever since.

In Genesis, Satan targeted Eve, not Adam, to instill doubt and make her question whether God really had their best interests in mind. He deceived her and persuaded her to doubt what she already knew to be true—that God loves her, desires a relationship with her, and that He gave them the entire garden to enjoy except for one tree because it would not be in their best interest to eat from it. Satan's talk with Eve in the garden of Eden was the first recorded incident of gaslighting. Satan intentionally deceived Eve into thinking that something horrific was good. As is his nature, Satan deceived Eve with the promise of something good, and it ended up being to her detriment and to his gain. Unfortunately, Adam, who was standing right beside Eve, never spoke up or protected her. Adam did not take responsibility for his own actions. He simply blamed the entire episode and his own sin on Eve. Satan accomplished his goal of destroying their relationship with one another and with God using trickery and deception, and he has been deceiving women (and men) through his minions, including abusers, ever since.

The Continued Attack on Women

Since Eve, Satan has launched a full-fledged attack on women. Around the world, women are the most likely to be in positions that are powerless, vulnerable, and in poverty. They are subject to the horrors of rape, slavery, sexual abuse and harassment, poverty, human trafficking, discrimination, domestic abuse, kidnapping, and a whole host of other atrocities in far greater numbers than men. Fear is another of Satan's most powerful weapons against women. Often the fear comes from within. She fears she isn't pretty enough or thin enough or wealthy enough. She fears she will never get married or that no one will love her or that she must give sex to get a man to like her. She fears she will end up alone as a poor bag lady, and she fears that she will have no friends unless she conforms to the crowd. She fears what others think of her—that she is too much or not enough. She fears retaliation if she exposes the truth, and she fears leaving her abuser. The list goes on and on and on. These are all the results of Satan's deliberate and targeted attacks on women. Once Satan has control over a woman, either by a traumatic act or through fear, she is paralyzed, and it takes Herculean efforts to bring her out of his clutches.

Satan—the Predator

The Bible tells us, "Be alert and of sober mind. Your enemy the devil prowls around like a roaring lion looking for someone to devour" (1 Peter 5:8). Women are in a spiritual battle, and Satan is looking for ways to attack. We need to be mindful of his ways, recognize the attacks when they come, and be ready for battle.

Lions are predators. They survey a herd of antelope, sizing up the fast and strong, and the slow and weak. They specifically target the weak and vulnerable, saving the strong and swift for another day. In the same way, Satan preys on women who are spiritually weak and vulnerable. He targets those who are not confident in their spiritual identity, who don't have a strong relationship with Jesus, or who are not intimately familiar with and grounded in God's Word. He picks on those with big hearts but who are not discerning or wise, those with childhood wounds of abuse and rejection from which they have never healed, and the lonely and wounded. But he also preys on Christian women who, although strong in their faith, naïvely do not recognize the evil and manipulation.

Women—the Prey

A woman who lacks spiritual faith or is spiritually weak and vulnerable can be easily swayed by Satan's ploys—illegal drug use, alcohol and prescription drug abuse, adultery, sexual promiscuity, prostitution, criminal acts, dangerous acquaintances, intimate relationships with dangerous men, going with the crowd, gang membership, etc. It takes little effort on Satan's part to ensnare someone who is already spiritually weak and vulnerable and make her completely useless for God's work. A woman involved in these activities is simply trying to survive; she is not working on being God's hands and feet to others.

However, a Christian woman who is strong in her faith, who has a relationship with her Lord and Savior Jesus Christ, who spends time in God's Word, and who tries to be God's hands and feet on earth is a threat to Satan, and he knows it. It will take a lot more effort to bring her down so that she is useless for doing God's work. A strong Christian woman will not typically be swayed by the lure of drug and alcohol abuse, adultery, prostitution, illegal activities, or partnering with someone who is a known criminal or gang member. Satan must be more creative to destroy her. And so, in order to get to her, Satan infiltrates her home through her husband (or husband-to-be). Once Satan has control of her husband, her husband will do Satan's bidding in all-out efforts to destroy her, his children, his whole family, his career, his finances, his health, and eventually, himself.

Satan's Strategy to Destroy the Christian Family

How can this happen? Satan has a well-planned strategy. While his biggest weapon against women is fear, his biggest weapon against men is pride. It is not the kind of pride we have when our kids work hard, do well, and show good character, but the kind of pride that says, "I'm better than others." Pride that says, "I don't have to follow the rules." Pride that says, "I should have what I want when I want it and how I want it." Pride that says, "I'm a Christian because I go to church," even though he uses church as a social club and has no relationship with God. Pride that uses people for selfish gain instead of cherishes people as gifts. Pride that values getting his way over doing what's right. Pride that wins at all costs rather than values a relationship. Pride that puts others down to make himself look good. Pride that selfishly climbs to the top and takes the spoils, while sacrificing his family and friends on the altar of success. Pride that views women as objects to use rather than partners to treasure. Pride that leads to abuse. Pride that leads to being a predator.

Once Satan has control over a man through pride and he has become a narcissist, sociopath, psychopath, or other predatory abuser, even Herculean efforts generally are ineffective in pulling him out of Satan's clutches. After all, his methods of abuse, coupled with the fact that he always wins and always gets his way, work quite well for him. He sees no need to change. He also has no idea that Satan has control and will use him to destroy his wife, his family, his career, his finances, and himself.

And so Satan's minion, filled with pride, prowls for his next victim—a lovely Christian woman who practices the spiritual disciplines of prayer, Bible study, and attending church, and who extols the virtues of a Christian woman. She is kind, patient, giving, forgiving, joyful, peaceful, nurturing, encouraging, uncynical, unjudgmental, and looks for the best in others. She clearly does not have her radar up for a narcissist, sociopath, psychopath, or other abuser. She probably doesn't even know what those terms mean. She shows the qualities of a woman who walks with the Lord—except for one: she lacks the ability to discern God's true children from imposters. She is naïve to Satan's ploys and the spiritual battle raging around her. Instead, she has taken to heart the words of Paul: "Whatever is true, whatever is noble, whatever is right, whatever is pure, whatever is lovely, whatever is admirable—if anything is excellent or praiseworthy—think about such things" (Philippians 4:8). And although she walks with the Lord, she does not recognize the spiritual warfare swirling around her or realize that she is the target of one of Satan's most convincing and deceitful creatures—the charming narcissist, sociopath, psychopath, or other abuser.

Once the SNAP has love-bombed his target and convinced her to become his wife, Satan's efforts to destroy her start in earnest.[124] Satan is invited into her home through her husband's pornography, viewing of violent and sexually explicit movies, playing of violent video games, and his social media feeds. Her husband rolls out the red carpet for Satan to enter her home through his browsing of the dark web and unsavory websites, through his constant feed of political news and hate talk, and through his texts and emails to his paramours and girlfriends. The constant barrage of Satan's voice through the media in the home convinces him that violence, hateful speech, and sexual abuse is not only normal, but is what he is entitled to. Rather than encouraging and building up his wife and children, he tries to destroy them. His efforts, through Satan's promptings, turn from love-bombing to devaluing and abusing her, and often the children as well, turning their home into a spiritually toxic wasteland that attacks the spirits of all who live there, and all they come in contact with. It is only a matter of time until the poison rises to an unsustainable level and either the Christian wife leaves, he leaves, or one or both of them dies often at the hands of the other.

Not satisfied with destroying his family, Satan is also working on destroying his career and finances. With the same contempt he holds for his wife, the abuser is busy bringing his abuse and toxicity to work. Many abusers have difficulty holding down jobs in environments that require cooperation and respect for authority and others for success. Rather, they tend to look for leadership positions in which they act charming and respectful to their superiors, while being abusive to underlings as they climb the corporate ladder. This can lead to a meteoric early rise in their career. Eventually, however, their abuse tends to catch up with them—in sexual harassment lawsuits, poor employee morale and productivity, excessive employee turnover, or other signs of extreme stress in the workplace. Satan uses abusers to bring destruction to employees in the workplace, as well as their own destruction. Their actions often lead to their firing, or if the employer is benevolent, they are allowed to tell the outside world they "resigned to pursue other interests" or took "early retirement." In some cases, SNAPs bring down an entire company, causing financial disruption to thousands of people. Many abusers go through several jobs during their careers, as they are hired and fired multiple times. Because larger corporations impose more rules for properly interacting with fellow employees or clients, many abusers choose to open their own business where they can be their own boss and make their own rules, or they work for a business owned by a family member.

Because abusers are often fired from their positions, they often pay a hefty financial price for their on-the-job abuse. However, unlike healthy people who take responsibility for their own actions and learn from the part that they played in their own termination, abusers neither take responsibility nor learn from their mistakes. As a result, their financial condition, which is largely tied to their employment, deteriorates over time as they hop from job to job.

An abuser's excessive pride and arrogance, fueled by Satan, also deceives him into investing in risky business ventures with the allure of getting rich quickly. Narcissists think so highly of themselves that they deceive themselves into thinking their past success is all due to their efforts rather than God's blessings. Thus, they believe any investment or venture they are involved in will be highly successful, if for no other reason than that they are involved. They truly believe that they have the Midas touch. An abuser will squander a disproportionate share of his net worth on high-risk business ventures that often fail. He will do this without the knowledge or approval of his wife, who is usually the voice of prudence and reason. Even among the wealthy, Satan often succeeds in bringing abusers to financial ruin.

---

[124] See chapter 3, "The Three Phases of a Romantic Abusive Relationship" and chapter 4, "The Cycle of Abuse within a Relationship."

In addition to setting his sights on destroying an abuser's wife, family, career, and finances, Satan is busy in his attempts to destroy the abuser's health. When a person is filled with negative emotions, it takes a toll on his body. Hatred and rage lead to a downward spiral of more hatred and rage, increasing cortisol and adrenaline hormones in the human body, breaking down nervous, immune and endocrine systems, and leading to severe physical and mental health issues. Over time, due to the increased levels of these hormones, many abusers succumb to a host of physical health problems at an earlier age than most, including heart disease, weight gain, headaches, and digestive problems. Abusers also tend to have mental health problems, including anxiety, depression, obsessive thinking, and paranoia. Abuse goes hand in hand with drug and alcohol use and addictions, which often leads to alcoholism, liver disease and drug abuse issues.

After Satan has used the abuser to destroy his wife, family, career, finances, and physical and mental health, unless the abuser repents and humbly turns to God, Satan will destroy the abuser himself—both physically and spiritually. The abuser does not even realize that he is being used as a tool of Satan, who will then turn on the abuser when he is done destroying others. All too often, an abuser's life ends in suicide or a murder/suicide, as his hatred overcomes his reason and he ends his and/or his victim's life by his own hands. Sadly, statistics reveal that more than 1,200 people die in murder/suicides each in year, 72 percent of which were committed by an intimate partner, and 90 percent of which were committed by a man.[125] But even if an abuser dies by other causes, without repentance he is spiritually doomed and bound for eternity outside the presence of God. Although God is a God of love, He is also a God of justice, and one can be sure that an abuser will be held accountable for his actions by a just God.

David observed the self-destruction of wicked people 3,000 years ago: "But look how the wicked hatch evil, conceive trouble, give birth to lies! They make a pit, dig it all out, and then fall right into the hole that they've made! The trouble they cause will come back on their own heads; the violence they commit will come down on their own skulls" (Psalm 7:14–16 CEB). "The Lord is known by his acts of justice; the wicked are ensnared by the work of their hands" (Psalm 9:16). "The wicked draw the sword and bend the bow to bring down the poor and needy, to slay those whose ways are upright. But their swords will pierce their own hearts, and their bows will be broken" (Psalm 37:14–15).

> Kerry: Patrick left his position as a high-priced litigator at a Chicago law firm (I suspect he was fired), had two divorces, was an alcoholic, was evicted from his home in Lake Forest, was held in contempt of court for refusing to pay child support, and yet spent thousands of dollars at bars every month. On January 10, 2019, Patrick committed suicide. As the events of the days leading up to his death unfolded, I realized how fragile my safety was and what he was capable of doing. This could have been a murder/suicide if I had not escaped and stayed away. I am a true survivor. Ironically, his favorite pub in Lake Forest has dedicated a seat to him. To me, he was an abuser; to his pub friends, he was the life of the party.
>
> John: My biological dad shot his wife and then himself. What a tragic end to a life that was devoid of authentic relationships. I had always hoped for a relationship with him, but he wanted nothing to do with me or my sister. In the end, I realize God protected us. I would have had a very different life if he had been my role model.

---

[125] "More than 1,200 Americans Die in Murder-Suicides Each Year, VPC Study Finds" (Violence Policy Center, October 29, 2015), vpc.org/press/more-than-1200-americans-die-in-murder-suicides-each-year-vpc-study-finds/.

Joan: Tory had difficulty holding down a job and had congestive heart failure while in his 30s. The combination of drugs, alcohol, and crazy lifestyle have taken their toll.

Sally: My own sister-in-law committed suicide with three little ones at home. Her life was so awful, and her husband was horribly abusive. She saw no way out.

Note: During the writing of this book, after her divorce from her abuser was finalized, Lydia took her own life in 2019. She will be missed by her daughter and friends.

Freedom to Choose Good or Evil

Many women ask God, "Why is this happening to me?" or "Why are You doing this to me, God?" But this is the wrong question. When we realize that we have been placed in the middle of a war zone, we recognize that God is not causing the abuse at all. Rather, the abuse is caused by someone who has chosen to follow Satan's ways, not God's. God gives us all free will to choose His ways or Satan's ways. If God forced us to choose Him, it would not be a choice at all. We would be merely puppets on a string. We know God is love and God is good. We know He wants the best for us (Jeremiah 29:11) and wants a relationship with us. But God is a gentleman. He will not force Himself on someone who does not want Him. Therefore, since the beginning of mankind, some have chosen evil, while others have chosen goodness. God's plan and hope is that we would all choose Him and choose goodness.

This freedom to choose evil, while living among those who choose God, is explained in the parables of Jesus. In the parable of the weeds, Jesus explains that the kingdom of heaven is like a man who sowed good wheat seed in his field, and his enemy came in the night and sowed weeds among the wheat. Rather than pulling up all the weeds, which would have destroyed the wheat, the good farmer allowed them both to grow up together until harvest time when he would gather the wheat and burn the weeds. Jesus explained that in the parable, God is the farmer and God's people are the good wheat, while the enemy is Satan and the weeds are Satan's people. God allows His people and the devil's people to coexist for a time while they are on earth, but in the end, God will gather His people to Himself and will send Satan's people away into a blazing furnace (Matthew 13:24–30; 36–43). God allows narcissists, sociopaths, psychopaths, and other abusers who have chosen to reject Him to live among those who have chosen to follow Him, but in the end, they will be held accountable.

Likewise, in the parable of the sower, Jesus explains that the kingdom of heaven is like a farmer who sows seed. Some of the seed lands on the hard path and it never takes root, some lands on rocky soil and withers because it has no roots, some lands in the thorns and gets choked out, and some lands on good, fertile soil and produces a great crop. The farmer sowing the seed represents God spreading His good news, and the soil represents the different condition of the hearts that hear it (Matthew 13:1–23). God gives the same message to everyone, but not everyone's heart accepts His gifts. Only those whose hearts are open and prepared will receive God's Word and produce godly fruit. SNAPs have such hard hearts that they do not accept God's message, even though they may pretend to by sitting in a pew on Sundays.

Abuse Is Not from God

Some women mistakenly believe that the abuse came from God to teach them a lesson, or so that somehow God would be glorified in it. Some even believe this pain and suffering is God's gift so that they can be more like Him. That is hogwash and not biblical. Stating that abuse came from God to teach us or so He would be glorified is akin to saying that a doctor broke his daughter's arm so that she would learn a lesson and he would be glorified as a magnificent doctor. That would be child abuse! God is not a child abuser. Because God is good, God is the giver of good gifts. We know that all good gifts come from Him (James 1:17). Abuse is evil and from Satan. Abuse is not from God. However, God is a God of redemption, and He can miraculously take what others meant for evil and use it for good (Genesis 50:20). God can and will bring good out of an abusive situation for those who love Him (Romans 8:28).

How Should We Respond?

How then should we respond? Many women pray that God will soften their husband's heart and magically change him into a good person. That rarely happens. David tells us that wicked people have been wicked their entire lives. "Even from birth the wicked go astray; from the womb they are wayward, spreading lies" (Psalm 58:3). This is supported by modern research. Adult sociopaths—that is, adults with antisocial personality disorder—all had conduct disorder (the official term for sociopathic behavior in children) as children.[126] The book of Daniel informs us that the wicked remain wicked: "Many will be purified, made spotless and refined, but the wicked will continue to be wicked. None of the wicked will understand, but those who are wise will understand" (Daniel 12:10). Jeremiah tell us that a wicked person changing is as unlikely as a leopard changing its spots: "Can an Ethiopian change his skin or a leopard its spots? Neither can you do good who are accustomed to doing evil" (Jeremiah 13:23).

In all the Bible, less than a handful of prideful men who were bent on evil humbled themselves and changed for good, and the change only occurred after God inflicted dire consequences on them to humble their prideful hearts. Manasseh, king of Judah, finally humbled himself before God, but only after he was led away to Assyria with a hook in his nose and shackles on his feet (2 Chronicles 33). King Nebuchadnezzar of Babylon finally humbled himself before God, but only after God took away his kingdom, turned him insane, and made him eat grass like an ox for seven years (Daniel 4:28–37). Paul turned to God after persecuting Christians, but only after God blinded him for three days and gave him a three-year time-out (Acts 9; Galatians 1:18).

Instructions from Jesus and Paul on Handling Flagrant, Severe, Unrepentant Sin

These examples, as well as recent research, inform us that if an abuser has any chance of repenting, it is only through severe consequences and God's intervention. Therefore Jesus gives specific instructions on how to handle difficult people who claim to be believers and yet sin against a fellow believer. The process is essentially an appeals process, going to higher and higher levels of authority to gain justice. His instructions to first-century believers are just as relevant to modern-day women with problem husbands. First, Jesus instructs a believer who has been sinned against to go privately to the perpetrator and (with gentleness and humility) show him his fault. Any believer who is sensitive to the Holy Spirit's promptings will repent at this point (Matthew 18:15). Thus, *if it is safe*, a woman whose husband has sinned against her should first go to her husband privately. A Spirit-filled husband will be prompted to repent, and the relationship can be repaired. Second, Jesus goes on to say that if the perpetrator does not repent, the victim should then take one or two other witnesses along to convince him of his sin and to repent (Matthew 18:16). A true believer would clearly repent when two or three people tell him he is

---

[126] "Antisocial Personality Disorder," The Recovery Village, last updated January 28, 2020, https://www.therecoveryvillage.com/mental-health/antisocial-personality-disorder/#gref

sinning. Thus, in modern-day language, a woman who cannot convince her husband that he has sinned against her, *if it is safe*, should consult with a counselor or two to work with her husband in repenting and engaging in healthy behavior. If her husband is a true believer, the Holy Spirit will convict him of his sin, and he will humble himself and repent. Third, Jesus continues His instructions and states that if the perpetrator will still not listen to the two or three witnesses, then the victim should take the matter to the church leaders (Matthew 18:17). Clearly, the hope is that even someone who is rather dull to the moving of the Holy Spirit should listen to church leaders, whose authority he is under, and repent. In a modern-day setting, *if it is safe*, a woman should bring the matter to her pastor and elders, who should then require repentance.[127] It should be noted here that some pastors and elders are misinformed, misled, lack courage, or perhaps are abusers themselves and do not support victims of domestic abuse. If that is the case, a woman should not allow a pastor or elder to convince her that abuse is ever acceptable. She must then find a safe church.[128] Finally, Jesus states that if the perpetrator won't even listen to the church leaders, he should be excommunicated from the body of believers (Matthew 18:17). These consequences are to be imposed in the hope that they will bring the perpetrator to a place of humility and repentance. In a contemporary setting, the woman is within her rights to ask the church to excommunicate her husband and forbid his attendance so the church is a safe place for her to worship.

Following the instructions of Jesus, Paul instructed the Corinthians to excommunicate and have nothing to do with people who claim to be Christians but continue to engage in severe, unrepentant, flagrant sin:

> I wrote to you in my letter not to associate with sexually immoral people—not at all meaning the people of this world who are immoral, or the greedy and swindlers, or idolaters. In that case you would have to leave this world. But now I am writing to you that you must not associate with anyone who claims to be a brother or sister but is sexually immoral or greedy, an idolater or slanderer, a drunkard or swindler. Do not even eat with such people. What business is it of mine to judge those outside the church? Are you not to judge those inside? God will judge those outside. "Expel the wicked person from among you." (1 Corinthians 5:9–13)

Paul gives similar instructions to Timothy and Titus. Paul warns Timothy, a young leader of the church in Ephesus, of SNAPs in the church. His is one of the best descriptions ever written:

> But mark this: There will be terrible times in the last days. People will be lovers of themselves, lovers of money, boastful, proud, abusive, disobedient to their parents, ungrateful, unholy, without love, unforgiving, slanderous, without self-control, brutal, not lovers of the good, treacherous, rash, conceited, lovers of pleasure rather than lovers of God—having a form of godliness but denying its power. Have nothing to do with such people. They are the kind who worm their way into homes and gain control over gullible women. . . . They are men of depraved minds, who, as far as the faith is concerned, are rejected. (2 Timothy 3:1–6, 8)

To Titus, Paul warns, "Warn a divisive person once, and then warn them a second time. After that, have nothing to do with them. You may be sure that such people are warped and sinful; they are self-condemned" (Titus 3:10–11).

Only through the consequences of being publicly removed from the benefits of a group of believers can there

---

[127] See chapter 35 on "How the Church Should Respond to Domestic Abuse" for further details.
[128] See chapter 35 on "Top Mistakes Churches Make in Responding to Domestic Abuse."

be any hope that an abuser would humble himself enough to repent, if he can repent at all. When he instructed believers to "have nothing to do with them," Paul did not make an exception for spouses, because to do so would subject her to a sentence of lifelong abuse. Rather, Paul was so emphatic about having nothing to do with abusers that he stated, "Do not even eat with such people" (1 Corinthians 5:11). Like Jesus, Paul's instructions were given with two things in mind: (1) to keep the victim and the church safe from the abuse, lies, and dissension caused by toxic people, and (2) to provide severe consequences that are necessary for a change of heart in the hope that the perpetrator will humble himself and repent.

Don't Beg and Plead

Many women beg and plead with their husbands to be kind and do the right thing. That rarely happens either. In most cases, God walks away from the wicked people of the world and allows them to continue down their wicked path of destruction. The author of Romans tell us that "God abandoned them to do whatever shameful things their hearts desired" and that "God abandoned them to their shameful desires" (Romans 1:24, 26 NLT). He continues describing how God deals with the wicked and their end:

> Since they though it foolish to acknowledge God, he abandoned them to their foolish thinking and let them do things that should never be done. Their lives became full of every kind of wickedness, sin, greed, hate, envy, murder, quarreling, deception, malicious behavior, and gossip. They are backstabbers, haters of God, insolent, proud, and boastful. They invent new ways of sinning, and they disobey their parents. They refuse to understand, break their promises, are heartless, and have no mercy. They know God's justice requires that those who do these things deserve to die, yet they do them anyway. Worse yet, they encourage others to do them, too. (Romans 1:28–32 NLT)

Recognize the Truth

Like David, Jeremiah, and Daniel, Jesus had a similar response to the Pharisees, Sadducees, and other religious leaders who appeared righteous, but who were wicked and were plotting His death in their hearts. He did not beg and plead for them to soften their hard hearts. As experts in Jewish law, they knew the right thing to do, but they simply had evil hearts too full of pride and too hard to penetrate. Instead, Jesus called them out on their wickedness, calling them "hypocrites," "white-washed tombs," "snakes," a "brood of vipers" (Matthew 23:13–33) and belonging to their father, the devil, who is a murderer and liar (John 8:44). He rightfully pointed out that people are like trees: a person is recognized by the fruit of his or her life, just like a tree is recognized by its fruit. A good person bears good deeds, words, and attitudes, while a bad person bears wicked deeds, words, and attitudes. "Make a tree good and its fruit will be good, or make a tree bad and its fruit will be bad, for a tree is recognized by its fruit. You brood of vipers, how can you who are evil say anything good? For the mouth speaks what the heart is full of. A good man brings good things out of the good stored up in him, and an evil man brings evil things out of the evil stored up in him" (Matthew 12:33–35). Rather than begging and pleading for them to act kindly and accept His words, Jesus recognized the Pharisees for the wicked people they were, spoke the truth, and had nothing to do with them. We would all be wise to do the same.

The Big, Bold Prayer and Examples of the Saints

The saints of old give us good examples of what to do when we are faced with wicked people who are trying to bring us down. Throughout history, when God's people were persecuted and under fire from people intent on harming and even destroying them, God's people made a big, bold prayer. The big, bold prayer consists of two parts: first, they reminded themselves of God's faithfulness, of His miracles, and of His power and love for His people. Second, they asked for boldness and strength to fight the battle. They sought supernatural help from the Lord to win. We can find examples of the big, bold prayer throughout the Bible. When Peter and the disciples were called into the Sanhedrin, they did not pray that the persecution would go away. Rather, they reminded themselves that God made the heavens and earth, that He spoke through David, and that He is all-powerful. They prayed for great boldness and more miracles. God answered their prayer with the filling of the Holy Spirit and the courage to speak boldly (Acts 4:24–31).

When Ezra made the long, dangerous journey back to Jerusalem to rebuild the temple, he didn't seek the king's protection. Rather, he proclaimed a fast for God's people so they could all join together in a big, bold prayer and fasting to ask God for safe passage (Ezra 8:21–23). A few years later, when Nehemiah was met with great opposition as he rebuilt the wall of Jerusalem, he, too, proclaimed a big, bold prayer. He reminded Israel that God was great and awesome, that God would fight for them, and that they should fight for their families. The Israelites built the wall with a trowel in one hand and a sword in the other. They were always prepared to fight, but kept working on the task before them (Nehemiah 4). Nehemiah did not pray for an easy fix. He knew the job to be done, and he got after it. He prayed for God to bring the opposers and ridiculers to justice (Nehemiah 4:4), and he prayed for strength to accomplish the task (Nehemiah 6:9). God answered his prayer; the wall was built, and Nehemiah's detractors were silenced.

Elisha was a prophet who could see into the spiritual realm. He saw the angels and demons fighting, just as he saw the earthly armies fighting. His ability to see God's angels fighting on his behalf, knowing that God controlled the outcome, filled him with confidence even against tremendous odds. In one battle, his servant saw that the enemy army with horses and chariots had surrounded them, and he was terrified. Elisha calmly responded, "Don't be afraid. Those who are with us are more than those who are with them" (2 Kings 6:16). He prayed that the eyes of his servant would be opened to the spirit world so he could see what Elisha saw. When the servant's eyes were opened to the spiritual realm, he saw God's angel armies of horses and chariots of fire. Then he prayed that God would strike the enemy army with blindness, and God answered his prayer. It was a complete victory.

Throughout history, God's people have met with opposition from Satan. We are no exception. The big, bold prayer—a reminder of God's faithfulness in the past and a plea for boldness, courage to face the fight, and justice—is a necessary weapon of battle.

Chapter 31

Redemption and the Spiritual Journey of the Exodus: From Bondage, through the Desert, to the Promised Land

Oftentimes church leaders will ask me what redemption looks like in the context of domestic abuse. I have two answers and one warning from Scripture. In almost all cases, God's redemption looks like the exodus, when God, through Moses, stepped in, rescued His beloved, led them through a desert, and then placed them in a promised land flowing with milk and honey. Notice that God did not change Pharaoh's evil heart, but He did rescue His people. On rare occasions, God will change the heart of the abuser. God will intervene and strike the wicked person with such severe consequences that the person has nowhere else to go but to God. In the end, it is still their option to choose God or continue their downward spiral. I could only unearth three persons in the Bible whom God chose to deal with in this way: Paul, King Nebuchadnezzar, and King Manasseh. Whether redemption comes by way of a rescue mission or the transformed heart of the abuser, it's important to know that when God redeems a situation, He puts His people in positions that are better than they were before.

Finally, Scripture warns us that we must be careful not to go back to an abuser whose heart God has not changed. The Judges 19–20 account of the Levite and his concubine is a heartbreaking story of a woman whose abuser persuaded her to return to him and was murdered. We will look at each of these examples from Scripture.

Moses and the Exodus: How God Rescues a Victim of Abuse

The exodus is an especially good example for women escaping the oppression of an abusive relationship. After all, what abused wife is not like the Israelite slaves, poor and powerless in a land of plenty? And what abusive husband is not like Pharaoh, who never turned from his evil, who didn't care about his slaves but certainly didn't want to let them go, and who even increased the abuse when they tried to leave? Powerless and unable to break free from their chains of bondage, God delivered His people and performed the most extraordinary rescue mission of all time. And He does the same for women leaving the chains of bondage today.

Moses had one of the most extraordinary relationships with God. God and Moses met and spoke together regularly—friend to friend. Moses had a slow and reluctant beginning. He was not at all enthusiastic about leading the Israelites out of Egypt. In fact, he asked God to send someone else. However, after seeing God's hand as He methodically conducted his rescue mission—including ten plagues, the death of the firstborn of all the Egyptians and their livestock, the Egyptians incredulously giving up their gold and silver to the Israelites to get them out of their country, and God's presence in the form of a cloud by day and fire by night—his trust in the Lord was second to none. God promised to be with Moses as he led His people to the promised land. Moses looked forward with great anticipation to the promised land and to the miracles God would do to get them there. When trapped between the Egyptian army and the Red Sea, Moses didn't flinch. The Israelites were terrified, questionied their decision to leave, and wanted to go back to Egypt. But Moses knew that God was about to do a miracle to deliver His people, and he proclaimed: "Do not be afraid. Stand firm and you will see the deliverance the LORD will bring you today. The Egyptians you see today you will never see again. The LORD will fight for you; you need only be still" (Exodus 14:13–14). God parted the Red Sea, rescued His people, destroyed the Egyptians, and the rest is history.

Moses's big, bold prayer was to know God. He knew that he needed an intimate relationship with God to have the strength to lead the people into the promised land. "Moses said to the LORD, 'You have been telling me, "Lead these people," but you have not let me know whom you will send with me. You have said, "I know you by name and you have found favor with me." If you are pleased with me, teach me your ways so I may know you and continue to find favor with you. Remember that this nation is your people'" (Exodus 33:12–13). The Lord was gracious to Moses, and promised that He Himself, the Lord Almighty, would be Moses's constant companion into the land of rest that God had promised. "The LORD replied, 'My Presence will go with you, and I will give you rest'" (Exodus 33:14). I am sure that Moses, like many of us, would have liked God to have given him a detailed road map of exactly where to go and when, but he got something better—God promised to go with him.

Unfortunately, the Israelites were always looking backward to Egypt, in fear of what lay ahead. "Maybe it wasn't so bad after all. We had food and clothes and shelter. At least we weren't going to die in this awful desert or be slaughtered by giants," they grumbled. Fear is one of Satan's most effective weapons, and he used it frequently on the Israelites because they didn't have the relationship with God that Moses did. But Moses relied on God's promise and anticipated the promised land.

Joshua, Moses's successor, had the same amazing faith that Moses had and trusted in God's promise to be with him and to conquer the promised land. When Joshua and Caleb and ten others were sent on a spy mission into Canaan, ten returned saying they couldn't take over the land because there were giants living there and the Israelites would not win against them. The ten focused on Satan's plot to thwart God's plan by filling them with fear. This negative report of the new land demolished the faith of the Israelites, made them question God's goodness, caused them to accuse God of taking them out of Egypt only to be killed by the enemy, and made them all want to go back to Egypt. Only Joshua and Caleb remembered all the miracles they had seen God do right before their eyes. They boldly stood on God's promises that He would continue to do miracles, be with them, and fight for them. Joshua and Caleb told the entire assembly they should boldly forge ahead and take the land: "The land we traveled through and explored is a wonderful land! And if the LORD is pleased with us, he will bring us safely into that land and give it to us. It is a rich land flowing with milk and honey. Do not rebel against the LORD, and don't be afraid of the people of the land. They are only helpless prey to us! They have no protection, but the Lord is with us! Don't be afraid of them!" (Numbers 14:7–9 NLT). Had the Israelites believed Joshua and Caleb and believed in God's promises, their trip from Egypt to the promised land would have lasted only a few weeks. But because of their disbelief, despite having seen God's many miracles, the Israelites were forced to wander in the desert for forty years, until an entire generation had died off. Only Joshua and Caleb lived to conquer the new land.

When Moses finally died and Joshua was named his successor, the Lord spoke to him directly and equipped him with all he needed to complete the daunting task ahead:

> Moses my servant is dead. Now then, you and all these people, get ready to cross the Jordan River into the land I am about to give to them—to the Israelites. I will give you every place where you set your foot, as I promised Moses. Your territory will extend from the desert to Lebanon, and from the great river, the Euphrates—all the Hittite country—to the Mediterranean Sea in the west. No one will be able to stand against you all the days of your life. *As I was with Moses, so I will be with you; I will never leave you nor forsake you. Be strong and courageous*, because you will lead these people to inherit the land I swore to their ancestors to give them. *Be strong and very courageous*. Be careful to obey all the law my servant Moses gave you; do not turn from it to the right or to the left, that you may be successful wherever you go. Keep this Book of the Law always on your lips; meditate on it day and night, so that you may be careful to do everything written in it. Then you will be prosperous and successful. Have I not commanded you? *Be strong and courageous. Do not be afraid; do not be discouraged, for the Lord your God will be with you wherever you go.*" (Joshua 1:2–9 emphasis added)

Just so it sunk in, God told Joshua three times that He would be with him and never leave him. And because God would always be with Joshua, God told Joshua three times to be strong and courageous. What's to be afraid of when the Creator of the Universe and Maker of Miracles is on your side? And for emphasis, God specifically told Joshua to not be afraid or discouraged, knowing that fear and discouragement are the devil's primary weapons. God told Joshua to know His Word backward and forward and to follow it so he would be successful in everything he did.

The first town to conquer was Jericho. When Joshua took the city of Jericho, God used His unique spiritual weapons to win the battle. He did not use swords or horses and chariots. He used music and shouts of praise and marching. God told the army to march around the city with the priests playing the trumpets in front of the ark of the covenant, and when it was time, to give a loud shout with the trumpet blast. Then the walls of the city would crumble and the Israelites would take the city. It was an unlikely battle strategy, but Joshua knew it was a spiritual battle, not just a physical battle, and he followed orders. The walls crumbled to the praises of God.

Like Moses and Joshua, an abused woman is called to rescue herself and her children. She must recognize that Satan will try to stop her in her tracks with fear of the unknown and discouragement over the long and difficult journey. Like Pharaoh, her abuser does not care about her. He only cares that she services his needs. But he also doesn't want to let her go. Controlled by Satan, the abuser will escalate the abuse when she leaves in the hope of getting her to stay. And like Pharaoh, his heart will not change; he will continue his wickedness without a second thought about her, and he will find a replacement to serve his selfish needs. Like the Israelites, she may look back and be tempted to return to the abuser.

But as a woman of God, she must prepare for the battle to come. First, she must know God intimately to be successful for the hard journey ahead. That means she must spend time with her Savior, recognize His voice, know His Word, and know His ways.

Second, she must know in her heart of hearts that He is always with her, because that is what He has promised. Even when she can't feel Him, even without a roadmap, even when she feels lost and out of her comfort zone, God will be with her because she is His beloved daughter.

Third, she must look forward and depend on His promise of a good plan for her life. She can be confident He will fight her battles and bring her to a place of rest. She is on a journey from slavery to freedom, and whether it's the Israelites wandering the desert, slaves on the Underground Railroad, or a woman escaping domestic abuse, the road from bondage to liberty will be long and difficult—but worth it. The path to healing is much shorter when looking forward and anticipating what God will do. But as the Israelites found out, it is extremely long and may last a lifetime if one keeps looking back.

Fourth, she must be an active participant with God. When He says go forth and conquer, she needs to jump into action. God does fight our battles, but He also requires our participation. Just like Canaan, the promised land of rest is inhabited by giants that must be overcome. Perhaps those giants are doing something she has never done before, such as going back to school, moving to a new town, changing careers, facing childhood trauma, becoming the breadwinner of the family, letting go of toxic people in her life, making new safe friends, speaking out about the abuse, speaking up for herself, demanding a fair divorce settlement, or establishing healthy boundaries. God promises to go with her to conquer the giants in her new land of peace and rest.

Finally, she must know that the battle will be won and that Satan will be conquered to the praises and worship of God. Satan can't stand praise to God—it's like poison to him. When we feel Satan's oppression and the heat of battle, and yet praise God in the midst of it, Satan goes into hiding. Not only does praising God turn our focus away from Satan's snares and toward God, but it opens the heavens and moves mountains in the spiritual realm. God inhabits the praises of His people (Psalm 22:3). We bring His Presence when we loudly praise and worship Him—and Satan runs at the sound. Praise, worship and thanksgiving, even in the mess, crushes the fear, anxiety, and doubt that Satan worms into our minds. Try it for yourself and feel the wave of freedom it brings.

When we are up against wicked people, our response should not be to beg and plead with the abuser to change, or to expect God to miraculously make them into good people. That's not how God operates. We must recognize the spiritual battle we are in, remove ourselves from the evil, bravely acknowledge the truth, and recognize domestic abuse as the wickedness that it is. Pray a big, bold prayer for strength, courage to fight the battle, and justice. Like Moses and Joshua, stand on God's promises, look forward to what He will do, and put on the entire armor of God. That is the road to freedom.

On Rare Occasions, Redemption Looks like the Conversion of Paul

Christians, who are naturally drawn to the notion of redemption, often look to the conversion of Paul in holding out hope that a SNAP's heart can be changed and a marriage saved. Of course, our omnipotent God can do anything, including changing hearts, but most of the time He chooses not to. The author of Romans tells us that God allows the wicked to continue down their path of destruction (Romans 1:18–32). Paul was the only person in the New Testament whom God chose to hit with such serious consequences that he finally turned his heart away from persecuting Christians to becoming one.

The success rate of most current perpetrator-counseling programs hovers near zero percent.[129] Batterer inter-

---

[129] *What Works to Reduce Recidivism by Domestic Violence Offenders?* (Washington State Institute for Public Policy, January 2013), https://www.wsipp.wa.gov/ReportFile/1119/Wsipp_What-Works-to-Reduce-Recidivism-by-Domestic-Violence-Offenders_Full-Report.pdf.

vention programs have virtually no effect on reducing domestic violence recidivism. Domestic violence has the highest recidivism rate of violent crimes, and there is no evidence that individual therapy stops violent men from being violent.[130] This dismal statistic is testimony to the biblical principle that the wicked continue their wicked ways, even when surrounded by good people trying to help them. Mental health professionals also attest that people with narcissistic personality disorder, sociopaths, and psychopaths have permanent personality disorders that are not treatable or curable.

Cajoling, extending grace, appealing to his conscience or better nature, or even attempting to make him feel guilt does not change the heart of an abuser. Only consequences humble an abuser enough that he repents. Paul had heard the same message of love and goodwill from Jesus as all the other hundreds of disciples who had chosen to follow Jesus. Even Jesus did not change his heart. What changed his heart were ramifications so dire that he had nowhere else to go but God. God struck Paul with blindness for three days and essentially put Paul in a three-year "time-out" away from Jerusalem and any other form of support before Paul was ready to serve God wholeheartedly. Abusers don't change without consequences so severe that they are forced to rethink their way of life and conclude it is better to change than to lose everything. In this respect, abusers are like substance abuse addicts, who must hit rock bottom before they change.

Paul used his experience to caution abusers who claimed to be believers, but who remained unrepentant and continued their evil and abusive ways. Paul commanded church leaders to excommunicate them from the church, and he commanded believers to have nothing to do with them, in the hope that they would turn back to Christ (1 Corinthians 5; 2 Timothy 3; Titus 3:10–11). This matches Jesus's teaching in Matthew 18:15–17.

Even severe ramifications do not often change hearts. After all, it remains one's personal choice to change. God does not step in like a cosmic puppeteer and pull strings so we are forced to choose good over evil. God always gives us the choice to follow Him, and the majority choose not to. We see this in the story of the Israelites in the Old Testament. They had been warned for centuries to repent and turn back to God or suffer dire consequences, but they refused. Even after they were plundered by their enemies and sent into exile in Assyria and Babylon, most did not return to God. Only a small remnant—less than 10 percent—turned to God. We also see this in abusive marriages in which the abuser loses his wife, his children, his job, his money, his house, and his health all in one fell swoop, but still refuses to change or accept responsibility for the destruction he leaves in his wake.

In the Bible we see only three people who qualify as narcissists, sociopaths, or psychopaths turn to God. Two are found in the Old Testament. Again, it took severe consequences for the turnaround. God warned Babylon's King Nebuchadnezzar in a dream to repent of his wicked ways. God extended grace by warning him in advance, yet it had no effect on the king. God struck him with insanity and forced him out of his palace to live with the animals. For seven years, he ate grass like the oxen while his nails became like claws before he repented of his sins, praised God, and turned from his wicked ways. When he repented, he humbled himself and praised, exalted, and glorified God (Daniel 4). A changed life is evidence of genuine repentance.

King Manasseh, one of Israel's most wicked kings, sacrificed his own children to pagan gods. God warned him to change his ways, to no avail. So the Lord brought an enemy army who took Manasseh away to Assyria with a hook in his nose and shackles on his feet. Facing the prospect of spending the rest of his days in an enemy

---

[130] Sandra Horley, "The New Domestic Violence Scheme That Focuses on Abusers, Not Victims, Is One of the Worst Ideas We've Ever Had," *Independent*, February 18, 2016, https://www.independent.co.uk/voices/the-new-domestic-violence-scheme-that-focuses-on-abusers-not-victims-is-one-of-the-worst-ideas-weve-a6881436.html.

prison cell, Manasseh finally humbled himself, and God graciously allowed him to return to Israel. Evidence of Manasseh's repentance is seen in his changed life: he rebuilt the outer wall of the city of David, he removed the foreign gods as well as their images and altars, he restored the altar and commanded the country to serve only the Lord, and he made offerings and sacrifices to the Lord (2 Chronicles 33:1–18).

In the New Testament, Paul serves as a shining, albeit rare, example of what a truly repentant heart and redeemed life looks like. Paul went from a brutal killer of Christians to a humble preacher of the gospel, a compassionate shepherd of his sheep, a fearless defender of the faith, and the author of much of the New Testament. Look at what he writes to his young friend Timothy, the pastor at the church of Ephesus:

> I thank Christ Jesus our Lord, who has given me strength, that he considered me trustworthy, appointing me to his service. Even though I was once a blasphemer and a persecutor and a violent man, I was shown mercy because I acted in ignorance and unbelief. The grace of our Lord was poured out on me abundantly, along with the faith and love that are in Christ Jesus.
>
> Here is a trustworthy saying that deserves full acceptance: Christ Jesus came into the world to save sinners—of whom I am the worst. But for that very reason I was shown mercy so that in me, the worst of sinners, Christ Jesus might display his immense patience as an example for those who would believe in him and receive eternal life. Now to the King eternal, immortal, invisible, the only God, be honor and glory for ever and ever. Amen. (1 Timothy 1:12–17)

A woman in an abusive relationship needs to see a Paul-like transformation before she considers reconciling with her husband or partner. Anything less is not a transformation from God. When God changes a heart, a former abuser will have these characteristics: (1) he confesses his wrongdoing for everyone to hear (note that Paul's letter to Timothy was intended to be passed around to the churches and became part of the Bible); (2) he gives all the credit to Jesus for saving him; (3) his actions are the polar opposite of his previous behavior; he goes from selfish and violent to loving and gentle; (4) his attitude is transformed from prideful and arrogant to humble and grateful, giving God all the honor and glory and credit; (5) he admits his prideful attitude of the past; (6) the fruit of the Spirit is abundant in his life; (7) change has come about because God imposed severe consequences; (8) the change is permanent, not a temporary shift to manipulate his spouse to return to the relationship; (9) he does not demand forgiveness or reconciliation; he recognizes it may be too late to save his marriage, and he wants the best for his former wife or partner; (10) he seeks to restore that which he has destroyed.

God's redemption will always put His people in a better place than before. If God has redeemed an abuser, the transformation will be abundantly clear to everyone—there will be no doubt whether his heart has changed for the better. He will be different, and all his relationships will be different. A woman hoping to reconcile with her husband or partner should insist on a God-initiated transformation for a significant period *before* returning to the relationship. Anything less—including promises to change—is only a tactic of manipulation to get her to return to abuse. The next story from Scripture explains why.

Reconciliation without God's Redemption is Disastrous

Many Christians so desperately desire to save a marriage that they will advise a woman to return to an abuser in the hope that he will change. They surmise he will reciprocate the grace she has extended to him. This approach is naïve and unbiblical at best, and is extremely dangerous for the woman. Unless God has transformed the abuser's heart, the abuse will escalate when she returns. The woman may return under the false assumption that since the abuser knows that she left due to his abuse, he will now be nicer to her. However, that assumption is misguided and naïve. In reality, the abuser will either be determined to punish her for leaving or will recognize that she left in spite of his prior abuses and will increase the abuse to ensure she won't leave again.

Judges 19 and 20 describe a horrific domestic abuser whose heart was never transformed. The husband, a Levite, one of God's handpicked priests, was so self-consumed that he allowed his concubine to be gang-raped and killed by an angry mob. Of all people, the Levite should have been most godly. As a concubine, the woman belonged to the man but did not have the rights of a wife. In this lopsided relationship, he was her husband, but she was only his sex slave. The concubine left the Levite and went back to her father's house. This was unusual for the time; we can only assume her husband was so abusive that she returned to her father's house for protection. Her only other option to support herself was prostitution. After four months, her husband came for her, "talked kindly" to her, ate and drank and yukked it up with his father-in-law, and convinced both the concubine and her dad that she should go back with him.

Instead of leaving in the morning when they could have traveled home safely in one day, the Levite insisted on leaving later in the day. They would have to find a place to stay overnight. The travelers spent the night in an unfamiliar village, in the house of a stranger who offered them shelter. The townspeople gathered around the house, demanding the Levite come out so they could rape him. Fearful for his life and unconcerned about his concubine, he gave her to the angry mob to be raped. Knowing the harm that would come to her, her husband put her in harm's way, clearing the way for the townspeople to inflict the actual harm. She was gang-raped all night, and then she dragged herself to the front doorstep of the house in which her husband was staying, and she died. When he opened the door in the morning and saw her on the front step, he had no remorse or guilt. In fact, he barked an order to her to get up and go, not realizing she was dead. Angry at his loss of property, but not distraught at the loss of life or remorseful for his actions, he threw her body over his donkey and didn't even give her the respect of a proper burial. Instead, he cut up his concubine into twelve pieces and sent the parts to the leaders of all the twelve tribes of Israel.

When the tribe leaders came together and asked him what had happened, he played the self-righteous victim, lied, and deceived the leaders. He took no responsibility for her rape and death, blaming the townspeople for his loss. He then incited a battle between the tribe of Benjamin and the rest of Israel, involving over 425,000 soldiers and causing over 65,000 casualties. The battle nearly exterminated the entire tribe of Benjamin. To make matters worse, since the women of the tribe of Benjamin had been killed in the war, the few male survivors from the tribe of Benjamin went to other territories and forcibly kidnapped virgins to be their wives. Like all abusers, he left pain and disaster in his wake. The ripple effects of his abuse had virtually no end.

The story of the Levite and his concubine is like the story of any abused woman who returns to her abuser when God has not transformed his heart. Like the Levite, the abuser is a liar and deceiver and is controlling. He blames others for the problems he creates, doesn't protect his wife or care about her, has no conscience, and plays the pity card and the self-righteous card when it suits him. He creates conflict (even when he is the one at fault), has no regard for the human cost of his selfish ambition, and wants to appear righteous in front of others, regardless of the cost. Many married women who have lived with domestic abuse often feel like a concubine, not a wife. They have no marital rights, are used only for the gratification of their husband, and are a wife in name only. When she leaves her husband, she often goes to a relative or close friend to escape the abuse. The abuser tracks her down, comes after her, and demands that she return to the marriage. But his heart has not changed. He has not suffered any consequences for his actions, save for a wayward wife who, in his mind, is easily replaceable anyway. He's not willing to change his ways, and he just wants her to come back so that things will go back to normal.

He will use whatever method is necessary to convince her and her family she should return. If he thinks he has a chance of getting her back, he will sweet-talk her with false apologies, professions of love, and claims to be better. But underneath he has no remorse or repentance. He will turn on the charm with her family and friends—he'll have a drink, engage in idle chitchat and laughter, then stay for dinner and tell them how much he loves his wife and wants her back. They will be charmed by this master deceiver and tell her things like, "He's such a nice guy. Why don't you give it a try again?" Or, "Look, he's here; he must really love you deep down. Give him another chance." Or, "He's so charming. He can't be that bad." Or, "Think about the kids. They need their dad."

The abused wife eventually caves under the pressure. *After all*, she thinks, *I really don't want a divorce, the kids miss their dad, he came all this way to get me back so he must love me, and maybe he will learn a lesson and change from all of this.*

She so wants to make the marriage work that she doesn't require him to repent before she returns. She doesn't demand that he make a public confession of wrongdoing, engage in serious individual counseling, or have a significant period of separation to see if he has actually changed his attitude and actions. Instead, she returns to the relationship and hopes that this time he really has changed.

Unfortunately, because there have been no consequences, no repentance, and no transformation on the abuser's part, after a short period of good behavior, the abuse returns even worse than before. When he doesn't get his way or adversity hits (and it always does), his true colors will be shown. In fact, he only cares for himself, and he will do whatever it takes to protect himself. *Besides*, he thinks, *she's the one at fault—she left. She deserves to be punished. I need to teach her a lesson so she never leaves again.* He will either inflict the abuse himself or intentionally put her in harm's way so that others can inflict the abuse. When she is harmed and leaves him, either by death or by divorce, the abuser lies, blames her and others for the problems he created, and accepts no responsibility. If she dies, he plays the victim and claims that others or an accident are at fault. If she divorces him, he plays the victim as the poor abandoned husband, blames her for leaving him, and falsely accuses her of everything from affairs to mental illness in order to deflect his responsibility. He will create conflict, especially among their churchgoing acquaintances, pitting them against each other and her.

A woman who returns to an abuser who has not repented will eventually die an emotional and spiritual death, and perhaps even a physical death, due to continued and escalated abuse. We were never designed to exist in toxic relationships. All relationships with a SNAP end badly—very badly. They leave a wake of pain and broken lives. Once a woman leaves a relationship, without the transforming work of God in the abuser, it is of monumental importance to not return.

Chapter 32

The Armor of God You Will Need for the Fight

No one relishes a fight, especially with someone in their family with the will and means to hurt them. That is one reason women stay in abusive marriages far longer than they should.

There is a weapon for every fight. You don't bring a knife to a gun fight, and you don't fight a spiritual battle with weapons for a physical war. Paul's letter to the Ephesians defines the weapons for the spiritual and emotional battles a woman confronts when leaving an abusive relationship.

Spiritual Armor

> Finally, be strong in the Lord and in his mighty power. Put on the full armor of God, so that you can take your stand against the devil's schemes. For our struggle is not against flesh and blood, but against the rulers, against the authorities, against the powers of this dark world and against the spiritual forces of evil in the heavenly realms. Therefore put on the full armor of God, so that when the day of evil comes, you may be able to stand your ground, and after you have done everything, to stand. Stand firm then, with the belt of truth buckled around your waist, with the breastplate of righteousness in place, and with your feet fitted with the readiness that comes from the gospel of peace. In addition to all this, take up the shield of faith, with which you can extinguish all the flaming arrows of the evil one. Take the helmet of salvation and the sword of the Spirit, which is the word of God. (Ephesians 6:10–17)

Spiritual Tactical Maneuvers

> And pray in the Spirit on all occasions with all kinds of prayers and requests. With this in mind, be alert and always keep on praying for all the Lord's people. Pray also for me, that whenever I speak, words may be given me so that I will fearlessly make known the mystery of the gospel, for which I am an ambassador in chains. Pray that I may declare it fearlessly, as I should. (Ephesians 6:18–20)

The Spiritual Battle

Paul reminds us that the devil and his demons are at work, plotting and scheming, making this a spiritual battle. We tend to think our fight is with the abuser, but behind the abuser is Satan, who, unbeknown to the abuser, is using the abuser to get to God's daughter. Paul says the day of evil *will* come. He admonishes us to put on the armor of God so that *when,* not *if,* the day of evil comes, we can stand. None of God's people are immune from Satan's plots. He doesn't encourage us to go looking for it. No, the fight will come to us. That's how Satan works. But when we put on God's armor, we will still be standing when the fight is over.

Paul also reminds us we are God's children, daughters of the King of Kings and Lord of Lords, the Maker of the Universe, the Creator, and the Almighty One with infinite power. Therefore, we have infinite power because God lives in us. He encourages us to be strong in the Lord and His mighty power. Satan is no match for God, and women leaving an abuser must remind themselves that God is on their side. Because He is, they can be bold in the battle.

In World War II, the world was engaged in a battle against an evil, narcissistic, sociopathic despot who had taken over Germany and was intent on taking over the world. America entered the war because it was a war the world could not afford to lose—a war against evil in every sense of the word. School teachers, farmers, factory workers, bank tellers, and gentle, peace-loving men from all walks of life left their families, joined the armed forces, and learned to shoot a gun to stop the onslaught of the Nazis. They did not want to fight, but they fought anyway because losing that war was not an option. The consequences of losing to the Nazis were, even to this day, unfathomable. These peaceable men-turned-soldiers were scared to fight, but they fought anyway—and that is the very definition of bravery. When the war was over, the soldiers and marines, pilots and sailors took off their uniforms and went back to their schools and farms, factories and banks, and peaceful, gentle former lives. They were never the same, and most of them tried to never talk about the war. The memories were too traumatic and painful. But they fought when they had to so they had a life to come back to.

In much the same way, a gentle woman of faith must gear up for the war of leaving an abuser because it is a war against evil that she cannot lose. The only differences between Hitler and the average domestic abuser are the resources at his disposal and his degree of influence and power. She must fight for herself and her children. She must fight through her fear. And when the battle is over and she is still standing, she can go back to her gentle, peaceful life. But for a time, she must be a warrior.

The Belt of Truth

The belt of truth is the first weapon she must don. A woman leaving an abusive spouse must be truthful in the face of the lies he is sure to spread. But even more importantly, she must identify and break agreement with Satan's lies and replace them with and rely on God's truth. We discuss this process in greater detail in chapters 41–44. Satan has saturated our culture with lies that are the opposite of God's truth. Men, women, and children suffer from believing his lies. Healing, strength, and power can only come when a woman's perspective is aligned with God's. What comes to her mind when a woman thinks about God is the most important thing about her.[131] The author of Romans tells us to "be transformed by the renewing of your mind" (Romans 12:2). The renewed mind thinks like God. She must have the mind of God.

For example, Satan (through her abuser) has told her she is nothing without her husband and that she won't be able to survive without him. He convinced her that she is unlovable and worthless, and that there is nothing about her that anyone would love. A woman who believes this is defeated and hopeless, and her spirit is near death. She accepts abuse and whatever crumbs her abuser gives her, but God's truth says she is a beloved daughter

---

[131] A. W. Tozer, "What comes into our minds when we think about God is the most important thing about us," https://www.goodreads.com/author/quotes/1082290.A_W_Tozer.

of the King of Kings, that she is wondrously and wonderfully made in His image, that God is always with her giving her power and strength, that she is capable, and that there are a million good things in her that good, godly people will recognize and affirm and love. When a woman believes this truth, she is calm and confident, resting in the peace that her Papa God loves her and wants nothing but the best for her. She holds herself like royalty, standing tall, regal, and strong as the daughter of the King. When others insult her, she does not let it deter her, knowing that her identity does not depend on the opinion of others, but on the fact that she is a princess and has access to the infinite resources and love of her Father, the King. She expects nothing less than love, respect, and excellence from herself and those around her.

The Breastplate of Righteousness.

Breastplates of old were designed to protect the heart and vital organs. The bulletproof flak jacket is the modern-day equivalent. Being righteous in the face of evil protects not only our hearts, but our entirety, from becoming as evil as those we fight.

We all must give an accounting for our words, deeds, and attitudes. The unrighteous will eventually reap the consequences of their decisions, and Satan will be laughing with delight as more are added to his lair of eternal damnation. One of the best ways to combat Satan is to simply refuse to stoop to his level and the level of his lackeys. Doing the right thing confounds Satan and confuses the abuser.

Abusers bait their victims. They cheat, lie, and do nasty things to get a rise out of them. It's a game for them. When the victim takes the bait and explodes at his bad behavior, even retaliating with the same bad behavior, the abuser will say, "See, I told you she was crazy!" Of course, the others around will not know the baiting that led up to it. They only see the explosion. But the woman who remains calm, who doesn't fall for the bait, and who simply goes on consistently being righteous will prevail. It doesn't mean that she shouldn't protect herself from the abuser's schemes. If he is lying to the court, hiding assets, and falsifying his income to avoid his responsibilities, she must protect herself, get to the truth, and enforce the law. Likewise, she needs to protect herself and her children from physical abuse. She is right to remove herself immediately, report him to law enforcement, and get an order of protection, but she should not engage in the same malicious schemes he does.

Satan loves when he can get a child of God to wrestle in the muck of sin and unrighteousness with one of his underlings. When both people are controlled by Satan, no one can tell the difference between the good guy and the bad guy. The author of Romans tells us, "Do not repay anyone evil for evil. Be careful to do what is right in the eyes of everyone. . . . Do not take revenge, my dear friends, but leave room for God's wrath, for it is written: 'It is mine to avenge; I will repay,' says the Lord" (Romans 12:17, 19). Wearing the breastplate of righteousness will protect the victim's heart from being dragged into the wickedness of the abuser.

Feet Fitted with the Readiness of the Gospel of Peace

This weapon is a mouthful. Let's unpack it as it relates to a victim of domestic abuse.

First, we should be ready to move when God calls us into action, and we should do so resting in the peace that God has a plan. For a woman living in domestic abuse, timing is important. She may have many reasons for staying in the relationship longer than she would like—lack of finances, a special-needs child, an aging parent, lack of a job, threats from her abuser, etc. However, during the relationship, she can be planning her departure, so that when the time is right she will be willing and able to follow God's calling from abuse to freedom. Planning may include squirreling money away so she and her children can live, pursuing education, gaining full employment, obtaining services for her special-needs child, putting together a safety plan, and a host of other things. But when God reveals the optimum moment, she must act.

Throughout history, God has worked collaboratively with His people to bring about change. He called Abram (whose name was later changed to Abraham) out of his homeland and told him to go on a long journey to Canaan. God promised to be with him and to make his descendants into God's people, as numerous as the stars. But to gain the promise—to work with God—Abraham had to act. He had to leave his comfortable home, journey for an uncertain duration to a foreign land, and start life anew. If only it were that easy for the woman escaping domestic abuse. At least Abraham didn't have someone trying to destroy him. The victim's journey is more like Moses's. God called him to bring Abraham's numerous descendants out of bondage from a narcissistic sociopath who tried to destroy them as they were attempting to leave, and told him to go on a long journey to Canaan. God promised to be with him and to fight the inhabitants of Canaan, who also tried to destroy them as they came. But to gain the promise of the amazing rescue and the promised land, Moses, too, had to act. He had to leave his comfortable life of a shepherd and confront a crazy man who made his life even worse. He had to lead an unwilling and grumbling people out of freedom and fight the giants in the new land before starting life anew.

When God calls us to action, he gives us a huge promise. He promises that He Himself will be with us and will guide us along the way. Sometimes we feel that we are not fully equipped to fulfill His calling. God doesn't always call the equipped, but He always equips those He calls. Therefore, we must listen to His voice, take time to know Him intimately, and obey so we can hear where He is guiding us and how we should get there.

When God calls a woman to leave abuse, He promises that He Himself will be with her and guide her along the way. Like Moses and Abraham, she must spend time with God, hearing His voice and knowing His ways. He will equip her for the journey and the fight, but she must act. This is a partnership with Almighty God. She must expectantly watch and see the amazing ways that God will go before her as she steps out in faith.

Second, God calls us to a gospel of peace. The author of Romans exhorts us, "If it is possible, as far as it depends on you, live at peace with everyone" (Romans 12:18). It is not possible for abusers to live at peace; they are constantly starting unpeaceful and ungodly conflicts. However, a woman of God should not create conflicts or engage in the conflicts he starts. There is simply no winning with toxic people. It is best to have no contact with them, or if she must have contact because of their children, to avoid controversial subjects. If they share children (and she does not have an order of protection or restraining order that limits communication), communication should be limited strictly to matters concerning the children. Rehashing old conflicts or trying to convince the abuser that he is abusive serves no purpose, as the abuser will never admit that he may be wrong or that there may be a different way to do things. If she must engage in small talk, it should be kept to benign things like the weather and sports. Living at peace with an abuser in one's life is exceedingly difficult. It will be up to her to keep the peace.

God wants us to live in peace, if possible. God is the author of peace. Making peace is a divine endeavor. Jesus Himself says, "Blessed are the peacemakers, for they shall be called children of God" (Matthew 5:9). If peace can be achieved, a family shall be blessed indeed.

Third, God wants our hearts to be at peace because we rest in Him and in the knowledge that He will carry us through. Being at peace is a strategic weapon in the warfare against the Enemy. The Enemy wants a woman to be anxious and so emotionally unstable that she is unable to serve the Lord, raise her children, or concentrate at work. Satan is quite successful, in that nearly 80 percent of abused women have suffered severe negative consequences at work,[132] including being fired. However, a woman at peace knows that God fights for her and she will be victorious. In this way, she stops Satan in his tracks.

The Shield of Faith

Enemy arrows, properly aimed, kill. Before modern warfare, flaming arrows were even more damaging. Dipped in pitch and set on fire, flaming arrows wreaked maximum destruction, burning houses, ships, and entire villages. Some were designed with hollow bolts and filled with a mixture of sulfur, resin, tar, and hemp soaked in oil. Just like the physical arrows, Satan's flaming arrows can turn a life into a blazing conflagration of devastation. Paul told us to use our shields of faith to fight Satan's flaming arrows and prevent mass destruction.

The Roman shield was a defensive weapon approximately two feet wide and four feet tall. It could protect a soldier from the deadly arrows of the enemy. Likewise, a woman's faith in God—her certainty of what she knows to be true about her Lord and Savior (Hebrews 11:1)—will protect her from the ruin that Satan and her abuser have planned for her.

An abuser delights in scheming to destroy any partner that leaves him (Psalm 38:12). He digs a pit for her to fall into, and he draws an arrow aimed at her heart and anything that is dear to her. But, as Proverbs points out, the wicked are ensnared by their own traps, while good people run the other way, glad to escape (Proverbs 29:6). David must have felt much like a woman escaping abuse: even though he was a man after God's own heart and had done nothing to harm Saul, Saul turned on him and hunted him down. While running from the wicked people who tried to kill him, David prayed they would fall into the traps they had set for him (Psalm 141:10). David's prayers were answered, and Saul eventually was injured in battle and took his own life. David's prayers in Psalm 140 and 141 that God would protect him, avenge him, and that the wicked would fall into their own traps are also appropriate prayers for a woman running from her abuser.

Helmet of Salvation

Another of Satan's tactics to demoralize and discourage a woman stuck in abuse is whispering words of doubt and deceit: *You're not good enough. You can't stand up to your abuser. He will destroy you; you're not strong enough. You can't do this. No one will love you; everyone hates you. God isn't going to fight for you. Your future will be nothing without him. You aren't smart enough to go back to school; you will be a homeless bag lady. You'd better go back to him.* A helmet protects one's head and mind from the enemy's attacks, and God's helmet of salvation protects His daughter from Satan's attacks on her mind.

With salvation comes the knowledge of Jesus as Lord. She may have walked with Jesus for a very long time, but when she goes through the battle of leaving an abuser, a woman will also know Him as her:

- Savior: the one who not only saves her soul, but also saves her from her enemy (Psalm 18:2; Luke 1:47)
- Rescuer: the one who rescues her from the enemy's evil plots (Isaiah 43:1–7)
- Jehovah Jirah: "the Lord will provide," even in difficult circumstances (Genesis 22:14)
- Yahweh Nissi: "the Lord is My Banner," He is her protection, leadership, and deliverance (Exodus 17:15)
- Shelter: she can go to Him to escape the attacks of the enemy (Psalm 46:1–6)

---

[132] *How Does Domestic Violence Impact People at Work?* (Canadian Labour Congress, October 22, 2019), at https://canadianlabour.ca/uncategorized/how-does-domestic-violence-impact-people-work/.

The Armor of God You Will Need for the Fight

- Stronghold: He gives her strength to withstand the devil's schemes (Psalm 6:1–6)
- Fortress: He is a safe fortification in times of trouble (Psalm 91:2)
- Refuge: a quiet sanctuary of rest in a time of strife and upheaval (Psalm 91:2)
- Deliverer: He will take her out of bondage into a safe place (Psalm 18:2; Psalm 116)
- Strength: He gives strength in battle and upholds her with His hand (Nehemiah 8:10; Isaiah 41:10; Psalm 28:7–8)

Armed with this knowledge, she can take the thoughts that the Enemy puts in her mind, extinguish them, and replace them with the truth of God. Paul tells us to do this in his letter to the church in Corinth when he states, "We demolish arguments and every pretension that sets itself up against the knowledge of God, and we take captive every thought to make it obedient to Christ" (2 Corinthians 10:5). How does she do this? By knowing the Word of God—the sword of the Spirit—and speaking truth out loud over her life and into those around her.

The Sword of the Spirit—the Word of God

The only offensive weapon in the arsenal for a spiritual battle is the sword of the Spirit, which is God's Word, the Bible. Like any warrior going into battle, the person using this weapon must know his weapon inside and out and know how to use it. It would do no good for a warrior to go into battle not knowing the intricacies and inner workings of his gun. In fact, soldiers in battle know their guns so well that they can take them apart, clean them, and put them back together in the dark—while they are blindfolded, and they can do it in a matter of seconds. They spend countless hours at the gun range doing drills and target practice so that when the real conflict comes, their instincts and training take over. There is no time for wondering how their weapon works in the heat of battle.

God's Word Is Her Weapon

Just as a warrior must know his weapon, a woman of God must know her Bible. She must know the context and proper application of a text so that when the conflict comes and Satan tries to deceive or attack her, she knows exactly what God has to say about the matter. For example, when her abuser is telling her she is worthless, she knows that God loved her so much that He sent His Son for her (John 3:16). When her abuser twists the Scripture and demands that she submit to him by doing everything that he selfishly wants, she knows that God calls both husbands and wives to defer to and support each other out of their love for Christ as an act of giving and love. God's Word does not allow the husband to demand submission for his every whim, but requires him to support and love his wife to the point of laying down his life for her (Ephesians 5:21–33). When her abuser demands that she "forgive and forget" his many abuses for which he is unrepentant, she knows that Scripture requires true repentance for reconciliation (Luke 17:3–4). When her abuser twists Psalm 103:12 and claims that God has separated his sins from him "as far as the east is from the west" and demands forgiveness and that she return to the abusive relationship, she knows that God mandates repentance for His forgiveness and that even sins that God has forgiven have lasting and severe consequences (2 Samuel 12:1–14). When her abuser tells her she is a second-class citizen and must keep herself covered and not talk or be a leader in church, she knows her abuser is taking 1 Corinthians 14 out of context and that Paul was addressing a particular problem in the first-century church in Corinth concerning a lack of order in their worship services. She also knows numerous godly women are mentioned in the Bible who had positions of leadership, including Deborah, Miriam, Huldah, Noadiah, Isaiah's wife, Esther, Anna, Tabitha, Junia, Phoebe, and Priscilla.

Studying her Bible as a domestic abuse survivor will open her eyes to a whole new way of appreciating biblical guidance in this area and in seeing God's love and respect for women, especially those who have suffered abuse at the hands of men.

Biblical Examples of Abusive Narcissists, Sociopaths, and Psychopaths

A woman who has seen domestic abuse firsthand will recognize the abuser tactics in the ancient abusers, as the tactics are as old as time itself. It will help her see evil for what it is in the abuser in her own life.

Pharaoh escalated his cruelty to the Israelites when Moses tried to rescue them from bondage, and even pursued them after he had let them go free, only to see God part the Red Sea for the Israelites and let the Egyptians drown. Pharaoh demonstrates the tactic that all abusers use—escalating abuse when a victim attempts to leave.

King Saul turned on David, who was best friends with his son Jonathon, and hunted down David, even though David had done nothing but support his king. Saul demonstrates the abuser's tactic of rage and vindictiveness, even to those who have done no wrong. King Ahab and his wife, Queen Jezebel, killed God's priests, worshiped Baal, and even killed a neighbor to get his land when he refused to sell it to them. Athaliah, the daughter of King Ahab and Queen Jezebel, killed her own grandchildren and took over the throne herself. When one grandchild escaped her mass murder and was crowned the next king, she accused the people who saved him of treason, demonstrating the abuser's tactic of projection (2 Kings 11). These sociopaths demonstrate the murderous lengths to which abusers will go to get their way at the expense of others.

Babylonian King Nebuchadnezzar was arrogant and boastful. He invaded Israel, made people worship him, and threw Shadrach, Meshach, and Abednego into the fire when they refused to worship him. His boasting and demands to be worshiped are abusive tactics of narcissists.

The Levite described in Judges 19 and 20 who gave his concubine to be gang-raped and killed by an angry mob, just after he had convinced her to return to him, is another cautionary tale of the escalating abuse that happens to a woman who returns to an abuser whose heart has not been changed by God. (See chapter 31 for more details.) Any woman who has gone back to her abuser after he sweet-talked her and her family into returning, and then escalated the abuse, will relate to this story. Anyone who has experienced her abuser lying and blaming others for the harm he caused and stirring up division and dissension among people will also relate.

King David's son Amnon burned with lust for his half sister Tamar. He pretended to be sick, called for her to take care of him, manipulated a way to be alone with her, and then raped her. As soon as he was done, his heart turned against her and he hated her. He then discarded her without any emotions and no consideration of how he had defiled her and ruined her life. He simply sent her away and wanted nothing to do with her. When she told him that he should marry her, according to Jewish law, he refused (2 Samuel 13). A woman who has been raped or coerced into sleeping with or marrying her boyfriend, only to have him turn on her once he was sexually satisfied and discard her like yesterday's newspaper, will relate to Tamar. The cycle of abuse was present even 3,000 years ago.

Women who see themselves in the pages of the Bible can see that God is just as displeased with abusers now as He was then. Simply knowing this is a step in the healing process.

God Honors Women Who Honor Him

A woman looking at the Bible through the eyes of domestic abuse will see that God honored a handful of women who might, at first glance, appear to have a sullied reputation. But from God's perspective, they worshiped and obeyed Him and became an important part of His family. The victim of domestic abuse usually feels embarrassed and marginalized. She should be encouraged to know that God does indeed have a place for her in His family—and in the front row. For example, in Matthew's genealogy of Jesus, God doesn't mention the "good girls" who are in the direct lineage of Jesus, yet He points out those who were looked at askance and gives them special recognition for raising godly children, even after enduring abuse or being discarded by society.

The first woman mentioned is Tamar. Tamar had married Judah's son Er, but he was so wicked that God struck him down. According to law, Tamar was responsible for carrying on the family line. Because she and the firstborn son had no child together, Tamar was required to marry his younger brother Onan, the "kinsman-redeemer," and Onan was required to bring up the firstborn child as his brother's son to carry on the family line (Deuteronomy 25:5–10). Onan, as the closest kinsman, was required to redeem the family line. But Tamar and Onan also had no children, and God struck down Onan, too, because he was also wicked. According to law, Tamar was then required to marry Judah's third son, Shelah, the next-in-line kinsman-redeemer. Judah promised Tamar that Shelah would marry her, but then Judah reneged on his promise and would not give him to her in marriage. Because of Judah's deceitfulness, Tamar was forced to live as a widow in her father's house, with no hope of a husband to provide for her. She was forbidden to remarry outside the family because she had the duty to carry on the family line, yet she was not given a husband promised by her father-in-law. She was financially abused and socially ostracized. So Tamar took matters into her own hands. Disguised as a prostitute, she approached the remaining kinsman-redeemer—Judah himself. She became pregnant by Judah, who, although originally ready to kill her for being guilty of prostitution, recognized that she was more righteous than he was because he had refused to give her a husband, and she had fulfilled her duty of carrying on the family line through him. Judah raised the children, but never slept with Tamar again. We can only assume that she led a lonely life without ever knowing the love of a good husband (Genesis 38). However, God honored her for her faithfulness and willingness to follow Him. She was renowned, as she is even mentioned in a blessing on Ruth (Ruth 4:11–12).

The second woman mentioned in the genealogy of Jesus is Rahab, the prostitute who lived in Jericho and saved the lives of the Israelite spies when they came to spy on Jericho. In exchange for hiding the spies from the king of Jericho, she asked them to protect her and her family. One can only imagine her life. Perhaps she was forced into prostitution because a man had rejected her. Perhaps she had been engaged to be married, but he had left her at the altar or had taken her virginity so that no one else wanted her. But Rahab had heard of the Lord's miracles—the escape from Egypt, the parting of the Red Sea, and Israel's victory in battle. She knew this God of the Israelites was the true God, not the silly wooden and metal idols they had in Jericho. She wanted the God of Israel to be her God and to be part of God's people (Joshua 2). She was not born a Jew, but she claimed the God of Israel as her own. After the Israelites took Jericho, they rescued Rahab and her family, who came to live with them. Rahab married Salmon, and they raised a kind and generous son named Boaz. Rahab's faith was so extraordinary that she is also included in Hebrews 11 among the great men and women of faith. People saw a prostitute, but God saw a strong woman of faith who recognized Him as the one true God, loved her family, took risks to save God's people, and would be a fine great-great-grandmother to the future King David.

The third woman mentioned in Christ's genealogy is Ruth, the wife of Boaz, Rahab's son. An entire book is written about her. Ruth was from Moab, and the Jews were forbidden to marry Moabites. Yet she was married to the son of Naomi and Elimelech. Her husband, his brother, and her father-in-law all died, leaving all their wives as widows with no way to support themselves. Naomi urged her to go back to her own family and remarry, but Ruth had seen the God of Israel through her mother-in-law. Like Rahab, she was not born a Jew, but she wanted Jehovah as her God too. Ruth refused to leave her mother-in-law and adopted Naomi's God as her own and Naomi's people as her own. They both moved back to Israel, so poor that they had to beg for food. But Boaz, her kinsman-redeemer, was kind to her, married her, bought the family farm, and supported both her and Naomi. Boaz was likely taught by his mother, Rahab, a former prostitute, the importance of kindness and to look past the exterior of a woman to see into her heart. Most people saw only a poor, foreign widow, but God saw a strong woman who loved Him and His people and her mother-in-law so much that she would not leave her.

The fourth woman distinguished in the genealogy of Jesus is Bathsheba, wife of King David and mother to King Solomon. Much has been written and preached about David's relationship with Bathsheba, a woman married to one of David's most loyal and accomplished military leaders. King David was in a position of absolute power, and he used that power for his own selfish gratification, with complete disregard for Bathsheba, Uriah her husband, his other wives, and the consequences of his sin. David demanded that Bathsheba be brought to him, and he raped her. She had no choice in the matter. When she told him that she was pregnant with his child, David tried to cover it up to avoid the embarrassment and punishment for his crime (death by stoning) by arranging for Bathsheba to sleep with Uriah so that it would look like the child was her husband's. When that didn't work, he put out a hit on Uriah, immediately took Bathsheba as his wife, and took the term "cover-up" to a whole new level. Of course, Bathsheba was silenced in the whole affair. How could she possibly accuse the king of such heinous behavior? The prophet Nathan, ahead of his time for the #MeToo movement, correctly called out David on his sexually abusive behavior and murder, prophesying that the baby that he and Bathsheba conceived would die. Poor Bathsheba was raped and impregnated by a power-hungry king, lost her beloved and noble husband to murder, was forced to marry the murderer of her husband, lost the baby, was added to David's harem, and was forever wrongfully blamed for the scandal that was brought on the house of David. God saw her plight, and although He did not bring her husband or baby back to life, He blessed her with a son, Solomon, who became the wisest and wealthiest man in the world.

And finally, Mary was honored as the mother of Jesus. Mary was a poor, unwed teenager when the angel Gabriel announced that she would become pregnant by the Holy Spirit and would carry the Son of God. She was engaged to be married, but the whole "pregnant by the Holy Spirit" story that she told her soon-to-be husband and family was so farfetched that they didn't believe her. And who could blame them? Of course, Joseph finally came around and married her due to a vision he received from God, but others didn't believe her crazy tale—she was forever the object of scorn and scandal. Jesus was revered throughout Israel as a great teacher, but rejected by those in His own hometown who knew His scandalous family history. "Isn't this the carpenter's son? Isn't his mother's name Mary?" they snickered behind His back (Matthew 13:55). Others saw a promiscuous poverty-ridden teenager who got knocked up, but at least had the good luck of a decent guy taking pity on her and marrying her. But God saw a young woman who had a pure heart, who walked with Him, who on faith agreed to take on the task He entrusted to her, and who was the only woman in the world worthy of the enormous job of being the mother of Jesus.

Abused women often feel they have no future. They feel they have already messed up their lives beyond hope. We can see from these honored women of the Bible, and from stories throughout the Bible, that God is very good at working with plan B because so often we have already screwed up plan A. He has plans to bless us, no matter how far beyond redemption a woman thinks she is.

Spiritual Weapons Directly against Satan

Domestic abuse is the Enemy's intentional attack on women delivered through an abuser. Women facing this attack from Satan must be fully armed with the weapons God has supplied in Scripture.

Fleeing from Evil

The first weapon against the Enemy is to get out from under the abuse. A woman in domestic abuse is in a battle with evil. Her abuser is controlled by the Enemy as surely as those belonging to Christ are filled with the Holy Spirit. The first thing she must do for her safety and sanity, and those of her children, is to remove herself from the abuser. The Word of God instructs us to do this. Numerous passages exhort God's followers to stay away from or flee from evil and evil people, including Psalm 37:27; Proverbs 1:15, 4:15; Romans 16:17; 1 Corinthians 5:11–13; 1 Timothy 6:20; 2 Timothy 3:1–5; Titus 3:9–10; and 1 Thessalonians 5:22. Paul asks, "What do righteousness and wickedness have in common? Or what fellowship can light have with darkness?" (2 Corinthians 6:14).

Jesus foretold of the evil that would come to His followers, telling us, "When you are persecuted in one place, flee to another" (Matthew 10:23). The Lord's Prayer asks God to "deliver us from evil" (Matthew 6:13 KJV). This requires a woman to break agreement with the Enemy who wants her to stay in abuse, and execute an escape plan to get out, trusting that God will deliver her. Yes, God can and will deliver us from evil, but it requires our participation, obedience, and willingness to act. In every instance where God delivered His people, believers had to obey God's call to action—whether it was Abraham, Moses, Joshua, Caleb, Gideon, Deborah, Jael, David, Elijah, Elisha, Isaiah, Paul, Peter, or Jesus Himself. We are called to take action to remove ourselves from evil.

Rebuke and Ejection

Another direct weapon against Satan is rebuking him and casting him and his demons out. Jesus has authority over everything, including Satan and his demons (Matthew 28:18), and He has given us His authority over Satan and his demons, the powers of darkness (Luke 10:19). Satan and his demons simply must obey when we use the authority of Jesus's name. Jesus states, "And these signs will accompany those who believe: In my name they will drive out demons" (Mark 16:17). Jesus sent out the twelve disciples and gave them authority to preach and cast out demons (Mark 3:14–15). He also gave authority to the seventy-two followers to cast out demons and "overcome all the power of the enemy" (Luke 10:17–19). When the seventy-two came back and reported that even demons submitted to them in Jesus's name, Jesus responded that when they did so, He "saw Satan fall like lightning from heaven." In other words, Jesus and His soldiers had defeated Satan and his demons. Jesus sends us out with the same mission.

Even after a woman has physically removed herself from evil, enemy attacks come upon women in domestic abuse in the form of anxiety, depression, rejection, fear, and timidity. She feels overwhelmed with uncertainty, hopelessness, worry, nervousness, and sadness. Her heart is burdened with feelings of unworthiness, anger, agitation, and lack of patience. Physically, she experiences nightmares, stomach aches, tightness around her neck, headaches, insomnia, tightness in her chest, heart issues, and digestive tract issues. These are also the symptoms of post-traumatic stress as a result of trauma. These negative responses are not from God. They are not merely biological and emotional responses. They are from the Enemy. How do we know this? We know God is the giver of all *good* gifts (James 1:17). We know the Enemy's mission statement is to steal, kill, and destroy (John 10:10), but Christ came to destroy the works of the devil (1 John 3:8) and to give us abundant life (John 10:10).

When these Enemy attacks occur, either directly to a woman or to someone she loves, a woman whose faith is in Christ can meet them head on. Rather than simply praying to God and asking God to work, she must address the Enemy and, under the authority of the name of Jesus, rebuke him and cast him out. For example, she can and should state, "Satan, I rebuke you in the name of Jesus Christ. Under the authority of Jesus, I command you and your demons to leave and never come back. I break agreement with the spirits of [fear/anxiety/depression/despair/etc.] and command these spirits to leave and never come back. I am a child of the Almighty God, Yahweh, the King of Kings and Lord of Lords, and you have no authority here. In the name of Jesus, I rebuke you and your demons and cast you out of this mind, out of this body, and out of this house." This woman or whoever is being prayed over will immediately feel a lifting of the evil spirits that have been tormenting her.

> Dirk: After two years in black ops that ended with an injury on a combat mission, followed by many years married to an abuser, I had nightmares every night for nearly thirty years. There was no way I could stop them. I hated to fall asleep at night because I knew the nightmares of combat would return. When I married my current wife (after two abusive marriages), as a godly woman full of the Holy Spirit, she recognized them as attacks from the Enemy. When I slept one night, she prayed over me, rebuked Satan and his demons, and commanded them to leave. I have not had a nightmare since. Praise God!
>
> After a men's retreat in which I felt the Holy Spirit moving in a powerful way, the next day the Enemy was on the attack. I felt anxious, nervous, upset, and completely out of sorts. I didn't realize that Satan often attacks right after we have an encounter with God to keep us from fulfilling our calling. My wife recognized it and again prayed for me. She rebuked Satan and his demons, broke agreement with the spirits of anxiety, nervousness, and all the other crazy things I was feeling, and cast them out of me and our home. I immediately felt a lifting of all the heaviness on me. What a relief!

Praise and Worship in Music

Praise and worship music opens a portal to the heavenlies to usher in the Spirit of God and His heavenly hosts. This beautiful gift of God lifts our spirits and moves our hearts like nothing else. Satan hates when we praise and worship God in song. He especially hates it when we praise and worship God in the middle of a crisis that Satan has brought about to destroy us. It's like Satan is allergic to our songs and thanksgiving and flees to avoid it.

Martin Luther put it this way: "Music is a fair and lovely gift of God which has often wakened and moved me to the joy of preaching. . . . Music drives away the Devil and makes people gay. . . . Next to the Word of God, only music deserves to be extolled as the mistress and governess of the feelings of the human heart. We know that, to the devils, music is distasteful and insufferable. My heart bubbles up and overflows in response to music, which has so often refreshed me and delivered me from dire plagues."[133]

Eighteenth century English theologian William Law also encourages us to sing:

---

[133] Roland H. Bainton, *Here I Stand: A Life of Martin Luther* (Nashville, TN: Abingdon Press, 2013), 352.

> Just as singing is a natural effect of joy in the heart, so it has also a natural power of rendering the heart joyful. . . . There is nothing that so clears a way for your prayers, nothing that so disperses dullness of heart, nothing that so purifies the soul from poor and little passions, nothing that so opens heaven, or carries your heart so near it, as these songs of praise. They create a sense and delight in God, they awaken holy desires, they teach you how to ask, and they prevail with God to give. They kindle a holy flame, they turn your heart into an altar, your prayers into incense, and carry them as a sweet-smelling savor to the throne of grace.[134]

Praise and worship is such a strong weapon that the Bible recounts stories where the only weapon used to defeat the enemy was the praise and worship of God in song. When Joshua overtook Jericho, he did so not with bows and arrows, but with shouts and trumpet blasts. And the walls of this fortress city crashed to the ground (Joshua 6). When King Jehoshaphat was being attacked, the Holy Spirit came upon Jahaziel with a message to the Israelites: "Don't be afraid or discouraged by this great army because the battle isn't yours. It belongs to God! . . . You don't need to fight this battle. Just take your places, stand ready, and watch how the LORD, who is with you, will deliver you" (2 Chronicles 20:15, 17 CEB). Then King Jehoshaphat worshiped God, and Israel's choir praised the Lord with music. The next day King Jehoshaphat put the choir and musicians *in front* of the soldiers as they marched to battle. Now that's faith! They broke into praise, singing, "Give thanks to the LORD because his faithful love lasts forever!" and God launched a surprise attack on their enemies and defeated them. We sing the same powerful song even to this day in our modern praise and worship music.

Paul and Silas knew the strength of singing as a weapon of warfare when they spent their time in the Philippian prison singing and praying while other prisoners listened (Acts 16). As they sang, God sent an earthquake, the doors of the prison flung open, and the fetters holding them in chains were unfastened.

When God fights our enemies, He does so to the sound of holy music. Isaiah predicted that the fall of Assyria would be by God's own mighty hand, attended by His battle song: "And every crack that is made in the foundation wall, which the Lord will bring down upon him, will be accompanied by timbrels and lyres. The LORD will raise his arm and fight against Assyria in battle" (Isaiah 30:32 CEB).

The more we sing praises and the more we worship, the more the heavens are opened, the more God's Spirit surrounds us, the more our hearts are lifted, and the farther away the Enemy flees. Just try feeling oppressed when you are in church, surrounded by hundreds of other worshipers, singing your heart out to our Almighty God and enveloped by the Holy Spirit. It's nearly impossible. When the Enemy attacks, singing out loud (not just silently) to Christian music—especially praise and worship music—is a strong way to neutralize him.

Calling Angel Armies

God has given us His heavenly angels to fight our battles against evil forces. We might not see them, but they are fighting with us and for us. A woman combating domestic abuse fights Satan and his demons by asking the Lord of Hosts to send His angel armies to fight for her and protect her.

The author of Hebrews describes angels as "ministering spirits sent to serve those who will inherit salvation" (Hebrews 1:14). The mighty archangel Michael is the commander of God's angel armies against the forces of Satan. The Bible states that Michael argued with the devil and rebuked him (Jude 1:9), fought the leader of the Persian kingdom (Satan) during the time of Daniel (Daniel 10:12–13), serves as the guardian and protector of God's people (Daniel 12:1), and will defeat Satan in the final battle (Revelation 12:7–9).

---

[134] William Law, *A Serious Call to a Devout and Holy Life* (Alachua, FL: Bridge-Logos, 2008), 183–200.

Few of us have the gift of seeing into the spirit realm where the battles between God's angels and Satan's demons take place. However, Elisha had this amazing gift and it brought him courage, strength, and peace knowing that those who were on his side were greater than those on the Enemy's side. At one time, he was surrounded by enemy forces. Elisha and his servant awoke one morning to survey an army of enemy horses and chariots from Aram surrounding their city. His servant shook with fear for their impending doom and asked Elisha what they should do. "Don't be afraid. Those who are with us are more than those who are with them," was Elisha's calm reply (2 Kings 6:16). At this point, his assistant must have thought Elisha delusional, and he likely started to look for an escape route. But Elisha asked the Lord to open his assistant's eyes so that he could see into the spirit world like Elisha could. When he looked out from their hiding place again, he could see what Elisha had seen: on the mountains surrounding the city there stood mighty angel armies with horses and chariots of fire standing at the ready to protect Elisha. What a sight it must have been! At Elisha's request, God struck the enemy's army with blindness.

We, too, have angel armies on our side ready to protect us and fight for us. The Lord God Almighty waits for us to request their deployment.

Tactical Maneuvers

In addition to the armor of God, Paul outlines tactical maneuvers that every warrior needs in order to successfully accomplish her mission.

Pray without Ceasing

Entire books have been written about one of our strongest weapons—prayer. Our prayers are precious to the Lord. He wants to hear our prayers in the same way a father wants to hear from his child. They move His heart, and just as importantly, they move our heart. But prayer is so much more than simply making requests of God. It's a time of two-way communication with our heavenly Daddy and commander of our mission. Prayer is a time to pour out our hearts and to hear His words of comfort, a time to ask questions and to receive answers, a time to seek Him and to be delighted when we find that He has always been seeking us. In prayer, we ask for direction and listen as He guides our steps. We reveal ourselves to Him and He reveals Himself to us in ways we never could have imagined. We remind ourselves of His faithfulness of the past, and He reminds us of His promises for the future. When we thank Him for His blessings, God reveals His gifts of encouragement throughout this difficult time. When we ask that His will be done, we see His will unfold. When we pray that His kingdom come, God reveals that we are an integral part of bringing the goodness of His kingdom. As we pray for boldness and strength against enemy forces, we discover that God is making us into a warrior princess. As we ask for the impossible, we see God moving in ways that are better than our minds could fathom. Sometimes, prayer is a time when our crushed and battered hearts don't even know what to say to God but "Help me"—and to see God, the Rescuer and Redeemer, do nothing short of a rescue mission. It's a time to just soak in His presence and let His Spirit wash over us.

In his passage outlining the weapons of spiritual warfare in Ephesians 6, Paul tells us to pray without ceasing because we need to be grounded and connected to God every day to withstand the constant barrage of the Enemy. Soldiers in combat need to be in constant communication with their commanding officer. An extended time of prayer and Scripture in the morning, before even getting out of bed, is the best way for a woman in the battle to ensure that she has connected to God and is able to weather the daily assaults from her abuser.

Midnight Prayer

At times God will want the undivided attention of a woman in battle because He has something important to say to her. He will often try to get her attention at 2:00 a.m. because her mind is filled with distractions other times. It is also very likely that she is already awake in the early morning hours because women in the midst of the battle often have insomnia. If God is trying either to get her attention by waking her or she cannot sleep due to the concerns of the day, she would do well to sit up, listen intently, and write down whatever she feels the Lord is saying to her. His voice usually comes as encouraging, uplifting thoughts or words or a compelling feeling. For some it comes in the form of a vision or a single word. She can confirm the message is from the Lord with Scripture, because He will not say anything contrary to His Word. When sleepless nights abound, reading the Psalms, praying, and writing words of thankfulness in a journal can often bring the peace that a woman needs to sleep.

Prayer Changes Us

We often view prayer as a cosmic vending machine in which we make a request and expect our treat to magically arrive. God doesn't usually work like that. When we pray for a Mercedes-Benz with a million dollars in the front seat, we should not be disappointed when it doesn't arrive in our driveway. Prayer molds our hearts so that they reflect the heart of God. Prayer changes us so that we can genuinely ask for His will to be done. Prayer shapes our will to God's. Prayer takes our focus off our troubles and puts it on God, where it should be.

I am reminded of the story of a young preacher who accepted a position of senior pastor at a church, only to find it was in a state of division and tumult with constant infighting. He became discouraged as he focused his attention on solving the latest acrimonious skirmish between congregants and himself. He was losing ground, and fast. Sensing his downward spiral, an older woman came to his office and asked him to look at the old picture of Daniel in the lion's den that hung on his wall. "Where is Daniel looking? At the lions or at God?" she asked the pastor. "At God," he replied. "That is where you should look, too, pastor, when you are surrounded by lions," said the wise woman.

During a battle, we often are focused solely on ourselves and the lions circling around us. However, our proper focus should be on God, and prayer gets us there.

Praying Scripture

God loves when we pray His own words back to Him. Praying the words of Scripture is a powerful way to remind us of God's promises and faithfulness. Nearly any place in Scripture will provide words to pray. The Psalms are a great place to start. David had his own run-in with a sociopath, King Saul. Even though David had only blessed Saul, Saul turned on David and was trying to kill him. David spent a significant portion of his early years trying to escape from Saul, who, with his army, relentlessly pursued David across Israel.

A woman escaping from an abusive husband can certainly relate to David's plight and prayers. For example, in Psalm 35, David pleads with God, "Contend, Lord, with those who contend with me; fight against those who fight against me. Take up shield and armor; arise and come to my aid. Brandish spear and javelin against those who pursue me. Say to me, 'I am your salvation'" (Psalm 35:1–3). What an appropriate prayer for a woman in a spiritual battle while leaving an abuser! In the remainder of Psalm 35, David describes the betrayal of a close friend, which echoes the pain of the betrayal of an abusive husband. Psalms 140 and 141 also ask God to protect and avenge one who has done no wrong.

Many times we need to remind ourselves that God is on our side. In that case, we can pray the words of Scripture back to God: "Father, I know you are always with me, I know you go before me, and I know your right hand guides me [Psalm 139], but right now, I am afraid. I know that my spirit of fear doesn't come from You, because You give us the spirit of power and love and a sound mind [2 Timothy 1:7]. I ask that Your Spirit overcome me in a bold new way so that I can be strong and courageous and not afraid, knowing that You are on my side and will fight my battles and will be victorious" (Joshua 1:9–10).

The Big, Bold Prayer

The big, bold prayer (see chapter 30) is another powerful prayer. This prayer, reminding us of God's faithfulness in the past, and a plea for courage to face the fight and to bring about justice, is a strong battle weapon.

Praying in the Spirit

Sometimes we are so crushed and distraught that we don't even know what to say. This is when, as Paul puts it, "praying in the Spirit" is the perfect prayer. When we pray in the Spirit, we use the heavenly language given to us when we have been baptized in the Spirit. The Bible calls this "speaking in tongues" (Mark 16:17; Acts 2; 1 Corinthians 12; 1 Corinthians 14). The Holy Spirit intercedes for us, edifies us, and gives us the right words, even though we may not understand the words we speak since they are a heavenly language.

Prayer Journal

A prayer journal is an excellent weapon against the Enemy. It is a good place to thank the Lord for His blessings, make requests, pour out one's heart, and record what God has put on our heart. Looking back through the prayer journal will remind the writer of God's faithfulness and goodness, His answers to prayer, and His guidance over time. As we see God's answers to our prayers, our faith, confidence, and maturity in Him grows, knowing that He will be just as faithful in future trials as He has been in the past.

Constant Communication with the Commanding Officer

Every special ops soldier going into enemy territory on a dangerous rescue mission needs to have constant communication with his commanding officer (CO) and fellow soldiers. The goal, of course, is to extract the target of the rescue mission from enemy territory and bring her back safely to her homeland. The soldier needs advance planning with his CO, intel on the enemy, orders on the right timing—whether to wait or go in—and information on unseen traps along the way. A rogue special ops soldier, one who is out of communication with his CO and does not have the support of his team, will have difficulty completing the mission and will likely be captured by the enemy. In the same way, a woman going through the dangerous spiritual battle of leaving an abuser, as well as the treacherous physical, emotional, legal, and financial battles, needs to be in constant communication with God, her CO. She also needs to remain in communication with her fellow spiritual brothers and sisters who are part of the rescue mission. The only difference between a woman escaping abuse and the special ops soldier is that she is also the target of the rescue mission, and she must cooperate and communicate with God to succeed.

The Armor of God You Will Need for the Fight

> Charlotte: I was a strong Christian prior to leaving my abusive husband. But going through the divorce process, with the abuse escalating and Satan reveling in it, I needed to be connected to God in a way I never was before. I started each day with two hours in prayer, Scripture, and journaling to get myself centered before the onslaught of the day. In the days I didn't do this, Satan managed to get me rattled and off my game. I continue this practice even now, years later, as I help other women leave abusive marriages. I started journaling my prayers, a practice that I had let go by the wayside when I was married to my abuser. It was so strengthening to my faith to reread my journals and see how faithful God was in answering my prayers and encouraging me. I came to hear and recognize His voice in ways that I never had before—whether it was calling me to be a warrior, warning me of a trick my abuser had planned, or lovingly reminding me that I was His beloved daughter and that He was with me. And during those many sleepless nights, I was able to read Scripture, write down what God was tenderly saying to me, and finally get some sleep, knowing that Papa God had me in His arms. Now when I can't sleep, I know God has something He wants to tell me. So I sleepily sit up in bed, grab my journal that sits on my nightstand with my Bible, and write down what God puts on my heart. When He's done talking, I can fall asleep with the assurance that my heavenly Dad, the Creator of the Universe, wanted to talk to me. How cool is that?

Be Alert and Watch for the Enemy

Paul had a bullseye on his back because he was on fire for God. Because he was such a high-priority target of Satan, he started riots, was beat up, and was thrown in prison or driven out of town everywhere he went. Paul warns us to be alert for Satan's schemes. Peter puts it this way: "Be alert and of sober mind. Your enemy the devil prowls around like a roaring lion looking for someone to devour. Resist him, standing firm in the faith, because you know that the family of believers throughout the world is undergoing the same kind of sufferings" (1 Peter 5:8–9).

One of the first rules of engagement is to know your enemy. A woman escaping an abuser must be alert and know that her abuser is scheming, manipulating, lying, slandering, stealing, hiding, and deceiving—all to destroy her, and oftentimes her children as well. She needs to anticipate his ongoing evil acts and act wisely to protect herself and her children. Knowing that abusers are unwilling or unable to do the right thing and that they will set a trap for an unsuspecting wife like a predator sets a trap for prey will help a woman act in ways that protect her and her children. Anything that sounds like a favor from an abuser is almost always a trap.

> Ellen: I was diagnosed with cancer and needed a double mastectomy, radiation, and chemo to live. My boyfriend at the time insisted that we get married five days before my scheduled surgery, claiming that he couldn't care for me if we didn't get married. Although he claimed he loved me and wanted to marry me, he was simply using me to get a green card, his citizenship, and take over my finances in the hope I wouldn't survive.

> Charlotte: I discovered that anytime my husband offered to do me a favor, it was really a trap. Some examples are him asking me to quit work and then foisting an onerous prenuptial agreement on me the day before the wedding, offering to repay a student loan and then making me pay him back twice the amount, buying birthday presents for me and then selling them and pocketing the cash, claiming that his own prenuptial agreement was unenforceable during the divorce, and breaching

multiple elements of the divorce agreement. After the divorce, he "offered to help" by paying for my health insurance and deducting it from my monthly maintenance. I had learned my lesson by then and declined his offers to "help."

Kerry: I was happy to help my husband's children, my stepchildren, by putting them on my corporate health insurance. However, fourteen months after the wedding, after my husband cracked my skull open on a coffee table, I was forced to leave and file for divorce. He insisted that I keep his children on my health insurance. Fortunately, the judge ordered them off my insurance plan. Even though he was a successful lawyer and had made a six-figure income for decades, I actually paid him to get a divorce. It was worth it just to be free.

Support Others in Prayer and in Word and Deed

Paul asks believers to support other believers with their prayers. We also know that whenever possible, believers should also support others with words and deeds, because faith without good works is dead faith (James 2:26).

One of the pillars of the warrior ethos of the US Army is "I will never leave a fallen comrade." "No man left behind" is not just a catchy motto. It is a solemn promise made to each other that even if they die, their brothers in arms will do everything in their power to bring them home. I have a similar motto for the women I represent and counsel: "No woman left behind." I will do all in my power to bring her and her children out of the bondage of abuse and into a land of freedom, peace, and respect. That sometimes means extracting them from their home, picking them up at a local hotel where they have been hiding, taking them to the courthouse for an order of protection, transporting them to an emergency shelter, taking on a case pro bono, helping them move, shopping for furniture for a new home, dropping everything to listen to their story, giving Christmas presents to the children, encouraging them, and even opening up my home for temporary emergency housing. At the very least, it always means praying for them.

Something happens when we focus our attention on supporting others and praying for others: we feel better because we are not focused on ourselves. When we are going through a valley, we are in danger of being so me-focused that we become depressed, anxiety-ridden, and self-centered. When we focus on God and on others, the Holy Spirit lifts us out of our pit, and our spirits are recalibrated to where they ought to be. It is no wonder that Paul puts our focus where it should be—on God and others.

Pray to Be Fearless and Bold

Paul does not end this passage on spiritual weaponry by asking others to pray that the battle disappear or that it becomes easier, or even that he gets released from prison. As one of God's generals on earth, he knows better than that. He knows the battle between good and evil for the hearts and minds of people will continue, and at a time that only God has ordained, God will be victorious and Satan will be defeated. We know the end of the story. God wins. But in the meantime, Satan will try to take as many as he can down with him. So as he sits in a prison with chains on, Paul asks that people pray for his boldness, that he would fearlessly proclaim the gospel. Peter and John also asked to be made fearless and bold as they made their stand before the Sanhedrin, who had threatened them and forbid them from talking about Jesus. "Now, Lord, consider their threats and enable your servants to speak your word with great boldness" (Acts 4:29). God gave them His Spirit of fearlessness and enabled them to speak boldly about the gospel.

Fearlessness—that is the number one quality a woman escaping domestic abuse needs. She needs to leave her abuser knowing that, even as she walks into the unknown, her Almighty God is fighting for her and will lead her, and carry her if necessary, into the promised land that He has prepared for her. On the other hand, Satan wants to fill her with fear so she is paralyzed and unable to move. Satan wants to fill her with doubt so she questions her every move. Satan wants her to be timid so she cowers and submits at the threats of her abuser. We know that God does not give us the spirit of fear or timidity, but of power, love, and self-control (2 Timothy 1:7). Throughout the Bible, God tells His people not to be afraid, but to be fearless. Why? Because His people are all super strong or super smart or super wealthy? No. Because the Almighty God, the Creator of the Universe, the Alpha and Omega, the one who parts the Red Sea and sends manna and causes enemy armies to annihilate themselves goes with them!

I often ask the women I counsel what they would be like if they knew they were born into royalty with a father king who has endless wealth, who is determined to pass his kingdom on to his children, and who sends a security detail to clean things up whenever one of them gets into a skirmish with an unsavory sort. Would they have their feelings hurt if they were insulted by a disagreeable commoner? Would they run and hide if a common thug threatened them? Would they be fearful if a regular Joe tried to take away their vast fortune? Of course not. Knowing that she is a daughter of the king makes all the difference. She pays no attention to insults—she is a princess and the insulter is an idiot. She gives no heed to threats—she has the king's army and the secret service protecting her. She ignores silly schemes to take her inheritance—the king's wealth is beyond measure and she is secure as an heir.

The response of a daughter of the King of Kings should be no less. The King of Kings and Lord of Lords goes with His daughters. He fights for them. He protects them. He rescues them, and He has a vast storehouse of blessings waiting for them. Daughters of the King—know *who* you are, know *whose* you are, and be fearless.

Chapter 33

The Only Opinion That Counts is God's

WOMEN LEAVING (OR TRYING to leave) an abusive marriage or relationship are often paralyzed with fear because of what others may think of them. Often times, she is so concerned about what others will think that she wastes a great deal of mental energy and is ridden with anxiety. Mental health professionals who counsel women escaping abusive marriages state that sometimes even more traumatizing than the abuse is the betrayal of close friends, family, and church leaders who either don't want to get involved, are not interested in listening to her, refuse to offer empathy or support, or actually side with the abuser. Such responses can be devastating.

Women, by nature, define themselves by their relationships. They often identify themselves as a wife, mother, grandmother, daughter, sister, a favorite aunt, a close friend, or an active church leader or member. Even professional women do not often find their primary identity in their vocation, which changes throughout their life, but in their deep, intimate, long-term relationships.

When friends or family turn against her or are apathetic to her plight, a woman leaving an abusive relationship may be under the illusion that if they only knew the truth, they would come to her aid, or at least come to her side. She then attempts to tell her story to persuade them that she, not her abuser, is the innocent victim. This is usually a mistake.

As we mentioned in chapter 21, people support an abuser for three reasons: (1) they are deceived by his charm and lies; (2) they are intimidated by him; or (3) they have a similar moral compass. A woman's family and close friends know her godly character. If former friends choose to support the abuser, unless they are deceived or intimidated, they have chosen to associate with someone who shares their values. No evidence or information will likely convince them to change teams. At this point, it is best to accept that they do not have her best interests at heart, and probably never did, and it is probably best to let the relationship go. She misjudged their character in the same way she misjudged her husband and assumed they were better people than they are. Since a woman in an abusive relationship naturally looks for the best in people, overlooking serious character flaws is a common mistake. A divorce will show the true colors of so-called friends. Those who share the abuser's values will naturally gravitate to him, while those whose moral compass is more like hers will side with her. As Scripture tells us, bad people are repulsed by good people, and good people have an aversion to evil ones. "The righteous detest the dishonest; the wicked detest the upright" (Proverbs 29:27). Leaving an abuser is a good time for "culling the herd" of friends and surrounding herself with only good, godly people who appreciate her and have her best interest in mind.

Divorce is a difficult time for relationships with children as well. As discussed in previous chapters, bonds with children can be stretched due to the actions of an abuser. The wise mother doesn't let the feelings of her children determine her self-worth. Rather, she looks to God for her self-worth and exudes confidence. She prays for their hearts to turn to Him, waiting expectantly for His answer. Over time, true characters are revealed, and the relationships between a mom and her children are usually restored.

Betrayal hurts. It's one thing to be attacked by known enemies; it's entirely different to be betrayed by friends and loved ones. King David wrote of the heartache of the betrayal by a close friend in Psalm 55. David writes:

> Listen to my prayer, O God,
> do not ignore my plea;
> hear me and answer me.
> My thoughts trouble me and I am distraught
> because of what my enemy is saying,
> because of the threats of the wicked;
> for they bring down suffering on me
> and assail me in their anger.
>
> My heart is in anguish within me;
> the terrors of death have fallen on me.
> Fear and trembling have beset me;
> horror has overwhelmed me.
> I said, "Oh, that I had the wings of a dove!
> I would fly away and be at rest.
> I would flee far away
> and stay in the desert;
> I would hurry to my place of shelter,
> far from the tempest and storm."
>
> Lord, confuse the wicked, confound their words,
> for I see violence and strife in the city.
> Day and night they prowl about on its walls;
> malice and abuse are within it.
> Destructive forces are at work in the city;
> threats and lies never leave its streets.
>
> If an enemy were insulting me,
> I could endure it;
> if a foe were rising against me,
> I could hide.
> But it is you, a man like myself,

> my companion, my close friend,
> with whom I once enjoyed sweet fellowship
> at the house of God,
> as we walked about
> among the worshipers.
>
> Let death take my enemies by surprise;
> let them go down alive to the realm of the dead,
> for evil finds lodging among them.
>
> As for me, I call to God,
> and the Lord saves me.
> Evening, morning and noon
> I cry out in distress,
> and he hears my voice.
> He rescues me unharmed
> from the battle waged against me,
> even though many oppose me.
> God, who is enthroned from of old,
> who does not change—
> he will hear them and humble them,
> because they have no fear of God.
>
> My companion attacks his friends;
> he violates his covenant.
> His talk is smooth as butter,
> yet war is in his heart;
> his words are more soothing than oil,
> yet they are drawn swords.
>
> Cast your cares on the Lord
> and he will sustain you;
> he will never let
> the righteous be shaken.
> But you, God, will bring down the wicked
> into the pit of decay;
> the bloodthirsty and deceitful
> will not live out half their days.
>
> But as for me, I trust in you.

It's easy to fall into despair when betrayed by someone we once viewed as a close friend. Like David, a wise woman will use this time of upheaval to seek God's truth to sustain her rather than the opinion of others. When a woman comes to the point where God's thoughts about her are all that matter, she will be free indeed, and she will have learned an important lesson that will uphold her for the rest of her life.

The Only Opinion That Counts is God's

As we discuss more fully in chapters 41–44, when a woman replaces Satan's lies and fully accepts God truth, the truth sets her free! She no longer is chained to the opinions of others, because the opinion of God is the only one that matters to her. Her view of herself is not tied to what others think, because she knows that God thinks she is terrific. The insults slung by her abuser and his stooges deflect off her like water off a duck's back because she knows they are lies from Satan and that God delights in her and sings songs over her. Her decisions are not made in fear wondering what others may think about her; rather, her decisions are made in confidence by seeking God's will for her life and aligning herself with His will. She no longer seeks to fill up the empty cup of her soul with the approval of others; instead, her cup is continually overflowing with God's Spirit and His approval. She has plenty of grace to give to others, even when it's not returned. She doesn't walk with her head bowed in shame because of the slander of others; rather, she walks with her head held high knowing that Father God knows the truth and she is walking in His path. She no longer feels the need to defend herself; instead, she knows that she is a lioness daughter of the Lion of Judah—and a lion doesn't need defending. She no longer is fearful of what others think about her; rather, she walks in regal confidence knowing that her heavenly Father, the King of Kings, is beaming with pride and telling all the heavenly hosts, "There she goes. That's my girl!"

Chapter 34

What Does the Bible Really Say About Divorcing an Abuser?

WOMEN OF FAITH HAVE an especially difficult time reconciling their vows of "'til death do us part" with the fact that their abuser has repeatedly and unrepentantly breached his vows to "love, honor, and cherish" to such an extent that divorce is the only solution. Few women want a divorce; they want a husband who loves them. They don't want to disappoint God or incur His wrath with a divorce. Divorce is a last resort. The stigma of divorce, along with misinformation from an abuser about how God views divorce, prompts Christian women to stay in abusive marriages significantly longer than women with no faith affiliation.[135]

What does the Bible really say about divorce? Is a woman in an abusive marriage obligated to stay until she or her abuser dies or she is killed by her abuser, or does God's love value her person over the institute of marriage, allowing for a divorce in cases of abuse?

There is a great deal of debate over divorce in Christian circles, including legitimate and illegitimate rationales for divorce. God's divine intention for marriage is found in Ephesians 5. Both spouses are called to support each other out of love for Christ (Ephesians 5:21 TPT). A husband is called to love his wife with the same sacrificial love that Christ has for His church, and a wife is called to support and be devoted to her husband (vv. 22–33 TPT). The Passion Translation is used here using the word *support* rather than *submit*, due to the misinterpretation used to justify abuse by demanding submission to an abuser. When God's design for marriage is demonstrated between a husband and wife, it is a little bit of heaven here on earth. However, if what God designed for our good has been twisted into a prison of abuse, we would do well to consider the following arguments allowing for divorce in cases of abuse.

Divorce Mitigates the Damaging Power of Evil

God's original plan for marriage was a masterpiece of two harmonious souls living in love and unity and serving God together as man and wife for the remainder of their lives. But after Adam and Eve sinned, God's

---
[135] Anne B. Doll, "Domestic Violence in the Church," Gordon Conwell University blog, October 17, 2016, https://www.gordonconwell.edu/blog/domestic-violence-in-the-church/.

beautiful design for marriage was twisted. Divorce was permitted, starting in the Old Testament (see Deuteronomy 24:1–4). To protect the injured spouse, the Father graciously allows divorce where sin has shattered the union of husband and wife (Matthew 19:8). Forcing a woman to stay in an abusive marriage is sentencing her to a life of spiritual, emotional, and sometimes physical death. Jesus, who came to give us abundant life, loves His children too much to sentence them to a life filled with constant evil.

Some people incorrectly assume that divorce is sin. While divorce is unfortunate and is always the *result* of sin, divorce *itself* is not necessarily sinful. Not everyone in a divorce situation is guilty of sin. In cases involving abuse, one party is clearly guilty and one innocent. Divorce is often the only option, and the lesser of two bad outcomes.[136] Research shows that the leading cause of divorce in people over forty, the majority of whom are in long-term marriages, is physical, verbal, or emotional abuse.[137]

Both Old and New Testaments offer remedies in the event of sin. They were designed to restore the victim and deter sin. The remedies were proportionate to the sin. For example, if a person stole his neighbor's property, he was required to pay him back the property plus 20 percent (Leviticus 6:1–5). The remedy for lying and falsely claiming that a woman was not a virgin was a beating and one hundred shekels (Deuteronomy 22:13–19). The redress for an unsolved murder was to break the neck of a heifer and pay for the atonement of the unsolved murder with the blood of the heifer (Deuteronomy 21:1–9). Kidnapping a fellow Israelite and selling him into slavery was punishable by death (Deuteronomy 24:7). Likewise, divorce was allowed when a husband sinned by being unkind to his wife, when hearts were hardened and not turned toward one's spouse (Deuteronomy 24:1–4).

The fact that God provided remedies for sin does not mean that He encourages or approves of the remedy as a way of life. God did not want His people to go around breaking the necks of cows, paying huge amounts of money, divorcing, beating, or killing people willy-nilly, yet He provided these as means to contain sin.

The point is that God allowed for divorce as the gentlest way to alleviate the sin that had arisen during a marriage. Allowing the parties to separate when they no longer were able to fulfill the promise to love, protect, and care for each other was God's most gracious way to protect the innocent spouse and to deal with the sin that had infiltrated the relationship.

John Calvin summarized it this way: God "did not lay down a law about divorces, so as to give them the seal of his approbation, but as the wickedness of men could not be restrained in any other way, he applied what was the most admissible remedy."[138] Many of God's laws are concessions to contain the effects of sin, and we should be grateful that, in His grace, the Lord seeks to mitigate the damaging power of evil.

An Abusive Marriage Cannot Serve Any Purpose of a Godly Marriage

The primary purposes of a God-ordained marriage are to (1) provide a picture of His love for us in the love that a husband has for his wife (Ephesians 5:21–33), (2) serve and glorify God together as a couple (Matthew 18:20), and (3) raise children in the love of the Lord (Malachi 2:15; Deuteronomy 6:6–7). Secondary purposes include (4) providing the affection, love, and companionship, as well as a co-laborer, that we need for an abun-

---

[136] See also "When God Allows Divorce," Ligonier Ministries, n.d. at https://www.ligonier.org/learn/devotionals/when-god-allows-divorce/.

[137] "The Divorce Experience: A Study of Divorce at Midlife and Beyond," *AARP*, 2004, 20–21, https://www.aarp.org/content/dam/aarp/research/surveys_statistics/general/2014/divorce.doi.10.26419%252Fres.00061.001.pdf.

[138] "Hard Hearts and Divorce," Ligonier Ministries, n.d. https://www.ligonier.org/learn/devotionals/hard-hearts-and-divorce/.

dant life (Amos 3:3; Ecclesiastes 4:9–12), (5) physical enjoyment (Hebrews 13:4; Song of Songs), and (6) the physical, emotional, and spiritual protection of a husband over his wife and children (Malachi 2:16; Ephesians 5:25).[139]

An abusive marriage can never serve any of the purposes of a marriage designed by God. In fact, an abusive marriage has been twisted by Satan to achieve the opposite of God's purposes. Satan cannot create anything on his own, but he can certainly take the good things that God has made and turn them into evil. Indeed, an abusive marriage is not a marriage at all, but rather resembles a master-and-slave relationship.

Abusers Do Not Intend to Enter into a Godly Marriage

Abusers have no intention of entering a God-ordained marriage. The wife of an abuser was deceived and defrauded by an imposter and liar who had no intention of keeping the marriage vows to love, honor, and cherish her. Instead, his goal was to control and abuse his power. In most cases, the abuse starts immediately after the wedding when the hook is set. (See traits of a sociopath/psychopath in chapter 3.) Unlike a healthy marriage in which a couple experiences the normal highs and lows of life, abusers plan their abuse and unfaithfulness even before the marriage begins. Abuse doesn't just happen. It is planned.

An abuser is incapable of emotional intimacy, empathy, and loving others as defined in Scripture and in healthy relationships. Therefore, he uses others, including his spouse. Although he does not love her, he uses the word *love* to deceive and defraud her into a marriage to meet his selfish needs. His wife is expendable to him, and he plans to discard and replace her when she is no longer useful.

For a marriage to be considered valid in the Catholic Church, both parties must, among other things, intend to be faithful to each other and intend the good of each other.[140] Fraud, deception, coercion, error about the quality of a person (you intended to marry someone who possessed or did not possess a certain quality, such as religious convictions, freedom from disease, or arrest record), lack of intention to be faithful or act for the good of the other, and psychological disorders are all grounds for annulment in the Catholic Church, as well as grounds for annulment in most civil courts. Fortunately, Catholic law and civil law recognize that a marriage to an abuser is not a true marriage and allow for a judgment that invalidates a marriage from the beginning.

Civil Divorce Recognizes That Marriage Is Already Terminated

A civil and legal relationship set up by a governmental authority should not be confused with a true marriage ordained by God. A legal divorce finalized in a court of law is simply a recognition that the marriage relationship is already severed as a result of the abuser breaching his marriage covenant. The legal judgment entered by the court sets forth the financial arrangements, legal and contractual obligations that the parties have to each other, and the parenting arrangement for the children. By the time a divorce is started in the court system, the vows have long been violated and the actual marriage has long been severed.

In the Catholic Church, an annulment recognizes that a marriage may be valid civilly by the courts, yet not considered valid according to canon law. A declaration of annulment has no effect on the legitimacy of the

---

[139] See also "Embracing God's Purposes for Marriage," *Family Life*, n.d., https://www.familylife.com/articles/topics/marriage/staying-married/gods-plan-for-marriage/embracing-gods-purposes-for-marriage/.

[140] "Annulment," United States Conference of Catholic Bishops, n.d., http://www.usccb.org/issues-and-action/marriage-and-family/marriage/annulment/index.cfm.

children born of the union or parental responsibilities, as the parents were presumed to be married at the time of the child's birth.[141]

God Divorced Israel

Many who argue that divorce is a sin do not realize that God Himself divorced Israel because their hearts had turned away from Him. God, of course, cannot sin, and His actions were an entirely appropriate response to Israel's rejection of Him.

In the Old Testament, God made two covenants with Israel. The first was a unilateral covenant that the Messiah would come. Under a unilateral covenant, one side is required to keep his promise regardless of the actions of the other side. Despite Israel's rejection of God, God kept His covenant to bring a Messiah when Jesus Christ arrived on the scene.

God also set forth a bilateral covenant with Israel in which God would extend His blessings to Israel if and only if they kept God's commandments. If Israel did not keep its end of the covenant, it would receive God's curses (Deuteronomy 28–30). Under a bilateral covenant, each side is required to keep its promises. If one side does not keep its promises, the other side is released from keeping its promises. Israel was God's bride, and God was her husband (Isaiah 54:5–6; Jeremiah 3:14; 31:32). However, over time, Israel wanted nothing to do with God. She did not love, honor, or cherish her husband. She worshiped other gods and gave them child sacrifices, engaged in other sins of the worst sort, and ignored God's pleas to come back to Him. She wanted the benefits of being God's beloved—His protection, blessings, and mercies—but she didn't want all the obligations that came with being called His bride. Many times God pleaded, *I don't need all these silly sacrifices. I just want your heart. I want your love. I want you to know Me* (see Psalm 51:15–17 and Hosea 6:6). But Israel's heart was far away. After many years of God patiently appealing for His wayward bride to come back into a relationship with Him, God divorced Israel for her continuing, unrepentant sin, her hardness of heart, and her spiritual unfaithfulness (Isaiah 50:1; Jeremiah 3:8). And when He divorced her, He withdrew His protection, blessings, and mercies from Israel. God did not sin when He divorced Israel, but His divorce acknowledged that the relationship had been severed because of Israel's continuing, unrepentant, serious sin.

God Himself set the example of how a woman should act in response to a husband whose heart is hard and who refuses to be in a loving relationship with her: she should patiently request that he return to the relationship and turn his heart toward her. Like God, her heart pleads with her husband, "I don't need your gifts or a big house or fancy cars. I just want your heart. I want your love. I want you to know me." However, if his heart continues to be hardened and he continues in unrepentant sin in violation of his marriage vows, the marriage relationship has been irretrievably severed and she is no longer bound by her marriage vows. Like God, a wife does not sin when she divorces a husband who refuses to repent and whose heart is set against her.

God Commanded Divorce

Not only did God divorce Himself from Israel, but God has *commanded* divorce to separate God-loving people from evildoers to ensure His purposes for marriage and family. God commanded 113 Israelite husbands to divorce their pagan wives (Ezra 10:10). Israel had violated God's laws and married pagans. As a result, Israel turned its back on God and engaged in all the evil practices of the pagans around them, such as worshiping other

---

[141] "Annulment," United States Conference of Catholic Bishops.

gods, sexual immorality, and child sacrifice. When God divorced Israel and withdrew His hand of protection, they were carried away to Assyria and Babylon. Having just returned to Israel from exile in Babylon, the people of Israel were under strict orders not to marry pagans so history would not repeat itself. Despite this, 113 Israelites chose to marry pagans who engaged in practices abhorrent to God.

The prophet Malachi put it like this: "Judah has been unfaithful. A detestable thing has been committed in Israel and in Jerusalem: Judah has desecrated the sanctuary the Lord loves by marrying women who worship a foreign god. As for the man who does this, whoever he may be, may the Lord remove him from the tents of Jacob—even though he brings an offering to the Lord Almighty" (Malachi 2:11–12).

God was not upset that His people had married women of another nation. God doesn't discriminate because of a person's nationality or race or color. He welcomed Rahab and Ruth into the family bloodline, even though they were from foreign countries, because they had chosen to worship the one true God. The Lord was upset because the women the Israelites had married continued in their pagan ways. In short, they were wicked.

Of course, God never commands us to sin. God did not sin or order His people to sin when He directed the Israelites to divorce evil people. He commanded divorce to protect His people from evil. Divorcing an evil person is not sin, but divorce is always the result of sin.

Again, God sets the example when a woman finds herself in a marriage with a wicked husband: she should give him the option to change his ways or go their separate ways to protect herself and her children.

The Context of "God Hates Divorce"

Malachi 2:16 has long been used to keep women in bondage to an abuser, with the phrase "God hates divorce." However, other translations of the passage taken in context state the following:

> And this is another thing you do: you cover the Lord's altar with tears, with weeping and groaning, because He no longer respects your offerings or receives them gladly from your hands. Yet you ask, "For what reason?" Because the Lord has been a witness between you and the wife of your youth. You have acted treacherously against her, though she was your marriage partner and your wife by covenant. Didn't the one God make us with a remnant of His life-breath? And what does the One seek? A godly offspring. So watch yourselves carefully, and do not act treacherously against the wife of your youth. (Malachi 2:13–15 HCSB)

> "The man who hates and divorces his wife," says the Lord, the God of Israel, "does violence to the one he should protect," says the Lord Almighty. (Malachi 2:16 NIV)

Those who use this Scripture to keep women in abusive relationships ignore the entire context. The passage addresses men, rebuking them for being unkind and cruel to their wives, including but not limited to divorcing her for no reason. It goes on to reprimand them for violating their obligation to protect—not oppress—their wives. This passage states that God is a witness to the marriage vows; He is a witness to how a man treats his wife and his spiritual and physical unfaithfulness and treachery. Therefore, when a man deals with his wife treacherously, and divorces her because he hates her, he does violence to his wife because he is charged with protecting her. The passage ends with a command to men to be faithful to their wives. Based on the context, we know this means both spiritually and physically.

Other translations condemn when a man acts "deceitfully," "treacherously," "unjustly," "unfaithfully," "violently," and "cruelly" toward his wife.

The prophet Malachi admonishes men to treat their wives well, not treacherously. It does not prohibit all divorce, but it does condemn a man who divorces his wife treacherously or out of hatred. It is important to bring this passage into context by looking at the Bible in its entirety and all the other things that God hates that make divorce an unfortunate necessity. The following are just a few passages that give us insight into the heart of God:

> There are six things the LORD hates, seven that are detestable to him: haughty eyes, a lying tongue, hands that shed innocent blood, a heart that devises wicked schemes, feet that are quick to rush to evil, a false witness who pours out lies, and a person who stirs up conflict in the community. (Proverbs 6:16–19)

> The LORD detests dishonest scales. (Proverbs 11:1)

> The LORD detests those whose hearts are perverse. (Proverbs 11:20)

> The acts of the flesh are obvious: sexual immorality, impurity and debauchery; idolatry and witchcraft; hatred, discord, jealousy, fits of rage, selfish ambition, dissensions, factions and envy; drunkenness, orgies, and the like. I warn you, as I did before, that those who live like this will not inherit the kingdom of God. (Galatians 5:19–21)

> For of this you can be sure: No immoral, impure or greedy person—such a person is an idolater—has any inheritance in the kingdom of Christ and of God. (Ephesians 5:5)

It is important to get the proper lesson from this passage in Malachi and not drop pithy quotes out of context. The entire book of Malachi is God warning about hard, unloving hearts. To be sure, God does not like divorce. God doesn't like divorce for the same reasons no one else likes divorce: because divorce is the result of horrific sin that rips apart a family, divorce inflicts wounds and leaves painful emotional scars that may never heal, and it leaves people, especially women and children, financially devastated. But more importantly, God hates the sins that characterize an abuser and are the reasons for divorce from an abusive man. So God tells men in this passage in Malachi to man up, be godly men, and start treating their wives as they should.

Have Nothing to Do with Them

Scripture often refers to separating from evildoers and those who profess to be believers but persist in serious, unrepentant sin. In 2 Timothy 3:1–5, Paul provides a perfect description of abusers who profess to be Christians: "There will be terrible times in the last days. People will be lovers of themselves, lovers of money, boastful, proud, abusive, disobedient to their parents, ungrateful, unholy, without love, unforgiving, slanderous, without self-control, brutal, not lovers of the good, treacherous, rash, conceited, lovers of pleasure rather than lovers of God—having a form of godliness but denying its power." Paul tells Christians to "have nothing to do with such people" (v. 5). He makes no exceptions for wives. Matthew 18:15–17, 1 Corinthians 5, and Titus 3:10–11 also give firm instructions to Christians to remove unrepentant people engaged in serious sin from their lives by having nothing to do with them.

Indeed, Paul does *not* instruct: "Have nothing to do with them, except for their wives, who must stay with an evil man who is intent on destroying her, her family, her spirit, and her body. Everyone else, leave him alone. He's trouble, and will make your life miserable. As for the wife, too bad for you; you are commanded to stay and be abused for the rest of your life." Such an instruction would be against the very nature of God, who has compassion on the weak and powerless (Proverbs 31:8–9), who came to destroy the works of Satan (1 John 3:8), and who gives us an abundant life (John 10:10). Unlike God, the nature of Satan and his puppets (including abusers) is to steal, kill, and destroy (John 10:10). Contrary to popular belief that commanding a woman to stay with her abusive husband is a godly thing to do to save a marriage, telling a wife to stay with an abuser is a demonic instruction that Satan himself revels in.

Flee from Evil and Danger

Many references in the Bible command us to flee from evil and danger (e.g., Proverbs 22:3, 10). When Saul turned on David and tried to kill him, David fled and went into hiding. David did some unusual things to escape: he broke the rules and ate the temple bread reserved only for the priests (1 Samuel 21:1–9); he spent sixteen months in hiding in the land of the Philistines, enemies of Israel, pretending to change alliances (1 Samuel 27); he was not entirely truthful (1 Samuel 21:1–9); and he even pretended to be insane at one point (1 Samuel 21:10–15). Far from condemning David, Jesus applauded David for his actions and used them as a lesson to the Pharisees to value human need over rituals. In numerous psalms, David pours his heart out to God as he flees from his oppressors and prays for the Lord's deliverance from his enemies (Psalm 28, 35, 36, 37, 55, 56, 57, 58, 59, 69, 71, 73, 120, 140, 141).

One must sometimes go to great lengths to escape evil and protect themselves and others, especially if they are being pursued. The time a woman leaves abuse is dangerous. A woman may need to go into hiding; she may need to take some funds that are normally reserved for other purposes; she may need to withhold information; she may need to pretend that she is someone she's not; and she may even need to tell a white lie to her abuser or others.

When lives and safety are at stake, there is no moral compunction to tell an enemy the information that will lead to someone's demise. A lie is defined as intentionally telling an untruth to someone who has the right to know the truth. Enemies of God who are intent on destroying others do not have the right to know the truth. Therefore, not telling the truth to one of God's enemies to protect yourself or another is not a lie. If her abuser asks a woman her whereabouts or that of her children when she has fled for their safety, she should feel no guilt whatsoever in not telling him. This may cause her a great deal of distress and guilt—however, God puts the needs of His daughters above the desires of evil people. Importantly, Rahab the prostitute did not tell the king of Jericho the truth when he asked where she was hiding Israel's spies (Joshua 2), yet she is honored in Matthew 1 as part of the lineage of Jesus and in Hebrews 11 as one of the pillars of faith. David fibbed when he was escaping a madman, yet Jesus used him as a moral lesson. And numerous people who hid Jews during World War II did not tell the truth about their whereabouts to the Nazis, yet they are hailed as heroes. In each case, God's enemies were intent on doing harm and had no right to know the truth. Those who protected others from evil were God's instruments in fighting Satan.

The Lord's Prayer asks God to "deliver us from the evil one" (Matthew 6:13). Taking refuge from the danger and evil of domestic abuse, and asking God's help in doing so, is scriptural.

Separate from Evil

In 2 Corinthians, Paul warns Christians about being married to unbelievers:

> Do not be yoked together with unbelievers. For what do righteousness and wickedness have in common? Or what fellowship can light have with darkness? What harmony is there between Christ and Belial [i.e., Satan]? Or what does a believer have in common with an unbeliever? What agreement is there between the temple of God and idols? For we are the temple of the living God. As God has said: "I will live with them and walk among them, and I will be their God, and they will be my people." Therefore, "Come out from them and be separate, says the Lord." (2 Corinthians 6:14–17)

Like Ezra, who commanded the Israelites who had married pagan women to divorce them, Paul recognized the need for God's people to not marry—and to be separated from—wicked people. Abusers are predators who prey on kind, giving, and forgiving Christian women who should not be married to them in the first place. If a Christian woman finds herself with a SNAP, she has been duped by a master manipulator, and she needs to separate herself from her abuser.

Jesus Settles a Dispute between the House of Hillel and the House of Shammai

Many people use a passage in Matthew 19 to justify forcing a woman to stay in an abusive marriage if the abuser has not committed adultery. They claim that a person can divorce a spouse only if the spouse has engaged in sex with another person. This misinterpretation of the Scriptures takes Jesus's words out of context.

In Matthew 19, Jesus was asked to solve an ongoing philosophical dispute among the Pharisees between the House of Hillel and the House of Shammai on the interpretation of Deuteronomy 24, regarding the definition of *indecency* as a valid cause for divorce. The Hillelites held that under Deuteronomy 24 divorce for any reason whatsoever was allowed, even for trivial reasons, such as a wife burning the toast, while the Shammaites claimed that divorce was commanded only for adultery. (The Greek word for adultery is *moicheia*.) Jesus reprimanded both in His answer, reminding them that God's design for marriage was for a man and woman to live together as one in unity. Jesus rebuked them for looking for approved reasons to divorce, rather than focusing on the purpose of marriage. He stated that Deuteronomy 24 did not *command* divorce on either grounds, but *allowed* it because of men's hard-heartedness to their wives. However, He stated that divorce was not God's ideal. He further condemned the Hillelites's claim that any trivial reason for divorce is valid, and He condemned the Shammaites's position that only adultery is a valid ground for divorce. Jesus stated that sexual immorality (using the Greek word *porneia*) is <u>one</u> legitimate ground for divorce in addition to adultery (*moicheia*). The word *porneia* that Jesus used for sexual immorality, from which we get the word *pornography*, included all forms of sexual immorality, not simply adultery. *Porneia* encompasses illicit sex, including sodomy, incest, prostitution, bestiality, marital rape, pornography, adultery, defiling one's spouse or children by subjecting them to viewing pornography or recreating it, or any kind of sex that is outside of God's design for us. However, Jesus did not condemn other grounds of divorce found in Exodus 21:10–11 that were not up for debate. Therefore, we can infer that these other grounds continued to be valid grounds for divorce.

Under Moses's law, a man was responsible for his wife's food, clothing, and other marital rights of peace, permanence, and security. In Jewish court cases that arose from this passage, wives were granted divorce for their husband's cruelty, disrespect, abuse, humiliation, failure to provide her food and clothing, and sexual neglect. These grounds continue to be valid, biblical grounds for divorce.

It is vitally important to recognize that one of the traits of abusers is *porneia*. Because they view people as objects to use for their selfish gains, not individuals made in God's image to cherish, abusers regularly engage in illicit sex, sodomy, incest, prostitution, bestiality, marital rape, non-marital rape, adultery, pornography, defiling his spouse, and sex outside of God's design. Even if the abuser doesn't engage in *porneia* (which would be highly unusual), we incorrectly interpret Jesus's answer as allowing divorce only for adultery, when, in fact, Jesus recognized many traditional reasons for divorce, encouraging us to focus on the divine purpose of marriage.[142]

Abuse, Neglect, Desertion, Hardness of Heart

In 1 Corinthians 7:12–15, Paul discusses divorce from an unbeliever: "If the unbeliever leaves, let it be so. The brother or the sister is not bound in such circumstances; God has called us to live in peace" (1 Corinthians 7:15). Verse 15 can be misinterpreted as requiring a victim to stay in a marriage unless her abuser abandons her. Since most abusers do not leave a marriage, but relish in exerting power and control over the victim, even demanding the leaving victim to return to the marriage only to relive the abuse again and again, this misinterpretation condemns a woman to a prison of abuse in her own home.

Correctly interpreted, verse 15 allows divorce in a situation in which an abuser has so destroyed the marriage covenant that it caused a separation between the parties and the victim is forced to leave. The key question, then, is not "Who walked out?" but "Who caused the separation?" Perhaps a more accurate translation of verse 15 is "If an unbeliever causes separation, let there be divorce." Constructive desertion, which is effectively covered by verse 15, is an ancient ground for divorce under English law when one spouse is so ill-treated that the victim is justified in leaving the abusive spouse. Thus, verse 15 allows divorce in cases of abuse, neglect, desertion, or such hardness of heart toward the other spouse that the marriage covenant has been breached and the victim is forced to separate from the abuser.

In 1 Corinthians 7:12, Paul says this about divorce: "If any brother has a wife who is not a believer and she is willing to live with him, he must not divorce her." This can be misinterpreted to mean that a victim must stay with an abusive spouse if the abuser is willing to stay in the marriage. Again, this interpretation would sentence a victim to a life of abuse, as abusers are seldom willing to give up power and control over their spouse or their money. The word *willing* is the Greek word *syneudoeko*, which means to join in approval with, approve of, sympathize with, applaud, be pleased together with, be like-minded with, agree, and consent. In short, in this context, it carries the idea of respecting, honoring, blessing, being in harmony with, and uplifting the spouse and the marriage. Since abusers are intent on disrespecting, dishonoring, destroying, creating division with, and harming the spouse, this verse cannot be correctly interpreted to command a spouse to stay with an abuser.[143]

Some abusers claim to be Christians, and therefore argue that 1 Corinthians 7:12–15 does not apply to them because it only applies to nonbelievers. Thus, they argue that the victim has no justifiable reason for divorce. However, it is doubtful that any abuser who continues to abuse a spouse or children without repentance is a true Christian. Thankfully, Scripture provides us with guidance on how to know the difference. 1 John 3:6–10

---

[142] Barbara Roberts, *Not Under Bondage: Biblical Divorce for Abuse, Adultery and Desertion* (Ballarat, Australia: Maschil Press, 2008), 79–88.
[143] Roberts, *Not Under Bondage*, 37–44.

is clear in how to recognize children of God compared to children of Satan: children of God do not continue in unrepentant sin, while children of Satan do not do what is right and do not love their brother and sister.

Jesus Did Not Value Institutions over People

Those who insist that women stay in an abusive marriage at all costs value the institution of marriage over people made in God's image. This is against the teachings of Jesus, who always valued people above institutions. For example, Jesus often healed people on the Sabbath, even though the Sabbath was a day set apart by God to rest (Luke 6:6–10; 13:10–17). He even ate grain from a field on the Sabbath and was wrongly accused of harvesting, and thereby working, on the Sabbath (Mark 2:23–28). Jesus was intent on doing good, regardless of whether doing good was on the Sabbath or anytime else. Jesus insisted that the Sabbath was made to benefit people, not the other way around (Mark 2:27). God ordained the Sabbath, yes. But He explained that when the man-made rules surrounding the Sabbath are so twisted that they no longer benefit the people they were designed to help, then something is wrong. Those rules should be broken because they no longer reflect God's design for the Sabbath.

Likewise, marriage, which was ordained by God, was designed to be a blessing to the people in the marriage. Like the Sabbath, marriage was made to benefit people, not the other way around. But when a marriage is so destructive and the man-made rules surrounding marriage have become so contorted that they require the destruction of one person to keep a marriage going, something is terribly wrong. Those rules should be broken because they no longer reflect God's design for marriage.

Advice for Normal Marriages versus Advice for Abusive Marriages

Much of the Bible's directions for marriage are like many Christian marriage books now on the market. They are geared toward emotionally healthy Christians—Spirit-filled people with goodwill toward each other and who desire the best for their spouse, and couples who experience the normal ups and downs of marriage. These resources are full of great advice for decent people. They don't recommend divorce as a first step, but encourage kindness, faithfulness, turning one's heart toward their spouse, protection, and unity of spirit that comes with a Christian marriage.

Neither the Bible's general passages regarding marriage nor Christian marriage books address marriage to a SNAP, who is intentionally destroying his spouse, shows no repentance, and who has chosen to be controlled by Satan. In such situations, the Bible warns us to flee from evil and separate ourselves from evil people, and books that are specially written to address abusive relationships tell us the same thing.

Divorce is generally viewed as the last option, when all other options to make a marriage work have failed. However, for the woman living with a narcissist, sociopath, psychopath, or other abuser, divorce is the only viable option.

Chapter 35

Biblical Best Practices for the Church: How to Support the Victim and Hold the Abuser Accountable

As people of faith, we are called to support the oppressed, those who cannot speak for themselves, the widow, and the orphan (Psalm 68:5, 82:3, 146:9, Proverbs 23:10, 31:8–9; James 1:27). How much more, then, are we called to support those whose husbands and fathers are actively and intentionally abusing them?

The way a pastor responds to a domestic abuse victim has a huge impact. Pastors are viewed as God's representatives with tremendous moral authority speaking on God's behalf. With an appropriate response from her pastor, an abused woman can begin to heal, while an inappropriate response can cause further devastation and prolong the abuse.

While everyone sins and falls short of God's standards, SNAPs make sinning a lifestyle for which they show no remorse or repentance. Scripture is clear that those who continue in unrepentant sin and do not love others are not God's children.

> No one who lives in him keeps on sinning. No one who continues to sin has either seen him or known him. Dear children, do not let anyone lead you astray. The one who does what is right is righteous, just as he is righteous. The one who does what is sinful is of the devil, because the devil has been sinning from the beginning. The reason the Son of God appeared was to destroy the devil's work. No one who is born of God will continue to sin, because God's seed remains in them; they cannot go on sinning, because they have been born of God. This is how we know who the children of God are and who the children of the devil are: Anyone who does not do what is right is not God's child, nor is anyone who does not love their brother and sister. (1 John 3:6–10)

Scripture warns us to stay far away from people who call themselves Christians but are unrepentant of serious, egregious, ongoing abusive behavior. In fact, Paul considered greed and other flagrant, unrepentant sin in so-called Christians so serious that he instructed churches to take disciplinary action, excommunicate them from their congregation, and have nothing to do with them. In his first letter to the church in Corinth, Paul rebuked the church for continuing to accept a person as a member of the congregation who was engaged in serious sexual sin with his stepmother:

> So call a meeting, and when you gather together in the name of our Lord Jesus, and you know my spirit is present with you in the infinite power of our Lord Jesus, release this man over to Satan for the destruction of his rebellious flesh, in hope that his spirit may be rescued and restored in the day of the Lord. Boasting over your tolerance of sin is inappropriate. Don't you see that even a small compromise with sin permeates the entire fellowship, just as a little leaven permeates a batch of dough? . . . But now I'm writing to you so that you would exclude from your fellowship anyone who calls himself a fellow believer and practices sexual immorality, or is consumed with greed, or is an idolater, or is verbally abusive or a drunkard or a swindler. Don't mingle with them or even have a meal with someone like that. What right do I have to pronounce judgment on unbelievers? That's God's responsibility. But those who are inside the church family are our responsibility to discern and judge. So it's your duty to remove that wicked one from among you. (1 Corinthians 5:4–6, 11–13 TPT)

Again, in giving advice to Timothy, the young pastor at the church in Ephesus, Paul warned:

> Understand that the last days will be dangerous times. People will be selfish and love money. They will be the kind of people who brag and who are proud. They will slander others, and they will be disobedient to their parents. They will be ungrateful, unholy, unloving, contrary, and critical. They will be without self-control and brutal, and they won't love what is good. They will be people who are disloyal, reckless, and conceited. They will love pleasure instead of loving God. They will look like they are religious but deny God's power. Avoid people like this. (2 Timothy 3:1–5 CEB)

Paul further warns that they will slither and worm their way into households to control women (2 Timothy 3:6). These passages practically set forth the clinical definition of narcissistic personality disorder, sociopathy, and psychopathy.

The notes in the NIV Study Bible are instructive to church leaders. Church leaders are called to excommunicate the unrepentant abuser from the church community in the hope that he will repent. God always disciplines with the intent of redemption, as should we. However, God understands that evil people will not change unless there are consequences—severe consequences—that will humble their prideful hearts. But even with consequences, the majority of wicked hearts will not repent and turn to God. The story of the Israelites who did not repent even after years of warnings and a seventy-year exile is testament to this. But even if the abuser doesn't repent, church discipline is needed (1) to protect the innocent victims (usually the wife and children) so they can safely worship without running into their abuser, (2) to keep the church from being divided with some taking the side of the abuser and others taking the side of the wife, (3) to protect others from being the abuser's next victim, (4) to be an example of how seriously God takes sin, and (5) perhaps most importantly, as an institution of moral authority to demonstrate to people inside and outside the church that God stands with the oppressed and the righteous and against the wicked.

Clergy and counselors are first responders. A woman of faith will often approach her pastor or counselor at her church to make her marriage more tolerable. These women often have nowhere else to go because any funds spent to see a mental health professional will be discovered by the SNAP, and the wife will be subject to retaliation. However, pastors often lack training in the area of narcissism, sociopathy, psychopathy, and other forms of abuse. In a 2014 Lifeway survey, 60 percent of pastors stated that they did not receive adequate education in seminary to prepare them for addressing domestic abuse. By 2018, after the start of the #MeToo Movement, the percentage of pastors who felt they had not received adequate seminary training to address domestic abuse had improved to only 55 percent.[144]

Therefore, many clergy make the mistake of assuming the SNAP is a reasonable person of good intentions, and that with some counseling sessions, the pastor or counselor can convince him to treat his wife and family in an equitable manner. In the 2018 Lifeway survey, 70 percent of pastors admitted to using marital counseling to address domestic abuse.[145] This approach will not be successful. The SNAP is not a reasonable person with good intentions. He is evil disguised as a "good Christian" or a "good Catholic." The SNAP will lie to the pastor just as easily as he does to his wife, and without a twinge of remorse. Likewise, well-meaning but misguided and ill-equipped counselors who do not have specialized training in domestic violence can exacerbate the trauma and the violence. These are among the many reasons that the National Domestic Violence Hotline and the American Psychological Association strongly recommend that couples in abusive relationship do *not* participate in marital counseling.[146]

Pastors must inform themselves about domestic abuse in all its forms and the typical tactics of abusers, and they need to be wary of being played by the SNAP, who will make every effort to appear victimized and penitent to the clergy, while being vindictive to his spouse when church leaders are not looking. A good place to start is by taking the forty-hour domestic violence training program sponsored by many states. Pastors also need to be protective of their flock and mindful of the damage and division that the abuser will do to the church if they allow him to continue attending. As indicated in the Scripture, unrepentant, intentional, flagrant sin is not only destructive to the individual victims, but it also divides the church.

The biblically based response to a woman who is a victim of domestic abuse can be summarized in three words: listen, support, refer. A more detailed outline of how the church should address domestic abuse in a congregation is set forth below.

Thirteen Ways a Pastor Can Support a Victim of Domestic or Sexual Violence

1. Listen, Believe, and Validate.

When a woman approaches a pastor or church leader and shares that she is a victim of domestic abuse, they should listen, believe, and validate her in a compassionate and caring way. It has taken a lot of courage for her to reach out to an authority figure. She has likely been hiding the abuse for years. She may be panic-stricken, emotionally dysregulated, and shaking. She may seem overwhelmed, paralyzed with fear, and not know what to do. People who have lived with constant abuse suffer post-traumatic stress and have trouble concentrating and

---

[144] "Domestic and Gender-Based Violence: Pastor's' Attitudes and Actions," *Lifeway Research*, 2018, http://lifewayresearch.com/wp-content/uploads/2018/09/Domestic-Violence-Research-Report.pdf.
[145] "Domestic and Gender-Based Violence," Lifeway Research.
[146] "Why We Don't Recommend Couples Counseling for Abusive Relationships," National Domestic Violence Hotline, August 1, 2014, https://www.thehotline.org/2014/08/01/why-we-dont-recommend-couples-counseling-for-abusive-relationships/; "Intimate Partner Abuse and Relationship Violence," https://www.apa.org/about/division/activities/partner-abuse.pdf.

seeing a way out. Her stories will likely sound so fantastical that they seem out of a movie. The stories are very likely true.

2. Assure Her That Abuse Is Always a Choice and Is Not Her Fault.

A pastor should assure her, regardless of what her abuser has told her, and regardless of his excuses or justifications for his behavior, that she did not cause the abuse and the Scriptures do not condone abuse—ever. Abuse is always a choice.

3. Affirm.

A pastor should affirm her efforts to be a faithful wife and keep her family intact. She feels like a failure, and she believes that she is responsible for her failing marriage. She feels that if she was just nicer, or less sensitive, or smarter, or thinner, or had bigger breasts, that her husband would be crazy about her—like he was when they were dating. Her abuser has repeatedly told her that she is the problem—she is too sensitive, too stupid, too crazy, too fat, too skinny, too whatever. A pastor should affirm to her that she is not the problem, but the abuser has the problem and very likely will not change.

4. Ensure Safety and Safe Housing.

Many women and children escaping domestic abuse are physically unsafe and have no safe place to live. Because her abuser has ensured that she has no access to funds, most victims are unable to secure a separate apartment, and most abusers will not voluntarily leave the house. A pastor must make sure she and her children are safe. Offer temporary housing or funds to secure housing if she needs it. Offer her the support of families who have been trained in domestic abuse to walk alongside her and support her and her family. This is a great congregational ministry. If a church doesn't have a domestic abuse congregational ministry, refer her to the local domestic abuse shelter that offers housing and counseling.

5. Legal Mandatory Reporting.

Clergy are mandated reporters in most states. If children are involved, clergy have a legal duty to report known or suspected abuse or neglect to the Department of Children and Family Services (or the applicable state agency) immediately.[147] Mandatory reporters are required to report immediately, not after consultation with a committee or others. Some pastors are hesitant to report because they have not conducted an investigation and are not completely certain that abuse has occurred. However, complete certainty is not the standard for reporting. Reporting is required if the mandated reporter has a "reasonable cause" to believe the child may be an abused child. A child or nonabusive parent reporting abuse to the pastor is reasonable cause. The agency is responsible for investigating, not the church. Further, reporting is required whether they are being directly abused or if they are witnessing abuse. Some states have recently passed laws that require all mandated reporters to take continuing education on reporting and domestic abuse.

The pastor should let the victim know that it is not un-Christian to use our laws to protect herself and her

---

[147] In Illinois, the mandated reporter statute is 325 ILCS 5/1 et seq. To consult the requirements in your state, contact local legal counsel or visit RAINN (Rape, Abuse & Incest National Network) at https://apps.rainn.org/policy/?gclid=Cj0KCQjwyPbzBRDsARIsAFh15JbUgsSaqkc3bnGJka1Phcb_mgBArkzrtYVl8gBWoDeS53kGpFxGIIEaApkuEALw_wcB.

children, and that if she does not call DCFS, pastors are mandatory reporters and he must call DCFS. The pastor should sit with her while she makes the phone call to DCFS.

6. Help Obtain an Order of Protection.

A pastor should advise a woman experiencing physical abuse, sexual abuse, stalking, or harassment that she can obtain an emergency order of protection from the local county court. In an emergency hearing, she will be heard by a judge and the order will be issued the same day. The abuser will then be served by a sheriff on an emergency basis. If the victim must see an abuser before he has been served, for her safety she should not mention the order of protection and should act as if nothing is out of the ordinary until the sheriff can remove him. An order of protection offers several remedies to protect her and the children. For further details on orders of protection, see chapter 25, "Have a Safety Plan."

Most women are terrified to go to court to obtain an order of protection. They understandably fear the retaliation by the abuser. Some fear that it is un-Christian to involve the courts. However, abuse will continue to escalate without it, and will generally decrease when the abuser knows that his victim is willing to take legal action and others are watching. The pastor or a pro bono attorney from the church should offer to go with her to court to file for the order of protection and let her know that it is not against biblical principles to use our laws to protect herself and her children. In my county, Lake County, Illinois, the courthouse is located in downtown Waukegan. An office directly outside the courtroom where orders of protection are heard, entitled D100, is staffed by A Safe Place, a domestic violence organization that can help her complete the petition and provide legal advocacy.

7. Encourage Reporting Abuse to Law Enforcement.

Women in abusive relationships seldom involve law enforcement for fear of retaliation. She fears that if he is let out of custody, or if the charges do not stick, the abuser will come after her. Her fears are well-founded. Abusers are vindictive. If she is still with the abuser, the pastor should advise her to call the police during an abusive incident. If the police catch the abuser in action, they can arrest him. Then the victim should immediately obtain an order of protection, as the abuser may be released from custody. If an incident has already occurred, getting an order of protection first, and then reporting the incident to local police is advisable. The pastor should offer to go with her to file the police report.

8. Refer to Domestic Abuse Counselors and Services.

Most pastors and counselors are not experts in domestic violence, and most victims need multiple forms of assistance. Almost every woman will need specialized trauma counseling, along with a support group and legal services. Many will also need housing, career services, child care, and financial counseling. Several may also need temporary food stamps, health insurance, transportation, and immigration assistance. Essentially, women escaping abuse need nearly everything one might need to start a new life from scratch again. Domestic abuse organizations often provide, or belong to a network of organizations that can provide, many or most of the specialized services a survivor of domestic abuse will need to heal and restart her life. These services are usually provided free of charge or at a greatly reduced cost. She may feel that she needs a pastor's approval to seek counseling and other services, as some women are hesitant to seek counseling outside the church. To ensure that she and her children receive the help they need, a wise pastor will refer her to local domestic abuse counselors and organizations, or sexual abuse counselors and organizations, as appropriate. He will encourage her and her children to seek these services from professionals who are trained experts in domestic and sexual abuse.

In Lake County, Illinois, A Safe Place offers individual and group counseling, supervised child visitation and exchanges, and emergency and long-term housing to victims of domestic abuse. Zacharias Center offers free counseling to victims of sexual abuse and assault.

9. Refer to Legal Counsel.

Women in abuse almost always need legal counsel. As discussed in chapter 34, marriage to an abuser is not a Christian marriage. The religious marriage covenant has been broken by the abuser, and a civil divorce is merely a civil legality that recognizes that the spiritual marriage covenant has already been broken. If she is not married, she will need legal counsel if she has children with the abuser to secure child support and custody and to otherwise disentangle herself. In any case, she will likely need legal counsel to protect her, assist in obtaining an order of protection or in shepherding her through criminal proceedings if her abuser has been arrested on criminal charges. She can be assured that her abuser will lawyer up.

To ensure that a woman and her children are protected legally, financially, and physically, a caring and astute pastor will assure her that divorce from an abuser is not contrary to Scripture (see chapter 34), reaffirm that God Himself instituted governments, courts, and laws for the protection of people (see Romans 13), and refer her to competent legal counsel who is familiar with domestic abuse issues.

Support the victim if she chooses to divorce her abuser. She will be looking to her pastor for his blessing, even if she doesn't ask him outright. She needs to know that her pastor approves of her seeking a divorce. Support her, knowing that divorce is the only other choice to abuse.

10. Refer Her to Separate Counseling, Not Marital Counseling.

A pastor who hears that a marriage is in trouble will often leap to the conclusion that marital counseling will keep the couple together. It is a natural for pastors to encourage couples to reconcile and to believe that, if only the difficult person could hear the gospel message of Jesus, redemption and reconciliation would occur. The wife might also ask the pastor to provide marital counseling in the hope that it will save her marriage. Even the abuser may ask the pastor for marital counseling.

However, as noted previously, marital counseling is not indicated and is not appropriate in domestic abuse cases. Indeed, it is often dangerous and is an opportunity for the abuser to continue the abuse. The victim needs separate counseling with specialized domestic abuse counselors to help her heal, understand domestic abuse, and set healthy boundaries. The abuser may benefit from perpetrator counseling that attempts to get the abuser to understand abuse and its negative effects, take accountability for his destructive actions, and make long-term positive changes. However, counseling will not be effective for individuals with a permanent personality disorder who have no conscience, show no remorse, and really don't want to change. Counseling will simply make them smarter abusers with new lingo to continue abusing her and manipulate the counselor, the pastor, and the system.[148]

---

[148] Jennifer Young, "Are Batterer Intervention Programs Killing Women?" *Safe Relationships Magazine,* October 30, 2018, https://saferelationshipsmagazine.com/is-batterer-intervention-programs-killing-women.

Marital counseling and marriage books are appropriate for normal marital issues, such as different communication styles and different parenting styles. However, marital counseling is *not* appropriate for abuse.

11. Make Check-Ins and Give Financial Assistance.

Check in with her from time to time and be patient. Don't be surprised if she returns to her abuser, as most women return several times in the hope of making her marriage work. When she is ready, she will leave permanently. Until then, offer support, not judgment. Since almost all women have been victims of financial abuse, she will likely need financial assistance.

Treat her with the compassion you would a widow who has just lost her husband. Our society, and especially our churches, offer kindness and compassion to a woman who loses her husband by death. A widow is usually surrounded by her family, her husband's family, and her church family in her time of grief. She is greeted with casseroles, visitors, cards, flowers, and friends offering condolences and regaling happy times together. But a woman who has lost her husband by divorce has a very different experience. Like the widow, she has lost a marriage that she did not want to lose, but had no other choice. Unlike the widow, she is socially ostracized and treated as a leper or a harlot rather than as a human being deserving of compassion. And unlike the widow, she has the ongoing pain of an ex-husband who continues to abuse and harass her. Many counselors and women report that divorce from an abuser is more stressful and leaves more emotional, financial, and physical scars than the death of a husband.[149]

12. Conduct Biblical Conflict Resolution and Impose Separation and Church Discipline.

It is imperative for a pastor and his elders to conduct biblical conflict resolution and impose separation and church discipline in matters involving domestic abuse. Churches are loathe to do this, but Scripture does not give us the option to ignore those commands we find less desirable to obey. The steps for this process are outlined in detail later in this chapter.

13. Undergo Training.

For a more complete understanding of domestic abuse and how to respond appropriately, I highly recommend taking the forty-hour training course offered in nearly every state. In Illinois, the training is sponsored and certified by the Illinois Coalition Against Domestic Violence (ICADV) and is offered several times a year by numerous organizations that combat domestic abuse. In addition to the National Coalition Against Domestic Violence, each state has its own Coalition Against Domestic Violence. A Google search will reveal many organizations that offer training in connection with their state coalition.[150]

---

[149] Brooke Randoph, "Divorce Is Worse than Death," Brooke Randolph, Licensed Mental Health Counselor, March 5, 2015, http://brooke-randolph.com/Blog/Divorce_is_Worse_than_Death; Jane Brody, "Divorce's Stress Exacts Long-Term Health Toll," *NY Times*, December 13, 1983, section C, 1; "The Divorce Experience," *AARP*, 27–28.

[150] The National Coalition Against Domestic Violence can be contacted at www.ncadv.org. The Illinois Coalition Against Domestic Violence can be contacted at www.ilcadv.org. The National Domestic Violence Hotline can be contacted at www.thehotline.org.

Biblical Conflict Resolution, Separation, and Church Discipline

The Bible provides a roadmap for imposing conflict resolution, separation, and church discipline in cases of severe and unrepentant sin by a church member who claims he is a believer. These steps are not elective; they are commands. It is an unpleasant process, and the pastor who has the courage to take these steps will get pushback from the abuser and his cronies. The church may face a decrease in membership and giving. However, we are not called to take the easy way out or to cave under pressure from the Enemy. We are called to defend the sheep of our flocks, not provide a safe haven for wolves. That takes courage.

Jesus outlines the steps to take when a believer sins against another believer:

> If your brother or sister sins, go and point out their fault, just between the two of you. If they listen to you, you have won them over. But if they will not listen, take one or two others along, so that "every matter may be established by the testimony of two or three witnesses." If they still refuse to listen, tell it to the church; and if they refuse to listen even to the church, treat them as you would a pagan or a tax collector. (Matthew 18:15–17)

Biblical conflict resolution requires a believer to approach a wrongdoer in love to point out serious sin. The goal is reconciliation or, if reconciliation is not possible, separation. Jesus recognizes that we all have conflicts on occasion and we all need healthy conflict-resolution skills. In His love, He gave us the outline for conflict resolution. Jesus also realized that, in love, sometimes we must even rebuke others with the dual goals of repenting and being reconciled to God and to each other. However, Jesus also recognized that not all people will repent, and in these cases, separation is needed.

Four Steps of Biblical Conflict Resolution

To carry out Jesus's model of conflict resolution, a wise believer takes the following steps:

Step One

The one who has been wronged lovingly approaches the person who has wronged her, explains the sin, and humbly requests repentance and reconciliation. If the wrongdoer is truly repentant and both desire reconciliation, then reconciliation can occur. This approach works for most reasonable people with hearts attuned to the Holy Spirit.

Step Two

If the wrongdoer does not repent, the one who has been wronged takes one or two others who are wise (perhaps a friend or pastor or counselor), approaches the wrongdoer, explains the sin again, and humbly asks for repentance and reconciliation. The idea is that if the wrongdoer won't listen to the reason of one person, perhaps the logic of two or three people who have reputations for honor and reason will convince him to change his position, repent, and be reconciled. If repentance is gained, then reconciliation can occur and the conflict has been resolved. This approach usually works for people who are stubborn and need additional convincing of their sin, but who essentially want reconciliation with God and others.

Step Three

If the wrongdoer still doesn't repent, the person who has been wronged discusses the situation with the church pastor and leaders. The church leaders approach the wrongdoer with the victim, explain the sin, and ask the wrongdoer to repent and be reconciled. Because both believers are under the moral authority of the church, which is required to act to support the weak and oppressed and to do justice, the full authority of the local church will convince a hard heart to repent.

Step Four

Finally, if the wrongdoer still doesn't repent, the church steps in to support the oppressed victim and removes the wrongdoer from the congregation. The notion here is that if a person is so hard of heart that he will not repent of his sin with the urging of the one he has wronged and the entire church, he is not seeking God. He is actually on Satan's team actively harming others, and only serious consequences (including losing his church and community of social and spiritual support) will ever enable him to humble his heart to repent and seek God—if repentance is ever to happen at all.

Jesus, like Paul in 1 Corinthians 5 and 2 Timothy 3, recognized that some hearts are so hard they will not repent. But if, by a miracle, they do, it is only because serious consequences have brought them to a place of humility before God, which is a necessary requirement for repentance and reconciliation. Jesus outlined these steps because He knew that pride—a sense of entitlement to such an extent that they believe God's rules don't apply to them—is the true reason behind sin and conflicts.

The Old Testament and both Jesus and Paul make it clear that the church's role in conflict resolution is not optional. The church has an essential role to play in supporting the oppressed and weak, in ushering in healing, in bringing repentance if possible, in keeping divisions among members at bay, and in standing as the moral authority of how God sees the situation. A church does not have the option of turning a blind eye to the plight of the oppressed or allowing parishioners with continued, unrepentant, serious sin to continue to worship with the congregation.

Four Steps of Biblical Conflict Resolution as Applied in Domestic Abuse Situations

Step One: Approaching the Abuser. If the church is following Jesus's mandate, by the time a woman approaches her pastor for assistance, she has already taken the first step of privately approaching her abusive husband to resolve the conflict with no results. She has likely attempted conflict resolution dozens of times, only to be rebuffed. Direct attempts at one-on-one conflict resolution with an abuser are simply ineffective because their hearts are far away from God, as we discussed in chapter 14. She may also have already taken the second step of approaching the abuser with one or two witnesses by seeking the advice of a counselor or therapist.

Steps Two and Three: Approaching the Abuser with Witnesses and Involving Church Leadership. Taking the next step will take courage, as exposing the acts of an abuser to others invites retaliation and further abuse. Given the danger that victims are often in, along with the severity of the sin, it is advisable that church leadership be aware of the matter and act, if necessary. Thus, the second step involving one or two witnesses approaching the abuser, and the third step involving church leadership approaching the abuser, may be combined. Therefore, after checking with the victim to ensure she wants involvement from the pastor and that she is safe, a pastor should approach the abuser with another church leader to point out the harmful sin, and to encourage him to repent, and enter into a long-term (six months to a year) domestic abuse perpetrator counseling program to unlearn abusive behavior. Marriage counseling is counter-indicated in situations involving abuse, and it does more harm to the victim. The perpetrator has a lifetime of unlearning to do, and if the miracle of repentance is to occur, it is only because he wants to and is willing to make radical changes. It is also important at this time that the victim seek separate counseling with domestic abuse counselors to strengthen her, to help her understand that she is not the problem, and to encourage her to do whatever she needs to do to provide a healthy and safe environment for herself and her children, regardless of whether the abuser sincerely repents.

The relationship may be irretrievably broken, and she may need to move on without him, even if he does repent. Once the marriage vows have been violated by an abuser, a victim is under no obligation to reconcile. A wise, Spirit-filled pastor recognizes this and will allow her to make her own decisions about reconciling without pressure from the pastor. Likewise, the abuser needs to repent for his own salvation and relationship with God, regardless of whether his wife is willing to reconcile. Repentance does not guarantee reconciliation, but it certainly is required for reconciliation. Again, with an abuser, it is highly unlikely that he will repent, even with the urging of others. He may apologize to look good in front of the pastor and others, but these expressions will likely be insincere. He may even be on good behavior for a little while, until the next eruption. And in so doing, he perpetuates the cycle of abuse that has become ingrained in him (see chapter 4). At some point, he will likely retaliate because his wife has exposed his secrets.

During this phase, the abuser should be separated from his wife or partner and from the church. This forced separation from the church may require the approval of the governing body of the church, such as the board of elders or deacons. The separation is necessary for the victim's safety. This period provides the distance and safe environment for her and her family to begin healing away from the constant demands of the abuser, who will be exerting pressure on her to return. The abuser's separation from the congregation is needed for the unity of the congregation because the abuser will cause division among the church as he spreads lies about the victim and attempts to get people on his side and against her. Separating the abuser from the congregation ensures the victim and her children a safe and supportive place of worship without the fear of facing her abuser. These forced separations—from both the abuser's biological family and his church family—are necessary if the abuser is ever to repent. Abusers rarely change, but if a change occurs, it is *only* because of consequences. With a forced separation from his family and social network—all of whom are aware of the abuse and who condemn his abusive actions—there is a miniscule amount of hope that a miracle might happen and that he might humble himself and repent. However, if a church imposes no consequences, there is virtually no hope of repentance. When a church chooses to ignore the biblical mandate of church discipline of an abusive member, it foregoes the possibility of seeing a miracle and being a vessel that brings about repentance and reconciliation to God.

What Genuine Repentance Looks Like

The Bible describes true repentance. Genuine repentance must be demonstrated before ending the period of separation. True biblical repentance requires the following:

Genuine Confession of Abuse

First, true repentance requires an abuser to openly confess that his actions were wrong, apologize, and take full responsibility for his wrong deeds. The apostle Paul provides a model when he openly admits his heinous sin, makes no excuses, and gives Jesus the credit for saving him. In his first letter to Timothy, Paul states:

> Even though I was once a blasphemer and a persecutor and a violent man, I was shown mercy because I acted in ignorance and unbelief. . . . Here is a trustworthy saying that deserves full acceptance: Christ Jesus came into the world to save sinners—of whom I am the worst. But for that very reason I was shown mercy so that in me, the worst of sinners, Christ Jesus might display his immense patience as an example for those who would believe in him and receive eternal life. (1 Timothy 1:13, 15–16)

James, the brother of Jesus, tells us to "confess your sins to each other and pray for each other so that you may be healed" (James 5:16). A genuine confession of sin and repentance is a necessary and first step toward the healing of the abuser and his victim. A truly repentant confession does *not* include the statement that "mistakes were made." This is a non-apology and takes no responsibility for intentionally harmful actions. Intentional actions designed to harm another person are not mistakes. Mistakes are unintentional actions that were done with one purpose to benefit another, but an unintentional harmful consequence occurred instead. For example, a mistake occurs when someone gives another person a piece of chocolate with nuts with the intent of giving that person a benefit, but it harms that person because the giver does not know that she is allergic to nuts. An abuser will give his wife chocolate with nuts, knowing that she is allergic to nuts. A mistake occurs when a husband thinks his wife is in the back of the van when he leaves, much like Kevin was accidentally left at home in the movie *Home Alone*. An abuser will leave his wife on the street and leave, knowing she is not in the van.

A truly repentant confession also does not include the statement, "I'm sorry you feel offended." This is also a non-apology that takes no responsibility for deliberately destructive actions. This statement blames the victim for being offended by an action that was done with the purpose to offend and harm.

Finally, a truly repentant confession does not include a statement that minimizes, justifies, rationalizes, excuses, defends, diminishes, or otherwise explains away bad behavior. Confession of wrongdoing and humbly admitting sin without excuse is the first step toward repentance.

Public Confession of Abuse

Second, true repentance requires the abuser to openly and publicly confess his purposefully harmful actions to the victim and all the others he has hurt. Ideally, this confession to all affected will occur at the same time. Again, Paul provides the example of repentance. He did not secretly admit his sins to God while publicly claiming his innocence. He included his confessions in his letters that were shared with the churches, and he spoke publicly of his past sinful actions.

He commanded the church at Ephesus to do the same: "Have nothing to do with the fruitless deeds of darkness, but rather expose them. It is shameful even to mention what the disobedient do in secret. But everything exposed by the light becomes visible—and everything that is illuminated becomes a light. This is why it is said: 'Wake up, sleeper, rise from the dead, and Christ will shine on you'" (Ephesians 5:11–14). Paul knew that exposing sin is a sign of humble repentance, a changed heart, and an illuminating example of hope for others.

Public confession shows that an abuser's heart has changed, while private confessions do not. A person whose heart has been changed will want to shout from the rooftops how Jesus has rescued him and changed him. Much like John Newton, the author of the beloved hymn "Amazing Grace," a transformed person will give glory to God and announce, "Amazing grace, how sweet the sound that saved a wretch like me! I once was lost, but now am found; was blind, but now I see." For those churches worried about a slander or defamation lawsuit brought by the abuser, a public confession by the abuser himself, rather than exposure by the clergy, eliminates the elements required to sustain a slander suit.

However, all too often, abusers hedge their bets. An abuser whose heart has not changed will insincerely confess his wrongdoings to his spouse in private in the hope of getting her to return to the relationship. Publicly, he is lying, blaming, and slandering her to others to alienate them from her and to recruit them to his team of supporters. In this way, he calculates that if she doesn't return to the relationship, she will have not a support network, and he will have his group of minions who have turned against her.

Complete a Perpetrator Counseling Program with Real Changes

Third, true repentance requires an abuser to attend, complete, embrace, and graduate from an extensive domestic violence perpetrator counseling program and show true life-transforming change. These programs often last six months or more and are designed to unlearn the destructive mindset and actions that abusers have learned and have often perfected during their lives. Unfortunately, perpetrator treatment programs usually fail in changing abusers because most abusers simply don't want to change, and they are unwilling to listen to advice or accept instruction from others.

The book of Proverbs gives us the blueprint for wisdom. True repentance results in humility and wisdom. The wise listen to advice (Proverbs 12:15), have a group of wise advisors (Proverbs 11:14), listen to advice and accept discipline (Proverbs 19:20), accept instruction (Proverbs 10:8), don't stir up conflict (Proverbs 28:25), and trust in the Lord and His wisdom rather than their own (Proverbs 28:26).

Those who have not repented will reject the advice and instruction of counselors and will continue to destroy the lives of those around them. Only those who have truly repented are willing to undertake extensive counseling with domestic abuse experts, admit their own folly, and accept instruction and advice from others.

Restitution Plus

Fourth, true repentance requires an abuser to make restitution to his victim for the losses he has caused. True repentance will put in the heart of the abuser a desire to not just make her whole again, but to make her better than before the damage he inflicted. These losses may include medical bills, broken personal items, or hotel bills or rent if she needed to flee her home for safety. Her losses may include a lost job or other lost financial opportunity. True repentance will cause the abuser to repay her for these financial losses, and then some.

In the Old Testament, when someone realized his guilt, the law required him to confess his sin and make full restitution plus 20 percent (Leviticus 6:1–7; Numbers 5:6–7). Sincere repentance results in a payment that makes the victim whole, plus an additional 20 percent payment for her pain, suffering, inconvenience, and emotional distress of being wronged.

In addition to financial losses, a victim's losses will likely include broken relationships caused by the abuser's efforts to divide people and alienate them from his victim. True repentance requires an abuser to do everything in his power to restore the broken relationships that he has caused and make them better than before.

When someone throws a baseball through a window, simply saying "I'm sorry" is insufficient to show repentance. Genuine repentance requires the wrongdoer to also replace the broken window with an even better window than before. In the same way, true repentance after domestic abuse requires the abuser to restore the victim to wholeness and put her in a better place than she was before the abuse.

Overcoming the Narcissist, Sociopath, Psychopath, and other Domestic Abusers

Permanent Change in Attitude and Behavior

Fifth, genuine repentance requires a change in attitude from pride and arrogance to humility and service, and a change in behavior from abusive to supportive and encouraging on a consistent basis for the remainder of his life. To clearly see whether repentance is sincere, the transformation needs to be evident and consistent for at least two consecutive years.

Again, the apostle Paul's life is instructive. When Jesus Christ got ahold of Paul, his transformation was evident in a completely changed life. Paul went from persecuting and killing Christians to loving them, teaching and serving them, and preaching the love of Christ with everything he had until his last breath. Repentance will be evident when a similar changed life is seen in a former abuser.

The sin of pride is at the root of domestic abuse. Pride is evidenced by arrogance, haughtiness, no need for God or others, viewing oneself as better than God and one's fellow man, and having no need or respect for God, His laws, and others. St. Augustine called pride the "original sin," the "beginning of all sin," and the sin from which all others arise.[151] C. S. Lewis labeled pride "the utmost evil."[152] The underlying sin of all abuse is pride. The Bible is replete with examples of prideful, wicked people who turned their backs on God. In the description of nearly every wicked king of Israel, pride reared its ugly head once the king had become successful and established his kingdom in opposition to God.

The Bible is clear on where God stands when it comes to pride. God opposes the proud (James 4:6). God hates pride, arrogance, evil behavior, and perverse speech (Proverbs 8:13). God detests all the proud of heart (Proverbs 16:5).

God also warns of the destructive results of pride, and He commands us to be humble. In his pride, a wicked man does not seek God (Psalm 10:4). "Where there is strife, there is pride" (Proverbs 13:10). "Haughty eyes and a proud heart—the unplowed field of the wicked—produce sin" (Proverbs 21:4).

God's Word commands us to be humble to avoid the destruction that pride brings. Do nothing out of selfish ambition, but be humble (Philippians 2:3).

Thus, true repentance requires, at its very core, setting aside pride and putting on humility, which results in a life that is transformed from abuse to the service of others.

All five elements of sincere repentance are necessary prior to allowing an abuser back in a congregation, or back into a marriage if the wife is willing to reconcile. Far too often, churches do not follow these steps, and it is the victim, not the abuser, who must leave the church for her safety. Requiring separation and sincere repentance will allow the victim and her children to safely attend her congregation, be surrounded by supportive church members, and not be in fear of being harassed by her abuser at her house of worship. It also sends a clear message to the children, the congregation, people outside the church, and the abuser that the abuse is wrong and is not condoned by the church.

A victim is often so wishing to restore her family that she is swayed by an abuser's demands and crocodile tears and is willing to reconcile without seeing true repentance. This will result in further and exacerbated abuse.[153] A prudent pastor will strongly encourage the victim to require these changes prior to allowing the abuser back in the family home.

---

[151] Paul Griffiths, *Lying: An Augustinian Theology of Duplicity* (Eugene, OR: Wipf and Stock Publishers, 2008), 59, 61 (quoting St. Augustine's remarks on Sirach 10:12–13); "Works of Augustine: Pride," *Augnet*, n.d., www.augnet.org/en/works-of-augustine/his-ideas/2328-pride/.

[152] C. S. Lewis, *Mere Christianity* (New York: HarperCollins Publishing, 2001), 121–122.

[153] See chapter 31 for the biblical account of a woman who returned to an unrepentant abuser in Judges 19–20.

Abusers who are unwilling to take these steps are not truly repentant. An astute pastor will be wary of abusers who "apologize" and cry crocodile tears, but do not want to undergo these steps.

Step Four. Removal from the Congregation. If the abuser still does not repent as outlined in steps two and three, the fourth step of biblical discipline requires removing the abuser from the congregation and prohibiting him from attending the congregation unless genuine repentance is demonstrated. Clearly, once a situation involves removal by the senior pastor and governing body, it is evident that the heart of the abuser is hard and turned away from God and his spouse. There is little chance that an abuser will change. However, all discipline should be done with the hope that in time, the consequences imposed will be instrumental in turning the abuser to God. Redemption is always God's hope.

Removing an abuser from church membership and prohibiting him from attending worship or other church functions is not simply a suggestion, but is a command in both the Old and New Testaments. The Old Testament requires wicked people to be excommunicated from the community in Deuteronomy 17:7, 12, Numbers 15:30, Ezra 10:8, Exodus 12:15, Leviticus 7:20, and Leviticus 17:9. Proverbs tells us, "Do not make friends with a hot-tempered person, do not associate with one easily angered, or you may learn his ways and get yourself ensnared" (Proverbs 22:24–25)

In addition to the passages in 1 Corinthians 5, 2 Timothy 3, and Matthew 18, the writers of the New Testament warn us of divisive people:

> Warn a divisive person once, and then warn them a second time. After that, have nothing to do with them. You may be sure that such people are warped and sinful; they are self-condemned. (Titus 3:10–11)

> I urge you, brothers and sisters, to watch out for those who cause divisions and put obstacles in your way that are contrary to the teaching you have learned. Keep away from them. For such people are not serving our Lord Christ, but their own appetites. By smooth talk and flattery they deceive the minds of naïve people. (Romans 16:17–18)

Reasons a Church Must Get Involved

Although the church's disciplinary action cannot guarantee a change of heart, the failure to impose severe consequences guarantees the abuse will continue. Since SNAPs have no internal self-control mechanism, good behavior is only the result of external measures, such as the authority of the courts or a disciplinary body. In rare cases, the shame and isolation that comes as a result of such actions may humble the SNAP and prompt him to repent. This is, of course, the hope and goal of church discipline.

Even if the disciplinary action does not change the SNAP, it is necessary for other reasons. First, it protects the victim from continued physical and verbal assaults, as SNAPs are less likely to abuse a victim once their bad behavior is exposed and they know they are being watched.

Second, it sends a clear message to the church members that the victim is not at fault, and it protects the victim from the character assassination and smear campaign the SNAP will inevitably engage in. SNAP behavior is predictable, and one thing is absolutely guaranteed—the SNAP does not want to look bad in front of this social group, and he will play the victim and make false accusations against his spouse as soon as she leaves. Church disciplinary action protects the victim from the social ostracizing and demands of silence that inevitably result when the abuser and his allies are left unfettered. It informs the congregation that the leaders are on the side of the victim, not the abuser. This support is immeasurable to the victim.

Third, churches should be a safe environment for those who come to worship, and church discipline protects the victim from being forced to choose between leaving her religious community or facing her abuser. When a church remains neutral and the SNAP suffers no public consequences, he inevitably remains at the church, playing the victim, continuing the character assassinations against his wife, and gaining the support of others while the wife leaves the church to avoid the danger of facing her abuser and enduring the severe anxiety and further abuse that it brings.

Fourth, disciplinary action sends a strong message to the children of the abuser that his actions are not acceptable. Just as the behavior of a SNAP is utterly predictable, so is the behavior of their children. As discussed in chapters 7, 22, and 23, older children are prone to side with the abusive father when their mother leaves the marriage, and even more so if the church or synagogue fails to take a strong public stand to support the mother. Having her own children whom she is trying to protect turn against her is, of course, heart-wrenching for a mother. Only when a strong message is sent by a social group with moral authority, such as the church or synagogue, denouncing the SNAP's action, will children take the side of their mother. It is important for children of all ages to see that their place of worship take a stand for righteousness. Far too often, young people leave the church and reject God altogether when they observe church leaders who do not have the courage to stand against evil.

Fifth, by their very nature, churches and synagogues decree a moral law. One of the essential functions of the church and synagogue is to distinguish right behaviors and attitudes from evil. The Christian church ought to stand boldly on God's side of righteousness, even when it's unpleasant, uphold standards of behavior within their congregations, and defend and protect the defenseless. The consequences when the church refuses to act like the church are evident in the sexual abuse scandal in the Catholic Church. This is but one sad example of church leadership fully aware of the sexual abuse at the hands of its clergy, but refusing to impart consequences or church discipline on the abusers, and demanding silence of those exposing the abuse—-or suffer the consequences. Evil breeds in silence. Thus, Paul called for publicly exposing sin so the sheer weight of the shame halts the abuser. Without consequences, without the truth being exposed, and without the church willing to take a stand, the evil of abuse breeds. For the churches which are concerned about a potential lawsuit brought by an abuser, the courts have consistently held that churches can operate their churches according to the tenants of their own religion, such as setting standards for membership, attendance or excommunication, without interference from the secular courts.

Finally, church discipline that validates the wife's experience, upholds her actions to save her marriage and hold her husband accountable, and makes a moral declaration that abuse is not acceptable is incredibly healing to the victim. By the time a woman seeks the counsel of clergy, she is at a point of questioning her sanity and her faith. Without a church or synagogue taking a strong stand that the abuser's actions are not acceptable, that the SNAP breached the covenant of marriage, and that she is not wrong to hold him accountable, the wife will struggle emotionally for years with unhealed wounds, PTSD, and even suicidal thoughts. However, with the support of her church or synagogue leaders, a woman is able to see things in the proper perspective and heal from the trauma much more quickly.

Attempting to be neutral is, in effect, taking the side of the SNAP and abuse. The abuse will continue. Churches and synagogues must stand on the side of righteousness.

Chapter 36

The Common Mistakes Churches and Pastors Make

As important as it is for the church to address domestic abuse biblically, equally important is avoiding common mistakes. To many faithful worshipers, pastors stand in the place of God as His mouthpiece here on earth. Their words and actions have import and influence far beyond other mortals. As God's representative and leader of a church, a pastor stands as a moral authority. His words and actions can encourage, support, and heal a victim of abuse and her family, or wreak further devastation and destroy a family, leaving her with unimaginable guilt and shame.

Perhaps no other matter is as important for a pastor to get right than how he addresses domestic violence in his congregation. Escaping from domestic abuse and leaving an abuser is, hands down, the most devastating, gut-wrenching experience most women will ever live through. As leaders in the spiritual community, pastors and other church leaders are held to a higher standard of accountability than the rest of the flock to get it right (James 3:1).

A search of the internet, news stories, and websites that address domestic abuse reveal that many pastors approach the subject in a way that is not only painful to victims of abuse, but also emboldens the abuser to continue and escalate the abuse. One youth pastor who sexually assaulted a high school girl under his care received a standing ovation from his church when he revealed his sexual assault (complete with an obligatory apology) to his congregation.[154] My own experience as a survivor of domestic abuse, and as an attorney and counselor who has represented dozens of domestic abuse survivors, supports the stories of millions of other women: pastors often do not get this right. Whether it is because of their ignorance of domestic violence or intentional actions to harm and silence those who dare speak up, many clergy side with the abuser rather than the victim. Sadly, some pastors are some of the most egregious abusers themselves, and they abuse with the full backing of their church, who turn against the pastor's wife when she exposes the truth.

---

[154] Kyle Swenson, "A Pastor Admitted a Past 'Sexual Incident' with a Teen, Saying He was 'Deeply Sorry,'" *The Washington Post*, January 10, 2018, https://www.washingtonpost.com/news/morning—mix/wp/2018/01/10/a-pastor-admitted-a-past-sexual-incident-with-a-teen-his-congregation-gave-him-a-standing-ovation/.

At best, well-meaning but uninformed pastors often unintentionally harm the victim, the abuser, and the church. To remain neutral, apathetic churches do nothing, essentially siding with the abuser. A duel between an abuser and his victim is fundamentally a match between a tiger and a bunny. The tiger will rip the bunny to shreds if someone stronger than the tiger doesn't intervene on the bunny's behalf. Thus, taking a neutral position in a match between a tiger and a bunny is siding with the tiger. At worst, some patriarchal, misogynist pastors actively support the abuser, cover up the abuse, and silence the abused. In any case, far too often, churches take steps or fail to take steps that leave the victim devastated, the abuser unrepentant and far from God, and a church divided.

Thirteen Common Mistakes That Churches and Pastors Make Regarding Domestic Abuse in Their Congregations

1. Fooled by Charm, Failure to Recognize Domestic Abuse as Evil

Some clergy make the mistake of being fooled by the charming, outgoing, charismatic personality of the abuser. The abuser may be a leader at work or in the community. He relishes the limelight and admiration, and he wants to appear as a pillar of the community. Although clergy usually have good intentions, they often do not want to admit that someone in their congregation who appears normal is an instrument of evil. Often clergy fail to recognize that the victim (and now the clergy) is in a real spiritual battle of good versus evil.

Many clergy do not want to admit that evil is the appropriate characteristic of domestic abuse, and that the father of evil is Satan, who has the abuser in his clutches. Satan's mission statement is quite clear—he has come to steal, kill, and destroy (John 10:10), and families are clearly in his crosshairs. Domestic abuse "steals, kills, and destroys" a family like nothing else. Satan masquerades as an angel of light. Likewise, abuse is perpetrated by one who appears outwardly as an "angel of light" (2 Corinthians 11:13–14), but is characterized by lies and destructiveness (2 Timothy 3:1–8).

Instead of calling abuse the evil it is, abuse is called an "incident," a "mistake," a "strong personality," or some watered-down version that does not recognize the evil nature of the intentional, systematic, multi-tactic destruction by the abuser of the ones he should protect.

We, and particularly leaders in the church, must be very careful not to call evil good, and good evil. The God who defends the widows and the fatherless will demand an accounting from those who do.

> Woe to those who call evil good
>   and good evil,
> who put darkness for light
>   and light for darkness,
> who put bitter for sweet
>   and sweet for bitter. . . .
> Who acquit the guilty for a bribe,
>   but deny justice to the innocent.
> Therefore, as tongues of fire lick up straw
>   and as dry grass sinks down in the flames,
> so their roots will decay
>   and their flowers blow away like dust;
> for they have rejected the law of the LORD Almighty

> and spurned the word of the Holy One of Israel.
> Therefore the Lord's anger burns against his people;
> his hand is raised and he strikes them down. (Isaiah 5:20, 23–25)

2. Fooled by False Apologies and Lies

Some clergy make the mistake of being fooled by the abuser's false apologies, promises of being a changed man, and lies. Abusers feign apologies and promise they have changed to get their victims to return to the abusive marriage and to get into the good graces of the pastors and church. These false apologies have always worked before to get her to come back, and abusers count on them working again—on the victim and on the pastors.

In addition to false apologies and feigned promises of changing, abusers lie to pastors, just as they have lied to their wives. When questioned by a pastor, abusers deny, justify, or mitigate the abuse to exonerate themselves. Abusers blame the victim and will falsely accuse her of any number of things to escape exposure. Abusers will falsely accuse others of the things they are most guilty of themselves (a tactic called projection), the most common being claims of adultery, mental instability, and abuse.

Some pastors even write letters of recommendation to the court or serve as character witnesses during hearings for orders of protection or criminal matters. They expound upon the long-term church membership of the abuser and his active volunteerism in efforts to reduce the punishment of the abuser's bad behavior. Nothing can be more betraying to a victim than for her own pastor to testify on behalf of her abuser when she is trying to seek protection.

Lying is a primary characteristic of any abuser. A naïve pastor will be swayed, but a discerning pastor will recognize the deceit that has become second nature to an abuser.

3. Not Believing Her

Far too many pastors make the mistake of not believing and not validating the victim. The stories of most victims are so heinous and atrocious that they sound like a Hollywood horror film made from some deranged writer's imagination rather than the story of a churchgoing family. Pastors simply don't believe the abused spouse when she tells him of the atrocities done at the hand of her husband, choosing instead to believe the lies of the abuser. On the other hand, many women downplay the abuse, leaving pastors to question why she would ever want to leave in the first place.

Disbelieving, insensitive pastors make the mistake of asking questions or making comments along the lines of: "If it was so bad, why did you stay so long?" "Are you sure you aren't exaggerating? He's such a nice guy." "That is crazy. He wouldn't do something like that."

Many pastors are worried that the victim is making false allegations as she finally shares the truth of the abuse she has hidden for years. However, a pastor should be more worried about all the women in his congregation who have not come forward. As any law enforcement officer understands, domestic abuse is not only the most commonly reported matter to police, but along with child abuse, it is also one of most underreported matters.[155] Victims are far more likely to hide abuse than to expose it.

For pastors who continue to be concerned about false allegations, here are some points to ponder.

---

[155] Lauren Rohr, "How Children's Advocacy Centers Help Reduce Trauma for Child Abuse Victims," *Daily Herald*, September 2, 2019, https://www.dailyherald.com/news/20190902/how-childrens-advocacy-centers-help-reduce-trauma-for-child-abuse-victims (quoting Mike Nerheim, Lake County, Illinois, state's attorney).

Considerations before Concluding Her Allegation of Abuse Is False

We have the Spirit of truth. We have the Holy Spirit for discernment. If we have doubts about the veracity of a testimony, we should earnestly inform ourselves about domestic abuse as much as possible, seeking truth from the Holy Spirit, the Spirit of truth.

The majority of claims of abuse are true. Most researchers state that false claims make up only 2 to 6 percent of claims.[156] In other words, statistically speaking across all circumstances, among women of all faiths or no faith at all, claims of abuse are true 94 to 98 percent of the time. It is fair to presume that a woman who is a faithful follower of Christ, is not previously known to be a liar, and is not previously known to have a mental illness is making a true claim. However, it is prudent to be mindful of things that arise that would damage credibility.

Domestic abuse is by far the most prevalent crime, but it is also the most underreported crime.[157] It's far more likely there are cases of unreported domestic and sexual abuse than overreported abuse. Here are some sobering statistics:

- Out of 1,000 rapes, only 230 are ever reported to police, only 46 of these lead to an arrest, only 9 are referred to prosecutors for a criminal trial, only 5 will lead to a felony conviction, and only 4 result in incarceration of the rapist. Therefore, 99.6 percent of rapists go free without any repercussions. The primary reasons for not reporting include fear of retaliation, assuming that the police would not do anything to help, or believing that it was a personal matter.[158]
- In a marriage or long-term relationship, 68 percent of women who are in abusive relationships are also raped by their partners, and 80 percent of these women are raped repeatedly. When rape occurs within a marriage or long-term relationship, only 6 percent of women ever report the rape, and only 8 percent of women seek a protective order.[159]
- With respect to childhood sexual abuse, approximately one in four girls and one in six boys will experience childhood sexual abuse, but only 1.8 in 1,000 cases of actual childhood sexual abuse are ever reported.[160]
- Abusive parents are far more likely to seek sole custody of children compared to nonviolent parents, and they are successful 70 percent of the time.[161]
- A Safe Place, the organization in Lake County, Illinois, that serves thousands of victims of domestic violence each year, is successful in obtaining an order of protection for its clients in approximately 95 percent of cases. In other words, in nearly every instance, an objective, reasonable judge in a court of law believed the person to be credible and that their allegations supported court-ordered legal protection.

---

[156] D. Lisak, et al., "False Allegations of Sexual Assault: An Analysis of Ten Years of Reported Cases," PubMed, December 16, 2010, National Library of Medicine—National Institutes of Health, doi:10.1177/1077801210387747. See also Lisa Lazard, "Here's the Truth about False Accusations of Sexual Violence," Independent, November 27, 2917, https://www.independent.co.uk/voices/false-sexual-violence-assault-rape-allegations-truth-rare-international-day-for-the-elimination-of-a8077876.html.
[157] Rohr, Children's Advocacy Centers.
[158] "The Criminal Justice System: Statistics," RAINN, n.d., https://www.rainn.org/statistics/criminal-justice-system.
[159] Lauren R. Taylor and Nicole Gaskin-Laniyan, "Sexual Assault in Abusive Relationships," National Institute of Justice, February 1, 2007, https://www.nij.gov/journals/256/Pages/sexual—assault.aspx.
[160] www.amjudges.org/publications/courtrv/cr35-1/CR35-1McDonald.pdf.
[161] "False Allegations of Abuse—or Not?" Colorado Coalition Against Domestic Violence, n.d., https://www.violence-freecolorado.org/wp—content/uploads/2013/11/CCADV—CCASA—Fact—Sheet—on—Myth—of—False—Allegations_updated—2.21.14.pdf.

- False rape claims have similar characteristics: they are usually bizarre forms of cruelty that don't make sense, and false claims are usually made by people with a criminal history, or a specific type of mental illness known as factitious disorder (related to Munchausen syndrome) that compels them to say they've been assaulted in dramatic ways.[162]

Consider the Totality of the Circumstances
- A woman's identity is usually wrapped up in her relationships as wife, mother, friend, sister, etc. A Christian woman's identity is based on her relationship with Jesus and her faithfulness to His calling and commands. Women are inclined to stay in abuse and suffer a great deal to keep a family together; they usually leave only when the abuse comes to a point that is unsustainable or their children are affected.
- Women rarely want to leave a man who loves them and is a good father and a good husband. What would be the motive?
- Women in abusive relationships are also victims of financial abuse in 99 percent of cases, yet they are willing to live in poverty or a far lower standard of living to get out of abuse. She has nothing to gain financially from false allegations.
- Does she have a history of lying? Does she have a criminal record? Does she have a history of making up fictitious stories of victimization? If not, she is likely among the 94 to 98 percent of women making true allegations.
- Does she have a history as a responsible, godly woman? Is she sweet, kind, giving, forgiving, lovely, generous, without guile, and loyal? These are the traits that abusers look for.
- What are his external characteristics? Abusers are often friendly, outgoing, charismatic, well-dressed, attractive, arrogant, prideful, in positions of leadership, wealthy, concerned about appearances, generous, and volunteer when it makes them look good to others. They have Jekyll/Hyde personalities—they appear one way to others, and completely different to their spouse.
- It is probably better to err on the side of supporting a victim than supporting an abuser.

4. Blaming Her

Too many pastors make the mistake of blaming the victim for her own abuse. They mistakenly believe that she did or didn't do something to provoke his abuse.

Disbelieving, insensitive pastors ask questions or make comments that cast doubt on the victim's abilities and behaviors and hold her responsible for the abuser's actions. Comments from real-life pastors include: "What did you do to provoke him to do that?"; "He would like you more if you lost thirty pounds and dressed nicer"; and "Well, if you would stay home and make sure dinner was on the table when he got home, he would be happier with you."

Like the comments that reveal unbelief on the pastor's part, these types of comments demonstrate an enormous ignorance of domestic abuse and an uncaring, unloving, un-Christlike response that clearly indicates the pastor supports and justifies the actions of the abuser.

The victim is silenced and blamed yet again, this time by her own pastor. The blame for the abuser's behavior is put on the victim rather than on the abuser. Contrary to the belief of some pastors, abusers choose to abuse

---

[162] Sandra Newman, "I've Studied False Rape Claims: The Accusation against Kavanaugh Doesn't Fit the Profile," *Vox*, September 18, 2018, https://www.vox.com/first-person/2018/9/18/17874504/kavanaugh-assault-allegation-christine-blasey-ford.

because that is their nature, not because of anything his partner has done or not done. An abuser chooses to abuse regardless of her appearance, abilities, or behavior.

As a result, the victim is further victimized by an unsupportive clergy who wrongly blames her for her husband's choice to abuse. The result of this is nothing short of emotional devastation. The very church that teaches her to love, be kind, and support those in need is the same church that refuses to put those characteristics into practice. This is hypocrisy in its highest form. Many victims state that the lack of support of their church and pastor is worse than the actual abuse.

As a result, the victim, who likely has made Herculean efforts to be a faithful wife and keep her family intact, feels betrayed and rejected by her husband, her pastor, her church, and her God. She believes that she, rather than the abuser, is the problem. She learns that the church is not a safe place, so she must keep the abuse silent. She is likely distraught, depressed, or even suicidal. She feels completely alone, and sadly, she is. The only one who hears her cry is God, but His ambassadors on this earth have utterly failed her.[163]

5. Demanding Submission or Return to Abusive Relationship

Some clergy make the mistake of telling her that for her husband to change, she must submit to her husband more, pray more, return to the relationship, and be a better wife. This takes Ephesians 5:22 out of context. God is clear that the role of the husband is to love his wife with the same sacrificial love that Christ has for us. In domestic abuse, an abuser has chosen to abuse and violate his marriage vows. Nothing she has done has caused it, and nothing she does will change it. Some clergy make the mistake of telling her that her husband will be won over if she has a gentle and quiet spirit. This takes 1 Peter 3:1–6 out of context.

Again, both responses, or anything like them, reveals an ignorance of domestic abuse, an ignorance of the nature of abusers, and a deep misunderstanding of Scripture. This misguided and dangerous advice puts the victim back in harm's way, doesn't hold the abuser accountable, and puts the blame on the victim. Scripture also tells us to run from evil, which many pastors ignore. Putting it bluntly, abuse is evil. A husband who abuses his wife is an abuser, and abusers choose to abuse, regardless of what she does.[164]

6. Criticism for Leaving the Abuser, Advising a Life of Bondage to Abuse

Some clergy make the mistake of criticizing the victim for separating or leaving the marriage. They inform her that the only escape from a marriage for a Christian woman is if the husband has committed adultery (taking Matthew 5:32 and Matthew 19:9 out of context) or if he is a non-Christian and wants a divorce (taking 1 Corinthians 7:12–13 out of context). They state that "God hates divorce" (taking Malachi 2:16 out of context), telling her that God will be angry or disappointed if she violates her marriage vows and gets a divorce.

This advice shows a deeply flawed understanding of the Scriptures and an enormous lack of theological comprehension. For a more complete discussion on the biblical support for separating from or divorcing an abuser, see chapter 34.

However, even using these Scriptures, we find justification for separation and divorce. We know that the

---

[163] Joshua Pease, "The Sin of Silence," *The Washington Post*, May 31, 2018, https://www.washingtonpost.com/news/posteverything/wp/2018/05/31/feature/the-epidemic-of-denial-about-sexual-abuse-in-the-evangelical-church/?utm_term=.5311ab9ca49f.

[164] Aaron Earis, "5 Myths the Church Often Believes about Domestic Violence," Facts & Trends, October 25, 2018, trends.net/2018/10/25/5-myths-the-church-often-believes-about-domestic-violence/.

majority of abusers are sexually deviant, habitual pornography users and have repeated affairs. All types of sexual immorality—not just adultery—are condemned throughout the Scriptures and are specifically condemned by Jesus in Matthew 5:27–28. Further, Scripture informs us that a true follower of God cannot also be an unrepentant, continuous abuser (1 John 3:6–10; Galatians 5:19–20). If the abuser so destroys the marriage relationship that he causes a separation, then divorce is allowed under 1 Corinthians 7:12–13. In Malachi 2, the prophet was issuing a warning to men who have dealt treacherously and unfaithfully with their wives, have failed to protect them, and have then divorced them, leaving their wives with no income or protection. The passage is not a prohibition on a woman protecting herself through obtaining a divorce, but a warning to abusers.

If an abuser is masquerading as a church member or attender, you can be sure that it is because he is using the church as a camouflage, a social club or a networking opportunity. Sitting in a pew no more makes a person a Christian than sitting in a garage makes a person a car.

This misguided advice from her pastor causes the victim to either return to an abusive relationship and continue to be traumatized, or divorce and suffer the shame of feeling that God no longer loves her and that her congregation is against her.

7. Failure to Recognize Abuse, Danger, or Damage to Victims

Some clergy fail to recognize the many tactics of abuse, and thus do not recognize that their congregant is in real danger. Many victims of abuse do not consider themselves as abused. She actually needs the help of a pastor or counselor to open her eyes and correctly identify what she is experiencing as abuse. Many victims and pastors only think of abuse as being hit, stabbed, or shot. Therefore, they don't even consider seeking the services of a local domestic abuse organization for emergency shelter and help. Sadly, Christian women, more so than others, are in denial about the abuse that is happening to them.[165] They mistakenly assume that, because they are women of faith, they are in a Christian marriage. Christian women, on average, stay in an abusive marriage 33 percent longer than non-Christian women.[166]

Other pastors make the mistake of not realizing that once a woman leaves an abusive relationship, she is significantly more likely to be the victim of a homicide, or at least of exacerbated abuse and stalking, than if she stays in an abusive relationship. As a result, the pastors don't appreciate the danger she is in and do not ensure that she and her children are safe.

Many pastors fail to recognize the emotional, physical, and financial devastation and upheaval that women are in, and therefore fail to provide support. They fail to understand that when a victim leaves, she usually has no access to funds, yet must somehow find safe housing for herself and her children while still getting the children to school, keeping them involved in extracurricular activities, going to work, feeding them, providing for their ongoing expenses, and providing a safe environment for her children while she is emotionally devastated. They do not recognize that she very likely feels very alone without any supportive people from her congregation, as most congregations do not have a domestic violence congregational ministry. They fail to appreciate the dynamics of abuse and that the abuser is busy trying to alienate her from her support network with a smear and slander campaign.

---

[165] Roberts, *Not Under Bondage,* 26.
[166] Roberts, 42.

8. Failure to Report Abuse to Authorities

An alarming number of clergy do not realize they are legally mandated reporters in most states and are duty bound to report child abuse to state authorities. Compounding the issue, many do not know what is considered child abuse. Some clergy do not know that immediate reporting is required if they have a reasonable cause to believe that the children themselves are being abused or are witnessing the abuse.

Rather than immediately reporting to state authorities when they have reasonable cause to believe a child has been abused (often as a result of a mother exposing her husband's abuse of her and the children), some clergy want to check with the abuser first to confirm the story, confer with a committee, or conduct their own investigation of the allegations rather than allow DCFS or law enforcement to do so. These clergy are concerned that they will hurt the abuser's feelings or damage his reputation if they report the abuse. As a result, when clergy conduct their own investigations prior to reporting to proper authorities, abusers will deny, justify, or mitigate the allegations and falsely blame the victim; the clergy are swayed by the lies, and the abuse doesn't get reported. Church investigations can be conducted in due time, but mandated reporting is required immediately.

Further, clergy often mistake a finding of "unfounded" by DCFS as a finding that no abuse occurred and that the victim was lying. A finding of "unfounded" by DCFS merely means that the agency could not find enough credible evidence to support a finding of abuse, not that the abuse did not occur. Abusers deny, justify, or mitigate the allegations, especially when questioned by authorities and when serious consequences are involved. DCFS in nearly every state is understaffed and undertrained, and they do not always follow up on leads.[167] Many states keep families together at all costs, regardless of reports of abuse. Each year thousands of children who have been reported to DCFS are killed or die, despite a report of their abuse deemed "unfounded" or not investigated at all. In Illinois alone, 123 children who had been actively in contact with DCFS died in 2019.[168]

Some clergy make the mistake of thinking it is un-Christian to use secular laws, rather than religious laws pursuant to a clergy and congregational inquiry, to address domestic abuse in their congregation. However, laws are instituted by those in authority for our good, and people of faith are required to submit to our governmental authorities, provided the law is not in direct conflict with God (Romans 13:1–7).

When clergy fail to comply with their legal duty to report child abuse to authorities, families are put in danger. Without an order of protection, a DCFS investigation, or a *guardian ad litem* report indicating the abuser is dangerous, the courts will often place children in the sole custody or joint custody of the abuser. Indeed, agencies are so overburdened that even with reports, children are often put in the custody of abusers. Abusive fathers are more than twice as likely as nonabusive fathers to demand sole custody of the children, just to spite the other parent.[169] Abusers will drag on the custody fight for so long, costing the other parent so much in legal costs, time away from work, and emotional distress, that the abusers usually win. Sadly, numerous studies show

---

[167] Daniel Heimpel, "LA Police Failed to Investigate 4,000 Serious Child Abuse Reports in 2018 and 2019. Why?," *Los Angeles Daily News*, October 20, 2019, https://www.dailynews.com/2019/10/20/la-police-failed-to-investigate-4000-serious-child-abuse-reports-in-2018-and-2019-why/.

[168] Sophia Green, "123 Children Died in 2019 Despite Contact with Illinois DCFS, Agency Inspector General Finds," *Chicago Tribune*, January 6, 2020, https://www.chicagotribune.com/news/breaking/ct-illinois-child-welfare-deaths-2019-20200106-hbrzua2rsbd3rfyeoogwqmjfgi-story.html.

[169] *Violence and the Family: Report of the American Psychological Association Presidential Task Force on Violence and the Family* (American Psychological Association: Washington, DC, 1996).

that when abusers demand sole custody, they are awarded sole or joint custody in the majority of cases.[170] Courts are unfortunately gender biased toward men, are generally prejudiced against women, discount the seriousness of abuse, do not believe a woman's claims of abuse, and often punish women who dare to raise concerns about their children's safety.[171] Even with court-ordered parenting agreements, abusers flagrantly disregard custody and parenting arrangements, making co-parenting impossible.

9. Failure to Advise Order of Protection or Ensure a Safe Home

Many clergy are unaware of legal protections for victims of domestic abuse. Therefore, they fail to advise a victim to obtain an emergency order of protection. As noted in chapter 25, short of incarceration, an order of protection is the best legal form of protection a victim can obtain. Without an order of protection, the victim will continue to be abused by the abuser. Even with an order of protection, the abuser may abuse the court system to destroy the victim emotionally and financially. Even with an order of protection, victims have been killed by their abusers, so she must remain vigilant. However, without an order of protection, abuse will certainly continue and escalate.

Without an order of protection, in order to have a safe place to live, the victim is forced to choose between several untenable options. The following are the typical chain of events that occur when a woman is in danger and needs to separate immediately, but does not have an order of protection:

The first option is to leave the family home with the children and live in a shelter, with family/friends, or rent an apartment (if she has the money). As a result, the children are forced away from their home, school, friends, and activities. The children will want to know why they are being taken from their home, requiring the mother to respond. The children will not want to believe her if they have not been the targets of his abuse. Older children almost always turn against their mother for upsetting the home, unless they have been the victim of severe abuse. The abuser will demand to see his children, and will likely file a petition in court that his wife has kidnapped the children, demanding sole custody of the children. It is likely that he will stalk them, demand to know where she lives, and continue to harass and abuse her. The abuser will often seek an order of protection, falsely claiming that he is the victim rather than the abuser. If she rents a home or apartment, the victim will use precious funds that she will need in the future to support herself and her children and fight the legal onslaught that will be coming.

The second option, if the children have not been the target of abuse, is to leave the family home without the older children and live in a shelter, with family/friends, or rent an apartment (if she has the money). In this case, the older children (teenagers/young adults) stay in the marital home and can continue life with school, friends, and activities intact. However, again, the children will demand to know from the father why their mother has left. Because the children are with the abuser, he will lie in an attempt to turn the children against their mother and will play the victim of the poor abandoned single father. He will tell the children that their mother abandoned them, had an affair, is crazy, has mental health issues, etc., and will otherwise alienate her children from her. Again, in this case, older children almost always turn against their mother for upsetting the home unless they themselves have been the victim of severe abuse. The abuser will argue in court that the mother abandoned the children and will demand sole custody of the children.

---

[170] For a summary of numerous research studies on child custody, abuse and gender bias, see Stephanie Dallam, "Are 'Good Enough' Parents Losing Custody to Abusive Ex-Partners?," Leadership Council on Child Abuse and Interpersonal Violence, n.d., www.leadershipcouncil.org/1/pas/dv.html.

[171] Dallam, "Are 'Good Enough' Parents Losing Custody to Abusive Ex-Partners?"

The third option is staying in the marital home with the abuser and children. Staying is not safe physically or emotionally, but is sometimes the only option for a woman without funds and without a support network. In this case, the abuse and parental alienation will escalate, and it will become particularly cruel in the event of a divorce.

In many cases, when the victim does not seek an order of protection, the abuser will bide his time, waiting for her to defend herself when he attacks her in the hope that she will leave a scratch or bruise. He may even scratch or bruise himself. He will then seek an order of protection for himself, lie, and claim to be the victim, with the scratch or bruise as proof of his wife's "attack." It is likely that the court will issue an emergency order of protection since they are issued without giving the opposing party notice. She will then be removed from the family home with no funds, no place to go, and no contact with her children. It will take Herculean efforts (and a great deal in legal fees) to get the courts to recognize that the abuser is lying and playing the victim.

As for the children, the abuser will continue to alienate the children from their mother by calling her names and disrespecting her in front of the children, usurping her maternal authority, telling the children she is worthless and need not be listened to, and even physically abusing her in front of the children. Like a pack of wolves turning against the weakest member, the children will often abuse their mother in the same way their father does.

10. Discourage Police Involvement after Criminal Behavior

Some clergy are unable or unwilling to identify criminal behavior and downplay a criminal act as an unfortunate incident. When criminal behavior is not taken seriously, clergy fail to ensure the safety of the victim and her children—the very ones whom they are charged to protect. Some pastors make the mistake of not advising a victim that she can and should report crimes to the police, while, even worse, others even discourage her from doing so. This is inexcusable, but far too prevalent.

Infamously, Paige Patterson, while president of Southeastern Baptist Seminary, discouraged a female student from reporting her rape to the police. Instead, he advised her to take no legal actions and just forgive the rapist.[172] This is unpardonable.

Pastors who give this advice show a deep misunderstanding of the God who commands us to do justice (Micah 6:8), to protect widows and orphans and the oppressed (James 1:27; Isaiah 1:17), who hates sin and violence (Proverbs 6:16–19), and who encourages the concept of human forgiveness. (Forgiveness is discussed in further detail in chapter 37.) Scripture is replete with God-given laws whose purpose was to protect the oppressed and administer justice. (See the books of Numbers and Deuteronomy.) Likewise, God gives us secular authorities and laws to protect and to provide justice (Romans 13:1–7). Pastors who suggest that Christians should not take advantage of laws to protect themselves from evil and to gain justice have a warped concept of God and our mission to usher in God's kingdom of righteousness, justice, and love here on earth.

11. Offer Marital Counseling, Failure to Refer to Domestic Abuse Counselors

Many pastors fail to refer abuse victims to professionals specifically trained in counseling victims of domestic and sexual abuse. This demonstrates an ignorance of the victim's special needs. Many counselors do not have adequate training to counsel victims of abuse, narcissists, sociopaths, and psychopaths. Many marriage coun-

---

[172] Kate Shellnutt, "Paige Patterson Fired by Southwestern, Stripped of Retirement Benefits," *Christianity Today*, May 30, 2018, https://www.christianitytoday.com/news/2018/may/paige-patterson-fired-southwestern-baptist-seminary-sbc.html.

selors focus on the normal marital issues of relatively healthy individuals. However, the trauma that arises from domestic and sexual abuse is substantially more severe with respect to the characteristics of abuse, the tactics of the abuser, the effect on the victim, and the dynamics of how it plays out. A trauma-based, sensitive therapist who is trained in abuse is necessary for the victim to heal.

Many pastors make the mistake of engaging in marital counseling with the goal of reconciliation. When pastors take on the role of marital counselor with a skilled narcissist, sociopath, psychopath, or other abuser, they themselves are played by the abuser. The abuser is unrepentant, gives false apologies to appear like the good guy to the pastor, lies and downplays the abuse, and is using the pastor to get the wife to return to the abusive marriage. As a result, the victim and her children don't heal, and the abuser continues to play games with the victim, the clergy, and the congregation.

Some pastors will even ghostwrite apology letters or love letters on behalf of the abuser in their efforts to get the couple back together. This should never be done. It perpetuates the abuser's fraud. He appears contrite when he is not, and the victim is even more confused at the dichotomy between his behavior and his purported remorse.

Mental health professionals almost universally agree that marital counseling is *not* recommended for people in abusive relationships. Marital counseling assumes that both parties are at least partially responsible for the marital troubles; however, in abusive situations, the abuser is entirely responsible for his abusive behavior and sees no reason to change. Abusers use marital counseling to blame the victim and further justify their abusive behavior. Separate, individual counseling with experts in domestic and sexual abuse is needed for both the victim and the perpetrator—for the victim so she can heal and become strong, and for the perpetrator in the hope that he will repent, although repentance is rare. The goal of the counseling should not be reconciliation, but for the two individuals to become healthy apart from one another.

12. *Failure to Recognize That Abusers are Sociopaths, Psychopaths, or Narcissists*

Few pastors are trained to identify abusers as people with permanent, untreatable, incurable mental illness. (See the first section for a more complete discussion of the typical personality disorders of abusers.) The majority of abusers are undiagnosed. While secular psychiatrists and psychologists identify the collection of purposeful actions intended to harm others with secular labels of mental illness and disorders, believers recognize the abuser's behavior as serious, unrepentant evil.

Further, pastors often make the mistake of treating abusers as if they were emotionally healthy, fully functioning individuals. They may appeal to their good nature or conscience, their sense of right and wrong, or remorse for the damage done to the victim—all in an attempt to get the abuser to adopt healthy behaviors. As noted previously, such appeals are fruitless because abusers lack the conscience, empathy, or remorse found in healthy persons. Unlike healthy individuals, who feel good when they help others, these disordered individuals get an emotional buzz from hurting others and being vindictive. In their game of cat and mouse, abusers feel especially pleased with themselves when they can get away with covertly hurting their victims while simultaneously looking good in front of others whom they wish to impress, thereby making their victim appear unreasonable.

13. *Failure to Impose Church Discipline*

Unfortunately, many clergy fail to follow scriptural directions to impose congregational discipline on those who practice flagrant, unrepentant, continuous, and serious sin as set forth in various New Testament passages.

Scripture requires the congregational leaders to expel the unrepentant abuser from the congregation to protect the victim, stand on the side of righteousness, and show that the congregation stands on the side of the innocent and oppressed. Excommunication also stops divisiveness caused by the abuser and, hopefully (although it rarely happens), brings the abuser to a point where he humbles himself, repents, and is reunited with God and others.

Some clergy offer excuses for not following the biblical mandate of imposing church discipline. The excuses are far and wide: the church and/or its leaders may be sued by the abuser; the abuser won't change anyway, so why bother; the church has a policy of allowing attendance for everyone; the church doesn't want to get involved; the church doesn't want to embarrass or expose the abuser; it's the job of police and courts, not the church, to discipline the abuser; the church must forgive the abuser and let him back in the congregation; the church doesn't believe the victim; the church wants to extend grace; the church doesn't believe the abuse is that bad; the church forgives the abuser; everyone sins; etc. None of these is an adequate reason for refusing to follow the Bible mandate of imposing church discipline.

If pastors and churches rest on these excuses for failing to follow God's Word, they are hypocrites and cowards, and they are certainly undeserving of a leadership position in a church. Christ calls believers to take up their cross and follow Him. Jesus never said that following His commands would be easy; in fact, He guarantees that we will have trouble in this world. After all, if the hypocritical religious leaders of His day rejected God as He walked among them, how much more will modern-day leaders reject Jesus's followers in their own churches? They will be held accountable for their actions and inactions. Whoever knows the right thing to do, yet fails to do it, is guilty of sin (James 4:17).

When clergy and congregational leaders do not impose church discipline, evil wins. In the eloquent words usually attributed to the great statesman Edmund Burke, "The only thing necessary for the triumph of evil is for good men to do nothing." When clergy fail in their duties to protect their flock, they allow an inescapable, unfettered chain reaction of further abuse.[173] When clergy and congregational leaders do nothing, the following chain of events inevitably results:

- The abuser *will* engage in a smear campaign of lies and false accusations against his victim to friends, family, congregants, and the community to vilify her, socially ostracize her, make himself look innocent, and gain supporters. His flying monkeys will add to the abuse and smear campaign. Most will believe the abuser and turn against the innocent victim, leaving her completely alone and without emotional support. Women often report that the betrayal of their pastor, church, friends, and family is worse than the betrayal and abuse of their spouse.
- The abuser *will* engage in a smear campaign of lies and false accusations against his victim to her children and stepchildren to vilify her, turn her children against her, cut off emotional support, destroy her relationship with her children (all part of parental alienation), hurt the victim, and make himself look innocent of any wrongdoing. The children are then pushed into "survival mode" and forced by the abuser to choose between parents. To survive and resolve the cognitive dissonance, they will believe the abuser and align with their father, turning against the mother. This is emotionally gut-wrenching for the mother, who has tried her entire life to protect her children from their father's abuse. It is so devastating to have her own children turn against her that, far too many times, an abuser's parental alienation leads

---

[173] The details are found in chapters 20–30 and elsewhere in this book.

to the victim's suicide or attempted suicide. Parental alienation is a form of emotional child abuse and results in severe short-term and long-term negative effects on the children.
- The abuser *will* play the pity card. He will play the victim to get sympathy. Many naïve church members, including many pastors, will believe him and turn against the real victim.
- He *will* cut off her income and access to all financial resources.
- When the victim exposes the truth of the abuse, the abuser's minions *will* shun her and try to silence her. They will tell her it is "un-Christian" or "unkind" to say negative things about him, that she needs to forgive and forget, and that her abuser has "moved on" and she needs to move on too. However, the victim is suffering post-traumatic stress and grief due to years of trauma and the fact that her children, friends, family, and congregation have rejected her and sided with a monster.
- Because the abuser incurs no consequences for his behavior, and because he is embraced by church leaders and members who have fallen for his lies and take pity on him, he *will* be emboldened and become even more arrogant and abusive. After all, he has gotten away with abuse, and nothing is more exciting for an abuser than getting away with evil while looking good in front of a pastor! He *will* believe his own lies, and in his own mind, will become a self-righteous victim of his wife, who he *will* believe wronged him. He *will* continue the abuse against his victim (when others aren't looking), and he *will* continue the lies, denial, justification, minimization, and blaming the victim for his abuse. He *will not* take responsibility for his actions or repent—and he *will not* reconcile with God. He will continue his path of overwhelming pride and evil, with the blessing of his church. But sadly, at the end of his days when he stands before his Maker, he will be one of those to whom God will say, "I never knew you. Away from me, you evildoers!" (Matthew 7:23).
- Because there has been no congregational discipline, he *will* claim the church as "his" territory. He will continue attending the same church, using the church as a camouflage to give him a cloak of respectability—while he continues his campaign of abuse against his spouse/ex-spouse when others aren't looking. He will use his church attendance to lure in his next spouse, and she will be swept into the orbit of his life, while she abandons hers. He may even become "super-volunteer" and become very involved in church activities to complete his image. Others assume that he is a "good guy"—which is exactly the persona he wants to project.
- Because the abuser has claimed the church as his territory (along with friends, family, coworkers, country club, the house, the furniture, and everything else), the wife is forced out because the church is not a safe place for her. The betrayal by her church family is so complete that many women never step into a church again, and the betrayal they feel from God often leads many women to reject God altogether. If she does want to continue worshiping with other believers, she must find another church family.

Imagine, if you will, a father with a lovely young daughter who cries out to her father that she has just broken up with her boyfriend because she had been raped and hit and called all sorts of horrible names. The police say there is not enough evidence to press charges, so her abuser will incur no consequences. She rightly expects that her dad will believe her, embrace her and protect her. But incredulously, he continues to invite the former boyfriend over for football games and a family dinner every Sunday. She rightfully feels betrayed not only by her boyfriend but also her dad, both men she has trusted and loved - both men who should protect her. Now she is forced to move out of her own house to avoid seeing her rapist in her home. She will never return home, even after the boyfriend has moved on to a fresh new girlfriend. This scenario seems unimaginable. But it is precisely what a pastor does when he continues to invite an abuser to the house of God each Sunday.

Oftentimes, she will need to move out of her own town and start a new life because she has been slandered and socially shunned by the community and because the abuser will always be a direct threat to her. Running into her abuser, particularly when he has incurred no consequences and has become extremely arrogant and self-righteous, often triggers post-traumatic stress symptoms in the victim of anxiety, panic attacks, extreme fear, headaches, migraines, heart palpitations, gastro-intestinal issues, and the overall inability to function normally.

> Charlotte: Like so many other women whom I know, my church could have written the book on what *not* to do in a case of abuse. I had served in many ministries, including on the board of deacons at the church, on the Board of Regents of a Christian seminary and university, and on the board of a Christian institute. As I leader, I knew eyes were watching, and I did not want anyone's faith to falter because of me. I wanted to do this right. The senior pastor, with no comfort or emotion, delegated my case to the executive director, who was not ordained and had no background in counseling or domestic abuse. For a year we went through marriage counseling, and the executive director tried to get us to reconcile—he even ghostwrote letters of apology for Tim. Tim admitted to the executive director that he had done all the abuses I accused him of and had written in a long letter, but he lied and told church members that I had a mental illness, abandoned my family, and left because I had an affair. The church leadership knew of his slander, but never told him or his church friends to stop spreading lies. My former mentor and friends refused to talk to me, and they spread Tim's lies word for word. My children and stepchildren turned against me. To ensure they knew I was not lying, I showed the pastor photographs that Tim took of his own sexual abuse and rape when he tied me with belts to the four corners of his bed. I also showed the pastor evidence of his parental alienation and evidence of his violations of our parenting agreement. I produced transcripts of Tim's own deposition, DCFS interview, and public records that showed his lying under oath. I provided a copy of an order of protection, a permanent restraining order, and a court order finding him in violation of the divorce agreement and owing *more than $1 million* in back payments. Despite the mountain of evidence, the church leadership allowed him and Didi, his girlfriend he was seeing when we were married, to continue attending church and even host church-sponsored parties at Tim's house, where so much of my abuse took place. His face is on the church web page, and they are featured smiling on the church Facebook page for a recent trip to Turkey with the pastor. The church's support of him only emboldened him to escalate his parental alienation and his physical, emotional, and financial abuse. It was not safe to be around him, so I was forced to leave and find a new church. I moved thirty minutes away so that I would not have to run into him around town. The final straw came when the senior pastor allowed Tim and Didi to get remarried in church with the blessings of the church—after the pastor had originally told me that he would not allow it. My church betrayed me, my pastor betrayed me, but God never did. He has blessed me and healed me, despite my old church.

What Is a Victim to Do When Her Church Fails Her?

What is a woman to do when her church fails her? Sadly, attempting to convince the pastor or church leaders who have already pledged their allegiance to abusers that they should support the victim, not the abuser, will likely fall on deaf ears. Of course, a church or pastor will not come flat out and say, "Sorry, honey. We are supporting the abuser on this one, and you, the victim, are out of luck. Go find another church, or don't. We really don't care about you." No, churches who support abusers are much more slick-tongued than that. They will make it sound like they are the righteous ones, and she is in the wrong. In the patriarchal systems found in most churches, males typically hold all or most of the positions of power and influence, from senior pastor through governing bodies. They will blanket their betrayal of her in eloquent words like, "We are extending grace to him," "All have sinned and fallen short of the glory of God," "It's not our place or policy to exclude people from our worship service. If we only let perfect people in, we would have an empty church," "We are a compassionate congregation that follows the principle of forgiveness," or "We don't support abusers. He apologized, and we must forgive as God forgives us."

In so doing, the church extends what German theologian Dietrich Bonhoeffer called "cheap grace" in his classic book, *The Cost of Discipleship*. Cheap grace is the deadly enemy of the church. Bonhoeffer knew the cost of discipleship—he stood against the Nazi regime and publicly challenged Hitler when the rest of the German church was silent. He paid for his stand with his life. Cheap grace is "the preaching of forgiveness without requiring repentance, baptism without church discipline, communion without confession. Cheap grace is grace without discipleship, grace without the cross, grace without Jesus Christ."[174] With cheap grace, so-called Christians can live any way they want since Christ has already paid the price. It is what a church does when it embraces an abuser and forces a victim out. What a church needs is costly grace—the real kind of grace that comes from God. "Costly grace is the sanctuary of God; it has to be protected from the world, and not thrown to the dogs. . . . Costly grace confronts us as a gracious call to follow Jesus, it comes as a word of forgiveness to the broken spirit and the contrite heart. It is costly because it compels a man to submit to the yoke of Christ and follow him; it is grace because Jesus says: 'My yoke is easy and my burden is light.'"[175] Cheap grace is the divine "get out of jail free" card for the unrepentant abuser, who believes that his sins—past, present, and future—are forgiven and his purported Christian beliefs give him license to keep sinning without consequence.

Bonhoeffer correctly stated, "Silence in the face of evil is itself evil: God will not hold us guiltless. Not to speak is to speak. Not to act is to act."[176] Pastors and churches who stand silent when abuse is in their midst embrace evil itself. God will not hold them guiltless.

A generation before Bonhoeffer, William Booth, the founder of the Salvation Army, warned us precisely of churches that embrace the abuser while letting the victim flail in the wind and fend for herself alone. In his wisdom, Booth proclaimed, "The chief dangers that confront the coming century will be religion without the Holy Ghost, Christianity without Christ, forgiveness without repentance, salvation without regeneration, politics without God, and heaven without hell."[177]

A church that fails to impose church discipline on an abuser is a church without the leading of the Holy Spirit and lacking in sound theological doctrine. God always stands against the violent, and He always stands with the oppressed, the widows, and the orphans. How much more does He stand against abusive husbands who leave their wives as widows, but continue to attack them, and leave their children as orphans, but continue to use them as pawns in their vindictive chess game of punishing the wives who escape their abuse?

A woman who finds herself in such a church needs to kick their dust from her feet (Matthew 10:14) and find

---

[174] Dietrich Bonhoeffer, *The Cost of Discipleship* (New York: McMillan, 1995), 44–45.
[175] Bonhoeffer, *Discipleship*, 45.
[176] Dietrich Bonhoeffer Quotes, https://www.goodreads.com/author/quotes/29333.Dietrich_Bonhoeffer?page=2.
[177] William Booth Quotes, https://www.goodreads.com/quotes/328694-i-consider-that-the-chief-dangers-which-confront-the-coming.

a different family of believers who are led by the Holy Spirit, are theologically sound and emotionally mature, demonstrate kindness and compassion, understand domestic abuse, and welcome those in need. Talking to the pastor or elders about where the church stands on these issues will reveal a great deal, as will observing how a single woman who is a newcomer is treated. These kinds of churches are out there, but one must look for them. Jesus designed us for community, and He designed church communities for us and for healing.

Most importantly, a woman whose church has supported an abuser must not mistake the attitude of the church for the attitude of God. The church is full of imperfect, broken human beings who often poorly represent the image of God. Even the leaders are not beyond human frailties. She must know that God is with her and for her, and that He loves her and her children. We must not mistake the failings of people for the nature of God.

PART III

Recovering from Abuse

THE EFFECTS OF CONTINUED abuse, especially over many years, have serious negative effects on women. We were designed to be in loving, life-giving, affirming, encouraging, trusting relationships. We were never designed to be under attack in our family relationships. When we are attacked, our bodies and our minds develop coping mechanisms to help us through the danger, but if these coping tools continue into the long term, they become unhealthy. Make no mistake, removing oneself from an abusive relationship will be the hardest thing most women will ever do. The attacks from an abuser will be unparalleled by anyone else in her life. The effects of abuse are far-reaching and affect nearly every area of life, which is why healing and recovering is so important. I tell each of my clients that healing must be her number one priority so she can be the amazing woman God designed her to be. Women need to be healthy emotionally, spiritually, physically, sexually, and financially for themselves and for their children, who are watching their every step on how to overcome and be resilient to life's challenges.

Unhealthy women cause a great deal of worry and stress to their children, who sometimes feel they need to take on the role of the parent for their needy mother. It is a role reversal in which the child is the stronger one who takes care of his or her weak mother. This is not a good situation.

In contrast, healthy women are a great blessing for their children, both during their formative years and as adults. An emotionally healthy woman provides the support her children need without being needy or feeling left behind when her children eventually spread their wings, leave the home, and make their own lives. Children observe adults to see what relationships should look like and how to respond in an abusive relationship. Daughters are watching their mothers to see what a woman should expect from a man and how she can choose to be strong and healthy. Sons look to their mothers to see how they should treat a future wife with love and respect, while protecting and caring for her. Mothers are role models for both their daughters and their sons.

Women who are spiritually unhealthy pass along their misperceptions about God to their children. She may incorrectly perceive that God is angry with her or even caused the abuse to punish her. Nothing could be further from the truth. Her heart is spiritually empty, and she cannot give her children what she doesn't have. But a woman who is spiritually healthy recognizes that God loves His children, that we will have spiritual battles in this world, and that God is with us fighting those battles. She will equip her children with this knowledge and the spiritual tools to win their own battles. She will be so full of the Holy Spirit that her heart will be overflowing so she can fill up those around her with love, encouragement, and blessings.

Women who are physically unhealthy require additional care. Children often will become the caretaker to their mother to the detriment of their own lives. Conversely, a physically healthy woman is ready to take on challenges and spend quality time with her children, which gives them confidence to take on life and share good memories of beautiful times together.

Women who are financially unhealthy are unable to provide for themselves or their children. Extreme poverty may make children feel unworthy, and they do not have the opportunities to thrive. As they become adults, children worry about their mother and often end up supporting her. However, a financially healthy woman blesses her children with financial blessings, educational opportunities, a safe home, healthy food, travel, a down payment on a first house, and even spoiling the grandkids a little when they come along. Healthy parents bestow blessings on children, grandchildren, and future generations in God's perfect plan.

When women are sexually unhealthy, they often pass along their unhealthy sexual attitudes to their children. These women may become promiscuous or, on the other extreme, never trust another person enough to allow anyone to come close to them. A woman with a healthy view of sexuality will model God's perfect plan for her children, and at the appropriate time, will explain it.

In Part 3, we explore the third "R" of the "3 R's" of an abusive relationship—recovery! This section is the most exciting part of the whole book! In it, we discuss how a woman can recover, heal, and become the person God designed her to be.

CHAPTER 37

The Target of a Narcissist, Sociopath, Psychopath, or Other Domestic Abuser

SOCIETY PICTURES THE VICTIM of an abuser as a poor, uneducated, minority woman from the wrong side of the tracks. But domestic abuse happens across all demographic, social-economic, and education levels. Churchgoing women are as likely to be the target of an abuser as nonbelievers.

However, most share common characteristics. As we discussed earlier, almost all of the women who find themselves as victims of domestic abuse are caring, kind, generous, trusting, trustworthy, cooperative, giving, and forgiving. They are extremely empathetic, conscientious, compassionate, honest, straightforward, humble, faithful, tolerant, and resilient. They are supportive, gentle, even-tempered, tender, sentimental, loving, responsible, conscientious, self-disciplined, intentional, accepting of others, self-accepting, and resourceful. They love deeply, form strong attachments, and put a great deal of value and investment into relationships.[178] These are wonderful traits for anyone to have. In fact, they are the same traits for which the Scriptures state we should strive.

Jesus commands us to love one another, and Paul provides a helpful description: "Love is patient, love is kind. It does not envy, it does not boast, it is not proud. It does not dishonor others, it is not self-seeking, it is not easily angered, it keeps no record of wrongs. Love does not delight in evil but rejoices with the truth. It always protects, always trusts, always hopes, always perseveres" (1 Corinthians 13:4–7). Jesus commands His followers to be full of the Holy Spirit, and Paul describes what that looks like: "But the fruit of the Spirit is love, joy, peace, forbearance, kindness, goodness, faithfulness, gentleness and self-control" (Galatians 5:22–23).

The problem is not with the women who have these delightful traits, but with the men with whom they share their lives. These are exemplary qualities when paired with an emotionally healthy partner who shares similar traits, but in a relationship with a narcissist, sociopath, psychopath, or other abuser who targets women with these traits to gain power and control over her, it leads to misery. The key is not for a woman to change, but for her to wisely and prudently share her life and these wonderful qualities only with people who are worthy of her.

---

[178] Sandra Brown, *Women Who Love Psychopaths* (Penrose, NC: Mask Publishing, 2018), 233–300.

The one quality missing from women who find themselves targets of abuse is discernment—the ability to tell good from evil, truth from lies, good intentions from bad, and integrity from hypocrisy. Discernment, a sign of spiritual and emotional maturity, is particularly important for women to develop. Women tend to be more vulnerable to abusers, and the damage inflicted on women when caught in the web of abuse is especially devastating.

However, we shouldn't beat ourselves up or feel guilty for the inability to discern a narcissist, sociopath, psychopath, or other abuser. No little girl is trained to recognize the signs of a SNAP. Most of us don't know what one is until we inadvertently walk into the SNAP's buzz saw of life and come out the other side feeling like we've been chopped into a million pieces. SNAPs are professional con artists and masters of deception. Our church families would do well to train our young ladies (and men) to recognize the signs of an abuser.

Women, especially Christian women, are culturally trained to be "the nice girl." From the time we are little girls, women are trained not to judge others harshly, to turn the other cheek when wronged, not to be loud or make a scene if mistreated, not to stand up for ourselves when wronged, and to be polite at all times. We are trained to look for "whatever is noble, whatever is right, whatever is pure, whatever is lovely, whatever is admirable—if anything is excellent or praiseworthy," and to think of these things (Philippians 4:8–9). Many women, especially victims of abuse, don't see the evil in others because they don't have that in themselves. Therefore, they mistakenly project their innocent motives on others because they are only looking for the good in others.

From an early age, women may even be criticized for noticing or acknowledging bad behavior or downright cruelty in others. "Oh, don't say that about poor Johnny. I'm sure he is a lovely boy; he is just having a bad day. Boys will be boys," an older woman might say to a young girl who expresses her opinion that Johnny, the sociopath in the making, is a horrible human being because he just drowned a puppy. Little Suzie has been told so many times that "boys will be boys" and to excuse their bad behavior, that later, when she is in high school and her first date puts his hands up her shirt and down her pants, she will be too fearful to make a scene or stand up for herself because she fears she will be ridiculed at school, and her date is "just being a boy." Still later, when her husband rapes her after a heated argument, she will be filled with shame and simply keep it to herself, especially after her misinformed pastor tells her that meeting her husband's sexual needs is her duty.

On the other hand, the boy whose unacceptable behavior has been excused again and again from an early age learns that he can do just about anything with impunity under the guise of "that's just what boys do." As an adult, he takes what he wants, when he wants, and how he wants from those sweet, kind, Christian women who will allow him to do so.

The author of Hebrews deemed discernment so necessary to the Christian faith that he criticized the first-century believers for being naïve and immature in their faith:

> "We have much to say about this, but it is hard to make it clear to you because you no longer try to understand. In fact, though by this time you ought to be teachers, you need someone to teach you the elementary truths of God's word all over again. You need milk, not solid food! Anyone who lives on milk, being still an infant, is not acquainted with the teaching about righteousness. But solid food is for the mature, who by constant use have trained themselves to distinguish good from evil." (Hebrews 5:11–14)

Unfortunately, a woman without discernment or without the courage to practice discernment is not as particular about a marriage partner as God would like her to be. God's purpose for marriage is to be an example to the world of His great love for us. Marriage is the venue to raise children in the love of the Lord, to protect and

The Target of a Narcissist, Sociopath, Psychopath, or Other Domestic Abuser

provide for the wife and children, and to serve the Lord and others. This is a tall order. It requires two people with great spiritual and emotional maturity to build a marriage that fulfills God's purposes.

Sadly, many women of faith do not require enough of a partner before they say, "I do." They overlook obvious, serious character flaws, forgive egregious sins without repentance, and are too willing to marry someone who is not seeking the Lord with all his heart. Women tell themselves many things to justify their choice of mate: "No one is perfect—I can't wait forever," or "Those affairs he had were in the past. I'm sure he won't do that with me," or "He said he was over his heroin addiction. He's a Christian, so we must be good now," or "I know he hasn't gone to church for the last ten years, but at least he goes to church with me now," or "How bad could it be? I'm going to be nice to him, and he'll be nice to me back. It's pretty easy," or "I will take the kids to church myself; he doesn't have to go if he doesn't want to," or "I can still be a good Christian and grow in my faith, even if he isn't." Every person I have counseled or represented had doubts in the back of their mind that they justified, excused, or otherwise defended before marrying an abuser.

Paul warns Timothy that abusers seek out and slither their way into the lives of naïve women lacking discernment: "They are the kind who worm their way into homes and gain control over gullible women" (2 Timothy 3:6).

Many people mistakenly believe that abusers only target women who are unsuccessful or who are victims of childhood abuse because they are easy targets. However, abusers also target women who are successful because they are more of a challenge to bring down. It is relatively easy to control and demoralize a woman who already has self-doubts, is familiar with patterns of abuse, harbors feelings of inadequacy, and believes that she is unworthy of being treated with love and respect. But to an abuser, the challenge of bringing down an attractive, intelligent, educated, successful, confident woman and turning her into a fearful, cowering, insecure creature who is under his thumb is exciting. To him, it is an intoxicating game of power.

Many women have also succumbed to the notion that the women who are partners of abusers are codependents. This myth is also untrue in most cases. Prior to their relationship with the abuser, most women were not overcome with the self-doubt and low self-esteem that plague people who suffer with codependency or dependency. In fact, many women had healthy self-confidence prior to the SNAP turning her into a puddle of doubt, anxiety, and lack of self-worth. Women who have been targeted by an abuser are often agreeable, conscientious, and invest deeply in relationships. The problem lies not in these traits, but with the abuser who exploits them.

Sandra Brown, who has made it her life's work to study pathological love relationships and to help the women who find themselves in them, explained the superlative traits that accompany the women who are targets of abusers:

> What I hope is abundantly clear is that Super Traits are a group of personality tendencies that make for a beautiful person. The traits are those any normal man would feel blessed to have in his partner. The traits of a kind, compassionate, and integrity-oriented person have only been problematic in the hands of antagonistic, manipulative, and juvenile Darkness. Super Traits aren't the problem. It is personality disorders/psychopathy that dismantle normal psyches into piles of ashes. It is personality disorder that the DSM cites as "unable to sustain positive nonmanipulative change" generated from neurological deficits that result in the inability to be empathetic or intimate. If Super Traits are present in a normal relationship, there's more than enough to provide the fertile ground from which love can grow and be sustained.[179]

---

[179] Sandra Brown, *Women Who Love Psychopaths* (Mask Publishing, 2018), 266.

Abusers target women with wonderful characteristics. To a healthy person, these are traits to be celebrated and cherished. To an abuser, these traits yell, "Sucker!" Women with these wonderful characteristics need not change them, but they do need to be sure they develop a healthy dose of discernment from the Holy Spirit. They must be willing to listen to the Lord and wait for the man God intended for them rather than settle for something less.

Chapter 38

Effects of Abuse on Women

THE EFFECTS ON WOMEN who live with abuse are far-reaching and deep-seated. A woman who doesn't think she is affected or who doesn't make healing a top priority will continue to feel the negative effects for years. In this chapter, we discuss the most common effects of abuse.

Post-Traumatic Stress Disorder

Numerous studies have found what most women know instinctively: those in abusive situations suffer post-traumatic stress disorder (PTSD). Cortisol is a hormone produced when we are under extreme stress, and it gives us the "fight or flight" response needed to respond to a dangerous situation. Women who live in continued trauma produce an abundance of cortisol, which can cause a rewiring of their brains. The cumulative effects of trauma from living in domestic abuse can have long-lasting effects, even after leaving an abusive relationship.[180]

Indeed, while earlier studies showed that up to 84 percent of abused women suffered PTSD, a 2008 study showed that an astounding 100 percent of women who were subjected to physical, sexual, and emotional abuse suffered abuse-induced PTSD, with more than 87 percent of women experiencing moderate to severe PTSD.[181] In comparison, approximately 8.7 percent of people in the United States will suffer PTSD at some point during the course of a lifetime, while during any twelve-month period, approximately 3.5 percent of adults will suffer from PTSD.[182]

PTSD occurs when a person has personally experienced or witnessed an actual or threatened death, violence resulting in an injury, or sexual violence. These are all considered traumatic events. Symptoms impair a victim's ability to function in social situations, at work, at home, and in other important aspects of life. Symptoms include (1) recurrent, involuntary, intrusive distressing memories of the traumatic event (these uninvited rumi-

---

[180] A. Kippert, "How Trauma Rewires the Brain," DomesticShelters.org, Aug. 8, 2016, https://www.domesticshelters.org/articles/health/how-trauma-rewires-the-brain.

[181] Mindy B. Mechanic, Teri L. Weaver, and Patricia A. Resick, "Mental Health Consequences of Intimate Partner Abuse: A Multidimensional Assessment of Four Different Forms of Abuse," *Violence Against Women* 14, no. 6:634–654 (June 2008), doi:10.1177/1077801208319283.

[182] American Psychiatric Association, *Diagnostic and Statistical Manual of Mental Disorders (DSM-5)*, (2013), p. 271–280.

nations can take up most of a woman's waking thoughts so that she feels as if she has hit "rewind" all day); (2) recurrent distressing dreams relating to the traumatic event; (3) flashbacks in which the victim feels or acts as if the traumatic event is recurring; or (4) intense or prolonged psychological distress or marked psychological reactions at internal or external cues that symbolize or resemble the traumatic event (for example, if the abuser used a hammer to inflict harm, the victim may show serious distress when seeing a hammer in a hardware store).[183]

Symptoms can also include persistent efforts to avoid (1) distressing memories, thoughts, or feelings about the event; or (2) people, places, conversations, activities, objects, or situations that bring up distressing memories, thoughts, or feelings about the traumatic event.[184]

Other symptoms of PTSD can include distorted feelings and thoughts such as (1) the inability to remember certain aspects of the traumatic event caused by dissociative amnesia; (2) persistent and exaggerated negative beliefs about herself or others (for example, believing "I am a bad person," or "I am ruined forever," or "No one is a good person and no man can be trusted," or "The entire world is a dangerous place."); (3) persistent distorted thoughts that lead her to blame herself for the traumatic event (for example, "I caused this," or "If I had been a better wife, he wouldn't have hit me," or "If I had gone to counseling and gotten some tools, I could have changed him."); (4) persistent fear, horror, shame, guilt, or other negative emotions; (5) diminished interest and participation in significant activities, such as getting together with friends and family, work or career, hobbies, etc.; (6) feelings of detachment or estrangement from others; and (7) the persistent inability to feel happiness, love, joy, satisfaction, and other positive emotions.[185]

Further, symptoms can include distorted reactions to everyday life, such as (1) irritable behavior and angry outbursts with little or no provocation (such as verbal or physical aggression toward others, pets, or objects); (2) reckless or self-destructive behavior (such as speeding or drinking to excess); (3) hypervigilance (for example, being overly suspicious of the actions of others); (4) an exaggerated startle response (for example, jumpiness to a telephone ring or alarm clock); (5) difficulty concentrating (such as forgetting a known phone number or name, not remembering schedules like picking up children from a soccer practice, or failing to focus or meet work deadlines); and (6) difficulty falling or staying asleep.[186]

The more severe the abuse, and the longer the woman has been in an abusive situation, the more severe the PTSD.[187] Because abused women are subject to multiple, frequent, and sometimes unrelenting trauma both during and after an abusive relationship, the impact of the abuse is cumulative.[188]

Ongoing harassment and abuse by the abuser, which is typical even after a woman leaves an abusive relationship, causes PTSD symptoms to continue long after a divorce is final. Continuous contact with an abuser who has received no punishment or consequences for his abuse also extends the symptoms of PTSD.[189] Both situations happen in nearly every instance in which a woman and her abuser (the ex-husband) have shared custody of the children. Abusers seldom suffer consequences for their behavior, and the courts usually force the parents to share custody, thus causing continuous contact between a woman and the abuser at least until the children turn eighteen or graduate from high school. Both situations also happen in every case in which a church refuses to

---

[183] *DSM-5*, 271–280.
[184] *DSM-5*, 271–280.
[185] *DSM-5*, 271–280.
[186] *DSM-5*, 271–280.
[187] *DSM-5*, 278.
[188] Mechanic, Weaver, and Resick, "Mental Health Consequences," Violence Against Women 14 (July 2008), no. 6, DOI: 10.1177/1077801208319283
[189] *DSM-5*, 271–280.

impose church discipline and remove the abuser from the congregation, resulting in contact between the woman and her abuser during worship and at church events. This typically results in the wife leaving the church since it is no longer safe.

While many people might assume that only physical abuse causes PTSD, all forms of abuse—psychological, physical abuse, and sexual abuse—cause PTSD.[190] Harassment, verbal and emotional abuse, dominance, isolation, and stalking are all independent causes of PTSD. Stalking and harassment, in particular, can be a cause of hypervigilance because of the unpredictable nature of this type of trauma.[191]

Women with PTSD are 80 percent more likely than others to suffer from depression, bipolar disorder, anxiety disorder, or substance abuse. Women with PTSD are also more likely to commit suicide.

Depression

Most women in abusive relationships also suffer depression. The more severe and longer lasting the abuse, the more severe and longer lasting the depression. And like PTSD, each kind of abuse causes depression. Emotional and verbal abuse, especially taunting and degrading, which denigrates a woman's self-worth and self-esteem, leads to depression, even without other forms of abuse. Likewise, controlling behaviors such as harassment, stalking, dominance, and isolation, particularly after a woman has left the abusive relationship, demoralizes a woman and leaves her feeling hopeless, leading to depression that continues long after a woman has left an abuser.[192]

In the 2008 study of the effects of abuse on women, 93.9 percent of women experienced depression ranging from mild to severe, with 76 percent suffering moderate to severe depression. Most abused women suffer from both PTSD and depression.[193]

Trauma Bonds

Almost every woman in an abusive relationship develops trauma bonds, a strong emotional attachment between a victim and her abuser that is formed as a result of the cycle of abuse. Trauma bonds are similar to the Stockholm Syndrome, in which a victim of a kidnapping or other traumatic event forms feelings of trust or affection toward her kidnappers. Trauma bonds are strengthened by the abuser's love-bombing actions in the beginning phase of the relationship and the intermittent periods of good behavior and promises to change during the abusive phase of the relationship. During these times of affectionate behavior, her body produces oxytocin, a hormone that bonds her to her abuser. Even after she leaves, a woman misses her abuser and longs to be with him. She may still hold out hope that things can change. The yearning for him is similar to a drug addict going through withdrawal and longing for another hit. Trauma bonds are so strong that many women end up returning to their abuser multiple times, despite acknowledging that he is abusive. Physical and emotional separation from an abuser is required to break trauma bonds. Because oxytocin can stay in a woman's body for up to six months, she needs to break all contact and communication with her abuser, emotionally distance herself, and recognize him for what he is – a predator.

---

[190] Mechanic, Weaver, and Resick, "Mental Health Consequences."
[191] Mechanic, Weaver, and Resick, "Mental Health Consequences."
[192] Mechanic, Weaver, and Resick, "Mental Health Consequences."
[193] Mechanic, Weaver, and Resick, "Mental Health Consequences."

Inability to Establish Economic Self-Sufficiency

Economic self-sufficiency means being able to meet everyday costs of living without relying on public assistance or the generosity of others. It requires a steady, living wage, which depends on job stability and employability. Those seeking employability are seriously undermined by an abuser because an abuser often forbids his partner from continuing her education or training, working full-time, or working at all, and he engages in disruptive behaviors that sabotage her career. Job stability and employability also require transportation and childcare. These are undermined when an abuser prohibits a woman from using a car and refuses to help with childcare. In addition, women who are targets of abuse may not be able to afford a reliable vehicle or dependable childcare.[194]

Financial abuse is prevalent in 99 percent of abusive relationships.[195] The majority of women in abusive relationships suffer negative effects in their jobs as a result of domestic abuse, including the inability to concentrate on the tasks at hand, fatigue and sleep deprivation, and being forced to take time off for injuries and emotional distress relating to themselves and their children. Victims of domestic abuse lose eight million days of paid work per year. Domestic violence costs the US economy more than $8.3 billion each year, of which $5.8 billion is for medical and mental health services, and $2.5 is due to lower productivity.[196] Over a lifetime, the average woman who is a victim of domestic violence suffers a loss of approximately $103,767, while the average man who is a victim of domestic violence suffers a loss of $23,414. The collective national cost over a lifetime, including lost wages, lost productivity, injuries, criminal justice costs, lost property and damage, and other costs total $3.6 trillion.[197]

Inability to Establish Financial Stability

Financial stability includes not only the ability to meet day-to-day expenses, but also having assets to leverage in times of hardship, meet financial goals, and build long-term securities. As we've observed, abusers prohibit their wives from having access to financial assets. Without access to funds, women lack sufficient funds to leave an abusive relationship, secure safe housing, provide for the educational and extracurricular activities for themselves and their children, and provide the necessities of life for themselves and their children.[198]

Physical Ailments

Abused women are also more likely to develop severe health issues as a result of the abuse. Women in abusive relationships are 70 percent more likely to develop heart disease, 80 percent more likely to suffer from a stroke, and 60 percent more likely to suffer from asthma.[199] Domestic abuse is a leading cause of adolescent pregnancy,

---

[194] Adams, "Measuring the Effects of Domestic Violence," 1–3.
[195] Adams, "Measuring the Effects of Domestic Violence," 1.
[196] Robert Pearl, "Domestic Violence: The Secret Killer That Costs $8.3 Billion Annually," *Forbes*, December 5, 2013, https://www.forbes.com/sites/robertpearl/2013/12/05/domestic-violence-the-secret-killer-that-costs-8-3-billion-annually/#100c9a7b4681.
[197] Center for Disease Control, "Preventing Intimate Partner Violence Fact Sheet," https://www.cdc.gov/violenceprevention/pdf/IPV-Factsheet.pdf.
[198] Adams, "Measuring the Effects of Domestic Violence," 1–3.
[199] Pearl, "Domestic Violence."

unintended pregnancy, miscarriage, stillbirth, intrauterine hemorrhaging, sexually transmitted disease, nutritional deficiency, abdominal pain, gastrointestinal problems, neurological disorders, chronic pain, disability, hypertension, cancer, and cardiovascular diseases.[200] Approximately 3 to 13 percent of all pregnancies are due to intimate partner abuse.[201] The stress caused by the trauma of abuse shows up in seemingly endless ways. Many women report that the stress of the abuse causes an "anxiety cough," which is a constant cough that occurs when under stress. The cough tends to reduce after a few months of being away from an abuser. Other women report that even their fine motor skills have been affected by the abuse, resulting in altered handwriting and difficulty in sewing, painting, or other activities that requires fine motor skills. Many women also report frequent and severe headaches and nightmares.

Substance Abuse

Domestic abuse results in increased smoking and increased alcohol and drug abuse among women, who use substances as a coping mechanism.[202]

Suicide

Many women feel so hopeless, helpless, and alone that they decide to end their own life. As many as 23 percent of domestic abuse survivors have attempted suicide, compared to only 3 percent among the general population with no prior domestic abuse experience. Women who experience prolonged abuse, more frequent abuse, more severe abuse, PTSD, childhood trauma, depression, or substance abuse suffer from suicide at higher rates than others. Verbal and emotional abuse, as well as physical and sexual abuse, are connected to higher rates of suicide.[203]

Death

Tragically, husbands, boyfriends and family members were responsible for approximately 47 percent of the homicides of women around the world in 2012, while wives or girlfriends were responsible for only 6 percent of the homicides of men.[204] By 2017, that number had jumped to 58 percent, making domestic abuse the most common killer of women.[205] Two-thirds of all family-related homicide victims were female, meaning that abusers target even female children more than they do male children.[206] Of course, a wife or girlfriend is not the only target of an abuser's wrath. Twenty percent of homicides caused by abusive spouses or intimate partners were

---

[200] National Coalition Against Domestic Violence (NCADV), "Statistics," https://ncadv.org/statistics.
[201] Jacquelyn C. Campbell, "Health Consequences of Intimate Partner Violence," *Lancet* 13, no. 359 (April 13, 2002), https://www.ncbi.nlm.nih.gov/pubmed/11965295?dopt=Abstract.
[202] CDC, "Preventing Intimate Partner Violence Fact Sheet," https://www.cdc.gov/violenceprevention/pdf/IPV-Factsheet.pdf.
[203] "Domestic Violence Survivors at Higher Risk for Suicide," DomesticShelters.org, June 8, 2016, https://www.domesticshelters.org/articles/health/domestic-violence-survivors-at-higher-risk-for-suicide.
[204] United Nations Office on Drugs and Crime, *Global Study on Homicide 2013*, https://www.unodc.org/documents/gsh/pdfs/2014_GLOBAL_HOMICIDE_BOOK_web.pdf.
[205] UN Office on Drugs and Crime, *Global Study*.
[206] UN Office on Drugs and Crime, *Global Study*.

family members, friends, neighbors, law enforcement responders, bystanders, or people who tried to intervene.[207]

Seventy-two percent of all murder-suicides are committed by a spouse or other intimate partner, and 94 percent of the victims of murder-suicides are female.[208]

Despite its damaging effects, survivors of domestic abuse can anticipate a life of peace and blessings once they leave their abuser. As we read in the coming chapters, we have a tremendous ability to heal from abuse and to lead a life full of meaning, purpose, and healthy relationships that God has designed for us.

---

[207] NCADV, "Statistics."
[208] NCADV, "Statistics."

CHAPTER 39

Effects of Abuse on Children

TO THRIVE AND DEVELOP properly, children need a safe and secure environment with loving parents and free of abuse. When children grow up in safe and loving homes, they develop physically, socially, verbally, cognitively, academically, emotionally, and neurobiologically in healthy ways.

Brain development and functional capacity depend on an extraordinary set and sequence of developmental and environmental experiences that affect how the human genome (the sum of all our genes) is expressed, which in turn affects cell function.[209] Optimal brain development and function occur when children are raised in a safe and loving environment.

However, when children are themselves victims of domestic abuse, or they witness abuse, there are significant and disastrous short- and long-term effects. Childhood abuse impacts memory function and cognition, as well as social attachment and the ability to regulate moods. More importantly, abuse affects the brain's ability to grow new neurons (neurogenesis). Children who have PTSD as a result of abuse have smaller brains, altered brain structures in the cerebellum and prefrontal cortex, altered EEG activity in the prefrontal cortex, difficulty regulating their sympathetic nervous system, increased cortisol and norepinephrine (stress hormone) levels, and increased resting heart rates. Child abuse can even affect the way the human genome is expressed, which affects the functioning of the genes. In general, child abuse leads to many negative differences in the structure and physiology of the brain, resulting in diminished functioning and negative behaviors.[210]

Like adults, children can also develop PTSD as a result of abuse directed at them or watching abuse of others. Factors affecting whether the child will develop PTSD and its severity include how traumatic the event was, how close the child was to the event, how long the trauma lasted, whether the trauma was repetitive or happened only once, the child's own resiliency, and whether the child received support from family and friends.

Children with PTSD feel emotional and physical distress when they are exposed to situations that remind them of the abuse, and some children relive the abuse in their minds. They may have nightmares, while also

---

[209] R. F. Anda, et al., "The Enduring Effects of Childhood Abuse and Related Adverse Experiences in Childhood," *European Archives of Psychiatry and Clinical Neuroscience* 256, no.174 (November 2005): 174–186, https://doi.org/10.1007/s00406-005-0624-4.

[210] R. F. Anda, "The Enduring Effects of Childhood Abuse," 174–186.

wrestling with disturbing memories during the day. They may also have trouble sleeping, remain on guard and hypervigilant, lose interest in things they enjoyed, or have trouble being affectionate. They often feel depressed or agitated, nervous or jittery, detached or numb, and fearful or anxious. They frequently feel angry or out of control, and they may be more aggressive or violent. These children can experience flashbacks of the abuse, lose touch with reality, and even reenact an abusive event. Children with PTSD may experience problems in school, have difficulty concentrating, and worry about dying at a young age. They sometimes wet the bed, suck their thumb, and experience headaches or stomachaches. To avoid memories and flashbacks, they often stay away from places or situations that bring back bad memories. PTSD also increases the risk for other mental health issues such as depression, anxiety, and suicidal thoughts.

Children from violent homes are more likely to abuse substances like drugs and alcohol, experience teenage pregnancies, and engage in criminal behavior. As Maslow's hierarchy reminds us, we all need to feel loved and accepted and be assured we have a place where we belong. When children do not have that sense of belonging in their own families, they find other ways to meet that need. Teens of abuse look for ways to dull the pain of feeling rejected and unloved by the people who should love and protect them, so they drown themselves in drugs, alcohol, and other addictive behaviors. Teens look to a gang, a lover, or a group of friends who take drugs together. However, these are poor substitutes for a family.

Abuse also damages social development and the ability to form connections with others. Children from abusive homes tend to lose the ability to empathize since they don't experience it from others. Some feel isolated, and they cannot have friends at their home like other teens do. Many are unable to make friends easily due to feelings of inadequacy and shame. Others are unable to determine what is acceptable behavior since it has not been modeled for them, and this inhibits their ability to make genuine connections with others.

Children, like adults, have a strong need to feel part of a family. Young and vulnerable, they recognize that they are completely dependent upon their parents. Sometimes this need to feel accepted is so great that it trumps the need for safety. We see this when a child is abused, yet still clings to his abuser in the hope of being accepted and loved. Like adults, children experience cognitive dissonance when they want to believe that their father is good and loving, but they experience his abuse. Like their mothers, they may make excuses for their father—he had a bad day at work, I made him angry, I shouldn't be so needy. They continue to believe that deep down he loves them. Many children, even into adulthood, still strive to have some relationship with a father who has been abusive to their mother, although adult children often seem less likely to want to carry on a relationship when they themselves have been victims of abuse.

Children see far more abuse than we think they do. Many women report they have tried to keep abuse away from the children, only to find that the children are aware. In a study on rape within a marriage, researchers found that nearly 90 percent of the children whose mothers had been physically assaulted or both physically and sexually assaulted had seen the abuse against their mothers. Teenage children of sexually abused moms had significantly more behavioral problems than others.[211]

Children often repeat the patterns of abuse they see in their own home. The single biggest predictor of whether a child will grow up to be either a victim or a perpetrator of abuse is whether he or she grew up in an abusive home. Boys who witness their mother being abused are ten times more likely to abuse a female partner

---

[211] Lauren R. Taylor and Nicole Gaskin-Laniyan, "Sexual Assault in Abusive Relationships," National Institute of Justice (NIJ), February 1, 2007, https://nij.ojp.gov/topics/articles/sexual-assault-abusive-relationships.

as an adult, while girls who see their father abusing their mother are six times more likely to become a partner to an abuser as an adult.[212]

Intimate partner abuse and child abuse go hand in hand. Most abusers are "equal opportunity" abusers and will perpetrate abuse on intimate partners, children, the elderly, pets, employees, and others who are in a position of less power. While it is difficult to determine with precision how many children experience child abuse while their mothers experience intimate partner abuse, studies estimate that 30 to 60 percent of abusers who abuse their intimate partners also abuse children.[213]

In many instances, children who report abuse to family members are not believed or are told to be quiet. Reports of abuse in a family are often silenced because if the abuser was exposed, the family would be forced to act against another family member, which is very uncomfortable. The abuser may be the sole breadwinner of the family, and the family would then lose financial support and may even become homeless if he was exposed. Or the abuser may be a favorite uncle or grandfather, and excluding him from the family would cause a division in the family between those who support the adult and those who support the child. Many people find it easier to silence or attack the credibility of a child so that they can maintain the status quo.

When children are silenced or not believed, they learn that they should keep the abuse to themselves. After all, if their own family did not support them, they cannot expect anyone else to. They feel unloved, unworthy, shame, and guilt. They learn that they cannot trust others, and this causes significant problems in adult relationships.

Silencing children who witnessed abuse or have been abused results in fewer reports to law enforcement, fewer convictions, and more abusers who have no repercussions for their actions, who are then emboldened to continue the abuse and repeat it on other children. While domestic abuse concerning intimate partners is both the most reported and yet the most underreported crime, abuse against children is even less reported. For example, a national survey found that 20 percent of women and 16 percent of men were sexually abused as children. These numbers indicate that childhood sexual abuse is common. Yet only 1.8 cases of out of 1,000 (far less than even 1 percent of the population) are ever reported.[214] Clearly, childhood abuse is extremely underreported.

One may assume that DCFS and other governmental agencies and professionals charged with protecting children would do all in their power to protect our children. However, the assumption of protection is often misplaced. Each year, hundreds of children die at the hands of someone they know, most often a father or other male relative or male friend or acquaintance.[215] Each year, children are killed by a parent after a judge forces the child to have visitation or custody with an abuser. Each year, children are killed by a parent, even though the DCFS has found the reports to be "unfounded." Each year, the pleas of thousands of concerned mothers are ignored by judges who force children to spend time with an abusive father. Mothers must either comply with the court order or risk violating a court order and going to jail, which then puts the child in the sole custody of the

---

[212] Office on Women's Health, *Effects of Domestic Violence on Children*, n.d., https://www.womenshealth.gov/relationships-and-safety/domestic-violence/effects-domestic-violence-children.
[213] National Domestic Violence Hotline, *Get the Facts & Figures*, n.d. http://www.thehotline.org/resources/statistics/.
[214] Merrilyn McDonald, "The Myth of Epidemic False Allegations of Sexual Abuse in Divorce Cases," *Court Review* (Spring 1998), as quoted in "Confirmed: Custody Courts Fail Children," https://barrygoldstein.net/articles/confirmed-custody-courts-fail-children.
[215] James Alan Fox, "Homicide Trends in the United States," Bureau of Justice Statistics, https://www.bjs.gov/content/pub/pdf/htius.pdf.

abuser. Ironically, in a divorce, the abuser, not the healthy parent, usually demands sole custody of the child in the court system. And in most cases, the abusive parent will be successful.[216]

Even when a mother knows that her child is subject to abuse, she may not have the strength to leave her abuser, the child's father. She may believe that it is better for the child to have both parents in an intact marriage than to leave and have a broken home where they would struggle to survive financially. Or she may believe that if she stays in the marriage, she can at least protect the child while she is there, but with a divorce she would be forced by a court to share custody of the child with the abuser. Or the father may have threatened to harm her or the child if she leaves, so she stays. There is no easy way out, and the court system, DCFS, governmental protection agencies, the church, and the extended family unit all seem geared to support the abusers rather than protect the children or their mother.

While the road to healing seems long for both the mother and her children, it is not impossible. Our bodies are designed to heal, and with the right approach, our minds and emotions can heal as well.

---

[216] Colorado Coalition Against Domestic Violence, "False Allegations of Abuse or Not? Understanding the Reality of Domestic Violence & Sexual Assault," n.d., https://www.violencefreecolorado.org/wp-content/uploads/2013/11/CCADV-CCASA-Fact-Sheet-on-Myth-of-False-Allegations_updated-2.21.14.pdf.

Chapter 40

A New Perspective

Most women coming out of an abusive relationship are emotionally, physically, and financially exhausted. She has serious doubts if she can ever heal and be whole again. She may feel like she could never trust a man or be in a relationship again. She doesn't trust her own senses. *If I was so wrong about my husband, I must not be able to read anyone at all to tell if they are good or evil* is a common thought. She wonders if she will ever be able to hold down a job, buy a house, reenter a social group, recover the torn relationships with her children and family, go back to school, or enjoy living again. She wonders if anyone even likes her, or if she is worthy of being loved. She may doubt her abilities in the things she had been very good at before she was run over by an abuser. She may wonder if she is good at anything anymore.

She may blame herself for not seeing the warning signs before she got into an abusive relationship. She may be overcome with guilt about why she did not get herself and her children out earlier, or she may feel guilty about divorcing and forcing her children to be children from a "broken household" of divorce. She misses the children incredibly when they are at their father's house. Her home is quiet, and she is lonely when they are gone. She may still feel that if she had gone to counseling, or had been nicer, or had done something different, he would have changed—or at least changed enough so that she could have "saved" the marriage.

But most of all, she feels fear—fear of the future, fear of the unknown, fear that she will get into another bad relationship, fear that her children will always be mad at her for breaking up their home, fear that her children will grow up and leave forever, fear that none of her friends will understand, fear that she will spend the rest of her life alone, fear that God is mad at her, fear that her church is mad at her, fear of facing the world alone, fear of getting out into the world, fear of having to get a job, fear of having to support herself alone, fear of having to deal with all the house issues by herself, fear of him being vindictive and taking her kids away, fear of him hurting the children, fear of him appearing at her doorstep and beating her or raping her like he used to do, and more. In sum, she is in fear of having no money, in fear of being alone, in fear of being a bag lady, and in fear of him.

And then there's God. *Wasn't He watching? Why did He let this happen to me? He must have sent this to punish me. I must have deserved it. But I'm a Christian. Bad things aren't supposed to happen to Christians! Look at all the things I did for God! Didn't He see those? Wasn't I supposed to love, love, love? And turn the other cheek? And forgive? And that's what I did! This is so not fair! Does God care? Does God even exist?*

To get to the other side—to get to a place of healing and wholeness, peace and rest, courage and strength, thankfulness and joy, and faith in a God who loves us—we must let go of the misperceptions and lies that have taken over our thoughts.

But we can't just let go of the lies—we must put something in their place. When we simply sweep our minds clean of the garbage and the lies, our minds are empty, and something else will take their place. Jesus tells us that when a demon leaves a person, it goes through arid places seeking rest, and then returns to the person, finding, like a house, that it is empty and swept clean. The demon then returns with other demons and makes the person worse than in the first place (Matthew 12:43–45; Luke 11:24–26). Likewise, we can't just clean out our minds from the spirits and lies of the Enemy. We must replace the lies and fill our minds with the truth—God's truth. And when our minds are full of God's truth, there is no room for the Enemy's lies to slip in. They are quickly identified as lies and rejected.

Our human perspective, skewed by years of abuse in a world so broken, is flawed. We likely have believed hundreds or perhaps thousands of lies. One by one, we must identify and reject the lies we have believed and replace them with God's perspective—God's truth about who He is, how He loves us, His promises, His design for us, and the good plans He has for us. One by one, the chains holding us are broken and we move toward freedom. One by one, we begin to see things as God sees them, our wounds are healed, and our spirits are restored. And once we finally embrace God's perspective, we have healing.

I return to David's perspective time and time again. He was betrayed by his friends and family to whom he had been loyal. He was hunted down, scorned, slandered, nearly killed, tossed out of his own home, on the run, and in hiding from people who wanted to kill him. A woman coming out of an abusive marriage can relate. She feels crushed by the unfairness and cruelty of it all. But David did not dwell on the why. In many psalms, he accounts for the terrible mistreatment he encountered at the hands of others, and his shattered heart cries out. He makes no bones about asking God to avenge him and to crush the wicked. But he doesn't wallow there. At the end of those psalms, he recalls God's faithful provision and protection and thanks God for rescuing him. And then he tells anyone who has been rescued to tell their story of the God who rescues and redeems in order to give others hope and healing.

> Let the redeemed of the Lord tell their story—those He redeemed from the hand of the foe. . . .
> Some sat in darkness, in utter darkness, prisoners suffering in iron chains. . . .
> Then they cried to the Lord in their trouble, and he saved them from their distress.
> He brought them out of darkness, the utter darkness, and broke away their chains.
> Let them give thanks to the Lord for his unfailing love and his wonderful deeds for mankind,
> for he breaks down gates of bronze and cuts through bars of iron. . . .
> He sent out his word and healed them; he rescued them from the grave. (Psalm 107:2, 10, 13–16, 20)

God naturally wired our bodies and our brains for self-healing. Every cut eventually forms a scab, and the skin heals over. Once a broken bone is set, doctors let nature take its course as the bone heals. After surgery, the patient is left to heal on her own. Without outside threats or violence, our bodies gravitate to a state of health. Likewise, our emotional and mental health gravitates toward healing when we are in a safe environment. Even after stress-filled experiences such as abuse, natural disasters, conflicts, war, and the like, our minds can return to a state of health. Remarkably, healing starts almost immediately when a woman gets out of an abusive situation and into a safe place surrounded by healthy people.

The author of Romans encourages us, "Do not conform to the pattern of this world, but be transformed by the renewing of your mind. Then you will be able to test and approve what God's will is—his good, pleasing, and perfect will" (Romans 12:2). Knowing God's will starts with being transformed, and transformation starts with renewing our minds. When we renew our minds, replacing former thoughts with God's perspective, everything changes—our perspective and worldview, our actions and attitudes, our habits and physical well-being, and our emotional well-being. Everything changes when we allow God to heal and renew our minds.

We are finding that science supports the notion that we can be transformed when we allow God to renew our minds. In his book *Anatomy of the Soul*, Christian neuroscientist Curt Thompson explains the science of how spiritual practices, interaction with Scripture, and positive connections with other empathetic, kindhearted people can rewire our brains, alter brain patterns, use new neuropathways, and lead us to become more like the people God intended us to be. Dr. Thompson shows scientifically what the author of Romans wrote 2,000 years ago—how to be transformed by the renewing of our minds. Likewise, in his book *The God-Shaped Brain*, Christian psychiatrist Timothy Jennings unveils how our brains, our bodies, and our relationships thrive when we have a healthy and accurate understanding of who God is. His book explores how neuroscience and Scripture can bring healing and transformation. Similarly, in the book *How God Changes Your Brain*, Dr. Andrew Newberg and therapist Mark Robert Waldman explain how our thoughts about God and our spiritual disciplines can change our brain processes and enhance our mental, physical, and spiritual health.

Jesus triumphantly stated His mission on earth: He has come to set the captives free and release the oppressed (Luke 4:18).

If you are a woman healing from domestic abuse, your Papa God sees you and is doing a rescue mission on you. You are a beloved daughter of the King of Kings. The Lord of Lords will stop at nothing to get you out of the prison you have been held in and lead you to the promised land. Satan has tried to destroy you and your children and has used your husband to do it. Satan knows that if you become the woman that God intended you to be, you will be a force to be reckoned with, and you will bring God's kingdom to earth. That would mess up the devil's plans of taking down you and your family. But God has seen His daughter, and He says to the Enemy, "Oh no, you are *not* taking this one. She is *My* girl! She is *My* daughter! I love her and she is *Mine*!" Watch God break down every door, cut through every chain, trample on anyone, walk through every fire, fight every battle, extinguish every stronghold, and destroy every bar that is holding you in prison. Feel your spirit become whole again as God's loving words heal you and speak to your heart. And when you stand on the other side of the valley of darkness, have the blessing of telling your story and being the catalyst for other women to come out of the darkness and be healed.

I have a battle cry that I adapted from the US military: no woman left behind. I will work tirelessly to get a woman out of abuse, healed, and into the promised land. Overwhelmingly, the women I have counseled and represented who have left an abuser and have done the painstaking work of identifying the lies they believed, rejecting them and replacing them with God's truth, have gone on to heal and lead lives of blessings, rest, and peace. Be a woman who chooses God's perspective. The God of the universe is waiting for you.

Chapter 41

Lies about God and the Truth That We Are His Beloved

The first step in healing is identifying the lies that we have been believing for so long. Whether the lie comes from the mouth of the abuser, the abuser's supporters, our family of origin, our children, our pastor, our church, tradition, *Cosmopolitan* magazine, or someplace else in today's culture, lies always originate with the devil, the father of lies (John 8:44). Lies and deceit are his character, and the character of every person within his clutches. Satan's character does not change; he has always been and always will be a liar and a deceiver. Sadly, the character of every person on the Enemy's team will not change either, because Satan's character runs through him. We should not expect an abuser to change his character. I typically counsel each of my clients that she will know when her abuser is lying because his lips are moving. Satan's first recorded conversation was with a woman and was fraught with lies and deceit to make her question God's goodness, all to her demise. Satan has been targeting women with the same tactics and goals ever since.

The next step in healing is rejecting the lies and replacing them with God's truth. We don't want to stop with merely identifying the lies. We need to eliminate them from our thoughts and hearts and replace them with God's perspective. Truth is the nature of God's character, and the character of every person who is filled with the Holy Spirit. The first spiritual weapon that Paul mentions is truth. Paul says, "Stand firm then, with the belt of truth buckled around your waist" (Ephesians 6:14). Paul is not merely referring to us telling the truth (although that is clearly something we should do). Paul is referring to God's truth as a weapon to battle against the lies, schemes, manipulations, and deceit of Satan and those who stand with him.

In one of his discussions with the Pharisees, Jesus states that the reason the Pharisees don't listen to Him is because they do not belong to God, and therefore cannot hear Him. They belong to the devil and cannot hear the truth of God, because there is no truth in them. Jesus called them out as liars, murderers, and sons of the devil, and He called out Satan as the father of lies and a murderer. Lying, Jesus said, is the devil's "native language" (John 8:31–47). It is also the native language of any abuser and of all who espouse Satan's way of thinking. A woman may have been pleading with her husband for years, trying to open his eyes to the destruction that he has caused and trying to get him to listen to her and change his ways. But he cannot hear her. It is no use. Like the Pharisees, he belongs to the devil hook, line, and sinker, and he cannot recognize the truth. He is deceived by the lies of Satan, and he even believes his own lies.

However, Jesus tells those who believe Him, "If you hold to my teaching, you are really my disciples. Then you will know the truth, and the truth will set you free" (John 8:31–32). Free from what? For the woman who has lived with domestic abuse, free from thinking that she is stuck, unworthy of being loved, and believing she is "lesser than." Free from shame and guilt and the false notion that she will be nothing if she leaves. Free from believing that she can marry a man who rejects God without suffering the consequences. Free from feeling that God is mad at her. Free from PTSD. Free from being scared of what everyone thinks about her. Free from fear. Free from believing she is not good enough for anyone or even God to love her.

Jesus calls Himself the Way, the Truth, and the Life. God's truth leads to life—abundant, joy-filled life—the life that God has called you to and designed you for. Let's get busy rejecting the lies and start embracing God's truth.

Below are some of the many lies that women in abusive relationships have believed, and the truth that needs to replace the lie—the truth that leads to healing.

If you are a woman living with abuse, as you go through these lies I encourage you to pray the following prayer out loud. Our voice has power. God spoke the earth into being with His words. When we are fighting a spiritual battle, using our voice to proclaim God's truth and break agreement with Satan and his lies is imperative. We can feel free to pray this prayer multiple times, whenever you discover a lie that you have believed and now need to reject so that you can heal, whenever you need to be free from the oppression of Satan's favorite tools—fear, doubt, and anxiety. We have no authority on our own, but Jesus has all authority to cast out Satan and his demons, and He has given that authority to us. Satan and his minions have no choice but to obey the King of Kings and Lord of Lords. Therefore, we invoke the name of Jesus to break strongholds and crash through the darkness into the shining light of God's healing and truth.

> Prayer for Healing: Father, I break agreement with the lie of Satan that (name the lie). I reject that lie and accept the truth of your Word that (name the truth). I repent of my wrong beliefs and for not trusting You. Fill me with Your Spirit, Your presence, and Your wisdom. Bring me to see things as You see them, to hear things as You hear them, and to think only Your thoughts. Heal me and make me whole again. Satan, I rebuke you and reject you and your lies. I cast out you and all your demons and banish you forever. You have no place in me. I belong to Christ. I cast out the spirit of (unbelief, anxiety, fear, infirmity, lying, doubt, etc.) I command you to leave, in the name and with the authority of Jesus Christ.

Rejecting the Lies about God, Replacing Them with God's Truth

A. W. Tozer, a well-known theologian of the last century, said that what we think about God is the most important thing about us. Think about that. The most important part of who we are—our personality and thought processes, how we make decisions, what we do with our lives, how we treat others, what our relationships look like—depends on what we think about God.

What we think about God informs our relationship with Him and our relationships with others. If we think He is distant, uninvolved, and unresponsive, we will believe that He has no compassion for us and we are on our own. This inaccurate kind of thinking can lead to great anxiety: if God is not on our side or working for our good, then it's all up to each of us to make life work. It can also result in a parenting and marriage style that is distant and unresponsive, lacking compassion, and leading to anxiety in our families.

But if we view God as close by and rooting for us, we have the confidence that the all-powerful God is always near, that we can go to Him with prayer requests, and that He wants the best for us and will help us win our battles. With this accurate view of God, we also bring this idea of a loving, close relationship into our human relationships with our spouse, children, and others. We want the best for others and we help others because God does that for us.

If we think God is a wrathful ruler, we may believe that Christianity is just a bunch of rules that should be followed. This kind of detrimental thought process can lead to legalism without compassion in ourselves and in our relationships.

But if we think God is a compassionate Father rather than a ruling tyrant, we rest in His love and care, knowing that if we are acting in love, we are acting like our Father. With this beneficial view of God, we know that while we make mistakes, we are becoming more like God when we strive to know Him and be more like Him. We are far more compassionate with others in our lives when we view God as compassionate with us.

If we believe that God is constantly looking for ways to punish us, we might think that every bad thing that occurs is God punishing us for something. This way of improper thinking can fill us with fear that God is mad at us and that we deserve whatever abuse we get, and that leads to hopelessness. This can result in destructive human relationships in which some are always playing the blame game and looking for a gotcha moment, while others feel they deserve the blame and abuse they receive for failing to be perfect.

However, if we believe that God is constantly looking for ways to encourage us and give us blessings, and that because of the Fall, we are in a spiritual battle and the Enemy is constantly looking for ways to derail us, we properly can attribute the good gifts in life to God, and the evil to the Enemy. With this proper perspective, we can properly prepare and equip ourselves for the spiritual battle. We also recognize that neither the blame game nor accepting abuse is healthy in interpersonal relationships. Rather, we have healthy relationships that are characterized by encouraging each other and establishing appropriate boundaries.

If we are of the opinion that God only loves us if we are good enough, we may believe that we must earn God's favor and work our way into heaven. This line of inaccurate thinking negates the power of grace on the cross and causes us to forget how desperately we need Jesus. It steals the joy that only comes when one is so overwhelmed with thankfulness to God for His rescue mission that our only response is praise, worship, and doing kind things for others. If we think we must earn love, our human relationships are not built on real love, but rather are manipulative relationships in which affection is meted out or withheld based on how the other pleases us or risks being trampled on.

But if we know that God loves us no matter what, that we cannot earn our way to heaven, and that Jesus did all the work on the cross in the Great Exchange where we laid on Him all our sins and He gave us His righteousness, we feel secure in the love of our Father God and understand how completely dependent we are on Jesus. When we fully understand the magnitude of God's love and what He has done for us, the only appropriate response is praise, worship, and becoming His hands and feet, bringing love to earth out of a grateful heart.

The following are a few of the lies that we believe about God, and the truth that sets us free.

Lies about God and the Truth That We Are His Beloved

Lie: I'm insignificant. God doesn't really care about me. He has bigger things to think about.

Truth: God thinks about you all the time. He's crazy about you!

So many women are under the misconception that we don't matter to God. *He has more important things to think about than my little life. He's got the conflict in the Middle East, the Somalian refugees, the Turks and the Kurds, the world economy—that's weighty stuff. My stuff is far too small to complain about or pray about. I don't really matter all that much to Him—especially after all the wrong stuff I have done and the mess I have made of my life. I am a worm.*

The truth is that God is crazy about us! He made us! We are His daughters! And like a loving father, He loves us, encourages us, cheers for us, teaches us, corrects us when we are off course, and thinks about us all the time! Nothing is too small for Him. Yes, He is dealing with world peace, but because He is God, He is also very concerned with our lives. Apparently, people in the time of Jesus had the same misconception. That is why Jesus tells us that the very hairs on our heads are numbered and that every sparrow is known to Him (Matthew 10:29–31).

Psalm 139, however, includes my favorite passage about God's thoughts toward us. David knew God was always thinking about him. What a wonderful, comforting thought that even when we are not thinking about our heavenly Dad, we are always on His mind and in His thoughts, pulling on the strings of His heart. We are Daddy's girls.

> How precious it is, Lord, to realize that you are thinking about me constantly!
> I can't even count how many times a day your thoughts turn toward me.
> And when I waken in the morning, you are still thinking of me! (Psalm 139:17–18 TLB)

Lie: I'm scared about the future. If I leave, it will be horrible.

Truth: God is with you. He has a magnificent plan for your life, and He has planned you from the beginning of time. Be fearless, knowing that the King of Kings goes with you.

Many times, what holds a woman in an abusive marriage is the fear of the unknown. The Enemy puts doubts in her mind: *How will I survive? How will I get a job? Will I become a bag lady? What will happen to my children? How will I live being all alone?* And then the Enemy answers those questions to keep her in bondage: *You won't survive. You won't get a job. You will become a bag lady. Your children will be taken away from you. You can't live by yourself.* While the marriage is unbearable, at least it is something she knows. The fear of the unknown is paralyzing.

The truth is, God's got this. And God's got you. Throughout the Bible, people were paralyzed with fear of the unknown when they did not believe God's promises, but the people who depended on God and believed in His promises amid uncertainty were fearless. There is nothing more life-changing than deciding to leave an abuser, set out into the great unknown, and make a new life for yourself in a new place. Ask the people of Israel. When they left Egypt, only Moses, Joshua, and Caleb had the faith in God's promises needed to withstand the attacks from Pharaoh, to persevere through the desert, and to fight the giants in the land that God had promised to them.

God knows that human nature fears the unknown. Throughout the Bible, whenever one of God's angels arrives with a word from God, the first thing the messenger says is, "Don't be afraid" (e.g., Matthew 28:5–6; Luke

1:30–31; Luke 2:10). As humans, we are a pretty timid bunch; we have a lot of self-doubt and insecurities. But God knows this. After all, He made us! He knows our nature.

God also knows that Satan preys on our insecurities and instills fear in us. In fact, fear is one of Satan's favorite weapons to use on victims of abuse (while pride is his favorite weapon to use on abusers). The Bible tells us that our insecurity, fear, and timidity is not from God, but from the Enemy: "For the Spirit God gave us does not make us timid, but gives us power, love and self-discipline" (2 Timothy 1:7).

So when God calls us out of bondage into unfamiliar territory, He also promises that He will be with us in our journey and that He will fight the giants that we must battle as we claim the land of peace. God gives us the same commands and the same promises that He gave Joshua and Moses before him:

> I will give you every place where you set your foot, as I promised Moses. . . . No one will be able to stand against you all the days of your life. As I was with Moses, so I will be with you; I will never leave you nor forsake you. Be strong and courageous, because you will lead these people to inherit the land I swore to their ancestors to give them. Be strong and very courageous. Be careful to obey all the law my servant Moses gave you; do not turn from it to the right or to the left, that you may be successful wherever you go. Keep this Book of the Law always on your lips; meditate on it day and night, so that you may be careful to do everything written in it. Then you will be prosperous and successful. Have I not commanded you? Be strong and courageous. Do not be afraid; do not be discouraged, for the Lord your God will be with you wherever you go. (Joshua 1:3, 5–9)

God does not give any of us a map with directions and step-by-step instructions, although we often wish He did. Instead, He wants us to seek Him and have a relationship with Him so that He will talk to us Himself, like He did to Moses and Joshua. God also does not promise that we won't have difficulties. In fact, it's pretty sure that wherever we go, we will have giants to battle, just like the giants in the land of Canaan. We are on a rescue mission for ourselves and our children, not a stroll through the park. What He does promise is better than any map or set of instructions. He promises to be with us, and He promises to fight our battles.

Because God is on our side, He commands us to be strong, courageous, undiscouraged, and fearless. In short, we are on God's SEAL Team Six, and He calls us to be a badass.

He also gives us guidelines that will give us success and prosperity—obey His laws unswervingly, meditate on God's Word day and night, and proclaim it out loud. When we embark on this mission, we need to be constantly in touch with our commanding officer, or the mission will go sideways: we must be in our Bible constantly. We must be in direct communication with God and listen for His voice. We must do what He says, and we must use our voices to loudly proclaim God's promises and rebuke Satan's attacks.

God has a fantastic plan for your life, far better than you can ever imagine. "For I know the plans I have for you, . . . plans to prosper you and not to harm you, plans to give you a hope and a future" (Jeremiah 29:11).

God knew about you and designed and planned for you, even before you were conceived. He has been planning for you since the beginning of time. King David, who was familiar with dealing with people trying to destroy him, had one of closest relationships with the Lord of anyone who has walked the planet.

> My frame was not hidden from you
> > when I was made in the secret place,
> > when I was woven together in the depths of the earth.

> Your eyes saw my unformed body;
>> all the days ordained for me were written in your book
>> before one of them came to be. (Psalm 139:15–16)

When we are in a relationship with an abuser, we are under a cloud of evil that keeps us from prospering and fulfilling God's plan for our lives. In an abusive marriage, we are under the influence of oppression and tyranny that comes with wickedness, and we simply cannot thrive or be the person God designed us to be. But when we come out from under the cloud of evil and the influence of oppression, when we are in constant communication with God, and when we are strong and courageous because we rely on His promises, we thrive—because God's promises can then come to fruition.

Invariably, when I see women escape their abusers and stay in God's Word and claim His promises, I see them bloom. It is as if a tiny flower thirsty for water has had an umbrella over it removed, and God's blessings can now rain down on her unhindered.

Lie: I'm all alone.

Truth: God is with you wherever you go.

A woman in an abusive marriage or relationship often feels completely alone. One signature move of nearly every abuser is isolating her from her family, friends, and often from coworkers and her church network. An abuser ensures that her life revolves around him. They see *his* friends, they go to *his* church (if they go at all), they hang out with *his* family, they move into *his* home, life revolves around *his* career, they do activities that *he* enjoys, they support *his* school, and they attend *his* charitable and social events. When the marriage is over, the abuser will ensure that all his family and other connections stay with him. A woman often feels abandoned by everyone, including God.

But the truth is, God is always with her. When we lean into God in a lonely, difficult season, we come to know Him in a way that is nearly impossible when all things are going swimmingly in our lives. In fact, many women of faith state that in going through a divorce from a SNAP, their relationship with God became much closer and the process forced them to mature spiritually.

Trials always change us. The crucible of adversity makes us either bitter or better. Choose to be better.

King David came to know God intimately. His trials stretched his faith and developed a spiritual maturity that a life of ease could not. His eloquent poetry reveals a heart that knows and loves God in a very real, personal way. David's words apply equally to us. There is no place we can go where God's Spirit will not be with us. We, too, can have the same intimate relationship with God that David had.

> You hem me in behind and before,
>> and you lay your hand upon me.
>
> Such knowledge is too wonderful for me,
>> too lofty for me to attain.
>
> Where can I go from your Spirit?
>> Where can I flee from your presence?
>
> If I go up to the heavens, you are there;
>> if I make my bed in the depths, you are there.

> If I rise on the wings of the dawn,
>   if I settle on the far side of the sea,
> even there your hand will guide me,
>   your right hand will hold me fast. (Psalm 139:5–10)

Lie: I am unloved and unlovable.

Truth: God's banner over you is love. He delights in you. He rejoices over you. He sings songs over you! He is crazy about you!

Women in abusive marriages and relationships feel unloved and unlovable, primarily because their husbands have told them that so many times that they eventually believe the lie. However, they let the voice of their abuser drown out the voice of God and of the people who cherish them.

Women in abusive marriages have some of the biggest hearts on the planet and are dearly loved by God and adored by nearly everyone—except their abusers. They are generous of spirit and are giving and kind almost to a fault. It is high time we replace the voice of the Enemy and let the thundering voice of the Almighty fill our hearts with His comfort.

Imagine a new daddy cradling his infant daughter, cooing over her, singing soothing lullabies to her, looking into her face, marveling at her tiny hands, and star struck at how exquisitely her little eyes shine in the soft glow of the nursery. She hasn't even done anything yet—she's not a star athlete or a straight A student or a music prodigy, but he is head over heels in love with her just because she is his little girl. He is giddy with delight. Over her crib, he has hung a big sign that looks like a pink ribbon that says, "Daddy loves you." The sign will stay there in her room even after she has moved away and started a family of her own as a constant reminder that Daddy loved her first, last, and always. And if his little girl is ever in danger, he will break down any doors, go to any lengths, fight any bad guys, and travel to the ends of the earth to make sure that she comes home safely.

This is how our heavenly Father feels about His daughters. He adores us, He delights in us, He rescues us, He sings songs over us, and His banner over us is "Daddy loves you," not for anything we have done, but because we are His. Let His voice be the one you hear.

> He has brought me to his banquet hall, and his banner over me is love. (Song of Songs 2:4 NASB)

> Do not fear; Zion, let not your hands be weak.
> The LORD your God in your midst,
> The Mighty One, will save;
> He will rejoice over you with gladness, [He will take great delight in you (NIV)]
> He will quiet you with His love,
> He will rejoice over you with singing. [he will renew you in his love (NRSV)] (Zephaniah 3:16–17 NKJV)

> See what great love the Father has lavished on us, that we should be called children of God! And that is what we are! The reason the world does not know us is that it did not know him. (1 John 3:1)

Lie: Why me? Why did God do this to me?

Truth: God doesn't send abuse. Everyone goes through trials in this fallen world.

Many women who have been in abusive marriages and relationships are mad, or at least confused, about why God allowed her abuse to occur. *Why me? Why did God do this to me? Why did God allow this? Why couldn't I sail through life without any difficulties and suffering?* They are under the misconception that everyone else in the world has no suffering, or at least none as bad as hers, and that God should have stopped hers.

Everyone on the planet will suffer. A review of any newspaper reveals tremendous anguish and suffering at the hands of others, through accidents, or because of natural disasters. People are killed, raped, maimed, cheated, stolen from, fired without cause, harassed, stalked, and verbally abused. Earthquakes, hurricanes, wildfires, snowstorms, mudslides, tornadoes, and wild animals cause injury and death to people and damage to property. A review of the Bible will reveal the same thing.

We must be careful not to call good evil, and evil good. We must be careful not to believe that evil gifts are from a good God, or that good gifts are from the Enemy. God does not send evil and disasters to hurt His people. If He did, He would be an abusive father to His children. God wants to bless His children and give them an abundant life.

So what causes abuse? Who sends all the evil in the world? Let's give credit where credit is due. Satan is in the business of causing death and destruction. His mission statement is to "steal and kill and destroy" (John 10:10). God wants the best for us, but like a good father, He allows us the ability to choose to be in relationship with Him or reject Him. That's called free will. He doesn't force us to love Him, He doesn't zap us into being good people, and He doesn't make us puppets so that we have no choice but to follow Him. He gives everyone a brain and the ability to choose Him or the devil—and those are essentially the only choices we have: good or evil. And ever since Adam and Eve chose to reject Him, we have lived in a fallen world full of the consequences of sin.

Some of the consequences are a result of our own sin, like when we land up in traffic court because we violated the traffic rules and drove 60 miles per hour in a 30 mile-per-hour zone. Some of the consequences are a result of others' sin, like when we suffer abuse at the hands of a SNAP. Some of the consequences are a result of natural disasters, like when our home is damaged by a hurricane. Sadly, even mother nature has been adversely affected by the Fall, resulting in death, decay, and calamities that cause misery to humans and animals. Creation looks forward to a new heaven and a new earth, just as we do, when we are all free from death, decay, and pain. Paul tells us:

> For the creation waits with eager longing for the revealing of the children of God; for the creation was subjected to futility, not of its own will but by the will of the one who subjected it, in hope that the creation itself will be set free from its bondage to decay and will obtain the freedom of the glory of the children of God. We know that the whole creation has been groaning in labor pains until now; and not only the creation, but we ourselves, who have the first fruits of the Spirit, groan inwardly while we wait for adoption, the redemption of our bodies. (Romans 8:19–23)

We all endure the groaning of life in a fallen world and look eagerly toward that day when we know there will be no more tears or sorrows.

Therefore, let's not accuse God of abuse. He is not to blame. Evil is Satan's realm, but God does give us something to stand up to Satan's schemes. God gives us His power, authority, and armor to fight the forces of evil. The Bible is a story of God's love for His people being challenged repeatedly by the evil of Satan. But in every battle and every imprisonment, God equips His people to fight the evil that is attacking them. Whether it is Noah seeking shelter in the ark from the flood, Joseph finding favor with Pharaoh after being sold into slavery by his family, the children of Israel being led out of bondage from Egypt, Joshua taking Jericho to the sound of trumpets and praise, the Israelites victoriously battling the neighboring countries in Canaan, Daniel and his friends finding favor with King Nebuchadnezzar in the land of Babylon, the remnant overcoming those who would stop the rebuilding of the Jerusalem wall and temple, Paul being released from prison by an earthquake and angel armies, or Peter standing up against the Sanhedrin with boldness, God doesn't stop the onslaught of the evil ones. But He does equip His loved ones to stand firm against evil in battle. And in the end, God is victorious.

God uses the same battle techniques today. In the face of the evil of domestic abuse, He equips His daughters for battle, and He brings His angel armies, both the heavenly hosts and His earthly angels sans wings, to fight for her freedom. And at the end of a woman's battle with abuse, God has won, and she is the victor.

Warrior daughter of the warrior King, let us equip ourselves for battle. Let us be bold as we come before the very throne of God and receive from Him strength and boldness in the crusade for freedom—and let us rejoice in the victory that comes.

Lie: God gave me this abuse to teach me patience, to punish me or something. After all, God gives us suffering.

Truth: God does not give us suffering. However, He will use it and bring good from it.

One of the biggest lies that people of all backgrounds believe is that God gives us suffering and misery to teach or punish us, or just because He can. This is a corollary to the previous lie that God sends abuse. I attended one Christian's woman's conference in which the speaker's entire premise was, "Your pain is your gift from God." She told a group of women—who collectively had suffered miscarriage, cancer, domestic abuse, the death of a child or a husband, and a whole host of other atrocities—that their sufferings were God's gifts to them. We then had written assignments that forced us to wallow in our pain, and hers, the entire day. This is simply hogwash. I walked out.

God does not send suffering to teach or punish or to show off His power. God wants to give us an abundant life, not a broken one (John 10:10). We all experience misery and suffering because we live in a fallen, broken world in which Satan is doing all he can to destroy us. It is only by God's blessings that are holding back Satan's attacks that we can conduct our lives at all.

However, God will take whatever we have been through and use it for our good. He promises that. One of my favorite verses is Romans 8:28: "And we know that in all things God works for the good of those who love him, who have been called according to his purpose." It is a good verse to commit to memory. Scripture does not state that all things are good. In fact, some things are very, very bad. But God does promise us that He is working for our good in all things if we love Him. Even when we don't see Him, even when things look dismal, He is behind the scenes working to bring about blessings for us.

Many women can relate to the story of Joseph in the Bible. Joseph was betrayed by his own family, sold into slavery, and ended up all alone in another country. Yet through all this, God was with him, blessed him enormously, and gave him a powerful position. A seven-year famine struck the region, but God had given Joseph the wisdom to store grain. His own family, who had betrayed him, came to buy grain so they would not starve.

When Joseph revealed his identity to his brothers, they feared he would take revenge on them. Joseph, however, realized that God had used their evil to bring about blessings: "You intended to harm me, but God intended it for good" (Genesis 50:20).

Sometimes women misinterpret Scripture to mean that God is sending suffering, as if it is His will that we suffer. Scripture's intent is to warn us that suffering will come as a part of being a Christian in a world in which the Enemy has not yet been neutralized, not to tell us that suffering is God's will for us. The New Testament is replete with references to suffering and persecution, but none of them state that it is coming from God. For example, Jesus warned us that He sends us out to a dangerous world, like sheep among wolves, and that we will face persecution and suffering just as He did. Evil people didn't accept Him, and therefore they won't accept us (Matthew 10). Nothing infers that God approves of the persecution and suffering; rather, it is a warning of what to expect. In fact, Jesus instructs us that when we are persecuted in one place, we should flee to another (Matthew 10:23). If persecution was really God's will for us, He would tell us to stay there and take it, not flee. Likewise, Paul told Timothy, "Everyone who wants to live a godly life in Christ Jesus will be persecuted" (2 Timothy 3:12). Paul's statement that we will face persecution is not a statement of God's will for us, but is rather a statement of a sad fact of life when we want to live godly lives. Someone in the Enemy's camp will always take a stand against what is good.

What about God disciplining His children? Hebrews 12:6 says that God disciplines those He loves. Is He sending abuse to punish me? The word *discipline* means to teach, not punish. Jesus's twelve best friends were called His disciples because He was teaching them, not punishing them. God does teach us, but only with the intent of bringing us closer to Him, to increase our faith, to better equip us, and to make us more like Him, not to harm us. God teaches and uplifts; Satan harms and destroys.

But what about the Old Testament and God's wrath? In the Old Testament, the Israelites did not have the Holy Spirit to guide them as we do today. Despite His warnings, they rejected God repeatedly until God finally let them have their way, and He withdrew His blessings so they would repent and turn to Him. God always used punishment in the Old Testament to turn hearts back to Him. It is important to keep in mind that the people of Israel were practicing child sacrifices, orgies, and prostitution—unimaginably evil, horrible, and destructive practices—even to their own families. They had no justice, even in the courts of law. Eventually, God will punish those who completely reject Him and refuse to repent. The punishment will certainly come in the next life, if not in this one, as we all will be held accountable for our deeds and words.

A Christian woman in an abusive relationship does not come close to the child sacrifices and other degenerate practices of the people of Israel who completely rejected God. She has the Holy Spirit to guide her. And when the Holy Spirit convicts us of sin, He does so in a way that is affirming, uplifting, and positive, never destructive of our spirit or our body. For example, if we are short with a spouse, the Holy Spirit will put on our heart that we lost our temper, acted out of line, and need to confess and ask our spouse for forgiveness so our relationship can be restored. His end game is always love and restoration. The Holy Spirit will not instruct our spouse to beat us, lock us in the basement, or make us spend the night in the car as punishment. That is not love; that is not restoration. That is hate and destruction.

Lie: This is a fight between me and my abuser/(soon-to-be) ex-husband.

Truth: This is a spiritual battle and an assault from Satan.

A woman in an abusive marriage is often so focused on the conflict with her abuser that she fails to realize that the battle is bigger than her and her husband.

She is most likely involved in the biggest spiritual battle of her life. For most women, nothing will even come close to the spiritual warfare that takes place when she takes a stand against evil and says, "No more!" Satan will then unleash his fury. She is a threat to him. He knows that when a woman of God is fully engaged with a faith that is as strong and bold as the saints, she is unstoppable. After all, Satan had Paul on his side at one point, and look what happened after God got ahold of him. He wrote much of the New Testament, started a bunch of churches, trained thousands of new Christians, and over the course of the last two thousand years, taught billions of Christians about God, pushed back the forces of darkness, and changed the planet for the better. The devil really doesn't want that to happen again. (See chapters 32, 33, and 34 for a more detailed discussion of the spiritual battle, the spiritual journey, and the armor of God.)

For the woman leaving domestic abuse, it's imperative to change her mindset from the meek-and-mild, sweet-yet-fearful church lady to a fearless warrior. She is in a war she must win, and God is fighting on her side. Her focus must switch from her husband (who is only being used as a tool of the devil) to the real cause of the fight. Her mantra must be, "Not today, Satan. Not ever. Not me, not my kids, not my dog, not my cat, not my neighborhood. Not now. Not ever."

I love *Star Wars*, not just for the great costumes, far-fetched alien creatures, and one of the best soundtracks of all time, but I also love it because it portrays the battle going on in the universe that gets played out in each of our lives. Out there, somewhere, is an unseeable Force that gives the Jedi knights unbelievable power to do good. The more they study the Force, the more they train with Jedi masters, the more they practice using the power of the Force, the more they gain powers of the Force to accomplish good. The Force gives them the power to move starships, fight battles, and change people's minds. Out there somewhere is also the Dark Side, another unseeable force that gives the bad guys incredible powers and the ability to manipulate situations, lie, steal power, destroy planets, and pretend they are the upright, honorable leaders of parliament at the same time. The universe is engaged in a constant struggle between the Force and its armies, and the Dark Side and its enemy combatants. Eventually, the good guys win because the Force is stronger than the Dark Side, but the victory is not without a struggle.

As a daughter of the King of Kings, know that the Force is strong in you. And when you defeat the Dark Side, there is nothing that will arise that will be even close to the battle you have just won. You will emerge stronger than steel and more courageous than a lion. A boss is grumpy? No problem, you defeated the Dark Side. A drama queen is in the PTA? Not an issue that you are even willing to waste your time on; you defeated the Dark Side. You lost your job? God's got this; you defeated the Dark Side.

May the Force be with you.

> For our struggle is not against flesh and blood, but against the rulers, against the authorities, against the powers of this dark world and against the spiritual forces of evil in the heavenly realms. (Ephesians 6:12)

Lie: Our weapons in the battle are legal briefs, police, the judge, the lawyers, the social workers, the guardians, etc.

Truth: Our weapons are spiritual: truth, righteousness, salvation, faith, God's Word, prayer in the Spirit.

Far too many women rely only on the earthly weapons of battle: lawyers, judges, police, social workers, child guardians, etc. They are under the false notion that if they lawyer up, they will win the fight, or at least break even. They don't even consider the other, more powerful, weapons they have at their disposal.

We live in a physical world, so we must use these earthly weapons to fight our earthly battle. But there is also a spiritual battle going on, and for that we must wield our spiritual weapons of truth, righteousness, salvation, faith, the Word of God, prayer in the Holy Spirit, peace, and movement. Long after the physical battle is over and the assets are divided, the maintenance and child support are determined, and parenting rights and responsibilities are established, the spiritual battle will rage on. And for this, we must be fully equipped. (See chapter 32 for "The Armor of God You Will Need for the Fight.")

> Finally, be strong in the Lord and in his mighty power. Put on the full armor of God, so that you can take your stand against the devil's schemes. For our struggle is not against flesh and blood, but against the rulers, against the authorities, against the powers of this dark world and against the spiritual forces of evil in the heavenly realms. Therefore put on the full armor of God, so that when the day of evil comes, you may be able to stand your ground, and after you have done everything, to stand. Stand firm then, with the belt of truth buckled around your waist, with the breastplate of righteousness in place, and with your feet fitted with the readiness that comes from the gospel of peace. In addition to all this, take up the shield of faith, with which you can extinguish all the flaming arrows of the evil one. Take the helmet of salvation and the sword of the Spirit, which is the word of God. And pray in the Spirit on all occasions with all kinds of prayers and requests. With this in mind, be alert and always keep on praying for all the Lord's people. (Ephesians 6:10–18)

Lie: I don't think God's promises apply to me. I have no hope.

Truth: God always keeps His promises.

So many women caught in abuse feel they have no hope, that God doesn't keep His promises. They profess to be women of faith, but read the Bible more as a storybook than as a collection of real-life stories of how God worked miracles and kept His promises to those He loves. God is still keeping His promises to us today. God promises to give us hope.

In today's nomenclature, the human definition of *hope* means little more than a wish. As a Chicagoan, I hope that the Cubs will win the World Series again, and I hope that it won't take 108 years like the last time. But given their history, I'm not holding my breath to see it again in my lifetime. However, in God's dictionary, *hope* means looking forward to something that we know will happen with great expectation. We don't just wish God is strong enough or loves us enough to keep His promises. We know that He is all powerful and that He loves us like crazy, so we know that He will keep His promises, and we look forward to seeing Him in action.

He promises that He will never leave us or forsake us (Deuteronomy 31:6; Hebrews 13:5), and He promises that His grace is sufficient for our needs (2 Corinthians 12:9). We don't just wish that those promises were true. We can take those to the bank.

Every woman has lies that she has believed about God. I invite you to set aside some time with God and write down all the lies you have believed about Him. Then next to the lie, write down the truth about God and back it up with a Scripture verse or two. Let His Spirit speak to your heart, and let His presence soak into your soul, until you believe His truth and reject the lies. Pray out loud the prayer for healing that was given earlier in this chapter. Then cross out the lie on the paper, leaving only the truth. Now look forward with great expectation to what God is going to do!

Chapter 42

Lies That Get a Woman into Abuse, and the Truth about Relationships

How does a woman who loves the Lord and has so many wonderful qualities end up with an abuser? How does a girl who dreams of having a loving Christian family find herself as a prisoner in her own home? Lies. She believes the lies that the abuser says, that society tells her, and that her own misperceptions whisper to her. She misinterprets Scripture and listens to others who misunderstand God's purpose for marriage. She lacks discernment – the ability to recognize good from evil and distinguish truth from lies. She has been deceived by the great Deceiver who has wormed his way into her thoughts and convinced her that not following God's way will not be that bad – that choosing someone who has not chosen God will not have dire consequences. In this chapter we discuss just a few of the lies women believe that pave the pathway for an abusive relationship, and the truth that God has to say about relationships that are healthy for us as well as honoring to Him.

Lie: I need to have a man in my life to make me complete. I didn't want to be lonely.

Truth: God made us to be in relationship with others, specifically good, healthy relationships with others, and to choose those wisely.

Our first and foremost relationship, however, should be with God as we strive to be more like Him. After that, if God has a spouse planned for us, we should choose as our life partner a person whose first and foremost relationship is with God and who is striving to be more like Him.

> Above all else, guard your heart, for everything you do flows from it. (Proverbs 4:23)

> I have this against you, that you have left your first love. (Revelation 2:4 NJKV)

Lie: He must love me when he wants to have sex with me.

Truth: Abusers use sex to get their victims bonded to them; it is not love.

Lies That Get a Woman into Abuse, and the Truth about Relationships

The hormone oxytocin that bonds a woman to the person with whom she has sex is activated regardless of the man's character or intentions. God intended the bond of sexual union to sustain us through the ups and downs of marriage, but Satan has usurped the original intent and uses oxytocin to bond women to abusers.

Abusers are sexually promiscuous and use sex early in a relationship so his victim becomes attached to him, which puts him in control. For an abuser, sex has nothing to do with love. Sex with anyone satisfies an immediate need for sex, just like a cheeseburger (or any other food) meets an immediate need for hunger. If you or I were hungry but only had twenty minutes for lunch, we might love filet mignon, but we wouldn't feel guilty about grabbing a quick burger instead of going to our favorite steak place. In the same way, when an abuser is hungry for sex, he wants it immediately, and anyone will do. He doesn't feel guilty about using whoever he happens to be with to satisfy that craving.

However, real love waits. Love is patient. Love wants the best for the other person; love is not selfish or demanding. Love sees the person inside the body, not just the body. Love is a heart connection. Love knows that sharing one's body is an act of giving. Love does not demand or require sex before the other person is ready to give of themselves. And love never takes.

> For this reason a man shall leave his father and his mother, and be joined to his wife; and they shall become one flesh. (Genesis 2:24 NASB)

> Love is patient, love is kind and is not jealous; love does not brag and is not arrogant, does not act unbecomingly; it does not seek its own. (1 Corinthians 13:4–5 NASB)

Lie: He says such complimentary things to me. He says we are soul mates. He says he never found anyone as wonderful as I am. He says we are so alike. And it is all going so quickly. It must be love.

Truth: Abusers love-bomb to get their victims emotionally attached to them.

An abuser pretends to be someone he is not, and he flatters his victim to quickly ensure that she forms an emotional attachment to him; however, he is not attached to her. His over-the-top romantic words and actions are not love—they are intentional deceit used make him look good and to worm his way into her life. The abuser masquerades as someone too good to be true, and she cannot believe her good fortune that someone this wonderful would be interested in her. But he will take off his mask after she is emotionally and financially hooked, and it is difficult to escape.

True love takes its time to get to know the other person from the inside out. It doesn't rush things, and it doesn't flatter. True love admires, appreciates, and affirms another person, but it doesn't offer superficial flattery. (See chapter 3, "Three Phases of a Romantic Relationship with a Narcissist, Sociopath, Psychopath, or other Abuser.")

> For such people are false apostles, deceitful workers, masquerading as apostles of Christ. And no wonder, for Satan himself masquerades as an angel of light. It is not surprising, then, if his servants also masquerade as servants of righteousness. Their end will be what their actions deserve. (2 Corinthians 11:13–15)

Lie: It's okay if I choose a spouse who doesn't know God or who needs some work. No one is perfect. I can love him enough to change him.

Truth: A spouse needs to be a co-laborer with you to fulfill God's purpose for a great marriage.

Many Christian women are under the illusion that the person they choose to spend their lives with, the person who will be the father of their children and the grandfather to their grandchildren, the person who will determine the financial, emotional, physical, and spiritual trajectory of their lives, can be someone who doesn't know God or who has some serious emotional or addiction issues. Oftentimes a woman of faith has a rescuer mentality. She believes that she can rescue a man like she rescues lost puppies. Believing this lie has serious consequences. Unlike with the puppies, she discovers that the person she married never matures and constantly needs rescuing. She has married a child who refuses to become a responsible, mature man. Anytime we act within God's will, we receive His blessings, but whenever we act outside of God's will, we do not get His best blessings.

God wants only the best for us. He has a beautiful purpose for marriage that will result in peace and joy when we embrace His purpose and make our decisions in line with His plans. Marriage is designed (1) to be a reflection of God's love for the world; (2) to love and serve God, each other, the family, and the community; (3) to raise godly children; (4) to protect and provide for the wife and children; and (5) to provide emotional, spiritual, and physical support for each other. God's purposes can only be fulfilled with two emotionally and spiritually mature people.

Imagine that your father is the king of a country and has appointed you to rule over a region of his country. You are responsible for the well-being of the citizens, for protecting them from internal and external enemies, for ensuring the financial stability of the people, for ensuring morally sound and safe communities and laws, and for ensuring that you have an heir who will be kind, generous, and will take his or her responsibilities to the citizens seriously. You recognize the weight of your purpose and that you are a steward of such a profound responsibility. However, it is a great responsibility to bear alone, and you need someone who can share in your sense of purpose, your loyalty to your father, and in your responsibilities. Who do you choose?

Daughter of the King of Kings, you are a princess who has been anointed by your heavenly Father to rule a kingdom here on earth. You have been given a sphere of influence in your home, family, community, and work. Choose a prince who is worthy to co-rule with you. Choose someone who is wholeheartedly seeking to be like the King of Kings, whose life reflects His values, who shares your sense of purpose of bringing heaven's kingdom to earth, and who is spiritually and emotionally mature enough to understand the responsibilities of living for others and to fulfill God's purpose for marriage.

A marriage is not the place to do rescue work. Save your charity work for charity. You cannot love a deeply flawed person or one who rejects God enough to change him. Only God can change hearts, and our efforts will only result in frustration, contempt, and hurt feelings. For a successful marriage, heart, emotions, and spirituality must be properly aligned. A good marriage is a marriage of equals, not of one trying to rescue or correct serious flaws in the other. A healthy marriage requires two mature, healthy people. If two people don't love and admire each other the way they are, without any changes, then those two people together are not good candidates for marriage to each other.

> Do not be yoked together with unbelievers. For what do righteousness and wickedness have in common? Or what fellowship can light have with darkness? What harmony is there between Christ and Belial [Satan]? Or what does a believer have in common with an unbeliever? What agreement

is there between the temple of God and idols? For we are the temple of the living God. As God has said:

"I will live with them and walk among them,
and I will be their God, and they will be my people."
Therefore, "Come out from them and be separate, says the Lord.
Touch no unclean thing and I will receive you."
And, "I will be a Father to you,
and you will be my sons and daughters,
says the Lord Almighty." (2 Corinthians 6:14–18)

Lie: The little things he says and does don't mean anything. Underneath, he's a nice person.

Truth: The "little" things that a person says and does are a reflection of their heart.

Many times, a woman will overlook the "little" things a boyfriend says and does. She will rationalize, justify, minimize, believe as a joke, or flat out deny the seemingly small actions such as offending words or misogynistic attitudes. Despite these obvious signs, she will still believe that he is a genuinely decent person deep down. This is a mistake.

The truth is that the smaller things are reflective of a person's heart. A person with a good, kind, respectful, loving heart is good, kind, respectful, and loving in the little things as well as the big things, in jokes as well as serious matters, to the waitress as well as the CEO, and when tipping the bellhop as well as giving Christmas presents. A Christfollower puts God's principles into action when going back and paying for what was overlooked in his grocery cart as well as living up to his obligations under a million-dollar contract at his company, in the way he treats a stray dog as well as the stranger, and with a little money as well as a lot of money. How he acts in the little things toward others is how he will act in the bigger things with the woman he marries.

Often, a woman coming out of the fog of an abusive relationship will look back. With 20/20 hindsight, she realizes the man she married exhibited small (or perhaps large) red flags that she overlooked when they were dating. These were indicative of a deeper pathological personality that emerged after they were married.

Jesus informs us of the truth of the human heart. Look at how people handle the little things, because whoever can be trusted with a little can be trusted with a lot, and whoever is cheating on the little things will also cheat on the big things.

> Whoever can be trusted with very little can also be trusted with much, and whoever is dishonest with very little will also be dishonest with much. So if you have not been trustworthy in handling worldly wealth, who will trust you with true riches? And if you have not been trustworthy with someone else's property, who will give you property of your own? (Luke 16:10–12)

Lie: He's under a lot of stress; that's why he does what he does. He just had a bad day. It's too much to expect him to be perfect. Deep down, he's a decent person.

Truth: Stress and adversity reveal one's true nature

American novelist James Lane Allen wrote, "Adversity does not build character, it reveals it."[217] A person's

---

[217] James Lane Allen Quotes and Sayings, InspiringQuotes, https://www.inspiringquotes.us/author/1849-james-lane-allen.

true nature emerges in stressful situations. Anyone can pretend to be a decent person for a few hours at a cocktail party, a date, or some other event requiring social etiquette. But the real character emerges under stress. What does he do when telling the truth will cost him money? What does he do when acting ethically may mean he loses his job? What does he do when he finds something that isn't his? What does he do when he doesn't get what he wants? What does he do when he is under a deadline at work? What does he do when someone he is close to is in the hospital and needs his help, but he has a heavy workload? What does he do when no one else is looking?

Military training is a crucible to determine how people will act under hardship. Only those who can respond well under pressure qualify for elite fighting forces such as the Army Rangers, Navy SEALs, Green Berets, Delta Forces, and other special forces units. These highly skilled warriors must be physically strong and mentally tough to complete their missions. Their training puts them under tremendous physical, emotional, and psychological stress. Why? Because the true nature of the person is revealed under such adversity.

When you want to know who the real person is beneath the exterior of the abuser, it's the person who reveals himself when the heat is on.

Lie: I know he may be mean to others, but he will always be nice to me.

Truth: When he has his emotional and financial hooks in, he will treat you like he treats others.

According to Dear Abby, "The best index to a person's character is how he treats people who can't do him any good, and how he treats people who can't fight back."[218]

Abusers are cowards. They pick on people who are weaker than them and who they look down on—which is nearly everyone who isn't more powerful or richer than they are. They view themselves as superior to everyone else, and view kindness as weakness. This skewed perception gives them permission to mistreat others. Notice how your prospective partner treats those he views as inferior. He will eventually treat his romantic partner the same way.

Lie: His (ex)wife/ex-girlfriend must be horrible based on all the things he said about her. The poor guy, no wonder he broke up with her.

Truth: Talk to his (ex)wife/girlfriend before you believe him. He will say the same horrible things about you when you break up.

Lying is one of the primary characteristics of an abuser, particularly when it makes him look good and deflects blame to someone else. Undertaking a smear and slander campaign against his former partner or wife and playing the victim after a breakup is guaranteed. In fact, an abuser is sometimes still very much married to his wife when he comes upon a new love interest, so he will often tell the new woman that he is separated, in the middle of a divorce, or divorced. The best way for a woman to determine a more realistic romantic history is to ask to talk to his former wife or girlfriend before she starts dating. If he won't let the new woman in his life talk to his former spouse or girlfriend, he is probably hiding something.

Just keep in mind that whatever he tries to pull on his spouse or girlfriend before you, he will do to you.

---

[218] Abigail Van Buren, GoodReads, https://www.goodreads.com/quotes/9940-the-best-index-to-a-person-s-character-is-how-he.

Lies That Get a Woman into Abuse, and the Truth about Relationships

Lie: No one else will love me. I had better get married to him; at least he will take me.

Truth: You are a daughter of the King of Kings and Lord of Lords! You are beautifully and wonderfully made (Psalm 139:14)! God wants the best for you. If marriage is in God's plans for your best life (and it usually is), God has a wonderful person picked out just for you who will love you and build a beautiful life together with you. Wait for him.

When an abuser tells a woman that no one else will love her and that she should be thrilled that he has shown pity on her, this lie is particularly dangerous. It makes a woman settle for nearly anyone who has shown an interest in her, just so she doesn't spend the rest of her life alone and unloved.

Anyone who tells a woman this does not love her. Dear one, God made you uniquely, unlike anyone else on the planet. And that is a good thing. He made you beautifully and wonderfully! He planned you before you were even conceived! Read Psalm 139 and see how amazing you are. And if He has planned a mate for you (and He usually has), He made someone else on the planet who is unique and beautiful and wonderful who will appreciate you and how God made you. Don't buy the lie that no one else will love you and that you should settle for the schmuck who just told you that. Wait for the one whom God brings who is head-over-heels crazy about you.

Lie: The Bible says, "All have sinned and fallen short of the glory of God." I am imperfect too. I would be a hypocrite to expect perfection in my husband.

Truth: All have sinned, but those seeking after God have repented of their sin and do not make sin a habit or a lifestyle. Abusers are unrepentant and have a lifestyle of sin.

Of course, we have all sinned. But a true follower of Christ is convicted of his sins, seeks to obey God's words, and doesn't continue sinning as a habit or lifestyle. One can see the fruit of the Holy Spirit in his life—in his decisions and in how he treats others. His life is marked by the fruit of the Spirit, along with wisdom and humility—hallmarks of Christ followers (Galatians 5:22–23; Proverbs 1:7; Philippians 2:3–4).

Abusers, on the other hand, ignore God's Word, do not listen to the Holy Spirit because the Holy Spirit is not in them, and continue in their sin. They lack godly wisdom, humility, and the fruit of the Holy Spirit. Instead, they leave destruction in their wake caused by sexual immorality, impurity, debauchery, greed, idolatry, hatred, discord, jealousy, anger and fits of rage, selfish ambition, dissensions, factions, envy, drunkenness, and similar unhealthy characteristics (Galatians 5:19–21). Paul warns that those who live like this bite and devour each other and destroy others (Galatians 5:15).

Requiring our spouse and our closest friends to be true followers of Christ is not being hypocritical. It is being obedient to God, and it protects us and our children from the inevitable harm that comes from those who are God's enemies.

Lie: I should have seen it coming. How did I not see it? I must be an idiot. How could I be so stupid? I am overwhelmed with guilt.

Truth: Abusers are skillful, professional liars who are experts at deceit.

A woman in an abusive relationship often feels tremendous guilt for not having identified an abuser before she got involved, and certainly before she married him. She likely had some vague, uneasy feeling that something wasn't right, but she couldn't put her finger on it. She probably had never studied the symptoms of narcissism, sociopathy, psychopathy, or other disorders that would have enabled her to identify him as an abuser. Clearly, most women have not been brought up expecting to run into people with such serious and dangerous conditions. Our first response when we get to know someone is not to do a complete background check and interview every teacher since kindergarten to determine their mental stability. Little girls are brought up on Disney movies and dreaming about meeting their Prince Charming and playing "wedding day" in mama's white dress and high heels.

The blame for the deceit falls squarely on the abuser, not the victim. The abuser intentionally deceived her and went to great lengths to do so. In hindsight, after learning about domestic abuse, going through it themselves, and putting the pieces of the puzzle together, most women can look back and identify behaviors, words, and attitudes that were indicative of deeper issues. But at the time, with no knowledge of domestic abuse, her innocence and trusting nature made her an easy target for the abuser's craftiness and deceit.

Even mental health professionals with doctorate degrees, including psychologists and psychiatrists, have been fooled, as have those whose training puts them on alert for bad guys, such as police and detectives. Doctors, lawyers, judges, CEOs, PhDs, and pastors all have fallen for narcissists, sociopaths, psychopaths, and other abusers. Training and education seem to have little impact when a woman herself is in a romantic relationship. Women usually want a marriage and family more than anything else, and we put our natural defenses on pause when romance starts to flourish. Intelligence is no match for the treachery of a SNAP. He is far more evil than women are smart.

Women in abusive relationships have believed many lies that led to them choosing an abusive partner. The ones in this chapter are just a few. I encourage you to spend some time identifying the lies that led you into an abusive relationship. Write them down and then write down the truth next to them. Pray the prayer of healing found in the prior chapter, and cross out the lies, leaving only the truth.

Chapter 43

Lies That Keep a Woman in Abuse and the Truth That Sets Her Free

As we've noted, Christian women tend to stay in abusive marriages longer than women without a faith. Faith commitments run deep. We do not give up on people or relationships without putting everything we have into them. We certainly don't want to look back and say, "If only I had tried harder, it would have worked out." We want to be able to look ourselves in the mirror every day and say, "I gave it 120 percent. There is nothing more I could have done to make it work."

Yet most women will hear the mocking sound of the abuser or his minions, people unfamiliar with domestic abuse, or even a pastor saying, "If it was so bad, why didn't you just leave?" Even well-meaning people can let this slip out. They have no comprehension of how difficult it is to leave an abuser, as if leaving an abusive marriage is as simple as quitting a job. They ask the wrong question to the wrong person. They should be asking the abuser, "If you are a human being, why are you abusing your wife?"

The following are a few of the many lies that women believe that keep them in abusive marriages or relationships.

Lie: My husband was so nice when we dated; I don't know what happened. I know that we can get back to that if I just pray, and if I am nicer to him. Our marriage will be good when he gets back to that wonderful Prince Charming that he used to be.

Truth: Recognize your abuser for what he is—he is a predator who put on an act when you were dating to deceive you and capture you.

Often a woman stays in an abusive marriage with the false hope that with enough prayer, or if she is just a bit nicer, her husband will return to the person she knew when he was trying to win her affections. However, abusers are predators looking for prey; they pretend to be someone they are not to lure their target into trusting them, and then they finally capture their victim. Once the target is captured, usually on a wedding day, the predator drops his act of luring her in, and his true character is revealed. Once the relationship ends, he will repeat the pattern with his next victim. This pattern occurs in every romantic relationship with an abuser. There is no going back to the happy days of dating when he was nice. (See chapter 3: The Three Phases of a Romantic Relationship with a Narcissist, Sociopath, Psychopath, or Other Abuser.)

> For such people are false apostles, deceitful workers, masquerading as apostles of Christ. And no wonder, for Satan himself masquerades as an angel of light. It is not surprising, then, if his servants also masquerade as servants of righteousness. Their end will be what their actions deserve. (2 Corinthians 11:13–15)

> Be alert and of sober mind. Your enemy the devil prowls around like a roaring lion looking for someone to devour. Resist him, standing firm in the faith, because you know that the family of believers throughout the world is undergoing the same kind of sufferings. (1 Peter 5:8–9)

Lie: My abuser can change with therapy.

Truth: You can't change the nature of Satan any more than you can change the nature of God.

A common misconception is that abusers can and will change with therapy. Therapy is not effective for most abusers because they don't see the need for change. They view themselves as right, and everyone around them as wrong. They do not accept responsibility for the problems they have, and they blame others or circumstances for the difficulties they have created. Abuse is always a choice, yet they either don't recognize their actions as abusive, or they feel entitled to act that way.

They have completely rejected God and His commands. They do not want to hear what God or anyone else has to say. Abusers are under the influence of Satan, just like a true believer is under the influence of God. We cannot change the nature of God, who is always good; nor can we change the nature of Satan, who is always evil. Thus, we cannot change the nature of someone sold out to God to make him evil, nor can we change the nature of someone sold out to Satan to make him good. While God is all powerful and can do anything, He chooses to let people choose Him rather than make them puppets. He allows people to reject Him, and He allows them to fall deeper and deeper into depravity, if that is their choice. This is the notion of free will. God doesn't force anyone into changing. We are free to choose Him or reject Him.

The Bible recognizes that the wicked have been wicked and will remain wicked because they have chosen evil and have rejected God. We should too.

> But when grace is shown to the wicked, they do not learn righteousness; even in a land of uprightness they go on doing evil and do not regard the majesty of the Lord. (Isaiah 26:10)

> Even from birth the wicked go astray; from the womb they are wayward, spreading lies. Their venom is like the venom of a snake, like that of a cobra that has stopped its ears, that will not heed the tune of the charmer, however skillful the enchanter may be. (Psalm 58:3–5)

> Can the Ethiopian change his skin or the leopard its spots? Neither can you do good who are accustomed to doing evil. (Jeremiah 13:23)

> Many will be purified, made spotless and refined, but the wicked will continue to be wicked. None of the wicked will understand, but those who are wise will understand. (Daniel 12:10)

LIES THAT KEEP A WOMAN IN ABUSE AND THE TRUTH THAT SETS HER FREE

Lie: If I am nice, he will return the kindness.

Truth: Don't be fooled into extending kindness to abusers.

A common lie that women tell themselves is that if they are nice to their abuser, he will return the favor. They believe that even if he isn't naturally kind, he will feel guilty enough to return her kindness. However, abusers view kindness as weakness, and they will only take advantage of it and use it against their victim. They do not appreciate or reciprocate kindness. This is especially true when a divorce has been filed. Many women don't want to file for a much-needed order of protection, or even temporary maintenance, because they don't want to damage their husband's reputation, make it more difficult for him to obtain or maintain a job, or cause undue financial stress. They extend grace. However, that will backfire on her. He will continue and even escalate the abuse and will make every attempt to destroy her financially.

When dealing with an abuser, we must realize that he will not return a kindness and that he will use any kindness we extend against us. Knowing this, we must be "wise as serpents and innocent as doves" (Matthew 10:16 NRSV). In other words, we must develop discernment—the ability to detect motives—and establish proper boundaries to protect ourselves and those we love. We should not return evil for evil, as revenge is for God to do, and it is forbidden by Scripture (Proverbs 20:22; 1 Peter 3:9; Romans 12:17). However, neither should we put ourselves in a position to be exploited.

Jesus warned those in abusive situations to maintain healthy boundaries—to stop showing kindness to people who don't appreciate it—because they will attack the very people who extended the kindness. We would be wise to follow His sage advice:

> Don't waste what is holy on people who are unholy. Don't throw your pearls to pigs! They will trample the pearls, then turn and attack you. (Matthew 7:6 NLT)

Lie: I must be a bad Christian, a bad mother, and just a horrible person. My husband says that all the time. I just can't seem to do anything right. He is never pleased with me. I'm a failure.

Truth: Know your identity: you are a child of God, a daughter of the King of Kings.

Abusers are liars. An abuser says things that destroy others to feel better about himself. He can't see the good in others because he does not have good in himself, and he has been blinded from seeing the light in others. He only sees what is in himself—and that is darkness.

When we hear general insults like this, attacking our person, we know they are lies from Satan. Satan's attacks are unsubstantiated, nebulous hits to our soul and spirit designed to steal our joy, kill our spirit, and destroy our lives.

The truth is that God thinks we are so fantastic because He made us just the way we are—we are wondrously and wonderfully made in His image. God thinks we are so wonderful that He sent His Son and calls us His children. Of course, we are not perfect, but He has exchanged His perfectness for our imperfections on the cross. Like a good dad, He sees us for the good that is in us and the women we are becoming. Our King says to His daughters, "You are my girl, and I will hold this crown over your head until I have finished my good works in you! You will wear this crown as My daughter, a princess, perfect and lovely in My sight, equipped to do all the good works that I have designed and assigned to you."

In contrast to Satan's assault on our being, God is always encouraging us. If the Holy Spirit needs to convict us of sin, He does so with surgical precision designed to bring us closer to righteousness. We never hear, "You're a horrible person" from the Holy Spirit. Rather, He will speak to us in a whisper, identifying our specific sin and giving us direction on what we need to do. For example, we may hear, "You lost your temper with Susie today, and all she wanted was some of your time before she went to school because she's nervous about a math test. She's hurt. You need to reassure her that you love her, tell her that you are sorry for losing your temper, and ask for her forgiveness. A hug and an ice cream cone are also in order."

When we fully comprehend our identity as children of God and know in our heart of hearts that we are the beloved daughters of the King of Kings, Satan's lies have no power over us. And that is freedom!

> See what great love the Father has lavished on us, that we should be called children of God! And that is what we are! The reason the world does not know us is that it did not know him. (1 John 3:1)

Lie: What will all the neighbors and friends at church think of me if I leave this abusive marriage? He will lie and blame it all on me. They will think I'm horrible, too, and I will have no friends.

Truth: Your identity is a child of God, a daughter of the King of Kings. It doesn't matter what friends and neighbors think.

Many times, a woman will be paralyzed by what friends and neighbors will think if she leaves her abuser. She doesn't want to lose friends, and a woman will often stay in an abusive marriage because she doesn't want to lose her social circle. Once a petition for divorce is filed, the abuser will engage in a smear and slander campaign, telling lies and blaming his wife for the breakdown of the marriage. Inevitably, many will be fooled by the lies of the abuser and side with him. A woman leaving an abuser will lose "friends"—guaranteed. Sometimes the loss of people she thought were friends is more painful than losing her husband.

A woman's identity, however, is in her standing as a child of God, not in what her fickle friends say she is. If friends side with an abuser, they are not true friends and don't have her best interests in mind. It is time to develop true friendships with people who love her, appreciate her godly character, and have her best interests in mind. She does not need shallow acquaintances who leave when she is no longer willing to put up with her husband's abuse. Sometimes we misjudge people and think they are better than they really are. We might consider someone a friend, when that person is merely an acquaintance who doesn't care that much about us. Superficial friends become apparent during a divorce from an abuser, as people reveal their true character. Although it can be painful, viewing this shift in relationships as a welcome revelation of their less-than-stellar character, instead of the loss of a real friendship, can ease the disappointment. Just as God revealed to us the true character of the abuser, in that we were sleeping with the enemy, God reveals to us the true character of others.

When we get to the point where the only opinion we care about is God's, that is freedom. When we are at that point, we have the God-given confidence that we are on the right path. And if other people seeking the Lord want to come with us on that journey in friendship, that's wonderful. But if not, it gives us the ability to break emotional ties to unhealthy relationships.

Lie: I'm not good enough. Everyone else does amazing things, but not me.

Truth: God made you wonderfully just the way you are to do things no one else can do. Don't compare yourself to others. They are on a different journey with a different purpose and different gifts.

Comparison is the killer of joy. As we scroll through the Facebook feed or hear of a colleague's promotion or learn of a high school classmate-turned-millionaire, we naturally compare ourselves to others. When we compare ourselves to others, we either feel better than them, and therefore superior, which is not healthy, or we feel they are better than us, and therefore we are inferior to them, which is not healthy. Either way, comparison is not good.

God created you in a unique, marvelous way, equipped you with a special combination of abilities and gifts and experiences that no one else has, and has designed you to do a job that no one else can do. When we pray, "Your kingdom come, your will be done on earth as it is in heaven," we acknowledge that we are part of God's plan in bringing His kingdom to earth. Jesus started the process by His work—the miracles and healing and kicking out demons that brought God's kingdom to earth—and we get to continue His mission. Our job is to find out how He made us, what our assignment is, and get to work.

When God made the animals, He gave each one special abilities. The geese are great flyers, the cheetahs are amazing runners, and the dolphins are excellent swimmers. We would never think of entering a goose or a dolphin in a footrace against a cheetah. Geese and dolphins are not made for running. Likewise, it would be foolish to enter a goose or cheetah in competition with a dolphin. While they can swim, geese and cheetahs are not made for speed in the water. And in a flying race, it would be impossible to enter a dolphin or cheetah to compete with a goose. They may be able to jump, but they cannot fly. The cheetah does not feel inferior that he can't swim or fly, the goose is perfectly content not swimming underwater or running, and the dolphin does not feel like a failure because he cannot fly or run. They each know what they are made to do, and they know they do it well.

The point is, God made each one of us for a special mission on this earth. When we compare ourselves to someone else who has a different mission and a different set of attributes to complete that mission, we must remember that we are on a different path. God has people in mind that only we can reach, there are problems that only we can solve, and there are some hearts that only we can heal.

Spending time with God to hear His heart, to discover the distinctive ways He made us, and to ask Him to reveal His plan for our lives will keep us focused on God and will comfort us, knowing we are in the center of His will for our lives. And that is the perfect place.

> God, You created all of my intricate parts—inside and outside. You knit me together inside my mother's womb. Thank You for making me the way You did! I praise You because I am wondrously and wonderfully made in Your image. You know me so well, and Your design is beautiful and perfect. (Psalm 139:13–14 paraphrased)

Lie: I have tried to be a good wife and mother and a good Christian, but my husband doesn't see it. He just criticizes everything I do. Why can't he see the good in me? Why can't he hear me? Why can't he love me? And his family and friends don't like me either. What's wrong with me?

Truth: Evil people detest good people, and good people detest evil people.

SNAPs look at people as a means to an end. The only value a person has to an abuser is how that person can serve his needs. Because an abuser does not have God's love and Holy Spirit within, he does not see or appreciate God's presence in others, except to the extent that it serves his purposes.

A woman in an abusive marriage often finds that her in-laws don't like her, and her husband's friends aren't crazy about her either. Her husband's children also hold her at arm's length, if they are not downright mean to her.

We each have intrinsic value because God made us in His image. A Christian woman in an abusive marriage is usually an exceptional wife, mother, daughter, friend, sister, coworker, volunteer, etc. She must be because she is making up for all her abuser's deficiencies. She is both mother and father. She must be a role model to her children who overcomes the negative influence of the abuser; she must be responsible because he is so irresponsible. The list goes on. She almost always has super traits. As we mentioned in chapter 37, almost all women who find themselves as victims of domestic abuse are caring, kind, generous, trusting, cooperative, giving, forgiving, extremely empathetic, conscientious, compassionate, honest, resilient, sentimental, loving, responsible, and resourceful. They love deeply, form strong attachments, and put a great deal of value and investment into relationships. However, the abuser won't appreciate, affirm, encourage, or uplift his wife for these wonderful Christian traits—but he will use them to his advantage.

We should not be surprised that abusers and their minions don't love or appreciate the amazing godly women who are their wives. An abuser might have used the L-word on his wedding day to seal the deal, and even occasionally after that, but abusers don't love—they use. Good repels evil. Evil people detest good people (Proverbs 29:27). Once the scales fall from our eyes, and we recognize the abuser for what he is, we will also find that the opposite is true: Good people detest evil people (Proverbs 29:27).

Jesus warned us that wicked people filled with darkness will hate good people filled with God's light:

> If the world hates you, keep in mind that it hated me first. If you belonged to the world, it would love you as its own. As it is, you do not belong to the world, but I have chosen you out of the world. That is why the world hates you. Remember what I told you: "A servant is not greater than his master." If they persecuted me, they will persecute you also. If they obeyed my teaching, they will obey yours also. They will treat you this way because of my name, for they do not know the one who sent me. If I had not come and spoken to them, they would not be guilty of sin; but now they have no excuse for their sin. Whoever hates me hates my Father as well. If I had not done among them the works no one else did, they would not be guilty of sin. As it is, they have seen, and yet they have hated both me and my Father. But this is to fulfill what is written in their Law: "They hated me without reason." (John 15:18–25)

Almost every woman in an abusive relationship is a people pleaser. We want others to like us, and sometimes we go to great lengths to prove to others that we are worthy of their love and affection, even after our efforts have been rebuffed again and again. We are so desperate to win the approval of others that we lose ourselves in the process.

Jesus has a better way. If someone doesn't like us, be proud! Why? Because people of darkness see the light of the Father in us and are repelled by our goodness! That's a good thing! We shouldn't try to please everyone. The only person whose opinion counts is God's! That's who we should try to please. Good people with the Holy Spirit in them will sense the goodness of the Holy Spirit in us and be drawn to us. Those are the people we want to surround ourselves with, not the ones who don't like us. We need to stop wasting our time trying to get people to like us, and only spend our time with those who view us as God views us—a treasure.

Jesus had great advice for what to do when people reject us: "If anyone will not welcome you or listen to your words, leave that home or town and shake the dust off your feet. Truly I tell you, it will be more bearable for Sodom and Gomorrah on the day of judgment than for that town" (Matthew 10:14–15).

Instead of pining and hoping and wishing that our abuser, the in-laws, the stepchildren, or his lackeys like us, Jesus tells us to leave the home and even the town of the abuser and his supporters. Move out and move on. Jesus doesn't tell us to plead and beg with toxic people who abuse and reject us in the hope of gaining their approval. He recognizes that some hearts do not want to hear what God has to say and do not see the good in His people. Jesus encourages us to set healthy boundaries that will protect us from toxic people. His advice here is similar to the advice He gave in the Sermon on the Mount when establishing healthy boundaries: "Do not give what is holy to the dogs; nor cast your pearls before swine, lest they trample them under their feet, and turn and tear you in pieces" (Matthew 7:6 NKJV).

Save your good deeds for people who are deserving of you and the Lord who is in you. "Whatever town or village you enter, search there for some worthy person and stay at their house until you leave. As you enter the home, give it your greeting. If the home is deserving, let your peace rest on it; if it is not, let your peace return to you" (Matthew 10:11–13).

Lie: I am as nice as I can be. Why doesn't he like me?

Truth: Evil people don't like good people—that's why your abuser didn't like you.

Jesus explained that evil people hate good people. While good people are attracted to the good in others, Satan's followers are repelled by the good in us. Remember when an abuser calls us "the devil" that the Pharisees called Jesus that too.

> You will be hated by everyone because of me, but the one who stands firm to the end will be saved. When you are persecuted in one place, flee to another. Truly I tell you, you will not finish going through the towns of Israel before the Son of Man comes. The student is not above the teacher, nor a servant above his master. It is enough for students to be like their teachers, and servants like their masters. If the head of the house has been called Beelzebul, how much more the members of his household! (Matthew 10:22–25)

Lie: My abuser is a decent person underneath it all.

Truth: God's people do not continue in unrepentant sin because the Holy Spirit convicts them. Abusers belong to Satan. You belong to God.

One of the most common lies we hold on to is that our abuser is a decent person, despite all evidence to the contrary. On occasion, particularly around those he wants to impress, an abuser can act respectable for a while. However, his actions are self-serving. Good behavior is always calculated to get something he wants. These intermittent actions of seeming decency interspersed among heinous behavior cause a cognitive dissonance in our minds: *Is he the nice person he appears to be on an occasional basis, or is he the monster that he is to me when no one else is looking?* Cognitive dissonance occurs when we try to hold two opposite things in our mind that cannot both be true at the same time. Our minds cannot hold our opinion that our husband is a good man who down deep actually loves us, and the truth that he has done many horrible, abusive things for which he is not repentant. Our brains look to resolve this dissonance. The easiest way for us to resolve the dissonance is to conclude that our abuser is a decent person. In this way, we can continue to stay married to him and hold out hope that he will, in fact, arrive at a time when his decency far outweighs the out-of-character periods of abusive behavior.

Here's the truth: an evil person will sometimes pretend to act like a good person, but a good person will never pretend to act like an evil one. A woman can view her partner's actions over time in an objective manner and determine whether he is good or not. Those on God's side will have a life brimming over with words and deeds that exude the fruit of the Holy Spirit and will be surrounded by people who have been blessed by being in their presence. Those on Satan's side will have a life with words and deeds that exemplify the fruit of the flesh and leave broken and hurting girlfriends, wives, children, coworkers, and business partners in their wake. One cannot claim to know God and be abusive to his fellow man. Period.

> Dear children, do not let anyone lead you astray. The one who does what is right is righteous, just as he is righteous. The one who does what is sinful is of the devil, because the devil has been sinning from the beginning. The reason the Son of God appeared was to destroy the devil's work. No one who is born of God will continue to sin, because God's seed remains in them; they cannot go on sinning, because they have been born of God. This is how we know who the children of God are and who the children of the devil are: Anyone who does not do what is right is not God's child, nor is anyone who does not love their brother and sister. . . . Anyone who hates a brother or sister is a murderer, and you know that no murderer has eternal life residing in him. (1 John 3:7–10, 15)

Lie: Love is patient and endures forever, so I must stay, because that's what love does.

Truth: Love wants what is healthy for everyone and loves the truth. Putting up with abuse is not healthy for you, your children, or your abuser. God calls husbands to love their wives. If they don't, it is their sin, not yours.

Many women have been fooled into believing that love simply puts up with abuse forever. They see Jesus's suffering on the cross and assume that suffering at the hands of an abusive husband is what we are called to do. An abuser may even rub it in with a Bible verse, "Love is patient," or claim that love lasts forever. He may even charge, "If you loved me, you would accept me as I am and stop trying to change me," or "This is who I am. You must love me—you're my wife."

All these well-used lines come from the lips of abusers who don't love their partner or wife, all to maintain control over them and convince them to stay in abusive relationships. They are also classic examples of spiritual abuse. Be aware that anyone who starts a sentence with, "If you loved me, you would [fill in the blank of something self-serving the person wants you to do]" is a manipulator.

Love wants the best for everyone. Love wants truth, respect, and trust. Relationships that are not built with these characteristics are unhealthy relationships. One party uses power to control the other.

As a mother, it would not be loving for me to do nothing as I watch my child bully another child, hit his sister, run into the street, call me horrible names, or spend his allowance on cigarettes. These actions would be emotionally, physically, or financially dangerous for my child, for others, and for me. The loving thing to do would be for me to correct my child and teach him the right way. If I don't, these actions will continue into adulthood. In a similar way, it is not loving to do nothing when a spouse bullies, hits others, engages in reckless activities that can cause harm to himself or others, calls his family horrible names, or squanders a good deal of money foolishly on unhealthy or unnecessary things. In abusive marriages, when an abusive spouse shows no intention of repentance after being patiently and respectfully corrected in the spirit of hoped-for repentance and reconciliation, the loving thing to do is to remove oneself from the abuse. Fleeing from evil is commanded by the Bible for the protection of the believer and her family, and in the hope that the wrongdoer will, because of consequences, repent and turn back to God (1 Corinthians 5).

Lies That Keep a Woman in Abuse and the Truth That Sets Her Free

Lie: He tells me he loves me, so it must be true, even when he doesn't show it.

Truth: Love always wants what is best for the other person. If what you have doesn't look like 1 Corinthians 13 when you insert his name for "love," then it's not love.

A woman in an abusive marriage commonly believes the lie that her husband tells her: "I love you"—even when his action, words, and attitudes indicate he doesn't care about her.

Abusers use the three little words "I love you" to manipulate others. An abuser knows that a woman wants more than anything to be loved and to hear those words. Men have a deep need to be respected. When a man feels respected by others—that is, when he feels that others look to him for guidance, as an expert, as someone with competence who has what it takes to succeed, as someone who makes wise decisions and has good judgment—he thrives. However, every woman has a deep need to be loved and cherished. When a woman feels loved—that is, when she feels treasured, that she is the apple of someone's eye, that she can move the heart of her beloved, that he will do whatever it takes to protect her, that she is irreplaceable—she blossoms. It is no wonder that God's Word calls for men to love their wives and for women to respect their husbands. "Love" and "respect"—these are the words women and men need to hear.

But for an abuser who knows that his wife wants to hear the L-word, he will use the word "love" even as he abuses her, just to keep her in the relationship. For example, he may say, "I'm hitting you because I love you. If I didn't love you, I wouldn't be so jealous when you look at other men." He doesn't mean that he loves her; it's just another tool in his toolbox to keep her in line.

Love is always interested in what is best for the other person. Paul describes godly love in his letter to the church at Corinth. To test if someone loves another person, insert that person's name in 1 Corinthians 13:4–8 wherever you see the word "love." If that describes your spouse, you are experiencing Christlike love. If not, what you have is not love. It's something, but it's not love.

> Love is patient, love is kind. It does not envy, it does not boast, it is not proud. It does not dishonor others, it is not self-seeking, it is not easily angered, it keeps no record of wrongs. Love does not delight in evil but rejoices with the truth. It always protects, always trusts, always hopes, always perseveres. Love never fails. (1 Corinthians 13:4–8)

> Charlotte: After twenty-one years of marriage, I had to face the fact that my husband never loved me. He loved his money, he loved himself, he loved prestige, and he loved power, but he had never loved me. I put his name in the passage from 1 Corinthians 13 and just laughed at what came out. It did not describe him at all—in fact, he was the exact opposite. "Tim is patient. Tim is kind. Tim does not envy. Tim does not boast. Tim is not proud. Tim does not dishonor others. Tim is not self-seeking. Tim is not easily angered. Tim keeps no record of wrongs. Tim does not delight in evil. Tim rejoices with the truth. Tim always protects [me]. Tim always trusts [me]. Tim always hopes [for me]. Tim always perseveres [for me]. Tim never fails." Ha! Not one of those descriptions was true. I had to recognize that from the moment we started dating, our relationship was a complete sham. Despite him occasionally dropping the L-word, I was never loved. I needed to leave.

Lie: He must be a Christian, because he says he is, so I must need to stay with him.

Truth: You can tell if he is a Christian by ample evidence of the fruit of the Spirit. Otherwise, he is not a Christian.

Overcoming the Narcissist, Sociopath, Psychopath, and other Domestic Abusers

Abusers who prey on Christian women will usually claim to be Christian to persuade them to date and eventually marry them. An abuser knows that a woman whose faith is important to her will have the characteristics he needs to manipulate, deceive, and abuse her for an extended period. When she tries to leave, he will pull out the Bible verses that "God hates divorce" (Malachi 2:16) and that if he is a believer and wants to stay in the marriage, she can't leave (1 Corinthians 7:13). Naïve Christian women will fall for him and the verses pulled out of context.

There is an old saying: If Christianity was a crime, would your life have enough evidence beyond a reasonable doubt to convict you? If a wife doesn't see in her husband ample fruit of the Holy Spirit (see Galatians 5:22–23), the first of which is love (see 1 Corinthians 13:4–7), he is not a Christian. The fruit of the Spirit comes supernaturally when the Holy Spirit invades our lives. An apple tree naturally produces apples simply because it is an apple tree, and that is the nature of an apple tree. The apple tree doesn't work on it; it doesn't think about it; it doesn't have a twelve-step plan to produce apples. It's in the DNA of the apple tree to produce apples, just like it's in the DNA of a pear to produce pears, and it's in the DNA of an oak tree to produce acorns. Likewise, when the DNA of the Holy Spirit takes over because we belong to Christ, we produce love, joy, peace, patience, kindness, goodness, faithfulness, gentleness and self-control. The more Holy Spirit we have—that is, the more of God's presence we have in our lives—the more bountiful the fruit.

The opposite is also true, the more DNA of the Enemy's spirit a person has in his life, the more that person will produce bad fruit. It is a natural outcropping of the Enemy's presence in his life.

Similar to the love test, to determine if a husband is a genuine Christian, insert his name in the passages below describing the fruit of the Spirit, the fruit of the flesh, and the description of an abuser to see which description best fits. The marital relationship is unique among all human relationships—we see the best and the worst in a spouse. We see far more than what a spouse is willing to share with others. If your husband fits the description of an abuser and evidences fruits of the flesh rather than exuding the fruit of the Spirit, beware.

> But the fruit of the Spirit is love, joy, peace, forbearance, kindness, goodness, faithfulness, gentleness and self-control. (Galatians 5:22–23)

> The acts of the flesh are obvious: sexual immorality, impurity and debauchery; idolatry and witchcraft; hatred, discord, jealousy, fits of rage, selfish ambition, dissensions, factions and envy; drunkenness, orgies, and the like. I warn you, as I did before, that those who live like this will not inherit the kingdom of God. (Galatians 5:19–21)

> There will be terrible times in the last days. People will be lovers of themselves, lovers of money, boastful, proud, abusive, disobedient to their parents, ungrateful, unholy, without love, unforgiving, slanderous, without self-control, brutal, not lovers of the good, treacherous, rash, conceited, lovers of pleasure rather than lovers of God—having a form of godliness but denying its power. Have nothing to do with such people. They are the kind who worm their way into homes and gain control over gullible women, who are loaded down with sins and are swayed by all kinds of evil desires, always learning but never able to come to a knowledge of the truth. Just as Jannes and Jambres opposed Moses, so also these teachers oppose the truth. They are men of depraved minds, who, as far as the faith is concerned, are rejected. (2 Timothy 3:1–8)

> Charlotte: At the same time I did the "love test," I had to ask myself if my husband was even a Christian. He sat in a pew and liked socializing with his country club friends who went to church

with us, but I did not see the fruit of the Spirit in him. "Is Tim overflowing with love? Joy? Peace? Patience? Kindness? Goodness? Faithfulness? Gentleness? Self-control?" No. Sadly, not one characteristic of the Holy Spirit was evident in his life when we were together, or life before I knew him. And they are certainly not now either. Sadly, Paul's description of an abuser in 2 Timothy 3 and Galatians 5:19–21 were accurate portrayals of how Tim lived his life. He prided himself on being "mean and nasty." After the divorce, I heard many stories from his former business associates and our former nannies about how he had mistreated them. Those and his antics during the divorce led me to conclude that he couldn't possibly be a Christian—no follower of Christ would ever act that way. He was a practical atheist—he uses the church for a social club, but he acts like there is no God. He will have a rude awakening when this life is over and he comes face to face with God.

Lie: If I just keep praying, God will zap him and change him.

Truth: God allows evil people to continue in their evil ways, but He equips His people to have the strength to leave.

Many Christian women believe the lie that if they keep praying, God will touch their abusive husband with His magic wand and *Presto!* the abuser's heart will miraculously change from evil to good. This one lie keeps many Christian women in the bondage of an abusive marriage for years.

God allows each of us to accept or reject Him, to be good or evil. While He may pursue us, and He often does, it is up to each one to decide to accept or reject His invitation. He doesn't go around with a heavenly magic wand zapping the bad out of people (although if I had a superpower, this would be my choice). Our hearts must be open to accept His righteous ways. Jesus is the perfect example of the heart of God. He was kind and compassionate, healed people, drove out demons, fed thousands of people with a kid's lunch, and turned water into wine. Yet despite these miracles, many rejected Him. When the Pharisees and Sadducees rejected Him, and even plotted to kill Him, Jesus did not beg and plead with them or cower in fear (as women often do with their abusing husbands). Jesus knew they had heard the truth just like everyone else and had chosen evil over good. They knew they were in the wrong. He simply pointed out their sin and left them to their own sin. We would do well to do the same.

Throughout the Old and New Testaments, evil people continued choosing evil, and God let them do so. That is what free will is all about. We can make our own decisions. Evil people rarely choose to change their ways, but if they do, it is only because of the severe consequences that God or the laws of nature inflict that make it more painful to continue in the ways of evil than to switch to the good side.

God lets malevolent people wallow in their wicked ways so they eventually become even worse, but He equips His own to stand against evil and flee from the wicked. Rather than hoping and praying for an abuser to change, the wise woman of faith will instead pray for the boldness, courage, wisdom, strength, and protection to stand against abuse and leave an abusive husband to his own sinful ways.

On the rare occasion an abuser repents, one can recognize the signs of true repentance when he willingly does all of the following: (1) apologizes and confesses to all his sins; (2) confesses publicly to his wife, children, friends, pastors, and church family; (3) completes a perpetrator counseling program that lasts at least six months; (4) reimburses her for all her losses at the cost plus 20 percent, and restores all her relationships that he destroyed; (5) demonstrates a clear change of attitude and behaviors for two years; and (6) accepts "no" as an answer and does not demand forgiveness, reconciliation, or to be allowed back in the church. These are set forth in more detail in chapter 35, "Biblical Best Practices on How the Church Can Support the Victim and Hold the Abuser Accountable."

God's method of dealing with wicked people who reject Him is set forth in Romans 1:

> The wrath of God is being revealed from heaven against all the godlessness and wickedness of people, who suppress the truth by their wickedness, since what may be known about God is plain to them, because God has made it plain to them. For since the creation of the world God's invisible qualities—his eternal power and divine nature—have been clearly seen, being understood from what has been made, so that people are without excuse. For although they knew God, they neither glorified him as God nor gave thanks to him, but their thinking became futile and their foolish hearts were darkened. Although they claimed to be wise, they became fools and exchanged the glory of the immortal God for images made to look like a mortal human being and birds and animals and reptiles. Therefore God gave them over in the sinful desires of their hearts to sexual impurity for the degrading of their bodies with one another. They exchanged the truth about God for a lie, and worshiped and served created things rather than the Creator—who is forever praised. Amen. Because of this, God gave them over to shameful lusts. . . . Furthermore, just as they did not think it worthwhile to retain the knowledge of God, so God gave them over to a depraved mind, so that they do what ought not to be done. They have become filled with every kind of wickedness, evil, greed and depravity. They are full of envy, murder, strife, deceit and malice. They are gossips, slanderers, God-haters, insolent, arrogant and boastful; they invent ways of doing evil; they disobey their parents; they have no understanding, no fidelity, no love, no mercy. Although they know God's righteous decree that those who do such things deserve death, they not only continue to do these very things but also approve of those who practice them. (Romans 1:18–26; 28–32)

Lie: I must be doing something wrong. The Bible tells me to look at the log in my eye before trying to get the speck out of someone else's eye. I must be the problem.

Truth: Take responsibility for your contributions to the problem, but don't take responsibility for other's contributions to the problem.

Women of faith overwhelmingly feel responsible for problems that they have not created. Yes, we need to look at ourselves first to see how we may have contributed to an issue, and we should not place blame on others when we have created difficulty ourselves. If we have trouble with anger, a critical spirit, lack of joy, divisiveness, overspending, pride, lying, or other issues that contribute to relationship strains, we need to correct them. However, after doing an honest assessment, we should not blame ourselves for the problems that are created by others. To take the blame for the actions or attitudes of others is not biblical, and it is a misinterpretation of Matthew 7:5 that exhorts us to take the log out of our own eye before we take the speck out of another's. There is never any excuse for abuse, particularly physical and sexual abuse.

What are the lies that have kept you in an abusive relationship? Write them down. Are you ready to replace them with truth? Next to the lies, write the truth. Now cross out the lie and let the truth soak in. What are you going to do with the truth?

Chapter 44

Lies That Inhibit Healing and the Truth That Heals

Even after leaving an abuser, almost every woman finds healing difficult. A run-in with a narcissist, sociopath, or psychopath leaves everyone in his wake damaged. However, healing is possible and needs to be the number one priority of a woman leaving the clutches of these pathological con men. Below are some of the lies that women believe that can keep them from healing and the truth that will set them free.

Lie: I am still emotionally attached to my abuser. I expect him to act like a decent human being, even though his mean words and actions still hurt me.

Truth: To heal, you must disengage emotionally from an abuser. Break all soul ties and trauma bonds. You give power to an abuser when you continue to expect him to act like a decent person and allow his words to affect you.

Almost every woman of faith is devastated when her former husband or soon-to-be former husband engages in the games of dirty pool that abusers do when a woman leaves. She believes the lie that he will treat her in the same respectful and honest manner that she will treat him. She believes the lie that he wishes her well as she leaves. She believes the lie that her abuser will not punch below the belt because she worked to put him through grad school, raised his kids, took care of his ailing elderly parents, and never left his side when he was sick. She believes the lie that her abuser feels guilty about his past behavior now that she has left and will at least try to make up for it by treating her fairly now. However, each day she is overwhelmed by his vindictiveness, which seems to know no bounds. And each vicious word and every malicious act is another cut to an already gaping wound in her heart. She simply wants to get away and live in peace; she did not expect to be attacked as she puts up the white flag in surrender and retreats.

Women must emotionally disengage from abusers to have any hope of healing. As the scales fall from her eyes and she recognizes her abuser for what he is, for her own self-preservation she must break the emotional and spiritual ties that have bound them together. Otherwise, she will continue to feel incredible hurt and disappointment from an abuser who delights in inflicting pain.

When a woman is in an abusive relationship, trauma bonds are formed. Trauma bonds occur because of the cycle of abuse: an abuser causes a great deal of harm, then seems to solve the problem he created by temporarily giving his partner the needed love, affection, and perhaps an apology. Makeup sex may be part of the cycle, causing her body to produce oxytocin, which in turn causes further bonding to her abuser. This cycle occurs repeatedly, causing a victim to be physiologically, psychologically, and biochemically bonded to her abuser. Even after a woman leaves an abuser physically, she is often still emotionally bonded to him and hopes that they can be friends in peace. Although she knows that he is abusive, she misses him and aches with the same intensity that a drug addict feels when he goes through withdrawal. She keeps hoping that he will act kindly to her, even though acting "kindly" is the furthest thing from his intentions. Trauma bonds must be broken to heal.

By their very nature, trauma bonds, which bond a victim to her abuser, are inspired by the Enemy. Satan has God's daughters marked as targets and uses trauma bonds to keep them from healing and from being the women that God has designed them to be. Do not let him win! God has given us authority over the Enemy through Jesus. Jesus promises that all power and authority has been given to Him from God, and He gives us that same power and authority when we use it in His will and in His name. Satan has no choice but to obey. So we command the trauma bonds, including the emotional and spiritual bonds and anything else that ties us to an abuser, to be broken in the name of Jesus. We use our voices, out loud, to break the bonds and declare healing. Our voices used in the authority of Jesus have power in this spiritual battle.

Jesus commanded His disciples, including us, to do great miracles in His name, including driving out the Enemy. We have the same authority that Jesus has, and the same authority He gave His disciples. Use it!

Heal the sick, raise the dead, cleanse those who have leprosy, drive out demons. (Matthew 10:8)

Prayer for breaking bonds:

Father, I thank You and praise You for Your goodness. I thank You for Your power and authority that You give us in the name of Jesus through Your Holy Spirit. I repent from any doubt and agreement with Satan. Satan, I break all agreement with you. I break all trauma bonds, and all emotional bonds, all spiritual bonds that you have used to tie me to [insert name here]. You have no place in me. I am a child of God and of the Lord of Lords. I command you and all your demons to leave, to go back where you came from, and to never return. I command this in the name and under the authority of Jesus.

Lie: My ex-husband and I can still be friends. I can have contact with my ex-husband and his friends, and it won't affect me.

Truth: Contact with an abuser is dangerous. Have no contact with an abuser or his supporters.

Many Christian women are under the misconception that they can still retain some kind of friendship or relationship with their abusive former husbands. After all, that would be best for the kids, they convince themselves. They are also under the misunderstanding that they can still have communication or contact with their former abusive husbands or their lackeys, and they will not be negatively affected. Believing these lies is unrealistic and dangerous.

A woman and her abusive ex-husband are unable to be friends or have any kind of relationship. This is not because of her, but because of him. He will always be dangerous to her. Every interaction and every communication from him will be toxic and negative. His very nature is toxic, dangerous, and directed at harming her. An abusive ex-husband is like a sharp knife: every interaction will result in a cut that reopens a wound so that it cannot heal. Her only hope of healing is staying far away from the knife and having no contact. If she has children with him and she is forced by the court to interact with him, then she should only interact to the extent that she must concerning facts about the children. Anything more will be used against her. An abuser will often send a text or email full of insults and false accusations along with something about the children. Don't take the bait. Simply ignore the garbage, and if a response is necessary, respond only to the factual matters regarding the children.

Abusers will recruit others to carry out their dirty work. These supporters that continue the abuser's insults and verbal abuse, even in his absence, are often referred to as "flying monkeys," named after the disdainful creatures who carried out the work of the Wicked Witch in the movie *The Wizard of Oz*. Every interaction with an abuser's minions will also be negative. Stay away from these unsafe people. They will have to give an accounting for their actions, just as the abuser will.

The Bible informs us in many passages to "flee from evil" and "have nothing to do with" abusers or their supporters. This is for our own protection.

> If anyone comes to you and does not bring this teaching, do not take them into your house or welcome them. Anyone who welcomes them shares in their wicked work. (2 John 10–11)
>
> Do what is good and run from evil so that you may live! Then the Lord God of Heaven's Armies will be your helper, just as you have claimed. (Amos 5:14 NLT)
>
> As you enter the home, give it your greeting. If the home is deserving, let your peace rest on it; if it is not, let your peace return to you. If anyone will not welcome you or listen to your words, leave that home or town and shake the dust off your feet. (Matthew 10:12–14)

See also Proverbs 13:20; 1 Corinthians 15:33; Psalm 1:1; Proverbs 14:7; Psalm 26:4–5; and Proverbs 22:24–25.

Lie: If I just explain one more time to my ex-husband how abusive he is, the lightbulb will finally go on in his head, he will finally understand how difficult he has been, and he will finally apologize and be easier to deal with.

Truth: An abuser will never get it. Save your breath.

Often a Christian woman will keep trying to argue with her abusive ex-husband about the abuse in their marriage under the false impression that if she just keeps explaining how horrible he has been, he will finally understand, apologize, and change his ways. This is ridiculous.

If he was going to change, he would have done so long before he lost his wife and a whole lot of money in a divorce. Constantly bringing up the past only antagonizes him and will bring about further vindictive abuse.

Women who have left an abusive marriage want closure. In any other relationship that ends, one party will usually, upon retrospect, accept responsibility for his or her bad behavior that caused an irretrievable breakdown in the relationship. Other times, the parties agree that their goals have become different and it is best to go their separate ways. Women who have been abused want some sort of acknowledgement from their abuser that he was a jerk, that he caused the breakdown of their marriage, and an apology. She will never get these. She will never get closure from him.

The best course of action is to have no contact with an abuser and rest in the peace that God sees all things and requires an accounting of everyone's words and deeds.

Lie: I will always live in fear, doubt, and anxiety.

Truth: Fear, doubt, and anxiety are Satan's best weapons against you. God's presence comes when you praise Him—and Satan runs.

Most women who have left an abusive mate live in constant fear of him coming to harm her or inflict further verbal and emotional abuse. They question if they are doing the right thing and feel an overarching sense of anxiety about nearly every aspect of life. A woman coming out of abuse believes the lie that this will be her new normal as she struggles to move on with life.

Fear, doubt, and anxiety are the greatest weapons Satan uses against women to keep them from healing. God doesn't give us those negative emotions; Satan does. God gives us power, confidence, love, and a reasonable mind, not one overcome with fear and anxiety.

If we are in physical danger, we need to take steps to combat it. Fear is a natural defense in the face of imminent danger. It prompts us to either fight or run. Due to the increased danger a woman faces when she leaves an abuser, she must always be mindful of her surroundings and take appropriate precautions.

However, an overall sense of anxiety, doubt, or fear when she is no longer in real danger is unhealthy and can leave her paralyzed. In these instances, the best spiritual weapon is praising God and thanking Him for His blessings, especially with praise and worship music. Satan hates music and hates when we praise and worship God, especially when the Enemy is trying so hard to bring us down. He is allergic to our praises and will leave when God's presence invades the room. Our praise and thanksgiving usher in God's Spirit, and Satan has no choice but to leave. When we praise and worship Him, His Spirit fills the atmosphere.

We can also command anxiety, doubt, and fear to leave. These are from Satan, and we have the authority, in the name of Jesus, to make these, and all of Satan's weapons, leave.

> For God has not given us a spirit of fear, but of power and of love and of a sound mind. (2 Timothy 1:7 NKJV)

> But you are holy, you who inhabit the praises of Israel. (Psalm 22:3 WEB)

Prayer for breaking anxiety, doubt, and fear (with praise and worship music blasting):

> Father, I praise You and worship You. You are amazing! You made the universe from nothing, You spoke and the world and all that is in it came to be, You parted the Red Sea, You are the maker of miracles, and nothing, absolutely nothing, is too powerful for You. Thank You for Your many blessings that are too numerous to name [name a few of them here]. I thank You for Your faithfulness, even amid this struggle with [name your ex-husband]. Lord, send me more of Your Spirit and more of Your presence. Let it invade the atmosphere and drive out anything that is not from You. Satan, I rebuke you and your spirits of anxiety, doubt, and fear [and any other negative emotions that are holding you]. I break agreement with you. You have no place here. I command you and your spirits

of anxiety, doubt, and fear to leave and never come back, in the name and under the authority of Jesus Christ. I proclaim I am a child of God, a daughter of the King of Kings. Amen.

Lie: The quality of people I hang around doesn't have that much effect on me.
Truth: The quality of people you are with has a huge effect on you! Healing happens when you surround yourself with good people who see the good in you and speak truth.

Occasionally, a Christian woman believes herself to be so strong that she believes the quality of the people she surrounds herself with does not have to be stellar because she is unaffected by them. This is utter foolishness.

We are all affected by those around us, and those around us are affected by us. We are designed to be in healthy relationships with each other. However, for us to be in a healthy relationship, both parties need to be healthy. A woman coming out of an abusive relationship must be especially careful to surround herself with healthy people, as she is particularly vulnerable and needs healthy, uplifting, encouraging people in her life to help her heal. When she is fully healed, she can go out and change the world, but when she is recovering from an abusive relationship, she needs to heal in the comfort of a safe environment.

> How good and pleasant it is when God's people live together in unity! (Psalm 133:1)

> And let us consider how we may spur one another on toward love and good deeds, not giving up meeting together, as some are in the habit of doing, but encouraging one another—and all the more as you see the Day approaching. (Hebrews 10:24–25)

Lie: I can go back to the same hectic lifestyle that I came from. I can handle it.
Truth: A woman recovering from domestic abuse needs to adopt a life that is gentle to herself and others in order to heal.

Oftentimes, a woman in an abusive marriage has been doing everything to make the marriage work. She may have a challenging career, do all the errands for the entire household, take care of the children and aging parents, volunteer with the PTA and church, and run the household, all while she is trying to please an abuser who cannot be pleased. She likely has bought into the lie that she can do it all, and that she must do it all. She has a to-do list for each day, and she takes great satisfaction in crossing things off the list and getting things done. She prides herself in gutting through the tough stuff like a champ.

Now, however, she must adopt a gentle lifestyle. She must be kind to herself and gentle with her children and those who depend on her so she can fully heal. She has been through trauma, she has PTSD, and she needs to bathe in a nourishing lifestyle, not a depleting one. Since she has been charging hard for so long, she likely requires a change in lifestyle.

At the very least, creating a space for healing means ensuring that her home is peaceful, loving, and pleasing to the eye. This includes enveloping herself in soothing, calming colors, comfortable couches, flowers, soft music, pleasing aromas such as scented candles, a cozy place to gather with friends and family, uplifting artwork, and plenty of natural sunlight. It might also mean moving out of the hustle and bustle of the city to the relative calm of a suburb or small town. A home with a garden, green meadows, or overlooking a body of water creates a sense of calm that is conducive to prayer, meditation, and healing. Most of us need far more green and blue space, and a woman healing from abuse needs a great deal. No wonder many people head to the seashore, the mountains, or the great outdoors for vacation; surrounding ourselves in natural beauty centers, calms, and restores us.

However, homes require maintenance. A woman leaving abuse may want to keep the large single-family home in which she raised her children. But with it comes a lawn that needs mowing, a driveway that needs re-coating, snow that needs plowing, plumbing that leaks, siding that needs painting, a roof that needs replacing, and a great deal of cleaning. A woman may consider downsizing to a more manageable home in which at least the outdoor maintenance is taken care of by a home owner's association. Renting an apartment for six months to a year after the divorce is final is often a wise option. It gives a woman time to heal in a home in which all the maintenance is taken care of, and it gives her time to consider where she would like to live long-term.

Being gentle with oneself includes taking time for self-care. This may include little perks that a woman in abuse generally foregoes, such as an occasional massage, a soak in a hot bath, a manicure or pedicure, spending time with a good book and cup of her favorite tea, sleeping late on the weekends, a walk in the park, a trip to the local museum or aquarium, watching sunsets or sunrises, watching a movie that she gets to choose, a fire in the fireplace, playing or listening to her favorite music, taking in a show, or spending time with girlfriends. It certainly includes taking care of her health, including keeping regular doctor and dentist appointments.

Creating a gentle place for healing may include finding a job with a short commute rather than spending more than an hour in traffic. It may also include switching out of a job that has a great deal of pressure and conflict to one with less pressure and little conflict.

Perhaps creating a gentle place for healing includes moving in (at least temporarily) with supportive parents who can surround a woman with emotional support, ease the financial burden of maintaining a home, provide occasional free childcare, and give the children an opportunity to bond with their grandparents. Such an arrangement is also healthy for grandparents, who feel more connected to their children and grandchildren. In many cultures, multiple generations live together. Unfortunately, in North America we have an aversion to this multi-generational living arrangement that can provide so many benefits for all involved if everyone is relatively healthy emotionally.

An essential part of creating a gentle life is reducing conflict and tension. Therefore, a woman may need to eliminate or reduce the number of toxic people in her life, such as the friend who takes advantage, the coworker who is a constant complainer, or the family member who always feels she must give advice.

Creating a gentle space requires surrounding oneself with beauty and creativity. God gives us the ability to create things of beauty, but far too often we stop creating because of criticism, self-doubt, feeling we aren't good enough, the busyness of life, or the need to support ourselves and our families. Creating things, as we were designed to do, uses a different part of the brain and is healing. Playing an instrument, painting a picture, writing poetry, drafting prose, crafting, sculpting, composing music, and other creative activities all use the right half of our brain and release the healing creativity that we need to restore our souls.

Lie: I am all alone in this battle. I feel like giving up. Death would be better.

Truth: Satan wants you to give up. God is with you in the spiritual battle. Put your armor on! Don't let Satan win! God has already won; expect a victory, expect miracles, and expect angel armies!

The struggle to break free from an abuser is difficult, and women feel so hopeless that some consider taking their own lives. They believe they cannot fight an abuser who is using every possible tactic to take away their children, home, money, dignity, friends, career, and the life they worked so hard to create. Being betrayed by someone she has loved and who claimed to love her is so painful that she believes the lie that death would be better. Sadly, far too many women take their own lives to stop the pain.

Suicidal thoughts are from the Enemy, who is on a mission is to steal, kill, and destroy God's daughters. A woman needs to know she is under attack from the Evil One and that God is fighting for her in a battle that she cannot even see. Oftentimes, a woman can be strong for her children or others, but not for herself. If she cannot be strong enough for herself, she must at least be strong for her children, who would have only an abusive parent if she were no longer here. Sometimes a woman can fight for God or her children, but does not have the fortitude to fight on behalf of herself. If that is the case, she must recognize that the real enemy is Satan, not her husband. Taking her life is letting Satan win, and deciding to live is choosing to defeat Satan and honor God. In effect, she needs to muster up her fighting spirit and say, "Oh no, Satan, not today. Today you will not win. Hell, no." This perspective must give her the fortitude needed to put on her spiritual armor and defeat the Enemy.

A woman escaping abuse is truly like Moses leading his people from the bondage of Pharaoh to the promised land. Like Moses, she must look forward, not back, and know that the Lord will fight for her.

> Moses answered the people, "Do not be afraid. Stand firm and you will see the deliverance the Lord will bring you today. The Egyptians you see today you will never see again. The Lord will fight for you; you need only to be still." (Exodus 14:13–14)

Not only will God equip her, but He has angel armies fighting on her behalf, and God Himself will fight for her. One of my favorite Old Testament stories is the story of Elisha, who was being hunted down by a foreign king trying to kill him. Unlike his servant, Elisha was not afraid because he had the gift of being able to see the spiritual world. He saw the angel armies and chariots of fire that God had sent on his behalf. He also had complete confidence that God would grant his request to defeat the enemy. He knew he had been called by the living, Almighty God who would ensure that his earthly mission would be complete. The same angel armies fighting for Elisha are fighting on behalf of one of God's daughters escaping domestic abuse. Envision the heavenly hosts surrounding His child and fighting on her behalf.

> "Go, find out where [Elisha] is," the king ordered, "so I can send men and capture him." The report came back: "He is in Dothan." Then he sent horses and chariots and a strong force there. They went by night and surrounded the city. When the servant of the man of God got up and went out early the next morning, an army with horses and chariots had surrounded the city. "Oh no, my lord! What shall we do?" the servant asked. "Don't be afraid," the prophet answered. "Those who are with us are more than those who are with them." And Elisha prayed, "Open his eyes, Lord, so that he may see." Then the Lord opened the servant's eyes, and he looked and saw the hills full of horses and chariots of fire all around Elisha. As the enemy came down toward him, Elisha prayed to the Lord, "Strike this army with blindness." So he struck them with blindness, as Elisha had asked. (2 Kings 6:13–18)

God Himself, the Mighty Warrior who is mighty to save, will fight for His daughters. Another of my favorite visions of the Bible is in Isaiah 63. I can just imagine God, our Warrior and Rescuer, walking to us, His beloved, in His bloodstained robes after doing battle for us, saving us from our enemy—whether it be an attacking and abusive spouse or Satan himself. We see Him in the distance, and as He comes into view, we can see His sword with the blood of the Enemy on it, the look of combat on His face, and His deliberate walk of victory. It is finished. He has fought for His daughter and won.

So often, a woman escaping abuse feels all alone. Her church, her friends, and her children, her family have all deserted her or have not wanted to get involved. Yet imagine the warrior God taking matters into His hands and fighting for His beloved, redeeming her, rescuing her, and saving her because of His unending love for her. It is the Lord Almighty (El-Shaddai), the Lord our Redeemer (Jehovah Gaal), our Rescuer, the Lord our Savior (Yeshua) who fights for her and is mighty to save.

> Who is this coming from Edom, from Bozrah, with his garments stained crimson?
> Who is this, robed in splendor, striding forward in the greatness of his strength?
> "It is I, proclaiming victory, mighty to save."
> Why are your garments red, like those of one treading the winepress?
> "I have trodden the winepress alone; from the nations no one was with me.
> I trampled them in my anger and trod them down in my wrath;
> their blood spattered my garments, and I stained all my clothing.
> It was for me the day of vengeance; the year for me to redeem had come.
> I looked, but there was no one to help, I was appalled that no one gave support;
> so my own arm achieved salvation for me, and my own wrath sustained me." (Isaiah 63:1–5)

Far from being alone, a daughter of the King has the Creator of the Universe fighting on her behalf.

Lie: I can't do this. I'm not strong enough.

Truth: Be fearless! God makes you courageous and is with you in your battle.

Many women believe the lie that they are not strong enough to overcome the pain of abuse. As a result, many return to their abuser several times. She simply doesn't believe she is able to leave, or she believes it will be better if she returns. It is never better after a woman returns to her abuser.

Even though a woman feels weak and unable to leave, get through the court battle, and stand up to his constant taunts and continued abuse, God will give her the courage and strength she needs. She must look to Him for strength, nourish herself with God's Word every day, and spend significant time each day listening to Him. And sometimes she must draw on the strength of others until she is strong enough to stand on her own. God's provision of strength during this time comes in surprising ways: He may provide a support group, a counselor, a domestic abuse shelter, or a friend who herself has experienced abuse and will walk with her. God's strength may come in the form of strong legal counsel, a helpful police officer, an influential friend, or an understanding prosecutor. God's wisdom may be found in a website, a book, or articles. His provision for her may come in the form of financial assistance, a safe house, loving parents or siblings, or any number of ways in which God will make an appearance to give her strength and encouragement and to let her know that He is with her. For a season, she can lean on the courage of others to get her through the valley. But as she soaks in God's presence and hears His words, that strength and courage will become her own as God pours out His Spirit of might and power into her.

> Have you not known? Have you not heard?
> The Lord is the everlasting God,
>   the Creator of the ends of the earth.
> He does not faint or grow weary;
>   his understanding is unsearchable.
> He gives power to the faint,

> and to him who has no might he increases strength.
> Even youths shall faint and be weary,
>   and young men shall fall exhausted;
> but they who wait for the LORD shall renew their strength;
>   they shall mount up with wings like eagles;
> they shall run and not be weary;
>   they shall walk and not faint. (Isaiah 40:28–31 ESV)

> The Sovereign LORD is my strength;
>   he make my feet like the feet of a deer,
>   he enables me to tread on the heights. (Habakkuk 3:19)

He gives His daughters who are escaping bondage and heading to their promised land the same promise and directives He gave Joshua. These are not options. If we want God's promises and want to be successful, we need to read and meditate on the Bible daily, do what it says, hear God speak to us through His Word, and listen as He specifically reveals Himself to us. As we go through our battle, He doesn't give us a to-do list, but He gives us something even better—He promises to be with us:

> Be strong and very courageous. Be careful to obey all the law my servant Moses gave you; do not turn from it to the right or to the left, that you may be successful wherever you go. Keep this Book of the Law always on your lips; meditate on it day and night, so that you may be careful to do everything written in it. Then you will be prosperous and successful. Have I not commanded you? Be strong and courageous. Do not be afraid; do not be discouraged, for the LORD your God will be with you wherever you go. (Joshua 1:7–9)

Lie: If God were on my side, all of this would go away. That's what I should pray for.

Truth: We will all go through trials. The evil people in the world hated Jesus and His goodness, and they will hate us too. Pray for boldness in the trial.

Many women are under the misconception that they should pray for their troubles to go away. She mistakenly believes the lie that if God were for her, she would not have these troubles in her life.

The truth is that we will all have troubles in our earthly life. No one gets through this life unscathed. That doesn't mean God is against us. Satan is alive and well. The same type of people who hated God's Son, Jesus, will hate His daughters.

However, having a spiritual battle doesn't mean we should pray that the troubles simply evaporate. Rather, we should pray for God to give us the boldness and courage to speak fearlessly and to fight courageously.

> If the world hates you, keep in mind that it hated me first. If you belonged to the world, it would love you as its own. As it is, you do not belong to the world, but I have chosen you out of the world. That is why the world hates you. Remember what I told you: "A servant is not greater than his master." If they persecuted me, they will persecute you also. (John 15:18–20)

> Pray also for me, that whenever I speak, words may be given me so that I will fearlessly make known

the mystery of the gospel, for which I am an ambassador in chains. Pray that I may declare it fearlessly, as I should. (Ephesians 6:19–20)

Lie: I will never be able to rebuild my life. It's too hard. My ex-husband is putting up roadblocks every step of the way.

Truth: Pray for protection, fearlessness, boldness, strength, and that God would avenge you. Fight for your family. Wield a spiritual weapon (and if necessary, a physical weapon) in one hand and work hard to rebuild with the other, knowing that God is with you.

It is hard to rebuild when an abuser has demolished a woman's life and continues his attempts to destroy her at every turn. Satan whispers the lie that you will never be able to rebuild and live an abundant life.

But God will give boldness and strength in the rebuilding process when we ask. My example for perseverance under pressure is Nehemiah. Nehemiah was a doer. He got things done, even in the face of extreme opposition. His mission was to rebuild the walls of Jerusalem with a tiny tribe of Jews who had been exiled in Babylon for seventy years and were now returning to their demolished homeland to rebuild their lives. Despite the opposition, Nehemiah never lost track of his mission. He prayed a big, bold prayer asking the Lord to avenge the opposition, and he told the Jews to be fearless, remember their God, and get to the task of fighting for their families and rebuilding their lives by holding a sword in one hand and working with the other. And in record time, fifty-two days, they rebuilt the city walls and were able to restart their lives.

Any woman recovering from domestic abuse may feel like Nehemiah. She has a mission to rebuild her life, and she will face extreme opposition from her abuser, his supporters, and sometimes even the church. Like Nehemiah, she must fight for her family and hold a spiritual weapon in one hand while working with the other to rebuild. As the Israelites did, she will need to stand guard to protect herself and her children. And like Nehemiah, she would do well to pray a big, bold prayer that God would strengthen her hands, embolden her heart, and avenge her.

> When Sanballat heard that we were rebuilding the wall, he became angry and was greatly incensed. He ridiculed the Jews, and in the presence of his associates and the army of Samaria, he said, "What are those feeble Jews doing? Will they restore their wall? Will they offer sacrifices? Will they finish in a day? Can they bring the stones back to life from those heaps of rubble—burned as they are?"
>
> Tobiah the Ammonite, who was at his side, said, "What they are building—even a fox climbing up on it would break down their wall of stones!"
>
> Hear us, our God, for we are despised. Turn their insults back on their own heads. Give them over as plunder in a land of captivity. Do not cover up their guilt or blot out their sins from your sight, for they have thrown insults in the face of the builders.
>
> So we rebuilt the wall till all of it reached half its height, for the people worked with all their heart.
>
> But when Sanballat, Tobiah, the Arabs, the Ammonites and the people of Ashdod heard that the repairs to Jerusalem's walls had gone ahead and that the gaps were being closed, they were very angry. They all plotted together to come and fight against Jerusalem and stir up trouble against it. But we prayed to our God and posted a guard day and night to meet this threat.
>
> Meanwhile, the people in Judah said, "The strength of the laborers is giving out, and there is so much rubble that we cannot rebuild the wall."
>
> Also our enemies said, "Before they know it or see us, we will be right there among them and will kill them and put an end to the work."

> Then the Jews who lived near them came and told us ten times over, "Wherever you turn, they will attack us."
>
> Therefore I stationed some of the people behind the lowest points of the wall at the exposed places, posting them by families, with their swords, spears and bows. After I looked things over, I stood up and said to the nobles, the officials and the rest of the people, "Don't be afraid of them. Remember the Lord, who is great and awesome, and fight for your families, your sons and your daughters, your wives and your homes."
>
> When our enemies heard that we were aware of their plot and that God had frustrated it, we all returned to the wall, each to our own work.
>
> From that day on, half of my men did the work, while the other half were equipped with spears, shields, bows and armor. The officers posted themselves behind all the people of Judah who were building the wall. Those who carried materials did their work with one hand and held a weapon in the other, and each of the builders wore his sword at his side as he worked. But the man who sounded the trumpet stayed with me.
>
> Then I said to the nobles, the officials and the rest of the people, "The work is extensive and spread out, and we are widely separated from each other along the wall. Wherever you hear the sound of the trumpet, join us there. Our God will fight for us!"
>
> So we continued the work with half the men holding spears, from the first light of dawn till the stars came out. At that time I also said to the people, "Have every man and his helper stay inside Jerusalem at night, so they can serve us as guards by night and as workers by day." Neither I nor my brothers nor my men nor the guards with me took off our clothes; each had his weapon, even when he went for water. (Nehemiah 4)

Lie: I am afraid of my abuser; my mind seems so scrambled and confused. I cannot concentrate. I cannot work. I cannot think straight. I am so forgetful. I will never be myself again.

Truth: Fear and a confused mind are from the Enemy. They are the natural result of trauma. Fearlessness, peace, and a sound mind are from God. With healing and time away from the abuser, God loosens the Enemy's grasp, and the ability to see things clearly will return.

Trauma and abuse have many detrimental effects, one of which is the inability to concentrate and to see things clearly, as well as forgetfulness. Stress reduces cognitive functioning. Many women believe they will always be in such a fog.

To the contrary; when a woman gets out of the relationship and is no longer subject to the daily confusion, attacks, and abuse of her husband, she can see things more clearly, and her cognitive functioning returns. Once a woman is out of the daily craziness, with hindsight she can start putting together the pieces of the puzzle that seemed so scrambled for years. Her husband has woven a web of deception and lies, and like an insect, she was caught in the web. Only when she is out of the relationship will the scales fall from her eyes, and she will recognize his actions as abusive and self-serving. Once she realizes that he was doing Satan's bidding, his actions start to make sense. Eventually, spending time in God's Word, surrounding herself with wise and godly people, and making healing a top priority, the confusion will lift, she will be able to see clearly what happened, and will find a way to move forward. By being involved in meaningful activities and fulfilling work, she can focus her attention on positive things rather than rewinding the abuse tape in her mind.

> For God is not the author of confusion, but of peace. (1 Corinthians 14:33 KJV)

> For God has not given us a spirit of fear, but of power and of love and of a sound mind. (2 Timothy 1:7 NKJV)

Lie: My life is so messed up. It will never be good.

Truth: God is working behind the scenes and will use all your experiences, even the bad ones, for good and to be a blessing.

Satan constantly whispers in our ears: "You aren't good enough. You are messed up. Your life is a mess. It will never get better." His goal is to defeat us. Don't let him.

Abuse is a horrible thing to go through, but God can use it to mold, shape, and mature a woman, and bring blessings out of the experience. Satan always twists the good things that God has given us and uses them for evil, but God takes the bad things that Satan has used against us and uses them for good.

> And we know that in all things God works for the good of those who love him, who have been called according to his purpose. (Romans 8:28)

> But as for you, you meant evil against me; but God meant it for good, in order to bring it about as it is this day, to save many people alive. (Genesis 50:20 NKJV)

Lie: I must get busy doing something. I need to get a job and get moving again.

Truth: A period of healing and restoration is needed. Soak in the Lord's presence. Let His Holy Spirit heal and restore; take time to heal, slow down, live gently, and depend on His guidance and promises. Thank Him for His blessings, and spend lots of time in God's Word. When He is ready, and when you are ready, He will call you to your next assignment.

Oftentimes, a woman coming out of domestic abuse and a long divorce will want to keep herself busy. Before, she might have been busy serving and waiting on her demanding husband. Perhaps she is used to gaining self-esteem by producing and crossing things off her to-do list. She probably had to prove her worth in her marriage by doing, even though it was never enough to please her spouse. Now she wants to fill up her empty days with something that will make her feel worthwhile again. If Satan can keep her busy with mindless things that take her focus off healing, he is happy to keep her from being the woman God designed her to be.

What every woman needs is a time of rest—a time of healing and just being, a time of soaking in the Lord's presence. She needs time to be nourished in God's cathedral of the great outdoors, to be thankful for His provision during the dark days and the rescue mission that He accomplished. Researchers now confirm what King David knew centuries ago: we need time outdoors to restore our minds and bodies. When she is sufficiently healed, God will give her the next mission.

> The LORD is my shepherd;
> I shall not want.
> He makes me to lie down in green pastures;
> He leads me beside the still waters.
> He restores my soul;
> He leads me in the paths of righteousness
> For His name's sake.

Lies That Inhibit Healing and the Truth That Heals

Yea, though I walk through the valley of the shadow of death,
I will fear no evil;
For You are with me;
Your rod and Your staff, they comfort me.
You prepare a table before me in the presence of my enemies;
You anoint my head with oil;
My cup runs over.
Surely goodness and mercy shall follow me
All the days of my life;
And I will dwell in the house of the Lord
Forever. (Psalm 23 NKJV)

Charlotte: When I finally came out of two years of hiding from my abuser and moved into a house twenty miles away, I wanted to get back to living life at breakneck speed. I had all but stopped practicing law because of the stress of the divorce and Tim's ongoing physical and emotional abuse. But I didn't know what the Lord wanted me to do. Every day I asked God to give me direction. One day, when I was just relaxing in the backyard on a beautiful summer day, God brought to mind Psalm 23 and explained it clearly to me.

"'The Lord is my shepherd; I shall not want.' Do you see? I have provided for you. My grace is sufficient. You have all you need. 'He makes me to lie down in green pastures.' Look around you at the horse pastures and white fences that surround you. Look at this lush green grass in your own backyard. I have brought you here. 'He leads me beside still waters.' Do you notice this beautiful pond that is in your very own backyard? You even named it Peace Pond because it is so quiet and peaceful. I send the geese and ducks and even the muskrat and turtles. When you were looking at houses, you asked Me for a home on the water. I heard your prayer. I led you here. 'He restores my soul.' Slow down for a time. I am restoring your soul in this peaceful, green place by the water. And when you are healed, I will give you a new assignment. But for now, spend time with Me. Let Me heal you. Let Me restore you. Let Me put the broken pieces back together and make you whole. I need you to be completely healed, and I need you to have unwavering faith in Me because your next assignment—it's gonna be *big*!"

Lie: Everyone is generally good—I trust everyone and share openly. Or: Everyone is bad—I will never trust again.

Truth: God tells us to be mature, discerning Christians who distinguish good from evil.

Women who have been in abusive relationships generally believe lies on either extreme. Prior to the abusive relationship, she believes that everyone is good. This Pollyanna outlook is likely one of the reasons she got into the abusive relationship in the first place. She was a trusting person and easily trusted everyone. She believed the lie that a person who was, in fact, evil was good. However, after the relationship ended, she believes that everyone—or at least every man—is evil. She doesn't trust her ability to judge a person's character and has resolved to never trust anyone again. She has built an impregnable wall so that she will never get hurt. Both extremes are unhealthy.

The truth is there are some good and godly people, and there are some truly wicked people. Most are somewhere in between. In any case, it is wise to take some time in determining someone's character and wait to trust someone until they've earned it. It is also important to recognize that there are degrees of trust. We may trust that someone won't steal our car, but we may not be able to trust that he will help pack when our elderly parents need to move closer so that we can care for them as they age.

It is wise to think of our hearts like a house. We have walls and doors and windows and fences around our house. These are boundaries established for our protection. We don't let complete strangers come in and help themselves to the fridge and the silver. Strangers stay outside or on the sidewalk. When someone knocks on the front door, we only let them inside if we know and trust them. Only our close circle of trusted friends or family are invited to stay and live with us. And only a person with whom we are very intimate is given the combination to the safe with the jewelry and silver and bearer bonds.

But a naïve woman who easily trusts a man because he shows interest in her, without proving his trustworthiness, is like someone who lets a complete stranger into her home and gives him the combination to the safe simply because he knocked on the front door and asked to come in and make himself at home. That is foolish and leads to destruction.

On the other hand, a bitter woman who refuses to trust anyone is like someone who has built a castle fortress with a moat around it. It isolates the castle owner from everyone, including those who are good and kind, because no one can even come close. The castle owner sinks further and further into isolation, loneliness, bitterness, and depression. That is foolish and leads to destruction from within.

Neither scenario reflects the abundant life lived in community with good people that God has designed as the best life for us.

Instead, God calls us to guard our hearts and be discerning and prudent in our relationships. God knows that the heart is where our joy of life comes from. Who we let into our heart determines the course of our lives—so we need to be extremely careful who we let in. Our heart is our most precious God-given gift. We must be sure that the person to whom we entrust our heart is worthy of that trust.

We get to know someone's character over time. We see the fruit of his life and observe how he treats others—especially when he thinks no one is looking. We watch how he spends his money and time, and we listen to see if his words honor God. We are careful to see if his actions match his words; we wait to see if he is dependable and follows through on his promises. We consider whether he acts in our best interests or only his own. And little by little, if that person proves to be a godly person, we learn that we can entrust our heart to him. However, over time, if we see that the person is not a godly person, we learn that we should not trust him.

> Watch over your heart with all diligence, for from it flow the springs of life. (Proverbs 4:23 NASB)

Other translations of Proverbs 4:23 also give great insight:

Above all else, guard your affections. For they influence everything else in your life. (TLB)

Above all else, guard your heart, for everything you do flows from it. (NIV)

I am sending you out like sheep among wolves. Therefore be as shrewd as snakes and as innocent as doves. (Matthew 10:16)

In fact, though by this time you ought to be teachers, you need someone to teach you the elementary truths of God's word all over again. You need milk, not solid food! Anyone who lives on milk, being still an infant, is not acquainted with the teaching about righteousness. But solid food is for the mature, who by constant use have trained themselves to distinguish good from evil. (Hebrews 5:12–14)

Lie: Why does my husband do these horrible things? He must do them for a reason.

Truth: Satan is the one who controls your husband.

A common question from a woman who has been in an abusive relationship is *Why? Why does he yell at me? Why does he hit me? Why is he so mean? Why is he lying about me? Why is he turning my kids against me? Why did he get fired? Why does he squander money? Why won't he pay the mortgage? Why doesn't he stop his addictions? Why doesn't he see his own kids?*

She believes her abuser does things for a reason. She doesn't know what the reason is because his actions don't make sense to her, but she assumes there is some underlying logic.

The truth is that an abuser is under the control of Satan. One cannot change the nature of Satan any more than one can change the nature of God. Satan's mission is to steal, kill, and destroy. He uses people to destroy other people. Once Satan has a man in his clutches, that man will destroy his own family—his wife and children; he will destroy his own career and finances. He will even destroy his own body and himself, without even knowing it.

As an attorney and a domestic violence professional, I see the same pattern time after time. A man becomes successful and powerful, which results in an increased attitude of superiority. He grooms and marries someone whom he thinks will serve his needs, but he doesn't really love her. After the wedding, he becomes abusive, and it escalates over the years. He has several addictions—alcohol, drugs, smoking, pornography, sex, prostitutes, affairs, buying things above his means—that make him feel important. His pride makes him feel superior to everyone, and he treats them abusively. Despite requests, he refuses to change, because in his pride, the problem is not with him, but with others. His wife leaves after many years, but he already been grooming a replacement while they were married, and he quickly remarries so he continues to have someone to serve his needs. His boss fires him for being abusive to employees and causing poor morale. He desperately needs another job to prove to himself that he is superior, but he struggles to find another job because he thinks most jobs are beneath him, and others know his abusive reputation. His pride has led him to foolishly squander his money on status symbols that he cannot afford or investments that he believes he cannot fail in. He loses big financially—a crush to his ego, which has always used money as a yardstick for self-importance. The constant toxicity in his life (generated by himself), combined with his addictions, lead to serious health issues, and his health takes a big decline. He refuses to make required maintenance and child support payments, and he is found in contempt of court. He loses his second (and possibly third) wife for the same reasons he lost his first wife. At the end of this life, he has lost his wives, meaningful relationships with his children, his money, his home, his health, and any reputation as a decent person. Finally, when he dies, an unrepentant abuser still full of pride and arrogance, he is not allowed to enter the kingdom of heaven. (In my relatively short time representing domestic abuse victims, I have even known two abusers who killed themselves, one of whom killed his wife shortly before he killed himself.) Satan has destroyed everything in his life, and finally his soul. All the while, the abuser has been full of pride and hubris, claiming that he lives life, as Frank Sinatra sings, "my way." He thinks he answers to no one, including God, not realizing that he is a slave to Satan.

> You are slaves of the one you obey—whether you are slaves to sin, which leads to death, or to obedience, which leads to righteousness. (Romans 6:16)

Lie: I must have deserved the abuse. It must have been something I did. If I had only done things differently, our marriage would have been saved.

Truth: He would have been abusive regardless of what you did or didn't do. There is nothing you did or didn't do that could have changed the outcome. All relationships with abusers end badly.

A woman will often carry great guilt and shame, believing that if only she had been a better wife, or been more understanding, or been more sexy, or gone to counseling, her husband would not have abused her and their marriage could have been saved. This is a lie straight from Satan and the abuser's lips.

All relationships with an abuser end badly. His nature is an abuser, and he would have been abusive regardless of what you did. No amount of counseling would have changed the outcome. In fact, he would be abusive regardless of who his wife was, how beautiful she was, how wealthy she was, or how nice she was. By way of example, stunningly beautiful supermodel Christie Brinkley was married at one point to architect Peter Cook, who was diagnosed with NPD by a court-appointed psychiatrist. In typical narcissistic behavior, Peter Cook was addicted to internet porn, had an affair with a eighteen-year-old, projected his misbehavior on his wife—calling her a narcissist—and used his children as pawns in their acrimonious divorce. His second marriage ended in divorce after his second wife discovered photos and videos of him with a prostitute. The latest news is that Cook, in his sixties, is engaged to a twenty-one-year-old woman, younger than his own children.

Lie: We can co-parent our children. It's best for them if we continue to be a coordinated mom and dad.

Truth: Co-parenting with an abuser is impossible.

Many women still try to co-parent and coordinate activities for the children with their abuser, thinking that this is the best approach to child-rearing. However, her attempts are constantly thwarted by the abuser. Her plans are sabotaged; the abuser undermines her and alienates her from the children. He tries to control every situation and ruin events, and the abuser provokes her so that when she finally has had enough, he makes her look crazy in front of the children.

Co-parenting with an abuser is nearly impossible, especially during or after a divorce. To the abuser, anything involving the children is a competition, and he will make sure their mother loses. Even if an abuser "ghosts" his family, he feels he wins the competition by saddling his former wife with all the costs and responsibilities of raising the children, while he has none. A mom should have her rules at her home, and dad will have his rules at his home. If the children are old enough, mom should plan things with them by talking directly to them, not coordinate with their father, who will sabotage any plans.

Lie: I can't tell when my abuser is lying and when he is telling the truth. I would like to be able to trust him.

Truth: When his lips are moving, he's lying.

Lying is a characteristic of narcissists, sociopaths, psychopaths, and other abusers. Especially during or after a divorce, if his lips are moving, he's lying.

LIES THAT INHIBIT HEALING AND THE TRUTH THAT HEALS

Lie: Maybe it wasn't so bad, really. I could go back. He keeps asking me to come back.

Truth: It was bad. Returning to an unrepentant abuser will result in increased abuse.

Oftentimes, a woman who has left an abuser will be tempted to return to the marriage. She is overwhelmed by loneliness, the financial stress of supporting herself, the trauma bonds that connect her to her husband, and the fear of the unknown. She may look back and wish that she hadn't left, or she may convince herself that it wasn't that bad. If he is actively abusing her, he lets her know that it will all stop if she just returns. Or perhaps he has claimed that he is sorry and has promised that he has changed.

Women who leave abusive relationships often experience abuse amnesia. They forget or minimize the abuse they endured and tend to remember only the good times. Abuse amnesia is a coping response so that the victim is not overwhelmed by the memories of abuse. To counter this mechanism, a wise woman will make a written list of all the incidents of abuse, including the approximate dates, so that that she can take an accounting of what she endured and remember why she left.

Invariably, when a woman returns to an abuser who has not repented (see chapter 35 regarding the signs of true repentance), the abuser escalates the abuse. From his perspective, he has crossed all reasonable boundaries and abused her, yet she still came back to him. Now it's a game. He will up the stakes and will cross even more boundaries to see how much she will take and still stay with him. If she leaves again, he will see if he can convince her to return. And they will play the same game again.

Lie: If I am a real Christian, I must forgive, forget, trust, and reconcile with my husband, and I must not take him to court for his criminal actions, violating court orders, or breaching our divorce and parenting agreements.

Truth: God requires repentance to forgive, forget, and be back in relationship. He does not ask us to do more than He does. Forgiving does not mean you forget, trust, declare the act is okay, reconcile, or return to the relationship. That would not be wise. It means you leave the avenging to God.

An abuser will try to convince his victim she must forgive him, forget the abuse, trust him, and reconcile with him. Many women believe that, because she is a Christian, she must comply. "Forgiveness" is a word that is grossly misunderstood and is misused by Satan to keep women in bondage.

Human forgiveness does not mean the victim must now trust the perpetrator, restore the relationship, forget the wrong, or perceive the wrong acts to be acceptable. Trusting an abuser would be foolish. Even if we could forgive a pedophile, we would never let that person around a child. Forgiveness does not mean that we leave our common sense at the door. Human forgiveness means that the victim allows God to do the avenging and that she gives up the right to get revenge for the wrong. "Repay no one evil for evil. . . . Beloved, never avenge yourselves, but leave it to the wrath of God; for it is written, 'Vengeance is mine, I will repay, says the Lord'" (Romans 12:17, 19 ESV, quoting Deuteronomy 32:35).

Forgiveness also does not mean that the victim should refrain from seeking justice from the civil and criminal courts. God is a God of justice, and He requires each of us to do justice (Micah 6:8) and to honor our obligations (Leviticus 6:4–7; Numbers 30:2; Galatians 3:15). The author of Romans tells us that courts and governments have been established to further justice. People of faith should avail themselves of the protections that have been afforded by our justice system. Further, they should do all they can to ensure that the laws we do enact are just.

> Let everyone be subject to the governing authorities, for there is no authority except that which God has established. The authorities that exist have been established by God. Consequently, whoever rebels against the authority is rebelling against what God has instituted, and those who do so will bring judgment on themselves. . . . For the one in authority is God's servant for your good. But if you do wrong, be afraid, for rulers do not bear the sword for no reason. They are God's servants, agents of wrath to bring punishment on the wrongdoer. Therefore, it is necessary to submit to the authorities, not only because of possible punishment but also as a matter of conscience. (Romans 13:1–2, 4–5)

When a bank forgives a loan, it takes an accounting of precisely the amount that it is forgiving—to the penny. Likewise, forgiveness requires that the victim take a full inventory of the wrongful acts that he or she is forgiving. We don't forget those acts—to the contrary, we know full well all the offenses that are the subject of our forgiveness.

God requires repentance before He forgives. That is the message throughout the Bible. When hearts are truly repentant and turn to God, God's forgiveness includes a restored relationship with Him (1 Kings 8:47; 2 Chronicles 6:37; Proverbs 1:23; Isaiah 30:15; 59:20; Jeremiah 15:19; 18:18; Ezekiel 18:30, 32; 33:12; Hosea 14:1; Matthew 3:2, 8, 11; 4:17; 11:20–21; Luke 5:32; Acts 2:38; 3:19; 2 Peter 3:9; Revelation 2:5; etc.). However, sin always has consequences. Even though God forgives, our sin carries a cost. King David found this out when he had an affair with Bathsheba and murdered her husband. He repented and God forgave him, but he paid a terrible price. The first child he had with Bathsheba died as an infant. David's kingdom was overthrown by his own son, who then forced David's concubines to have sex with him in public, just as David had done to Bathsheba in private.

God doesn't require more of us than He requires of Himself. If a relationship is to be restored, there must first be true repentance. If your brother sins, rebuke him; and *if he repents*, forgive him (Luke 17:3). The victim must recognize that trust is the basis of every relationship. Once trust is breached, it is extremely difficult to restore. Sin always has consequences, and the consequences of abuse are legion. When a husband has violated his marriage vows, even if he repents, a wife is not required to trust him, restore a relationship with him, forget the abuse, or declare that a wrong is now all right.

If someone is truly repentant, he does not demand forgiveness. Forgiveness cannot be demanded by the abuser. His job is to make things right without demands or strings attached. If he demands forgiveness, he has not repented.

Forgiveness takes time and the Holy Spirit. It is a process. It is a particularly long process when it involves an abusive marriage because the abuser continues to sin against his victims. In other situations involving a one-time occurrence, such as when someone steals something or hits another car, forgiveness tends to be easier. The one-time sin is not recurring, the negative consequences are generally known, further pain is not inflicted, and the victim has the opportunity to heal. However, when it comes to abusive marriages, the abuse is ongoing even after the marriage has ended. In fact, the abuse increases when the victim leaves, and the losses she suffers as a result of his abuse continue for years afterward.

Forgiveness in abusive marriages is also difficult because the abuser is not repentant. He is unremorseful. It is likely that in all her other relationships, when another person has sinned against her, a woman of faith has managed to reconcile, come to some agreement, heard an apology, and had closure. However, with an abuser, she will never have closure. He will not offer a true apology, take responsibility for his wrongdoing, or change his ways. A woman of faith must then make her own closure with God, who sees all things. She must come to recognize that God does not approve of her abuser's behavior, that God does not want her to stay in abuse, that God has provided a way out, and that, either in this life or the next, God will hold him accountable.

Unforgiveness is an ugly thing. Much like a cancer, it remains hidden inside, but it grows when it is fed, and it becomes so toxic that it can consume the host that it is living in. Its fruit is bitterness, anger, acrimony, and revenge (which almost always backfires). It has been said that unforgiveness is like drinking a poison and expecting the other person to die. This is not the abundant life that God envisions for His daughters. God came to set the captives free—and holding on to bitterness means that a woman is still held captive by her abuser. Her prison door has been opened, but she will not walk out.

In the end, forgiveness is not for the wrongdoer, but for the victim. Forgiveness enables her to be free of bitterness and live out the abundant life that God has planned for her, comforted by the knowledge that God's got this and will hold her abuser accountable.

Lie: Divorce is a sin.

Truth: The abuse that breached the marriage covenant is a sin. The divorce simply recognizes that the covenant has been irretrievably breached.

Women of faith stay in abusive marriages longer than women without faith, partly because they believe the lie that divorce is a sin. After a divorce from an abuser, they often hide in shame and guilt, and many churches continue to push even more shame and guilt on them because many people falsely believe that divorce is a sin.

On the contrary, divorce from an abusive husband is not a sin. God commands that we run from evil and have nothing to do with people who are involved in continuous, intentional, unrepentant, serious sin (1 Corinthians 5; 2 Timothy 3:1–9; Titus 3:10; etc.). Marriage the way God intended is a mutually beneficial, life-giving, supportive, loving, encouraging relationship. Abuse is a serious breach of the marriage vows. A civil divorce recognized by the government merely recognizes that the marriage relationship no longer exists due to the abuser's breach.

Even God divorced Israel when their hearts turned away from Him (Jeremiah 3:8; Isaiah 50:1). Further, after some of the Israelites ignored God's specific commandments not to marry pagan wives, God commanded that the Israelites divorce their pagan wives (Ezra 10). God doesn't sin. Therefore, when He divorced Israel for rejecting Him, and when He commanded divorce from people who rejected Him, He did not sin. And neither do we when we divorce an abuser who has utterly rejected God. (For a more detailed explanation of what the Bible says about divorce, see chapter 34.)

Lie: I should move on. That's what he did. His friends are mocking me because I haven't moved on.

Truth: Grieving takes time. It takes time to heal your heart, recover your finances, and start over from scratch. You will move on when you are ready.

The world gives people about ninety seconds to grieve a loss, and then it expects them to move on with a stiff upper lip and a plastic smile as if nothing had happened. If nothing else, it makes people extremely uncomfortable when they are around someone who is hurt and sad. I even heard a seminary student/Bible study leader say callously after someone shared that she had recently lost someone close to her, "Well, the Lord says we should be joyful in all things!" We, as a society, don't do well with grief.

When emotionally healthy people who love greatly experience a major loss, their grief is profound because their love is profound, and therefore their loss is profound. It takes time to heal, even from the anticipated life losses—for example, the death of an aged parent or an ill spouse, the loss of a close relationship, or a move away from family and friends. We are bound with grief because of our fierce love for people who have been close to us and whose lives were intertwined with ours.

The death of a marriage by divorce is no less a loss and cause for grief than the death of a marriage due to the death of a spouse. In fact, when a spouse dies, the surviving spouse is most often supported by friends, family, and her support network. This at least provides some comfort to the grieving widow, and most people give her grace and time for the natural grieving process.

But when a marriage ends by divorce, the reaction from others is far less empathetic and much more judgmental. And when a marriage to an abuser ends by divorce, the wife is sure to endure continued abuse from the abuser and his flying monkeys, as well as shunning from former friends, family, and church members. In addition to grieving the loss of a marriage, she grieves the fact that her life was a complete sham and that her husband never loved her. Further, she grieves losses that many widows do not experience—the loss of her home, her town, her physical safety, her finances, her in-laws, her friends, her children, her career, her health, and the years she lost with him. Her grief is no less profound than the widow's, but she typically has no emotional support. Many women who have experienced both divorce and widowhood state that a divorce is more stressful than losing a husband by death.

A period of grieving is natural whenever we experience a loss. Experts tell us there are five general stages to grief, but they are not necessarily experienced in order, and we tend to bounce around and go back to previous stages. We may move two steps forward one day and one step back the next.

The first stage is denial. When we finally realize that we have been living with an abuser who doesn't care about us and that we must get out, we are in shock and deny reality. We also tend to isolate ourselves. We don't want to believe that we live in abuse and that the only way out is divorce. We don't want to give up the lives that we have built. Denial helps us cope with the loss at a pace that we can accept. It's nature's way of giving us only as much as we can handle. Slowly, as we recognize the reality of the loss, we can move forward past the first wave of pain.

The second stage is anger. "How could he do this to me? How could he do this to us?" We cannot understand why he just can't be nice to his own family. Underneath the anger is pain. This type of anger is healthy; it is a righteous anger at the injustice done by an evil person who destroys his own family. In some cases, it may be the first time a woman has experienced anger, because during the marriage she was not allowed to express any negative emotions. Her abuser only wanted her to worship him and be happy to do so.

The third stage of grief is bargaining. We try to make a deal with God, or with anyone else who might be able to help, to stave off the inevitable so that life will go back to normal. "I will devote the rest of my life to You, Lord, if You will just save my marriage." We may go through a series of "if only" statements that are attempts to bargain: If only we had gone to more counseling . . . If only I had been nicer . . . If only the pastors would have talked to him earlier . . . We may feel guilty and believe there was something that we could have done to make him less abusive and save the marriage.

The fourth stage of grief is depression, when grief enters us on a deeper level than we could have imagined and feels like it will last forever. The intense sadness sometimes leaves us wondering if life is worth going on alone. Children are always a blessing from God, but they are a particular blessing at this time because we know they depend on us and we know we must go on and not give up hope, if not for our sake, at least for theirs. Depression is not an abnormal sign of mental illness; rather, it is an appropriate response to great loss. It is the great valley of the healing journey that one must go through to get to the other side of redemption.

The last stage of grief is acceptance, when we accept the reality of the new normal and adjust accordingly. We accept that relationships have shifted, roles have changed, and the old has passed away never to return, and we start to accept the new—new friendships, new communities, a new home, a new job, a new sense of purpose, a new budget, and perhaps even a new love, if we dare. We begin to live again, and perhaps use our experience to help others.

While there are essentially five stages, the following diagram helps us recognize the many different emotions and dynamics experienced within those five stages.

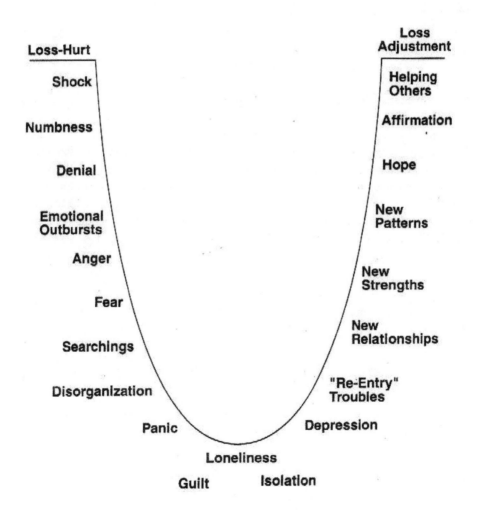

STAGES OF GRIEF

On average, it takes a woman approximately half of the years that she spent in an abusive relationship to recover fully. Thus, if she was in a twenty-year marriage, it will likely take ten years to recover. However, God, the Great Healer, can do miracles that no counselor, psychologist, or therapist can do. When we actively participate in His redemptive process of healing our wounds—when we allow Him to invade our hearts with His Spirit, invite Him to transform our perspective by rejecting lies and replacing them with His Truth, soak in His Presence as we read His Word and listen to what He reveals to us, and surround ourselves with godly people—our healing happens more rapidly.

An abuser moves on quickly and feels little, if any, grief because he has never loved greatly. In fact, he never loved at all. The loss of a spouse is no great loss to him because he views them as expendable and interchangeable—one is as good as the other as long as she serves his needs. Thus, rather than experiencing grief, he is angry that he may be forced by a court to divide assets (which he views as all his) and to pay maintenance and child support (which he views as undeserving), and he will put all his efforts into fighting monetary payments.

It is almost impossible to imagine someone so callous as to mock a widow for her grief, but the abuser and his minions will mock a victim of domestic abuse for her grief. They all belong in the camp of wicked people who should be avoided at all costs.

> Charlotte: After literally fleeing my home with only an overnight bag after years of emotional, physical, and sexual abuse—where my husband literally tied my hands and feet to the four corners of his four-poster bed and left me for hours, and where he intermittently raped me—I needed a time of healing. After a period, I felt God calling me to use my law career to help other women escape domestic abuse. For years, I had sent a monthly inspirational devotional email to some people. In one of them, I announced that I was starting my own law firm to focus on helping women escape domestic abuse. I received tons of congratulations and accolades on the decision. However, one of Tim's cronies who was still on the email list asked to be removed and another sent a long attacking email that, among other things, essentially called me a liar and mocked me for not moving on like my abuser had. It was the most scathing email I had ever received in my life—and I had considered this person a spiritual mentor and friend. She was also a longtime member of our church, and her husband, Tim's close friend, was a former deacon. "If your life had been as bad as you portrayed in your divorce decree, why did you stick it out for twenty years? . . . Your past ex-husband has moved on. . . . You APPEAR to have moved on—but you have NOT moved on. Judy (K****)"

Fortunately, I had healed enough to not let it terribly affect me, but I now know that when anyone attacks a domestic abuse survivor for trying to help others, that person is abusive.

Lie: Everything triggers me. I will never get over it. Everything that reminds me of his abuse sends me into a panic attack: a loud noise, hearing someone yelling, hearing loud footsteps coming down the hallway, thunder, firecrackers.

Truth: Our flight or fight response takes over when things remind us of past trauma. Using the cognitive part of our brain to talk to the unconscious part of our brain helps to calm us.

When we have been traumatized, things that remind us of the trauma will often cause the autonomic nervous system to respond with a flight or fight response. If the abuser yelled at us, we will be triggered by yelling; if we heard his footsteps down the hall as he made his way to the bedroom to sexually abuse us, we will be triggered by loud footsteps; if we heard gunfire, we may be triggered by thunder or firecrackers.

The fight or flight response is an unconscious response that prepares us to either run from or fight a perceived harmful situation or attack. A flush of hormones is released that creates a boost of energy, and we physically react with, among other things, accelerated heart and lung action, paling or flushing, inhibition of the stomach and intestines, constriction of blood vessels in many body parts with dilation of the blood vessels to the muscles, inhibition of tear and saliva production, dilated pupils, loss of hearing, tunnel vision, and shaking.

Even when we are not in danger, we can react to triggers that are associated with previous trauma. For example, the yelling may be simply cheering at a football game, footsteps down the hall may merely be those of a coworker in heels, thunder is from a storm, and firecrackers are part of a fun Fourth of July celebration.

So how do we enjoy our lives without panic attacks from everyday events?

Fortunately, God gave us two sides of our brain—He gave us both an unconscious side, which reacts without our telling it to, and a conscious side, in which we decide what to think or do. To overcome our panic attacks, the conscious part of our brain must step up to the plate and tell our unconscious side that there is no real threat, so it can settle down and return to normal.

For example, if a woman hears footsteps coming down a hallway at work, she might have this conversation with herself: "I know I hear footsteps, and I feel myself getting anxious because every time I heard footsteps in our house, he was walking down the hallway into our bedroom, and it wasn't pretty after that. But I know that is behind me now. He is not here. Those are not his footsteps. Those are the footsteps of my coworker Andy, and Andy is a very nice person who is just going down the hallway for a meeting. Nothing is going to harm me. I can sit here and relax and not worry."

As she talks to herself and reminds herself that she is not in danger, her anxiety will subside and she will return to a resting state. It may take several minutes. As she repeats this exercise every time she is triggered, over time her body's response will return to normal and she can enjoy life again.

Lie: I should be over my anxiety when I have to see him. Why am I not over this?

Truth: He will always be perceived as a direct threat because he is.

A woman leaving domestic abuse would like to think that over time, she will be able to see her abusive ex-husband at the typical family functions, such as their children's graduations and weddings, without a great deal of anxiety. However, he has been a direct threat to her in the past, and he will continue to be a direct threat because of his vindictive character. She will likely experience a fight or flight response every time she must encounter him.

However, like the triggers, there are ways to reduce the anxiety when she is around him.

First, a woman must be sure that he is not dangerous before she is physically near him. To their peril, many women ignore their gut that screams: *Leave now!* If he has physically assaulted her, used or threatened to use a weapon, stalked, or sexually assaulted her in the past, there is good reason never to trust him again. She should never be alone with this person, and she should be extremely careful when she is in a crowd with him.

Second, if he is with people he wants to impress, he will likely be on better behavior than if he is with strangers or alone with her.

Third, like we do with triggers, the conscious side of her brain will need to have a conversation with the unconscious side of her brain to talk her off the ledge so she can function. For example, she may need to say to herself, "I know he is your abuser and he is now standing here in front of you; however, this is a wedding for your child. You want your child to have a wonderful day, and you are willing to make sure that, as long as it relates to you, she does. You are surrounded by people whom he knows; you are surrounded by your family and friends. He will be on good behavior if people are around. So settle down, let your daughter enjoy her day, and you enjoy her day too. And when the crowd thins down, you will leave so you are never alone with him."

Lie: Where was God when all this was going on? He deserted me.

Truth: When you think back and imagine where God was, He was helping you escape.

Sometimes when a woman looks back on her abuse or on abuse she experienced as a child, she comes to the incorrect conclusion that God deserted her during her time of need. This is believing a lie.

By virtue of the fact that you are reading this book, you are a survivor. God has done a rescue mission on you! God did not cause the evil that happened to you, but He certainly set you free!

By imagining the abusive event or series of events, and envisioning where God was and how He was working at that time, we can more clearly see that God was working behind the scenes accomplishing His redemptive work through people, sending messages, and setting up events to move us toward freedom.

For example, as an attorney representing survivors of domestic abuse, I have heard many women share that, looking back, they see that God had prompted them to leave the abusive relationship many times, but they ignored Him until He sent a message loud and clear. In each incident of abuse, they felt the urge to leave or even heard a whisper warning them to go, but they dismissed the soft voice of the Holy Spirit imploring them to leave. As the abuse escalated, so did God's promptings to flee. Finally, the abuser did something so vicious, so over-the-top, so beyond the pale, that it got their attention—and God's clear and direct message to find safety was heeded.

> Charlotte: For years, I ignored the Holy Spirit's promptings. I ignored Him when I saw signs even before the wedding that Tim was not a godly man. And I ignored the Holy Spirit's warnings to protect myself after the wedding. After the rape and stalking, I finally listened when He said I needed to get out now. During the divorce, I realized that God had used the prenuptial agreement, as painful as it had been, as my provision, because Tim argued that he didn't owe me a dime.

> Kerry: There were many promptings by God along the way that I should get out, but I so wanted to make my marriage work. Patrick was moody and an alcoholic and abusive. But the night that he slammed my head against the table and said I deserved it, I knew God had told me in no uncertain terms to leave.

> Dirk: Everyone I know who has been through an abusive marriage, including me, had a feeling in their gut before the wedding that they were making a big mistake. I think we all ignored the warnings by the Holy Spirit, both before and after the wedding. I finally left when I was so wracked with anxiety that I couldn't swallow my food anymore. That was God's clear sign that I needed to leave.

Lie: God was nowhere to be found when I went through traumatic experiences in my childhood and early adulthood.

Truth: God was right there. He rescued you.

Just like the traumatic events during a marriage, many people look back on a traumatic event in their childhood or early adulthood and assume that God had deserted them. Oftentimes, people are haunted by a traumatic event for years. They may even mark a date on their calendar reminding themselves of the event each year and reliving it in their minds. This unresolved trauma can inhibit healing and cause them to make poor choices in partners and in life. Our skewed perception and failure to heal clouds our judgment of the past, present, and future.

In truth, God was right there doing a rescue mission. Soldiers who have been in combat often refer to their "Alive Day." It is a day when, by all natural accounts, they should have been dead—but somehow they survived. This is the day that God intervened in the natural order of events and worked a miracle. Rather than looking at past traumatic events as days to wallow in our grief, women would do well to envision where God was and how He orchestrated her rescue mission. When she properly perceives that day, she can celebrate that day as her "Alive Day"—the day her Papa God, Mighty to Save, broke down doors, cut through chains, and performed a miracle to rescue His beloved daughter.

The people of Israel, no strangers to traumatic events, celebrated their Alive Days with feasting and making an altar. Jacob built an altar and named it Bethel after God protected him from Esau (Genesis 35). The Israelites celebrated Passover as a reminder of God's rescue mission out of Egypt. They celebrated Purim as a reminder of God's rescue mission during the time of Esther. We would do well to copy their customs and celebrate God's faithfulness rather than wallow in remembering Satan's schemes.

Doing the hard work of remembering past trauma and identifying the lies that shaped her worldview will often help a woman discover why she made poor choices in partners. Poor marriage choices can often be traced back to a traumatic event or series of events that remained unresolved and unhealed. When we replace the lies with the truth, the scars from our past can heal and we can make better choices for our future.

> Ellen: One of the most traumatic events in my life was when I was a child and some children pushed me off a dock into a lake, even though I couldn't swim. The water was over my head, and I was drowning, but the other children didn't know what to do. Finally, a man passing by saw me and saved me. For years I was so traumatized that I couldn't go by water, and I felt that God had left me during that horrific experience. But recently, as part of a spiritual healing exercise, I remembered the event and imagined where God was during that time. I realized that God was there all the time—He was in the man who dove into the water and rescued me! Perhaps feeling rejected by my friends and by God was part of the reason I chose abusive husbands. I felt so alone that I married anyone who paid me some attention rather than seeking out a man who sought after God.

> Dirk: When I was in black ops, one of our missions went terribly wrong. We were given the wrong coordinates and ended up surrounded by enemy fire. My CO was wounded and trapped—his leg was broken, and he couldn't make it back to the chopper. Our orders were to leave anyone who couldn't make it back. No one had any dog tags or identification on our missions—we were not supposed to exist. The man left behind had a cyanide pill to take so if he wasn't killed by enemy fire, he would die before the enemy could torture him and extract information. As the chopper was taking off, I strapped on as much ammo as I could, grabbed my M16, and jumped out to get to my CO. I knew we would both be left behind, but I couldn't let him die alone. I figured I would take out as many bad guys as I could before we died. To my amazement, I saw the chopper take off and then come back down—disobeying all protocols. The guys yelled at us to run in while they covered us with firepower. I put my CO on my back and ran as fast as I could. We both made it back to the helo, and it took off.

I am sure that the trauma of being in combat was a big part of the reason why I was in abusive marriages. I had to give up black ops due to an injury—that's another story. When I got out, I just wanted to settle down to a peaceful, normal life as soon as possible. I settled for the first woman I met. What a mistake!

March 16 is a date that haunted me for thirty years. I dreaded it as it approached, but my new wife explained to me that God worked a miracle that day and did a rescue mission on me and my CO because He loved me and had a purpose for my life. I now celebrate that day, and all my Alive Days, because I see God's hand at work in my life. Rejecting the lies and replacing them with God's truth has healed me—not only from the combat trauma, but also from two abusive marriages.

Charlotte: When I was about thirteen years old, I was diagnosed with scoliosis and had to wear a full-body Milwaukee brace for more than two years. It was a rough experience being an ugly duckling, teased, and ostracized in high school. I thought for sure I would never be asked out on a date, much less have someone interested enough to marry me. When I finally got out of the brace, I was surprised that anyone asked me out. My dad, who was loving but overprotective, got rid of anyone I was dating. In no uncertain terms, he told them to leave, but I did not know of these conversations until years later. So I couldn't understand why my boyfriends just ghosted me when things were going so well. I thought, *What in the world do I have to do to keep a man?* Between the insecurity caused by the brace and the multiple rejections from people I cared for, I was the perfect target for an abuser. I was willing to put up with nearly anything to have a relationship. I now have a wonderful marriage with a godly man, but it took a lot of work to heal and to understand why I kept choosing abusive men.

Tina: I was sexually abused as a child, even though my parents went to church. After my parents divorced, my mom went on to have three more abusive marriages. My dad was married multiple times too. Like my mom, I just wanted a man who loved me, but I ended up marrying someone just like my dad.

CHAPTER 45

Practical Steps toward Healing

Transforming our perspective into God's by rejecting the lies and replacing them with God's truth is perhaps the most important step toward healing. In addition, a woman can take practical steps, which I summarize below, to encourage healing. However, a woman should not feel compelled to do all of them at once. Healing happens over time. Day by day, step by step, and piece by piece, she and God will build a new life together. One day she will discover that she is no longer in pain, that her first thought in the morning and her last thought at night is not about her abuser. She will be smiling and enjoying life again. She has experienced firsthand Jehovah Raphe, the Lord our Healer.

A beautiful thing happens when we ask God to be part of our healing journey. God is a God of redemption. When God redeems a life, He doesn't just put it back like it was before—He makes it *better*. We have a relationship with Him like we have never had before. When He makes a promise, we take it to the bank because we have seen Him fulfill all His promises before. We know who we are, and we know *whose* we are—and nothing and no one can shake that. We are healthier emotionally and physically. We are surrounded by good, kind, godly people. We are blessed with financial opportunities that we have never had before. God opens His storehouses of heaven and pours out His blessings. Time and time again, I have seen women blossom as they leave the toxic, evil cloud of their abuser behind and walk into the light, holding on to God's hand. Jehovah Gaal—the Lord our Redeemer indeed!

Prayer

There is simply no substitute for spending long periods of time alone with God, soaking in His Presence, listening to His whispers, and sharing your heart. Many people approach prayer as a cosmic grocery list of things to ask for within five minutes or less. God wants a relationship with us. Good relationships are built by spending time together, listening to each other, sharing both the big things and the small. It's no different with God. Just like every good dad wants to spend time with his kids, our heavenly Dad wants time with us.

Some people wonder why we should bother with prayer. If God already knows the future, why bother to ask Him to change His mind? Prayer is a time when our hearts become more aligned with His. As He speaks to us, and we speak to Him, His will becomes our will. Jesus said that if we ask anything in God's will, it will be answered. Prayer, then, is a time for our will to conform with His and to ask that His will be done. Throughout the Bible, the saints of old pleaded with God and moved His heart. We, too, move the heart of God. God hears the prayers of the righteous (Proverbs 15:29; James 5:16; 1 Peter 3:12).

Spending an hour or so with God each morning before starting the day keeps us centered and equipped to fight off the arrows that Satan will launch against us that day. Spending some time before we fall asleep at night gives us the comfort that God is still with us, even as we nod off to sleep. It's much like a toddler falling asleep on his father's chest as he hears the rhythm of his dad's heart and the soothing sound of his voice at bedtime. Rather than feeling guilty if we fall asleep during our bedtime prayers, I suspect God likes that the last words on our lips are to Him as we drift into blessed rest from the day.

We, like David, can know the peaceful slumber that comes from God, even in the midst of a trial: "Know this: the Lord takes care of the faithful. . . . I will lie down and fall asleep in peace because you alone, Lord, let me live in safety" (Psalm 4:3, 8 CEB).

Many people wonder how they can hear God's voice, and whether He talks to us at all. I believe God uses all forms of communication to communicate with us. He is not limited by human language. He speaks to some people in dreams, and to others a picture may come to mind. Sometimes we get full sentences that are impressed on us, while other times just a single word comes to mind out of the blue. To some, He communicates with a song; to others, He speaks as they write or read. Nature is a favorite form of communication—what better way to say "I love you" than a gorgeous sunset every night, or a rainbow, or a flower? Whatever our preferred form of communication, God knows it and will use it. Like a radio that has different frequencies, God will find whatever frequency our hearts are tuned to and broadcast His heart to us.

The more we listen to and act on God's voice, the more we recognize the voice of God among the many other voices clamoring for our attention. Sometimes it's a noisy world, and God needs our full attention, so He talks to us in the middle of the night when there are no other noises competing for our attention. I have learned that when I cannot fall asleep, or when I wake in the middle of the night, God has something He wants to say to me. In the past, I have tried to bargain with Him and have asked Him to wait until morning to tell me what He wants to say, but He doesn't want to wait until then. I know better now—He will not let me sleep until we have a conversation. So I turn on the light, sit up in bed, get out my journal that I keep by the side of my bed, and write down God's midnight whispers. Sometimes it fills three or four pages of my journal, and other times just half a page. I am always amazed that the Creator of the Universe has something He wants to say specifically to me. How precious! And when He is done talking, I can then drift off to sleep.

Prayer is when God gives us our assignments, tells us that He loves us, encourages us, lets us know that He is with us, reveals Himself to us, and reminds us of His promises.

Reading the Bible

Just like there is no substitute for prayer, there is no substitute for spending large chunks of time in the Bible. The Bible is a 1,200-page love letter from God, full of promises, wisdom, practical advice, solid rules to live by, information about Him, and most of all, descriptions of how very much He loves us. The Bible is where God reveals Himself and His redemptive purpose. The study application versions bring context and explanations when we need them.

The Bible says, "For the word of God is living and active, sharper than any two-edged sword, piercing to the division of soul and of spirit, of joints and of marrow, and discerning the thoughts and intentions of the heart"

(Hebrews 4:12 ESV). This means that the Bible speaks to us in a real way in every situation, and it exposes not only our innermost intentions, but also the intentions of others. We can read the same passage ten times, but in the midst of a struggle, the words come alive and resolve our problem in a way they may never have done before.

I had read the Bible regularly before I fled my abuser, but when I started reading the Bible from the perspective of a domestic abuse survivor and looked for what God had to say to *me* at that time, passages I had never noticed before practically jumped off the page. For the first time, I was able to understand the type of toxic, abusive person the authors warned of. Jesus, Paul, Peter, David, Solomon, and others described the innermost intentions of my abuser (and other abusers) to a T—intentions that had been carefully hidden behind a web of lies and deception of which I still don't know the full extent. As I pored over its pages, the Bible spoke to me and clearly divided good from bad, righteousness from evil, and God's children from Satan's. The Bible cleared up my misunderstandings and unequivocally explained to me how a domestic abuse survivor should respond to abuse and her abuser—and it also clearly explained how the church should deal with abuse and abusers. All the fuzziness and confusion I had been living in when I was married to an abuser cleared up when I dug deep into God's Word.

Rather than the words from my abuser ringing in my ears and stinging my heart, when I read the Bible, God's words told me that He delights in me, He sings songs over me, He made me wonderfully and wondrously just the way I am, He uniquely equipped me with amazing gifts to do His works, and He called me for a purpose. While my abuser tried his best to drive my children away with his lies and slander, in the Bible, God promised to bring my children back from the north, south, east, and west—and I held on to those promises until He did. Rather than thinking I had to stay with an abuser, God's Word explained that I was justified in expecting love rather than abuse. Contrary to my misunderstanding that I needed to explain my innocence to my abuser's cronies, the Bible explained that those who support him share his moral compass. My fears about the future were replaced by God's promises of blessings that became a reality.

Journaling

Writing down our thoughts, God's whispers, those "aha" moments when the lightbulb goes off in our heads, things we learn as we read the Bible, revelations from God, prayers, answers to those prayers, and all the things we are thankful for is a huge tool for healing. Journals both collect our thoughts and inspire new ones. Nearly every inspirational leader journals his or her thoughts.

Healing occurs when we write the intricacies of our thought processes, the details of our answers to prayers, the minutiae of the piece-by-piece, thought-by-thought transformation that takes place in our hearts and minds. This detailed journaling is far different from the short, factual scribbles of making a diary or calendar of dates and events of the day. The Bible encourages us to "work out our faith with fear and trembling" because God is at work in our hearts to transform our will and our actions to fulfill His divine purpose (Philippians 2:12). What does that mean? I believe it encourages us to humbly wrestle with the difficult issues we need to wrap our mind around, to seek to understand God's perspective, and to pursue God with everything we have as we work out in our own mind God's hard-to-understand secrets. God promises that when we seek Him with all our heart, we will find Him (Jeremiah 29:13). He's hiding in plain view, but those who don't care about Him will not bother to seek Him. Only when we care enough to look fervently for Him, because our very life depends on it, will He reveal Himself to us. Journaling this process ensures that we have worked it through. Journaling also helps calm our swirling brains by putting our reflections on paper so we can stop ruminating.

Many nights I have not been able to sleep because I have a thought, an epiphany, a memory, or a word from God, and my mind seems to be on a constant rewind and replay. My journal helps me get the thoughts out of my mind and onto paper so I can finally sleep.

Journaling what God reveals to us—our discoveries of God's nature and the prayers He answers—strengthens our faith. When we reread our journal later, we are reminded of His faithfulness, and our faith is strengthened again and again. And gradually, we heal and move closer to the wholeness, the shalom, that God desires for us.

Write Your Story

Even if no one else reads it, it is important to write down our story. The details of the abuse, the confusion, the fear, and the mess—all of it. This may take some time. It is likely too overwhelming to write all at once.

However, it is important that we remember. Writing our story reminds us of why we left, keeps us from ever going back, and makes it real. When our story is only swirling around in our mind, it can be so horrific and seem so unreal that we sometimes doubt that it ever happened. Our memories play tricks on us at night as we rewind and replay the abuse. We spend our waking hours with intrusive thoughts about the abuse and our abuser. Putting those memories and thoughts on paper helps calm us. As we write, we transfer our thoughts from our minds to the paper, and our brains feel the release from the pressure of holding our secret. Our brains no longer need to be the keeper of the facts—the historian of our story—because it is now written for the ages, and our uninvited memories of the abuse will abate over time.

The Bible tells us to take captive every thought and make them obedient to Christ. But uninvited thoughts of the abuse fill our minds even after the trauma is over. Journaling and writing help take captive the invading thoughts of abuse and our abuser. Imagine those thoughts in a cartoon bubble that is flushed down the toilet, and then consciously refocus your mind on something positive.

Tell Your Story

Telling your story to a safe, supportive, empathetic person is another healing technique. Science shows that verbalizing an experience not only changes us and paves the way to healing, but it also changes the other person and leads to a deeper relationship. Of course, we must make sure that anyone to whom we entrust our story is worthy of the privilege. Supporters of our abuser and so-called friends who did not want to get involved are not safe and are not worthy of being entrusted with our story. It is very likely that anyone who entrusts her story to a minion of her abuser will not receive the support or empathy that she seeks. She will be mocked, criticized, and falsely attacked. These people have a warped moral compass and should be avoided.

Many women who have been through abuse want to help others. After you have healed, you may at some point wish to tell your story publicly as an advocate for victims of abuse. If you choose to go public with your story, you will want to end on a note of victory to give others encouragement. Women in the battle need a story with a good ending to give them strength. When I speak publicly, I always include a message of hope and give glory to God for His rescue mission. Reminding people of God's amazing love for us is my favorite subject. I stand with the psalmist who says, "Your love, God, is my song, and I'll sing it! I'm forever telling everyone how faithful you are. I'll never quit telling the story of your love" (Psalm 89:1–2 MSG).

Volunteer

Volunteering has amazing psychological and physical healing power that rivals or exceeds medication, meditation, or exercise. Volunteering reduces blood pressure, depression, anxiety, and stress while increasing our optimism and sense of purpose. Physiologically, volunteering releases oxytocin, the hormone responsible for bonding connections between people. Volunteers report feeling more energized, more clear-minded, and more relaxed when they volunteer.

One of the many dangers of going through abuse is becoming extremely self-focused and constantly dwelling on our own problems. This can spiral downward into depression and self-pity. Such self-focus is not healthy and is not how God wants us to approach life. God wants us to be God- and other-focused. His two most important commandments are to love God and love others. They are intertwined—we can't love God without loving others. Volunteering is a practical way to do both. As we focus on helping others, it helps us keep our mind off ourselves and puts our own problems in perspective. Volunteering through an organized entity with a mission we believe in reduces social isolation, gives us meaningful work with a purpose that is bigger than ourselves, and can lead to significant friendships with like-minded people.

Altruism has been found to light up the reward centers of our brain in the same way that good food and sex do. In short, helping others gives us the natural high that our brains are wired for.

Exercise

Abuse and its aftermath are physically, mentally, and emotionally draining. Exercising has amazing healing powers. First, exercise acts as a natural antidepressant. As we exercise, our bodies release endorphins that raise our spirits and reduce depression and stress. Exercise also gives us more energy. The hardest part of exercising is the first few minutes. It's so much easier to curl up on the couch. Walking is a good way to start, and in time, we can increase our activity level.

Exercise also boosts immunity, lowers our chances of getting colds, and reduces stress-related health issues such as high blood pressure and heart disease. Exercise also increases overall health, keeps weight at a healthy level, and reduces the chances of developing type 2 diabetes and hormone-related cancers like some forms of breast cancer. Exercise rebuilds bone and muscle, reduces inflammation, and staves off osteoporosis—a condition for which women are particularly at risk. Women recovering from abuse often find it difficult to concentrate because most of their mental energy goes to surviving and countering the physical and verbal attacks. Difficulty concentrating is one of the many symptoms of PTSD. Exercise increases mental acuity and helps with concentration, improving cognitive functions.

Healthy Eating and Drinking

In the aftermath of a divorce from a SNAP, it is especially important to eat and drink things that are healthy and will boost our immune system. When we are under stress and have lost an important relationship, our immune system is compromised and we feel fatigued. This is not the time to ingest copious amounts of donuts, Twinkies, and Jack Daniels. Nor is it a time to starve due to nerves and lack of appetite. Good sources of protein, fresh fruits and vegetables, and plenty of water are needed to nourish our depleted bodies, help our cognitive functioning, increase our immune systems, and flush out toxins that gather in our systems during times of stress. Most of us know how to eat healthily, and there are numerous online articles and books about healthy eating.

Avoid food and drinks high in carbohydrates and sugars. These provide little nutritional value and will lead to a carbohydrate "crash" that will cause us to feel sleepy and lethargic. Sugar is a known factor in several maladies, including obesity, inflammation, and even dementia. Sugared sodas, juices, and alcoholic beverages are all extremely high in sugar and carbohydrates. If a woman feels like she needs a drink to calm down at the end of the day, a hot cup of tea is the perfect thing to sip on and is a good ending to the day. Fortunately for coffee lovers, coffee is high in antioxidants and can be a good start to the day, but the caffeine tends to keep people up at night.

How we eat is equally important as what we eat. Taking the time to gather around a table with your children in an unhurried evening of dinner, prayer, conversation, affirmation, and thankfulness feeds the body and the soul. Far too often, families do not take time to gather and reconnect. Children are running off to soccer practice or texting friends, and overworked parents are too tired to make dinner, much less conversation. Food is often either grabbed on the run while everyone goes their separate ways, or eaten in front of the television with little interaction, leaving families with no idea what goes on in the hearts and minds of each other. Family dinners together are essential to healing and connecting with loved ones.

Research confirms what wise parents and grandparents have known for centuries: family dinners eaten around a table without television, cell phones, or other distractions have healing benefits.[219] Family meals help maintain healthy weight and eating patterns and provide healthier foods. They connect families and contribute to traditions that tie families together and give them a sense of identity. More than any other activity, family meals provide a safe and secure environment to facilitate communication, share values and ideas, negotiate issues, impart wisdom, pass along family stories, ask questions, catch up on what is happening in each of their lives, discuss current events, and solve problems. Children who regularly eat meals with their family have lower incidents of depression, eating disorders, drug and alcohol use, high risk behaviors, sexual activity, television watching, and emotional and behavioral problems. They also tend to receive higher grades in school, have higher life satisfaction, experience better emotional health, and enjoy better relationships with their siblings and parents. Indeed, the benefits are so great that the position statement of the American College of Pediatricians states: "Given the protective factors that are conveyed to children and adolescents, pediatricians should encourage parents to make every effort to regularly gather around the 'Family Table' for meals."[220] Of course, adults enjoy the same benefits that come from the family table as children.

Being intentional is the key to meals that feed the body and the soul. Choose days and times that are convenient for the entire family so that there is plenty of time to relax together. Cooking together is a fun way to connect, choose healthy foods, learn to cook from each other, and try out recipes. Pray together. Encourage each other by having each person share one or two things that they appreciate about each other and what he is grateful for that day. Stimulate uplifting conversation by sharing the high of the day or pulling questions out of a bowl and have everyone around the table answer.

Mealtimes with an abuser are usually anything but pleasant. But with the abuser out of the picture and with some effort and intentionality, you can transform them into some of the most meaningful, healing, and enjoyable times to be with your children.

---

[219] Jane Anderson and Den Trumbull, "The Benefits of the Family Table," American College of Pediatricians, https://acpeds.org/position-statements/the-benefits-of-the-family-table.
[220] Anderson and Trumbull, "The Benefits of the Family Table."

Back to Nature

Being in God's cathedral—His beautiful creation—is healing. Scientists tell us that when we spend time in nature, it reduces depression, blood pressure, anxiety, aggression, and ADHD symptoms while increasing pain control, the immune system, and happiness. Physicians in Scotland are now even able to give patients a prescription to spend time in nature.[221]

Walking through a grove of one-thousand-year-old redwoods, strolling along the seashore at sunset, hiking in the majestic snow-covered mountains, and gazing at the stars bring us closer to their Creator. They give us a sense of awe at the power and creativity of God while also making us realize that our time here on earth is short in comparison to eternity and our physical being is quite small in contrast to the universe. Yet, when we notice the delicate features of a flower or the small sparrow, we are reminded that God dwells on the small details of our life just as He dwells on the details of a flower, and He knows every one of us just as He knows every sparrow. God is involved in the design of a rose just as He is involved in making the Milky Way. He is Lord of both the big and the small.

I am convinced that God made nature so beautiful for our pleasure and for His. Why else would He make a new sunset every night? Why else would He make thousands of varieties of flowers? Sometimes when I see a spectacular sunset or an amazing mountain from the top of a ski slope, I think He is just showing off. I usually give Him a thumbs up and a "Good job, God!" when I see one of His remarkable displays of art. We are reminded all around us how much He loves us. Do we always appreciate His daily artwork?

It is no wonder God does His best healing after trauma and His best preparation for service in the great outdoors. When Moses fled to Midian after he killed an Egyptian, he became a shepherd. For the next forty years, as He spoke to Moses in the solitude of the desert, God healed his heart and prepared him for his next assignment of rescuing Israel and leading them to the promised land.

God prepared David for his assignment as king of Israel in the sheep fields too. It was in the great outdoors that God gave him the courage to kill a lion, the bravery to protect his sheep, and the faith to rely on God's promises. In this training ground, David learned how to face Goliath without fear, how to lead a people, and how to hear God's voice.

For much of the Old Testament, God was a God of the fields. His people lived in tents and moved wherever God led them. They lived in nature, not in the cities. They were completely dependent upon God's provision for them. His Presence was in a cloud by day and in fire by night. He met with His earthly leaders in a tent, not a building. I suspect His outdoor wandering was by design, because when Israel became a people who lived in the cities with wealth and power, it was the beginning of the end.

When we are in nature, away from the noises of the world and the distractions of life, we can hear God speak to our hearts. God tells us to "Be still, and know that I am God" (Psalm 46:10). There is no better place to do that than in the quiet moments in the temple of nature. Just like a good father, God tells us just what we need to hear at that time. He soothes our anxious soul and calms our worried nerves. Surrounded by the beauty He created for our pleasure, He restores our spirit and equips us for our next assignment.

---

[221] Evan Fleischer, "Doctors in Scotland Can Now Prescribe Nature to Their Patients," Big Think, October 12, 2018, https://bigthink.com/personal-growth/doctors-in-shetland-can-now-prescribe-a-walk-in-nature.

Building Community

God has wired us to be in community. Research tells us that when hurting people are removed from a toxic environment and are surrounded with healthy people, they make great strides in healing, even without therapy or counseling.[222] We are wired for healthy relationships, and when we don't have a toxic person in our midst, we return to health.

A woman recovering from domestic abuse must often rebuild her entire community. Abusers vindictively try to destroy all relationships between their victim and her social network.

How does she build a safe community? The first step is finding a Bible-believing, spiritually mature, compassionate, Holy Spirit-filled, active church with a pastor who understands domestic abuse and toxic people. Joining a small group, Bible study, Sunday school class, or ministry will help one get connected on a more personal level than just pew sitting on Sundays. God expects us all to be participants in His church, not spectators.

The second step is finding a community of survivors of domestic abuse to walk with through recovery. Only people who have experienced domestic abuse can understand others who have gone through it. It is important for her to find her tribe who understands her. People who join support groups usually heal more rapidly than those who don't. Almost every county in every state has a domestic violence organization that provides counseling and support groups. Getting connected will help her heal and may even introduce her to a new group of friends. When the group sessions are no longer needed, the friendships will remain. She may even find that she wants to help others escape from domestic abuse, and she may find it a good place to volunteer.

The third step is getting to know your neighbors. Many of us live in communities where we don't know even our next-door neighbors. This leads to feelings of isolation and disconnectedness. If you have moved to a new location, take the first step of building community. Bring a homemade goodie or homegrown vegetables to your new neighbors, introduce yourself, and give them your name and contact information. Unless they are grumpy or toxic, they will appreciate the gesture. Host a potluck dinner and invite your neighbors. Good people will enjoy the social gathering, and those who don't want to know their neighbors will decline. You will quickly find out who your good neighbors are.

Good neighbors are a blessing. In small towns where neighbors know each other, it is common for neighbors to help each other with projects, bring over food when people are sick, bring over homegrown tomatoes from their garden, gather for potlucks, and take out the trash and watch the cat when folks are on vacation. Good neighbors are gifts from above.

The fourth step is to volunteer. As noted above, volunteering has many benefits. One of those benefits is belonging to a community of like-minded people with a common purpose. Good organizations value their volunteers and make volunteering a pleasant and meaningful experience. This alone is a conduit to healing.

The fifth step is to join a community organization or a professional organization. Community organizations like the Rotary Club, Kiwanis, Lions Club, Women's Club, and the like are nonprofit organizations whose purpose is to enhance the community. Joining a community organization is a good way to expand one's network in the local community. Most local organizations are part of a national organization, and so a woman can meet others from across the country. A professional organization will put her in touch with businesspeople or profes-

---

[222] Wayne Jonas, "How the Right Relationships Can Help You Heal," *Psychology Today*, November 30, 2018, https://www.psychologytoday.com/us/blog/how-healing-works/201811/how-the-right-relationships-can-help-you-heal; Robert C. Whitaker, "Relationships Heal," *Permanente Journal*, v. 20(1) (2016), 91–94, https://www.ncbi.nlm.nih.gov/pmc/articles/PMC4732802/.

sionals in the same field. Although deep friendships may not result from these types of organizations, certainly being with others in similar professions helps expand her network, helps her reputation in her field, and may even be helpful in finding a job.

Establishing Healthy Boundaries

Whether a relationship is romantic or platonic, establishing healthy boundaries is important for healing. We cannot control anyone but ourselves. Healthy boundaries are predetermined limits we set for ourselves. We cannot set boundaries on others—they will do what they do. But we can determine what we will or won't tolerate.

Many women find it hard to say no when asked to do a favor or volunteer. They feel they would be rude or impolite if they said no to a request. They conduct their lives based on what others might think about them. As a result, they find themselves overcommitted, stretched thin, used by others, and involved in activities and relationships they regret. Their emotional state is dependent upon the opinion of others rather than upon God's opinion of them.

We may erroneously believe that it is selfish to establish boundaries. However, the most generous and effective people set healthy boundaries that allow them to recharge their batteries, save time for the most important projects, focus on priorities, and accomplish their goals.

One way to establish healthy boundaries is to determine our priorities, the goals we want to accomplish, and the highest and best use of our time and skill sets. For example, if our priority is to become financially independent after a divorce and several years of not working in the marketplace, and if our goal is to get an upwardly mobile job using our college degree, we will need to establish boundaries in which we say no to requests to volunteer, and instead focus our efforts on updating skills and finding a position. If we have an accounting degree and wish to volunteer at church, we may establish a boundary by saying no when asked to volunteer on the decorating committee, but yes to the finance committee, because that is the highest and best use of our time and skill.

Sometimes our boundaries revolve around time. We can easily get overcommitted, when what we really need for ourselves and our children is downtime, a snuggle night on the couch watching movies, or soaking in the Word with God. When we don't put time for these on our calendars, other activities will fill the time. I start each morning with time in prayer, journaling, and reading God's Word. I need this time to connect with God because I know that Satan will start his attacks on my day as soon as I start moving. I don't plan anything that interferes with my morning reconnection with my Lord. I have commitments on many evenings, but I reserve a few nights a week just to recharge the batteries with some "deep couch sitting" with my husband. We must protect our time with boundaries.

All relationships, of course, need boundaries. For women coming out of domestic abuse, establishing appropriate boundaries in friendships and work and romantic relationships is difficult. However, setting and keeping boundaries becomes easier with time and practice.

For example, we may wish to establish a healthy boundary that we will not be in the same room with someone who is yelling at us, and therefore, we will leave the room when someone raises their voice. When anyone starts to engage in yelling rather than remaining calm, we can state, "I am happy to discuss the issue with you, but I will not be yelled at. When you can calm down and discuss the matter at hand in a calm, rational way, let me know. In the meantime, I will not discuss this with you or be in the same room with you." And then leave the room. Note that our boundary does not tell the other person what to do, but rather it determines what we will do. We cannot stop others from yelling, but we can control whether we will remain in the conversation and be yelled at.

We may establish a healthy boundary that we will not be in a relationship with someone who lies to us, and therefore, we will terminate contact with anyone who lies to us. If a client lies to his attorney, she can state, "I agreed to represent you upon the condition that you were honest with me. I must represent things about your case to the judge and to opposing counsel. If you are not honest with me, I find myself telling the judge and opposing counsel things that are not true. You have not been honest with me, and therefore, I can no longer represent you." If a friend lies to us, we can state, "The basis of any friendship is honesty and trust. I am disappointed that you were not honest with me, because it has broken the trust I had in you. I have a policy of requiring honesty from people I consider friends, and it grieves me that we can no longer have a friendship." We cannot control another person's lying (or from being upset when we break off the relationship), but we can control whether we will continue a relationship with someone who is not honest with us.

We will need to establish healthy boundaries that we will not be in a romantic relationship with someone who is controlling, jealous, manipulative, or shows any of the tactics or characteristics that abusers use. We will want to ensure we do not enter a romantic relationship with someone who has addiction problems, is a regular purveyor of pornography, is not a committed follower of Christ, or has a history of mental illness. These are indispensable boundaries that establish who we will or won't allow to be intimate with us and influence us.

Jesus, again, is our example for establishing boundaries. While He spent time preaching, teaching, and healing, He regularly withdrew from the crowds to spend time with His Father and restore His spirit in prayer. He surrounded Himself with an inner circle of friends who believed in Him and supported Him, and of those, He chose two to be His closest confidantes. We must do no less.

Establishing healthy boundaries is essential to leading an abundant life and being effective and efficient in the things we choose to do. It is important for women to decide ahead of time the things they will or won't do, the relationships they will or won't have, and the things they will or won't tolerate. When we don't decide these matters for ourselves in advance, we invariably find ourselves in unhealthy relationships and commitments from which it is difficult to extract ourselves.

Bible Study with Holy Spirit-Filled Women

We learn and heal in community. That is how God designed us. Being involved in a Bible study with spiritually mature, compassionate women who are seeking God, who are filled with the Holy Spirit, and who have themselves healed from difficult experiences will be a tremendous step toward healing. Not every Bible study has these secret ingredients. Some older women aren't spiritually mature. Some smart women are not compassionate. Some women know the Bible, but don't have the Holy Spirit. Some discerning women are not empathetic. Some women view Bible study as a social club or extension of their country club rather than a place to seek God and be more like Him. Ask God to lead you to the right group of women, and experience the healing that only comes from God working through the hands and feet of his beloved daughters.

> Charlotte: In my own journey, I knew I needed to be surrounded by good, kind women, but I had been hurt and disappointed when some women in the couples Bible study that I led supported my abusive ex-husband. I started attending a new church and was invited to a women's Bible study led by a beautiful, Holy Spirit-filled woman named Pam. I was very guarded during my first meeting,

and I said very little. I was watching to see if this was a safe group, or if it was filled with judgmental, catty, uncaring "church ladies" like the previous one. I was overwhelmed by the hearts of these women who poured into my aching soul, prayed for me, unveiled truths of heaven that I had never even imagined, and brought the presence of God. I will be forever grateful for this sanctuary of women baptized in and overflowing with the Holy Spirit.

Getting to Sleep

Most women in the aftermath of divorce from an abuser have a difficult time getting to sleep and staying asleep. Yet adequate sleep is imperative to good health. Try one of the following tactics until one or more work.

Hot tea before bed is good way to calm down and prepare for sleep. Herbal teas that contain chamomile, spearmint, or valerian root have soothing qualities that prepare our bodies for bed. Avoid caffeinated drinks, such as coffee, colas, and tea with caffeine. Colas, juices, desserts, and alcohol—such as wine and many liquors—have sugar in them, which can either keep us up or wake us up.

Proteins help the winding-down process, especially those with tryptophan, like turkey and milk. This is why we get that sleepy food coma after a big Thanksgiving meal. Peanut butter, which has both protein and fats, is a good bedtime snack.

Some women take natural products to help them sleep, like melatonin. Others rely on over-the-counter medications like sleeping aids and diphenhydramine (the chemical in Benadryl). A few must resort to prescription medications to get a restful night.

Lights often inhibit sleep. Screens, such as computer screens, TV screens, and phone screens, tend to keep us up at night. The blue light emitted by our devices reduces the production of melatonin, the hormone that controls our wake and sleep cycle. With less melatonin, our bodies find it harder to fall asleep and stay asleep. Our electronic gadgets also keep our brains engaged. When our brains are racing about the work we need to accomplish, the emails we need to send, or the latest news story, we find it hard to relax and switch our brains to sleep mode. Our devices are also noisy, and they wake us up at night with alerts of texts, emails, and calendar reminders. It is advised to stop all screen watching at least thirty minutes before getting into bed and to keep screened devices in silent mode, out of the bed, and out of reach.[223] The light from a clock by the side of a bed may also keep some people awake, so turning the clock away and putting out the lights is a good habit for sleeping as well.

Some people find that essential oils reduce anxiety, aid relaxation, stabilize blood pressure, and promote better sleep. Essential oils are usually used in a diffuser. Even if essential oils don't work for you, they will make your room smell lovely.[224]

Exercise is beneficial for a good night's sleep. Exercise increases our body's production of adenosine, a chemical that causes drowsiness, increases body temperature, and improves the wake and sleep cycle. These, in turn, reduce body temperature at night and allow for longer and deeper sleep.[225]

Ear plugs can be quite beneficial in drowning out distracting noises. Cocooning in quietness facilitates sleep.

Reading before bed helps many people drift off to sleep. A calming book, rather than a horror novel or crime

---

[223] "National Sleep Foundation, "Challenging Ways Technology Affects Your Sleep," at https://www.sleep.org/articles/ways-technology-affects-sleep/.

[224] National Sleep Foundation, "Do Essential Oils Promote Good Sleep?," https://www.sleep.org/articles/do-essential-oils-promote-good-sleep/.

[225] National Sleep Foundation, "Does Exercise Help or Hurt Sleep?," https://www.sleep.org/articles/does-exercise-help-or-hurt-sleep/.

news, is the preferable bedtime reading. On the many nights that I couldn't sleep, a midnight snack of peanut butter and crackers with milk, followed by writing in my journal and reading the psalms, did the trick.

Cultivating Thankfulness and Joy

Cultivating thankfulness is a key ingredient to bringing joy to your life. And let's face it, everyone needs more joy, especially those recovering from abuse. Researchers have discovered that being thankful is the key to more joy.[226] It's nearly impossible to be sad and depressed when you are thankful.

Be on the lookout for blessings, and remind yourself that each one is a gift from God. Oftentimes our blessings arrive just when we need them. God is known for His "just in time delivery" methods. And God often sends little signs of encouragement to let us know He is with us when we need it most. God knows when we are going to have one of those awful, very bad days, and during it He will give us a boost, an unexpected blessing, or a surprise pick-me-up to counteract the negativity. But we must be on the lookout, recognize God's gifts, and take the time to say, "Thank You, Lord!"

Research has confirmed that gratitude has a number of positive health benefits. Gratitude brings happiness, improves health, builds relationships, enhances our mood, and even changes the neural structures in our brains, leading us to feel happier and more content. Thankfulness increases our levels of dopamine and serotonin, two feel-good hormones. Gratitude releases toxic emotions, reduces pain, improves sleep, and reduces stress, anxiety, and depression. It also helps reduce our grief and increases our resilience during periods of loss.[227] In short, gratitude is, indeed, the key to joy.

It is hard to be thankful when we feel that our entire life has been hijacked and taken away by a crazy man. But we must remember that God is on a rescue mission. We cannot expect life to be the same. He is taking us out of bondage and into freedom. Like Harriet Tubman, we may feel as if we are on the Underground Railroad before we reach freedom, and even then, we must remake our life in a new land.

It helps to remember how God took care of the Israelites on their journey out of Egypt to the promised land. They no longer lived in the palace of Pharaoh, but God provided tents to live in, manna every day for food, water in the desert, and birds for protein. He guided them with His own presence, with a cloud by day and fire by night. He promised to be with them and to fight for them so they could take over the land He had promised to them. He demonstrated His power and faithfulness by a series of miracles to set them free from Pharaoh, and then took a "take no prisoners" policy by parting the Red Sea for His people and drowning their opponents. Yet still they complained and did not believe His promises, despite the miracles they saw every day. They were completely unappreciative of God's provisions, and even said it would have been better to stay in Egypt! Because of this, they wandered the desert for forty years, and none of their generation were allowed to enter the promised land. They died in the desert before reaching their land of rest. Joshua and Caleb, who believed God's promises and voted to fight for the promised land, were the only two allowed from that entire generation to enter Canaan. Even though they were eighty years old by the time they arrived, God had preserved them and blessed them, so they fought with men half their age.

We must be mindful to not be like the Israelites. I suspect that the more we are unappreciative and unthank-

---

[226] Brené Brown, "Brené Brown on Joy and Gratitude," Global Leadership Network, November 21, 2018, https://globalleadership.org/articles/leading-yourself/brene-brown-on-joy-and-gratitude/.
[227] Madhuleena Roy Chowdhury, "The Neuroscience of Gratitude and How It Affects Anxiety and Grief," May 12, 2020, https://positivepsychology.com/neuroscience-of-gratitude/.

ful, the longer our recovery from abuse will be, and some might never enter their promised land. If we remain bitter, we jeopardize our own healing and happiness. We need to be like Joshua and Caleb—we need to be thankful, filled with God's Spirit, and so excited about God's promises that we are ready to fight the giants and take our new land because we know that God is fighting on our side and we will not fail.

For example, perhaps we had to flee our house because it wasn't safe, but we can be thankful for that friend or domestic abuse shelter that provided a place to stay until we found permanent housing. Perhaps we were beaten, but we can be thankful that we had the good sense to call the police and they arrived and arrested the abuser. Perhaps our new home is smaller than our marital home, but we can be thankful that it is peaceful and full of love. Perhaps we have less money than when we were married, but we can be thankful that our income plus government services are sufficient to meet our needs. Perhaps we needed to say goodbye to toxic friends who supported our abuser, but we can be thankful that God revealed their true character and that He brought new people into our lives. Perhaps we had hoped to save our marriage, but we can be thankful that God brought us out when He did and that we are alive today. Regardless of our situation, we can always find something for which to be thankful.

Writing down those things we are thankful for is an important reminder of all we have to be grateful for, especially on those difficult days when everything seems sideways. I have adopted a Blessings Journal. In addition to my regular prayer journal, at least once a year I take an assessment of all the blessings God has showered me with. How wonderful it is to remember the people who make my life rich, the doors God has opened, and the resources the Lord has provided. It is impossible to be sad for very long when I bring out my Blessings Journal and remind myself of the Lord's limitless favor.

Writing in a daily gratitude journal is a great way to cultivate thankfulness. Every day, we can write at least five things we are thankful for. Sharing with our family what we are thankful for as we say grace before dinner is another way to practice gratitude. It also gives us an insight into the inner lives of each of our children. As we continue to do this, it becomes a habit, which then becomes a mindset, which then brings a lifestyle of joy and thankfulness.

Adopt a Pet

I believe God designed cats and dogs to be companions to us, to show us love, and to heal us. I cannot think of any other purpose to have an animal living in my house that I feed and care for, that has no chores or responsibilities, and that can't wait to see me every day. Dogs and cats are healing.

Scientists now know that dogs and cats provide physical and emotional health benefits for their owners.[228] These include lower blood pressure and stress levels. Pet owners are less likely to suffer from depression and isolation. In addition, they experience longer survival rates after a heart attack, need fewer visits to the doctor, get more exercise, and have lower triglyceride and cholesterol levels. Playing with a pet produces dopamine, oxytocin, and serotonin, hormones that enhance mood, facilitate bonding, and reduce stress. Interacting with a pet also reduces levels of cortisol, the stress hormone, resulting in lower stress levels, better heart function, and lower blood pressure. Cats and dogs provide companionship, unconditional love, and caring, which is particularly nice when these traits have been missing from your human relationships. Having a dog is a good way to meet others,

---

[228] "The Healing Power of Animals," *What's Your Grief*, March 28, 2017, https://whatsyourgrief.com/healing-power-of-animals/; Meg Daley Olmert, "Dog Good," *Psychology Today*, May 5, 2010, https://www.psychologytoday.com/us/blog/made-each-other/201005/dog-good.

whether by walking the dog, at a pet store, in a training class, or as a member of a dog club. Some breeds make ideal service dogs, and owners can meet others as their dog attends a senior center, nursing home, or children's center. Caring for a pet gives their human a sense of purpose and belonging, in addition to giving them a focus outside of themselves. Horses and equine therapy are also known to have healing benefits.

Of course, a pet should be chosen with full awareness of the needs of the species, breed, and individual pet. Cats generally require less maintenance than dogs, while dogs are generally more affectionate than cats.

In the end, choosing a rescue animal is often the best choice. The cost of a rescue from a shelter is reasonable compared to buying from a breeder. Rescued animals are often grateful to their humans for rescuing them, and they show a lifetime of love and affection. While we may rescue them, they also rescue us. That's how love works.

Education about Domestic Abuse

Educating ourselves about domestic abuse is healing. Oftentimes, a woman has no idea that she married a narcissist, sociopath, or psychopath or that she was in an abusive relationship. She just knows that nothing seems to be right and she doesn't know how to fix it. Educating herself about domestic abuse helps her understand what she went through, lets her know that it was not her fault, and facilitates the healing process. As she reads, she may finally feel understood. *"Yes, that's exactly what he did. Yes, that is just how I felt. It's good to know it's not just me."* It is important, of course, that the education comes from experts in the area of supporting victims and survivors of domestic abuse, not from someone who takes the side of the abuser or dismisses abuse as a minor offense or even the right of a husband.

See the Appendix for additional resources.

Listening to Music

Music is one of God's most beautiful gifts. It reaches us in ways that nothing else does. Praise and worship music is a spiritual weapon that defeats the devil and sends him packing. He hates to be around when we praise God, especially in the middle of our mess. If a woman is feeling anxious or stressed, this is Satan's grip. But when we burst into song and praise God, it changes the atmosphere: the Holy Spirit invades our space, Satan leaves, and our anxiety and stress are lifted.

A few of my favorite praise and worship songs that speak to the heart of a domestic abuse survivor are listed in the Appendix.

Uplifting music of any type is good for the soul. Personally, in addition to Christian praise and worship music and the old hymns, I sang and listened to a lot of country music during my recovery because hearing the country singers crooning about how much they loved their sweethearts gave me hope that there were still good men in the world. Obviously, music with violent lyrics or discordant, non-melodious music is not healing and should be avoided.

Playing and singing music is healing as well. Dusting off the piano keys, pulling your old saxophone out of the closet, or belting out "Respect" with Aretha Franklin uses a different part of our brain—a creative part that has healing powers.

Creating

Creativity of any sort uses a different part of our brain than the logic and reasoning that we normally use. As we create things, rather than simply sitting and taking things in, we use this creative region in our brain that has healing powers. God is creative—the whole world shouts His creativity, whether it is the varied topography, the thousands of different creatures, the uniqueness of every flower and tree, or the diversity among all of us humans. When God made us in His image, He designed us to be creative just like Him.

Creative artistic activities can include painting with acrylics or oils, pastels, watercolors, or any number of media, pottery, sculpting, or drawing with charcoal, pencils, or pens. Creative musical activities can include playing an instrument, composing music, or singing. For the tech savvy, creativity might look like photography, graphic design, or videography. For those who like to wear their creativity, jewelry making, weaving, sewing, knitting, or crocheting might be their activity of choice. For those who like to use their creative projects in their home, building furniture, wood carving, or crafting might be good options. For book lovers and writers, writing poetry or prose, journaling, or scrapbooking brings joy. Women who enjoy creating a beautiful home will find delight in decorating or redecorating their home. Those who are blessed with a green thumb will enjoy planning and planting a garden. And the chefs among us will find their creative outlook in creating new recipes, cooking, and baking. The options are virtually endless. Don't worry about being good or bad—just do it. You are in a no-judgment zone. It's fun to learn something new, and taking a class at a local studio, recreation center, or community college is a good way to be creative, learn, and meet new people. But most important of all, creativity leads to healing.

Read or Listen to Good Books

Reading quality books helps expand our minds and calm our souls. Because women who have been in abusive relationships need to heal spiritually, books about God can help reject the lies they've been told and replace them with truth.

Bill Johnson is one of those pastors and authors who has a vibrant church and sees God work miracles on a regular basis. He expects God to show up—and of course, He does! Bill Johnson heads up Bethel Church in Redding, California. His books were incredibly healing as I learned a better view of God and our purpose on this earth. *God Is Good: He's Better Than You Think* and *Hosting the Presence* are good ones to start with. He also has videos and seminars. Other folks who are on fire for the Lord and have written books include Danny Silk, Mike Bickle, and Heidi Baker, to name a few. A list of recommended reading is included in the Appendix.

Reading or rereading some of the classics is a good way to expand our minds and heal at the same time. Socrates, Plato, Homer, Tolstoy, C. S. Lewis, Henry Blackaby, Jane Austen, J. R. R. Tolkien, Mark Twain, Lewis Carroll, Louisa May Alcott, J. M. Barrie, Shakespeare, Robert Frost, George Washington, and Thomas Jefferson are just a few authors of the must-read classics.

Refuse to Be a Victim

Having the mindset of a victim will bring healing to a screeching halt. Refuse to adopt the victim mindset. We all know the person who has adopted the identity of a victim: she believes the world is against her, bad things happen only to her, and she has no control over what happens to her. She believes she cannot make a good decision, she can't do anything by herself, and all her problems are caused by someone else. Regardless of the outpouring of help she receives from others, she is constantly in a state of crisis, she complains incessantly about all her problems, she is helpless, she needs constant help and attention, and she seeks constant pity from others. She refuses to do the hard work of healing, claiming that she can't. In reality, she can—she simply won't. This is a woman who is still a little six-year-old girl and has not matured into a woman.

God does not want us to remain children. He wants us to be mature, spiritually wise adults who live in the fullness of God. Paul said that when he was a child, he thought and spoke and reasoned as a child, but when he became an adult, he put aside childish things (1 Corinthians 13:11). We, too, must put aside childish, helpless, "someone needs to take care of me because I can't" thinking. God has made us "more than conquerors" (Romans 8:37). We can do all things because God gives us His strength to do so (Philippians 4:13). Do we believe God's promises, or do we think the Bible is merely a fairy tale?

We get to choose our identity. We can choose whether we will be a victim and wallow in self-pity for the rest of our lives or whether we will be victors and partner with God to make an abundant life for ourselves and our children. We cannot change our past, but we can certainly start now and change our future.

The words we use can change how we think. Negative thinking leads to more negative thinking and a downward spiral into depression and victimhood. On the other hand, positive words open a path to victory over abuse. Posting positive words on sticky notes, surrounding yourself with inspirational quotes, positive self-talk, and claiming the promises of God out loud can literally rewire our brains and put ourselves on new, positive paths. And as God opens door after door, we can choose to be victors.

For robust discussions on how words can change our brains, read *Words Can Change Your Brain* and *How God Changes Your Brain* by Andrew Newberg and Mark Robert Waldman and *Anatomy of the Soul* by Curt Thompson.

No Contact with the Abuser

It cannot be emphasized enough. A woman who is in contact with her abuser cannot fully heal. Abusers will use every opportunity to be nasty, vindictive, and hurtful. Do not give them the opportunity.

The relationship between an abuser and his victim is like the relationship between a sharp knife and a finger. Every time a sharp knife comes in contact with the finger, it will cut and hurt the finger. It is the nature of the knife to cut because it is sharp; it is the nature of the finger to be cut because it is soft. If the knife continues to encounter the finger, it will continue to cut it, and the finger will never heal from its wound. In fact, the wound is likely to get infected and become worse due to the constant damage done by the knife, until the finger no longer functions as intended.

However, if the finger no longer meets the knife, it can heal. The finger may still have a scar where it was cut, but the wound has healed and the finger is useful again.

An abuser will always cut and damage when he encounters his victim—that is his nature. And the victim will always be hurt by the abuser—because she is human. Continued contact with an abuser will not allow her to heal. No contact will allow her to heal. Even though she will have a scar on her heart, it will no longer be a gaping wound.

Some women feel they need to get even with their abuser or make him look bad in front of others in revenge. This course of action will undoubtedly backfire. Abusers are far more cunning and devious than godly women are. Their Machiavellian instincts are finely honed. He will turn even her benevolent efforts against her, and much more so any efforts to get even. Jesus warned, "For the people of this world are more shrewd in dealing with their own kind than are the people of the light." (Luke 16:8) The best course of action is to stay far, far away.

As explained in more detail in chapter 28, if contact is required for children, try to arrange for communications to go through attorneys rather than directly. A court-approved email system is a far less desirable option. Keep communications simply to the facts. If the abuser continues his harassment, don't hesitate to bring it to the attention of the judge for a reprimand.

Creating a New Home

God designed the home to be a sanctuary of healing, acceptance, love, and peace. Sadly, for the woman recovering from domestic abuse, her former home was anything but. However, this is the time for her to make a home that she and God design and furnish together.

Most abusers want control of everything and want all the assets gained in the marriage—including the big family house and all the furniture. To them, it was all theirs anyway. To that I say, "Let them." Let him have the big house and the fancy furnishings; she can have the equivalent in cash. The family home is usually a lot to take care of for a newly single woman—it requires painting, mowing, shoveling, pruning, landscaping, planting, utilities, HOA dues, real estate taxes, repairs, maintenance, new appliances, new HVAC, new water heaters, and a new roof. And those are just the things we expect to happen. In addition, there is the occasional unexpected—a flood, a dead tree, a kitchen fire, a lightning strike, or a hail storm that requires a new roof. It all takes time and money.

The wise financial move for most women recovering from an abusive marriage is to take the cash and figure out *where* she wants to live and *how* she wants to live. It is likely that she will want to put some space between herself and her abuser; who wants to run into him at the local grocery store? To heal properly, she will want to adjust her lifestyle so that it is a gentle, healing lifestyle in a gentle, healing home in a gentle, healing community. The days of breakneck speed of life where everything and everyone swirls around the SNAP are over. For her to explore her options, she may want to rent for a year to determine what's best for her and her children. Renting also lets her off the hook for maintenance—she can simply call the landlord when the toilet breaks.

When she is ready to settle down, it can be in a home that speaks to her heart in a community where she feels at ease and safe. A wise woman will invite God to join her in shopping for a new home. After all, God already has a wonderful life planned for her and a lovely home picked out for her in one of His favorite neighborhoods that is just right for her. A wise woman seeks God's holy guidance when looking for a home, and He will reveal Himself to her when she earnestly seeks Him. Of course, it is wise to live *under* her means so that she can have a chance to save and have a reserve for when unexpected things arise. Making a budget is key to knowing how much she can afford.

Once she has her own home, it will need furnishing. The furnishings in the family home may have been expensive or something brought from college, but they all have memories of their life together. The kitchen table holds the memories of hundreds of arguments, and the master bedroom furniture will remind her of the sexual abuse. It's time to furnish her new home with things that she picks out that have no bad memories attached. The most economical (and fun) way is to look at resale shops, consignment stores, thrift shops, flea markets, and estate sales. She can furnish her entire home from these sources inexpensively in whatever style she chooses. The abuser probably doesn't know that furniture, rugs, lamps, art, designer kitchen equipment, china, crystal, and other furnishings just like his expensive furnishings that he insisted on keeping in the divorce are being sold for ten cents on the dollar. This is great for her, particularly if he overestimated the value of his furnishings (as abusers are wont to do) and she received an equivalent amount in cash.

If she is decorating on a budget (and who isn't?), there are lots of websites and magazines to get ideas so that she can do it herself. One popular website is www.houzz.com, which has hundreds of thousands of photos to browse through for any style, any room, or any outdoors. Unlike other websites that are typically just online stores, Houzz offers professional photos of the work of thousands of designers, in addition to resources where she can shop.

Once she moves into a home, she will want to make it her own. Almost every designer will say that a new coat of paint is the way to get the most bang for the buck. Soothing colors that can help calm frazzled nerves is a good start. If she has the time, painting (or anything that requires sanding, such as refinishing floors) before she moves the furniture in will avoid splatters, dust, and moving furniture multiple times, and will make it easier in the end. For the traditional home, a light pale yellow with white trim goes with nearly every color, and is an inviting, neutral backdrop for the classic styles of country French, Chippendale, Sheraton, French Empire, William and Mary, Queen Anne, Victorian, Hepplewhite, and Federal. I always say that nearly every traditional room needs a little touch of red—perhaps in a vase or pillow. In the bedroom, where soothing colors are preferred, instead of red, use a touch of black for the pop—perhaps in a lamp or accent piece of furniture. For the more modern or transitional home, shades of gray, taupe, and beige are quite popular now. A little pop of color—blues, reds, and turquoise are in vogue now—in a pillow, rug, or an accent piece keeps the "greige" from being too monochromatic.

When she is ready to start shopping for her home, www.estatesales.net is a website where people hosting estate sales can list the sale and upload photos of the items that are being offered for sale. Typically, professional estate sale companies advertise on it, but individual sellers can advertise too. It makes shopping for estate sales much more efficient, as shoppers can see the online listing and photos of items for sale and focus on those sales that are of the most interest. As a rule of thumb, many estate sales will allow some negotiation on price, especially if someone is buying a few items. I have found that about one-third off the asking price is the "sweet spot" if buying in bulk. Typically, after the first day, prices are slashed 50 percent to encourage shoppers. The items remaining at the end of an estate sale are often given to local donation sites and thrift stores, usually because the family is either moving or someone has died. In any event, the sellers will often sell things at a very good price to move it out.

Other good sources of reasonably priced furnishings are resale shops, consignment shops, and thrift stores. In the Chicago area, one of my favorite places to wander is Village Treasure House in Glenview (www.villagetreasurehouse.org.) The name is befitting, as it is a warehouse full of beautiful treasures from the lovely homes of Chicago's Northshore at very reasonable prices, and all their proceeds are donated to organizations that help women and children. Another favorite spot is Upscale Rummage Sale in Libertyville (www.upscalerummagesale.org), with an enormous warehouse filled with clothes, housewares, furniture, rugs, art, and furnishings. All proceeds go to support local charities. When I am in the area, I usually try to stop in Forest and Found in Lake Forest (www.forestandfound.com) and say hello to Diana, the proprietor. The shop always offers high quality clothes, as well as unique home furnishings and jewelry. Making the rounds, I try to catch Renew in Libertyville (www.renewfamilyconsignment.com). Renew is a for-profit consignment shop carrying furniture, home furnishings, designer handbags, upscale children's clothing and shoes, and sporting equipment. Finally, Sparrows Nest Thrift Stores have a number of quality thrift stores in the Chicago area (www.hosparrow.org) that donate to the Home of the Sparrow women's shelter.

Most towns will have a quality thrift store. If not, a trip to a larger town or purchasing online on eBay may be called for. Higher quality merchandise will usually be found in the more affluent towns from where the stores receive donations. In addition, many towns also have Goodwill and Salvation Army thrift stores, as well as Habitat for Humanity ReStores that sell home improvement items such as cabinets, sinks, toilets, appliances, and lighting fixtures in addition to furniture. Thrifting can be great fun, and in the end, she will have a gorgeous home that is ready to make beautiful memories at a reasonable price.

With homes come projects. She will want to obtain a good set of tools to keep her house and yard well maintained. These, too, can be purchased at garage sales and estate sales at reasonable prices. If she is not already handy, YouTube has videos on how to do nearly anything. It might also be a good idea to hire a reputable handyman for some projects.

Of course, when she finally has her home, she will want to thank the Lord for His provision and to ask Him to fill her home with love, peace, and good people. That is a prayer right in the center of His will. He will answer that prayer!

When I finally came out of hiding and was able to buy my home, I literally fell prostrate on the floor and thanked God for providing me with a safe and beautiful home to live in. I asked Him to use it for His purposes and His glory, and to fill it with good people. The Lord honored my request, and it has been a safe place of peace and love and rest for me and everyone who has walked through the doors. The Lord uses it as a safe house to give shelter to women and children who need an emergency place to stay, and each one has been a blessing to me. In European fashion, I named my home *Frieden Und Liebe Haus*, or FLH for short, meaning "House of Peace and Love" in German.

To put the finishing touch on her new home, she may want to hang a House Blessing in the foyer and host a House Blessing Gathering to thank the Lord for His provision and to bless her new home. I wrote my first House Blessing as a gift to a dear couple, the Kellers, who bought their first house together after she had left an abusive marriage many years prior:

A House Blessing

May your door be always open to family and friends,
May your foundation be solid rock in a world of sand.
May your roof be a shelter from the storms of life,
May your windows bring fresh breezes off the land.

May your kitchen be the heart of your home
Serving good food and good cheer.
May it nourish the body and the soul,
May it bless all who enter here.

May friends gather 'round your table
With laughter, food, and wine.
May precious memories of the life you share
Be made in the rooms where you dine.

May the bedrooms be the safe haven that renews
Tired bodies and tired minds.
May sweet, sweet rest and gentle sleep
Bring refreshment and renewal sublime.

May New Year's Eve and Christmas Day
And all the celebrations in between
Tie your hearts together with Love,
With cherished memories yet to be seen.

May the language of Love be spoken here
And the gift of Grace freely given.
May the Lord fill your Home with Faith, Hope, and Love.
On earth, may it be a glimpse of heaven.

A list of websites for home furnishings is included in the Appendix.

Making Steps toward Financial Security

Almost every woman recovering from an abusive marriage needs to take steps to recover financially. Abusers don't play fair during the marriage, and they certainly don't play fair during a divorce or after a marriage.

The first thing that is imperative for a woman to do is to ensure that her marital settlement agreement and parenting agreement provide for the proper amount of child and marital support and divides the marital assets equitably. Each state has a formula for the minimum amount of child support, marital support, and division of assets; however, abusers will always try to evade it. Abusers will purport poverty and claim that they have no assets and little income. It may seem like she needs to turn into Sherlock Holmes to uncover the truth, but it is important to do so for her financial future and that of her children. Her attorney can help her with subpoenas and discovery requests. If the purported amount of his income is unreasonably low, the court can impute his income based on what he should be making based on his level of education and experience. For example, if he has a master's degree in information technology with ten years of experience at a large company, but he only reports that he makes $15,000 a year, the court will assign him a salary that is commensurate with his education and experience using the Department of Labor guidelines.

Second, it is imperative for a woman to ensure that the child support, marital support, and asset division set forth in the marital settlement and parenting agreements are actually paid. Abusers will always disregard financial obligations if they think they can get away with it. One characteristic of abusers is their refusal to honor obligations. Sometimes, whether because of her giving nature, she feels guilty for being paid, she doesn't want to cause an inconvenience for him, it is too costly in legal fees, or she is intimidated, a woman will not require that her ex-husband pay the obligations in the divorce agreement. However, as an essential part of her healing, a woman must learn to financially protect herself and her children and hold her ex-husband accountable.

Third, making a budget is important so that a woman knows her financial condition, how much she needs to make, how much is available for living expenses, and how much she can put into savings. Many women have been removed from the budget process during their marriage, so it is doubly important to learn this important information. Putting pen to paper, establishing a budget, and keeping to the budget is important for every household. The post-divorce budget may be significantly smaller than the budget during a marriage. Therefore, it is important to find ways to both make extra money and save extra money.

For women who have stepped out of the workforce for a few years, it is important to find gainful employment that will pay the bills and provide some extra for savings or for those unexpected expenses. Getting back into the workforce can be a bit intimidating. If she needs new skills, such as computer skills or working with software such as Word or Excel, taking a course at a community college will help her gain skills and allow her to be around people in a learning environment. Since she is in a period of healing, it is wise to ease back into the work world and look for employment at a supportive organization in a position with a minimal amount of stress. Sometimes local not-for-profit organizations, such as churches, colleges, nursing homes, or local agencies, can provide a healthy, low-stress atmosphere for those returning to the workplace. Temporary agencies that match companies with workers are also good places to explore, since many employers will offer temporary workers full-time employment if they find the right person. For professionals, working with a search firm (also called a head-hunting firm) will make the job search more efficient.

If finding a job that pays well and suits her skill sets proves to be difficult, a woman may need to expand her horizons, be open to adventure, and look for unique opportunities. Rather than the regular 9 to 5 job, she may want to explore positions that provide housing and pay for her living expenses so she can save for her retirement. For example, if a woman enjoys young people, is single, and is able to relocate, she might want to explore being a sorority house mom or director (see www.greekhouse.net for a firm that matches sororities with applicants). The salary is approximately $30,000–$50,000 per year, and all food, housing, and car expenses are paid. Serving as a live-in nanny or governess allows her to use her mothering skills while enjoying the comfort of being surrounded by a family. Who doesn't love Mary Poppins? Another adventurous position is working on a cruise line, which has the additional bonus of providing a floating house and food while being far away from an abuser. While looking for a job with an ideal fit, a woman can explore part-time employment, such as substitute teaching, seasonal employment, working at a local store, marketing companies looking for consumer opinions, opportunities on craigslist, and the like. Starbucks, for example, offers benefits even to part-time workers. Working as an Uber or Lyft driver offers nearly immediate cash flow, while allowing a woman to set her own hours and geographic location. The options are nearly limitless when we open our options up to out-of-the-ordinary ventures.

Taking advantage of company-sponsored 401(k) retirement plans and individual retirement accounts is one of the smartest moves anyone can make. Putting money aside for retirement that will grow tax-free, especially if her company has a matching policy, is a smart financial decision that will reap benefits. She should start putting funds aside as soon as she is able.

Perhaps this is a time to further her education and change careers. Again, community colleges are excellent, reasonably priced institutions of higher education that can prepare her for a new career. Or it might be a good time to finish the bachelor's degree or master's degree that she has been working on. Most schools have online options that allow her to work and take online classes when it is convenient for her. In addition, almost all colleges have financial assistance, and some are even free. Thus, the published cost of most colleges is usually nowhere close to the cost actually paid by most students. Most colleges have a career services center for students that she can use to secure employment.

Saving costs on living expenses can be challenging, but not impossible. The biggest costs are usually housing, health insurance, childcare, and food. As women are working toward financial independence, they should not feel guilty about taking advantage of organizations and government programs that can provide a little short-term boost. When they get back on their feet, many women give back to others who need a helping hand. Online internet searches will be able to help her find cost savings on most of the large-ticket living expenses.

Some local domestic abuse shelters offer free housing, reduced cost housing, or assistance with housing costs. Other agencies may also offer housing assistance. Doing a Google search for "[your county's name] County Housing Authority" will put you in touch with your local agency that provides housing assistance. Some women find a roommate or another mom with children to split the costs of a home. House sharing has the additional bonus of providing companionship, emotional support, and free childcare for each other when needed.

Health insurance has become outrageously expensive for many. However, if a woman is unemployed or her employer does not provide health insurance and she meets the income qualifications, she can check into the government-sponsored health insurance programs—Medicaid or Children's Health Insurance Program (CHIP). In addition, Christian healthshare programs such as Medi-Share or Christian Healthshare Ministries offer healthcare sharing options at significantly less cost than traditional insurance. These healthsharing programs typically do not provide as extensive coverage as traditional insurance, however. For example, many do not cover wellness programs, preventative health treatments, psychological treatment, or out-of-wedlock pregnancies. In order to be eligible, members must typically represent that they do not engage in activities that fall outside the church guidelines. For example, members agree to not cohabitate with people of the opposite sex, drink to excess, or use recreational drugs.

When it comes to childcare, some women can arrange for a parent or relative to watch their children. Such an arrangement can create lifelong bonds between the childcare giver and the child. Others will use a neighbor who operates an informal childcare business from her home. These are often significantly less expensive than corporate-run, for-profit childcare companies such as Kindercare. Some local agencies, including the YWCA, offer childcare assistance for qualifying individuals.

With respect to savings on food, many local churches and organizations have food pantries with regular hours. The Supplemental Nutrition Assistance Program is a federally funded program, formerly known as food stamps, for low-income households. Many schools have programs that provide breakfasts and lunches. If a woman has enough room for a garden, she can grow her own fresh vegetables. For the more adventurous, many raise chickens for their own eggs.

Clothes, toys, and sporting goods that are slightly used but still in good condition can easily be found for greatly reduced prices at thrift stores, resale stores, consignment shops, garage sales, and estate sales. Once a woman realizes she and her children can look fantastic for pennies on the dollar compared to retail stores, she may never shop at retail again!

Reliable transportation is critical. However, one of the biggest financial mistakes women tend to make is to go out and buy a new car, which saddles them with large monthly car payments. A car's value depreciates 20 to 30 percent within the first year, and 40 to 60 percent after the first three years. After five years, the value has depreciated by at least 60 percent. Buying a good used car with low mileage and driving it until it dies is usually the most economical way. In addition, maintaining a car with oil changes every 5,000 miles and new tires every 30,000 to 50,000 miles (depending on the tires) should keep a car running well into the 150,000-mile mark or more.

Women recovering from abusive marriages have often been the "givers" to such an extent that when the abuser (the "taker") asked (or demanded), she gave up her career and financial security. Her life revolved around him. Even after the marriage, she finds it hard not to give of her limited resources to her adult children, her extended family, her friends, her church, and organizations seeking donations. It is important for women to understand that their own financial health is not only important to themselves, but also to their children. As mothers, we want to be a blessing to our children. One of the best ways to be a blessing is to be emotionally, physically, spiritually, sexually, and financially healthy so that our children don't worry about our future or theirs. Healing in these areas should be our number one priority after an abusive marriage. Therefore, it is important to say no to requests that deplete us of our money or time so that we can say yes to opportunities that will provide desperately needed finances. If a relative or church asks her to do a "favor" that requires a tremendous amount of time, which she should be spending on making money, she needs to give herself permission to say no.

In essence, making emotional, physical, spiritual, sexual, and financial healing our first priority can help us say "no" to a lot of mediocre or even good things so that we can say "yes" to the best things for ourselves and our children.

CHAPTER 46

Healing Our Children

Children's biggest fears are losing a parent and divorce. A divorce rips apart their world, and they struggle with their fears and feelings. Oftentimes children feel they are responsible for their parent's divorce. After all, the arguments were often about how to raise the children.

A mother must always be intentional about raising her children. Children don't just grow up into mature healthy adults without a mother's wisdom and guidance. However, mothers navigating the stormy waters of raising children during and after an abusive marriage have a burden not shared by women in healthy marriages. Therefore, she must be particularly intentional in raising children in this volatile environment. The primary role of a mother who has gone through domestic abuse is to assure her children that they are loved by her and by God, that she will always be in their lives, that God will provide for them, and that they were not the cause of divorce.

Many of the lies that women believe, which were discussed in chapters 41–44, are also the lies that children believe. A wise mother will help her children identify the lies that they have believed and help replace them with the truth.

Roles will vary based on the circumstances. While no two situations are alike, we know that abusers and their behavior are predictable, and we know that the effect of their abuse on children is predictable as well. Below are a few guidelines to keep in mind as we help our children heal.

Children Who Are Targets of Severe Abuse

A child who is the target of physical, sexual, or extreme emotional and verbal abuse will likely be relieved to be rescued from the abusive father. Safety is the top priority. It is important to protect the child, ensure that an order of protection is in place, and listen to the wishes of the child. This is easier when the abusive parent is facing incarceration for a crime. However, most abusers are never convicted or even charged with a crime. Thus, most abusers face no repercussions for their abuse.

Even when there has been abuse, courts will oftentimes try to reconcile the child with the abusive parent. This is beyond the comprehension of most people and flies in the face of common sense. In the opinion of most sensible people, a child should not be forced to visit a parent who has abused him or her. Nonetheless, the courts will be involved in the custody and visitation decision unless the father is incarcerated or dead. If visits with the child are ordered by the court, the mother needs to ensure that any court-ordered visits are safe. Supervised visitation under the watchful eye of a domestic violence visitation program, drug tests prior to visitation, and no overnight visits are a necessity when the child has been a victim of abuse. Children need to know that their mother is fighting for them and protecting them as much as humanly possible.

Oftentimes a court will appoint a guardian ad litem (GAL) or child representative to ensure that the best interests of the child are represented. The mother should feel free to share with the GAL or child representative anything that disturbs or concerns her. The children will also talk to the GAL or child representative. However, it is important that they share their own concerns, not just the concerns of their mother. GALs and child representatives have a great deal of influence in a courtroom, and they frown on any mother who coaches her children on what to say to them. Children sometimes want to talk directly to a judge; however, that is up to the discretion of the judge.

Children who are victims of abuse are hurting, and they need to replace the lies with truth, just like their mother does. They need a wise and compassionate mother to help them with this process. For example, a child needs to reject the lie that if he had been a better child, the abuse would not have happened. He needs to know that nothing he did justified abuse, and that abuse is never right. A child needs to reject the lie that he was the cause of the divorce and replace it with the truth that the abuse was the cause of the divorce. A child needs to reject the lie that there was something that he could have done to save the marriage and replace it with the truth that there was nothing anyone could have done to save the marriage. In short, the child needs to reject many of the same lies the mother does and replace them with the truth.

Children who themselves are victims of abuse also need a sensitive mother to walk them through and resolve the cognitive dissonance that comes with an abusive parent. For example, children want to believe that their father is a good man who loves his family, but his abuse informs them otherwise. The child must either ignore the facts or the definition of *good* so that he can still believe his father is a good man and loves his family, or the child concludes that his father is not the good man he thought he was. If he concludes that his father is not the good man he thought he was, he will likely feel compelled to protect himself and change his attitude and behavior toward his father.

A sensitive mother, with some coaching from a therapist, can ask the child questions so that the child comes to his own conclusions about the abuse and his father. For example, the following conversation might occur:

> Child: Mommy, why is Daddy so mean?
> Mom: I'm not sure. It's complicated. We know that people who love God are loving to others, but people who don't love God aren't loving to others. Why do you think Daddy is so mean?
> *Conversation ensues including the child's thoughts on abusive behavior.*
> Child: Doesn't he love us?
> Mother: You know what love looks like. We know from the Bible that love is patient and kind, not self-serving, not arrogant or boastful, it's always truthful and always does the right thing, and love always wants the best for the other person. When someone hits somebody else or yells at somebody else, is that showing love?
> *Conversation ensues on what loving and right behavior is and what abusive and wrong behavior is.*

However, mothers walk a fine line between helping children see their abusive father for who he really is so they can heal, and encouraging parental alienation. It is not healthy or healing to berate, curse, or rail against someone's parent. That child knows that half of his or her DNA came from the father, and the child will likely feel that he or she is bad and cursed if she is constantly told that the father is bad and cursed. If a child is told, "Your father is a good-for-nothing a**hole and should be shot," the child hears, "You are a good-for-nothing a**hole and should be shot." On the other hand, children should never be told excuses for an abuser's behavior, because there are no justifications for abuse, and such excuses will only confuse them. For example, if a child asks why his father was so mean, we must not say to a child, "Daddy ran us over because he was having a bad day, and we should not have been playing in the way when he drove in the driveway." There is no justification for a father running over his family, and they had every right to be in their own driveway. The most helpful and healing thing might be to say, "It is never right for anyone to lose their temper and hurt someone else, especially their own family. Families are supposed to love each other. You did nothing wrong. Daddy was wrong. When you grow up and become a daddy, you will know to do things better. Jesus is our example of how we need to treat and protect others."

Children of abuse will need to attend therapy with a skillful therapist who understands domestic abuse and trauma-informed therapy to express their concerns and to be given the tools they need to heal. At some point, perhaps when the child reaches adulthood, the child will need to decide whether they want a relationship with their father.

Children Who Are Not Themselves Victims of Severe Abuse

However, children who themselves have not been direct victims of physical, sexual, or severe emotional and verbal abuse can be more difficult for a mother to help heal. These children have not seen the extent of their father's abuse against their mother. And while a mother might expect her children to support her, they seldom do, especially when the children are teenagers or older. Indeed, children often side with their father against the mother.

Why do children support the abuser? When children turn against a loving parent and side with an abuser, parental alienation is occurring. As we discussed more fully in chapters 23 and 24, several dynamics explain this strange but all-too-common phenomenon. They are summarized here:

- The abusive father has already spoken to the children and spread lies about their mother, while the mother has not spoken about adult issues that should be kept among adults. Thus, the children hear only one side of a story. In our patriarchal society, the opinions and authority of fathers and men in general carry more weight than that of women. Children want to believe that their father is a good man and tells the truth; thus, they will often believe these lies without question.
- The father has been manipulating them with money, clothes, vacations, cars, and demands on their time, and the children are too immature to see the manipulation.
- An abusive father will play the pity card with his children, another form of well-thought-out manipulation. It is incredibly hard to be upset at someone you pity, and the abuser knows that.
- An abusive father will have virtually no house rules so that teenagers will naturally gravitate toward the house with fewer rules, compared to the mother's house with sensible house rules.
- An abusive father will devalue the mother, undermine her parental authority, breach the parenting

agreement, exclude her from all family events and decision-making, and try to eliminate her from the lives of the children. In effect, he will treat her as if she never existed.
- An abusive father will play on the insecurities of the children by telling them that the mother will be so poor that she will not be able to support them or that she has a mental illness and will be unable to care for them.
- An abusive father will threaten self-destructive or destructive behavior, like committing suicide, hurting the family pet, or refusing to pay for college, if the children do not do what he wants.
- An abusive father will quickly replace their mother with a girlfriend or new wife. The abuser will tell the replacement the same lies about his former wife that he told his children and others. Therefore, instead of a cooperative relationship between the mother and the new stepmother, the new stepmother carries the same animosity toward the mother of the children that the abusive father does.

Children involved in the dismantling of an abusive marriage are in survival mode. Many choose to side with the abuser to survive the turmoil. They must navigate the new relationships, hostility, and new communication (or lack of communication) patterns that the abuser imposes. Older children instinctively know who has the money and the power in the relationship. They do not want to be devalued, left with no means of support, and discarded by their father just like they have seen him do to their mother. They know that if they side with her, they will be. So some children side with the father for survival, not unlike the kids who side with the school bully so they won't get picked on, or the young women who dated Nazi troops when they invaded their country during World War II. They don't like the bullies, and they don't trust the bullies, but if they are on the side of the bullies, they won't get annihilated. Children know deep down that their mother, the safe parent, will always love them and take them back when they can resume normalized relations, but that their father will not. No one crosses an abuser without consequences. Even children know that.

Other children choose to support an abuser because it is the easiest way to resolve their cognitive dissonance. The children want to believe that their father is a good man; however, their mother's facts are the opposite of what they want to believe. If they can still believe that Dad is a good man, they can go along with their lives with very little change, but if they believe he is guilty of abuse against their mother, this will require them to either (1) acknowledge that their own father is a monster, and if they support him, by association, they are monsters too; or (2) distance themselves from the monster so they are not guilty by association. Either of these two actions is usually too much to bear, especially when they are financially dependent upon their father. Therefore, except for the most principled of young people who have a strong moral compass, most teenagers will resolve the cognitive dissonance in favor of continuing to view their father as a good guy. In order to do this, children need to accept his lies, dismiss the mother's accounting of the facts, justify his behavior, or conclude that she was exaggerating or lying.

Over time, as they grow older, children will likely see through their father's manipulative and controlling behavior and want to develop a closer relationship with their mother. However, they may never see the extent of the abuse against their mother since the abuser will likely want to continue to have them on his side. Therefore, the abuser will need to be on his good behavior, at least while his children are around him.

Some children will take up the torch of their father and continue the abuse on their mother. Unfortunately, children exposed to domestic abuse are more likely to be abusers themselves or to be victims of abusers. These children have learned abusive behaviors from their father and continue to use them on their mother. Sadly, these children share the same distorted moral compass of the father.

Some children choose to side with their father because they are deceived by his smooth talk. These likely are older children who are now out of the house and have forgotten how difficult he was to live with.

And some children choose to side with an abusive father because he has money and it is financially advantageous to the children to support him, regardless of what he has done. This seems to be the case with the children of at least one well-known figure, who support their father despite his many very public affairs, narcissism, bullying, misogynistic outlook, and the fact that his first wife (their mother) publicly accused him of raping her.

Occasionally, an emotionally mature child will navigate the stormy waters of a divorce and remain on good terms with both parents. This is more often the case when a child is an adult and is financially independent so that he does not need to worry about the financial repercussions from his father. This child usually understands the limitations of a narcissist, sociopath, psychopath, or other abuser and manages to maintain healthy boundaries while keeping a relationship with the abusive parent and the nonabusive parent. This child can be an influence for good on his less mature siblings, encouraging them to be more gracious to their mom and bringing them to a closer relationship.

Navigating the Minefield

So, what are some guidelines to navigate through the minefield of strained relationships in the aftermath of an abusive marriage? While each situation is unique, and it is best to seek the advice of a licensed therapist with extensive experience in counseling victims of domestic abuse, here are a few things to keep in mind:

Kids Are Not Our Confidants

As adults, we should not put the burden of adult issues onto our children or take them into our confidence. This is too much of a burden for children to bear. Each woman exiting an abusive relationship needs a trusted therapist and support group with whom to share her thoughts and concerns and obtain the tools for dealing with an abuser. Even if our children are adults, the abuser is still their father, and most of them love their father no matter what.

Kids Are Not Our Spouse

Some women run the risk of making their child a surrogate spouse, sharing things that only spouses should share with each other. Women can become emotionally dependent on a male child, and their lives revolve around the child like they revolved around the former husband. This is also too much of a burden for a child to bear. Regardless of the child's age, mothers need to be emotionally healthy and independent of their children.

Kids Need to Be Allowed to Grow Up

The sad reality is that many abusive marriages break up around the same time children become teenagers, go to college, and need to be independent. Some mothers long for the time when the children were little and dependent upon them, and so they try to keep control over teenagers who simply want to do what teenagers do—express some independence from their parents and get away from the mess at home. As long as they are with a healthy group of friends doing healthy things, kids need to start to become independent. Helicopter moms who control every aspect of their teenager's life do not do them any favors. Teens need to learn resilience, good decision-making, to do things for themselves, and grit. We also must be mindful of where we place blame. We cannot blame a teenager's normal quest for independence on our abuser's parental alienation.

Kids Need to Learn Resilience and Grit—and So Do We

Some of the most important things we can teach our children are resilience and grit. Resilience is the ability to overcome obstacles without being defeated. Grit is a corollary to resilience: the passion and perseverance to achieve long-term goals. Combined, they are the ability to overcome obstacles without being defeated and persisting with passion over a long period, even through failures, until success is achieved. According to researcher, best-selling author, and TED Talk celebrity Angela Duckworth, the number one factor that determines a person's success is not their socio-economic level, their intelligence, the grades they made in school, or the university they attended. The number one factor that determines a person's success in life is grit.[229] Not only do our kids need to learn grit, but so do we.

Fortunately, grit and resilience can be learned. How do we teach our kids and ourselves grit and resilience? First, help your child find his or her purpose. We each have been designed uniquely and wonderfully by our Creator for a mission that no one else on earth can do. God will use all our gifts, talents, skills, passions, and experiences for His redemptive purposes. Incredulously, He will use even our unpleasant experiences for His purposes. We can help our child discover his gifts, talents, skills, and passions and point out experiences that can help him or her realize God's purpose for Him. Until a child discovers his or her purpose, we can point out that God knows his purpose, that He will reveal it over time, and that He is working all things for good.

Second, encourage your child to conduct interviews with family or friends who demonstrate grit. Ask them how they set and achieved a big goal, overcame obstacles, refused to give up, and how they felt when they succeeded. These might be people who fought in a war or overcame a physical illness, abuse, or any number of obstacles.

Third, study people with grit. The Bible is full of them—Abraham, Moses, Joshua, David, Paul, and Peter, to name a few. Modern life is full of them too. Every successful person has had to overcome adversity.

Fourth, practice grit. Have your child choose a difficult goal that he will get feedback on and continue until he achieves the goal. It might be taking music lessons to become proficient at an instrument, running a mile under eight minutes, reading a challenging book, making money to buy something important, taking painting classes, etc. (Playing video games is not allowed as a goal.) Whatever it is, it will build passion because they chose it and perseverance because they cannot quit. When they succeed, or at least improve, it fosters confidence.

Fifth, help your child with problem-solving skills. When you ask your child what the hardest part of a problem is, you help them identify the biggest hurdle. We can then ask how they would fix or overcome the hard part. We should encourage them to formulate some solutions and probable outcomes for each. Even if we need to guide them, our children need to come up with answers themselves, not hear them from us. It helps them realize that almost every problem can be solved when they break it down into a series of smaller problems and take the time to think through them.

Sixth, help your child with overcoming obstacles. We all face obstacles—some temporary, some permanent; some are the result of our own actions, some the result of others' actions. Helping your child identify whether the obstacle he or she is wrestling with is temporary or permanent, how he has contributed to it, and how others

---

[229] Angela Duckworth, *Grit: The Power of Passion and Perseverance* (New York, NY: Scribner, 2016) 8.

have contributed to it will help him discover ways he might resolve it. He will likely find that most obstacles are temporary and that he contributed to them, which means that it is within his power to overcome them. For those obstacles caused by others, he can brainstorm about various solutions to try.

Grit and resilience are invaluable skills as we navigate the struggles of life. The earlier we help our children learn this, and the earlier we learn it ourselves, the better off we will all be.

Kids Will Be Used as Spies by Our Abuser

We know that abusers are vindictive and will use their own children to spy on their mom and report back. Kids are sometimes innocent spies, while older ones are often complicit in their dad's schemes. To the children, his questions may sound like innocent, thoughtful inquiries to see how Mom is doing or to create conversation. He will use every piece of information he can get against her.

How do we counter this? We don't tell our children anything that we don't want to go back to our abuser. This can be difficult, but imperative for our own protection. The easiest way to do this is to focus our conversations on our children, not ourselves. Children are, by their nature, self-absorbed. They love to talk about themselves, their lives, their friends, their school, their activities, etc. There is plenty to talk about when we focus on them, not ourselves.

Kids Share Their Frustrations and Anger with the "Safe" Parent

Mothers often get the brunt of our children's ire, frustrations, and wrath because we are the parent with whom they feel secure in our love sharing the good, the bad, and the ugly. They know that as the emotionally "safe" parent, we will always love and forgive them and will always take them back. David did the same thing with God. In many psalms, David expressed his anger and frustration to a good Father. David knew that God would understand his rantings and welcome him back with open arms after he blew off a little steam. Children save their good behavior for the toxic parent because they know he is unforgiving and that his affection is tied to performance. So when you get the unregulated emotions, be thankful and know you are the safe parent.

The Abuser Will Make the Kids into a Competition

During and after a divorce, an abuser will make everything about the kids into a competition with their mom in order to hurt her. He wants more time with them so she has less; he wants to spend less money on them so she must pay more; he wants to take them to the cool events so they like him more; etc. You can see his manipulation and the stress he puts on everyone, but the kids are often oblivious to it.

How do we deal with this? We don't take the bait. We know his game. As the Brits would say, we stay calm and carry on. Firmly state that the parenting agreement says XYZ, he will follow XYZ, and if he chooses to disregard it, he will hear from your attorney. After a few trips to court, paying lawyers $500 an hour, he may learn to behave.

Plan Things with the Kids First; Then, If Required, Consult with the Other Parent

An abuser will sabotage his ex-wife's plans with the children, particularly if she tries to coordinate plans with him first, as normal parents do. For example, if the mother wants to take the kids to a concert and tries to coordinate plans with their father before buying the tickets and telling the children, the abusive father will likely ask the kids to go to the concert with him and tell the mother they are already busy. To counteract his sabotage, the mother will want to discuss the concert with the children first, and then, only if she is required by the parenting agreement, tell the father of their upcoming plans. If the concert is during the father's parenting time, the children may be able to persuade him to trade time with her. If she is not required by the parenting agreement to inform him, she can simply make plans with the children and attend the concert during her time with the kids. Often times, in their excitement children will share the news of upcoming plans with the father, who then makes it difficult for them to attend. If the father has a history of ruining plans, she may need to keep the concert under wraps and surprise the children with concert tickets during her parenting time with them. This leaves a vindictive father with little opportunity to sabotage plans.

Don't Talk about the Abuser except When a Specific Question Is Asked

Mothers who have been abused will often want to share with their children why they left the marriage. After all, she doesn't want the children thinking she did not have legitimate reasons to divorce their dad. So that the children don't think that she left merely because he left the toilet seat up, she may be tempted to share the details of the abuse that justify her actions.

Further, abusers will tell lies and half-truths and will smear their former wife to the kids to garner favor. He will recount the litigation in a play-by-play, blow-by-blow, one-sided, self-serving story. He is circling the wagons, and he will do anything to get the kids on his team. The children will often come to Mom's house hurling false accusations at her that they have heard from their dad. "Dad said you [fill in the blank of whatever appalling thing that he made up]. How could you?" These false accusations automatically put the mother on the defensive, and she will feel the need to defend herself, to set the record straight, and to rattle off a list of horribles their abusive father committed.

It is usually a mistake to share with the children the details of abusive events leading up to a divorce. In fact, sharing their father's abuse with the children usually backfires on the mother. Due to the patriarchal authority in our society, especially in abusive families, the unfair fact remains that if their dad smears their mom, children will likely believe it and side with the dad. However, if the mom tells the truth about her abuse at the hands of their dad, she will be harshly criticized by the children, and the truth will be labeled as dad-bashing. Yet if she says nothing, the children will likely believe the lies of their dad: Mom had an affair; Mom abandoned them; Mom broke up their family; Mom has a mental illness . . . yada, yada, yada. In effect, it's damned if you tell and damned if you don't. Furthermore, children simply don't want to hear their parents bicker about each other.

So what is a mother to do? In my experience, it's important to do three things. First, remain calm and confident in front of the children. She knows exactly why she left. She is completely justified in leaving based on biblical principles and principles of human decency. Her departure from the marriage is based on his repeated, unrepentant violation of the marriage covenant. She did everything she could to save the marriage, and she does not need to explain it to anyone. Children need to see an air of confidence in their mother rather than a scared mouse intimidated by an angry tiger trying to defend her actions to everyone. An air of confidence signals to the children and others not to mess with her.

Second, unless her children ask direct a question, a mom should not talk about their abusive father or respond with stories of abuse when her children have false stories of "Well, Dad said . . ." Third, she should let them know that she will not engage in juvenile back-and-forth bashing. The matter is an adult matter and he should not put children in the middle; they have not heard the whole truth, and she will not discuss the matter (nor should their dad) unless they have a specific question to ask her. In that case, they should be prepared for the unvarnished, non-sugar-coated, ugly truth. That often stops the conversation in its tracks because children do not really want to hear the ugly truth about their dad. Deep down, they sense that the truth will be ghastly, and they don't want to follow up with a question. Plus, the confident tone of their mother shows them that she is not to be fooled with. However, if the children do follow up with a question, they have been forewarned that the truth is forthcoming.

A conversation in which there is no follow up into the abusive events might go something like this:

> Teenager: Dad says you filed for an order of protection just to be vindictive and to cause chaos at his wedding.
> Mother: I'm not going to respond to that. This is an adult matter, and your dad should not put you in the middle or even be discussing it with you. But if you would like to know the other 99 percent of the story, if you have a specific question, I will answer it. But if you ask me a specific question, you should be prepared for an honest answer, and it may not be pretty.
> Teenager: Hmmm. Okay, can you please pass the potatoes? (She really doesn't want to hear the truth, and she stops asking questions before she must hear the real story.)

Another conversation in which there is follow up questions might go something like this:

> Teenager: I heard that you left because you had an affair and that you abandoned us and filed for divorce just so you could get more money.
> Mother: We are not going to play that game. First, if you have a specific question, then ask it. But be prepared to hear the ugly, unvarnished truth. Otherwise, I am not going to give that comment the dignity of a response. Second, you need to tell me who told you. We are putting all our cards on the table here.
> Teenager: Okay. Dad told me. Did you leave because you had an affair?
> Mother: No, I didn't leave because of an affair. This is why I left. [Calmly explain the facts.] That is abusive. It is not loving. No one should be treated like that. That is a violation of every marriage vow to love, honor, and cherish. I have asked him several times to change, but Dad doesn't want to change, and that is his choice not to change. I have the self-respect to require love and respect in a marriage, and that is my choice. Dad's own behavior caused the divorce, but he is now trying to blame me so that you feel sorry for him. If someone treated you or your siblings like that, I would tell you to leave too. I'm sorry that this is the sad truth. However, if you don't believe me, I have documentation [photos, police reports, orders of protection, text messages, etc.]. If you want to see it, let me know, and I will show it to you. And here is the phone number to my [counselor/pastor/therapist, etc.]. Feel free to contact him/her and discuss it. I have already signed a waiver so that you can speak to him/her directly.
> Teenager: Are you abandoning us?
> Mother: No, I will never abandon you. I will always be your mother, I will always be in your life, I will always love you, I will always support you, and I will always be there when you need me. Just because I moved out of a house that wasn't safe for me doesn't mean I abandoned you. In fact, the prenup your dad demanded before the wedding says that our family home is really his house, not our house, and I must move out if there is a disagreement. So I didn't have much choice. If you want to see the prenup, let me know, and I will show you.
> Teenager: Are you divorcing just so you can get more money?

Mother: No. Divorce is governed by laws, and the law determines who gets what. The judge divides the property based on what is equitable to both sides, and there is a formula for child support and maintenance. Your dad insisted on a prenuptial agreement before we got married—it is a legal agreement that anticipates a divorce and decides in advance what each party will get in a divorce. So ours will be determined by the agreement your dad required. Again, if you want to see the prenup, let me know, and I will show it to you.

Teenager: Dad said you were taking our college money? Is that true?

Mother: I would never take your college money. Here are your college account statements. It is all there. And here is my bank account statement. You can see where I made a payment to your school.

Over time, hopefully, children will see that their father is not telling the truth and will stop bringing up his false accusations to their mother. In any event, unless specifically asked, the focus of conversations should not be on the abusive father, but on other positive things.

Kids Will Test You to See If You Love Them

Sometimes our children put our love to the test. In their minds, they think: *Mom said she loves me, but I doubt it. She will leave me if I act like this [fill in the blank on dreadful behavior].* Then they push the limits and behave badly to see if we still love them. Of course, we cannot approve of bad behavior, but we still love them— and we must tell them so.

For example, after our child behaves badly, we might say something along these lines: "Sarah, you know I don't approve of your smoking pot. That is illegal, and now your coach has kicked you off the team. Behavior always has consequences, and you are now paying the consequences of bad choices. I will always love you. I will not always approve of everything you do and every choice you make, but I will always love you."

Set and Maintain Boundaries

Boundaries are limits that you put in place that you can control. We cannot control others; we can't even control our children. But we can control ourselves and what we will or won't tolerate.

Kids will test our boundaries. At young ages, especially when there is significant stress, kids are still working on their self-control. Since they have seen their abusive father yell and scream at others when he is upset, they may assume that this is acceptable behavior. Teenagers and even young adults may yell and scream at their mother during the stress of a divorce. When this occurs, she would be advised to remain calm, let her child know that she loves him or her and that she will be happy to discuss the matter when the child is calm, and then leave the room so that everyone can take a breath and calm down.

Physically, when we are screaming and our emotions are elevated, we cannot hear when others are speaking to us, and we cannot engage in a rational discussion. Yelling never contributes to understanding or meaningful conversations. We must be calm to hear others. For a mother and her child to understand each other, they both need to be calm.

Sometimes, one of our children grows up to be an abuser himself. This happens far more often in families where one or both parents are abusers. This is a heartbreaking outcome for a mother who has tried to stop the generational pattern of abuse. The abusive adult child often rewrites history in his own mind, plays the victim, slanders his mother, turns others against her, and blames his mother for imagined offenses and lifelong problems that are the result of his own behaviors. He may also be physically violent. These behaviors are nearly identical to the behaviors seen in his abusive father. Setting healthy boundaries is particularly important in this situation, as it may be emotionally, physically, or financially dangerous for a mother to have a relationship with an abusive adult child.

It's Not about Winning an Argument; It's about Moving Forward with Understanding

Parents and children often make the mistake of trying to win an argument by pointing out the other's fault, explaining the other's illogical reasoning, elucidating why they are right and why the other person is wrong, and pointing out all the facts that prove their point. They mistakenly feel that if they win an argument, the other side will back down and admit defeat, and, after seeing the error of their ways, the strained relationship will somehow be restored. This approach will not restore a relationship.

The point to a conversation with a loved one is not to win or lose, but to understand the other person and go forward together in a shared relationship. Most arguments are not about facts, but feelings. It is important to dig deep to find the feelings and heal the pain underneath the anger. Both sides may feel misunderstood and have hurt feelings. Things that were not meant to be hurtful caused pain. Things might have been said that were not meant. An apology is in order when feelings have been hurt, even if unintentionally. A mother must set the example. For example, if a child has had her feelings hurt due to something her mother has said, an apology and attempt to repair the breach of relationship is called for.

The mother might say something along these lines: "Sweetie, I am so sorry that what I said hurt your feelings. I didn't mean to. I had meant it completely differently [explain how it was meant]. And I had no idea that you took it that way and that it hurt you. I am terribly sorry. I hope you can forgive me. I can't change the past, but we can make the future better than the past. From this time forward, I really would like to work on having the best relationship we can. We're not perfect, and we'll never be perfect, so we need to give each other lots of grace. I love you very much. I promise that I will always have your best interest in mind, even if it doesn't come out that way. So please forgive me when I don't say things right, and I will be more mindful of the words I choose and how it comes across. I'd like to start again. What do you say?"

Conversations are not about facts or about who was right or wrong. Conversations must be made with healing, understanding, and moving forward together in mind.

Let Your Kids Know They Are Loved and Valued—Even When the Relationship Is Strained

It is important to know your child's love language and to let them know they are loved and valued unconditionally. To some children, acts of service, such as taking them to their activities, making lunches, or taking their dog for a walk, says, "I love you." To others, words of affirmation and encouragement speak to their heart and let them know they are loved. Some kids respond to gifts as an expression of love. Others need a hug, a back rub, or cuddling on the couch to fill their love bucket. And many feel that just spending time together in a meaningful activity, such as cooking together, watching a movie, or attending their sporting or music events, says, "I love you." (Read Gary Chapman's *The Five Love Languages of Children* for ideas of how to show love to your children in a way they will understand.)

During and after a divorce from an abuser is a turbulent time. It is even more turbulent when it coincides with the children's teenage years. There may be times when a mother's children won't talk to her. They are angry at the situation and punish their mother with the prolonged silent treatment. As the safe parent, she will get the brunt of their ire because they often correctly sense that the abuser would retaliate if he was not properly worshiped by his children. Children often blame the parent who is leaving the marriage and upsetting their world, even when leaving is entirely justified. They likely have been manipulated by their father, or perhaps their mother did not handle a delicate situation well. In any event, children of high-conflict divorce often put space between themselves and their mother and shut down communications.

The silent treatment from her own children is incredibly painful for a mother. Even during times of non-communication and physical separation, children need to know that their mother loves them. A text a few times a week letting her child know she is thinking of him and she loves him is in order. Multiple texts a day may seem suffocating to a child who is trying to create some space, and a lack of texts may be perceived as not caring. But a short text once or twice a week will at least let the child know she is loved and valued, even during difficult times, until the relationship can be repaired. Ironically, even as a child puts up roadblocks to communications, the child often secretly hopes his mother loves him enough to pursue him.

Other times, children, especially teenagers, can be extremely demanding of their mother, even as they disrespect her. If they don't yet have a driver's license or access to a car, they demand taxi services, and they often use their mom like an ATM machine. They also want help with homework and shopping trips, and they make other demands of a mother's time and money, even as they spend more time with their father and are ill-mannered and rude to their mother.

Rather than being annoyed at these requests or telling them to ask their father, a wise mom will view them as opportunities to show the child that he or she is loved and valued. Of course, if a child is disrespectful, setting boundaries requiring proper manners is an appropriate condition for complying with a child's request. "I would love to take you to the mall as long as we can keep our communications positive and respectful" is a reasonable request. Car rides gives a mom time with her child—they can crank up the radio and sing along, talk about the day, stop for quick bite on the way, and grab an ice cream cone on the way back. Inviting friends along helps the conversation and brings the mother into the child's world. If a child's love language is acts of service, this says, "I love you."

Providing twenty dollars to go to the movies, grab pizza with friends, or buy a gift for a friend's birthday party will tell the child whose love language is gifts that her mom loves and values her. It is especially heartbreaking to hear parents try to get out of giving such a small amount by telling their child to ask the other parent. The child, who is totally dependent on his or her parents for support, hears, "You are not worth even twenty dollars to me. Go see if you can get your other parent to care about you." Unless a mother is genuinely close to the poverty level and cannot afford it, giving a child a reasonable allowance or some spending money will not make a difference in her lifestyle, but it will mean a lot to her child.

Helping with homework or going on shopping errands will speak to the child whose love language is acts of service. Encouraging texts, emails, Bible verses, cards, or notes tucked in their backpacks are good for all kids, but especially good for those whose love language is words of affirmation. Most kids who harbor some animosity will not ask for physical touch; however, offering to share a blanket or a back or foot rub while watching movies together on the couch can crack a tough exterior.

The important thing for any mother is to look for ways to let her children know that she loves and values them unconditionally. However that works is the right way. In time, when children know they are loved, the strained relationship between a child and his mother usually heals, and the relationship grows stronger as the child and the mother mature.

Find Time to Do Fun Things with Your Kids

Much of life is filled with commitments and obligations. This is true even for our children. For many kids, most of their time is spent meeting the obligations of school, homework, athletics, band or chorus, theater, lessons and tutors, and part-time jobs. It is important for moms to sneak a few minutes of fun into each week with their kids. It gives both moms and children something to look forward to, gives everyone a break from the unending responsibilities of modern life, picks up the spirits with laughter, and creates lasting memories.

It's important to intentionally create space where a mother and her children can participate in an activity together to facilitate bonding. Passive activities such as watching TV and video gaming do not facilitate bonding and are not encouraged. Further, the hazards of video gaming—including addiction, obesity, sleep deprivation, aggressiveness, and lack of social skills and exercise—do not justify making it a mother-child activity.

So how do we sneak fun into an otherwise busy schedule? One of the easiest ways is to take our kids out to lunch during the week. It gets them out of the school cafeteria and gives them a short treat with Mom. It also gives the kids a chance to be with Mom without having to share their whereabouts with Dad or be subject to his interrogation. Every other time the kids are with Mom, Dad knows all about it and pumps them for information about their mother when they return to his house. Lunchtime can be stress-free mother-child time. If it's okay with other parents, it's fun for the kids to bring a friend or two and give everyone a fun pick-me-up. This tradition can start in grammar school and continue through high school, and even continue during college breaks.

At home, we can plan an evening of cooking, painting, crafting, scrapbooking, playing music, singing, or something creative together. For kids who enjoy sports, a pickup game of basketball, catch with a baseball or football, frisbee, tennis, working out, golf, or jumping on the trampoline is a welcome break. Game night, where the family participates in card or board games, charades, or the like, is a wonderful wintertime way to have fun. Card games with questions is a good way to draw out children's thoughts in a playful way. For a quiet night, reading classic books out loud is a nice way to wind down. A hike in the woods, on the beach, or in the dog park with Fido gets everyone much-needed nature time.

For longer periods of time, staycation trips to the movies, the zoo or aquarium, a museum, a concert, a sporting event, a local festival, an art show, or anything your child is interested in provides fun extended time together. Taking a class together, such as learning a new musical instrument or Italian cooking or how to paint, is an enjoyable way to learn something new together.

Developing at least one thing you enjoy as a family will provide meaningful times together when relationships can be strengthened, not only as they are children, but also as they become adults and start their own families. It can also provide the basis for family vacations as you gather in beautiful places to enjoy shared activities and bond as a family. Family activities might be hiking, skiing, going to baseball games, playing music, tennis, golf, snorkeling, or any number of things. As long as it brings a family together in a healthy way, it is a good activity.

Assume the Abuser Will Lie and Hide Things about the Kids

We know that two primary characteristics of abusers are lying and deception. They will lie and deceive the mother of their children regarding the children to inflict further emotional pain and abuse on her. She must expect this and make extra effort to work around it.

Even with a parenting agreement requiring cooperation, she can anticipate that her ex-husband will not inform her when he takes the child to the doctor or dentist, makes arrangements for school activities and conferences, signs the child up for extracurricular activities, orders school pictures, or even takes the child to the emergency room. She can anticipate that her ex-husband will not provide the doctor, dentist, school, coach, teacher, or college with her contact information so that she will be left in the dark and miss important events in her child's life.

Because she can anticipate his deceitful behavior, she will need to contact the doctors, dentists, school, coaches, teachers, photographers, and college directly, inform them of the situation, provide her contact information, and ask that they inform her of important events and put her on all communication lists.

In addition, she can anticipate that her ex-husband will sabotage any plans that she tries to make with him involving the children. Again, an abuser will use this tactic to intentionally hurt their mother and to keep her from participating in important events in the lives of her children. To avoid this gamesmanship, she can speak directly with the children about planning important milestone events for them.

Further, she can anticipate that her abuser will refuse to provide travel information when her abuser takes the children on trips. Because travel information is generally not shared with the children, this information is generally difficult to obtain without getting attorneys involved and demanding the information set forth in the parenting agreement.

Do the Right Thing and Let the Kids See It

When we are under constant attack, we can be tempted to retaliate in kind and stoop to the level of our abuser. This is a mistake—and it usually backfires. The Bible admonishes us to not repay evil for evil (1 Peter 3:9; Romans 12:17). We must always be intentional about being a role model for our children. We do the right thing not because our abuser deserves it, but because that is who we are.

So what do we do? We show our kids how mature adults are supposed to act. For example, when our ex-husband sabotages our efforts and excludes us from a milestone celebration, the next time we plan a celebration with the children far in advance. Make sure they ask their father for a convenient date he will be available, and be sure that they know he is invited. He may not attend, and it is likely that he won't, given his prior bad behavior. However, the children will see that mature parents include the other in important events. The mother may want to say, "I'm sorry your dad chose not to come to your graduation party. But at least he knew he was invited, because that is just the right thing to do, and that's what mature parents do. Hopefully, he will come the next time." She doesn't need to rub it in that she was not invited to the prior event. They will get the point.

If the children are over eighteen and their father is required to help pay for costs, a mother can ask the children to assist by reminding him to pay. For example, a child may ask for a special graduation present, and the parents agree with the child that they will split the costs. If the abuser has left the mother holding the bag for the entire cost, she can ask the child to remind the father to pay her. It will likely take a few reminders. In this way, the mother is showing that mature people act responsibly, and it is also clear who is not being responsible.

The "Divorce-Activated" Dad

Many times an abusive husband will all but ignore his children during the marriage, preferring to make his wife take on all the responsibilities of raising children while he focuses on making money, furthering his career, hobbies, and other self-centered pursuits. However, when the inevitable divorce occurs, the previously uninvolved dad will suddenly demand parenting time or sole custody. He will take the children on lavish vacations, plan exciting events, buy expensive gifts, buy a house with a pool, and other moves aimed at getting his children to favor him over their mother. I call these fathers the "divorce-activated dads" or the "Disneyland dads." Their true intent is not the best interests of the children, but to ensure they are on his team.

It can be exasperating for a mother who has spent so much time and energy raising good children despite an absent father to see him suddenly swoop in and play the hero. She may prefer he continue his bad behavior so the children can see his true colors. However, the wise mother is intentional about doing what is best for her children, not seeking revenge. The good news is that the father is finally showing some interest in his children, albeit it took a divorce to bring it about and his intentions are not pure. The wise mother understands that if the children are safe, it is best for them to have a relationship with their father, regardless of how it comes about, and she will encourage the children to spend time with their father. However, she will approach the new relationship with due caution because she knows that it may not last and that she may need to pick up the pieces when the father reverts to his true nature.

On the other hand, some fathers continue to pursue their selfish pursuits and seldom spend time with their children, using the divorce as an excuse to dive into work or take up a new sport or activity. They are emotionally and physically unavailable to their children and tend to act more like a benevolent uncle than a father. The wise mother still understands that children need their father, and so she encourages the father-child relationship. However, she also understands the limitations of her ex-husband. She recognizes that even a part-time, benevolent uncle-type relationship with a child is better than no relationship, and she does what she can to foster their bond.

A mother will likely miss her children when they are with their father, and she may wish she had the money that their father has to lavish on them. However, while a wise mother acknowledges the less-than-honorable intentions of her abuser when he springs to life to become super dad after years of dormancy, or the part-time drop-in dad, as long as the children are safe, she will also encourage whatever relationship can be achieved because she understands that children need their father.

The Abuser Will Violate the Parenting Agreement

Abusers are predictable in that they can be expected to violate all agreements they enter. A parenting agreement and marital settlement agreement are no exceptions.

What's a mother to do with constant violations? The answer depends upon the type of violation and the circumstances. Financial violations involving child support or maintenance payments, refinancing or selling a house, or mortgage or vehicle-related breaches can and should be addressed to the court as soon as possible. When a woman waits too long to bring justice, she will often find herself in a worse financial position. For example, many marital settlement agreements require a wife to provide a quitclaim deed to the house (so that it is owned only in his name) and require a husband to refinance the house (so he is solely responsible for the mortgage). However, if she complies and quitclaims the house to her ex-husband, but her ex-husband doesn't refinance or sell the house, he may stop paying the mortgage. Then she will be liable on the mortgage because of his continued breach, but she won't have any ownership in the house because she complied. The abuser's breach of the mortgage and potential foreclosure by the bank will cause severe economic damage to her. Further, failure to pay child support or marital support makes it extremely difficult for a mother to provide the financial stability that children need. In many states, if a parent is required to bring an action to enforce child or marital support or brings a petition for contempt of court for a willful violation of child or marital support payments, the attorney's fees must be paid by the violator. Financial obligations should be remedied as soon as possible to prevent further financial harm.

However, what should she do if her ex-husband continuously brings the children home fifteen minutes late, or brings them home without feeding them dinner, or doesn't show up for visits? These minor violations may be frustrating and annoying, but she must consider the emotional and financial cost of bringing a court action to enforce the agreement. She may end up spending a great deal in legal fees with little to show. All violations should be carefully recorded. However, if she has requested compliance and he continues to violate the agreement, she may be better served by telling her divorce attorney, who can then send a letter to her ex-husband's divorce attorney and request compliance. At some point, the continual letters from his divorce attorney directing him to comply will cost money, and he may decide it is easier to just comply.

The proper responses to major violations concerning the children are harder to discern. For example, if a parenting agreement calls for fifty-fifty parenting time, but the father has determined to keep sole custody of a child, what is a mother to do? If the child is young, the mother has little choice but to seek enforcement of the parenting agreement by the courts. However, if the child is a teenager, the situation is more complicated. With such an egregious and willful violation, she knows severe parental alienation is at play. He has undermined the mother's authority, has told the child he does not need to spend time with his mother, has no house rules, has lied about the mother to alienate the child from her, and has told the child he can do whatever he wants. She is already dealing with a very strained relationship—and a father who is trying to sever it.

If she goes to court to enforce the parenting agreement, she very likely will have an angry teen on her hands who does not want to be with her and may even be abusive like his father. The teen will be put in the middle of an acrimonious situation, and she can be assured that the abusive ex-husband will escalate the parental alienation, blame the mother for taking him to court, and give a play-by-play of the proceedings to the child. The mother-child relationship may deteriorate, even though the court will likely enforce the parenting agreement.

She may wish to explore other ways of enforcing the agreement short of initiating court action. For example, she may wish to contact her attorney and request the attorney to contact opposing counsel and direct his client, the abuser, to comply with the parenting agreement.

On the other hand, she may also need to consider other ways to restore the relationship. For example, she may want to find stress-free ways to spend time together with her child, given the extreme parental alienation. For example, a mom taking her teen out for lunch once or twice a week during his school lunch hour is time they can spend together and reconnect without fear of being interrogated by Dad about time with his mom. Taking time to do things that her child enjoys (see above ideas for planning fun with a child) can also go a long way in restoring relationships. Rebuilding the heart connection so her child wants to spend time with her, rather than going through the court system, may be the best course of action.

Sometimes the wisdom of Solomon is the best advice for a mom amid severe parental alienation. Solomon was approached by two women who both claimed to be the mother of a child. When he suggested the women divide the baby in two, the true mother told Solomon to let the other mother have the child. She loved the child so much that she was willing to give the child up so that he might live. Solomon knew that only a mother's love would make such a sacrifice, and he awarded the child to the woman who was willing to give up the baby.

In a similar way, an abuser will often claim full or joint custody and put the children in the middle of his vindictive game. He will divide the children between the parents, sometimes even forcing them to testify or lie against their mother, without caring how cruel it is to the children or how negatively it will affect them. He doesn't particularly care about the children, but he does want to punish their mother because they are the most precious things in the world to her. Sometimes the most caring thing a mom can do for her teenage children when the abuser has put them in the middle is to refuse to fight and to let the other parent feel as if he has won. Sometimes when an abuser has won a custody battle, he won't even see the child. He just wanted to win against the mother. Once the child turns eighteen and heads off to college, and the abuser has less of a grip on the child, the mother can then work toward reestablishing the relationship.

> Charlotte: In my town of Lake Forest, in the spring of 2012 when I fled my home, three teenage boys threw themselves in front trains within a ninety-day span of time. One lad had such a terrible home life marked by strife and discord, and his divorced parents were so acrimonious, that separate funerals were held by the mother and the father in two separate churches. Imagine a mother and father who cannot even come together in one church to grieve over a son who, because of their own fighting, felt that life was no longer worth living. Reasonable people don't act that way. No one acts that way unless one person is abusive. I didn't want that to be the story of my teenage son. So when his father vindictively took 100 percent custody and acted like I had never existed, even though our parenting agreement required a fifty-fifty arrangement, I chose not to enforce the parenting agreement or put my son in the middle of a custody battle. I was the woman in Solomon's court battle who gave up her child to another parent for the sake of the child. The relationship with my son has healed since then, now that he is older and no longer under his father's iron-fisted control.

Co-parenting Is Impossible; the Best One Can Hope for Is Parallel Parenting

Many women make the common mistake of assuming that their abusive ex-husband will cooperate in co-parenting. A woman can expect her abuser to be uncooperative and controlling and to undermine her authority and sabotage her parenting efforts.

While cooperation and co-parenting with an abuser is impossible, the wise mother knows that parallel parenting is possible. With parallel parenting, each parent has his or her own house rules, and children are expected to live by the rules of the parent they are with. A parent is responsible for making day-to-day decisions regarding the children while that parent has custody. There is little communication or cooperation. The upside is that the mother has less contact with the abuser. She does not need to get the abuser's approval or cooperation for things the children do while in her custody, and the abuser cannot impose his demands on the children while they are not in his custody. The downside is that the parents have little communication or cooperation. The abuser will likely have a vastly different parenting style than the mother, and the children must constantly adjust to different house rules depending upon the parent they are with.

While parallel parenting is far from ideal, it is, in fact, usually the only viable option for the mother who has been in an abusive marriage.

Praying and Fasting for Our Kids

Perhaps the most important thing a mom can do for her kids is to pray for them. God promises to hear the prayers of the righteous and turn His face against the wicked (1 Peter 3:12). Prayer aligns our hearts with the heart of the Father. Prayer moves our hearts—and His. And God alone moves the hearts of those we love.

Fasting brings our prayers to a higher level. Fasting deepens our intimacy with God (Isaiah 58:1–14), gives us authority for breaking strongholds (Mark 9:29), humbles us so that we can have God's perspective (2 Chronicles 7:14), and gives us godly wisdom and understanding (Daniel 10:12).

A wise mother will pray and fast for the protection of her children from the Evil One. Satan is not satisfied with merely her ex-husband. He wants her children too. She prays God's words back to Him and claims the promises spoken of Isaiah:

> Father, I pray that no weapon formed against my children shall prosper, and every tongue that rises against them in judgment they shall condemn. This is the heritage of my children, the servants of the Lord, and their righteousness is from You, the Lord Almighty [Isaiah 54:17]. Protect their minds, their hearts, their souls, and their bodies from the arrows of the Evil One. I pray a hedge of protection with Your angel armies over each of them, from now until You bring them home.

A wise mother will pray and fast for discernment for her children, that they will be able to discern good from evil, that they can tell good intentions from manipulation and abuse, and that the scales will fall from their eyes so they can see all people, including their father, for who they are and their true character. She prays her heavenly Father's words back to Him, using the words of the saints:

> Father, teach my children to mature in their faith, to discern good from evil [Hebrews 5:14], and to recognize children of God by their righteousness and the children of the devil by their wickedness [1 John 3:7–9]. May they never mistake evil for good or good for evil [Isaiah 5:20]. May the scales fall from their eyes so that they will always see clearly, and may they always do justice, love mercy, and walk humbly in Your ways [Micah 6:8].

A wise mother will pray and fast that her children reject Satan's lies and replace them with God's truth, that God will reveal Himself to them, that they would know their identity as children of the King of Kings and who God says they are, and that that God would fill them with His presence. She prays the words of the Almighty God back to Him:

> Lord, teach my children to believe Your truth and to reject the enemy's lies. May You Yourself teach them and reveal Yourself to them. Instill in their heart of hearts their identity. They are Yours, sons and daughters of the King of Kings. May they know that You delight in them, sing songs over them [Zephaniah 3:17], love them [John 3:16], and made them wondrously and wonderfully in Your image [Psalm 139:14]. May Yours be the only opinion that matters to them.

A wise mother will pray and fast that God would turn the hearts of her prodigal children to Himself and to her, knowing that God alone is in the business of changing hearts, and that when their hearts are turned to God, they will also turn to their mother. She will claim the promises of Isaiah and Jesus Himself:

> Father, You have promised that anything we ask in Your will, You will hear our prayer [1 John 5:14]. I know that it is Your will that the hearts of my children turn to You [John 6:39–40]. Soften their hearts, pursue them relentlessly, and turn their hearts to You, first and foremost. And Lord, I know that when their hearts beat the same as Yours, they will turn their hearts to me [Exodus 20:12]. So, Lord, I ask that You turn their hearts to me as well. I claim Your promise that You will gather my

children from the north, south, east, and west and their hearts will return to You. And I thank You in advance for doing so [Isaiah 43:5–7].

A wise mother will adopt the attitude of Job, who offered sacrifices and repentance on behalf of his children in the event they had sinned and had not done so themselves.

> [Job's] sons used to hold feasts in their homes on their birthdays, and they would invite their three sisters to eat and drink with them. When a period of feasting had run its course, Job would make arrangements for them to be purified. Early in the morning he would sacrifice a burnt offering for each of them, thinking, "Perhaps my children have sinned and cursed God in their hearts." This was Job's regular custom. (Job 1:4–5)

She covers them with the redemption of Jesus and, with the authority as their mother, offers repentance on their behalf:

> God, I thank You for my children, and thank You that You have given me authority over them as their mother. With the authority as their mother, I repent on their behalf, and I ask that You forgive them for their sin and cleanse them from all unrighteousness. Bring their hearts into alignment with Yours, and may they walk in Your ways.

A wise mother will always speak goodness, truth, and life into her children, over her children, and about her children to others, and she will claim them for God's kingdom. She knows that Satan, the accuser, is always standing before God in the heavenly courts, accusing her and her children of sin. She will not add any ammunition to his accusations by speaking ill of her children. She will not allow Satan to accuse her child in the celestial courtroom: "Look—Johnny's own mother says he's a bad kid. He's a lost cause. Cut him loose, God, and let me have him." Her words echo the ancient words of the saints:

> Father, I speak goodness and life into these children that You have entrusted to me. They are Yours, and I claim them as sons and daughters of the Almighty God and King of Kings. They have known You since their early days, and I will hold a crown over their heads until they are fully mature and complete in You, and claim the crown in their own right as Your dearly beloved children. Lord, I ask You to fan into a raging fire the small flame that was ignited in their souls the day they came to know You. Mature them, complete them, and perfect them as only You can do. Thank You for the wonderful gifts, talents, skills, and attributes You gave each one. May they use them for Your glory.

Putting God First

As nurturers, some mothers may tend to overindulge their children because of the divorce they have lived through. They focus all their attention on the children, and the lives of the moms revolve around their children, their wants, their schedules, and their every little desire. The mother's work and relationships suffer as she constantly cancels commitments or moves schedules to accommodate the latest whim of a child. This makes for entitled, spoiled children who think the world should revolve around them.

Other mothers tend to focus on themselves and their happiness. They may try to fill the void left by the divorce with dating, going out, activities, or work. Their own pursuits take over their lives, while the children feel left out. This makes for depressed children who feel unloved and unvalued, who may act out just to get some attention.

What are we to do, then, if we can't focus on the child and we can't focus on ourselves? Turn your family's focus not to either the child or the parent, but to the Lord. Keeping your focus on God puts all relationships in proper alignment. Ask not what little Johnny or Mommy want, but what God wants our family to do.

With a God focus, we put all things in proper perspective. Sometimes we need to back off our work commitment or our social calendar because a child needs extra help or attention from Mom as he struggles through a rough patch. God would want us to focus on our child at that time because He cares about people, and at that time, our little one needs more love and attention than our social calendars do. At other times, we need to address a crisis at work or put time into making money, and we cannot attend all Susie's basketball games. God would want us to focus on work because we are to be excellent, dependable, and trustworthy in our commitments, particularly in times of crisis when others are depending on us. He also wants us to be fiscally responsible, good stewards of our resources, and financially supportive of ourselves and our children. Therefore, there is an appropriate time for making money.

Sometimes our children are over-scheduled and we need to allow them time to relax, be still with the Lord, read, and spend time with family. God wants a balance between activities and unscheduled time because that is how He made us. We need to spend time with Him, time at rest, time to create, time to wander in nature, and time to just lie on the grass and watch cloud animals float by. Other times, our children are uninvolved in any activities and spend hours wasted in front of video games and TV sets eating junk food. At these times we need to help them explore their gifts, talents, and passions. God wants us to get up and about because He gave each of us gifts, talents, and passions to use for our enjoyment, to help our communities, and to glorify Him. God is for an abundant, healthy life filled to the brim exploring the world He created for our pleasure—not an empty, unhealthy life addicted to a screen.

Placing our focus on God and His wisdom rather than on the whims of people helps the entire family to set proper boundaries, develop healthy lifestyles, instill correct priorities, and love the people God has entrusted to us so our children are brought up in the love and fear of the Lord.

Chapter 47

New Relationships

Most women coming out of an abusive marriage distrust their ability to accurately assess the character of others. A typical doubt might be: *After all, I thought my former husband was a nice guy when I married him, and look how awful he turned out to be. I am obviously a horrible judge of character.*

Being a person who is sold out for God and choosing a person who is sold out for God is essential for a truly happy, godly marriage. A fulfilling marriage is like an isosceles triangle with a man on one corner, a woman on another, and God at the top. As each person moves closer to God, they also move closer to each other. God wants the best life for us, but we need to actively be seeking His will when choosing a marriage partner and being a marriage partner. Knowing another person's character is paramount. When we surround ourselves with people of godly character, most things take care of themselves. We may not know what the future will hold, but we can be assured that whatever challenges we face, if we are facing them together with someone who is emotionally and spiritually mature, we will be okay.

How do we know someone's character? We observe, we ask questions, and we do a little detective work.

Observation

Observation is probably the easiest place to start. When you are with this person, is he respectful, kind, and considerate, or does he appear arrogant, prideful, and selfish? When you look over the attributes of healthy relationships as outlined in chapters 6, 8, 9, 10, and 11, does your relationship align with those characteristics? The basis of all true relationships is honesty and trust. Is he honest and trustworthy, or have you observed little white lies, excuses, and irresponsibility? Does he take his time to get to know you down deep inside, or does he want to rush into a physical relationship? Does he hold sexual intimacy as a sacred act, or is it just another normal activity that he has engaged in with many others? When he thinks you are not looking, is he kind and considerate to wait staff, service people, the elderly, the handicapped, and those who can do nothing to return a kindness, or does he lose his patience, talk down to them, and have an air of superiority? How does he talk about his mother, sisters, daughters, and other women in his life? Does he hold them in high esteem, or does he dismiss them as second-class citizens? How does he talk about his ex-spouses and girlfriends? Does he claim they are all crazy and it was all their fault, or does he take some responsibility for the breakdown in the relationship? Can you discuss difficult subjects or disagree, or are you afraid of his reaction? Does he value your opinion, or is he dismissive?

You will also want to observe his family and friends. Are his parents kind and accepting of you, or are they critical and unwelcoming? Does his family demonstrate a gracious spirit, or are they judgmental and cruel? Do his friends act like gentlemen and use appropriate language, or do they use profanity and act like cads?

Does his life exude the fruit of the Spirit, or are the fruits of the flesh more apparent? Do people speak well of him with stories of his generosity and acts of kindness, or do they share stories of selfishness, gouging others, a tough businessman, and being a hard-charging drinker? Does he leave blessings where he has been, or does he leave shattered and broken lives in his wake?

A wise woman will vet her potential partner with her friends and family, particularly those with a strong gift of discernment. She will ask them to observe him and ask him questions and share their impressions with her. If he is emotionally mature and has her best interests in mind, he will welcome this, knowing that they are simply protecting someone they love. Objective third parties who have her best interest in mind may see red flags that she overlooked.

Make a List

Sometimes a woman makes the mistake of falling for anyone who is interested in her. He chooses her, and she's all in. It is intoxicating to be wanted. We all want to be wanted, but in a healthy relationship, a woman chooses to be with a certain man, and a man chooses to be with a certain woman. It is a two-way, not a one-way choice.

But how do we choose the right person for us? The wise woman does a great deal of soul-searching to know who she is, what her purpose is, what she wants in a relationship, and who she needs in a marriage partner. This is a process she goes through with God. She also knows what an emotionally, physically, financially, sexually, and spiritually healthy relationship looks like. (See chapters 6–11.) Importantly, when she is not in a romantic relationship, she takes out a few sheets of paper and, with God's guidance, lists three categories: nonnegotiables she needs in a partner, things she won't tolerate in a partner, and things she prefers in a partner. In the first category, she lists all the nonnegotiable characteristics that she needs in a marriage and a potential partner. Equally important, in the second category, she will identify the characteristics she will not tolerate in a potential partner—such as addictions, a criminal background, or a serious, untreated mental illness. In the third category, she lists all the characteristics that she would like to have in a partner, but if he doesn't have one of these, it is not a deal-breaker.

Writing down what she needs in a partner and what she will not put up with in a partner solidifies the character of the person she is looking for. Far too often, when our non-negotiables are not written, they become flexible, and we settle for someone who is not now and never will be a good fit. For example, a woman who is called to be a missionary may be attracted to a handsome man with some wonderful characteristics, but then finds out that he has an alcohol addiction or a mental disorder. If she doesn't have a list or doesn't follow the list she has, she may end up with a marriage partner who will require a great deal of managing because of his addiction and/or disorder. It may be so overwhelming to deal with his issues that it takes her away from God's purpose for her life—that of foreign mission work. However, if she follows her list, she can wish him well and perhaps have a lasting friendship with him, knowing that he may be a good person, but he is not the ideal fit for her and what God has called her to do.

The non-negotiables should generally be based on values, character, health, and maturity. (See chapters 6–11 for descriptions of emotional, physical, financial, sexual, and spiritual maturity and health.) A godly woman needs a man who is sold out for God and is filled with the Holy Spirit. Therefore, kindness, honesty, and humility are just a few examples of the fruit of the Spirit, values, and characteristics that she will want to include on the "must have" list. In addition to someone who exudes the fruit of the Spirit found in Galatians 5 and the characteristics of love found in 1 Corinthians 13, she may need someone with a sense of humor and adventure and who is happy to work with her in a foreign country because she believes she has been called to mission work.

On the other hand, racist, porn-addicted, and convicted arsonist are examples of fruits of the flesh, values, and characteristics that a person will wish to include on the "must not have" list. While we may not know the future, the character of a person remains constant over time, and his character will determine how he will deal with whatever life may bring.

Paul warned the Corinthians to refrain from being "unequally yoked" with nonbelievers (2 Corinthians 6:14 KJV). Many people interpret this to mean that a Christian should not marry a non-Christian, but I believe it goes far beyond that. We should seek to be mature and healthy in all aspects of our lives, and we should seek a spouse who is equally spiritually, emotionally, physically, financially, and sexually healthy.

On the other hand, many things fall into the category of personal preference. They are nice to have, but do not rise to the level of a non-negotiable. For example, whether a person likes football or the theater, barbeque or French cuisine, or country or classical music are personal preferences. These types of differences can make a relationship interesting and expand our horizons.

God has a purpose for you. He wants the best for you. He has an ideal mate in mind for you, too, so this should be a Holy Spirit-led process.

Far too many people believe that they must find someone who is perfectly compatible. They want someone who shares their interest in sports or hobbies or music. However, many interests are personal preferences. It is far more important to find someone who shares the godly values and Christlike characteristics in your nonnegotiables than someone who shares a common interest in sports.

Ruth Bell Graham, who married Billy Graham, penned a beautiful poem about the person she was determined to marry. She originally thought she was going to be a missionary in China like her parents, but if she was going to marry someone, he had to fill very big shoes:

If I Marry

If I marry, he must be so tall that when he is on his knees,
he reaches all the way to heaven.
His shoulders must be broad enough to bear the burden of a
family.
His lips must be strong enough to smile, firm enough to say no,
and tender enough to kiss.
Love must be so deep that it takes its stand in Christ and so wide
that it takes in the whole lost world.
He must be active enough to save souls.

New Relationships

He must be big enough to be gentle and great enough to be thoughtful.
His arms must be strong enough to carry a little child.

Once a woman knows the character of a person she is looking for, she can then ask for God's guidance in finding a person who is the best fit for her. Far too many people fall in love with a person they believe is 90 percent of the person they want, and then they seek to change the final 10 percent to make them into their ideal spouse. Setting out to change a person into an ideal mate is a recipe for disaster. People don't change unless they want to, and they resent it when someone else tries to change them. With a list of non-negotiables that she and God have arrived at, a woman can guard her heart until God's ideal mate for her comes along.

Many women have a hard time coming up with the characteristics they want in a husband and father. I think it is much simpler than we make it out to be. Most of us who have come from abusive marriages grieve the fact that our husbands were not the role models whom we wanted for our sons and daughters. When our children came to us with a question, particularly one with undertones of morals and values, we wanted to say, "What would your father do? Do that." But we couldn't. Our former husbands did not have the Christlike character that we wanted in our children. Therefore, if we marry again, the man we choose should be the godly man about whom we can answer to our children and grandchildren, without hesitation, "What would your father do?"

Take It Slow

Lasting friendships develop slowly over time. They may start over a shared interest. Conversations often begin with clichés or shared facts, the lowest level of intimacy. As each person engages in the conversation on the same level of shared intimacy, the conversation slowly moves toward the next higher level of intimacy, such as sharing opinions, to see if the other person joins. If not, then we step back to a level of intimacy at which we both feel comfortable. (See chapter 6 for a discussion of emotionally healthy relationships and levels of intimacy.) Some relationships are destined to stay at a low level of intimacy. These are often labeled *acquaintances*. Other relationships, such as a healthy marriage, can reach the highest level of intimacy. A developing friendship is a slow, beautiful ballet as each person gets to know the other. Healthy, lifelong friendships develop over months and years.

Frequently, women who have been in abusive relationships reveal everything about themselves in the first date or two. They over trust and over share. Abusers and other toxic people tend to take advantage of that. Abusers often move quickly in securing their next victim. He tells his prey that she is the woman of his dreams, drops the L-word, and talks about marriage within a matter of weeks. It is important for trust to be earned prior to revealing ourselves. We don't show all our cards; we play them close to the vest until the other person has shown over time that he can be trusted. I like to use the analogy of dogs and cats. Oftentimes, women who have been in abusive relationships are like golden retrievers—loveable, beautiful, trusting people pleasers who are all too happy to befriend a perfect stranger, greet a burglar at the door and lead them to the silver, and want a belly rub. We need to be more like cats—they are elegant and loving, but they are wary at first and require complete trust from their humans before they will snuggle up to them or offer them their belly.

Red Flags

One easy way to determine an individual's potential for abusive behavior is how he responds to "no" when he wants something. A safe person will respect the individual's right to disagree, say no, or simply decline an invitation. However, a toxic person will not accept no for an answer. He will expect others to go along with his demands and will hound, cajole, guilt, verbally attack, or explode until you acquiesce to his expectations. A wise woman will say "no" occasionally as a test to see what her new beau does with it.

For example, if her new friend asks her to go to lunch on Wednesday, she will politely decline. A safe person will respond with, "Okay. Sorry you're tied up. Maybe we can try next week." A toxic person might respond with an attack, a guilt trip, an accusation, an insult, or all the above: "You say you want to date, but you're not making any effort. Here I asked you to a nice place and you turned me down. What's with that? Do you have a better offer? Am I not good enough? Whatever else you are doing can't be that important."

Red flags may not appear right away, as most people are on good behavior at first. Over time, as people reveal more of themselves, their true character usually shows through. The following are a few red flags that are indicative of a toxic and potentially dangerous person:

- Witnessed abuse or was abused as a child
- Displays violence against other people, animals, or things
- Enjoys watching violence in the media
- Habitually watches pornography
- Has a collection of guns
- Angers easily
- Abuses chemicals, alcohol, illegal drugs, recreational drugs, or prescription drugs
- Shows extreme jealousy of partner's friends, children, family, job, etc.
- Humiliates partner or others in public
- Isolates partner from family and friends
- Always needs to know his partner's whereabouts
- Expects partner to spend all her free time with him
- Becomes very angry when partner doesn't take his advice
- Has a dual personality—charming in public, abusive in private
- His partner is in fear when he becomes angry
- His partner feels like she is walking on eggshells and makes every attempt not to anger him
- Has definite opinions for male and female roles: males should be in control, strong, and show no emotions; women should be quiet, passive, and feminine
- Has an inconsistent job history
- Has been fired for abuse of employees
- Resorts to violence when he is angry
- Shows ownership and possessiveness of his partner
- Uses phrases like "I can't live without you," "You are the world to me," or "I want to take care of you"
- Pressures his partner to get married or live together
- Pressures, coerces, or forces his partner to have sex prematurely in the relationship, when she is not ready, or when she has other obligations

- Engages in sexual acts that are disrespectful, unloving, humiliating, or degrading
- Has no regard for the law
- Brags about past crimes, breaches of agreements, or treating others disrespectfully
- Drives recklessly
- Disregards the safety of others
- His partner is afraid of what he might do if she ends the relationship
- Has a record of arrests
- Has a reputation as a fighter, philanderer, swindler, or of vindictiveness
- Feels he has certain rights over his partner
- Doesn't want his partner to know about his past
- Hides things from his partner
- Refuses a simple request to use his phone because he is hiding something
- Keeps former partners separate from each other and current partner
- Blames former partners for the breakup and takes no responsibility: "She was a b***h," "She was crazy," or "She was the problem"
- Treats females in his family, at work, and elsewhere disrespectfully
- Insists on handling all the money, including his partner's
- Refuses to let his partner work outside the home or forces her to work
- Shows no regard for his partner's personal health
- Criticizes his partner often for appearance, weight, clothes, cooking, housekeeping, intelligence, being too sensitive, not earning enough, etc.
- Blames his partner for his problems
- Tries to control his partner's behavior

Ask Questions

While getting to know a person, it's important to ask a lot of questions. Some card games and books are designed to ask thought-provoking questions. These can reveal each party's thoughts and attitudes toward a variety of issues and what they value. A wise woman will make a game of it while keeping her eyes and ears open for red flags, values, attitudes, and thought patterns that are important to her. For example, one question might be, "If you could invite three people from history to have dinner with you, who would you invite?" The person who answers that question with "Jesus, George Washington, and Abraham Lincoln" will show different values than the person who answers with "Adolph Hitler, Mussolini, and Jack the Ripper."

A wise woman will also ask questions of his previous partners as to his character and what went sideways with their relationship. Even though it might be an uncomfortable conversation, she will ask him if she can talk to his ex-wife or ex-girlfriend. Of course, she does not need his permission to talk to a prior partner. However, how he answers the question will be revealing. If he refuses, he is very likely hiding something from her, which is a red flag in itself. The ex-wife or ex-girlfriend may have insights that will affect her decision to pursue the relationship.

A wise woman also asks questions of his family, his friends, his business partners, his pastor, and anyone else who knows him. She discreetly hides her questions in casual conversation so it doesn't sound like an interrogation.

Detective Work

In generations past, we usually got to know someone we were interested in because he lived in our same town and because we knew his family, friends, and business associates. If we didn't know him personally, we at least knew his reputation. But in the modern world, we often don't have that luxury, so we need to do a little detective work to protect ourselves.

The wise woman will conduct a background check using a readily available online service. She will check the public records for any lawsuits, orders of protection, criminal matters, marriages, parental allegations, or divorces. She will also make a FOIA (Freedom of Information Act) request of the local police station in places where he has lived to determine if there have been any police reports involving him.

Of course, Google and social media searches will often reveal important information. Asking friends, neighbors, and business associates who know him or know about him is also a wise move.

Billy Graham wisely said, "Nothing brings more joy than a good marriage, and nothing brings more misery than a bad marriage."[230] God wants the best for us, but we must follow His leading, not our own. Ignoring God's promptings got us into an abusive marriage in the first place. A wise woman will ensure that both her and her groom's hearts are aligned with God's and that God is an integral part of any marriage she enters.

---

[230] Billy Graham, "5 Pieces of Marriage Advice from Billy and Ruth Graham," Billy Graham Evangelistic Association, August 12, 2019, https://billygraham.org/story/5-pieces-of-marriage-advice-from-billy-and-ruth-graham/.

CHAPTER 48

God Our Father, Rescuer, Redeemer, Deliverer, Warrior, Restorer, Healer, and Avenger

Most of us will never go through anything in life as difficult as marriage and divorce from an abuser. It is, by far, the most gut-wrenching fight with evil that any of us will ever know. It is also a time when we come to know our heavenly Father as we never have before. Prior to this time, we may have had a love for the Lord, but being on the battlefield with one of Satan's skilled terrorists who is trying to destroy us and watching firsthand as God rescues us from the bondage of abuse is a humbling, awe-inspiring experience. We have front-row seats as we see God in action as He delivers us from evil, fights for us in the courtroom and beyond, avenges us, heals us, redeems us, and restores us to a place even better than before. The words from Scripture are no longer empty words of an ancient manuscript, but are living, breathing words describing our own experience with the Almighty God who personally moved the heavens for us, His daughters. We know firsthand His power to save. We sing, along with millions of others across the globe and with the audience of saints who have gone before, "How Great Thou Art," and we truly know how great a God we serve.

As we journey from abuse to an abundant life, declaring the Scriptures out loud and claiming God's promises in a strong voice are wonderful ways to remind ourselves that our God is in the battle with us and for us. Below are some of the names of God and powerful passages that resonate with women escaping abuse, as well as some of my reflections on them. How grateful I am that in His grace, the Lord packed His Word full of loving encouragement and promises for us, revealed His character, and preserved His Scriptures through the centuries. During my darkest days, I hung on to these passages like a sailor clinging for dear life to a mast in a storm. Our heavenly Father tells us who we are—we are His beloved, and He tells us that the promises of old are the same promises He makes to us (Galatians 3:14, 29). I encourage you to soak in God's presence and reflect on how these verses are not just promises to biblical characters, stories from the Bible, and ancient prayers, but they are promises to *you,* they are *your* story, and they are *your* prayers.

God—Our Good, Loving Father (Abba)

> See what great love the Father has lavished on us, that we should be called children of God! And that is what we are! (1 John 3:1)

> Let his banner over me be love. (Song of Songs 2:4)

> The Lord your God is with you,
>   the Mighty Warrior who saves.
> He will take great delight in you;
>   in his love he will no longer rebuke you,
> but will rejoice over you with singing. (Zephaniah 3:17)

I love that we have a father-daughter relationship with our heavenly Father. I am a daddy's girl. I adored my father, who is with the Lord now. He was one of the good ones, and I know he adored me. Much like an adoring earthly father, our heavenly Father delights in us. I can hear Him saying, "That's my girl!" He is not a distant or cold father, but a good, warm, loving father. What a privilege to call him Papa God.

God—Who Is Always with Us

> Be strong and very courageous. Be careful to obey all the law my servant Moses gave you; do not turn from it to the right or to the left, that you may be successful wherever you go. Keep this Book of the Law always on your lips; meditate on it day and night, so that you may be careful to do everything written in it. Then you will be prosperous and successful. Have I not commanded you? Be strong and courageous. Do not be afraid; do not be discouraged, for the Lord your God will be with you wherever you go. (Joshua 1:7–9)

Whenever I am doubtful or timid, I remember this verse. Much like Joshua coming out of Egypt and heading into the unknown land of the giants with only the assurance that God was on his side, God calls us to come out of bondage and go into unknown lands with giants with the assurance that He is on our side. As women, we tend to be more fearful than fearless. We like security. We worry about money, jobs, kids, relationships, getting into the right school, making the right next career move, and all that is unknown. A friend of mine who had served in combat and was in special ops helped me gain a new perspective. He doesn't seem to worry about anything. He explained, "When, by all reasonable accounts, you should be dead, and you find out by some miracle that you are, in fact, alive, it gives you unbelievable clarity. You are thankful to just be alive. All those little things of life that we worry about are just not that important. They will work out. God has brought you through alive thus far, and He will bring you through whatever you will face ahead." Amen.

God—Our Rescuer

> Therefore, say to the Israelites: "I am the Lord, and I will bring you out from under the yoke of the Egyptians. I will free you from being slaves to them, and I will redeem you with an outstretched arm and with mighty acts of judgment. I will take you as my own people, and I will be your God. Then you will know that I am the Lord your God, who brought you out from under the yoke of the Egyptians. And I will bring you to the land I swore with uplifted hand to give to Abraham, to Isaac

GOD OUR FATHER, RESCUER, REDEEMER, DELIVERER, WARRIOR, RESTORER, HEALER, AND AVENGER

and to Jacob. I will give it to you as a possession. I am the Lord." . . . Moses answered the people, "Do not be afraid. Stand firm and you will see the deliverance the Lord will bring you today. The Egyptians you see today you will never see again. The Lord will fight for you; you need only to be still. (Exodus 6:6–8; 14:13–14)

Rescue me, Lord, from evildoers;
    protect me from the violent,
who devise evil plans in their hearts
    and stir up war every day.
They make their tongues as sharp as a serpent's;
    the poison of vipers is on their lips.
Keep me safe, Lord, from the hands of the wicked;
    protect me from the violent,
    who devise ways to trip my feet.
The arrogant have hidden a snare for me;
    they have spread out the cords of their net
    and have set traps for me along my path.
I say to the Lord, "You are my God."
    Hear, Lord, my cry for mercy.
Sovereign Lord, my strong deliverer,
    you shield my head in the day of battle.
Do not grant the wicked their desires, Lord;
    do not let their plans succeed.
Those who surround me proudly rear their heads;
    may the mischief of their lips engulf them.
May burning coals fall on them;
    may they be thrown into the fire,
    into miry pits, never to rise.
May slanderers not be established in the land;
    may disaster hunt down the violent.
I know that the Lord secures justice for the poor
    and upholds the cause of the needy.
Surely the righteous will praise your name,
    and the upright will live in your presence. . . .
Keep me safe from the traps set by evildoers,
    from the snares they have laid for me.
Let the wicked fall into their own nets,
    while I pass by in safety. (Psalm 140; 141:9–10)

I had never thought of God being a rescuer until I needed rescuing from domestic abuse. He absolutely did a rescue mission on me. Like the children of Israel, it wasn't pretty, and it wasn't easy. I didn't always see His bigger plan, and I often looked back. But He took me out of bondage and put me in a place of rest and peace and freedom. I will be forever grateful.

God—Our Redeemer

> But now, this is what the L<small>ORD</small> says . . .
> "Do not fear, for I have redeemed you;
>   I have summoned you by name; you are mine.
> When you pass through the waters,
>   I will be with you;
> and when you pass through the rivers,
>   they will not sweep over you.
> When you walk through the fire,
>   you will not be burned;
>   the flames will not set you ablaze.
> For I am the L<small>ORD</small> your God,
>   the Holy One of Israel, your Savior;
> I give Egypt for your ransom,
>   Cush and Seba in your stead.
> Since you are precious and honored in my sight,
>   and because I love you,
> I will give people in exchange for you,
>   nations in exchange for your life.
> Do not be afraid, for I am with you;
>   I will bring your children from the east
>   and gather you from the west.
> I will say to the north, 'Give them up!'
>   and to the south, 'Do not hold them back.'
> Bring my sons from afar
>   and my daughters from the ends of the earth—
> everyone who is called by my name,
>   whom I created for my glory,
>   whom I formed and made."
> . . . This is what the L<small>ORD</small> says—
>   he who made a way through the sea,
>   a path through the mighty waters,
> who drew out the chariots and horses,
>   the army and reinforcements together,
> and they lay there, never to rise again,
>   extinguished, snuffed out like a wick:
> "Forget the former things;
>   do not dwell on the past.
> See, I am doing a new thing!
>   Now it springs up; do you not perceive it?
> I am making a way in the wilderness
>   and streams in the wasteland." (Isaiah 43:1–7, 16–19)

How sweet that God calls us by name and promises to be with us through the valley. He doesn't promise to take away our problems, but He promises to be with us. And that is what we need. I also love that God tells us to forget the former things and not to dwell on the past. We can get stuck there, but God is making a new life for those of us coming out of domestic abuse. He has great plans for us: He will open doors, make ways, provide streams of goodness, and give us a life we could not have even imagined before if we walk with Him.

God—Our Warrior

> Contend, Lord, with those who contend with me;
>   fight against those who fight against me.
> Take up shield and armor;
>   arise and come to my aid.
> Brandish spear and javelin
>   against those who pursue me.
> Say to me,
>   "I am your salvation."
> May those who seek my life
>   be disgraced and put to shame;
> may those who plot my ruin
>   be turned back in dismay.
> May they be like chaff before the wind,
>   with the angel of the Lord driving them away;
> may their path be dark and slippery,
>   with the angel of the Lord pursuing them.
> Since they hid their net for me without cause
>   and without cause dug a pit for me,
> may ruin overtake them by surprise—
>   may the net they hid entangle them,
>   may they fall into the pit, to their ruin.
> Then my soul will rejoice in the Lord
>   and delight in his salvation.
> My whole being will exclaim,
>   "Who is like you, Lord?
> You rescue the poor from those too strong for them,
>   the poor and needy from those who rob them." (Psalm 35:1–10)

> Arise, Lord, in your anger;
>   rise up against the rage of my enemies.
>   Awake, my God; decree justice. . . .
> Vindicate me, Lord, according to my righteousness,
>   according to my integrity, O Most High.
> Bring to an end the violence of the wicked
>   and make the righteous secure—
> you, the righteous God
>   who probes minds and hearts. (Psalm 7:6, 8–9)

I love the salms of David. They are my calming place when I can't sleep. David speaks from his heart to my heart and provides clarity for the abuse that I went through. He was a warrior for God, and he asked God to be a warrior for him and give him justice. Many of us forget that God is a warrior who fights for justice on our behalf. We tend to think of Him as all butterflies and rainbows, but He is also a God of justice. He is against anything that is against love. I would not want to be an abuser facing God's justice when He takes up His sword and fights for His girls.

God—Who Is Mighty to Save

> Who is this coming from Edom,
> > from Bozrah, with his garments stained crimson?
> Who is this, robed in splendor,
> > striding forward in the greatness of his strength?
> "It is I, proclaiming victory,
> > mighty to save."
> Why are your garments red,
> > like those of one treading the winepress?
> "I have trodden the winepress alone;
> > from the nations no one was with me.
> I trampled them in my anger
> > and trod them down in my wrath;
> their blood spattered my garments,
> > and I stained all my clothing.
> It was for me the day of vengeance;
> > the year for me to redeem had come.
> I looked, but there was no one to help,
> > I was appalled that no one gave support;
> so my own arm achieved salvation for me,
> > and my own wrath sustained me.
> I trampled the nations in my anger;
> > in my wrath I made them drunk
> > and poured their blood on the ground." (Isaiah 63:1–6)

This is such a picture for me. I can imagine a lone, strong warrior walking slowly on the horizon after battle, coming closer and closer to the walls of an ancient city. He is tired, but victorious. The people shout from the walls of the city and ask him who he is and what he has done. He responds, "God, Mighty to Save." He has been victorious in fighting for His beloved daughter. Satan wanted her. Satan wanted to keep her in bondage and put many of his minions and demons in the fight. But God fought for her. He is victorious, and she is out of domestic abuse. The soldiers ask God who fought with Him. Who was on His side? The warrior God replies that no one fought with Him for His daughter. All the people who should have fought for her didn't help. Not her husband, pastor, or friends; not her children, parents, or siblings; not even fellow church members, the courts, or law enforcement—not even her attorney. No one fought for her. They all either joined with Satan or sat on the sidelines and watched. So God alone fought for her and brought her out of domestic abuse. What a God we have!

God Our Father, Rescuer, Redeemer, Deliverer, Warrior, Restorer, Healer, and Avenger

God—Our Righteous Avenger

> Woe to you, destroyer,
> > you who have not been destroyed!
> Woe to you, betrayer,
> > you who have not been betrayed!
> When you stop destroying,
> > you will be destroyed;
> when you stop betraying,
> > you will be betrayed. (Isaiah 33:1)

> Do not drag me away with the wicked,
> > with those who do evil,
> who speak cordially with their neighbors
> > but harbor malice in their hearts.
> Repay them for their deeds
> > and for their evil work;
> repay them for what their hands have done
> > and bring back on them what they deserve.
> Because they have no regard for the deeds of the Lord
> > and what his hands have done,
> he will tear them down
> > and never build them up again. (Psalm 28:3–5)

> Surely God is good to Israel,
> > to those who are pure in heart.
> But as for me, my feet had almost slipped;
> > I had nearly lost my foothold.
> For I envied the arrogant
> > when I saw the prosperity of the wicked.
> They have no struggles;
> > their bodies are healthy and strong.
> They are free from common human burdens;
> > they are not plagued by human ills.
> Therefore pride is their necklace;
> > they clothe themselves with violence.
> From their callous hearts comes iniquity;
> > their evil imaginations have no limits.
> They scoff, and speak with malice;
> > with arrogance they threaten oppression.
> Their mouths lay claim to heaven,
> > and their tongues take possession of the earth.
> Therefore their people turn to them
> > and drink up waters in abundance.
> They say, "How would God know?
> > Does the Most High know anything?"

> This is what the wicked are like—
>   always free of care, they go on amassing wealth.
> Surely in vain I have kept my heart pure
>   and have washed my hands in innocence.
> All day long I have been afflicted,
>   and every morning brings new punishments.
> If I had spoken out like that,
>   I would have betrayed your children.
> When I tried to understand all this,
>   it troubled me deeply
> till I entered the sanctuary of God;
>   then I understood their final destiny.
> Surely you place them on slippery ground;
>   you cast them down to ruin.
> How suddenly are they destroyed,
>   completely swept away by terrors!
> They are like a dream when one awakes;
>   when you arise, Lord,
> you will despise them as fantasies.
>   When my heart was grieved
> and my spirit embittered,
>   I was senseless and ignorant;
> I was a brute beast before you.
>   Yet I am always with you;
> you hold me by my right hand.
>   You guide me with your counsel,
> and afterward you will take me into glory.
>   Whom have I in heaven but you?
> And earth has nothing I desire besides you.
>   My flesh and my heart may fail,
>   but God is the strength of my heart
>   and my portion forever.
> Those who are far from you will perish;
>   you destroy all who are unfaithful to you.
> But as for me, it is good to be near God.
>   I have made the Sovereign Lord my refuge;
>   I will tell of all your deeds. (Psalm 73)

So many times we wonder if wicked people ever receive justice. The Bible informs us that revenge is not ours to take. That is God's purview. As we watch the lives of abusers, we see that they are usually self-destructive. God is just, and whether in this world or in the next, we all will be held accountable for our words and actions.

God—Our Deliverer

> Do not fret because of those who are evil
>   or be envious of those who do wrong;

for like the grass they will soon wither,
    like green plants they will soon die away.
Trust in the Lord and do good;
    dwell in the land and enjoy safe pasture.
Take delight in the Lord,
    and he will give you the desires of your heart.
Commit your way to the Lord;
    trust in him and he will do this:
He will make your righteous reward shine like the dawn,
    your vindication like the noonday sun.
Be still before the Lord
    and wait patiently for him;
        do not fret when people succeed in their ways,
    when they carry out their wicked schemes.
Refrain from anger and turn from wrath;
    do not fret—it leads only to evil.
For those who are evil will be destroyed,
    but those who hope in the Lord will inherit the land.
A little while, and the wicked will be no more;
    though you look for them, they will not be found.
But the meek will inherit the land
    and enjoy peace and prosperity.
The wicked plot against the righteous
    and gnash their teeth at them;
    but the Lord laughs at the wicked,
    for he knows their day is coming.
The wicked draw the sword
    and bend the bow
        to bring down the poor and needy,
        to slay those whose ways are upright.
But their swords will pierce their own hearts,
    and their bows will be broken.
Better the little that the righteous have
    than the wealth of many wicked;
        for the power of the wicked will be broken,
    but the Lord upholds the righteous.
The blameless spend their days under the Lord's care,
    and their inheritance will endure forever.
In times of disaster they will not wither;
    in days of famine they will enjoy plenty.
But the wicked will perish:
Though the Lord's enemies are like the flowers of the field,
    they will be consumed, they will go up in smoke.
The wicked borrow and do not repay,
    but the righteous give generously;
    those the Lord blesses will inherit the land,

but those he curses will be destroyed.
The LORD makes firm the steps
   of the one who delights in him;
   though he may stumble, he will not fall,
   for the LORD upholds him with his hand.
I was young and now I am old,
   yet I have never seen the righteous forsaken
   or their children begging bread.
They are always generous and lend freely;
   their children will be a blessing.
Turn from evil and do good;
   then you will dwell in the land forever.
For the LORD loves the just
   and will not forsake his faithful ones.
Wrongdoers will be completely destroyed;
   the offspring of the wicked will perish.
The righteous will inherit the land
   and dwell in it forever.
The mouths of the righteous utter wisdom,
   and their tongues speak what is just.
The law of their God is in their hearts;
   their feet do not slip.
The wicked lie in wait for the righteous,
   intent on putting them to death;
but the LORD will not leave them in the power of the wicked
   or let them be condemned when brought to trial.
Hope in the LORD
   and keep his way.
He will exalt you to inherit the land;
   when the wicked are destroyed, you will see it.
I have seen a wicked and ruthless man
   flourishing like a luxuriant native tree,
   but he soon passed away and was no more;
   though I looked for him, he could not be found.
Consider the blameless, observe the upright;
   a future awaits those who seek peace.
But all sinners will be destroyed;
   there will be no future for the wicked.
The salvation of the righteous comes from the LORD;
   he is their stronghold in time of trouble.
The LORD helps them and delivers them;
   he delivers them from the wicked and saves them,
   because they take refuge in him. (Psalm 37)

God wants to give us the desires of our heart—after all, He put them there. He promises that when we put

Him first, then He will give us the desires of our heart, make our righteousness evident to all, vindicate us, and deliver us from the evil around us. How very true for the woman coming out of domestic abuse.

God—Our Refuge

> Have mercy on me, my God, have mercy on me,
>   for in you I take refuge.
> I will take refuge in the shadow of your wings
>   until the disaster has passed.
> I cry out to God Most High,
>   to God, who vindicates me.
> He sends from heaven and saves me,
>   rebuking those who hotly pursue me—
> God sends forth his love and his faithfulness.
> I am in the midst of lions;
>   I am forced to dwell among ravenous beasts—
> men whose teeth are spears and arrows,
>   whose tongues are sharp swords.
> Be exalted, O God, above the heavens;
>   let your glory be over all the earth.
> They spread a net for my feet—
>   I was bowed down in distress.
> They dug a pit in my path—
>   but they have fallen into it themselves.
> My heart, O God, is steadfast,
>   my heart is steadfast;
>   I will sing and make music.
> Awake, my soul!
>   Awake, harp and lyre!
>   I will awaken the dawn.
> I will praise you, Lord, among the nations;
>   I will sing of you among the peoples.
> For great is your love, reaching to the heavens;
>   your faithfulness reaches to the skies.
> Be exalted, O God, above the heavens;
>   let your glory be over all the earth. (Psalm 57)

As domestic abuse survivors, we often feel under siege. This wonderful passage promises that we can find our safety and refuge in Him and that abusers will fall into the same evil schemes that they plan for others.

God—Who Restores

> The Spirit of the Sovereign Lord is on me,
>   because the Lord has anointed me
>   to proclaim good news to the poor.
> He has sent me to bind up the brokenhearted,

> to proclaim freedom for the captives
> and release from darkness for the prisoners,
> to proclaim the year of the Lord's favor
> and the day of vengeance of our God,
> to comfort all who mourn,
> and provide for those who grieve in Zion—
> to bestow on them a crown of beauty
> instead of ashes,
> the oil of joy
> instead of mourning,
> and a garment of praise
> instead of a spirit of despair.
> They will be called oaks of righteousness,
> a planting of the Lord
> for the display of his splendor.
> They will rebuild the ancient ruins
> and restore the places long devastated;
> they will renew the ruined cities
> that have been devastated for generations.
> Strangers will shepherd your flocks;
> foreigners will work your fields and vineyards.
> And you will be called priests of the Lord,
> you will be named ministers of our God.
> You will feed on the wealth of nations,
> and in their riches you will boast.
> Instead of your shame
> you will receive a double portion,
> and instead of disgrace
> you will rejoice in your inheritance.
> And so you will inherit a double portion in your land,
> and everlasting joy will be yours.
> "For I, the Lord, love justice;
> I hate robbery and wrongdoing.
> In my faithfulness I will reward my people
> and make an everlasting covenant with them.
> Their descendants will be known among the nations
> and their offspring among the peoples.
> All who see them will acknowledge
> that they are a people the Lord has blessed." (Isaiah 61:1–9)

God restores us to a place that is even better than before. His restoration process is nothing short of miraculous. As with Job, those who follow Him through domestic abuse find that God blesses the second half of their life even more than the first. Their grief is replaced with the crown of a beautiful life; mourning for loss is replaced with joy; hopelessness is replaced with praise and thanksgiving. Without fail, the kind, good women of faith whom I counsel who leave domestic abuse and follow Him blossom under the blessings of the Lord.

God—Our Strength

> The Lord is the everlasting God,
>   the Creator of the ends of the earth.
> He will not grow tired or weary,
>   and his understanding no one can fathom.
> He gives strength to the weary
>   and increases the power of the weak.
> Even youths grow tired and weary,
>   and young men stumble and fall;
>   but those who hope in the Lord
>   will renew their strength.
> They will soar on wings like eagles;
>   they will run and not grow weary,
>   they will walk and not be faint. (Isaiah 40:28–31)

> The Sovereign Lord is my strength;
>   he make my feet like the feet of a deer,
>   he enables me to tread on the heights. (Habakkuk 3:19)

It is hard to even explain how God gives us His supernatural strength when we need it. I first experienced this when my father was elderly and in hospice. I was working full time, raising young children, and married to an abuser. But miraculously, I had the energy to move my parents close to me, see my dad every evening after work, arrange for visits with my mother and children, and not get sick with even a cold for the eighteen months that my dad was declining, even though the flu went through our family three times. When we are on a mission for Him, God gives us an extra measure of strength and nimbleness of foot that we need to complete our task. What a good Father!

God—Our Healer

> "In that day," declares the Lord Almighty,
>   "I will break the yoke off their necks
> and will tear off their bonds;
>   no longer will foreigners enslave them.
> Instead, they will serve the Lord their God
>   and David their king,
>   whom I will raise up for them.
> "So do not be afraid, Jacob my servant;
>   do not be dismayed, Israel,"
>   declares the Lord.
> "I will surely save you out of a distant place,
>   your descendants from the land of their exile.
> Jacob will again have peace and security,
>   and no one will make him afraid.
> I am with you and will save you,"
>   declares the Lord. . . .

> "But I will restore you to health
>   and heal your wounds,"
>   declares the LORD,
> "because you are called an outcast,
>   Zion for whom no one cares."
> This is what the LORD says:
> "I will restore the fortunes of Jacob's tents
>   and have compassion on his dwellings;
> the city will be rebuilt on her ruins,
>   and the palace will stand in its proper place.
> From them will come songs of thanksgiving
>   and the sound of rejoicing.
> I will add to their numbers,
>   and they will not be decreased;
> I will bring them honor,
>   and they will not be disdained. . . .
> "I have loved you with an everlasting love;
>   I have drawn you with unfailing kindness.
> I will build you up again,
>   and you, Virgin Israel, will be rebuilt. . . .
> They will be like a well-watered garden,
>   and they will sorrow no more.
> Then young women will dance and be glad,
>   young men and old as well.
> I will turn their mourning into gladness;
>   I will give them comfort and joy instead of sorrow.
> I will satisfy the priests with abundance,
>   and my people will be filled with my bounty,"
>   declares the LORD. (Jeremiah 30:8–11, 17–19; 31:3–4, 12–14)

Women coming out of abuse need a great deal of healing. God Himself heals us. God is love, and love heals. As we spend time with Him, as our hearts beat as one with His, as our minds are transformed into thinking like His, as we see with His eyes and hear with His ears, as we hear His whisper, "I love you, you are Mine," we heal. And in time, we find the joy in life again.

Psalms and Proverbs That Speak to Our Hearts

When our souls are in anguish, as they are when we struggle with domestic abuse, some of the most comforting words come from the Psalms and Proverbs. David himself wrestled with people who unjustly accused him, plotted evil against him, lied about him, manipulated him, and tried to take his life. In many psalms, David cries out to the Lord from the depths of despair, asks God to avenge his enemies, and in the end, praises God for rescuing him. The psalms are the cries of our own hearts as much as they were the cries of David's heart. They can be our own prayers. As we pray God's words back to Him, we can insert our name for David's and our enemies for David's enemies. On those nights when sleep will not come and daylight is far away, having a cup of tea in

God Our Father, Rescuer, Redeemer, Deliverer, Warrior, Restorer, Healer, and Avenger

bed while reading the Psalms and praying them back to God is a sure way to calm frazzled nerves and quiet an anxious heart until we can fall asleep with God's words on our lips.

David's son Solomon was gifted with wisdom, at least until he lost his way because he married numerous pagan women who caused him to drift from God. His proverbs are words to live by, especially in dealing with toxic people. I often wish I had read them and taken them to heart decades earlier.

While they are too voluminous to include in this book in their entirety, listed below are several passages from Psalms and Proverbs that speak to the heart of a woman overcoming domestic abuse.

Psalms: 7; 9; 10; 14; 17; 18; 20; 23; 27; 28; 31; 34; 35; 36; 37; 38; 41; 43; 44; 46; 53; 54; 55; 56; 57; 58; 59; 69; 71; 73; 77; 91; 92; 94; 101; 103; 109; 116; 120; 129; 139; 140; 141; 142; 143; 144; 146; 147.

Proverbs: 1:2, 8–33; 3:33; 4:23; 5:21–23; 6:12–19; 8:12–14; 9:7–8; 10:11–12, 18–19, 23–24, 31–32; 11:1–3, 5–6, 9, 16–17, 21, 29; 12:3, 10, 16, 18, 20, 26; 13:1, 10, 13, 20, 22; 14:7, 9, 14, 16–17; 15:12, 18, 25, 27–29: 16:4–5, 18, 27–29; 17:4, 13; 21:30; 22:10; 23:9; 25:5; 26:4; 27:12; 28:10, 25; 29:20, 22–23, 27; 30:20, 23; 31:28–29.

CHAPTER 49

Becoming the Woman God Designed You to Be

A WOMAN WHO HAS overcome domestic abuse will not be the same person she was before. Nor should she be. What were once gaping wounds in her heart preventing her from functioning have now healed and have become scars. Although she can function, the scars remain. To become all that God has planned for her, she needs to make healing her top priority. But then what? Where does she go from there?

For all the pain she endured to overcome domestic abuse, if she chooses to allow God to work in her, domestic abuse will also be the impetus to become the woman God designed her to be. God doesn't send abuse, but He will use all things for good and for His redemptive purposes. My dear friend Orley Herron, who is now with the Lord, often told me, "God has no wastebaskets. He will use everything you go through for His purposes." Becoming the woman God designed her to be starts with looking at what's in her wastebasket and understanding that God will use that for His redemptive purpose.

Use Trials to Get to Know the Father in an Intimate Way

Nothing brings us closer to our Lord than having nowhere else to go. When we come to the end of our ability to make things right, and when we are completely dependent upon God for strength, comfort, companionship, and provision, we get to know our heavenly Father in ways we never could when things are all roses and sunshine in our world.

In a recent documentary on the faith of missionaries in countries where Christians are persecuted, *The Insanity of God*, the members of a suffering, underground Chinese church said they never trust a pastor who hasn't spent time in prison for his faith. When Christians are beaten, tortured, and starved for their faith, they are utterly dependent upon God against Satan's attacks. An imprisoned pastor receives his PhD in theology directly from the Teacher.

If we choose, the trial of living through, escaping, and overcoming domestic abuse will bring us close to the heart of God. When we lose everything and everyone who matters to us because of our abuser, the only unwavering thing in our lives is our heavenly Father.

The earthly trappings we once held dear slowly lose their grip on us as we rely more and more on our heavenly Father for our significance and identity. When false friends betray us, we learn that the only opinion that matters is God's. When we must flee our home for safety, we find that God makes Himself at home in whatever refuge He provides for us. When we must leave our possessions behind in our flight to safety, we find we can live with much less. When our finances are significantly less and the abuse has taken such a toll that we cannot concentrate at work, we find that Jehovah Jireh (God our Provider) provides for us from unlikely sources. When our bodies are overcome with anxiety and stress-related illnesses, we find that Jehovah Rapha is truly God our Healer. When the silence from our church is deafening and we can no longer attend because our church allows our abuser to attend, we still hear the whispers of Abba Father saying, "I love you. Abuse is an abomination in My sight. My righteousness surrounds you like a cloak." When we are all alone, God fills us with His presence and speaks to our hearts in ways that comfort us.

Know That God Has Prepared You for Something Big

God doesn't give us small assignments. If our assignment was easy enough to do on our own strength, we wouldn't need God. God gives us God-size assignments so we are completely dependent upon Him. When we succeed, we will know the credit goes to God.

Moses was assigned to bring Israel out of slavery from the most powerful nation in the world. He could not do that by himself, and he knew that. But God called him to the task, so Moses knew that He would deliver. Moses wasn't sure how, but he knew that God would rescue them. God had been preparing Moses for this enormous undertaking since birth. Prior to his mission and throughout his mission, God spoke to Moses directly so Moses had a direct hotline to God. God knew Moses needed unwavering confidence in Him to lead His people on their journey. And God did not disappoint.

Likewise, the twelve apostles were called to tell the known world about Jesus. This was humanly impossible, but heavenly possible. Jesus had been preparing them for three years. During Jesus's earthly ministry and through the Holy Spirit, Jesus spoke directly with the apostles. God knew they would need steadfast faith to accomplish their task. Their confidence in Jesus's promises and their daily communication with God kept them going through difficult times.

Few of us are given the monumental tasks God gave Moses and the disciples. Not many of us are called to be on the world stage, but each of us is called to live an extraordinary life of purpose with God as our center. It is our task to find out our assignment and get after it. And when we find our assignment, we would do well to heed the words of Ruth Bell Graham: "My job is to take care of the possible and to trust God with the impossible."

When God has a big mission for us, we need big faith to go with it. We cannot expect God to give us a heaven-sized assignment with a human-sized faith. He doesn't want us to fail, and so, out of His gracious patience and provision, He waits until our faith grows big enough to take on His God-sized assignment. But how does God typically grow our faith? Our faith rarely grows when things are cushy and rosy. Our faith only grows when it is tested—and that is usually with trials.

We should be careful to not get too comfortable when our faith takes a leap to a higher level and we have completed our assignment. God will likely have another God-sized assignment that needs even more faith to accomplish. And how will we jump to the next level of faith that we need? Most likely through another trial.

After I had healed, I had hoped to teach full time or serve in the administration at the Christian university where I had served on the board of regents and taught as adjunct professor of business law. I love working with young people and investing in the next generation of leaders. I felt God was calling me away from my job at the law firm to serve at a university, but God had different plans. We had a conversation that went something like this:

God: I am calling you to use your legal skills in the courtroom to represent other women escaping domestic abuse.

Me: I really don't think I'm cut out to be a trial lawyer. You know I love young people, and they seem to like me, based on the student reviews. I want to go into teaching at a Christian college.

God: I have plenty of people who are qualified to teach at a Christian college. I don't have anyone else with your experience with domestic abuse (that I healed you from in record time, by the way), your law degree (which I gave you), your heart for others and for justice, and the resources that I have given you. I need you in the local courtroom to rescue women from bondage.

Me: I'm really not a fighter. Litigators are fighters. You know me. I just want everyone to get along.

God: I know you aren't a fighter. I will make you into a warrior Myself.

Me: I'm not a warrior.

God: I know you're not. I will make you into one. That way you will know it was Me when you become a warrior and set women free.

Me: Okay. You win. I got nothin'. I'll be your warrior for women. But it's gotta be all You. Fighting isn't in my nature.

God: Don't worry. I'm going with you. Now let's get after it.

Know Your Mission

One of the most important questions we can ask ourselves is, "What is my mission while I am here on earth?" The answer will determine the trajectory of your life. We each have an allotment of time on this planet—an unknown number of years. What will you do with the time God gives you? What did God uniquely prepare you to do? How did God uniquely equip you—what personality traits, passions, skills, gifts, talents, and experiences did He give you—to do a job that no one else can do, to reach people no one else can reach, and to make a difference that no one else can make?

Determining to find our mission and asking God to show us His direction for our next phase of life are crucial steps in becoming the women God designed us to be. This process will likely take time, perhaps years, to hear the heartbeat of the Father, sort out the special way He wired us, assess our experiences and skills and talents, and follow the direction of the Holy Spirit as He leads us to our next steps. We often wish that God would just give us an easy-to-use road map for our life that says, "Go right at the next stop. Then walk on that road for the next fifteen years and take a left." But that would take our relationship with God out of the equation—we would just look to the map for our guidance and not seek Him. It's much easier to follow a map than to spend time talking with God, getting to know Him, and listening to His calling on our life. However, God doesn't work like that. God wants an intimate relationship with us. He wants us to seek Him every day, and He wants to reveal Himself to us every day. He promises that we will find Him when we seek Him with all our hearts (Jeremiah 29:13), and He promises to always be with us (Joshua 1:9). Because of these promises, He commands us to be strong, courageous, and fearless (Joshua 1:9).

Bob Buford, the author of *Halftime* and the founder of the Halftime Institute, has some great ideas on how to determine God's purpose for our lives. Reading his book, taking self-assessments to discover the way God made me, and attending the Halftime Institute (twice) had a huge impact on how I chose to live the second half of my life. His motto, "from success to significance," has made a worldwide impact on how a generation of people have used their skill sets to further God's kingdom on earth.

Every good company has a mission statement. It tells why they exist. In a well-run company, everything they do should, in some way, further the mission. Every employee, from the president to the janitor, should know how they contribute to the mission. A mission statement focuses a company. It allows them to say no to a lot of opportunities that don't align with their mission so they can say yes to opportunities that further their mission. Otherwise, they lose focus and run the risk of not doing anything particularly well. For example, Apple's original mission statement in 1977 stated: "Apple is dedicated to the empowerment of man—to making personal computing accessible to each and every individual so as to help change the way we think, work, learn, and communicate."[231] In 2009, the acting CEO embellished on the original mission statement and stated, "We believe that we're on the face of the Earth to make great products, and that's not changing."[232] If the best-run grocery store chain in North America approached Apple and asked Apple to buy the grocery store company, Apple would say, "No, thanks. It's not in our mission statement." It's not that grocery stores are bad. In fact, they do a lot of good—like feeding people. But owning grocery stores is not in Apple's mission statement. Apple makes great products, and it doesn't want to lose its edge or assign people to work on a grocery store when they should be focused on the next innovative technology.

Every good company also has a vision statement. It identifies their long-term concept for the company. For example, Apple sees itself as the premier leader in personal device technology to empower people. "Apple leads the world in innovation with iPhone, iPad, Mac, Apple Watch, and Apple TV. Apple's four software platforms—iOS, macOS, watchOS, and tvOS—provide seamless experiences across all Apple devices and empower people with breakthrough services including the App Store, Apple Music, Apple Pay and iCloud."[233]

After the vision statement, every good company will have key values—values from which they will not waiver. Shortly after he founded Apple, a young, idealistic Steve Jobs published these core values in 1981:

- One person, one computer.
- We are going for it and we will set aggressive goals.
- We are all on the adventure together.
- We build products we believe in.
- We are here to make a positive difference in society, as well as make a profit.
- Each person is important; each has the opportunity and the obligation to make a difference.
- We are all in it together, win or lose.
- We are enthusiastic!
- We are creative; we set the pace.
- We want everyone to enjoy the adventure we are on together.
- We care about what we do.
- We want to create an environment in which Apple values flourish.[234]

Nearly thirty years and billions of dollars later, Apple expounded upon its original core values under new leadership, shifting the emphasis from people to products. In 2009, Apple published these values:

---

[231] Barbara Farfan, "What Is Apple's Mission Statement?" *The Balance Everyday*, November 20, 2019, https://www.thebalanceeveryday.com/apple-mission-statement-4068547.
[232] Farfan, "What Is Apple's Mission Statement?"
[233] Farfan, "What Is Apple's Mission Statement?"
[234] "Have Your Ever Read about Apple's Core Values?" *Think Marketing*, January 11, 2016, at https://thinkmarketingmagazine.com/apple-core-values/.

- We believe in the simple, not the complex.
- We believe that we need to own and control the primary technologies behind the products we make.
- We participate only in markets where we can make a significant contribution.
- We believe in saying no to thousands of projects so that we can really focus on the few that are truly important and meaningful to us.
- We believe in deep collaboration and cross-pollination of our groups, which allow us to innovate in a way that others cannot.
- We don't settle for anything less than excellence in every group in the company, and we have the self-honesty to admit when we're wrong and the courage to change.[235]

Finally, companies set goals, both long- and short-term, to help them achieve their mission and vision. Goals usually come in the form of budgets and marketing plans.

To help them stay true to their values, goals, mission, and vision, good companies employ a board of directors, people who help keep the ship steered in the right direction. Although boards are not involved in the day-to-day nitty gritty details of running a company, companies are accountable to their board of directors.

Mission and vision statements, along with written values and goals, are important for people too. I encourage every woman I counsel to do a great deal of soul-searching with God to determine her own mission statement and to write it down. I then encourage her to consult with God about what she wants her life to look like in ten or twenty years—the legacy she wants to leave—and to write a vision statement. After these important milestones are complete, I ask her to write down the key values that she will live by—her honor code. These are values that she holds dear and will not waiver from. Finally, I ask her to write several short- and long-term goals necessary to achieve her mission and vision statements. For example, if her ten-year goal is to own a thriving business, she also needs to set goals about where she needs to be in five years and in one year to achieve that goal. To meet her one-year goal, she needs to establish her six-month goal and what she needs to do each month to achieve her one-year goal. These are then reduced to weekly and daily goals. If you are a woman coming out of domestic abuse, I encourage you to do this exercise.

Once this is in place, I ask her to place them all in a prominent place, perhaps her office, so that she can see them every day and remind herself that she is part of God's great plan that is bigger than herself. They will encourage her on those days she needs an extra boost, and they will help her say no to good things so she can say yes to the best things that align with her mission. We are much more likely to achieve our purpose when we write these down and see them every day. Otherwise they tend to swirl around as nebulous clouds in our minds, blown here and there by the wind, and we tend to deal with short-term emergencies instead of focusing on our long-term purpose. Then I recommend gathering a few wise people for her personal board of directors whom she will meet with a few times each year and who will keep her accountable for staying on track.

We should not get discouraged when we don't immediately know our mission or hear God's voice for our next assignment. He will reveal it in His timing, which is frequently not our timing. If we don't hear God's voice calling us to a new assignment and releasing us from our current position, it means we need to wait and stay at our current position. When God calls us to a new task, He will also release us from our current task.

We should not get discouraged when God calls us to a new mission in a different season of life. When our children are young, they are a priority, and our mission will clearly include raising them up in the love and fear

---

[235] "Have You Ever Read about Apple's Core Values?" *Think Marketing*, 2016.

of the Lord. However, when our child-rearing obligations are over, God will likely call us to a new mission for which we are ideally suited.

I had been seeking God's direction for years, but had not heard a clear direction. So I stayed at my position in a law firm, although I needed to reduce my hours due to the stress of a divorce from an abuser. After the divorce and after I had spent nearly two years working on healing, God called me to open a law practice representing women who were escaping domestic abuse. At the same time, at the end of 2015, He released me from my position at my old law firm with an amicable parting of the ways. In April of 2016, I opened my law firm for women with the slogan, "Helping women overcome domestic abuse." Ironically, my first client attended my former church, the same church that supported my abuser. I don't advertise or even have a website, but since the day I opened my door, God has brought clients from local churches, domestic abuse shelters, and by word of mouth. I turn away more clients than I can take on. God confirms regularly that I am in the middle of His will for me at this time in my life. I will continue to serve Him by representing women escaping abuse until He calls me to another assignment.

By way of example, I have set below my life's mission and vision statement that I created in 2015. It hangs in my office right above my desk.

My Life Mission Statement

To serve God, my husband, my children, my neighbors, my church, and my community by:

- Loving God, spending time with Him, being filled with His presence
- Loving and honoring my husband, building a strong relationship with him, serving together with him
- Loving my children and future grandchildren by words of encouragement, wisdom, and deeds
- Reaching out to neighbors and building community
- Healing women coming out of abusive relationship with:
    » Legal services
    » Coaching
    » Writing a book
- Educating the church community regarding domestic abuse with:
    » Writing a book to use as a healing curriculum
    » Conducting seminars
    » Teaching church leaders and members
    » Using the media
    » Running the website and organization www.abusecare.org

God Our Redeemer and Restorer

I have found over and over that the women who have had the courage to leave an abusive marriage will thrive when they remove themselves from abuse, make healing a top priority, and focus on God and His purpose for their lives. God always wants to bless us, but it is hard for His blessings to get through when we are attached to an abuser and Satan is actively thwarting God's blessings. Once they come out from under the cloud of evil that surrounds an abuser, God can rain down His blessings. He is truly a Redeemer. God restores the years that the locusts have taken away (Joel 2:25).

When God is at work, He restores us to a better place than we were before. That looks different for each person, but time and time again, I have observed amazing restoration in the lives of women who have overcome abuse. He replaces our old houses filled with strife and discord with new homes filled with peace and His presence. He replaces our false friends with a new community of people who love God and speak truth and life into us. He replaces our dysfunctional church that supported our abuser with a community of believers filled with the Holy Spirit. He replaces our former jobs and careers with new positions that are focused on bringing His kingdom to earth. And many times, like the story of Abigail and David (1 Samuel 25), He replaces an abusive husband and toxic in-laws with a kind, godly husband who adores her and sweet in-laws who love her and affirm the good in her.

God's Grace Is Sufficient

Women of faith who find themselves recovering from domestic abuse did not anticipate their lives unfolding as they have. Most of us have dreamed of a beautiful wedding day with our Prince Charming, surrounded by friends and family, and followed by a home filled with happy children, a meaningful career, a successful husband, and a supportive community of church and other friends, culminating in a comfortable retirement, enjoying the blessings of grandmotherhood encircled by our adult children and grandchildren, and reflecting on a lifetime of happiness. We did not foresee a marriage filled with strife and abuse, a high-conflict divorce, a church and false friends who supported our abuser, children who sided with their father against us, a struggling career due to the stress of abuse, and leaving our homes. We did not foresee financial difficulties, constantly returning to court because of our abuser's violations of divorce and parenting agreements, and continued abuse and hostility even years after the marriage is over.

I suspect that Paul's life did not turn out as he had planned either. He was a prestigious Jewish Pharisee and an up-and-coming leader in the Jewish community when Jesus got ahold of him. He switched teams and then became the most prolific author of the New Testament, planted churches, and became a leader among the Christians. God allowed him to see a vision of heaven that no one else saw. Paul was also the source of riots, was thrown into prison, was insulted and persecuted, and was run out of town everywhere he went. He had some affliction he asked God to remove, but God did not. Paul explained his conversation with God like this:

> Therefore, in order to keep me from becoming conceited, I was given a thorn in my flesh, a messenger of Satan, to torment me. Three times I pleaded with the Lord to take it away from me. But he said to me, "My grace is sufficient for you, for my power is made perfect in weakness." Therefore I will boast all the more gladly about my weaknesses, so that Christ's power may rest on me. That is why, for Christ's sake, I delight in weaknesses, in insults, in hardships, in persecutions, in difficulties. For when I am weak, then I am strong. (2 Corinthians 12:7–10)

When I read this with new eyes in the aftermath of my divorce, the words jumped off the page. I, too, felt like I was given "a thorn in my flesh, a messenger of Satan, to torment me." Even after my divorce was final, the emotional, verbal, financial, and physical abuse from my ex-husband was constant. His insults never stopped, his parental alienation was constant, his slander campaign against me escalated, his violations of parenting and divorce agreements caused me to return to court numerous times (and is ongoing as I write), and I was forced to obtain an order of protection for my own safety. A woman with an abusive ex-husband often feels that she has a messenger of Satan tormenting her endlessly, because, well, she does.

But God's reply to Paul's messenger of Satan is His same reply to us: "My grace is sufficient for you. I will meet all your needs. You are weak and human, and you are no match for Satan. But I am with you, and you will see My power working through you and in you and going before you when you are dependent upon Me. Then you will know that it is Me, not you, who is all victorious. Lean on Me and watch Me do miracles on your behalf!" (2 Corinthians 12:9–10 paraphrased).

Our only proper response to God is Paul's response: "Okay, God. I see that my abuser, Satan's messenger and tormentor, is not going away. But I claim Your promise that Your grace will be enough for me, and Your strength and power will show up, even in my weakness, and You will prevail. So I'm going to focus on You and Your promises, because I will know that when I prevail, it is because of what You have done and Your power, not me. I am going to wait and watch expectantly for You. I'm not going to get sidelined by his insults, threats, emotional abuse, slander, parental alienation, refusal to pay, or anything else. I am going to do what I can and depend on You. I will watch You show up in a big way that I never could myself, so that I, too, can give You all the praise and glory! Amen" (2 Corinthians 12:7–10 paraphrased).

Know Your Identity

Nothing changes a person as much as knowing their identity. Her identity permeates everything she does and how she sees the world. Do you know that you are a daughter of the King of Kings? Have you heard you are a lioness of the Lion of Judah? Do you realize your heavenly Dad has immeasurable resources for you? Are you aware of just how loved you are?

We can often tell a person's identity just by how they hold themselves, what they wear, and how they walk and talk. Have you ever seen a person plodding along a sidewalk aimlessly, looking down with hunched shoulders, dirty, torn clothes, and disheveled hair? His speech reflects that he sees himself as a victim, and that is how he sees the world. That person does not think highly of himself. He has told himself he is not worthy and he has no particular purpose. On the other hand, have you ever seen a British royal attending an event? He is dressed immaculately, he holds himself straight, he is focused, he walks with purpose in his step, and his words are carefully measured to achieve his purpose. He knows he is royalty, and he knows he has a job to do and a crown to represent.

We, too, are royalty. We have a job to do and a heavenly crown to represent.

Sometimes, though, we forget that we are royalty. In Disney's movie *The Lion King*, Simba, the lion crown prince, had run away from home to escape his past and an evil relative who has taken over his kingdom. The wise man (or monkey in this case) Rafiki reminds Simba that his deceased father, Mufasa, the great lion king, lives in him. Mufasa lovingly speaks through the stars and reminds him who he is: "You have forgotten who you are, and so forgotten me. . . . You are more than what you have become. You must take your place. . . . Remember who you are. You are my son, and the one true king. Remember who you are." Simba's courage is stirred, and he returns to his kingdom, kicks out the bad guys, and returns peace and order. It was a task that only he, as the rightful heir to the throne, could do.

Like Simba, sometimes we need to be reminded that we are royalty. Daughter of the Lion of Judah, your Father lives in you. Do not forget who you are. You must take your place as the daughter of the one true King. Your kingdom—your family—was taken over by a bad guy. Only you can save your kingdom, kick out the bad guy, and bring peace and order. You are fully equipped to do so. Remember who you are.

To remind myself of the King I serve and the crown I represent, I have placed crowns around my house.

They remind me that I am a daughter of the King. In my office I have a sign that states, "You are a Lioness. Your Daddy is the Lion of Judah!" On the days when I might feel overwhelmed, I see reminders of God all around. He reminds me that He has brought me through my own fight victorious, and He reminds me that He has called me to the task before me to bring others to freedom—and that He goes with me. He reminds me that I am His and He is mine.

We often hear the expression that we are physical beings on a spiritual journey. This, however, is a misunderstanding of our journey. We are, in fact, spiritual beings on a physical journey while we spend a few short years on this earth. King David offers us the perspective that we are known and designed by God even before we were formed in the womb, and that every day of our physical lives was ordained before we were conceived (Psalm 139:13–16). We become alive in our physical bodies when God breathes His Spirit into us, and we return to our spiritual beings when His Spirit departs from our physical bodies (Psalm 104:29–30). Paul reminds us that our true citizenship, where our hearts call home, is not here on earth, but in heaven where our spirits find rest and peace in the glory of God (Philippians 3:20). We will always feel a bit out of place here on earth because this is not our home, and our restless spirits long to be home when our assignment is complete.

So how does the fact that we are spiritual beings on a physical journey on earth affect how we think and how we act? How does it remind us of our identity? Our best example is Jesus. He was on a mission to save the world, to defeat Satan, to comfort the brokenhearted, and to be a living, breathing, walking example of the nature of God. He knew His mission, He knew His identity, and He did not let anything get in the way of His mission. People insulted Him, but He did not let insults hurt His self-esteem. The Son of God understood that the insults came from ignorant people or from those who were on the Enemy's team. People rejected Him, but He did not let rejection deter Him from His mission. He brushed the dust off His feet and kept on teaching and preaching to those who accepted Him. Some people even praised him and wanted to crown Him king, but He did not let even accolades or a royal position sidetrack his mission. His knew His kingdom was not of this world, and he refused to be affected by the praise of men. Satan himself attempted to get Him off mission, testing Him to turn stones into bread and offering to give Him the world if He would just bow down and worship him. Jesus rejected temptation because He knew His calling, knew His identity, and knew who wins in the end. Jesus was even brought to trial, tortured, and killed, but it did not deter Him from His assignment.

Like Jesus, it is critical for us to know our mission, know our identity, and not let anything deter us from our task. When we are in a rut or have been insulted, rejected, or abused by our abuser or his minions, we can use Jesus as our example and imagine ourselves as a spiritual, heavenly being who has been sent to earth with a mission. And what is that mission? While individual assignments vary, our overall mission collectively is to collaborate with God to bring God's kingdom to earth so God's will is done on earth as it is in heaven (Matthew 6:10). Earth is not our destination; it is merely our temporary assignment before we head home. Knowing our identity—that is, knowing *whose* we are and why we are here—along with using our spiritual weapons, helps deflect the arrows of insults, rejection, temptations, and abuse that are hurled our way in an effort to deter us from our God-given calling. It also helps us to provide compassion and reflect God's character to others who are not as sure of their identity. And it makes us fearless.

From Victim to Victorious—Becoming Fearless

For most women, nothing in this world will be harder than going through, escaping, and overcoming domestic abuse. She may have been beaten down during the marriage, but once she has been healed by Jehovah

Rapha and believes in her identity as a daughter of the Lion of Judah, she will be transformed from a scared kitty cat to a roaring lioness. She will be a force to be reckoned with. Satan has known all along that when she grew into her strength, which God would impart to her, she would be a danger to Satan's plans, so she became a target of Satan's abuse. She is a threat to the Enemy when she becomes all that God has designed her to be.

In his book *Killing Lions*, John Eldredge outlines the coming-of-age tradition of one African tribe that requires a teenage boy to kill a lion before he is considered a man. This man-size quest intentionally prepares the young man with the confidence he needs for adulthood. After one endures the dangers of hunting, stalking, and killing a lion—with the claw marks on his chest to prove it—to protect his family and his community, nothing in the world will intimidate him.

Women who have overcome domestic abuse have killed their lion. We have slain the terrorist who has been assaulting us and our family, and we have the scars to prove it. After equipping ourselves with God's armor and strength and facing Satan head-on, God has gone before us and has fought for us, His daughters. We now stand victorious. Nothing on this earth can intimidate us, for we have seen firsthand Almighty God fight for us, provide for us, equip us, and defeat our Enemy. A difficult boss, a snarky remark, a move across the country, job deadlines, the loss of a job, aging parents, challenging children, a house fire, a financial crisis—whatever the challenge, we face these trials with courage and confidence, knowing our God is faithful and that through Him we have what it takes to overcome. When we overcome domestic abuse, our mindset moves from victim to victorious. God moves in us and strengthens and matures us, and we become fearless, as He designed us to be.

Gentle reader, if you have lived through domestic abuse, I pray this blessing and prayer over you:

You are the beloved daughter of the Almighty God and princess of the King of Kings. Remember who you are and whose you are. The Creator of the Universe has gone before you. He has sent His angel armies to fight for you. He conducted a rescue mission that took you out of the chains of abuse and set you in a place of rest. He is victorious. You are victorious. He is healing you even as you read this. He is equipping you for your next assignment.

Heavenly Father, I ask Your presence to invade Your daughter. I ask Your Holy Spirit to teach her about You and to guide her along Your paths. I ask You to reveal Yourself to her so that she knows without a shadow of a doubt that she is Yours, and that You are who You say You are. Impress upon her heart how You uniquely and wondrously designed her to do Your will on earth, and clarify her mission and assignment for her. Father, let Your presence be so felt in Your daughter that she knows that You are always with her. May she recognize Your voice and hear Your calling. May Your relationship be one of intimacy and daily talks and a true friendship. Replace the lies she has believed with Your truth. Remove all doubt from her mind. Heal her body and soul. Open Your storehouses of heaven and rain down Your blessings on her and her children. Be with her as she fulfills her mission to bring heaven to earth, and give her Your strength and courage and power so that she is *fearless*. Amen.

What's Your Story?

If this book has helped you with overcoming domestic abuse, I would love to hear from you.

Likewise, if you have a story of overcoming domestic abuse that you would like me to consider for including in a future book that will be a collection of powerful stories of overcoming, I would love to hear from you.

Finally, domestic abuse is a complicated topic. I tried to write a book that is as comprehensive as possible to be as helpful as possible to the reader. I am sure that I have missed some things. If you think there are additional topics that would be helpful that should be included in future editions, please drop me a line.

Charlene D. Quint
abusecarenow@gmail.com
PO Box 230
Lake Forest, IL 60045
www.abusecare.org

Appendix

Resources

National and Chicago-Area Organizations that Serve Victims of Domestic Violence

A Safe Place—Provides shelter, court advocacy, referrals, supervised visits and exchanges, and counseling for victims of domestic violence. Also provides abuser counseling and training for Certified Domestic Abuse Professionals. 2710 17th St, Zion, IL 60099; 847-741-7165. 24-hour hotline: 847-249-4450. www.asafeplaceforhelp.org

AbuseCare.org—Nondenominational, faith-based domestic abuse recovery organization that provides faith-based articles, resources, blogs, individual and group coaching to victims, and training, presentations, and workshops for pastors, church staff, and lay leaders. www.abusecare.org

Archdiocese of Chicago Family Ministries Domestic Violence Outreach—Headed by Fr. Charles Dahm, this outreach offers extensive resources, training, help in setting up a congregational ministry, and an Interfaith Guide https://pvm.archchicago.org/human-dignity-solidarity/domestic-violence-outreach

Catholic Charities—Nationwide network offering assistance to families in need and services for victims of abuse and elder abuse. Contact your local Catholic Charities for further information. https://www.catholiccharitiesusa.org/

Chicago Metropolitan Battered Women's Network—Provides programs and resources for victims of domestic violence. 1 East Wacker Dr., Suite 1630, Chicago, IL 60601; 312-527-0730. Illinois Domestic Violence Hotline: 877-863-6338. http://batteredwomensnetwork.org/

Cornerstone Counseling Center of Chicago—This faith-based, nonprofit counseling center offers counseling and personal development services to individuals of all ages, from a Christian perspective. They partner with Chicago-area schools, businesses, churches, and other community organizations to provide professional development training and are approved by the American Psychological Association as a training site for doctoral-level psychology students. https://chicagocounseling.org/

Counseling for Transitions—This Evanston, IL, counseling center focuses on helping women navigate through life transitions and toxic relationships. In addition to in-person services, it offers online counseling for residents of Illinois. https://counselingfortransitions.com/

Dental Care—This website lists free or reduced-price dental-care clinics nationwide. Many community colleges who offer dental hygiene classes offer free or reduced-price dental cleaning. Many dental schools also offer free or reduced-price dental cleaning. https://www.freedentalcare.us/

D100—The legal advocacy arm of A Safe Place to obtain Domestic Violence Orders of Protection, Civil No Contact Orders, and Stalking No Contact Orders, located in Lake County Courthouse near courtroom T-511, 18 N. County St., Waukegan, IL 60085; 847-360-6471.

Domestic Shelters—National online resource of nationwide hotlines, services, and articles for victims of domestic abuse. www.domesticshelters.org

Domestic Abuse Intervention Programs—Initiative to end violence. They provide training materials for communities and have developed the Duluth Model to reform the criminal justice system. The organization has also created a number of wheel illustrations (the Power and Control Wheel, the Equality Wheel, etc.) that have become widely used by professionals in the field of domestic violence. https://www.theduluthmodel.org/

Faith Trust Institute—National, multi-faith, multicultural training and education organization to end domestic violence. http://www.faithtrustinstitute.org/

Focus Ministries—Located in the Western suburbs of Chicago, offers faith-based counseling and training for pastors, students, lay persons, and professionals. http://www.focusministries1.org/

Food assistance—The national Supplemental Nutrition Assistance Program (SNAP), formerly known as food stamps, offers benefits to help with the purchase of food for the household for qualified persons with limited income. https://www.fns.usda.gov/snap/supplemental-nutrition-assistance-program

Food pantries—Almost every county has food pantries organized by local churches, townships, and nonprofit organizations. Search online for the local food pantries in your area.

Grace for My Heart—Online ministry written by author and pastor David Orrison on narcissists in the church. https://graceformyheart.wordpress.com/

Health and Human Services—Many counties have a health and human services department that offers health care, food assistance, child care assistance, home energy assistance, crisis intervention services, and/or child and elder abuse reporting lines. Search online for your local county's health and human service department.

Housing—Most counties have local housing authorities that provide housing assistance to qualified persons. Search online for your county's housing authority.

Illinois Coalition Against Domestic Violence—806 S. College St., Springfield, IL 62704; 217-789-2830. Help Line: 877-863-6338. www.ilcadv.org

The Institute for Relational Harm Reduction and Public Pathology Education—Offers articles, research, information, retreats, and other resources regarding understanding and healing from pathological relationships. http://saferelationshipsmagazine.com/

JCFS Chicago—Safer Synagogues and Synagogue Partnerships offers connections to support and services to member community synagogues in the Chicago area, 855-275-5237. https://www.jcfs.org/taxonomy/term/236

Lake County Sheriff's Office—Order of Protection information: https://www.lakecountyil.gov/1918/Order-of-Protection

Legal Counsel—Most law schools offer free legal representation through a legal clinic staffed by law students and supervised by lawyers. Many counties offer free legal services through nonprofit legal clinics. Search online for a local legal clinic near you.

Resources

Medical clinic—Many counties offer free health care clinics for qualified persons with limited income and no health insurance. Search online for your local county health department.

National Association of Free & Charitable Clinics—A nationwide directory of free health care clinics. https://www.nafcclinics.org/find-clinic

National Coalition Against Domestic Violence—National organization dedicated to supporting survivors of domestic violence, holding offenders accountable, and supporting advocates. https://www.ncadv.org/

National Domestic Violence Hotline—24-hour hotline: 800-299-7233. www.thehotline.org,

North Suburban Legal Aid Clinic—Provides pro bono legal services to low-income individuals in the areas of domestic violence, landlord-tenant disputes, and immigration issues. www.nslegalaid.org

Peaceful Families Project—Provides workshops, training, and resources for Muslim leaders to end domestic violence in Muslim families. www.peacefulfamilies.org

Restored—International, UK-based Christian alliance working to transform relationships and end violence against women. www.restoredrelationships.org

Salvation Army—Nationwide network that offers emergency and transitional shelters and counseling to victims of domestic violence and their children. https://www.salvationarmyusa.org/usn/stop-domestic-abuse/

Shalva—Offers domestic abuse counseling to the metropolitan Chicago Jewish community. 24-hour crisis line: 773-583-4673. www.shalvaonline.org

State Coalitions Against Domestic Violence—Most states have their own coalitions against domestic violence that provide resources for victims of domestic violence. This web page lists each state coalition and contact information. https://ncadv.org/state-coalitions

United States Conference of Catholic Bishops—Includes resources and the Catholic Church's position against domestic violence. http://www.usccb.org/issues-and-action/marriage-and-family/marriage/domestic-violence/

Unholy Charade—Ministry with articles and books by author and pastor Jeff Crippen, designed to expose domestic abusers hiding in the church and provide support and validation to abuse victims. https://unholycharade.com/

Willow Creek Care Center—Ministry associated with Willow Creek Church in the northwest suburbs of Chicago. Offers free or reduced-price counseling, vehicle and bike repairs, free vehicles and bikes to approved families, used clothing and shoes, food store, dental and vision care, employment services, English as a second language assistance, financial education, health screenings, legal aid, pregnancy tests and ultrasounds, temporary and permanent housing, and tax preparation. https://www.willowcreekcarecenter.org/

YWCA—The YWCA administers the child care–assistance program in Illinois and other states to help income-eligible parents pay for child care while they work or go to school. Contact your local YWCA for further information. https://www.ywca.org/

Zacharias Sexual Abuse Center—Provides counseling for victims of sexual assault and abuse. 4275 Old Grand Ave, Gurnee, IL 60031; 847-244-1187. 24-hour hotline 847-872-7799. www.zcenter.org

Books

Abuse in the Jewish Community, Michael Salamon PhD, Urim Publications (2011).

A Cry for Justice: How the Evil of Domestic Abuse Hides in Your Church, Jeff Crippen and Anna Wood, Calvary Press Publishing (2012).

Anatomy of the Soul: Surprising Connections between Neuroscience and Spiritual Practices That Can Transform Your Life and Relationships, Curt Thompson, Tyndale Momentum (2010).

Domestic Abuse and the Jewish Community: Perspectives from the First International Conference, Diane Gardsbane, Routledge (2005).

Domestic Violence: What Every Pastor Needs to Know, Al Miles, Fortress Press (2011).

The Emotionally Destructive Marriage: How to Find your Voice and Reclaim your Hope, Leslie Vernick, LCSW, Waterbrook, (2013).

The Emotionally Destructive Relationship: Seeing It, Stopping It, Surviving It, Leslie Vernick, LCSW, Harvest House (2007).

Freeing Yourself from the Narcissist in Your Life, Linda Martinez-Lewis, PhD, Penguin Books (2008).

God is Good: He's Better than You Think, Bill Johnson, Destiny Image (2018).

How God Changes Your Brain: Breakthrough Findings from a Leading Neuroscientist, Andrew Newberg and Mark Robert Waldman, Ballantine Books (2010).

I Promise to Hate, Despise and Abuse You Until Death Do Us Part, Andrea Oegler and Troy Martin, Bookend Publishers (2012).

Narcissism in the Church: A Heart of Stone in Christian Relationships, David Orrison, PhD (2019).

Not Under Bondage: Biblical Divorce for Abuse, Adultery and Desertion, Barbara Roberts, Maschil Press (2008).

Moving Out, Moving On: When a Relationship Goes Wrong Workbook, Susan Murphy-Milano, Kind Living Publishing (2005).

Seven Principles for Making Marriage Work, John Gottman and Nan Silver, Harmony Books (2015).

Seven Reasons Women Find Themselves in Abusive Relationships, John Shore (2012).

Seven Levels of Intimacy, Matthew Kelly, Fireside Books (2005).

Time's Up: How to Escape Abusive and Stalking Relationships Guide, Susan Murphy-Milano, Dog Ear Publishing (2010).

The Sociopath Next Door, Martha Stout, PhD, Harmony Books (2005).

Unholy Charade: Unmasking the Domestic Abuser in the Church, Jeff Crippen, Justice Keepers Publishing (2015).

The Verbally Abusive Relationship: How to Recognize It and How to Respond, Patricia Evans, Adams Media (2010).

Will I Ever Be Free of You? How to Navigate a High-Conflict Divorce from a Narcissist and Heal Your Family, Karyl McBride, PhD, Atria Books (2015).

Without Conscience: The Disturbing World of the Psychopaths Among Us, Robert D. Hare, PhD, Guilford Press (1993).

The Wizard of Oz and Other Narcissists: Coping with the One-Way Relationship in Work, Love, and Family, Eleanor Payson, MSW, Julian Day Publications (2002).

Women Who Love Psychopaths: Inside the Relationships of Inevitable Harm with Psychopaths, Sociopaths and Narcissists, Sandra L. Brown, Mask Publishing (2010).

Words Can Change Your Brain, Andrew Newberg and Mark Robert Waldman, Avery (2013).

Resources

Praise and Worship Music for Overcomers

"Amazing Grace (My Chains Are Gone)" by Chris Tomlin
"The Breakup Song (Fear You Don't Own Me)" by Francesca Battistelli
"Break Every Chain" by Hillsong Worship
"Chain Breaker" by Zach Williams
"Fear Is a Liar" by Zach Williams
"Giants Fall" by Francesca Battistelli
"Glorious Day" by Passion
"Good, Good Father" by Chris Tomlin
"Holy Spirit" by Kari Jobe
"The Lion and the Lamb" by Big Daddy Weave
"No Longer Slaves" by Zach Williams
"Oceans" by Hillsong United
"Overcomer" by Mandisa
"Praise You in the Storm" by Casting Crowns
"Rescue" by Lauren Daigle
"Rescue Story" by Zach Williams
"Resurrecting" by Elevation Worship
"Reckless Love" by Bethel Music
"Revelation Song" by Kari Jobe
"Spirit Break Out" by Jesus Culture
"This Is Amazing Grace" by Phil Wickham
"Way Maker" by Bethel Music
"What a Beautiful Name It Is" by Hillsong Worship
"Who You Say I Am" by Hillsong Worship
"Whom Shall I Fear (God of Angel Armies)" by Chris Tomlin
"You Say" by Lauren Daigle
"You Know My Name" by Tasha Cobbs Leonard

Classic Girl-Power Overcomer Songs

"Girl on Fire" by Alicia Keys
"Respect" by Aretha Franklin
"I Am Woman" by Helen Reddy
"I Miss Me More" by Kelsea Ballerini
"I'm Coming Out" by Dianna Ross
"I'm Every Woman" by Chaka Khan
"I Will Survive" by Gloria Gaynor
"Pretty Woman" by Roy Orbison
"Stronger" by Kelly Clarkson
"You Don't Own Me" by Lesley Gore
"You're So Vain" by Carly Simon

College and Scholarship Information

www.affordablecollegesonline.org
http://www.applyingtoschool.com/forms/ComCol-State.aspx—listing of community colleges by state
www.bestcolleges.com
https://www.collegeboard.org/—well known website for information on colleges, requirements, testing, searches
www.collegeconsensus.com
www.collegescholarships.com
www.fastweb.com
www.scholarships.com
www.scholarshipsforwomen.net
https://www.usnews.com/education/best-colleges/paying-for-college/slideshows/12-tuition-free-colleges—information on tuition free colleges

Nationwide and Chicago-Area Resources for Gently Used Appliances, Building Materials, Clothes, Shoes, Furniture, Home Furnishings, Home Goods, Toys, and Other Items

Estate Sales.net—Nationwide website for estate sales, featuring photographs of items for sale, and times, dates, and locations of sales. https://www.estatesales.net

Facebook Garage Sales—Nearly every community has its own Facebook page for sales of used individual items, estate sales, and garage sales.

Forest & Found—Upscale not-for-profit cozy thrift store in Lake Forest, IL, that donates 100 percent of profits to local charities. Offers clothes, shoes, furniture, home goods, and home furnishings. http://www.forestandfound.com/

Garage Sales.com—Nationwide website for garage sales. https://www.garagesales.com/

Garage Sale Finder—Nationwide website for garage sales. https://garagesalefinder.com/

Goodwill Thrift Stores—Nationwide network of not-for-profit thrift stores that supports Goodwill. Offers clothes, toys, books, furniture, home goods, and home furnishings. https://www.goodwill.org/locator/

Habitat for Humanity Restore—Nationwide network of not-for-profit home improvement thrift stores benefiting Habitat for Humanity. Offers new and gently used furniture, appliances, home goods, and building materials. https://www.habitat.org/restores

Let Go—A nationwide website for buying and selling secondhand items. Many items are simply free because the owners wants to get rid of them. Offers everything from kids shoes to cars. For safety reasons, bring a friend when going to someone's house to look at items. https://www.letgo.com/en-us

Love INC or **Love In the Name of Christ**—Nationwide ministry that works with local churches to provide thrift stores and needed assistance, including gently used furniture, home goods, and home furnishings. Check with your local Love INC for further information. https://www.loveinc.org/

Renew Family Consignment—Cozy, upscale consignment shop in the northern suburbs of Chicago. Offers upscale children's clothes, shoes, outerwear, sporting equipment, furniture, designer handbags, designer jewelry, and home furnishings. https://renewfamilyconsignment.com/

Salvation Army Family Stores—Nationwide network of thrift stores that support the Salvation Army. Offers a wide variety of gently used items. https://satruck.org/familystore

Resources

Sparrow's Nest Thrift Stores—Eight not-for-profit thrift stores located throughout the Chicago area that support Home of the Sparrow, a homeless shelter for women and children. Offers clothes, toys, books, furniture, home goods, mattresses, medical equipment (such as walkers, canes, etc.), and home furnishings. https://www.hosparrow.org/sparrows-nest-thrift-stores/

St. Vincent de Paul Thrift Stores—Nationwide network of thrift stores associated with the Society of St. Vincent de Paul, a Catholic lay charity. Offers a wide variety of gently used items. https://www.svdpusa.org/

Upscale Rummage & Furniture Warehouse—Huge not-for-profit thrift store located in a warehouse in the northern suburbs of Chicago that donates 100 percent of its profits to local charities. Offers a huge variety of clothing, shoes, home goods, holiday decorations, furniture, and home furnishings. https://upscalerummagesale.org/

Village Treasure House—Upscale, not-for-profit consignment shop in the northern suburbs of Chicago that donates 100 percent of its profits to local agencies benefiting women and children. Offers furniture, home goods, and home furnishings. https://www.villagetreasurehouse.org/

The Domestic Abuse Intervention Program in Duluth, Minnesota, has done a great deal of work with men who were battering their partners from a position of learned entitlement. What has become widely known as the Duluth Model developed a number of visual aids in the form of wheels to help visualize the tactics that are common to men who batter women. These wheels are commonly used by domestic abuse organizations throughout the country and the world. The images on the following pages are included with permission from the Domestic Abuse Intervention Program, to whom we owe a debt of gratitude.

Overcoming the Narcissist, Sociopath, Psychopath, and other Domestic Abusers

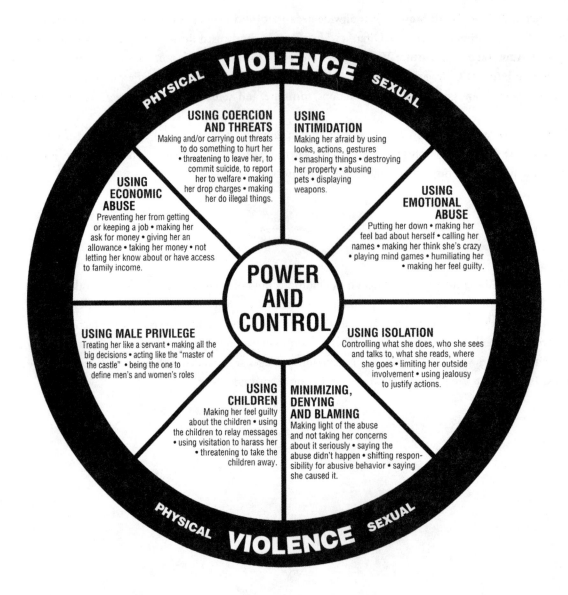

DOMESTIC ABUSE INTERVENTION PROGRAMS
202 East Superior Street
Duluth, Minnesota 55802
218-722-2781
www.theduluthmodel.org

Resources

Post Separation Power and Control Wheel

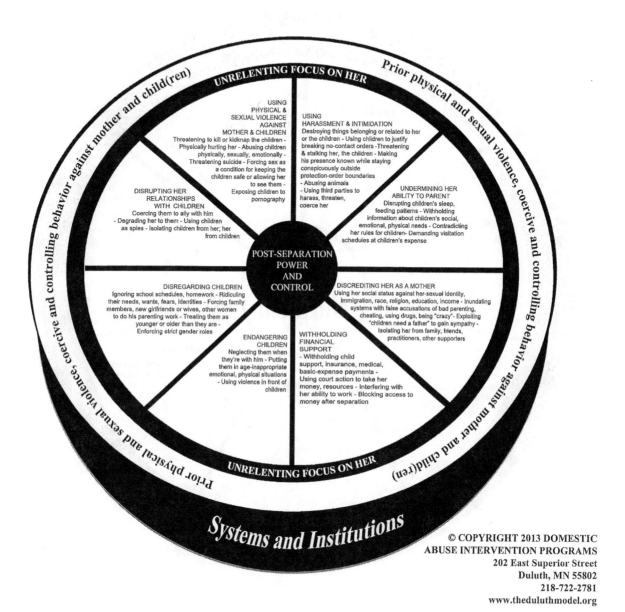

Overcoming the Narcissist, Sociopath, Psychopath, and other Domestic Abusers

Domestic Abuse Intervention Programs
202 East Superior Street
Duluth, MN 55802
218.722.2781
www.theduluthmodel.org

Resources

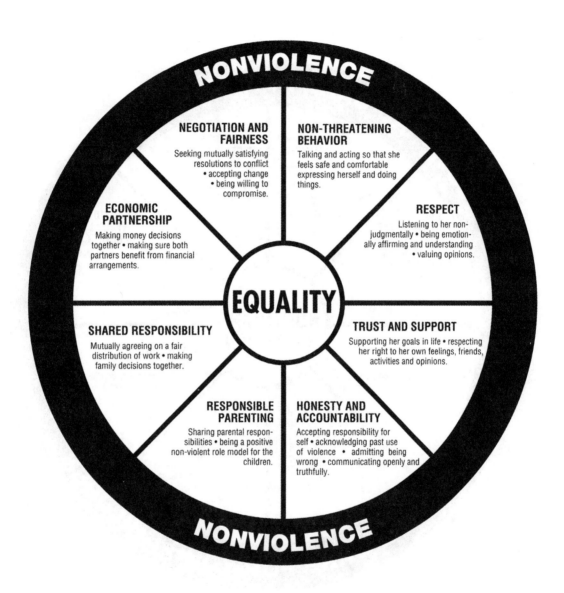

Overcoming the Narcissist, Sociopath, Psychopath, and other Domestic Abusers

DOMESTIC ABUSE INTERVENTION PROGRAMS
202 East Superior Street
Duluth, Minnesota 55802
218-722-2781
www.theduluthmodel.org

Order Information

To order additional copies of this book, please visit
www.redemption-press.com.
Also available on Amazon.com and BarnesandNoble.com
or by calling toll-free 1-844-2REDEEM.